shed by

CKPOLE BOOKS
Ritter Road
anicsburg, PA 17055

ed in the United States of America

ously published as *Outdoor Life's Complete Fish & Game Cookbook*

8 7 6 5 4 3 2 1

ISED EDITION

author would like to acknowledge material quoted from *Edible Plants and Animals,* reprinted by permission of
s on File, Inc.; Stackpole books for material from *Microwave Game & Fish Cookbook* by Paula J. Del Giudice;
ford Angier for material from his interesting book *Gourmet Cooking for Free,* published by Stackpole Books, North
lina Wildlife Resources Commission for a recipe from *Wildlife in North Carolina;* the University of Arizona Press
recipe from Juanita Tiger Kavena's book *Hopi Cookery;* B.A.S.S., Inc., and *Southern Outdoors* for material adapted
my article "How to Eat Good and Sleep Well" and for material from an editorial by Larry Teague; and *Sports
,* a division of the Hearts Corporation, for permission to quote a short article by Anderson DuPree. Also, the
or acknowledges material adapted from his articles and columns that originally appeared in *Gray's Sporting Journal,*
& Stream, Outdoor Life, Southern Outdoors, and *Sports Afield.* Other acknowledgments are made in the text as
opriate.

r Stackpole Books by A. D. Livingston: *Venison Cookbook, Wild Turkey Cookbook, Bass Cookbook, Trout Cookbook,
Saltwater Fish Cookbook*

eff, Bill, Jarrod, and James

ary of Congress Cataloging-in-Publication Data

ngston, A. D., 1932–
    Complete fish & game cookbook / A.D. Livingston.
        p.   cm.
    Includes index.
    ISBN 0-8117-0428-9
    1. Cookery (Game)   2. Cookery (Fish)   I. Title.
X751.L577   1996
41.6'9—dc20   96-14077
                                                    CIP

COMPLETE
FISH & GAM
COOKBOOK

A. D. Livingston

STACKPOLE
BOOKS

CONTENTS

PART TWO: BIRDS

PART THREE: GAME

INTRODUCTION

While headed west as a fairly young man some years ago, I learned by radio of a café in Winters, Texas, that served up buffalo steaks. After pulling off the road and circling Winters on the map, I decided to take a quick dogleg detour from my planned route. Back then, buffalo was hard to find.

Several hours later, I enjoyed a big buffalo T-bone, cooked medium rare. Licking my lips, I quickly paid up and hurried on toward El Paso. As I sped on for the next several hundred miles, however, I couldn't get the rich, red meat, which was a little sweeter than prime beef, out of my mind. Finally, I parked at Indian Mountain Lodge, a quaint adobe place, and wrote an article about the buffalo T-bone.

When the article came out in a magazine some months later, the owner of the café wrote me a letter. After thanking me nicely, he requested rather firmly that I write nothing else about his café. "Folks have come in here from twenty-seven states, and they have et every buffalo in this part of the country!"

Following the same line of thought, I at first had reservations about writing this book. Many of our game animals, birds, and fish are just too good (with proper handling) compared with supermarket foods! Moreover, wild game animals and birds are typically very low in fat compared with pen-raised chickens and feed-lot cattle, and the nutritional advantages of fish are well known and widely touted. Furthermore, wild game and birds are probably safer than domestic meats; I believe that, when properly handled, game is less likely to be infected with salmonella. In short, I feared that the regular hunters and fishermen would be joined by zealous gourmets, plump dieters, and gaunt, half-starved health-food nuts, so that folks from forty-eight states and Greenwich

Village would wind up chasing swamp rabbits in Louisiana, stalking elk in Wyoming, or angling for eelpout in northern Minnesota.

But I proceeded with the book, and made it fatter, when I considered that there are no doubt more wild turkey in this country now than there were thirty years ago. White-tailed deer and a number of other animals have also enjoyed population booms in many parts of the country. The reason is that modern game management programs, from state to state, as well as nationally and internationally for such migratory birds as the sandhill crane, have given us good hunting and fishing. It's true that some fish and game species are in trouble in some areas.

There are, of course, some sad stories in game management. But for the most part, hunting and fishing in North America are better now than before World War II.

Why? Because hunters and fishermen paid for it. The bill is not being footed by bird-watchers in sneakers or water skiers in swim-suits. We the hunters buy the hunting licenses, we the anglers buy the fishing licenses, and we the waterfowlers buy the duck stamps. More important, we pay the excise tax. Excise tax? Yes, excise tax. It's not a sales tax, which we also pay. It's not an income tax, which we also pay. It's not a duty on imports, which we also pay. It's not really a value added tax. It's an excise tax. Ten percent at the manufacturer's end. Guns and ammo are taxed even more. This tax pulls in millions and millions of dollars per year, and it is earmarked for the preservation and improvement of hunting and fishing in this country (although several attempts have been made to hijack the money for the general fund). Yes, we pay the bills for our sport—and good eating is our bonus.

—A. D. Livingston

PART ONE

FISH

1

FRIED FISH,
PLAIN AND FANCY

Frying is by far America's favorite way of cooking fish. The reason is simply that fried fish taste good, crunchy on the outside and soft in the middle. The trouble is that all cooks have their own preferred methods, batters, and so on. Once, for example, I had to stand between two guys, one from Connecticut and the other from California, as they disagreed on whether to shake fish in white flour or yellow cornmeal before frying them.

Back then, I myself championed good causes, such as the culinary superiority of the Tennessee hornyhead over ordinary fare like the New England brookie or the Northern California grunion. For flavor and crunch, nothing beats fresh, properly fried hornyheads, provided that fine-ground *white* cornmeal and *peanut* oil are used.

But I look for no argument in these pages and want to get on with a variety of recipes wide enough to suit everyone, North, South, East, and West. My personal favorite for fried fish is set forth next, along with my reasons for liking it. But catch lots of fish—and try everything.

Ninety Miles from Opp

Dick Wood, a talented advertising professional who is responsible for a lot of those pretty fishing tackle ads in the slick magazines, once told me that the late Lew Childre, the founder of the tackle firm, didn't trust or abide by any fisherman who wasn't born within a 90-mile radius of Opp, Alabama. As the crow flies, I'm certainly within that radius. Thus, I consider myself not only qualified but also trustworthy to say that you require only a short list of ingredients in order to fry the world's best fish.

3

good fresh fish
peanut oil
fine-ground white cornmeal
salt and pepper

Fillet or pan-dress the fish. Heat ¾ inch of peanut oil in a large skillet. Salt and pepper a few fish at a time, as you need them. Shake the fish in a bag of cornmeal, then fry in very hot peanut oil—at least 375 degrees, and preferably hotter, kept just short of the smoking point. (See the sidebar below for a discussion of hot cooking oil.) Drain the fish on brown paper grocery bags. Serve hot. If you have lots of folks to feed, start them eating before all the fish are cooked. You'll have to add more cooking oil if you have lots of fish to fry.

Serve the fish with corn bread and lots of good salad, coleslaw, or (my favorite) sliced fresh tomatoes.

The corn bread is made as follows: Mix cornmeal, salt, and pepper with hot water until it gets to a good "spooning" consistency. Let it sit for about 15 minutes or more, during which time it will firm up a bit. Then add a little peanut oil and mix. Heat oil in a skillet to medium heat (not nearly as hot as for the fish). Spoon the bread into the skillet. Cook until browned on both sides, turning once. Drain on a brown paper bag.

Because the corn bread takes longer to cook than the fish, it is a good idea to cook it first. Or use two skillets.

The success of this and most of the other fried fish recipes depends not so much on ingredients as on careful attention to detail. Thus, the following points are important:

1. The oil should be very hot while the fish are frying. I constantly adjust the heat while cooking, turning it up to high when new fish are put into the oil and turning it down a bit as the fish heat up. I use peanut oil because it has a high smoking point, no unpleasant flavor, and no cholesterol.

2. The fish should not be cooked too long. If your oil is at the right temperature, the fish

Too Hot?

I usually recommend that fish be fried in very hot oil, just short of the smoking point. But there are exceptions. Skate and ray, for example, contain lots of moisture and tend to pop violently if dropped into very hot oil. Roe sacs also tend to pop—sometimes explosively. So proceed with caution.

Also, a pan full of hot oil can be very dangerous if it catches on fire. Extinguish a grease fire with baking soda or a suitable fire extinguisher, or by covering the pan with a tight-fitting lid. *Do not* use water on a grease fire, and do not attempt to make a run for the door with a burning frying pan. It's better to smoke up the house than to risk burning yourself. Fall down with a pan full of burning oil and it could kill you—or burn up the house. Opening a door could cause the flames to blow back on you, burning your arm and face.

So . . . be careful with hot grease. Treat minor burns by holding the afflicted area under cold running water as soon as possible. Most serious burns should also be cooled quickly and, if possible, kept cold en route to a doctor or hospital.

will brown on the outside before they overcook on the inside. If the oil isn't hot enough, the fish will dry out while you are trying to brown the outside. In fact, some of the worst fish I've ever eaten were cooked by this recipe, but were fried in a large iron pot on a small camp stove. The stove simply would not get the oil hot enough.

3. The fish should be drained and left on absorbent paper. They'll be soggy if you take them out of the frying pan and pile them high on a platter. In fact, I serve fried fish on brown grocery bags.

4. The cornmeal should be very fine, like flour. Coarse, gritty meals simply won't work and won't stick to the fish, unless perhaps with the aid of whisked chicken egg or other goo.

5. Serve the fish hot.

Trout with Watercress or Parsley

Although this recipe is ideal for small brook trout, it can also be used for other small fish and for fillets. I consider the dish to be the classic sauté, although many variations are possible and many experts will argue hotly for the use of beef suet or bacon drippings instead of butter, or for cornmeal or other coatings instead of flour.

> small trout, dressed whole
> butter
> freshly squeezed lemon juice
> flour
> watercress or fresh parsley, chopped
> salt and pepper to taste

Dress the fish whole. Behead them if they are too long to fit into your skillet. Sprinkle the

> ## Brook Trout
>
> Small brook trout are best fried. They are the only trout that are really good fried without being scaled or skinned. Before frying them, wipe completely dry with paper towels. This keeps the skin intact and the fish whole in the pan.
> —*The Maine Way*

fish inside and out with lemon juice, salt, and pepper. Wait 15 minutes, then heat some butter in a skillet. Dredge the fish in flour, then sauté them on medium heat until they flake easily when tested with a fork. Remove the fish from the skillet. Then add to the skillet a little chopped watercress or parsley, lemon juice, and more butter if needed. Scrape up the pan dredgings and simmer, stirring as you go, to make a sauce.

Don't serve these fish with the usual hush puppies and french fries. Try sourdough bread, boiled new potatoes, and string beans. Serve the sauce over the boiled potatoes and fish. Garnish with a sprig or two of watercress or parsley and with a wedge of lemon.

Sautéed Trout

A few purists might smile politely whenever the likes of this writer starts arguing the merits of dusting fish with cornmeal or wheat flour. They might express an interest in the experimental use of flour from teff or amaranth, or meal from ground chick peas (garbanzo beans). They would probably laugh at claims made for powdered sugar-coated corn flakes—and would surely shudder at the very idea of dipping a good fish into a gooey batter. If pressed into the argument, these people will point out that a small trout (neither skinned nor scaled) crisps up and browns nicely without any coating whatsoever, provided that it isn't washed too vigorously.

Thus, all you need to sauté an undusted trout in camp is a little butter and salt. Or you may want to try the following recipe, adapted from my *Trout Cookbook*.

> 2 or 3 trout 9 or 10 inches long, dressed whole
> ½ cup milk
> 1 teaspoon salt
> 2 strips bacon
> 1 tablespoon white wine Worcestershire sauce
> 2 or 3 green onions, chopped with part of tops

Dissolve the salt in the milk, then dip the trout in the liquid, coating them all over. Fry the bacon in the skillet and remove it to drain. Heat the skillet until the bacon drippings are almost to the smoking point. Place the trout in the skillet and cook on both sides until it flakes easily when tested with a fork. It's best to turn the fish only once. If the fat gets too hot, remove the skillet from the heat for a minute or two and turn down the heat a little.

Put the fish onto a brown bag to drain. Sauté the chopped green onion in the remaining bacon grease for about 5 minutes. Stir the white wine Worcestershire sauce into what's left of the bacon grease. Add a little salt. Crumble the pieces of bacon and stir them in. Place the fish on plates and pour the sauce over them.

Italian Fried Spanish Mackerel

Here's a recipe that I enjoy using for Spanish mackerel, mullet, or other fatty fish from salt water. I use a lower frying temperature with this recipe because on high heat, the batter tends to burn before the fish gets done. Also, here I prefer to use a deep fryer instead of a frying pan.

> 2 pounds fillets
> cooking oil for deep frying
> 1 cup Italian bread crumbs
> 1 cup Parmesan cheese
> salt and pepper
> egg
> lemon

Rig for deep frying. Mix the bread crumbs and cheese. Salt and pepper the fillets, dip them in egg, roll them in the crumb mixture, and fry them until the flesh flakes easily and is golden brown. Slice a lemon or two for garnish. Feeds 4.

Small-Fry

This recipe is based on the "Indian Method of Cooking Small Fish," in *Bull Cook and Authentic Historical Recipes and Practices,* by George Leonard Herter and Berthe E. Herter. The authors say that (1) fish in some areas run small and (2) in some cases you must eat them to supplement your diet in order to survive.

Anyhow—poach, boil, or steam the fish for a few minutes, then flake the meat with a fork. Salt and pepper to taste. Heat up a little oil or butter in an Indian skillet. Add the fish and

Frying for 1 or 100

When I was planning this book, I thought I would get into a long-winded discourse on the merits of frying fish by different methods, such as pan frying or deep frying. There is a good deal of difference, of course, but I now think that the choice should be a practical one. For example, most people wouldn't want to heat up a deep fryer full of expensive oil to cook fish for one person. Thus, my advice is to choose a method that is suited to the number of people you have to feed.

Fish for one or two people can be sautéed in butter without making up batter or heating lots of oil.

Fish for three or four can easily be fried in a skillet, with oil from ⅛ to 1 inch deep, depending on how you like it and on how much fish you plan to cook. Of course, you can use a skillet to cook for more people simply by cooking in several batches, adding more oil as needed.

Fish for five to ten or more are best fried in a deep fryer, simply because it is quicker. It is also easier to tell when the fish is done; if a piece of fish floats, it's ready to eat.

Fish for a hundred or so people can be fried (usually outside) with special equipment. A large cast-iron pot, as was once used for washing clothes, works nicely if you can heat it properly. But be very careful; this much hot oil can be dangerous. Even larger pots can be used. For example, a local group of farmers fry fish for several hundred people in a large cast-iron vat that was made for scalding hogs.

sizzle until browned. Drain. Eat. Survive. Catch more fish.

Also try the next recipe for frying very small fish.

Flaked Fish Fry

A number of recipes for fritters, fish balls, patties, and so on are set forth in chapter 4, on fish flakes. But a little overlap is certainly justified here simply because fish patties are so good—and so easy to cook.

2 cups fish flakes
oil
2 large chicken eggs
salt and pepper

Boil or poach the fish for a few minutes, until it flakes easily with a fork. Drain. Salt and pepper to taste. Whisk the eggs, then mix with the fish. Spoon the mixture into the pan. (The mixture will be runny, but it will firm up as it cooks.) Fry in very hot oil for a couple of minutes, or until the fish is brown. The fish has already been cooked before flaking, so don't fry any longer than necessary to brown. Feeds 3 or 4.

With a simple fish flake recipe like this, I prefer to pan-fry the patties, using two spatulas to turn them gently. They can, however, be fried by any method, from griddle to deep fryer. The shape of the final product, from round to flat, will be influenced by the frying process and the depth of the oil used.

Note: In this recipe, the primary purpose of the egg is to hold the fish together while cooking it. I have purposely kept this recipe simple, but you can use everything from buttermilk to elderberry blossoms in fish patties and fritters. (See chapter 4 for more ideas.)

Beer Batter Fish Fingers

If you like a very crispy batter, here's one to try. I modified the idea from a more basic batter recipe that was published by the Oklahoma Wildlife Federation in *Wildlife Chef*:

2 or 3 pounds fish fingers or small whole
    fish
cooking oil for deep frying
½ cup melted butter
½ cup beer
2 large chicken eggs, separated
1 cup flour
½ cup cornstarch

Beat egg yolks and mix with beer and melted butter. Then stir in the flour and cornstarch. Whisk or beat the egg whites until they stiffen, then add to flour mixture. Heat oil on medium high in deep fryer. Salt and pepper the fish, then dip each piece into the batter. (Add the seasonings to the batter if you prefer.) Deep-fry until golden brown. Drain on absorbent paper or brown grocery bags before serving. Feeds 4 to 6.

Note: Medium high heat works best for this recipe. If the oil is too hot, the batter tends to pop away from the fish.

Shallow-Fried Pigfish (Grunt)

Here's an interesting fried fish recipe from a booklet called *Pigfish*, published by the UNC Sea Grant. (The fish is also known as the grunt.)

The Fish
    6 pigfish, about ¾ pound each
    6 tablespoons cornstarch
    3 tablespoons minced fresh ginger
    12 small whole green onions, coarsely
        chopped
    10 tablespoons oil
The Sauce
    6 tablespoons light soy sauce
    6 tablespoons dry sherry
    6 tablespoons red wine vinegar
    6 teaspoons sugar
    4 tablespoons sesame oil

Pan-dress the fish, score on a slant 3 times on each side, then dust well with cornstarch. Mix the sauce ingredients in a small bowl. Set aside. Heat a large, heavy skillet over high heat until very hot; add and heat the oil. Sauté the ginger and scallions for about 5 minutes over high heat, stirring constantly. Push the mixture to one side. Sear the fish for 1 minute on each side, turn the heat to low, and sauté each side for about 4 minutes, until crisp and brown. With the heat on high again, pour the sauce directly onto the fish, basting and turning them once as the sauce sizzles. Remove the fish with a spatula to a hot serving platter, spooning darkened ginger and scallions on top, and serve hot. Feeds 6 people.

Zesty Griddle Fish

Here's a tasty recipe that I use from time to time when I'm in a hurry to feed one or two people:

fish fillets
Zesty Italian dressing
salt
bread slices

Salt the fish fillets. Heat a griddle and pour a little Zesty Italian dressing onto the surface. Put the fillets in the middle of the griddle. With a wide spatula, move most of the dressing to the center. Tear bread slices in half and arrange them around the fish. Cook for 4 minutes, then turn the fish and bread. Cook the fish another 3 minutes, and remove them to a plate. Check the bread for toastiness.

Variations: Experiment with other clear salad dressings that contain about half olive oil. Many of the dressings contain a lot of vinegar, however, and won't behave like pure oil when heated. Creamy dressings may not work at frying and grilling temperatures.

Rockfish Wingo

If you like a golden, crunchy batter and sweet-tasting fish, try this one from my friend Carl Wingo of Woodbridge, Virginia. (That's Chesapeake Bay country, where "rockfish" is a popular name for the striped bass.)

> rockfish fillets
> salt
> 2 chicken eggs
> 1 tablespoon water
> frosted flakes
> cooking oil

If you have large fillets, cut them into fingers. Beat eggs with 1 tablespoon water added. (The water, Wingo says, breaks down the egg so that it isn't so globby.) Crunch up the frosted flakes. Heat the cooking oil. Salt the fillets, dip in egg, roll in frosted flake crumbs, and fry on medium high heat. Cook the fillets until they are golden brown, but be careful; the frosted flake batter will burn quickly.

Wingo says that his daughters love the

Chain Pickerel

Often called "jacks," these fish have a medium-low oil content and are considered very good by many people. The pickerel has a series of small bones that runs down each fillet, and these are difficult to deal with. Most people gash the fish with a sharp knife in one way or another, often with crosshatches. Then they fry them crisply—and eat bones and all.

sweetness in frosted flake batter, but for himself he prefers to mix half frosted flakes with half regular cornflakes. In any case, try frosted flake batter; the sugar caramelizes, thereby producing more crunch than ordinary batters.

Flatfish Parmesan

Here's a tasty dish that works well with thin fillets, such as those from flounder or other flatfish. (Fillets from rounder fish can be put between sheets of waxed paper and flattened a bit with a smooth mallet.)

> 2 pounds thin fillets
> 1 cup cooking oil
> ¾ cup fine cracker crumbs
> ¾ cup Parmesan cheese, grated
> 1 tablespoon onion juice
> 1 chicken egg
> salt and pepper

Stir the onion juice into the oil. Place the fish in a nonmetallic container, pour the oil mixture over them, and marinate in the refrigerator for about 2 hours. Drain the fillets, then sprinkle with salt and pepper. Heat the marinade oil in a skillet. Mix the cracker crumbs and cheese. Whisk the egg. Dip the fillets in the egg, roll them in the cracker crumb mixture, and quickly brown them in the hot marinade oil. (Add more oil if needed.) Eat the fish while hot. Feeds 4 or 5.

Potato Fried Fish

This tasty recipe requires onion soup mix that has been reduced almost to a powder. This is easily accomplished with a mortar and pestle—and lots of elbow grease—or by putting the mix in a cloth bag, or perhaps sandwiching it between sheets of waxed paper, and pounding it with the smooth part of a meat mallet.

   2 pounds fish fillets
   1 cup instant mashed potato flakes
   1 pack (2 envelopes) onion soup mix (2.6
      ounces)
   cooking oil
   1 chicken egg, lightly beaten
   salt and pepper

Pulverize the onion soup mix. Add the instant potatoes, mixing well. Heat the oil in a skillet or deep fryer. Salt and pepper the fillets, roll them in potato mix, dip in beaten egg, roll again in potato mix, and fry in oil at medium high heat until fillets are golden brown. Feeds 4 or 5.

Note: This batter burns quickly on high heat, so watch the fish closely.

Pan-Fried Jamaican Fish Steaks

Here's a good recipe for frying fish that are large enough to cut into steaks instead of filleting. Steaks can be cut with a knife, but an electric slicer works best. If you've got a 20-pound grouper, catfish, or something similar, ask your butcher to steak it for you.

The Fish
   2 pounds fish steaks, 1 inch thick
   cooking oil
   flour
   salt and pepper
The Topping
   1 clove garlic, minced
   1 small onion, sliced in rings
   ½ medium green pepper, sliced in rings
   ½ medium red pepper, sliced in rings
   ⅛ teaspoon cayenne pepper

Heat about 2 tablespoons of oil in a large skillet. Salt and pepper the fish steaks, shake

Thick or Thin?

Many of the thick and fancy batters for frying fish are nice and crunchy. But all such recipes should be tested before you cook them for guests. If you are a little off in mixing or cooking a recipe, the batter may come off the fish or burn, or both. Also, thick batters, no matter how tasty and crunchy they may be, tend to hold more grease than a light coating of meal or flour.

them in flour, and brown them in the skillet, about 6 minutes on each side. Carefully put fish steaks on a serving platter.

Add a little more oil to the skillet, if needed, and sauté the garlic, onion, green pepper, and red pepper for 5 or 6 minutes. Sprinkle with cayenne. Stir-fry on high heat for 3 minutes. Spoon the vegetables onto the fish. Serve hot. Feeds 4 to 6.

Apalachicola Fry

In many parts of the rural South, using flour instead of fine-ground white cornmeal for frying fish would be simply out of the question. Unthinkable. Flour is for frying chicken. Period. But I have a booklet titled *How to Fish for Snook*, which sets forth a recipe called "Spicy Apalachicola." Astoundingly, it calls for flour. I would have felt better about this if the booklet had been called *How to Catch Snook* instead of *How to Fish for Snook*, but I tried the recipe anyway, and I can recommend it here with the following reservations:

First, let me say that snook don't often roam as far north as Apalachicola, which is a fishing village in the Big Bend area of Florida's Gulf Coastline—but I wouldn't argue that point. Second, I don't know as fact that anyone in Apalachicola actually uses flour instead of corn-meal. But I do know that if anyone in this area, and as far north as Wewahitchka, chooses to use flour when frying fish, then they will damn well do so! And if they want to fish for snook in Dead Lakes, they'll do that, too.

In any case, the following recipe is unusual for southern fare not only because of the flour but also because mustard is used in an offbeat manner. I tried it and hereby confess that it's good.

fish
1 chicken egg
1 tablespoon prepared mustard
salt
flour
cooking oil for deep frying

Rig for deep frying, heating the oil to 375 degrees. Whisk the egg, then stir in the mustard. Salt the fillets, dip them in egg and mustard mixture, roll them in flour, and fry them in hot oil.

Pickerel Fillets Doria

Here's a recipe out of Winnipeg, Manitoba, which was sent to me from Saskatoon, Saskatchewan, by a fisheries ecologist. Besides being good, it makes interesting use of garlic clove and cucumber.

This recipe doesn't deal with the tiny bones found in pickerel and other pikes. You may therefore want to substitute boneless fillets. Or bone the pickerel.

6 pickerel fillets
1 large chicken egg
2 tablespoons milk
3 ounces fine bread crumbs
2 tablespoons cooking oil
1½ ounces butter (divided)
1 clove garlic
3 cucumbers
2 tablespoons chopped parsley
salt and pepper
flour

Beat a large egg and whisk in the milk. Salt the fillets, shake in flour, dip into the beaten egg mixture, and roll in bread crumbs.

California Grunion

As a rule of thumb, lean fish are better for frying than fatty fish. But this doesn't always hold. The little California grunion, for example, is very fatty but is very good when fried.

Heat the cooking oil and ½ ounce of butter, then sauté the whole garlic clove until it browns. Discard the garlic and sauté the pickerel fillets, turning once, until they are browned on each side. Drain the fillets on absorbent paper, preferably brown bags.

While the fish are cooking, peel the cucumber and cut it into 2-inch segments. Then cut each piece lengthwise into quarters. Melt 1 ounce of butter in a skillet and sauté the cucumber until the pieces are tender. Season the cucumber with salt and pepper, then serve on a platter with the fried fish fillets. Sprinkle the fish and cucumber with chopped parsley. Feeds 6.

Note: I confess that I haven't gone full course on this recipe. I'll eat most anything, at least once, but I have four good reasons for not eating cucumber, even for testing purposes.

First, the stuff simply doesn't agree with me. If I eat cucumber even in a salad I suffer an aftertaste for days.

Second, my wife once served up some cucumber soup for my dinner, even though *I* was on no diet. Cucumber soup. That was fifteen years ago, come July, and I have to use every opportunity to remind her of the fact. Within six months of the cucumber soup event, she made ham sandwiches for lunch—but she "forgot" to put the meat in mine, and was none too generous with the mayonnaise. Maybe she was trying to tell me something, and I still puzzle on it from time to time. And I remember to eat no cucumber, raw or cooked, in soup, salad, or fish, whatsoever.

Third, far too many people call cucumbers "cukes," which, for some reason, grates on my nerves, along with cute TV reporters and Richard Simmons calling vegetables "veggies."

Fourth? I don't want to seem fussy, but . . . well, a good, well-seasoned, deeply blackened cast-iron skillet is the only thing I like to fry fish in. A man's frying pan is a personal thing, and, frankly, I don't want any cucumbers in mine.

Trout Almandine

If you're looking for an elegant but easy fish dish to prepare, get some very good white wine and cook trout amandine, a classic dish that was popular in early American restaurants. A number of variations of the basic recipe can be found in many cookbooks and magazines. Here's one of my favorites, made with small fish. It can also be made with fillets from larger fish and is delicious when made with fillets of walleye.

The Fish

    4 to 6 small trout, about 8 ounces each

    ¼ cup half and half or light cream

    ¼ cup flour

    2 tablespoons cooking oil

    2 tablespoons butter

    1 chicken egg

    salt and pepper

The Topping

    ¼ cup slivered almonds

    ¼ cup butter

    2 tablespoons lemon juice

Gut the trout, leaving the heads and tails on. Whisk the egg and stir in the cream. Heat the oil and butter in a skillet. Salt and pepper the trout, roll them in flour, then dip them in the egg mixture. Sauté them in medium hot oil until the fish is golden in color and flakes easily. Place the trout on a warm serving platter.

Quickly, melt ¼ cup of butter in a pan and brown the almonds. Remove from heat and stir in lemon juice. Pour mixture over fish and eat at once. Serves 2 or 3.

Too Big to Eat?

Once I had the pleasure of fishing for several days with the late Lew Childre, a genius of the international fishing tackle trade, at his camp on the lower Apalachicola River in Florida. We were expecting Lew's advertising executive, a manufacturing representative from Japan, a lure maker, and other VIPs of the angling world. We were to have fish to eat that night before getting down to business.

Lew and I were expected to catch the bass, and we set out before sunup. On the third cast, just as the sun was peeping through the Spanish moss in the cypress trees, Lew caught a nice largemouth. About 5 pounds. Looked like another great day. "He's too big, Lew," I said. "Throw him back and let's catch some smaller fish to eat."

Holding the fish by the lower lip, Lew lowered it gently back into the Apalachicola.

Well, we plugged the banks. We pulled spinnerbaits across the flats. We jigged the depths. We flipped into logjams. We pushed back into the sloughs. All morning we fished without a strike. Lew held silent during our lunch. After eating, he said he would take me to a secret hole or two if I would promise not to show them to Shag Shahid. I promised and we headed up the Apalachicola at full throttle. At Lew's honey holes, we fished worms, crankbaits, spoons, and spinnerbaits. We fished them deep. We fished them shallow. We fished them far and wide, fast and slow. At 3 P.M., we still hadn't had another strike. We hadn't even seen a fish. At about 4:30, however, I threw a deep running crankbait across a point where a creek entered the Apalachicola. Wham. I connected with an 8-pounder.

After we had the fish safely in the net, Lew said, "I don't care how big he is. We're not going to throw him back!"

Catfish Buddy Platt

Here's a good one, from a friend of mine, for cooking catfish with a little more pep:

    catfish fillets
    Louisiana hot sauce (or Tabasco sauce)
    fine white cornmeal
    peanut oil
    salt

Put the catfish fillets in a dish or bowl and shake hot sauce on them. Let sit for 6 or 8 hours, turning several times. Heat the oil in deep fryer. Salt the fillets, then shake them in fine-ground cornmeal. (Note that the fish is not dipped in egg or milk before mealing.) Fry in very hot oil until brown. Do not overcook. Drain.

Serve hot with fresh corn bread and lots of green salad.

Buddy says that shaking the fish in a mixture of half flour and half meal will make it look pretty, but he usually uses pure meal. He is of more firm opinion about using only fine-ground meal, saying that medium or coarse meal tends to come off the fish and collect in the bottom of the deep fryer.

2

BAKING FISH

I'll be honest about it. Some of the worst fish I have ever eaten was baked. Usually, such sorry fare was the result of a weekend angler catching a lunker fish and wanting to show it off, whole, at the dining table. This circumstance is entirely understandable, and of course a whole baked fish, even with the head on, can be delicious. But proceed with caution—and don't count on your lunker for Sunday dinner unless you or your chef has experience in baking whole stuffed fish. The bigger the fish, the greater the hazard. Unless you are quite experienced in baking whole fish, your best bet is to fillet the larger fish or otherwise cut it down to size. If you want stuffing, it's best to put it between fillets.

On the other hand, some species, such as bluefish, are traditionally baked in certain areas, and some of the best fish I have ever eaten was baked. This chapter includes recipes for whole stuffed fish as well as baked fillets, steaks, and other pieces. (Also see the fish roll recipes in the next chapter.)

One final note: If you are baking a large fish, insert a meat thermometer into the fish at the thickest point, being careful that the probe end doesn't touch bone. Bake until the internal temperature is 140 to 150 degrees. This will ensure that the fish is done enough to eat safely but not too done to be succulent.

Fillets and Mushrooms

This dish is quite good and can be cooked with almost any fish. I prefer rather lean fillets, such as walleye or black bass, skinned and boneless.

2 pounds fish fillets
12 ounces fresh mushrooms, sliced

½ cup grated cheese
1 cup heavy cream
¼ cup butter
2 tablespoons flour
2 tablespoons sherry
1 teaspoon prepared mustard
salt and pepper

Preheat the oven to 400 degrees. Melt the butter in a skillet and sauté the mushrooms. Add the sherry and mustard. Stir in the flour until smooth. Bring to heat, then turn to simmer. Slowly stir in the cream. Salt and pepper to taste. Stir in the cheese.

Arrange the fish fillets in a well-greased baking dish. Pour the sauce over the fish, then bake for 20 minutes, or until fish flakes easily when tested with a fork. Hot, buttered French bread and French-cut green beans go nicely with this dish. Feeds 4 to 6.

Baked Bluefish

Although the bluefish isn't as highly touted in the South, one of my favorite recipes for the fish has been adapted here from *The Official Louisiana Seafood & Wild Game Cookbook*. The measures call for a 4-pound bluefish. This is the weight of the fish before it is filleted. In my interpretation, the French bread crumbs are made by crumbling some French bread. The Louisiana book listed 1 tablespoon of cayenne, but I took the liberty of reducing this measure to 1 teaspoon. If you feel frisky and have guests who like hot stuff, increase the measure at will.

4-pound bluefish, filleted
2 or 3 cups French bread crumbs
2 cups chopped fresh parsley
2 cups chopped fresh sweet basil
½ cup grated Parmesan
½ cup olive oil
5 tablespoons minced fresh garlic
1 teaspoon cayenne pepper
1 teaspoon salt
lemon slices (for garnish)

Preheat the oven to 350 degrees. Grease a baking dish large enough to hold the two fillets side by side. Sprinkle the salt and cayenne evenly over the fish. Baste the fillets with the olive oil, then place them in the baking dish. Mix the remaining olive oil with the rest of the ingredients, and top the fillets with the mixture. Bake in the center of the oven for 20 to 25 minutes, or until the fish flakes easily when tested with a fork. Serve with lemon slices, rice, vegetables, and French bread.

Baking Tip

Fish baked whole with the skin on tend to curl up. The longer the fish, the more likely it is to curl badly. Gashing, or scoring, the skin will help prevent curling; this should be done crosswise, or diagonally to the backbone. Scoring can also help in basting the fish, but it will also permit more of the natural juices to escape. Do not gash the fish all the way to the backbone (unless you're trying to cook it quickly); simply cutting through the skin is what helps prevent curling.

Chipper Drum

Here's an easy-to-fix and easy-to-remember recipe that I adapted from information provided by the Gulf and South Atlantic Fisheries Development Foundation. It calls for drum, but any suitable white-fleshed fillets can be used.

2 pounds drum fillets, skinless
½ cup creamy Caesar salad dressing
1 cup crushed potato chips
½ cup shredded sharp cheddar cheese
salt and pepper

Preheat the oven to 500 degrees. Place individual fillets between sheets of waxed paper and pound them flat, to about ¼ inch thickness. Salt and pepper the fillets, then dip them in salad dressing. Place the fillets, skin side down, in a wide, shallow, well-greased baking dish or pan. (If you're cooking larger measures, don't overlap the fillets; if your baking pan isn't wide enough to accommodate all of the fillets, try the broiling pan without its rack.) Sprinkle the potato chips on each fillet, then sprinkle the cheese evenly over chips. Bake for 10 or 15 minutes, or until the fish flakes easily. If the cheese hasn't begun to melt and brown, bake a little longer—but watch closely. Then carefully lift each fillet with a spatula and place it, cheese side up, onto individual serving plates. Feeds 4 to 6.

Easy Fish and Shrimp

This dish is not only easy to prepare and cheap, but also very, very tasty. Most any sort of fresh or frozen fish will work, but I prefer mild, white-meat fillets. Flounder works nicely. So do channel and blue catfish.

2 pounds boneless fillets
1 can cream of shrimp soup (10¾-ounce size)
8 ounces fresh mushrooms, sliced
4 ounces cheddar cheese, shredded
salt and pepper
paprika
butter or margarine

Preheat the oven to 375 degrees. Place fish fillets in a flat casserole dish that has been heavily greased with butter. Season with salt and pepper (go easy on the salt). Add the mushrooms. Pour the soup over all and spread it out smoothly. Distribute the cheese atop the soup, then sprinkle with paprika. Bake for 40 minutes.

Feeds 4 to 6.

Butterflied Trout with Dill Cream

This excellent recipe, adapted from *Sunset* magazine, requires both baking and broiling. It is cooked primarily by baking, then browned under a broiler.

6 (6- to 8-inch) trout
½ cup whipping cream
¼ cup dry white wine (or regular strength chicken broth)
2 tablespoons lemon juice
2 teaspoons minced fresh dill
fresh dill or parsley (garnish)
butter
salt
white pepper
lemon wedges (garnish)

Preheat the oven to 350 degrees. Arrange the trout in a 12-by-18-inch baking pan, well greased with butter. Sprinkle the fish with dill. Season with salt and pepper. Drizzle the wine (or chicken broth) and lemon juice over the fish. Put a sheet of aluminum foil loosely over pan and bake for about 15 minutes.

While the fish is baking, beat the whipping cream until it holds a peak. Take the fish out of the oven, then heat the broiler. Spoon the cream equally on each fish, put the fish back in the oven, and broil 2 inches from heat for about 3 minutes, or until the cream browns lightly.

Carefully transfer the fish to a warm platter. Garnish with lemon wedges and parsley, or with fresh dill. Feeds 6.

Creole Fish Fillets

In this recipe, fillets from mild-tasting fish such as flounder, channel catfish, smallmouth bass, or walleye are recommended.

Oven Frying?

There is much confusion of cooking terms, and even a simple concept like frying is not without misunderstanding, as for example the difference between a skillet and a griddle. "Oven frying" was not covered in the chapter about fried fish simply because I believe that anything cooked by this method is baked, not fried. But the term is widely used, and the results can be quite tasty.

The trick is to work with good fillets. Dip them in milk, salt and pepper to taste, and coat heavily with dry bread crumbs, cracker crumbs, crushed corn flakes, or some such dry ingredient. Then baste the fish with melted butter and put it into a 500-degree oven for 10 minutes or so, until the fish flakes easily when tested with a fork. If everything works right, the butter-basted batter will also absorb the juices from the fish and will be a golden brown color and nicely crisp when it is done.

Try the method—but don't call the result fried!

The Fish
    2 pounds boneless fillets
    1 medium onion, thinly sliced
    ¼ stick margarine
    salt and pepper
    several sprigs fresh parsley (garnish)
The Sauce
    ½ cup mayonnaise
    ¼ cup Creole mustard (or Dijon)
    ¼ cup sauterne
    ½ teaspoon Tabasco sauce

Preheat the oven to 300 degrees. Put the fish in an ovenproof shallow Pyrex serving dish, well greased. Sprinkle with salt and pepper. Cover with onion slices. Melt margarine, then pour it over the onions and fillets. Bake for 20 minutes.

While the fish is baking, make a sauce by mixing the mayonnaise, mustard, Tabasco sauce, and sauterne. After fish has cooked for 20 minutes, remove dish from oven. Heat the broiler. Cover the fish with the sauce, then put the dish under the broiler for a few minutes—just long enough to brown the top. Garnish with parsley. Feeds 4 to 6.

Baked Minted Trout

Here's a dish that I adapted from material sent to me by the New Hampshire Fish and Game Department:

    4 to 6 trout
    ½ cup milk
    ½ cup flour
    ½ cup fine bread crumbs
    ¼ cup melted butter
    ¼ teaspoon dried mint
    salt and pepper

Preheat the oven to 450 degrees. Melt the butter, stir in the dried mint, and let steep. Salt and pepper the fillets, dip them in milk, roll in flour, dip again in milk, roll in bread crumbs, and put carefully into a well-greased baking dish. Baste with minted butter. Bake for 10 to 12 minutes, or until the fish flakes easily when tested with a fork. Feeds 4 to 6.

Barbecued Fish Steaks

    2 pounds fish steaks (or fillets)
    ½ cup catsup
    ½ cup chili sauce
    ½ cup finely chopped onion
    ⅓ cup cooking oil
    2 tablespoons red wine vinegar
    2 tablespoons brown sugar
    1 tablespoon Worcestershire sauce
    1 clove garlic, minced
    ½ teaspoon Tabasco sauce
    salt and pepper

Preheat the oven to 350 degrees. Heat the oil in a skillet. Sauté the onion and garlic. Add the other ingredients, except for the fish, and simmer for 20 minutes. Grease a baking pan and place the fish steaks into it. Pour the sauce over the fish, then bake for about 20 minutes, or until fish flakes easily when tested with a fork. Serve with the sauce from the baking pan, steamed rice, and vegetables. Feeds 4 to 6.

Fish with Horseradish and Sour Cream

If you want something different for your fish fillets and have access to fresh horseradish, try the following dish. It's a Russian recipe that I

Bluefish

The bluefish has a dual reputation. Many folks in the Northeast rate it as purely excellent, whereas many folks in the Southeast treat it as a trash fish. The fish is high in oil content and has a rather dark meat. It is usually baked, broiled, or grilled.

adapted from *Uncommon Fruits & Vegetables: A Common Sense Guide*, by Elizabeth Schneider.

2 firm fish fillets, about ½ pound each
3 tablespoons sour cream
2½ tablespoons finely grated fresh
  horseradish
1 tablespoon lemon juice
1 teaspoon softened butter
salt and pepper

Adjust the rack in the oven so that the dish will be baked in the upper one-third section, then preheat the oven to 425 degrees. Select a baking dish that will hold the fish fillets rather tightly without overlapping. (The dish should also be suitable for serving.) Butter the baking dish and put the fillets into it.

Sprinkle the fillets with lemon juice, then rub with softened butter. Salt and pepper the fillets, then sprinkle evenly with the grated horseradish. Divide the sour cream equally for each fillet, then spread it to coat fillets.

Bake for 15 minutes, or until fish flakes easily when tested with a fork. Do not overcook. Serve with salad and vegetables. Feeds 2.

Fish Jekyll Island

Once I was a sort of editor at *Southern Living* magazine, which published lots of articles and books about foods. One of the best things that I got from that outfit was a recipe called Shrimp Dejonghe, which apparently came from Jekyll Island.

After leaving the magazine and taking a fling at free-lance writing, I got married and quickly had a family. Seldom did I have money to spare for shrimp, but during this good time I caught and ate more fish than I care to admit and therefore modified the recipe somewhat. Here goes:

2 pounds skinless fish fillets
1 cup soft bread crumbs
½ cup of butter
¼ cup sherry
1 tablespoon chopped parsley
2 cloves garlic, minced
salt
⅛ teaspoon cayenne pepper

Preheat the oven to 375 degrees. Cut the fillets into chunks about the size of shrimp, and put them into a well-greased casserole dish. Melt the butter. Mix butter with remaining ingredients, and spread the mixture over the fish. Bake for 20 minutes. When done, the topping should be a little brown, and fish should flake easily. Feeds 4 or 5.

Stuffed Fish with Almond Butter Sauce

Here's a recipe for stuffed fish that's hard to beat. Try it with smallmouth or largemouth bass, lake trout, or a mild saltwater fish, such as red snapper, which is especially good when baked whole.

The Fish
    4 or 5 pound bass or other good fish
    1 tablespoon butter
    salt
The Stuffing
    8 ounces fresh mushrooms, sliced
    1 medium onion, minced
    3 cups soft bread crumbs
    ½ cup butter
    ¼ cup slivered almonds, toasted
    juice of 1 lemon
    ¼ teaspoon celery seed
    salt and pepper
The Sauce
    ½ cup butter
    ¼ cup slivered almonds, toasted
    juice of 1 lemon

Clean the fish, leaving it whole (head on or off) for stuffing. Preheat oven to 425 degrees. To make the stuffing, melt ½ cup of butter in a skillet. Sauté the mushrooms and onions. Stir in remaining ingredients.

Spoon about 1 cup of this stuffing mixture into fish cavity. Put the stuffed fish into a well-greased baking pan of suitable size. Dot the fish with 1 tablespoon of butter and sprinkle with salt. Place the baking pan in the oven. Put the rest of the stuffing in a separate casserole dish and cook it along with the fish. Bake for about 25 minutes.

To make the sauce, melt ½ cup of butter in a small pan. Stir in the slivered almonds and lemon juice. Heat but do not boil. Pour the sauce over the fish just before eating. Feeds 4 to 6.

Huachinango Acapulco

One of my favorite fish dishes comes from south of the border. It's a fine dish for red snapper, black bass, or sea bass. The ingredients call for chili peppers. For best results, these should be about 4 inches long and mildly hot. The tiny peppers are far too hot for comfort and don't provide enough bulk.

    red snapper or other fish, about 5 pounds,
        head on
    ½ cup melted butter
    2 medium-large white onions, sliced
    2 medium-large tomatoes
    2 fresh red chili peppers
    2 fresh green chili peppers
    1 lemon or lime
    1 cup white wine
    ½ cup red wine
    salt and pepper

Scale and gut the fish, then sprinkle it inside and out with salt and pepper. Preheat the oven to 400 degrees. Peel and quarter the tomatoes. Seed and slice the chili peppers lengthwise. Grease a Pyrex or similar baking pan with part of the butter. Put the rest of the butter into the pan. Cover the bottom of the pan with pepper slices, then put a layer of sliced onions over the pepper. Place the fish on the onions. Squeeze the juice of a lemon or lime over the fish. Place the tomato quarters over the fish. Add both kinds of wine. Tear off a sheet of aluminum foil, grease the dull side of it with butter, and place it, butter side down, over the fish.

Bake for 15 minutes. Remove the aluminum foil, spoon some of the pan juice over the fish and tomatoes, and bake for another 15 minutes, or until the fish is done, basting from time to time. Carefully transfer the fish to a serving platter, then top it with onions, peppers, and pan drippings. The pan drippings have a wonderful flavor and are excellent when served over rice. Feeds 6 nicely.

Fiskgratin with Crawfish Sauce

This dish was developed by the Scandinavians over the years, probably using cod or some other cold-water ocean fish with freshwater crawfish. The sauce can also be made with a few shrimp—frozen, fresh, or canned—if you can't catch any crawfish.

The Fish
   2 pounds fish fillets
   3 cups mashed potatoes (seasoned to taste
      and rather stiff)
   ½ cup shredded Swiss cheese
   2 tablespoons melted butter
   1 teaspoon salt
   ½ teaspoon dill
   paprika
The Sauce
   1 cup crawfish tails, minced
   ¼ cup minced onion
   2 tablespoons butter
   2 tablespoons flour
   ½ teaspoon salt
   milk as needed to thin sauce
   2 chicken egg yolks, beaten
   1 tablespoon lemon juice
   ½ teaspoon dill weed

Preheat the oven to 425 degrees. Arrange the fish in a large, shallow baking dish or on an ovenproof platter. Sprinkle the fish with salt and dill weed. Cover the fillets with aluminum foil. Bake for 10 minutes. Take the dish out of the oven. Remove the aluminum foil, tilt the dish a little toward one corner, and spoon out any liquid that may have collected. Spoon 6 large dollops of mashed potatoes into each end of the dish. Drizzle the melted butter over the fish and potatoes. Return the dish, uncovered, to the oven for 10 minutes, or until fish flakes easily when tested with a fork. Sprinkle cheese and paprika over the potatoes, then return to the oven long enough for the cheese to melt.

To make the sauce, sauté the minced crawfish tails for 4 or 5 minutes in butter. Add the onion and cook until tender. Stir in the flour and salt. Add milk a little at a time, stirring constantly until the sauce thickens. Beat the egg yolks in a bowl. Add a small amount of the hot sauce to the egg yolks, stir, then add the yolks to the rest of the sauce, beating constantly. Add the crawfish, onions, lemon juice, and dill weed. Stir. Pour part of the sauce over the fish fillets, and put the rest into a serving dish. Feeds 4 or 5.

Fish Jambalaya Casserole

   2 cups cubed fish (skinless and boneless)
   1 cup cubed cured ham (precooked, prefer-
      ably baked)
   2 strips thin-sliced bacon
   2½ cups diced tomatoes (peeled)
   ½ cup chopped green pepper
   ½ cup chopped onion
   ½ clove garlic, finely chopped
   ¼ cup Italian bread crumbs
   ¼ cup Parmesan cheese, grated
   2 tablespoons melted butter
   2 tablespoons flour
   5 ounces extrathin spaghetti

Break the spaghetti in half, then cook it in salted water, following the directions on the package. Drain and rinse in cold water. Preheat the oven to 300 degrees. Cook the bacon in a large skillet; set aside. In the bacon drippings, cook the onion, garlic, and green pepper until the onions start to brown. Add the tomatoes. Stir in the flour. Cook and stir until the mixture thickens. Mix in a casserole dish with the ham, crumbled bacon, fish, and cooked spaghetti. Mix together the bread crumbs, cheese, and butter, then top the casserole with this mixture. Bake for 35 minutes. Feeds 5 or 6.

Microwave Fillets with Orange Sauce

I'm not too fond of microwave cookery, except for warming stuff up quickly. There are other opinions, however, and people interested in quick cooking ought to take a look at Paula J. Del Giudice's *Microwave Game & Fish Cookbook*, published by Stackpole Books. In any case, fish fillets are one of the easiest things to cook in a microwave.

  2 pounds fish fillets
  2 tablespoons frozen orange juice
    concentrate
  2 tablespoons soy sauce
  juice of 1 lemon
  1 tablespoon catsup
  2 cloves of garlic, mashed
  salt and pepper

Salt and pepper the fish fillets, then let them stand for a few minutes. Mix the orange juice concentrate, soy sauce, lemon juice, catsup, and garlic. Arrange the fish in a microwave-safe 7-by-12-inch glass baking dish, platter, or other

Muskellunge

The muskie can make good eating, especially when it is baked or broiled. Usually, fish of 10 pounds or less are considered to be better than larger ones. These fish are quite bony, so be careful, especially if you put the fish into a stew or chowder.

container suitable for serving. Pour the sauce over the fish and roll fish around, making sure that both sides are covered with sauce. Cover dish with plastic wrap. Microwave on high for 6 minutes, then test the fillets with a fork. If it doesn't flake easily, microwave on high for another 2 minutes. Let the fish stand for a few minutes, leaving plastic wrap over the dish, before serving. Feeds 4.

Easy Microwave Fillets

  2 pounds fish fillets, boneless
  2 tablespoons yogurt
  1 tablespoon prepared mustard
  ¼ teaspoon black pepper

Grease a wide, shallow, microwave-safe pan. Arrange the fish in it, preferably in a single layer. Mix the yogurt, mustard, and pepper, and spread the sauce over the fish. Cover with plastic wrap. Microwave on high for 8 minutes. Let stand, covered with the wrap, for 5 minutes. Feeds 4.

Dillpout (Microwaved or Baked)

I found this unusual dish in a booklet called *Eelpout (Burbot): The Fish Minnesotans Love to Hate*. It is quite good, and my wife is especially fond of the sauce. It calls for eelpout, but most any good fish can be used.

> 1 to 2 pounds eelpout fillets
> ¼ cup sour cream
> ¼ cup butter or margarine
> 1 teaspoon dill weed

Melt the butter in a small saucepan, then mix in the sour cream and dill weed. Arrange the fish fillets in a microwave-safe baking dish, placing the thicker edges and the larger pieces toward the outside of the dish, and overlapping thinner portions of the fillets so that the thickness will be more uniform. Pour the sour cream mixture over the fillets. Cover the dish with plastic wrap, piercing it to let out steam. Microwave the fish on high for 7 or 8 minutes.

If you prefer a regular oven, as I do, wrap the dish with aluminum foil and bake for 25 to 30 minutes at 350 degrees.

Feeds 2 to 4.

Fillets en Papillot

I've eaten a number of fish cooked in a paper sack and called some fancy name. But the best dish of this sort I've ever eaten wasn't in a New Orleans restaurant. It was cooked in my own oven, in a plastic baking bag. I agree that the brown paper or "parchment" might add a touch of quaintness, or something, for the sophisticate, but I've always been afraid that the things would catch on fire in the oven. Also, I've read that brown bags made from recycled paper can give off chemical tastes and might catch on fire.) In any case, the plastic baking bags available at any good supermarket will do just fine for this dish.

> 3 pounds good fish fillets, skinless
> ¼ cup melted butter
> 2 small bell peppers, cored and sliced into rings
> 2 medium onions, sliced into rings
> juice from 1 lemon
> salt and black pepper
> paprika (optional)
> lemon wedges (garnish)

Preheat the oven to 375 degrees. Baste the fillets with about half the melted butter mixed with about half the lemon juice, and sprinkle with salt and pepper. Put a plastic baking bag into an ovenproof dish or pan. Put the onion and pepper rings into the baking bag and then pour in the remaining lemon juice and melted butter. Carefully place the fish fillets on top of the vegetables. Close the bag and punch a few holes into it, following the directions on the package. Bake for 30 minutes.

The easiest way to serve this dish is to leave the bag in the baking dish. Slit the bag, then serve directly onto plates, sprinkling with paprika. Or carefully remove the fillets, arrange them on a platter, sprinkle with paprika, and put the vegetables around them. Garnish with lemon wedges. Feeds 5 or 6.

3

ROLL YOUR OWN

Once my wife and I lived in a little red-roofed house beside a blue water lake in Florida. It was in a rural area, a true fried-fish, grits, and watermelon place, on the outskirts of the Big Scrub. Our neighbor happened to come in one day while I was beating bass fillets on the kitchen counter. She dropped whatever she was chattering about and watched me, as though she had now seen everything.

"We roll them and bake them," my wife said, as though an explanation were necessary. "When they are flattened, they are easier to stuff."

"It also changes the texture," I said. "Makes the meat firmer."

The woman's silence said everything.

"You really ought to try it," my wife said, knowing full well that she wouldn't. But she *should*.

"What do you stuff them *with?*" the woman asked.

"With whatever you think will be good," my wife said. "We try all sorts of things."

"All sorts of things, huh?" the woman said, no doubt recalling some of my experiments with fish liver, pickled golden shiner, smoked spotted gar, prickly pear petals, and so on.

It's true. We used whatever sounded good and happened to be on hand. Often, we had

Grouper

There are a number of fish in the grouper family, most of which are purely excellent eating. They are medium low in oil content and have firm, white, mild flesh. Some of the groupers have bitter skin, however, so skin them. The groupers can be cooked in any style.

four or five kinds of stuffing at one meal, so that everybody got to try different ones. It was fun, and the kids loved it. I still feel that it is best to use your own imagination for fish rolls, simply because you'll enjoy it more that way.

In Florida, we normally used small bass about 12 inches long, but any mild flavored fish, such as walleye, will do.

Rolled Fillets

Place a skinned fillet on a piece of waxed paper on a smooth, solid surface such as a large wooden chopping block or your kitchen coun-tertop. Place another piece of waxed paper over the fillet. With a large wooden mallet, start pounding in the middle of the fillet and work toward either end. Pound the fillets until they are about ¼ to ½ inch thick. Proceed easily at first and lift the waxed paper after a few strokes to see how you are doing. After you've beaten half a dozen or so, you'll get the hang of it. If you don't have a wooden mallet, use a 2-by-4-foot board and a hammer. Cover the fillet with a sheet of waxed paper. Place the board firmly over the fillet, then pound the board with the hammer. After you've beaten all the fillets, set them aside. As a rule, allow at lease ¼ pound of fish fillets per person when the stuffing calls for

White Suckers and the Redhorse

I was brought up eating a little white sucker from small streams, and, when fried by ordinary methods, they were very tasty—once you got past the bones. I still rate them very, very good as table fare. Yet, I've read in other books that they are mushy and have no flavor! We also ate the larger redhorse sucker, and it too was good.

At the same time, local people used to almost spit out the words "pond sucker" as if it had a bad taste. I don't think I ever ate a pond sucker, and I'm not sure what they are. I bring the matter up in order to suggest that the sucker's habitat might well have a bearing on its flavor. The ones I eat come from cool streams in the fall, winter, or early spring. In fall or winter, the suckers are baited in holes and caught with hook and line. It's hard to tell when you're getting a bite, but you sure know it when you hang into one. In spring, the suckers are taken at night with net, seine, traps, or gig in shoal areas of small streams, where they spawn. In some sections of the country, a lot of people consider the spring sucker run just as much a part of the sportsman's calendar as the early fall dove season. A town in Missouri even has a spring festival in honor of the sucker run!

Many people call the sucker, especially the redhorse, "buffalo fish." There are dozens of species of such fish, and all of them are in the sucker family. The big-mouth buffalo has a rather good reputation in the Midwest as table fare, but, unfortunately, it is seldom taken on hook and line.

American Grayling

The American grayling has firm, white flesh of medium oil content. This fine fish can be cooked by any method.

other meat, and from ⅓ to ½ pound of fillets per person when the stuffing contains no other meat.

Preheat oven to 350 degrees. Mix the stuffing. Salt and pepper the fillets, then spread the stuffing evenly over each fillet. Roll each one carefully and pin with toothpicks. Put the rolls into a greased baking dish and bake for about 30 minutes.

In all the recipes in this chapter, you can put any remaining stuffing on top of the fillet rolls. If you stand the rolls on end, you can form a cup in the top and use this cavity to hold additional stuffing, or fill it, after cooking, with a topping such as sour cream. If you want to form a cup, start rolling from the small end of the fillet toward the big end. Try whatever topping sounds good with a particular stuffing. You can use the juices and drippings left in the baking dish either as a basting sauce or thickened into a gravy.

Italian Stuffing

1 cup ground beef, venison, or turtle
6 tablespoons spaghetti sauce
6 teaspoons finely chopped fresh
    mushrooms
Parmesan cheese

Brown the ground meat in a skillet. Cover 6 small fillets with the ground meat, spreading evenly. Put 1 tablespoon of spaghetti sauce and 1 teaspoon of finely chopped mushrooms over each fillet, and sprinkle with Parmesan cheese. Feeds 6.

Crab Stuffing

½ pound crabmeat
1 cup dry bread crumbs
¼ cup butter
2 tablespoons minced onion
1 tablespoon minced bell pepper
1 tablespoon minced celery
2 beaten chicken eggs
1 garlic clove, minced
1 teaspoon chopped parsley
salt and pepper to taste
1 lemon (garnish)

Snappers

The red snapper has a very good reputation as table fare, owing in part to its pretty red-orange skin. But the other snappers, such as the smaller mutton snapper and the larger black snapper, are also quite good. All of the snappers have a medium low oil content and can be cooked by most any reasonable method. They have rather meaty throats and heads, which can be used in soups and chowders.

Snook

There are several types of snooks, all of which are very good fish of medium oil content. They can be cooked by any method. Some varieties should be skinned instead of scaled.

Sauté the onion, celery, garlic, and bell pepper in butter until tender. Stir in the parsley, bread crumbs, eggs, salt, and pepper. Spread evenly over the fillets for rolling. Makes enough stuffing for 8 to 10 small fillets. Garnish with lemon wedges or slices.

Vegetable Stuffing

6 tablespoons chopped tomato
6 tablespoons chopped onion
6 tablespoons chopped mushrooms
6 teaspoons minced bell pepper

Put 1 tablespoon each of tomato, onion, and mushrooms on each fillet, then add 1 teaspoon of minced bell pepper. Or you can mix all the vegetables together and spread evenly. Makes enough stuffing for 6 small fillets.

Cream Cheese and Onion Soup Mix

3 ounces cream cheese
1 envelope onion soup mix (1.4-ounce size)
1 tablespoon finely chopped parsley
salt and pepper to taste

Mix all ingredients and spread evenly over fillets for rolling. Makes enough stuffing for 4 small fillets.

Variation: After stuffing, dip the fillet rolls into beaten eggs, then roll in bread crumbs or crushed cereal, drizzle with melted butter, and bake as usual. Watch closely so that the crumbs don't get too brown.

Tomato Paste Spread

tomato paste
Italian bread crumbs

Spread the tomato paste evenly over fillets, sprinkle with Italian bread crumbs, then roll.

Variation: Wrap a strip of thin bacon around each fillet roll and pin with a toothpick. Bake as usual, or until the bacon is brown and crisp.

Fried Green Tomato Stuffing

I'm fond of fried green tomatoes, and one of my favorite dishes is fillet rolls stuffed with fried green tomato slices.

green tomatoes
cooking oil
salt and pepper

Slice the green tomatoes thinly (about ¼ inch) and fry in hot oil until brown. Place fried tomatoes on fillets, sprinkle with salt and pepper, and roll as usual.

Variation: Wrap a slice of thin bacon around each fillet roll and pin with a toothpick. Bake as usual, or until bacon is brown and crisp.

Ham and Cheese Stuffing

thinly sliced pieces of boiled ham
grated cheddar cheese

Cover each fillet with a thin slice of ham
and sprinkle with grated cheese. One teaspoon
of cheese for each fillet will be about right.

Mushroom Stuffing

1 cup bass flakes (precooked or leftovers)
1 cup chopped mushrooms
1/3 cup milk
1 tablespoon flour
1 tablespoon parsley flakes
1/2 teaspoon dry mustard
1/2 teaspoon Worcestershire sauce
1 chicken egg, beaten
butter

Sauté the mushrooms and parsley in butter
for about 10 minutes. Mix in the fish flakes.
Add the milk and egg, then stir in all other
ingredients. Spread evenly over fillets. Makes
enough stuffing for 8 to 10 fillets.

White Perch

The white perch is often confused with
the white crappie, but they are in fact
two different fish. The white perch has
good white flesh, rather firm, and low in
oil content. It is rated very highly as
table fare. It thrives in the Northeast, on
down to Virginia, in both fresh and
brackish water.

Variation: If you want something a little
more impressive for company, try crabmeat or
chopped shrimp instead of bass flakes.

Asparagus Bundle

1 16-ounce can asparagus tips
1 can cream of celery soup (10¾-ounce
   size)
1 medium onion, minced
1 lemon
1 tablespoon Worcestershire sauce
Parmesan cheese
salt and pepper

The ingredients in this recipe are about right
for 5 or 6 fillets, but the stuffing procedure is a
little different from that used in the preceding
recipes. First, preheat the oven to 350 degrees.
Divide the asparagus heads into equal amounts,
making a bundle for each fillet. Roll a beaten
fillet around each bundle and place in an 8-by-
10-inch baking dish. Mix all other ingredients
and pour over the fillet and asparagus rolls.
Sprinkle liberally with Parmesan cheese. As in
the other recipes, bake for 30 minutes.

Variations: Try this recipe with cream
of mushroom soup or clam chowder. You can
also use tender French-cut beans instead of
asparagus.

Eggplant and Cream Cheese Stuffing

My wife has cooked some delicious batches of
bass rolls with eggplant stuffing, but unfortunately the recipes were not written down and
have escaped me. You might experiment with
any good eggplant puree stuffing or with thin

slices of fried eggplant. Or maybe with bundles of fried eggplant sticks. One reason that I forgot the recipes is that we quit experimenting when we came upon the following:

1 large eggplant
½ pound cream cheese (room temperature)
2 tablespoons finely chopped parsley
fine, dry bread crumbs
cooking oil

Preheat the oven to 350 degrees. Peel the eggplant and slice it to the thickness of your beaten fillets. Sprinkle the slices with salt and drain on absorbent paper for 20 or 30 minutes. Rinse and pat dry with absorbent paper.

Heat a little oil in a skillet and fry the eggplant slices until they are tender. Drain on absorbent paper.

Mash cream cheese with a fork and mix in parsley. Then spread cream cheese over fillets evenly, and top each fillet with one of the fried eggplant slices. Roll fillets in bread crumbs, put them into a suitable pan, and bake for 30 minutes.

This might well be my favorite fish dish!

4

FISH FLAKES

Once the IRS received an unsigned letter in which the writer confessed that he hadn't had a good night's sleep since cheating on his income tax some years earlier. "I'm enclosing $100 in cash money," he wrote. "If I still can't sleep, I'll send the balance."

I too have a guilty conscience, and I admit to midnight tossing and turning over the catch-and-release dilemma. On the one hand, I agree that anglers who release all of their catch of game fish, such as trout and bass, deserve some respect, and I would guess that most of them sleep soundly. On the other hand, I am inordinately fond of fresh fish and I find it difficult to fault myself or anyone else for keeping a few for the table. But, still, I suffer pangs of guilt whenever I slice the fillets off a fish and throw the rest away. On most fish, filleting leaves some meat that is very much worth getting. Besides being good, this bonus eating reduces

the grocery bill and helps eliminate the need for sleeping pills.

Scale the fish, gut it, and fillet it as usual. Set the fillets aside. Cut off the head. (Save that head as well as all the innards, putting them into the refrigerator or on ice for safekeeping.) Put what's left of the fish (backbone and ribs) into a pot and cover with water. Add 2 bay leaves. Bring the water to a boil and cook the fish for 6 or 8 minutes. Remove the fish from the water and drain. Flake the meat off the bones with a fork. The fish flakes can be refrigerated for use the next day or frozen for later use. Save the liquid to use as fish stock or fumet, in case you ever have time for French cooking.

After using some of the flaked fish in one of the recipes below, you will probably be able to sleep well enough. If not, get up in the middle of the night and boil the fish heads (keeping

31

the innards on ice). Flake off any meat you can find. Some fish, such as the red snapper and the largemouth bass, have quite a bit of meat on the throat, and larger fish also have a cheek of good size on either side of the head. Also, there is quite a bit of meat on the top of the head and in various cavities inside. The head meat is the best meat on the fish.

If you still can't sleep and feel up to further culinary adventures, you should know that still other parts of the head and innards are outright delicacies. Fishmongers usually keep these parts for themselves, but sportsmen who catch their own fish can also enjoy these unsung delicacies. Yet some people are a little queasy about such matters, and therefore I have decided to save the best parts for last. I hope that the recipes below and in the following chapters will sufficiently whet your appetite and inspire you to continue. If you can't wait, get the fish innards out of the refrigerator and go directly to chapter 10.

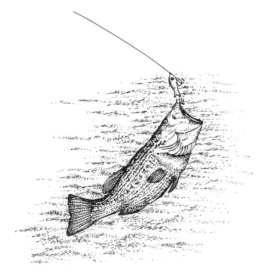

Easy Fish Patties

Here's a dish that I cook with fish flakes and either a griddle or a skillet. It's good in camp or at home, either as a light lunch or as part of a larger meal. The seasoned Italian bread crumbs are available in supermarkets. You can substitute ordinary dry bread crumbs, cracker crumbs, or a mixture of crumbs.

>2 cups cooked fish flakes
>1 cup seasoned Italian bread crumbs
>1 medium onion, minced
>2 large chicken eggs, whisked
>salt and pepper
>butter or margarine

Mix the fish, crumbs, onion, eggs, salt, and pepper. Shape handfuls of the mixture into patties about ¾ inch thick. Heat a little oil in a skillet or shallow griddle. Fry the patties until browned on both sides, turning once. The measures listed will serve 4 for a light lunch. Allow more for heavy eaters. I like these patties with sliced home-grown tomatoes and ice-cold green onions. Serve the green onions in a glass of ice water or on a platter of crushed ice.

Variations: Use regular bread crumbs and serve the patties with a thick sauce, such as Pickapepper or Chinese oyster sauce, or with ordinary American catsup.

Fish Patties with Sauce

Here's a dish that I like to cook for people who think they don't like fish. It works best with a mild, lean, white-fleshed fish.

Measures

A friend once asked me for a recipe for a fish flake and radish salad that I used to make (I've since lost the recipe). He commented later that it took too many fish to make a cup! I laughed, but his comments didn't quite sink in. At the time, most of my fish flakes were made from fish left from filleting. I didn't realize how much it takes to fill a cup until I went out on the lake to catch enough fish to fill a recipe. I quickly caught a 1-pound largemouth and I told myself that I could get off a cup and freeze the rest of it. Well, a fillet off the bass didn't even start to fill up the cup, and the second fillet came to the halfway mark. I took a fork and flaked the meat off the backbone, picked the ribs clean, and even got the meat off the head. Still, I came up a little short.

Exact yields per pound of fish are impossible simply because each kind of fish is different. I suspect also that the size of the fish will make a difference, in that the larger fish may have a higher average yield. Also, a cup of fish flakes can be loose or packed, with a considerable difference in weight. But, as a rule of thumb, you can figure on 1 cup of flakes per 1½ pounds of undressed fish. Also, 1 cup of fish flakes weighs from 6 to 8 ounces; therefore, 1 pound of boneless fillets should make at least 2 cups when flaked.

The Patties
    2 cups cooked fish flakes
    2 chicken eggs
    flour
    fine-ground white cornmeal
    1 teaspoon Worcestershire sauce
    peanut oil
    salt and pepper
The Sauce
    1 can tomato paste (6-ounce size)
    1 small onion, finely chopped
    ¼ cup vinegar
    ½ teaspoon Worcestershire sauce
    ¼ teaspoon Tabasco sauce
    salt and pepper
    water

Whisk the eggs, then mix with the fish flakes, along with the Worcestershire sauce. Stir in ⅓ cup of flour and ⅓ cup of cornmeal. Add salt and pepper and mix thoroughly. Form into patties. Mix together ½ cup of flour with ½ cup of cornmeal, then dredge patties in it. Heat about ½ inch of peanut oil in a large skillet. Fry the patties in hot oil on both sides until they are browned. Set aside to drain on absorbent paper.

To make the sauce, mix the tomato paste with 1 can of water in a small pan. Stir in the onion, vinegar, Worcestershire sauce, and Tabasco sauce. Bring to a quick boil, reduce heat, salt and pepper to taste, and simmer for a few minutes. Pour the sauce over the fish patties. Serve hot. Feeds 4.

Fish Flake Fritters

2 cups cooked fish flakes
1 chicken egg, lightly beaten
½ cup biscuit or pancake mix
1 tablespoon milk
1 onion, finely chopped
1 teaspoon Worcestershire sauce
cooking oil
salt and pepper

Mix the milk, egg, onion, Worcestershire sauce, salt, and pepper with the fish flakes. Thicken the mixture slowly with approximately ½ cup of biscuit or pancake mix until the mixture can be formed into patties. Fry in ½ inch of hot oil. Feeds 4.

Fillets with Whole-Thing Sauce

This dish, which calls for both fillets and flakes, is one of my favorites. Any mild fish can be used for this recipe, but I especially recommend black bass, walleye, or red snapper, in the 2-pound class.

2 pounds of boneless fish fillets
1 cup cooked fish flakes
8 green onions with part of tops
1 clove garlic, minced
1 cup half and half
1 cup grated cheddar (divided)
salt and pepper
butter

Heat a little butter in a saucepan. Chop the green onions with about half the tops. Sauté the onions and garlic in the butter for 3 or 4 minutes. Mash the fish flakes and add them to the saucepan. Cook on low heat for several minutes, stirring constantly. Reduce heat. Slowly stir in the half and half. Do not boil. Sprinkle on a little of the grated cheddar, stirring, until the sauce thickens. Remove the sauce from direct heat. Cover and keep it hot.

In a skillet, heat a little butter. Salt and pepper the fillets, then sauté them on one side for 4 minutes. Turn them and cook the other side for 3 minutes, or until the meat flakes easily when tested with a fork. Carefully remove the fillets and arrange them on plates or a serving platter. Sprinkle each fillet with grated cheddar, then pour the hot sauce over the cheese. Serve hot with French bread, salad, and vegetables.

Fish 'n' Eggs

Although I've probably cooked this dish a hundred ways, here's one of my standbys for breakfast or lunch:

2 cups cooked fish flakes
6 large chicken eggs
4 strips bacon
¼ cup finely chopped green onion with part of tops
salt and pepper

Fry the bacon in a skillet until crisp. Set aside until cool, then crumble. Sauté chopped green onion in the bacon drippings. Pour off excess bacon drippings. Lightly whisk the eggs in a bowl, then pour them into the skillet with the onions. Add the fish flakes and crumbled bacon. Stir over medium heat until the eggs set the way you like them. Salt and pepper to taste. Feeds 3 or 4 ordinary folks for breakfast—or 2 hungry anglers for lunch.

Griddle Omelet

Omelets are usually cooked in a special pan, but I am fond of this cheese omelet that is cooked in a flat 12-inch pancake griddle, first on top of the stove and then under the broiler. Here's how:

    4 chicken eggs
    1 cup cooked fish flakes
    1 strip bacon
    grated cheese
    salt and pepper

Adjust the oven rack so that it is very close to the heating unit, and preheat the broiler. Break the eggs into a bowl and whisk them lightly. Set aside. Heat the griddle on the stovetop and fry the strip of bacon until crisp. Crumble the bacon. Put the fish flakes onto the griddle and sauté them for 2 or 3 minutes. Add the eggs, stir with a spatula, and cook on low heat until eggs are partly set. Remove the griddle from stove top. Sprinkle the eggs lightly with the cheese, then put the griddle into the oven directly under the broiler. Broil until the cheese starts to soften. Sprinkle with crumbled bacon, then broil until the cheese browns on top.

Variations: These are infinite. Try other toppings such as chopped tomatoes or chopped onions on top of the eggs, with or without cheese.

Stuffed Tomatoes

This recipe will come in handy for a summer lunch, especially when you've got fresh tomatoes in the garden or from the local farmers' market.

    2 cups cooked fish flakes
    4 large vine-ripened tomatoes
    ¼ pound salt pork
    ½ cup finely chopped celery
    ¼ cup finely chopped mild onion
    1 tablespoon finely chopped parsley
    ½ cup mayonnaise
    Tabasco sauce

Cut the salt pork from the rind and dice the meat finely. Sauté the salt pork well in a frying pan, drain, and set aside. Core the tomatoes and chill. Mix the mayonnaise, onion, celery, parsley, fish flakes, and a little Tabasco sauce. Chill the mixture. When you are ready to serve, stuff the tomatoes with the fish flake mixture. Sprinkle each serving with salt pork bits. Place the stuffed tomatoes on lettuce leaves and serve with crackers.

Fish Flake Pie Littlejohn

Here's a good recipe that I adapted from *Coastal Carolina Cooking*. It was submitted to that publication by Frances Drane Inglis of Edenton, North Carolina, who says that it was passed down from one of her ancestors, Mary M. C. Littlejohn.

    1 whole fish, about 2½ pounds
    3 cups mashed potatoes (cooked)
    4 tablespoons butter
    6 tablespoons flour
    1 large chicken egg
    juice from ½ lemon
    1 heaping teaspoon anchovy paste
    salt and pepper
    3 cups water

Dress the fish, cut it up, and poach in water in a saucepan. Remove the fish to drain, retaining the liquid. Flake off the flesh with a fork. Put bones back into the saucepan, bring to a boil, and simmer in the liquid.

Melt the butter, add the flour, and mix well. Strain ¼ cup of fish stock from pan, add it to flour and butter, and stir until well mixed. Add the lemon juice, egg, anchovy paste, and fish. Salt and pepper to taste.

Preheat the oven to 350 degrees. In a deep 9-inch pie pan, spread half of the mashed pota-

toes (1½ cups). Spread fish mixture onto potatoes, then top with the rest of the mashed potatoes. Bake in the center of the oven for 20 minutes. I like to sprinkle the cooked pie with paprika, just for color, but the Outer Banks residents might not truck with this idea! Feeds 4 to 6.

Livingston's Favorite

This dish is very rich, but we like it as a main course together with a green salad and sourdough bread. It can also be served as a side dish, or with crackers as an appetizer. No matter how you serve it, you aren't likely to have any left over. If you do, freeze it for a rainy day. On one such rainy day, we served up a seafood dinner for some rather sophisticated international guests. Fearing that we wouldn't have enough food to feed everybody, I thawed and warmed up some leftovers of this dish. It took the menu honors away from such competition as stone crab claws! If you want to try it, here's what you need:

> 2 cups cooked fish flakes
> 1 large eggplant
> 1 bell pepper, chopped
> 2 medium onions, minced
> 2 medium tomatoes, peeled and diced
> 1 clove garlic, minced
> juice of 1 lemon
> 1 cup Italian bread crumbs
> Parmesan cheese
> salad oil
> salt and pepper

Peel the eggplant, wrap tightly in aluminum foil, and bake in preheated 400-degree oven for about 1 hour. While eggplant is cooling, pour a

℞ for Fish Bones

The time to look for fish bones is before a dish is cooked, and certainly before it is eaten. This is especially true of fish used in fish flake cookery. Anyone who is careful when dressing the fish and who understands where the trouble spots are with a particular species can take care of the bones.

But everybody who eats a lot of fish is likely to tangle with a bone or two at one time or another. Usually, this is not serious. I've never known anyone who had to be taken to a doctor because of a fish bone. But I'm sure it can happen, and having even a tiny bone stuck in your throat can scare the hell out of you. Usually, swallowing a large blob of bread will dislodge such a bone and it will go on down with the bread, where it is easily digested by stomach juices. But if two or three swallows of bread don't clear the bone, head for a doctor or the emergency room.

little salad oil in a skillet, heat, and sauté the pepper, onion, and garlic for about 10 minutes. Add the diced tomato and simmer for about 5 minutes. Transfer to a casserole dish of suitable size. Dice the eggplant and add to the other vegetables. Add ½ cup of the bread crumbs and the lemon juice. Stir carefully until the ingredients are mixed pretty well, adding salt and pepper to taste. Mix in the fish flakes. Baste with oil or melted butter, sprinkle with remaining bread crumbs, then sprinkle liberally with grated Parmesan cheese. Bake in 350-degree oven until the cheese begins to brown. Feeds 6 or 7.

Florida Hash

This old dish is best made with a large skillet (about 14 inches wide). With smaller pans, cook the measures below in two batches.

  2 cups cooked fish flakes
  4 cups diced potatoes
  1 cup chopped onion
  4 strips bacon
  1 teaspoon salt
  ½ teaspoon pepper
  ½ tablespoon vinegar

Dice enough peeled potatoes to yield 4 cups, boil until tender, drain, and set aside. Dice bacon and cook in a large skillet until it is almost done. Add the chopped onion, and cook until the onion and bacon start to brown. While bacon and onion cook, mix fish flakes, potatoes, salt, and pepper. Add to the skillet and spread evenly. Cook on medium heat until the bottom browns. Turn over and brown the other side.

Sprinkle lightly with vinegar and serve. This

Cod

Several kinds of cods and closely related fish are quite good, having lean, white meat. Although the fish is the source of cod liver oil, its flesh is quite low in oil content. Members of this family include Atlantic cod, Pacific cod, haddock, hakes, and freshwater burbot (also called ling).

dish goes nicely with a large salad or lots of sliced tomatoes. Serve for lunch or a light dinner. It also makes a hearty camp breakfast. Feeds 4 to 6.

Fish and Rice

  3 cups cooked fish flakes
  1 can tomatoes (16-ounce size)
  ½ cup grated cheese
  1 onion, chopped
  2 ribs celery, chopped
  ½ green bell pepper, chopped
  ½ red bell pepper, chopped
  rice (cooked separately)
  butter
  paprika
  salt and pepper

Preheat the oven to 350 degrees. Sauté the bell peppers, onion, and celery in butter. Mix in the fish flakes, cheese, tomatoes, salt, and pepper. Put the mixture into a well-greased casserole dish.

Bake for about 20 minutes, until the cheese has melted. Serve hot over rice. Sprinkle lightly with paprika. Feeds 5 or 6.

Fish Flake Casserole

Here's a tasty dish that I like to prepare when I've got only a modest amount of fish flakes.

    1 cup cooked fish flakes
    6 strips bacon
    1 large potato
    1 large tomato
    6 green onions with part of tops
    ½ cup plain yogurt
    Parmesan cheese, grated
    salt and pepper

Bring a little water to boil in a pan. Slice the potato into ¼-inch wheels and boil for 10 to 15 minutes, until tender. Fry the bacon and set it aside. Slice the tomato into ¼-inch pieces. Dice the green onions, including about half of the tops.

Preheat the oven to 400 degrees. Grease a shallow 8-by-10-inch casserole dish and place the potato slices in the bottom of it. Pour yogurt over the potato slices, then sprinkle evenly with fish flakes, onions, crumbled bacon, salt, and pepper. Cover with sliced tomato and sprinkle generously with cheese. Bake in the center of oven for 12 minutes.

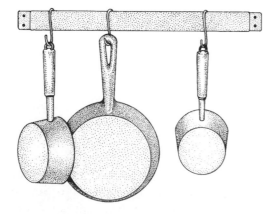

Serve with a spatula, maintaining the layered structure of the dish as much as possible.

Note: The measures in this recipe can be doubled or otherwise increased provided that a wider baking dish is used. For best results, do not overlap the potato slices on the bottom of the dish.

Sweet 'n' Sour Fish Balls

I usually make this dish with largemouth bass flakes, but any good fish with mild, flaky flesh will do nicely.

The Fish
    2 cups cooked fish flakes
    ½ cup peanut oil
    ½ cup water chestnuts, minced
    ¼ cup dry bread crumbs
    2 tablespoons soy sauce
    1 teaspoon ground ginger root
The Sauce
    1 can pineapple chunks and liquid
       (20-ounce size)
    1 bell pepper, diced
    ½ cup apple cider vinegar
    ¼ cup brown sugar
    2 tablespoons cornstarch

Heat the peanut oil in a large skillet. Mix fish, water chestnuts, bread crumbs, soy sauce, and ginger. Shape the mixture into about 25 small balls. Fry and stir the fish balls in hot oil until brown on all sides. Drain on absorbent paper (I use brown grocery bags).

To make the sauce, drain the pineapple juice and add enough water to make 1½ cups of liquid. Put the liquid into a large saucepan. Heat and add the vinegar, brown sugar, and cornstarch. Stir until well mixed and the liquid

Mako Shark

Low in oil content, the mako is highly regarded as table fare in some circles. Its flesh has a pleasant flavor and good texture. The fish can be cooked by most any method.

thickens. Add the pineapple chunks and green pepper. Stir and cook 6 or 7 minutes. Remove from the heat, then gently stir in fish balls. Serve over rice. Feeds 4 or 5.

Fish 'n' Potatoes

Anyone who likes baked potatoes will appreciate this one. Although it goes best as a side dish, I can make a light lunch of it, with a strip or two of bacon. It's a great way to use up leftovers.

cooked fish flakes
baked potatoes
cream or milk
chopped parsley
grated Cheddar cheese
salt and pepper

Bake the potatoes in the oven as usual. Then halve the potatoes lengthwise and scoop out the meat, being careful not to damage the skins. Mash the potato meat and mix with fish flakes, a little cream, salt, pepper, and parsley. Put the filling back into the potato skins. (Put any leftover filling in a small ovenproof bowl.) Sprinkle with grated cheddar. Broil close to the heat source until the cheddar melts.

Fish Spread

2 cups cooked fish flakes
3 tablespoons whipped margarine
$\frac{1}{3}$ cup grated onion
$\frac{1}{2}$ tablespoon white wine Worcestershire sauce
$\frac{1}{2}$ teaspoon celery salt
$\frac{1}{8}$ teaspoon cayenne pepper

In a bowl, mash the fish flakes and margarine together. Blend in the onion, white wine Worcestershire sauce, celery salt, and cayenne pepper. Be careful with the cayenne. Serve at room temperature as a dip or spread for chips or bread. Or refrigerate for several hours, slice, and eat on crackers.

Fish and Avocado Vinaigrette

My wife says this might be her favorite fish dish—and I don't argue. But I might add that we're both nuts about avocado.

2 large avocados
1 cup cooked fish flakes
6 slices thick bacon
$\frac{3}{4}$ cup chopped onion
juice from $\frac{1}{2}$ lemon
$\frac{1}{4}$ cup apple cider vinegar
1 teaspoon salt
$\frac{1}{4}$ teaspoon pepper
mayonnaise (optional)
paprika (optional)

Cook bacon in a skillet until well browned, remove, drain, and crumble. In 2 tablespoons of the bacon fat, sauté the onions for 5 minutes. Add the vinegar, crumbled bacon, lemon

Fish Flakes Save Freezer Space

If you've made a big catch and don't know quite what to do with all the fish, consider flaking and freezing. This quickly reduces a very large stringer into a few small packages. If you have a large batch, it's best to skin the fish, then boil or steam them until the flesh flakes easily. Cool the fish and flake off the meat with a fork.

I normally freeze fish flakes in units of 1 cup, because that amount seems to work in a lot of recipes. But units of 2 cups or more can be used, depending on your requirements. Just be sure to label the contents carefully. I like to use a Ziploc or similar zipper-close bag, simply because it's easy to use and freezes flat and very compactly. The key is to put the bag on a flat surface and smooth it out. Zip the bag closed, then open one corner and squeeze down on the bag, forcing out the air. I use a 7-by-4-inch bag that opens the long way.

juice, salt, and pepper. Cover and simmer for a few minutes. Gently mix in fish flakes.

Cut the avocados in half, remove the seeds, and scoop out meat in small chunks. Put equal amounts of avocado chunks in bowls, then spoon in the fish mixture. If desired, top with a tad of mayonnaise and sprinkle lightly with paprika.

Avocado Fish Dip

Anyone who likes guacamole dip will want to try this recipe. It can be made with leftover or freshly poached fish.

2 very ripe medium avocados
1 cup cooked fish flakes
juice of ½ lemon
¼ cup mayonnaise
1 tablespoon grated onion
⅛ teaspoon Tabasco sauce
salt to taste

Halve the avocados, remove the seeds, and spoon the meat into a bowl of suitable size. Add the fish flakes, lemon juice, mayonnaise, onion, Tabasco sauce, and a little salt. Mash and mix thoroughly. (Use a food processor if you wish.) Serve with crackers or chips.

Fish Flake Salad

2 cups cooked mild fish flakes
½ cup chopped celery (center pieces)
½ cup mayonnaise
½ cup finely chopped onion
2 tablespoons pickle relish
2 hard-boiled chicken eggs, chopped
salt
lettuce (optional)
paprika (optional)

Mix all ingredients except lettuce and paprika. Chill for several hours. Serve on lettuce leaves. Sprinkle with paprika.

I also like this dish, mixed with a little mayonnaise, as a spread for sandwiches on soft white bread. For best results, trim the crusty edges from the bread slices.

Easy Fish Chowder

1 cup cooked fish flakes
1 can condensed mushroom soup (10¾-
  ounce size)
1 soup can water
¼ cup finely chopped onions
a little butter
salt and pepper to taste

Sauté the onions for a few minutes in a little butter in a skillet. Put the condensed mushroom soup in a pan of suitable size, adding 1 can of water. Bring to heat but do not boil. Add the onions and butter. Stir in fish flakes. Salt and pepper to taste, then serve in bowls.

Variation: If you prefer a chowder with more of a seafood flavor, substitute canned clam chowder for the can of mushroom soup.

Kedgeree

Here's an old dish from the British Isles that was originally made with flaked salmon. It is one of my favorites, and I've made it with several kinds of fish, including leftover fried largemouth bass and smoked mullet.

2 cups cooked flaked fish
2 hard-boiled chicken eggs, chopped
¼ cup cream
1 tablespoon butter
1½ cups chopped onion
1 tablespoon chopped parsley
salt and pepper
1½ cups rice (cooked separately)

Cook the rice according to the directions on the package. Next, melt the butter in a skillet, then sauté the onion for a few minutes, until tender. Pour water into the bottom part of a double boiler, then put the onions, fish flakes, egg, parsley, and 1½ cups of cooked rice into the top part. Salt and pepper to taste. Bring to a boil. Add the cream, reduce heat, and stir. Cover and heat gently on low until the Kedgeree is hot. Serve immediately.

Fish Flake Loaf

This recipe is good with fish that are often called "coarse." Try steaming or poaching very fresh carp or buffalo fillets for about 10 minutes, then flaking the meat.

2 cups cooked fish flakes
½ cup bread crumbs
½ cup chopped celery with green tops
1 tablespoon chopped fresh parsley
1 medium to small onion, minced
juice of 1 lemon
1 cup whole milk
¼ cup butter
¼ cup flour
salt and pepper to taste

Sprinkle fish flakes with lemon juice. Preheat the oven to 350 degrees. Melt the butter in a skillet, then stir in the flour and milk with a wooden spoon; simmer and stir until the mixture thickens. Remove from heat, then add all the other ingredients. Pour out onto a smooth surface and form into a loaf. Place the loaf into a greased baking dish, then bake in the center of the oven for 30 minutes.

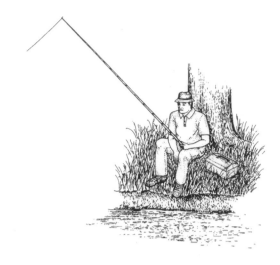

Fish Flake Soft Loaf

This recipe was a little difficult to name; it is not really firm enough to be called a loaf or gooey enough to be called a casserole. But it's mouth-watering. Try it—then call it whatever you like.

> 2 cups cooked fish flakes
> 16 crackers
> ¼ cup milk
> ¼ cup sauterne
> 1 tablespoon Worcestershire sauce
> garlic powder
> grated cheese
> melted butter
> salt and pepper to taste

Preheat the oven to 350 degrees. Roll or beat the crackers into fine crumbs. Mix the crumbs with ¼ cup of melted butter and the milk. Mix in fish flakes. Add the wine. Season with Worcestershire sauce, garlic powder, salt, and pepper. Form the mixture into a loaf in an oblong 1½-quart casserole dish. Pour 1 table-spoon of melted butter over loaf and top with grated cheese. Bake for 35 minutes. Feeds 4.

Fish Rolls

> 2 cups cooked fish flakes
> 1 medium onion, grated
> ½ bell pepper, grated
> biscuit mix
> milk
> salt and pepper

Mix the biscuit dough according to direc-tions on the package. Roll the dough to ¼ inch thick, forming an oval shape. Set aside. Preheat oven to 350 degrees. Mix the fish flakes, bell pepper, and onion with a little milk. Salt and pepper to taste. Spread the mixture evenly on a dough sheet. Roll together, forming a loaf. Cut the loaf every inch or so, but do not completely sever pieces. Bake on a well-greased pan for 15 to 20 minutes, or until the loaf is biscuit brown.

Note: I sometimes serve these fish rolls instead of regular bread with a fish casserole or similar dish. The loaf can also be topped with a mild cheese sauce or salsa.

5

BROILING FISH

Broiling is one of my favorite ways to cook fish, especially fatty species such as king mackerel. Usually, a fatty fish doesn't need much on it except a little salt to make a good meal. Lean fish, on the other hand, tend to be dry if broiled for very long, and these should be basted frequently with butter or sauce.

Like roasting and grilling, the term *broiling* has several meanings in cookery, depending on who you are talking to or what you are reading. In this book, to broil is to put fish or meat directly *under* the heat source. The best results are usually obtained by putting the meat or fish very close to the heat source, although there are some variations from one recipe to another. True broiling requires that the oven door be left open, so that the fish isn't baked as well as broiled. Broiling is by radiant heat; baking, by convective heat.

I usually prefer to broil fillets rather than whole fish, but this often presents a problem because tender fillets are difficult to turn over without breaking them apart. A double rack will work, and I sometimes use two small portable racks placed atop the main oven rack, with the fish sandwiched in between so that the entire unit can be flipped over. This chapter includes several recipes in which you won't have to turn the fish.

Broiled Crappie Fillets Paprika

This dish is half fried and half broiled. I cook it in a flat cast-iron skillet or griddle, using the stove top first, then switching to the broiler. By using this procedure, I avoid having to turn the fillets. It works nicely on delicate fillets, such as those from crappie.

Northern Shark

For many years, northern shark has been in high demand in Europe, especially Great Britain, where it is widely used in the traditional English fish 'n' chips. Northern shark has a white flesh containing some dark meat that provides a unique sweet, delicate flavor. Sharks do not have a skeletal structure, therefore there are no bones to contend with. Shark, when properly handled, gives off a slight ammonia odor because of a natural chemical occurrence. This odor dissipates during cooking; however, to remove the odor completely, you can marinate the shark in an acidic solution such as lemon juice or a vinegar-water solution. Northern shark is excellent for barbecuing, as the flesh will not fall apart.

—Nova Scotia Department of Fisheries

1 pound skinless fillets
1 tablespoons bacon drippings or butter
salt
paprika
lemon juice

Turn on the burner. Turn on the broiler. Brush fillets with bacon drippings or butter, then sprinkle with salt. Sauté them on one side on a flat griddle for 2 or 3 minutes (or less if griddle is hot to begin with). Then, without turning or moving the fillets, squeeze a little lemon juice on each fillet and sprinkle liberally with paprika. Put the whole griddle under the broiler very close to the heat source for 4 min-utes, or until the fish flakes easily when tested with a fork. Feeds 2.

Note: This technique will not work for large amounts of fish, unless you cook them in several batches. A similar method is to first heat a flat, well-greased broiling pan. Place the fillets in the pan, and quickly put the pan under the broiler, thus cooking both sides at once.

Marinated Shark Kabobs

Here's a recipe that I got from the Nova Scotia Department of Fisheries. It calls for northern shark, but amberjack or similar fish of rather firm flesh can be used, along with blackfin shark and others. The trick to shark cookery is to put the meat on ice as soon as it is caught. Some people remove the streak of dark meat that runs down either side, just under the skin, but this is not always necessary. As a rule, the key to the quality of shark is the presence of a strong ammonia smell.

1 pound northern shark fillets, cut into
    1-inch cubes
4 ounces fresh mushrooms
15 cherry tomatoes
$\frac{1}{2}$ cup lemon juice
$\frac{1}{2}$ cup vegetable oil
2 tablespoons chopped parsley
1 teaspoon dry mustard
1 clove garlic, minced
$\frac{1}{2}$ teaspoon salt
$\frac{1}{4}$ teaspoon pepper

Mix the oil, lemon juice, parsley, mustard, garlic, salt, and pepper in a large bowl. Stir. Add and toss the shark chunks. Refrigerate for 1 hour or longer. Just before cooking, add the mushrooms and tomatoes and toss.

Turn the oven broiler on, break out the kabob skewers, and grease a broiling rack. Place the rack so that kabobs will be 4 inches from the heat source. Drain the fish. Heat the marinade in a saucepan until it starts to boil, then turn off the heat. Make the kabobs by threading on a cherry tomato, a shark chunk, and a mushroom, in that order. Start and end with a cherry tomato. Broil 4 inches from the heat for 3 minutes. Baste. Broil 3 minutes. Baste and turn. Broil for another 3 minutes. Baste and broil for 2 more minutes, or until the fish flakes easily when tested with a fork. Feeds 2.

Mullet

The mullet is very high in iodine and mineral content. Usually, those mullet that are caught by sportsmen are taken with castnets, but more and more anglers are going for them with tiny bait and salmon egg hooks. Mullet should be dressed quickly and put on ice. Although they are high in oil content, fresh mullet are very good fried, broiled, grilled, or smoked. For best results, dress and ice down a mullet soon after catching it.

"If you plan to freeze mullet for more than a month," according to UNC Sea Grant, "remove the strip of dark meat that runs along the lateral line. You'll lose as much as a third of the meat, but it will be worth it because it will improve the taste of the meat when you pull it from the freezer. This dark meat is high in fatty acids, and it impairs freezer shelf life. The remaining white meat can be frozen for up to six months."

Broiled Fillets with Tangerine Sauce

Because I currently live in Alabama, it strikes me as being somewhat ironic that the following recipe from *Alabama Conservation,* a state publication, was sent to me from Florida! The Alabama people gave credit for the recipe to the National Marine Fisheries Service, Consumer Affairs Division. I don't know exactly who to thank, but I suspect that the Florida citrus folks had something to do with it. Anyhow, somebody, somewhere, came up with a good one, which (of course!) I have improved on somewhat.

The Fish
  2 pounds fillets
  2 tablespoons butter, melted
  2 tablespoons tangerine or orange juice
  ½ teaspoon salt
  ⅛ teaspoon pepper
The Sauce
  1 tangerine or orange, cut into chunks (see note below)
  ¼ cup butter
  1 cup tangerine or orange juice
  ½ cup sliced almonds
  ¼ cup white wine
  ¼ cup apple jelly
  ¼ cup lemon juice
  2 tablespoons cornstarch
  1 teaspoon grated tangerine or orange rind
  ¼ teaspoon Louisiana hot sauce (or Tabasco sauce)
  ⅛ teaspoon salt

Preheat the broiler. Combine the melted butter and tangerine juice. Place fish in a well-greased baking pan of suitable size. (The fillets

Rock Bass

The little rock bass gets excellent ratings in other books, but, frankly, I rate them as inferior to bluegill or black bass. The rock bass, and similar sunfish such as warmouth perch and Roanoke bass, are often called "goggle-eyes." In my opinion, they have a somewhat muddy flavor and are best when grilled.

should not overlap.) Brush the fish with butter and tangerine sauce, then sprinkle with salt and pepper. Broil 4 inches from the heat for 8 minutes, or until fish flakes easily when tested with a fork, depending on the thickness. Baste 2 or 3 times while cooking. Carefully remove the fillets, arranging them on a warm serving platter and keep warm while making the sauce.

To make the sauce, melt the butter in a saucepan. Sauté the almonds until they are browned a bit. In a bowl or other container, mix the cornstarch with ¼ cup of the tangerine juice; set aside. To the sautéed almonds, add the rest of the tangerine juice, wine, jelly, and lemon juice. Bring to a quick boil. Stir in the cornstarch mixture. Cook, stirring, until the mixture thickens. Reduce the heat. Stir in the hot sauce, salt, grated rind, and tangerine pieces. Remove the saucepan from the heat and serve sauce hot over the fish fillets. Feeds 4 to 6.

Note: Sections of orange or tangerine, cut into bite-size chunks, will be satisfactory in the recipe above. Neither the Alabama nor the Florida sharps mentioned it, but if you want the ultimate in flavor and texture, take the trouble to peel the thin skin off each section of the orange or tangerine. For peeling each section, I prefer to work with rather thick-skinned navel oranges.

Lemon Broiled Walleye

> walleye fillets, skinless (or other suitable fish)
> ½ cup melted butter
> ½ cup white wine Worcestershire sauce
> juice from 1 lemon
> salt and pepper

Preheat the broiler. Melt the butter in a saucepan, then stir in the lemon juice and white wine Worcestershire sauce. Salt and pepper fillets, arrange them on a broiling pan, and baste them with lemon sauce. Put the pan under the broiler, with the fish about 4 inches from the heat. Turn the fish after 4 minutes, and baste again with lemon sauce. Baste again after 2 or 3 minutes. The fish is done when it flakes easily with a fork.

Broiled White Perch Fillets

I developed this recipe with crappie, called "white perch" where I lived at the time. These fish yield a rather flat fillet about the size of a man's hand. The recipe would be good with any suitable mild fish, and it is especially suited for flatfish such as flounder. With long fish such as trout or bass, the recipe works better if you pound the fillet flat before cooking. Merely put the fillet between sheets of waxed paper and pound it with a mallet or the side of a heavy meat cleaver until it flattens to about ⅜ inch. Here's what you need:

boneless fillets
butter
garlic juice
Creole mustard (or Dijon)
salt
crackers

Preheat the broiler. For two small fillets, melt ¼ cup of butter in a small pan and add ¼ teaspoon garlic juice. (Increase the measures for more fish.) Swab a little of the butter onto the surface of a shallow skillet and cook fillets on medium high heat for 2 minutes. Transfer the fillets, without turning, to a piece of aluminum foil. Swab a little butter on each fillet, then sprinkle a little salt on top. Next, spread a tablespoon of Creole mustard on each fillet. Crumble 4 crackers into a saucer and pour the rest of the butter on them. Spread buttered crackers evenly on top of fillets.

Broil the fillets, close to heat source, for about 5 minutes, or until crackers are browned. Watch carefully so that crackers won't burn. It's not necessary to turn fillets because the bottom part was cooked in the skillet. When the fillets are browned on top, slide them off the aluminum foil directly onto the serving plate. (The aluminum foil facilitates handling the thin fillets without breaking them up.)

Paddlefish

Paddlefish are delicious and can be prepared in a variety of ways. When smoked, the meat is moist and delicious. Fried, it resembles catfish. The roe can be salted and dried for caviar, or fried in butter with a few minced shallots and served on toast.

To clean a paddlefish, hang it by the paddle, then cut the skin around the tail. Twist sharply on the tail to remove it, and pull out the attached notochord. Skin from the head down using pliers, then remove the entrails and head. The meat can be cut into fillets or steaks, but many people recommend trimming off the dark, reddish outer meat and using only the light-colored inner flesh.

—Keith Sutton in *Arkansas Game and Fish*, March-April 1987

Easy Broiled Bluefish

Some of the best recipes for fish are often quite simple. Here's one designed for bluefish fillets, but it's also good with other fillets or fish steaks:

2 pounds bluefish fillets
¼ cup butter
2 tablespoons Creole mustard (or Dijon)
juice of 1 lime
lime wedges (garnish)
salt and pepper

Dress and fillet the bluefish. Line a broiling pan of suitable size (it should hold the fish in a single layer) with aluminum foil. Preheat the broiler. Adjust the rack so that the fish will be 4 inches from the heat source. Grease the foil with a little butter. Salt and pepper fillets, then arrange them, skin side down, in the pan. Mix the melted butter with mustard and lime juice. Spread the mixture evenly over the fillets. Broil for 10 minutes, or until the fish flakes easily when tested with a fork. Baste several times with pan drippings. Serve hot, garnished with lime wedges. Feeds 4 to 6.

Saucy Parmesan Fillets

This dish should be made in a large skillet with an ovenproof handle.

2 pounds boneless fish fillets, skinned
1 can cream of shrimp soup (10¾-ounce size)
¼ cup sherry
¼ cup half and half
1 medium onion, diced
butter or margarine
salt and pepper
grated Parmesan cheese

In a saucepan, heat the shrimp soup. Stir in sherry and cream. Set aside. Turn on broiler so that it will be ready.

Heat butter in skillet, then sauté onion in butter or margarine. Add the fish fillets, sautéing for another 4 minutes. Sprinkle with salt and pepper. Pour in soup mixture. Sprinkle the top with cheese and put the skillet under the broiler for 5 or 6 minutes, or until the cheese is melted and fish flakes easily. Serves 4 to 6.

Mackerel

The king mackerel, the Spanish mackerel, the Pacific mackerel, chub mackerel, cero, sierra, and other mackerels are all high in oil content. They can be very good when broiled or grilled, but I do not recommend frying them. It's best to eat them fresh, simply because they do not freeze well. They have a smooth, finely scaled skin that should be scraped and washed.

Fish Lea & Perrins

If I could pronounce the name without twisting my tongue, I would no doubt give more word-of-mouth advertising for Worcestershire sauce. (A contributor to *The South Carolina Wildlife Cookbook,* Ben McC. Moise, called it "wurster sauce," and I confess, I sometimes resort to "rooser sauce" after having a drink or two.) In any case, I'm fond of the flavor, and the sauce goes nicely with some red-meat dishes. I was therefore excited in the local supermarket when a bottle of new white wine Worcestershire sauce caught my eye a few years back. Quickly I bought a bottle. Eagerly I tried their recipe for broiled fish. It's good stuff.

2 pounds boneless fish fillets
4 tablespoons white wine Worcestershire sauce
juice of 1 lime
salt and pepper

Salt and pepper the fillets. Combine the lime juice and white wine Worcestershire sauce. Broil the fish, basting frequently with sauce, until the flesh flakes easily with a fork. Do not overcook. Feeds 4 to 6.

Lemon–Glazed Lake Trout

The following recipe came from a booklet that was distributed by the Manitoba Export Corporation in Canada. Be sure to try it the next time you've got lake trout. Also, try it with catfish fillets.

    2 pounds lake trout fillets
    ¾ tablespoon prepared mustard
    juice of 1 large lemon
    ¼ teaspoon grated lemon rind
    ¼ cup brown sugar
    thin slices of lemon
    salt

Cut the fillets into serving-size pieces. Mix the mustard, lemon juice, lemon rind, and brown sugar. Marinate the fillets in the lemon mixture for half an hour. Preheat the broiler. Salt the fillets, place them on a greased rack within 3 or 4 inches from heat source, and baste with the sauce. Brown the fish on one side. Turn, baste heavily with the sauce, and brown. Top with thin lemon slices, then broil for another 2 minutes. Serve hot. Feeds 4 to 6.

Broiled Flatfish for Beginners

This recipe, at once simple and quite tasty, makes an excellent starter for people who haven't broiled fish before. Use fillets from a thin fish, such as flounder or crappie. The fillets for this dish should be no more than ½ inch thick so that they will cook through without having to be turned, which could tear them apart.

    flatfish fillets
    1 cup good mayonnaise
    1 tablespoon crushed dried dill weed
    ¼ cup minced onion
    1 teaspoon grated lemon peel
    salt and pepper
    paprika
    lemon wedges (garnish)

Several hours before cooking, mix the mayonnaise, dill weed, onion, and lemon peel. When you're ready to cook, preheat the broiler. Place the fish fillets on a well-greased oven-proof serving platter. Salt and pepper the fillets, then spread evenly with mayonnaise mixture. Broil very close to heat source for 4 or 5 minutes, or until the fish is browned on top, with the oven door open. If fish flakes easily when tested with a fork, take it out. If the fish isn't quite ready, turn off the broiler and close the oven door for a few minutes so that the fish will finish cooking. Sprinkle each serving with paprika and garnish with lemon wedges.

Northern Pike

The northern pike grows to be quite large, but those fish of under 6 pounds make the best table fare. Of medium oil content, the pike can be cooked by several methods. I recommend baking or broiling. These fish are quite bony.

Gulf Coast Trout Almandine

Along the American coast of the Gulf of Mexico, the weakfish or sea trout is called a "trout" or "speckled trout" or "spec." By whatever name, it is an excellent table fish, and this is an excellent way to prepare it. Fillets of another mild fish may also be used for this recipe.

The Fish
   2 pounds spec fillets
   ¼ cup flour
   2 tablespoons melted butter
   1 teaspoon salt
   1 teaspoon paprika
   ¼ teaspoon white pepper
The Sauce
   ½ cup sliced almonds
   2 tablespoons melted butter
   2 tablespoons freshly squeezed lemon juice
   1 tablespoon chopped parsley
   Louisiana hot sauce (or Tabasco sauce)

Preheat the broiler. Mix the flour, salt, pepper, and paprika. Roll the fish fillets in the flour mixture, then place them, skin down, in a well-greased baking pan or dish. The fillets should not overlap. Spread the melted butter equally on the fillets. Broil about 4 inches from heat source for 10 minutes, or until fish flakes easily when tested with a fork.

Meanwhile, sauté the almonds in butter, stirring until golden brown. Remove from heat. Add the lemon juice, parsley, and a few drops of hot sauce, to taste. Pour the sauce over the fish fillets. Serve hot. Feeds 4 or 5 people of moderate appetite.

Sauger

The sauger, a smaller cousin of the walleye, is an excellent freshwater fish that is of medium oil content and is very good table fare when cooked by any method. It's a fish of big waters, and the large impoundments on the Tennessee and other rivers have greatly expanded its habitat.

6

BOILED, POACHED, AND STEAMED FISH

If you enjoy the subtleties of French cooking or the mysteries of the Chinese, poached or steamed fish is for you. True Chinese or even French cooking is difficult in most parts of America because you can't get all the ingredients, although times are changing for the better and our supermarkets are becoming more international. In any case, I think the recipes in this chapter will satisfy almost all tastes—and anyone who thinks that poached, steamed, or boiled fish are too delicate should try the following hearty country recipe:

Puppy Drum and Potatoes

It might surprise many people to learn that the recently famous blackened redfish of Cajun cookery is really a drum. Most of the people up the Atlantic coast know the fish as a channel bass. But the people who live along the Outer Banks of North Carolina call a small one (less than 10 pounds) a "puppy drum."

The following recipe for puppy drum has been adapted here from *Coastal Carolina Cooking*. It came from Elizabeth Howard, who was born and raised on the island of Ocracoke, one of the more remote areas of the Outer Banks. Before the highway was built in 1957, the people on such islands as Ocracoke branded their hogs, cows, pigs, and horses, allowing them to roam free. Most of the homes were fenced in, and one islander commented that Ocracoke was one of the few places where the people were fenced in and the animals roamed free! Anyhow, several recipes in this fine regional book are similar to Puppy Drum and Potatoes, and it is a dish that I highly recommend. It's better, in my opinion, than burned "redfish." The original recipe specified fillets, but I prefer the fish diced like the potatoes. Suit yourself.

4- to 6-pound drum, filleted and diced
6 medium potatoes, peeled and diced
2 slices salt pork, diced
1 to 2 medium onions, diced
2 hard-boiled chicken eggs, sliced

Hard-boil the eggs and let them cool. Dice the onions and chill them. Boil the diced potatoes until they are tender. Pan-fry the salt pork until it is crisp, then let it sit in its own grease. Poach the diced fish (or fillets if you prefer) for about 10 minutes.

Put the potatoes and fish into separate serving bowls and mix the servings on each plate. Sprinkle each serving with salt pork and grease, top with chilled onions, and serve the sliced egg on the side. The above measures serve 4 to 6.

Cold Dilled Fish

fish fillets
crushed dill weed
1/2 cup sour cream
1 tablespoon lemon juice
salt and pepper
sprigs of parsley (garnish)

Add 1 teaspoon of dill to 1 quart of boiling water and poach fish fillets for 4 or 5 minutes. Do not overcook; the fillets are done when they flake easily when tested with a fork. Drain the fillets, salt and pepper to taste, and refrigerate for at least 30 minutes.

Make a sauce by mixing the sour cream, lemon juice, salt, and more crushed dill. Pour over the chilled fish, then garnish with sprigs of parsley. I like this dish with French bread and with ice cold green onions, served directly from ice water in a tall glass or similar container.

Tweed Kettle

Here's an old Scotch recipe from Edinburgh, where, I understand, the tail end of the salmon was considered to be the best. (I too have noticed that the tail part of some fish, such as the larger catfish, seems to be much better than the larger end, at least for some recipes.)

3-pound fresh salmon (undressed weight)
2 chopped green onions with part of tops
1 cup white wine
2 tablespoons chopped parsley
1/8 teaspoon mace
salt and pepper

Put the fish into a pot, cover it with water, bring to a quick boil, reduce heat, and simmer for 5 minutes. Remove the fish. Retain at least 1 cup of the liquid. Remove the skin from the salmon and bone it. Cut the meat into 2-inch cubes and season with salt, pepper, and mace. Put the fish into a suitable pan and add the reserved fish stock, wine, and green onions.

Salmon

There are several kinds of salmon, and all are quite good. Typically, they are high in oil content, but their flesh has a good flavor, texture, and color. Frying is not recommended for most salmon, although the coho and the sockeye are often cooked by that method. Salmon usually is best when grilled, broiled, smoked, or baked. It is also excellent when poached.

Bring to a light boil, reduce the heat, cover, and simmer for 10 minutes. Add the parsley. Feeds 3 or 4.

Easy Fish Newburg

2 pounds boneless fish fillets
1 can cream of shrimp soup (10¾-ounce size)
¼ cup sherry
¼ cup cream
salt and pepper

Poach the fillets until done. Salt and pepper to taste. In a saucepan, heat soup slowly. Stir in cream and sherry. Serve the sauce over fish. It's easy. It's good. Feeds 4 or 5.

Cold Fish with Avocado Mayonnaise

Here's an excellent dish for a hot summer day. It might well be my favorite recipe for poached fish, and for salmon steaks, but I am especially fond of avocado. The recipe below has been adapted from Bert Greene's excellent book *Greene on Greens.*

The Fish
2 pounds fish fillets or steaks
3 cups water
½ cup dry white wine
1 small onion
1 stalk celery
1 bay leaf
juice of ½ large lemon (or lime)
6 peppercorns
1 teaspoon salt

Weakfish

Often called sea trout, speckled trout, or "specs," the weakfish is quite popular as a gamefish and as table fare. Its meat is lean, white, and flaky. It can be cooked by any method. Several related fish— white trout, sand trout, spotted sea trout, and silver sea trout—are also quite good if prepared properly. Their flesh softens quickly, and for this reason many people do not eat them. But it is very good if it is dressed quickly, iced down, and cooked right away.

Avocado Mayonnaise
1 large avocado
1 cup mayonnaise
juice of ½ large lime (or lemon)
salt and ground white pepper
Garnish
1 lime peel, finely grated
lemon slices or wedges (optional)
sprigs of fresh parsley (optional)

Pour the water into a large skillet, Dutch oven, or other container suitable for poaching. Bring to a boil. Cut the celery into several large pieces and put them, along with the green tops, into the water. Cut onion in half and add it to the liquid, along with the wine, bay leaf, lemon juice, peppercorns, and salt. Let the liquid simmer for 5 minutes. Turn the heat up, then add the fish one piece at a time. Reduce the heat and poach for 5 minutes, or until the fish flakes easily when tested with a fork. (Thick fillets or steaks might take longer.) Take the fish up with a spatula and place it, carefully, on a serving platter. Cover the fish and refrigerate for at least 1 hour.

Cut the avocado in half and scoop out the meat with a spoon. Put it into a blender or food processor. Add the mayonnaise and lime juice. Puree the mixture. Mix in salt and white pepper to taste. Put the mixture into a serving bowl, cover, and refrigerate for at least 1 hour.

When you're ready to eat, grate the lime peel over the fish. (Use a fine grate on the outer part of the lime, and avoid cutting into the bitter white part of the inner rind.) For color, garnish with yellow lemon slices and with a few sprigs of fresh green parsley. Feeds 4 to 6.

Black Bass

The largemouth, smallmouth, spotted bass, and redeye are all very good eating, and I don't think that there is any difference in the taste of these fish. To be sure, the smallmouth has a better reputation, but this is probably because it is usually taken from better water. The fish are medium low in oil content and have white, flaky flesh.

I like variety in my foodstuffs, but if I were forced to pick one fish as table fare, I wouldn't have to ponder the matter for very long. New York angling editors notwithstanding, I would pick a black bass about 10 inches long, skinned or scaled. The larger bass aren't quite so good, at least partly because the texture is coarser.

Low-Salt Poached Fillets in Light Cream Sauce

I usually like quite a bit of seasoning on fish, but the following recipe from Lea & Perrins is good. It's even better with a little salt sprinkled on it, but of course individual servings can be salted to taste—or to low-sodium diet specifications.

2 pounds fish fillets
1 cup white wine Worcestershire sauce
¼ cup light cream (or half and half)
2 tablespoons unsalted butter

Melt the butter in a saucepan. Add the white wine Worcestershire sauce, bring to a light boil, reduce heat, and simmer for a few minutes. Stir in the cream. Keep warm. Poach the fillets in water for 4 or 5 minutes, or until fish flakes easily. Carefully place the fillets on a plate or platter. Top with cream sauce.

Grant Avenue Fillets

I've browsed around in a number of Chinese cookbooks over the years, looking for recipes for ducks and fish that can be cooked without special equipment and without all sorts of roots and seaweeds and stuff that I can't get. I finally gave up. But here's an excellent steamed-fish dish from San Francisco's Chinatown. It's good with flounder, mutton snapper, sea bass, or other mild fish with a low or medium oil content. Some fish, such as the largemouth bass, however, are quite flaky and are a little difficult to handle without tearing the fillets apart.

Sheepshead

The sheepshead has good white flesh of medium oil content. It can be prepared by most any method. *The Frank Davis Seafood Notebook* suggests that the sheepshead can be poached and then used in recipes that call for crabmeat.

2 pounds fish fillets
1/3 cup salad oil, heated
1/3 cup soy sauce
1/2 cup sliced green onions, including part of tops
4 whole green onions (with tops)
1 tablespoon grated fresh ginger root
2 teaspoons salt

Rig for steaming. Fix a rack with legs, or some sort of trivet with legs, into a roasting pan or some suitable container. Your container must hold about a quart of water and your rack must not be submerged. Ideally, the rack should hold all the fillets without overlapping. Also, you must have a cover for the container. When you've got the equipment ready, heat 1 quart of water to boiling. Arrange fillets on the rack and sprinkle them evenly with salt and grated ginger. Place whole green onions atop the fillets. Bring the water to a boil, cover tightly, and steam for 8 to 10 minutes or until fish flakes easily, depending on the thickness of the fillets.

Carefully transfer the fish to a heated serving platter. In a saucepan, heat the salad oil, mix in the soy sauce, and pour over the fish. Garnish with sliced green onions. Serves 4.

Soused Rainbow Trout

Here's a recipe that I got from the Freshwater Institute in Manitoba, Canada. Be sure to try it cold on a hot summer evening.

several pan-sized rainbow trout
1 quart boiling water
1½ cup white vinegar
3 stalks celery, thinly sliced
1 medium onion, thinly sliced
1 carrot, thinly sliced
3 tablespoons mixed pickling spice
1 tablespoon salt
2 peppercorns

To make a court bouillon or poaching liquid, mix all the ingredients except the fish in a suitable pan. Simmer for 15 minutes. Strain and retain the liquid. Dress the trout. Make diagonal incisions into the skin along each side of the fish. Butter a shallow pan of suitable size, then place the fish in it so that they do not touch. Pour enough court bouillon over the fish to almost cover it. Cover the fish with a well-buttered sheet of waxed paper. Bring the liquid to a boil, reduce the heat, and simmer for 7 to 10 minutes, or until the fish flakes easily when tested with a fork. Carefully transfer the fish to a serving dish. Pour the poaching liquid over the fish. Chill. Serve cold with French bread and good white wine.

Poached Fish with Egg Sauce

Some of the recipes for poached fish in many other books may seem simple at first glance, but can lead into a quagmire. References to basic sauces, white sauces, court bouillons, and

Dolphin

A popular saltwater gamefish, the dolphin, not to be confused with the porpoise (a mammal), is quite good and can be prepared by any method. For best results, the dolphin should be put on ice as soon as it is caught.

so on can lead to references within references—and sometimes it's hard to find your way back to where you started from. So if the recipe below seems a bit long, remember that it's all there in one place and, I hope, easy to follow.

The Fish
    2 pounds fish steaks (about ¾ inch thick) or
        fillets
    paprika
The Poaching Liquid
    2 cups water
    juice of 2 lemons
    1 small to medium onion, finely chopped
    1 tablespoon chopped parsley
    1 teaspoon salt
    1 bay leaf
The Egg Sauce
    1¼ cups milk
    ¼ cup butter
    2 hard-boiled chicken eggs, chopped
    2 tablespoons flour
    1 tablespoon chopped parsley
    1 teaspoon dry mustard
    ½ teaspoon salt
    ⅛ teaspoon pepper

Bring the water to boil in a saucepan, then add all other ingredients listed under Poaching Liquid. Simmer for 5 or 10 minutes. Grease a large skillet or other pan suitable for poaching the fish. Arrange fish in the pan and pour in the poaching liquid. Bring to a boil, reduce heat, cover, and let simmer for 6 to 10 minutes, or until fish flakes easily when tested with a fork. Carefully remove the fish to a hot serving platter.

To make the egg sauce, melt the butter in a saucepan. Stir in the flour, mustard, salt, and pepper. Stir in the milk slowly; cook and stir until the sauce is thick and smooth. Add the chopped eggs and parsley. Pour the sauce over the fish, then sprinkle with paprika. Eat while hot. Feeds 4 or 5.

Fillets in Cream Sauce

    3 pounds boneless and skinned fillets
    1 pint cream
    1 cup sliced green onions with part of tops
    1 cup sliced mushrooms
    ¼ cup chopped parsley
    ½ cup dry white wine
    salt and pepper

Mix the onions, mushrooms, and parsley, then spread them evenly over the bottom of a large skillet. Place the fillets over vegetables. (The fillets shouldn't overlap. If your skillet isn't big enough, use two pans or cook in two separate batches.) Pour in the wine. Bring to a quick boil, then cover pan, reduce heat, and simmer for 5 to 8 minutes, or until fish flakes easily when tested with a fork. Carefully remove fillets with a spatula, placing them in a serving dish. Salt and pepper to taste. Keep warm.

To make a sauce, add the cream to the skillet and bring to a slow boil. Reduce the heat a little, but keep the sauce boiling lightly until it turns a slightly golden color. Be careful; cooking the sauce too long will scorch it. Constant stirring with a wooden spoon helps. Pour the sauce over the fillets. Serve hot. Feeds 5 or 6.

Norm Lee's Steamed Fish Egg Rolls

Here's a recipe that I received from Mr. George Nelson, Sport Fishing Representative of Manitoba. In a letter to me, Nelson said, "Norm Lee's Fish Egg Rolls are excellent served hot with sweet and sour sauce and sesame seeds on top. They can be sliced like pinwheel sandwiches and served as hors d'oeuvres or whole to each guest as an entree to a Chinese dinner. I usually used sucker for this dish as the grinding of the fish eliminates the intermuscular bones."

In a note attached to the recipe, Nelson added, "Norm Lee is a well-known angler and chef from northern Manitoba. He is Chinese and all his cooking is slanted that way. Norm is in his 70s now . . . but he still wets a line and cooks his catch."

Unfortunately, Norm Lee neglected to write down the measures in his recipe for fish egg roll—or else he wanted to hold them secret.

Freshwater Drum

The freshwater drum is quite plentiful, but it is not highly prized as table fare. It is of medium oil content, but it tends to get dry and tough when cooked. It can, however, be good eating if properly prepared. Try a good poaching recipe or a chowder.

Thus, I experimented, like a chemist, and hashed this one out with my wife until we came up with the following mix. Since the recipe came from Canada, I first assumed that a blended whiskey was in order, but I confess that I promptly switched to Tennessee sour mash bourbon. Anyhow, here goes:

The Rolls
  1 cup minced fish
  2 medium chicken eggs
  ½ cup green onions, tops and all
  ½ bell pepper, green or red
  1 tablespoon butter
  1 tablespoon whiskey
  1 tablespoon soy sauce
  salt and pepper to taste
  ½ teaspoon garlic powder or 1 clove garlic, minced
  ¼ teaspoon Mei den (monosodium glutamate)

Melt the butter in a skillet on low heat. Beat the eggs and pour into the pan with the butter. While cooking, shake and jiggle the pan to keep the eggs from sticking. The eggs should have a large pancake shape. Slide out of pan onto a flat surface to cool.

Heat the water in a steamer. Mix the fish and all other ingredients into a paste. Spread the paste on the egg patty and roll it up. Secure with toothpicks or skewers. Steam the roll for 20 minutes. Slice and serve with sweet and sour sauce, prepared as follows:

The Sauce
  3 cups water
  2½ cups brown sugar
  1 cup white vinegar
  pickle juice (from a jar of pickles)
  cornstarch

Put the water, vinegar, and brown sugar in a saucepan. Bring to a boil, reduce the heat, and thicken with cornstarch. When the sauce becomes clear, add a little pickle juice. Pour the sauce over the fish rolls. Serves 5 or 6 as a side dish.

Walleye Veronique

This is an excellent dish, both tasty and attractive, to serve for special occasions. Break out your best china and polish up the silverware. Other mild fish can also be used for this dish.

2 pounds walleye fillets, skinned
1 cup seedless white grapes
1 cup dry white wine
3 tablespoons butter
1 tablespoon flour
juice of 1 large lemon
2 teaspoons salt
1/8 teaspoon white pepper
1/8 teaspoon cinnamon
1/8 teaspoon ground ginger
1/8 teaspoon dry mustard
paprika

Arrange the fillets in a large, greased skillet, preferably in one layer, and sprinkle them with lemon juice. In a small saucepan, mix and heat wine, grapes, white pepper, salt, cinnamon, ginger, and mustard. Pour the sauce over the fish fillets. Bring to simmer, cover the pan, and poach for 5 minutes.

Move the fish very carefully to an ovenproof serving platter. (I prefer two long spatulas to transfer—one slipped under the fillet, and the other placed on top to hold it.) Retain liquids and grapes. Preheat the broiler so that it will be ready. In a clean pan, melt the butter over medium heat. Blend in the flour, stirring with a wooden spoon. Add the retained liquid (but not the grapes) from the skillet. Cook until the sauce is smooth, stirring constantly. Pour the sauce over the fish fillets. Put the fillet platter under a hot broiler, very close to the heat source, and cook until the fillets are brown. Sprinkle with paprika, garnish with the grapes, and serve hot. Feeds 4 or 5.

7

FISH CHOWDERS, STEWS, AND SOUPS

Once I knew a schoolteacher, a very learned fellow, who had eight or nine children to feed and a wife who seemed to be perpetually pregnant. Money was his biggest problem. His salary simply wasn't large enough to go around. To class he wore combat boots and World War II khaki trousers and shirts, with a many-colored civilian tie for color and decorum. He wasn't ashamed of what he wore; rather, he enjoyed people's reactions to it.

Of necessity, he and his good wife were students of nutritional values, and he had decided that collard greens and fish were the ticket. He caught his own fish, and raised stalks of collards in his flower bed. The pot liquor from the collards (or from other cooked vegetables) was always saved for the fish stews—and once I saw him break up leftover corn bread and put it into a pot of stew, adding a good thick texture, flavor, and nutrition.

I don't have any of his recipes to report, and

I doubt that he ever made a fish stew the same way twice. But from this philosophic fellow I absorbed an attitude toward fish stews that goes beyond mere ingredients. I can only hope that some of his teachings are reflected in the following recipes.

Poor Boy's Gumbo

There are a lot of good gumbo recipes, most of which call for shrimp, crabmeat, and so on. It's simply not a poor man's dish anymore. In short, these ingredients can get quite expensive if you have to purchase them at today's prices. I have come up with a fish recipe that does quite well in taste as well as in texture. The trick is in cutting the fish into chunks, strips, and small diced pieces, as well as using flakes. Other than bony species such as pickerel, almost any kind of fish will work with this recipe, but a fish that isn't too soft or flaky works best. And, yes, a mixed catch also works.

½ pound fish fingers (2 inches long, ¾ inch thick)
½ pound fish chunks, 1 inch
½ pound diced fish, ¼ inch
1 cup (or less) fish flakes
2 cups chopped tomatoes
1 cup chopped okra
1 cup chopped onions
1 cup chopped celery
½ cup cooking oil
2 tablespoons flour
1 tablespoon parsley
juice of 1 lemon
2 garlic cloves, minced
2 bay leaves
salt and pepper
filé (optional)
rice (cooked separately)
water

Skin the fish, fillet it, and cut it into fingers, chunks, and dice. Simmer the head, backbone, and rib cage in some water in a boiler for about 20 minutes, then flake off the meat with a fork. Sprinkle the fish with a little lemon juice and refrigerate.

Heat the oil in a skillet, then sauté the onion, garlic, and celery for 4 or 5 minutes. Stir in the flour. Transfer to a large Dutch oven. Add the tomatoes and okra. Measure 1 quart of poaching liquid (if necessary, add enough fresh water to yield 1 quart), add it to the pot, and bring to a light boil, stirring in the parsley, flour, salt, pepper, and bay leaves. Cover the pot, reduce the heat, and simmer for 1 hour. Add the fish, cover, and simmer for 15 minutes. If you want a thick gumbo, add a little filé to individual servings in bowls. (Do not add filé to the whole pot while cooking gumbo or any other dish.) When you have each serving of gumbo thickened to taste, place a dollop of rice into the middle of each bowl. Serve hot. Feeds 6 to 8.

Quick Chowder

I wouldn't call this dish a recipe because it's so easy. I like it from time to time to use up a small amount of fish, but it also works with large batches.

fish flakes
canned clam chowder
salt and pepper

I don't have exact measures, but 1 cup of fish flakes to 1 can of soup would be reasonable. If the fish is cooked, flake it or dice it before mixing it with the soup. If raw, poach it a few minutes or sauté it in a pan with a tad of butter, then flake it or dice it. Heat the chowder. Add the fish. Salt and pepper to taste. I like quite a bit of black pepper, and I sprinkle it onto the chowder after I have put it into serving bowls.

Most of the canned chowders I've sampled

Try Lake Whitefish in Winter

Long valued by Indians and Eskimos, lake whitefish has only in the past few years been recognized by anglers and consumers for the fine fish that it is. . . . According to northern Indians, it is the perfect food. On a diet of whitefish, all goes well. Without it, ailments.

Lake whitefish has always been important as dog food in the North, where the Indians partially dry or "hang" it to make light work for the dogs who must carry it. A ten-day requirement for six dogs being 120 fish, weight is a consideration when the whitefish up there run to 8 pounds, of which 90 percent is water. . . .

The recent recognition of the lake whitefish is in measure due to the increasing popularity of ice-fishing, for the whitefish is a winter fish. In summer the bottom-feeding whitefish is fat and sluggish and as a fresh food and angling item it is best ignored.

Winter-caught whitefish is another matter. The post-spawning fish is leaner and hungrier and provides a good sport and tasty flesh.

—Frances MacIlquham,
Fish Cookery of North America

had a good flavor but were a little short in meat. Fish flakes will fix that nicely.

Variation: Add some sautéed mushrooms to the soup.

Florida Cracker Fish Chowder

Here's a favorite of mine. I adapted it from Marjorie Kinnan Rawlings's book *Cross Creek Cookery.* Mrs. Rawlings called it "Ed Hopkins' Fish Chowder," saying that "Ed was of the great amateur cooks of the world, and with the simplest Florida backwoods ingredients and a Dutch oven, turned out dishes so superlative that when I now prepare one, I grieve that Ed is not here to partake."

I have fished Cross Creek, which joins Orange Lake and Lake Lochloosa in central Florida. I've lived on the outskirts of the Big Scrub. I've read some of Mrs. Rawlings's writings, and I enjoyed the movie about Cross Creek. In fact, Rip Torn, who portrayed Marsh in the movie, did one of the best acting jobs that I've ever seen, and I fear it's his image that I see when I cook the following version of Mrs. Rawlings's version of "Ed Hopkins' Fish Chowder":

4 pounds fish fillets, skinned and boneless
½ pound salt pork
3 potatoes
3 medium onions
oyster crackers
light cream or half and half
butter
salt and pepper
water

Put some water on to heat. Dice the salt pork. Slice the potatoes and onions thinly. Place the salt pork in bottom of a large Dutch oven. Add a layer of fish, a layer of onion, a layer of potatoes, a layer of oyster crackers, a few small pieces of butter, and some salt and pepper. Repeat the layers in this order until everything but the cream is in the Dutch oven. Try to add the ingredients in proportion for three complete layers of everything.

Put the Dutch oven on high heat. Add enough hot water to bring the level to within 2 inches of the top of the ingredients. Reduce the heat to very low, cover tightly, and simmer for 45 minutes, at which time the water should be almost gone and the top layer of potatoes should be tender and ready to eat. Heat the cream and pour it over the chowder. Let the pot sit for a few minutes off the heat. If all goes well, the bottom should be browned, but not burned. Feeds 6 to 8.

Note: Do not stir this dish, and serve it so that the layers remain intact as much as possible.

Texas Shark Chili

If you don't believe this one, I've got proof. The recipe was sent to me, in a news release packet, by the Texas Parks and Wildlife Department on August 11, 1976, dateline Austin. I've still got the paper, complete with the Texas lone-star logo. After pointing out that Texas cooking has been called a potpourri of many cultures, the writers claimed that this chili is a "fine example of the blending of foods and flavors that represent Mexican, Indian, and Spanish

A Failure to Communicate

My father, when a dapper young man, owned and operated a grocery store, advertising plain foods and fancy. He even offered delivery service. A new young schoolteacher (later to be my mother) moved to town, called his store, and said she wanted 3 pounds of mullet, and that she wanted them dressed and delivered.

Well, my father picked out three of the best looking 1-pound mullet he had, dressed them nicely, and sent them to her right away. She sent a message back by the delivery boy that the package contained only 1½ pounds of fish whereas the bill showed 3 pounds. In short, she wanted what she paid for. My father wrapped up 1½ pounds of mullet heads, guts, scales, and bones, and had them delivered to her!

There was clearly a failure to communicate, and the same thing can happen in recipes if both writer and reader aren't careful. Sometimes a simple error can ruin a recipe. For example, a teaspoon of salt can be written or read as a tablespoon, a difference that can ruin a dish. (Such mistakes are more likely to happen, on the part of the writer, reader, and typesetter, when abbreviations are used. For this reason, I have written out "tablespoon" and "teaspoon" instead of using abbreviations in this book.) Another error of this type can occur when the writer calls for "1 cup cornflakes, finely crushed" and the reader proceeds with 1 cup of finely crushed cornflakes. By weight, 1 cup finely crushed cornflakes can have ten times as many grams as 1 cup cornflakes, finely crushed. Such a difference can make some dishes far too dry.

tastes." They go on, "It is rich in the onion and garlic the Spaniards used so well, the chili and oregano of the Aztecs, and our native beans and seafoods." I doubt that oregano is Aztec, but, here's the recipe:

2 pounds shark fillets (or other fresh fish)
1 can red kidney beans, undrained (16-ounce size)
1 can tomatoes, undrained (16-ounce size)
1 can tomato paste (6-ounce size)
2 cups sliced onions
1 cup diced green pepper
2 cloves garlic, minced
2 tablespoons margarine or cooking oil
1½ teaspoons chili powder
2 teaspoons salt
½ teaspoon oregano
¼ teaspoon pepper

Cut the skinned and boneless fillets into 1½-inch chunks. Heat the margarine or oil in a large skillet or Dutch oven. Sauté the onions, green pepper, and garlic for a few minutes. Stir in the chili powder, salt, pepper, and oregano. Add the kidney beans, tomatoes, and tomato paste. Bring to a light boil, then reduce the heat to very low. Simmer for 15 minutes. Add the fish. Cover and simmer for about 10 minutes, or until the fish flakes easily. Do not overcook.

Eat with corn bread (preferably jalapeño corn bread) and a tossed salad. Feeds 6 to 8.

Tennessee Cioppino

This dish clearly has attachments to California, and one report suggests that it was invented in San Francisco by an Italian. Another says that it came to California from Portugal. If you aren't familiar with cioppino but think that you want the real stuff, I suggest that first you boil a whole blue crab, put it into a bowl of catsup, and then try to eat it. Unless you chew the crab shell and all, you're clearly bound to have a mess on your hands, and if you feed your guests such a dish, they will need bibs and towels and finger bowls, or buckets, at the table. With the right partner, of course, it could be fun, like mud-wrestling after all of the children have gone to bed.

Anyhow, the traditional dish has a tomato base and contains crabs, prawns in the shell, clams in the shell, and so on, as well as fish. I have nothing against such fare, and I'm not all that opposed to shucking or picking at the table. I love to peel and eat boiled shrimp, for example, and of course I eat fried chicken with my fingers. But picking crab in tomato soup? Anyhow, some years ago I came up with a sensible and very inexpensive cioppino made from bass that I caught from the Elk River in Tennessee. (If you've got sophisticated guests coming to eat Tennessee cioppino, however, be sure to save the rib cages and the backbones to throw in for pickings, and add whole crawfish, if you've got them alive.)

3 pounds boneless bass fillets cut into easy-to-find chunks
2 pounds tomatoes, peeled and chopped
1 cup dry wine
1 large onion, sliced
1 bell pepper, chopped
6 green onions, chopped with tops
½ cup butter
8 ounces mushrooms, whole (optional)
2 cloves garlic, minced
2 tablespoons chopped parsley
salt and pepper
⅛ teaspoon Tabasco sauce (optional)

Striped Bass, White Bass— and Hybrids

The small white bass, a freshwater fish, is low in oil content and can be cooked by any method.

The larger striped bass, or rockfish, is a saltwater species that runs up rivers to spawn—and sometimes becomes landlocked in large man-made impoundments. Much larger than the white bass, the striper has rather dry flesh with low oil content. The larger stripers, over 10 pounds, have coarse flesh that is better when cooked in liquid rather than being fried, broiled, baked, or grilled. The literature of angling and fish cookery rates the striped bass quite highly, with a history going all the way back to Captain John Smith. I don't argue—but personally I'll take a black bass any day over any sort of striper.

The small white bass and the large striped bass are related and have been crossed in the laboratory, producing a hybrid that is being stocked in the nation's waters. These hybrids are called "sunshine bass" in Florida. My experience in eating hybrids is quite limited, and the opinion of my friends varies. But one thing is certain: An 8-pound hybrid is fun to catch.

Heat the butter in a Dutch oven or suitable pot, then sauté the onion slices, green onions, bell pepper, mushrooms, and garlic for about 5 minutes. Add the tomatoes, Tabasco sauce, parsley, salt, pepper, and wine. Bring to a boil. Add fish chunks, cover, reduce the heat to very low, and simmer for 15 minutes.

Serve the Tennessee cioppino in large soup bowls, along with sourdough bread and a hearty salad. Feeds 6 to 8.

Fish Spaghetti Stew

2 pounds boneless and skinless fish chunks
7 ounces uncooked spaghetti
1 can stewed tomatoes (14½-ounce size)
1 can tomato sauce (8-ounce size)
1 cup chopped onion
1 cup chopped celery
1 cup chopped mushrooms
1 clove minced garlic
½ cup butter or margarine
2 teaspoons salt
½ teaspoon black pepper
2 cups water
Parmesan cheese

In a large skillet (with a cover) or a Dutch oven, melt the butter or margarine. Add the onion, celery, mushrooms, and garlic, then sauté until the vegetables are tender, stirring as you go. Add the tomatoes, tomato sauce, salt, and pepper. Bring to a boil, reduce heat to very low, cover, and simmer for 20 minutes.

Put the water into a pan and bring to a boil. Add the spaghetti to the vegetables, increase the heat, and add the boiling water. Reduce the heat, cover, and cook for 10 minutes. Add the fish chunks, cover, and cook for another 10 minutes. Sprinkle Parmesan cheese over individual servings. Feeds 4 to 6.

Carteret County "Conch" Chowder

Bill and Eloise Pigott, according to *Coastal Carolina Cooking*, often cook together in their kitchen, and for the recipe below Bill makes the chowder and Eloise makes the dumplings. The result is said to be a Carteret County Classic, and, according to the book, "There is even a saying that goes along with the dish: 'If you ever eat conch chowder in Carteret County, you'll never want to leave.' Bill says that cleaning and tenderizing this abundant mollusk is time-consuming, but, he adds, the results are worth the effort. He admits that the conch, which is more accurately a whelk, has a strong flavor for which many folks have to acquire a taste."

The Chowder
 7 to 8 whelks, in the shell
 1 quart water
 1 or 2 thin slices salt pork
 2 or 3 potatoes, diced
 1 small onion, diced
 2 tablespoons butter
 ½ teaspoon salt
 ½ teaspoon pepper
 1 teaspoon thyme

Cornmeal Dumplings
 2 cups cornmeal
 ½ to 1 cup water
 1 teaspoon salt

Bill recommends freezing the whelks in the shell before trying to remove the meat. Thaw, then pull out the meat. Keep only the tough, cream-colored foot. Tenderize the meat for 10 minutes in a pressure cooker, or pound it thoroughly with a meat mallet.

After tenderizing, chop the whelk foot into small pieces. Put the whelk, water, salt pork, butter, salt, and pepper into a small saucepan. Bring to a boil, reduce heat to very low, cover, and simmer 1½ hours. Add potatoes, onions, and thyme, and simmer for 30 minutes. Meanwhile, make the dumplings by combining the cornmeal and salt in a mixing bowl, and stirring in just enough water to bind the mixture. Shape into small patties. Drop the dumplings around the edge of the chowder, simmer for another 15 minutes, and serve hot. Enjoy.

Note: Up on the Outer Banks, there is considerable controversy over how to make the best cornmeal dumplings. First you've got to decide on what texture and taste are best, and then on how to achieve these qualities. There are dozens of variations in method and

Yellow Perch

The yellow perch is an excellent panfish of medium low oil content. It is good cooked most any way, and it is very good when fried.

ingredients, but the recipe above is, in my opinion, the easiest as well as the best. But it's not really a dumpling—it's an ordinary Alabama corn dodger! If your meal isn't finely ground from whole corn, the dumplings might not hold together. Try mixing the cornmeal with some of the broth from the chowder instead of with water.

Bouillabaisse Louisiane

This is one of my favorites. I've eaten a number of variations, and some sources advise that small fish, such as smelt, be used in the dish. But I prefer boneless fillets, or chunks of fish, because I don't want any bones to slow me down. My recipe is based on the *Heritage Cook Book*. According to this text, the French, who settled Louisiana, had originally made the dish with a fish called *rascasse*. In their new home, they used red snapper. I normally use largemouth bass, or any other good fish I can catch.

> 2 pounds fillets, skinned and boneless
> 4 or 5 cups diced tomatoes
> 1 cup chicken broth (or fish stock)
> 2 tablespoons chopped fresh parsley
> ½ lemon, sliced
> 2 cloves garlic, minced
> 1 bay leaf, crumbled
> 1 teaspoon dried thyme
> 1 teaspoon salt
> ¼ teaspoon ground allspice
> ¼ teaspoon cayenne pepper
> ⅛ teaspoon ground saffron (optional)
> olive oil
> rice (cooked separately)

Redear

The redear, often called "shellcracker," is a sunfish with white flesh of low oil content. It is often fried. This fish is difficult to take with a fly, and it is usually caught with earthworms instead of crickets.

Lay the fillets out on a table or counter. Mix the parsley, garlic, bay leaf, thyme, salt, and allspice with 1 teaspoon olive oil. Stir. Spread mixture over the fillets.

In a large skillet or Dutch oven, heat 1 tablespoon of olive oil. Sauté onion for 5 minutes. Add the tomatoes, lemon slices, chicken broth, cayenne, and saffron. Add the fish fillets, bring to a light boil, reduce heat to very low, cover, and simmer for 10 minutes, or until the fillets flake easily when tested with a fork. Remove the lemon slices. Serve with rice. Feeds 5 or 6.

Note: I normally leave the saffron out of this recipe. It was probably a North African influence on the basic French recipe. Most French recipes for this dish call for all manner of liquids made from boiling fish heads and tails. This is fine if you're working with fresh fish, but if you're using frozen fillets, making the proper French stocks is just not practical. If you've got fish heads, bony parts, and fins, boil them in water, and use this liquid instead of the chicken broth.

New England Fish Chowder

There must be a thousand published variations of this chowder—and ten thousand unpublished versions. Here's one of my favorites:

2 pounds boneless fillets, skinned
¼ pound salt pork, diced
4 cups milk
4 cups fish stock or water
3 medium potatoes, diced
1 medium onion, diced
½ small green bell pepper, diced
½ small red bell pepper, diced
1 large stalk celery, tops and all, diced
1 carrot, diced
flour
butter
2 bay leaves
2 teaspoons salt
1 teaspoon black pepper (or to taste)
½ teaspoon tarragon

In a bowl, mix 1 tablespoon butter with 1 tablespoon flour. Mix in more and more flour, mashing with a fork, until the butter will take up no more. Then work in even more flour with your fingers. Form into small balls, then set aside to thicken the chowder when needed.

Put the water or fish stock (see the note to the previous recipe) into a small pan and heat to boiling. Cut the fish into 2-inch cubes. In a stove-top Dutch oven or suitable pot, sauté the salt pork. Remove the pork, but leave the pan drippings. Sauté the onions. Add potatoes, peppers, celery, and carrot. Pour in the boiling water or stock. Add the salt, black pepper, tarragon, and bay leaves. Bring to a boil, cover, reduce the heat to very low, and simmer for 20 minutes. Add the fish chunks, cover, and simmer for 20 minutes. Taste, adjusting salt and pepper, if desired. Add the milk. Heat to smoking—but do not boil. Add about half of the flour balls, continue heating for 5 minutes, and stir gently. Add more flour balls if a thicker chowder is desired. Stir in the salt pork. Serve hot with French bread. Feeds 6 to 8.

Daddy's Oyster Stew

My father cooked three dishes. One, he took care of squirrels that he figured were too tough for mother to handle; two, he fried salt mullet; and three, he always cooked oyster stew on Christmas Eve. I don't know how the exact date was set, but he always bought a burlap bag of oysters for the holidays, and the Christmas Eve oyster stew followed. Anyhow, his recipe is almost exactly like one that I found in *Coastal Carolina Cooking.*

According to that work, Sneads Ferry folks say that oyster stew is a cure-all for illnesses. Percy and Loraine Jenkins ran a café there for a number of years, and Percy's cooking won him a reputation of being an "angel of mercy." Often he took jars of his oyster stew to the sick, and some local folks believed the stew to be better than medicine. Loraine said, "If you get so sick you can't eat oyster stew, you're really sick."

1 quart oysters (not washed after shucking)
½ cup water
½ cup milk
¼ cup butter
½ teaspoon black pepper, freshly ground
saltine crackers, very fresh
salt to taste

For best results, shuck your own oysters and drop them one by one into a quart jar until it is filled, saving some of the liquor as you go. Usually, "bucket" oysters bought already shucked have been washed, which takes away much of the salty flavor. Also, get some fresh, crisp saltines. If yours are stale, put them in a slow oven for a few minutes.

Put the oysters and liquor from the container, butter, water, and pepper into a pot.

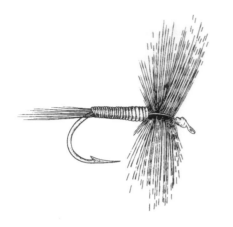

Bring to a boil, reduce heat, and simmer until the oysters start to curl on the edges. Reduce the heat, salt to taste, and stir in the milk. Heat to smoking, but do not boil. Serve in bowls, and have plenty of crackers on hand. Also, have a pepper mill for those who want lots of pepper, which, freshly ground, adds both taste and aroma to this dish. Feeds 6 to 8.

Minnesota-Style Chowder

I got this basic recipe from a booklet on eelpout (burbot) that was published by the University of Minnesota Sea Grant Extension Program. I tried it with channel catfish and found it to be very good. The recipe in the booklet did not call for pepper, but I took the liberty of adding some. I also changed the directions somewhat.

1½ pounds boneless fish, cut into chunks
2 cans creamed corn (17-ounce size)
2 cans chicken broth (13¾-ounce size)
2 cups half and half
1 cup milk
1 cup diced celery
½ cup dry white wine
¼ cup butter (divided)
1 large onion, chopped
1 clove garlic, minced
2 tablespoons flour
1½ teaspoon salt
1 teaspoon black pepper

Melt 2 tablespoons of the butter in a small saucepan, then sauté the onions, garlic, and celery for 5 minutes. Melt the rest of the butter in a Dutch oven. Stir in the flour until it is blended. Mix in the wine, simmer for 1 minute, and stir in the half and half and milk. After the mixture starts to thicken, stir in the chicken broth, corn, salt, and pepper. Add the sautéed onions, celery, and garlic. Simmer for 10 minutes—but don't bring to a boil. Add the fish chunks. Simmer for 10 more minutes, or until fish flakes easily. Feeds 6 to 8.

Variation: Try the above recipe with fish flakes or leftover fish instead of chunks.

8

APPETIZERS, SNACKS, AND FISH SANDWICHES

A number of the recipes set forth in other chapters could fit nicely here. A gourmet looking for hors d'oeuvres would surely turn to the chapter on fish roe, for example. The truth is that fish and seafood offer such variety that a whole book could easily be filled without exhausting the appetizer possibilities. If the recipes that follow whet the palate for a few dishes that can be used on occasion, fine. If they inspire the imagination or trigger the urge to experiment, so much the better.

Po' Boy's Pâté

Here is an inexpensive paté that can be made from any mild fish. I sometimes make it with fish flakes from the backbone and rib cage after filleting. This is also a good way to use leftovers. If the fish hasn't already been cooked, poach it for 10 minutes in water.

2 cups cooked fish flakes
½ cup butter
2 tablespoons white wine Worcestershire sauce
juice of 1 small lemon (1 tablespoon)
1 tablespoon grated onion
¼ teaspoon dry mustard
¼ teaspoon ground mace
⅛ teaspoon white pepper
⅛ teaspoon cayenne

Set butter out to soften. Mash the fish flakes with a fork. Put the butter in a mixer and cream. Add the white wine Worcestershire sauce, lemon juice, onion, white pepper, cayenne, mustard, and mace. Mix. Add the fish flakes. Mix until smooth. Put the mixture in an oblong serving dish or mold and refrigerate. Slice as needed and serve on crackers.

Note: We like the above recipe for lunch, eaten with crackers, along with chilled V-8 juice. It's also good as a sandwich spread when mixed with a little mayonnaise. Feeds 4 or 5 for lunch.

Walleye Cocktail

This dish is good as an appetizer, to be eaten before getting to a heavy meal. Walleye is ideal, but the cocktail can be made with any mild, flaky fish, such as black bass, grouper, or white perch.

The Fish
    2 cups cooked fish flakes
    ½ cup celery, very finely chopped
    ½ cup green onions, very finely chopped
    ¼ cup green pepper, very finely chopped
    ¼ cup fresh garden radishes, very finely
        chopped
    2 tablespoons capers
    salt and pepper to taste
Cocktail Sauce
    1 cup catsup
    ⅛ cup prepared horseradish
    juice of ½ lemon (make garnish slices with
        other half)
    ⅛ teaspoon Tabasco sauce

Mix the fish, celery, pepper, onions, radishes, capers, salt, and pepper. Chill. Serve on lettuce. Have plenty of thin crackers and cocktail sauce on hand. To make sauce, mix catsup, horseradish, lemon juice, and hot sauce. Refrigerate until ready to use. Serves 6 or 7 as an appetizer.

Smoked Fish Spread

    2 cups cooked smoked fish
    1 cup mayonnaise
    2 tablespoons minced onion
    2 tablespoons finely chopped celery
    2 tablespoons chopped parsley
    2 tablespoons pickle relish (or finely
        chopped sweet pickles)
    1 tablespoon prepared mustard
    1 garlic clove, minced
    ¼ teaspoon Worcestershire sauce

Mix the ingredients and chill for 2 hours. Spread on crackers. Or add a little more mayonnaise and use as a dip.

Hot Fish Sandwich

I prefer this sandwich made with fish fillets that have been sautéed without batter on them. Putting heavily battered fish between bread is a bit much of a good thing, in my opinion.

    fish fillets
    butter
    lemon juice
    mayonnaise (or tartar sauce)
    loaf bread
    salt and pepper

Salt and pepper the fillets, then sauté them in butter. Squeeze on a little lemon juice. Spread mayonnaise on the bread rather generously, then sandwich the fillets. For best results, the fillets should be hot and the bread soft.

Variations: Try the sandwich with broiled or grilled fish fillets.

Fish and Avocado Puree

It would be incorrect for me to call this dish a snack. It's an appetizer. The more I eat of it, the more I want, as long as it lasts!

2 very ripe avocados
1 cup cooked fish flakes
¼ cup mayonnaise
salt and pepper

Stone Roller

The stone roller, a small fish often called a "hornyhead," is very good when it is rolled in cornmeal and fried. A minnow, it seldom grows over 7 or 8 inches long, although it can reach 11 inches or more. In parts of Tennessee, the hornyhead is highly prized as table fare; some anglers fish for and catch it with tiny wet flies, although a small hook baited with a piece of earthworm is more commonly used. The stone roller's range is quite wide, and it can be taken in many other states from Texas up to Canada and east to the Carolinas. Catch some and try them as appetizers.

Cut the avocados in half, scoop out the meat, and mash with a fork. Mix in the fish, mayonnaise, salt, and pepper. Serve at room temperature, on thin wheat crackers. Serves 4 to 6 as an appetizer.

Zesty Spot Canapés

Here's a recipe that I got from the state of South Carolina some years ago, as published in *Saltwater Conservation*. It calls for spot, a saltwater panfish, but any good fish will do.

1 cup cooked spot flakes
3 tablespoons mayonnaise
½ cup finely chopped celery
½ cup butter or margarine, softened
3 tablespoons prepared horseradish
30 melba toast rounds or toast points
chopped parsley (garnish)

Mix the fish flakes, mayonnaise, and celery. In another bowl, mix the margarine and horseradish. Spread the margarine mixture over the toast, then top with the fish mixture. Garnish with chopped parsley. Makes 30 canapes.

Stuffed Cherry Tomatoes

The idea for this recipe, but not the exact ingredients, came from the Nova Scotia Department of Fisheries. I tried it with leftover baked bass, flaked, whereas the original calls for snow crab meat. (The snow crab, by the way, is found in the waters off Labrador down to the Gulf of Maine.)

1 to 1½ cups cooked fish flakes
36 cherry tomatoes
¼ cup good mayonnaise
¼ cup finely chopped celery
2 tablespoons freshly squeezed lemon juice
¼ teaspoon thyme
salt (optional)
Parmesan cheese

Slice the tops off the cherry tomatoes, then scoop out the pulp and seeds with a small spoon. (A grapefruit spoon with a cutting edge is great for this purpose.) Put the tomatoes upside down on absorbent paper to drain for at least 20 minutes. Mix the flaked fish with the celery, mayonnaise, lemon juice, salt, and thyme. Stuff this mixture into the cherry tomatoes. Before serving, sprinkle the tops with Parmesan cheese. Serve as hors d'oeuvres.

Fish Bowl

This dish is a tasty appetizer, but I can make a whole meal of it if I've got some ordinary saltine crackers to put the fish chunks on.

2 pounds fish fillets, skinned and boneless
½ cup minced green onions with part of
    tops
½ cup minced parsley
½ cup red wine vinegar
½ cup olive oil
2 tablespoons coarse, Creole-style mustard
    (or Dijon)
2 tablespoons good mayonnaise
1 teaspoon salt
¼ teaspoon black pepper
1 bay leaf
water

Poach the fish for a few minutes in water with a bay leaf. Refrigerate the fish in a serving bowl. After the fish fillets have chilled, cut them into bite-size chunks. Mix the onions, parsley, vinegar, oil, mustard, mayonnaise, salt, and pepper, pour the mixture over fish, and refrigerate for several hours. Eat with the aid of toothpicks. Serves 8 as an appetizer.

Catfish Bleu Appetizers

The recipe below, I understand, took third prize at the 11th Annual National Farm-Raised Catfish Cooking Contest. I got the recipe from the UNC Sea Grant Program.

The Fish
    2 pounds catfish fillets
    1 cup finely crushed cheese crackers
    ½ cup grated Parmesan cheese
    ½ cup butter or margarine, melted
    ¼ cup sesame seeds
    salt and pepper
The Dip
    1 cup sour cream
    ¼ cup crumbled bleu cheese
    ½ cup finely chopped onion
    ¼ teaspoon salt
    chopped parsley

To make the dip, combine the sour cream, bleu cheese, onion, and salt. Garnish with chopped parsley. Refrigerate while the fish are cooking.

Preheat the oven to 400 degrees. Salt and pepper fillets, then cut them into 1-inch cubes. Mix the cracker crumbs, Parmesan cheese, and sesame seeds. Dip the catfish cubes in the melted margarine, then roll in cracker crumb mixture, and place them about ½ inch apart on well-greased (or foil-lined) baking sheets. Bake for 20 minutes, or until fish is golden brown. Serve with dip. Makes about 6 dozen appetizers.

Low-Calorie Sandwich Snacks

    1 to 2 cups cooked fish flakes
    plain yogurt
    finely chopped watermelon rind pickles
    very fresh white bread

Mix the fish flakes and pickles. Stir in the yogurt until the desired consistency is reached. Trim the edges from the bread, and make the sandwiches. Quarter them by cutting from corner to corner.

Fish Strips

Fried fish is an American favorite for a meal, and it can also make a good appetizer. The trick is to use thin fish, cook it very quickly, and serve it very hot. It is best to eat fish strips as soon as they come out of the skillet or deep fryer, instead of keeping them warm on a heated platter. For best results, the fish should be on the firm side. The fillets will be cut into thin strips, and fish that flakes easily may tend to come apart on you.

    fish fillets, boneless
    peanut oil
    buttermilk
    fine-ground white cornmeal
    salt and pepper

Dolly Varden

The Dolly Varden, a char, is oily with pinkish red meat. It can be baked, broiled, or grilled and is a delicacy when smoked. If you serve it as an appetizer, remember the following trivia for conversation: The fish was named for Miss Dolly Varden, a character in Charles Dickens's *Barnaby Rudge* who wore a spotted pink dress.

Cut the fillets into strips ¼ inch thick and ½ inch wide. (Partly frozen fillets will slice easier.) Put the fish strips in a suitable glass container, then soak them in buttermilk for 30 minutes under refrigeration.

Heat the peanut oil in a skillet or deep fryer. Drain the fish strips, salt and pepper them to taste, and shake them in a bag with cornmeal. Fry the strips, a handful at a time, in very hot oil until the strips are golden brown—only 2 or 3 minutes if your oil is hot. Drain on brown bags.

Fish Spread on Water Chestnuts

The Chinese and some other oriental peoples often employ the principle of opposites in their daily life, as in sweet and sour foods. Here's one that's hot and cold, soft and crunchy:

    cooked fish flakes
    butter
    garlic salt
    canned whole water chestnuts

Cut each water chestnut in half, making 2 wheels. Chill. Melt a little butter in a small skillet, add fish flakes, and sprinkle with garlic salt to taste. Stir and bring to heat. Drain any excess butter. Put the fish in a serving dish that can be heated. Keep hot until ready to eat. Line a bowl with ice, then put the water chestnuts on it. With a spread knife, put a little of the hot buttered fish onto the cold water chestnuts, one at a time, and eat.

Fish Flake and Egg Sandwich

    1 pound boneless fish
    1 quart water
    3 hard-boiled eggs, chopped
    ½ cup chopped black olives
    ½ cup mayonnaise
    1 tablespoon prepared horseradish
    salt and pepper
    1 teaspoon dill weed
    rye bread

Heat the water in a large pan. Add the dill weed, then poach the fish until it flakes easily

with a fork. Flake the fish, then mix it with mayonnaise, olives, horseradish, eggs, salt, and pepper. Spread the mix generously on rye bread. Makes 4 to 6 sandwiches.

Bacon 'n' Fish

    boneless, skinned fish fillets
    bacon
    salt and pepper
    lemon

Cut the fillets into 1-inch pieces. Squeeze a little lemon juice on the fish, then refrigerate for 1 hour. Preheat the broiler. Wrap each piece of fish with ½ strip of bacon, then pin with a toothpick. Broil until the bacon is crisp on both sides.

Toasted Cream Cheese and Fish Sandwich

Once, long ago, I took a swivel stool at a drugstore lunch counter in Norfolk, Virginia. On the next stool sat Gary Cooper, eating a toasted cream cheese sandwich. I ordered one myself, and I've been a cream cheese fan ever since. Here's one of my favorite versions:

    1 cup cooked fish flakes
    8 ounces cream cheese, room temperature
    1 tablespoon mayonnaise
    1 tablespoon finely chopped olives
    white sandwich bread
    butter

Mix the fish, cream cheese, olives, and mayonnaise. Spread the mixture on bread, then put the two halves together. Butter one side of the sandwich lightly, then toast it under the broiler until brown. Turn, butter the other side, and brown. Eat at once.

Variation: Use smoked fish flakes and omit the chopped olives.

Mushrooms Stuffed with Fish

1 cup cooked fish flakes
12 ounces large mushrooms
½ cup butter (divided)
⅓ cup milk
1 tablespoon flour
1 tablespoon chopped fresh parsley
1 teaspoon white wine Worcestershire sauce
½ teaspoon lemon juice
½ teaspoon dry mustard
¼ teaspoon salt
⅛ teaspoon pepper
1 chicken egg yolk, beaten
grated Parmesan cheese

Remove and mince the mushroom stems. Melt ¼ cup of butter in a pan. Sauté the mushroom stems for a few minutes, then carefully stir in flour, salt, pepper, white wine Worcestershire, and mustard. Slowly add the milk, stirring constantly until the mixture thickens. Remove from the heat. Stir in the fish flakes, egg yolk, parsley, and lemon juice. Set aside.

Preheat oven to 400 degrees. Melt ¼ cup of butter in a skillet. Sauté mushroom caps for about 5 minutes. Drain. Stuff the caps with the fish mixture. Sprinkle the tops with cheese.

Place the stuffed mushrooms in a pan, and bake for about 15 minutes.

River Cats Taste Better

Although pond-raised catfish for the masses might be better than none at all, the old-time connoisseurs and many fishermen know that the best cats still come from clean, free-flowing streams. Part of the reason (I believe) has as much to do with texture as with flavor. All catfish have fine-grained flesh, and those raised in ponds tend to be downright mushy. Swift-water fish are firmer simply because they swim more. They have to work to find crawfish and other natural food, whereas many of the pond fish are fed pellets daily. In fact, some of the "cultured" catfish aren't even free to roam the length and breadth of the pond; they are penned up in cages or baskets. Not long ago a farmer told me that he raised 2,000 channel cats in a basket only 8 feet long by 4 feet wide. He was a hefty fellow with a large mortgage at the bank, so I didn't tell him that somebody ought to poke him in there with the catfish.

Fish Spread

I'm fond of eating various kinds of spreads on crackers, and here's one of my favorites:

1 cup finely flaked fish, precooked
6 ounces cream cheese
1 golf-ball size onion, grated
2 tablespoons white wine Worcestershire sauce
juice of ½ lemon
¼ teaspoon salt

Mix all the ingredients and chill. Spread on crackers.

Variations: Substitute 4 ounces of grated cheddar for the cream cheese and omit the lemon juice. If you're having a party and want a little color on your appetizers, put the spread into a small serving dish and sprinkle with paprika.

Fish Dogs

Here's a dish that children think is neat. It should be made from fairly large fish, and the fish *must* be boneless. The fingers should be about the size of jumbo wieners. I specify Vidalia onions, but any mild onions can be used.

    large fish fingers
    mayonnaise
    salt and pepper to taste
    hot dog buns
    chopped Vidalia onions (optional)
    water for poaching

Poach the fish fingers for a few minutes, until the meat flakes easily when tested with a fork. Drain. Salt and pepper to taste. To make a fish dog, spread some mayonnaise in a hot dog bun, then put a fish stick into it. Spread more mayonnaise on top. (You may want to use tartar sauce or catsup instead of the mayonnaise.) I like plenty of chopped onions on mine, but many children prefer to leave them off. In any case, it's best to have a hot piece of fish topped with cold sauce, and be sure that the bun is fresh and soft.

9

FISH ROE

"Are you going to eat *that?*" my son Bill asked, peeping into the skillet when I had my soft roe dish about half done.

Well, yes. If there is anything better than scrambled brains and eggs, it is soft roe and eggs. My wife loves the combination. But the boys won't touch it because it doesn't *look* right, and I usually fry ordinary roe for them to eat. But of course I know better than to fry roe that is too large and dry. Bluegill roe is my favorite for frying, and the boys always search for it when they dress the stunted "bream" that they bring home by the dozens from a nearby farm pond.

Everyone knows about caviar made from sturgeon roe, and of course a lot of coastal anglers already have favorite recipes for shad roe. But anyone who fishes at all should be aware that some other species have very, very good roe. One dangerous exception is the roe of the various garfishes, which is toxic to man. I understand also that the innards from the puffer can be deadly, and I therefore stay clear of their roe. But I've eaten excellent roe from a number of other fish, including largemouth bass.

"White roe" is another name for soft roe, or milt. Besides being good, it's also highly nutritious and is easily digested. White roe from mullet, which is available around the Gulf of Mexico in the fall, is one of my favorites, but carp, mackerel, shad, and other fish also have good white roe.

In any case, here are some of my favorite recipes for fish roe:

Scrambled Soft Roe and Eggs

soft roe
chicken eggs
green onions
butter
salt and pepper

Warning

None of the fish and game cookbooks that I have seen, or any other book that I know about, give fish roe the coverage it deserves. Typically, they set forth a recipe or two for shad roe, then indicate that other roe can be used. Don't believe it. *The roe of puffers and gars can be toxic. In fact, gar roe can have extremely dangerous stuff in it.*

Consider the following quote, which is from Dr. Donn E. Rosen, curator of the Department of Ichthyology at New York's Museum of Natural History. (The quote was published in a sidebar to an article by Janet H. Alexander in *Sports Afield,* February 1968.) "The roe of a species of fresh-water garfish is so dangerous to eat that the slightest taste on the tongue can be fatal. In its death-dealing qualities, it's similar to cyanide—no one ever survives."

But don't throw away your gar roe. It's one of the best bluegill baits that you can put onto a hook. (Apparently bluegill have become immune to the roe so that they can feed on it. Bluegill are, more than people realize, roe eaters and nest robbers.) When baiting up, use tiny salmon-egg hooks, or, since the gar eggs are quite sticky, bait with a gob of 'em.

Gar eggs can be frozen and used later for bait—but be sure that you mark the package properly before freezing. Draw a skull and crossbones on it.

Remove the chicken eggs from the refrigerator. After the eggs have reached room temperature, break them into a bowl and whisk them lightly. Melt a little butter in a skillet. Chop up some green onions, including about half the tops, and sauté them for a few minutes in butter. Add the soft roe, heat, and stir. Break up the roe, chopping it with a fork, as it cooks. Add the eggs and scramble everything, stirring constantly. Salt and pepper to taste. (Freshly ground pepper is best.) Serve hot with toast, bacon, and very cold tomatoes. Exact amounts of eggs and soft roe aren't critical, but as a rule, try about half egg and half roe.

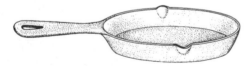

Roe 'n' Eggs

If you don't have any soft roe to cook the recipe above, or don't care for soft roe, then try this recipe with regular roe. Again, I haven't given any measures for the ingredients. Often this is a practical matter of putting whatever fish roe you have in with enough eggs to feed everybody. If you've got plenty of roe, however, use about half roe and half egg.

    roe
    4 cups water
    2 tablespoons vinegar
    chicken eggs
    butter
    salt and pepper

Heat the water and vinegar in a pan. Add fish roe, bring to a boil, reduce heat, and simmer for about 10 minutes. While roe is cooking, break the sacs and scatter the roe. If you are cooking a large batch of roe, increase the measures of water and vinegar, or add more water as needed. Roe will absorb water while cooking and will expand to about twice its original volume.

Strain the roe, then put it into a bowl with eggs. Whisk until mixed. Heat some butter in a skillet, then scramble the mixture until the eggs set. Salt and pepper to taste. For a delicious breakfast, serve with buttered toast and sliced tomatoes.

Bonus Small Fry

My boys are very, very fond of tiny roe of bluegills and other small panfish. If we are frying, we normally cook the bonus roe right along with the fish, in which case we use the same oil, batter, and seasoning.

This recipe is pretty much our standard recipe for fried fish, but I prefer bacon drippings for pan-frying a mess of small roe alone. This technique works best for small roe with sacs no longer than 3 inches; some larger roe tend to be far too dry when cooked by this method.

> small roe
> fine-ground cornmeal
> bacon drippings or other cooking oil
> salt and pepper

Salt and pepper the roe, then shake or roll it in cornmeal. Heat ⅛ inch of bacon drippings in skillet. Fry the roe on each side over medium heat for 5 minutes or so, depending on size. Some roe pop violently, so be careful if you fry on high heat; stand back and turn the

roe with a long fork. Do not overcook. Usually, a breaded or floured roe is done when the outside takes on a golden brown color. If you feel that you need to check inside, cut off a slice and look for any variation in color. The middle should look pretty much like the edges in color and texture.

Shad Roe with Sweet Potatoes

This is an unusual combination that I got from *Coastal Carolina Cooking*, which attributes

Fish Roe

Some say the best caviar is the roe of the sturgeon. Coastal Carolinians are sure to disagree. When prepared correctly, the fish eggs of mullet, menhaden, shad, and herring are just as tasty, they say.

The roe usually consist of two elongated saclike ovaries, covered with a connective membrane. The color varies according to species, ranging from yellow to orange to black.

The eggs of each species have a distinctive taste and texture. Descriptions of the variations in flavor will not suffice; you must try the roe for yourself. And even roe-lovers warn that it is a taste you have to acquire.

Most roe are good fried, baked, dried, or scrambled with eggs. If roe are plentiful, cooks often serve them alone as the main dish.

—*Coastal Carolina Cooking*

it to Jessie Savage of Morehead City, North Carolina:

   4 shad roe (about 1 pound)
   ½ cup cornmeal
   2 large sweet potatoes, peeled and sliced
   ½ teaspoon salt
   ½ teaspoon black pepper
   ½ cup vegetable oil or shortening (for sweet potatoes)
   vegetable oil for deep-frying

Rig for both deep frying and pan frying. Season the cornmeal with the salt and pepper, then roll or shake the fish roe carefully in the mixture. Deep-fry the roe until it is golden brown. Meanwhile, heat ½ cup vegetable oil in a skillet, and pan-fry the sweet potatoes over medium heat until they are browned on both sides. Serve the roe and potatoes together. Feeds 4.

Fried Roe

George Leonard Herter, coauthor of *Bull Cook and Authentic Historical Recipes and Practices,* says that he has never happened upon anything to eat as bad as fried fish roe. He probably got hold of some rather large roe that were cooked too long, which I admit can be dry, hard, grainy, and even difficult to swallow. These larger roe should be poached for a few minutes before frying. Poaching expands the eggs, making them more fluffy and moist. The poaching liquid is a mixture of 1 pint of water, ½ teaspoon salt, and juice of 1 lemon. Expand these measures if you've got lots of roe to cook.

After poaching, roll the roe in flour and fry it in cooking oil. Avoid high heat, which causes the roe to pop too much. (In fact, it's best to use a cover on the skillet.)

Don't overcook. If in doubt, cut into a roe and look at the cross section. If it is done, the center will be the same color and texture as the edges.

Pan-Fried Soft Roe

   soft roe
   cooking oil
   salt
   flour

Salt the soft roe, roll it in flour, and fry it in medium hot cooking oil until the outside is golden. Handle carefully. Overcooking, within reason, doesn't seem to hurt the quality very much. But soft roe does tend to shrink as it is cooked.

Variation: Forget the flour and oil. Salt the roe to taste and sauté in a little hot butter. Sprinkle with lemon juice and dust lightly with paprika.

Broiled Roe

I first became acquainted with broiled roe during 1968 at a rather elegant eating house on the Gulf Coast of Mississippi, near Pascagoula. My waiter told me how it was done.

   roe
   butter
   lemon juice
   salt
   water
   parsley (garnish)

Anyone for Sturgeon Marrow?

Just about everyone knows that the Russians make great caviar from the roe of large sturgeon, which can grow up to 2,500 pounds. But did you know that *vesiga*, made by drying the spinal marrow of the sturgeon, is also used in Russian cookery?

Steam the roe for 5 minutes. Make a basting sauce from butter, lemon juice, and salt. Broil the roe 2 inches from the heat source until done, turning once and basting. Carefully remove the roe from the broiling rack. With a sharp, thin knife, slice the roe in half lengthwise, then brush on some of the basting sauce lightly from one end to the other. Garnish with parsley.

Variations: You can poach or boil the roe instead of steaming. Very small roe can be broiled without prior preparation.

Cod Roe Ramekins

Here's an old Irish dish, *eochrai truis,* that I adapted from George L. Thomson's *Traditional Irish Recipes.*

½ pound boiled cod roe
1 cup milk
4 ounces bread crumbs
1 chicken egg
2 teaspoons chopped parsley
salt and pepper

Preheat the oven to 400 degrees. Mash the roe, then mix in the parsley, salt, and pepper. Add the bread crumbs. Beat the egg yolk, stir in the milk, and pour it over the bread crumbs. Let the mixture sit for about 10 minutes. Beat the egg white until it stands, and then fold it into the bread mixture. Grease some ramekins and spoon them nearly full of the mixture. Bake for about 15 minutes, or until golden brown.

Roe on Toast

This recipe is good for roe that is too large for cooking in the sac. My own guideline in this matter is that the eggs must be a good deal smaller than ⅛ inch.

roe (medium to large)
juice of 2 lemons
butter
bread slices
bread crumbs
salt
water
radish and parsley (garnish)

Tarpon

Although tarpon provide lots of protein for the peoples of Central America, it is not normally eaten in this country. The flesh is quite oily, tough, and none too good. The roe, on the other hand, is quite tasty.

Paddlefish

In the late 1800s, paddlefish were important commercially in the Mississippi Valley, valued for their tasty flesh and their eggs that sold as caviar. Around 2,500,000 pounds were harvested in 1899.

—*Arkansas Game and Fish Department*

Preheat the oven to 400 degrees. Heat a pan of water. Add most of the lemon juice and salt. Break the egg sacs and squeeze fish eggs into water. Boil lightly for 4 or 5 minutes. Strain and drain. Fry the bread and bread crumbs in butter. Spread the roe over bread, then sprinkle with fried bread crumbs and rest of the lemon juice. Put the bread on a baking sheet and bake for a few minutes, being careful not to burn the crumbs. Garnish with sliced red radish and parsley. If you don't have any parsley, try the radish tops.

Soft Roe Surprise

Here's a tasty dish that depends, in part, on a crispy outside and a soft inside:

    soft roe
    lemon juice
    butter
    chicken egg
    fine bread crumbs
    water
    salt

Poach the roe on low heat for a few minutes in a mixture of water, lemon juice, and salt. (Exact measures for the poaching liquid aren't too important, but try about 1 pint of water with the juice of 1 lemon and ½ teaspoon salt. Increase the measures if you have lots of roe to cook.) *Carefully* drain the roe, dip in beaten egg, roll in bread crumbs, and pan fry in hot butter until the outside is golden. Eat hot.

Note: If you've got lots of folks to feed, deep-fry the roe in a basket instead of pan-frying. Drain on absorbent paper before serving.

Variation: If you want to surprise your guests with a mystery appetizer, make balls of this dish. After poaching, cut the roe into sections with a sharp, thin knife. Dip, roll, and fry as above. Serve hot or warm.

Soft Roe with Fish Sauce

Soft roe, or milt, is very good when merely dusted with flour and sautéed in butter. A little lemon juice can be stirred into the pan drippings, thereby making a quick sauce. I also like the following recipe, which is adapted from a Thai recipe for pork brains. Soft roe, I might add, can be substituted for brains in most recipes—and is probably better.

Although most soft roe can be used, the males of some fish don't produce a large quantity of the stuff. Look for it in those fish that broadcast their eggs instead of depositing them in a nest like a black bass.

The recipe calls for fish sauce, which can be found in food shops that specialize in food from Southeast Asia. It is sometimes available in local supermarkets, usually imported from Thailand. Traditionally, the fish sauce is made by packing small fish with salt in wooden bar rels. The liquid that drips out is fish sauce. The Roman epicures also enjoyed a similar fish sauce, and some other famous sauces, such as Worcestershire, contain salted fish extract, often from anchovies. I have made the pure stuff from golden shiners packed into a wooden shotgun shell box with a drain hole in the bottom. What drips out is a mild form of fish sauce. For even stronger sauce, run the drippings through several times. (If you want Arab fish sauce, bury the box of salted fish in the warm sand for a few weeks.) Anyhow, fish sauce smells and tastes strong, but it is a wonderful ingredient for cooking and for use as a table sauce, if you like it as much as I do.

1½ to 2 cups soft roe
4 chicken eggs, beaten
2 green onions with tops, minced
2 tablespoons fish sauce (plus more for the table)
1 tablespoon all-purpose flour
¼ teaspoon black pepper
peanut oil

Mash the soft roe with the aid of a fork. Whisk the eggs and stir them into the soft roe, along with the minced onion, fish sauce, flour, and pepper. Heat a little peanut oil in 9-inch skillet or on a small griddle, then ladle in about ¼ of the fish mixture. (Or simply pour it in from the mixing bowl.) It will spread and cook like a pancake; use a spatula to help contain the outer edge a little. Cook the patty until the bottom is browned, then flip it over and brown the other side. Cook the rest of the mixture in the same way. Roll the patties and eat as is, or dip into a bowl of fish sauce or perhaps Pickapepper.

Roe and Bacon

Fish roe and bacon complement each other, whether you cook them together or separately. I prefer to cook mine together, usually by wrapping the bacon around the roe or, with smallish roe, by folding the bacon over the roe lengthwise. Bacon and roe are good fried without any other ingredients added, but I prefer a little salt and pepper with them. The combo can also be broiled, or put into a folding wire rack and grilled over coals.

Small roe can be fried, broiled, or grilled wrapped in bacon without any prior cooking, but large roe tend to be too dry unless they are first poached for a few minutes. (When poaching them, add a little salt and lemon juice to the water.)

If you choose to fry the bacon separately, use the drippings to cook the roe.

Soft Roe 'n' Bacon

This is a good dish to introduce somewhat skeptical folks to soft roe. If they are down-right squeamish, change the name to "bacon 'n' white roe." Here's all you need:

soft roe
bacon

Heat a skillet. Fold a strip of bacon over roe lengthwise and secure with a round toothpick.

Caring for Roe

For best results, roe should be removed from the fish as soon as possible and put on ice. As you remove the roe, be careful not to break or puncture the egg sac. Far too many good roe are cut with a knife when gutting the fish, thereby making the roe much more difficult to handle, store, cook, and eat. If you have experience and a good eye, you can usually tell before you dress a fish whether it is fat with roe.

If the fish aren't dressed soon after catching, then, needless to say, keeping them alive or quite cold will yield better roe.

Fresh roe can be kept in a refrigerator for several days or can be frozen. I prefer to freeze them in small containers of water, being careful to completely cover the roe. They can also be wrapped like cigars. Wrap them first with plastic film, then with aluminum foil.

(The roe can also be wrapped with a spiral of bacon, but this is a little harder to wrap and cook.) Fry on one side, then turn carefully and fry the other side.

Note: You can broil the roe and bacon instead of frying it, or put it into a hinged rack and grill over coals.

Baked Roe

This recipe (and this cooking technique) works best with medium to large roe, with sacs about 6 inches long.

roe
bacon
salt and pepper
lemon wedges (garnish)

Preheat oven to 350 degrees. Salt and pepper the roe, then place them close together (but not touching) on a shallow baking pan or sheet. Crosshatch with bacon strips. Bake for about 30 minutes, or until bacon begins to crispen. Serve with lemon wedges.

Caviar and Cheese

Most people eat caviar on dainty crackers or thinly sliced bread, maybe with a little lemon juice squeezed on top. I prefer mine with a slice of ordinary "hoop" cheese, which I usually buy unrefrigerated from a country grocery store. (This is a cheddar with a red rind around it, and is cut in wedges from a large wheel-shaped hoop.) I put the cheese on crackers, and the caviar atop the cheese. But of course all true connoisseurs know that the caviar, instead of being canned, must have been held at a temperature somewhere between 28 and 32 degrees for at least 5 months. Further, all true connoisseurs of hoop cheese know that it must be served at room temperature and, indeed, must not have been refrigerated at all.

Just as true wine must be made from grapes, not blackberries or elderberries, true caviar must be made from sturgeon roe, not carp roe or whitefish roe. Also like fine wine, good caviar is too difficult to perfect in home kitchens without special equipment. But I may be wrong, and you may want to consider the following opinion.

According to George Leonard Herter's *Bull Cook and Authentic Historical Recipes and Practices,* caviar was originally made in China from carp eggs. Genghis Khan, Herter said, took it to Russia, where sturgeon roe became popular because of its color. Herter says that sturgeon roe tastes no different from the roe of bluegill, walleye, and such when prepared "in the same manner." Carp roe, he says, still makes the best caviar. Here is what he recommends:

carp eggs
1 gallon water
2½ cups salt
1 teaspoon ground ginger
1 teaspoon dry mustard
⅙ ounce sodium nitrate
1/32 ounce sodium nitrite

Stir the salt into the water. Put an egg into the solution. If it floats, fine. If it sinks, add more salt until it does float. Stir the sodium nitrate, sodium nitrite, ginger, and mustard into the water. Cut the end off each roe sac and carefully squeeze the eggs into the salt-water solution. Leave the eggs in the salt solution, at room temperature, for 5 days. Strain the eggs and put them into glass jars. Keep

them under refrigeration (or frozen, Herter says) until you are ready to eat them.

Outer Banks Caviar

I've always felt that the Russians had the best of the caviar trade, but I have definitely acquired a taste for *batarekh,* which is an ancient treat that was enjoyed on the Nile long before Anthony and Cleopatra came barging along. Today the secret is known to a few gourmets in New York, Paris, and elsewhere, while the old salts on the Gulf Coast of Mexico and along the Outer Banks of North Carolina are said to walk around with salt roe in their pockets like candy.

The delicacy is usually made from the roe of mullet or cod. Get some very fresh roe, wash it, and drain, being careful not to tear the sacs. Roll the roe in salt, then place it on absorbent paper (I use brown grocery bags). Sprinkle more salt on it. Within a few minutes, the salt will start drawing the moisture from the roe. The paper must be changed every few hours. At each change, turn the roe over and sprinkle with more salt. Continue this for several days, until no more moisture is coming out and the paper doesn't have to be changed. Then hang the roe in a cool, airy place for several days, or put it on a well-ventilated rack. When it becomes dry and rather hard, it's ready to eat. Slice it very thinly, put it atop a small wheat cracker, and put one drop of fresh lemon juice on it.

To store *batarekh,* wrap each roe individually and refrigerate until you are ready to eat them. Dried salt roe will keep for several weeks.

Be warned that the dish does have a strong flavor, like caviar; it may be an acquired taste. I loved it from the start. But, to be honest, my wife still doesn't care much for it, and I can't even get my son Bill to try a taste of the stuff.

"It doesn't *look* good," Bill said, staring at one of the dry, salt-coated skin sacs.

Patiently I explained that *batarekh* is a delicacy from ancient Egypt—food for the Pharaohs.

"I don't want any," he said, quickly turning his head, not looking so good himself just then. "They look like . . . little mummies!"

Even for the sake of culinary research, I didn't ask Bill what he thought my famous scrambled soft roe and eggs looked like.

10

THE BEST PARTS

The greatest delicacy among the free foods, Dr. Vilhjulmur Stefansson, the explorer, always avowed to me, is ling liver.

—*Bradford Angier*

The New York editor of the first edition of this work wanted to throw out this chapter, fast, as if it could taint the rest of the work. Fortunately, I was able to convince him that he, like many other good Americans, would be throwing out the best eating.

I don't pretend to eat all the parts of the fish. I've never had much appetite for the eyeballs, for example, fish or otherwise. If the Asian gourmets want to eat 'em, that's fine with me, and I'll be glad to leave them in whenever I cook fish heads. I understand that some of the old Roman epicures ate mullet entrails, and that the French called the mullet the Woodcock of the Sea because they relished the entrails of that bird, if properly aged. Although I don't seek out the entrails, I'll have to point out that the big ends of small canned sardines often contain the liver, guts, and other innards. Who can deny that this is the best part of canned sardines?

Fish Throats

Some people who are knowledgeable about seafood won't pass up such offbeat but choice cuts as grouper or red snapper throats, and I read somewhere that the fishermen (or the fishmongers) kept these pieces for themselves. More and more, however, I see them on the menu at Florida restaurants. Almost any fish has a throat, and I have eaten quite a few off largemouth and smallmouth bass, which are purely excellent.

Throats are almost V shaped. They are cut from the front part of the fish, where the belly joins the gills. Usually, when most people behead a fish, they cut behind the collarbone and pectoral fin down to the backbone on both sides, then snap the backbone and pull off the head. This leaves the pectoral fins attached to the head, and the meat holding the fins is the throat. Skin it, cut it off from the head, remove

87

the fins, and you've got a good piece of fish. It can be sautéed, fried, baked, or whatever. String several onto a skewer, kabob-style, and cook them over coals. If you've got just a few, cook them along with the rest of the fish. If you've got enough for a mess, try them broiled, as follows:

> 1 pound fish throats
> ½ cup melted butter
> juice of 1 lemon
> salt and pepper

Combine the lemon juice and melted butter; pour over fish, and marinate for a while. Preheat the broiler. Arrange the throats on a rack in a broiler pan, baste them with lemon-butter mixture, and sprinkle them with salt and pepper. Position the rack about 4 inches from the heat. Broil for about 5 minutes on each side, until fish flakes easily, depending on the thickness. Feeds 2.

Be warned that throats have an unusual bone structure, so don't wolf these down too fast.

Sautéed Mullet Gizzards

The mullet eats large amounts of plant matter, which is digested in a pyloric stomach that is similar to the gizzard of a chicken. Recipes are hard to come by, but I found a good one in *The South Carolina Wildlife Cookbook*, to which it was submitted by James M. Bishop of the city of Charleston:

> mullet gizzards
> butter
> chopped parsley
> lemon juice
> salt

Split the gizzard and clean it inside and out. Heat the butter in a skillet, then sauté the gizzards, adding a little chopped parsley and lemon juice. I also like a touch of salt on gizzards of any sort, although Bishop didn't list the ingredient.

Liver Escoffier

Having a dislike for other kinds of liver doesn't necessarily mean that you won't relish fish liver. As George Leonard Herter once said, under a recipe called "Liver Escoffier" in his *Bull Cook and Authentic Historical Recipes and Practices,* "People who will not eat beef or pork liver are

---

Need Vitamins?

Burbot livers, like cod livers, are very large and high in vitamins. Burbot were harvested in Minnesota in the 1930s just for their livers. Rowell Laboratories of Baudette extracted the oil from the livers for a vitamin A and D supplement similar to cod liver oil. The oil was also used in the preparation of an ointment to promote wound healing. Scandinavians even consider burbot livers a delicacy. If you care to try it, boil the liver first to remove some of the oil, then fry it.

—University of Minnesota
Sea Grant Extension Program,
"Eelpout (Burbot): The Fish
Minnesotans Love to Hate"

crazy about fresh fish livers." To make this recipe, Herter goes on, "Take the fish livers and wash them well in water. Roll them lightly in flour and fry until done in butter. Salt and pepper to taste. I have eaten fish livers prepared this way for over thirty years and they are just wonderful. I prefer them to the fish itself by far and you will too, if you try them. They are one of the world's finest foods."

A dentist from Minnesota once wrote me, in response to an article I had published in *Gray's Sporting Journal,* that Herter was full of bullshit. I can't deny that, but, still, he may be right about fish liver—provided it is very fresh. The kinds I have eaten were quite mild and, I agree, were much better than beef or pork liver. More like chicken liver—but not quite as good as the mild, flat liver of the soft-shelled turtle. I have also eaten frog liver, which, I understand, is a delicacy in parts of South America. Livers of eels and lampreys are also highly regarded in some areas of the world.

Often a lean fish, such as cod, will have an oily liver that may be on the rich side for some tastes, in which case it should be poached in water before frying or cooking by some other means. On the other hand, some people relish a rich liver, and the burbot liver is considered to be a delicacy in Scandinavia. Since the burbot, or eelpout, is plentiful in Minnesota, maybe Herter was influenced by these livers. At one time, oil of burbot liver was processed commercially in Minnesota and sold like cod liver oil. It is very high in vitamins A and D. Today an annual eelpout festival is held on Leech Lake—but I'll bet even money that most of the livers go to waste. The liver from a related fish, the lingcod, is highly prized along the coast of the Northwest, and Alaskan natives are said to relish the liver of lingcod, either fried or raw. I can't go quite that far, however.

Heads or Tails?

A New York banker's daughter, who fished from the backwoods of Maine to the hills of West Virginia, argued with the son of a Utah Mormon, who fished from upper Baja to lower British Columbia, about whether to leave the heads on trout when you fry them. The one had no good reason for leaving the head on. Nor, on the other hand, did the other have a good reason for taking the head off. Does it matter?

Before long, both of them turned on me, although I set forth good reason for leaving the *tails* on fish. For flavor and crunch, nothing beats fresh, properly fried tails of yearling-size largemouth and smallmouth bass, and the tails as well as the fins of bluegills and crappie are truly great.

I don't care much for large fish tails, or fins, but note that the Chinese rate shark fins highly.

Rumaki

This appetizer is usually made with chicken liver halves. I like it with fish or turtle liver, prepared as follows.

livers
bacon
water chestnuts, halved
½ cup soy sauce
¼ cup sugar
¼ teaspoon black pepper
3 slices fresh ginger root

Watch Out for Puffer's Gall

Puffers are believed to be at their most toxic just before spawning, in late spring or early summer, but they are poisonous enough at any time for the old-time Japanese to have eaten them as a method of committing suicide. In Hawaii, where the word for puffer is *maki-maki* (deadly death), warriors used to use the gall of the fish to poison their spears. If you have a craving to live dangerously and can't wait to taste puffer, go to a first-class restaurant in Japan where there is a licensed "fugu cook." The meat is a delicacy there—but blowfish will be left strictly out of *my* pot.

—Janet H. Alexander,
Sports Afield, February 1968

for camp or shore lunch, by alternating bacon-wrapped liver with mushroom caps of suitable size.

Sautéed Fish Liver with Mushrooms

I haven't specified any measurements for the ingredients in this recipe because I always eyeball the liver, onions, and mushrooms. Equal parts, by volume, of liver, onions, and mushrooms would be about right.

fish liver
oil
vinegar
onion
mushrooms
bacon
salt and pepper

Mix a little oil and vinegar, in equal parts, and marinate the liver in the mixture for several hours under refrigeration. Fry the bacon until crisp in a skillet. Remove the bacon, drain, and break each strip into 3 or 4 pieces. Sauté the liver for about 4 or 5 minutes in the bacon drippings, turning once. Add the onions, mushrooms, salt, and pepper. Cook until tender, then drain off the grease and add bacon pieces. Serve hot.

Fish Liver and Chicken Eggs

Anyone who has a taste for liver but might be a little squeamish about trying *fish* liver might consider starting with the following recipe from the Middle East:

In a saucepan combine the soy sauce, sugar, pepper, and ginger root. Bring to a bubble, remove from heat, and let cool. Put the livers (cut into bite-size pieces, if necessary) into a nonmetallic container and pour the soy mixture over them, stir, and marinate for 30 minutes.

While waiting, cut some bacon strips in half, then sauté them in a skillet until limply done. Rig for grilling, preferably over charcoal or wood coals. Put each piece of liver onto half a strip of bacon, along with half a water chestnut. Overlap the bacon and secure with a round toothpick. Grill over hot coals until the bacon is crisp and ready to eat.

Variation: Make fish liver kabobs, maybe

All Aboard for Whale Tongue

Whale meat was not greatly esteemed by our grandfathers, but they did set some store by the tongue of the animal, usually salted, and Ambroise Paré says that "it is tender and delicious." They also appreciated whale fat which they ate "during Lent, with peas."

—*Larousse Gastronomique*

¼ pound fish livers
6 chicken eggs
6 strips bacon
1 tablespoon chopped parsley
½ teaspoon cinnamon
salt and pepper

Fry the bacon until crisp. Remove the bacon, crumble it, and set it aside. Sauté the fish liver in the bacon drippings for 4 or 5 minutes. Do not overcook. Pour off excess grease. Add the bacon to the liver, sprinkle with cinnamon, and mix quickly. Break the eggs over the liver and bacon mixture. Cook until the eggs set. Season with salt and pepper, then sprinkle with parsley. Eat while hot. Feeds 3 or 4.

Whitefish Livers for the General

Brigadier General Frank Dorn, author of *A General's Diary of Treasured Recipes,* said that he adapted this recipe, with a few minor additions, from a dish served up at Blue Bell Cafe in Saint Ignace on the Upper Peninsula of Michigan, where it was served during whitefish season.

8 to 10 whitefish livers
½ cup butter
½ pint dry white wine
½ cup brandy
2 tablespoons Worcestershire sauce
8 whole cloves
8 peppercorns
1 teaspoon caraway seeds
1 teaspoon ground ginger
4 bay leaves
⅛ teaspoon Tabasco
salt and pepper
flour

Mix all the ingredients except the livers in a saucepan, bring to heat, and simmer for 2 or 3 minutes. Add the livers. Remove the pan from the heat, cool, and place in the refrigerator for at least 6 hours. Then remove the livers from the sauce, drain them, and broil them under a preheated broiler until golden brown. Place on a heated serving platter.

Strain the sauce, return to the pan, then bring to a boil over medium low heat, stirring in a little flour to thicken it. Pour sauce over the livers before serving. Garnish with white radishes. Serve hot.

Saucing the Fish

Bleed a medium-sized lamprey. Keep the blood aside to flavor the sauce.

—*Larousse Gastronomique*

Fish Bones

Fish bones, often eaten in canned salmon and sardines, are an excellent source of calcium. I don't have a recipe, but I would like to point out that the Indians of the Northwest pulverized salmon bones and used them in pemmican, a mixture of dried meat (or dried fish), bear fat, and dried berries.

Fried Fish Sounds

Some fish don't have sounds, but many do. The sound is the air or swim bladder. I often save these when I am dressing fish to fry, but I've never eaten them as a main dish. Usually, I add them more or less as a conversation item. They are good, however.

> sounds
> fine-ground white cornmeal
> peanut oil
> salt and pepper

Cut the sounds loose when you dress the fish. Wash and drain them, sprinkle with salt and pepper, shake them in cornmeal, and fry them in hot peanut oil for a few minutes, until they begin to brown. Serve hot.

Newfoundland-Style Tongues and Sounds

The following recipe has been adapted from Frances MacIlquham's *Fish Cookery of North America.* Codfish is plentiful off the coast of Newfoundland, and it is the fish that was recommended in the recipe. Of course, other fish can also be used.

> 1 pound tongues and sounds
> milk
> ¼ pound salt pork
> 1 medium onion, minced
> 1 cup egg sauce (see chapter 17)
> parsley (garnish)

Wash the tongues and sounds in several changes of water, then put them in a glass container and soak them, under refrigeration, overnight in a mixture of half milk and half water. Then, simmer the tongues and sounds in a mixture of half milk and half water until they are tender. Drain. Cut the sounds into strips and slice the tongues open (especially from large fish).

While the tongues and sounds simmer, dice the salt pork and sauté it with the minced onion. Put the sounds, tongues, salt pork, and onion into a warm serving dish and mix. Heat the egg sauce and pour it over the dish. Garnish with parsley. Feeds 3 or 4.

The Virginia Housewife's Cod Sounds

Steep your sounds as you do the salt cod, and boil them in a large quantity of milk and water; when they are very tender and white, take them up, and drain the water out and skin them; then pour the egg sauce boiling hot over them, and serve them up.

—Mary Randolph, 1824

Cod Liver

The strong odor of cod liver oil may discourage some eaters from attacking the fish's liver, but it is luscious eating nevertheless, which does not recall the oil extracted from it.

—Waverley Root, *Food*

Fish Cheeks

Old farm boys like myself know that a chicken has got two choice pieces of meat on it, each about the size of the end of your thumb. They are located in the small of the back, one on either side. But you have to cut up your own chicken to get it. I've looked at a thousand chicken backs in various meat markets, thinking that I could luck into a whole package of backs with the choice bits. But they are never there. Somebody gets them at the packing house. Anyhow, to compare these choice bits to the rest of the chicken is similar to comparing tenderloin to the rest of the beef.

Fish also have two choice pieces of meat—the cheeks—one on either side of the head. They are often difficult to get at, however, and may not be worth the trouble on smaller fish. I normally skin the head partly, then cut the meat out carefully with a sharp knife. Once you have the cheek, cook it any way you see fit. Fry it or sauté it. If you've got only a few fish, it is best to mix throats, tongues, and cheeks.

If you don't want to take the trouble to gouge out the cheeks, cook the whole head, as in the next recipe.

Ojibway Feast

Ted Trueblood once wrote in *Field and Stream* about a group of Ojibway Indians in the vicinity of Lake Nipigon, Ontario, who seemed to prefer the heads of fish to the other parts. While Trueblood and his companion were frying or broiling the fish, mostly large brook trout and northern pike, the Indians were boiling the heads in salted water. Trueblood added that later he experimented successfully with boiled fish heads, and he also found that a head of a 10-pound salmon or other fish could be wrapped in aluminum foil and roasted in the coals of the campfire.

I too have experimented with fish heads of several sorts, often in stews, and I think they often contain the best meat on the fish. Of coarse, the throats of most fish, which may or may not be considered part of the head, contain quite a bit of meat. The fact is that the throat is usually removed along with the head. In addition to the throats, the cheeks each contain a small piece of delicious meat. On

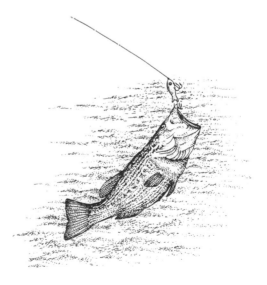

In Defense of the Mullet Bird

Students of judicial trivia might be interested in a bit that I found deep inside *McClane's New Standard Fishing Encyclopedia*. In Florida, McClane says, a commercial fisherman was charged with taking mullet out of season. The slick defense lawyer got a biologist to testify that only birds have gizzards. Because mullet have gizzards they must be birds. Birds are not covered by fishing seasons in the state of Florida. Case closed.

very large fish, these are sometimes cut out and cooked separately. There's also some good meat on top of the head, back toward the body, that's easy to get at. After that, the nibbling starts. Or rather, the picking. There are all sorts of cavities with meat in most fish, all very good eating.

The heads are best, I think, when they are cooked in a stew and gnawed or picked at the table. This is a messy business, however, and in polite company it might be best to flake off the meat and use it for any of the recipes in chapter 4. The best part of the head might be the eyeball, but most Americans simply won't go that far, and I won't either, as I stated earlier. I normally leave them in the head, however, in case anybody wants them.

11

FROGS

I've always heard that frog legs would jump about in the skillet, and even out of the skillet. And it's all true, up to a point. An old issue of *Sunset* magazine (March 1961), for example, says that chilling the legs in the refrigerator for a few hours will prevent them from twitching. Going further, the article cites one expert cook as saying that soaking them in cold milk not only will take the kick out of them but also will make them as tender as butter.

Well, I've eaten some river-swamp frogs of unbelievable size that could stand a little tenderizing, but I've also been in situations where I didn't want the kick taken out of them. In fact, I've been known to *help* a huge frog kick its way out of the skillet. Let me explain.

Once I went night fishing in the swamps of the Choctawhatchee River, not too far from a place called Crackerneck. With me was the best football player, for his size, that I've ever known. Later, he got a Ph.D. and wound up

being athletic director at a college. Anyhow, we had gone fishing, and had agreed to take only skillet, grease, a little meal, and salt for food. In other words, we had to catch fish to eat. At two in the morning, we hadn't caught a single fish. We hadn't even had a bite. Neither of us had eaten since noon the previous day, and we thought we were about to starve to death. Finally, we took our only flashlight, which was growing weak, and tried to shine fish or crawfish along the bank, hoping to dip them up with a net or hack them with a sheath knife. No luck. Finally, I heard a huge bullfrog bellow from a slough downstream. I knew where he was, and ever so carefully I stalked and caught him with my hands. I held him while the football player stabbed him in the head with the knife, which didn't immediately stop him from kicking.

Right off, the football player wanted to know if it was true that bullfrogs could jump

out of a skillet. The guy had already seemed a bit cautious about our potential fare, asking, for example, whether I thought we would have to eat any eels. I knew that I had a tough tenderfoot, so I started working on him, knowing by now that the frog was all the meat that we were going to get that night.

"If this frog ain't enough to fill us up," I said, while we were sloshing back to our campfire, "we'll head home come daylight and get Pa to cook us up a big mess of scrambled chicken eggs and hog brains."

He didn't want any hog brains for breakfast. Or any other time. Or chitterlings. He wasn't even sure now that he liked chicken eggs.

"We won't find a rattlesnake tonight," I said, "but we may run up on a big cottonmouth." He didn't want any snakes to eat, either.

By campfire, I carefully skinned the frog from head to toe. After gutting it, I held it up by the lower lip. It was big. The flesh was deathly white in the red glow of the campfire. It looked like a little man, with arms, legs, fingers, and long, long little toes with several joints. Silence came over the swamp, it seemed. Way off, a hoot owl hollered. I pretended to wash the frog while I picked carefully at the tendons in its back, near the hind legs. I was getting them ready for my trick.

"I . . . I thought you ate just the back legs," he said, finally.

"Oh, no, you eat the whole frog," I said. "As hungry as we are, we can't waste *any* of this fine frog. Except maybe the head. Frog brains ain't really big enough to fool with."

"They tell me those things will jump right out of the skillet," he said.

"Awh, there's nothing to that," I said, heating up the grease. Keeping the whole frog intact, I put a little salt on it and shook it in the sack of white meal for quite some time, waiting until I thought the grease was just right. "Here, I'll show you. He won't jump." Carefully, I held the frog by the lip with my left hand and grasped the leaders in its back between my right finger and thumb. Slowly, I lowered the frog's hind-leg toes into the hot grease, then tugged on the leaders in its back. The legs didn't merely twitch; they jumped up, and I helped lift the frog a bit with my left hand.

"Damn," he said.

"Let's try that again," I said, repeating the procedure. It jumped again as soon as its toes touched the hot grease. "We'd better stab this son-of-a-bitch again," I said, lowering his toes into the hot grease once more. He jumped again, but not as violently now. Maybe the leaders were pulling out.

"I don't want any frog," he said, turning his head.

So, that's how I got to eat the whole thing.

A year later, the guy got a football scholarship and went off to a small college somewhere in Louisiana. I don't think he went there because of the excellent frogging in that Sportsman's Paradise!

Anyhow, if you're short of meat and want your frogs to jump, leave the tendons intact and learn to work them properly. If you've got plenty of meat to go around, pull the leaders out before cooking the frogs. Salting the meat may cause it to twitch a bit, but the legs will stay in the skillet when the leaders are removed.

Here are a few recipes to try:

Dr. Stowell's Advice (or Dr. Wolfe's)

During the best of my frogging days, I worked for NASA in Huntsville, Alabama. While trying to figure out how to get to the moon ahead of the Russians, I sometimes had occasion to talk of good food to a German named Dr. Walter Wolfe, who lived at the local YMCA. I never did quite figure that one out, and I often wondered how he cooked Swedish meatballs and such at the Y. Anyhow, I made a bunch of notes on cooking and rocketry. Most of these notes were written on a green NASA memo form that had routing instructions, spaces or boxes for codes, boxes to check for action to be taken, and so on. My frog leg recipe is noted on such a green paper, MSFC–Form 183 (Rev. February 1961). I suppose that the form worked pretty well. We got to the moon, and I've still got the recipe. But I failed to note whether the information came from Dr. Wolfe or another friend of mine, Dr. Marion Stowell.

I suspect that Dr. Stowell should get the credit. She's from Quitman, Georgia, studied French in college, and spent a good deal of time in France. She didn't live at the Huntsville Y. And, to be brief, I'm almost certain that the recipe below is based on her advice. I remember that once I talked with her at some length about my larger frog legs getting a little stringy when they were fried, and I think that on the spot she gave me a list of ingredients used in the recipe below. I cooked the recipe several times back then, but after we got to the moon I slacked off somewhat on my frogging. Thus, over the years, I forgot some of the details. But I've recently put the recipe back together, and it's as good now as it ever was. Here goes:

Bullfrogs

Bullfrogs eat a great variety of foods, but require moving objects. Provision for moving food is one of the many difficulties in frog farming, which is not economically feasible. Crayfish and insects are important foods. Bullfrogs are opportunists, and sometimes gorge themselves on cicadas, grasshoppers, and meadow mice when these animals are locally abundant. Food items occasionally taken include young snapping turtles and fledgling red-winged blackbirds.
—*Frogs and Toads of Missouri*
    Missouri Department of Conservation

Frog fishermen sometimes use the frogs' love for live insects to an advantage. An artificial fly dangled or cast near a frog will sometimes get action.
—Texas Parks and Wildlife Department

2 pounds dressed frog, cut up
½ cup cream
¼ cup butter
¼ cup white wine
8 ounces mushrooms, sliced
1 medium onion, diced
2 tablespoons parsley
juice of 1 lemon
flour
salt and pepper

Heat the butter in a skillet, then sauté the frogs on low heat for 6 to 8 minutes, depending on size. Add the onions and mushrooms.

Salt and pepper to taste. Sauté for another 5 minutes. Sprinkle with a little flour. Add the wine and parsley. Cook for another 10 minutes. Reduce the heat, add lemon juice and cream, stir, and simmer for 5 minutes. Serve hot. Feeds 4 or 5.

Broiled Frog Legs

Frog legs can be very good when broiled, but they tend to dry out unless they are either marinated in oil or basted frequently. Here's what I recommend:

24 frog legs
½ cup olive oil
½ cup lemon juice (freshly squeezed)
1 tablespoon white wine Worcestershire
    sauce
1 tablespoon grated onion
1 tablespoon minced parsley
salt and pepper
paprika

Dress the frog legs, then put into a non-metallic container. Make a marinade of the olive oil, lemon juice, white wine Worcestershire sauce, onion, and parsley. Pour the marinade over frog legs, toss, and refrigerate for 4 hours. Preheat the broiler. Drain the frog legs.

Bring the leftover marinade to a boil in a saucepan, reduce heat, and save as a basting sauce. Salt and pepper the frog legs, then put them on a rack very close to the broiler. Cook for 4 or 5 minutes, baste, and turn. Cook for 4 or 5 minutes, baste, turn, sprinkle with a little paprika, and broil for 2 to 4 additional minutes, until tender. Serve hot.

Easy Sautéed Frog Legs

If you've got a few small frogs that you want to cook up without going to lots of trouble, try this:

frog legs
butter
salt and pepper
lemon juice

Salt and pepper the frog legs. Heat a little butter in a skillet. Sauté the frog legs for 6 to 8 minutes, until golden brown and tender. Reduce the heat, sprinkle a little lemon juice over the legs, and simmer for a few more minutes. Serve hot with hot French bread and vegetables.

Note: Don't let the simplicity of this recipe fool you. It can be very good, if you've got good, fresh frogs to work with. If you are using this dish as an appetizer, garnish the frog legs with a few sprigs of parsley before serving.

Fried Bullfrogs, Legs and All

It's really no joke. All of the frogs large enough to eat have some good meat on the front legs and along the backbone, and this is actually the *best* meat on the very large bullfrogs.

Although most frogs are fried by merely dipping them into flour or batter and then plopping them into hot oil until brown, I really can't recommend the method. But let me quickly add that I've probably eaten a hundred pounds of frogs fried exactly that way. They have a good flavor, but sometimes the texture isn't quite right. The meat can be stringy, and tends to get bigger when you chew it. This usually happens with very large frog legs, and I highly recommend that all large frogs be soaked for a while in lemon juice before frying, as in the following recipe:

frogs
flour
lemons
butter
salt and pepper

Skin the frogs, then cut off the hind legs and separate them. Cut off the front legs as a unit, and trim the belly flab from the back section. Put the meat into a glass container and squeeze lemon juice on it. (Use 1 large lemon per pound of meat.) Refrigerate for several hours.

Rinse the meat and let it drain. Heat the butter in a skillet. Salt and pepper the meat to taste, then dip, roll, or shake it in flour. Fry it in hot butter until golden brown.

Bullfrog Legs Piquant

Several New York editors have taken me to task, wanting to change my "bullfrog legs" to "frogs' legs" or "frog's legs," and they won't listen to the difference. Large bullfrog legs can be a little stringy when they are fried as usual, whereas the smaller frogs, such as the leopard frog, have legs more suited to frying. By whatever name, I highly recommend the following recipe for large bullfrog legs. The same text can be used for smaller frogs' legs if you will reduce the cooking time and add an *é* to the end of *Piquant* in the title, making it look more like French than American.

How Big Is It?

Too many recipes, especially those influenced by the French, call for a certain number of legs from frogs without giving any indication of exactly what kind of frog they are talking about. Edible frogs vary greatly in size. The highly prized red-legged frogs found west of the Sierra Cascade attains a maximum head-to-toe length of only 4½ inches. A full-grown American bullfrog, by comparison, can measure up to 18 inches. I've heard that they attain a weight of 7 pounds and can have as much edible meat as a small chicken. I've never seen one that big, but one night I gigged a huge bullfrog that had swallowed a full-grown sparrow! Other edible species, such as the leopard frog, fall somewhere in between the bullfrog and the red-legged frog. Obviously, any recipe that calls for a certain number of legs leaves a lot of room for miscalculation. The best bet is to go by pounds of meat, but I don't think I've ever seen a recipe that went this far. I'll eat ½ pound or more.

1 pound bullfrog legs
½ cup white wine Worcestershire sauce
½ cup butter
4 to 6 ounces fresh mushrooms, sliced
1 medium onion, minced
juice of 1 large lemon
½ tablespoon minced fresh parsley
salt and white pepper

Skin the bullfrog legs, separate them, sprinkle them with lemon juice, and let them sit for 30 minutes or longer. When you are ready to cook, sprinkle the frog legs with salt and pepper. Heat the butter in a large skillet. Sauté the bullfrog legs for about 10 minutes, turning once. Put the legs onto a plate. Add the onions, mushrooms, and parsley to the skillet. Sauté for 5 or 6 minutes. Stir in the white wine Worcestershire sauce, salt, and pepper. Put the legs back into the skillet and sprinkle on the minced parsley. Cover and simmer on very low heat for 10 minutes. At this time, the meat should be falling off the bones. Carefully put the frog legs onto a warm serving platter and pour the skillet sauce over them.

Serve over rice, along with French bread, vegetables, green salad of your choice, and rosé. If you are a wild foods enthusiast, try this recipe with cattails, tubers of arrowhead, water lily root, young unfurled leaves of pickerel weed, and so on, all taken from the frog pond.

Smoked Frogs

You can hot-smoke frogs in any sort of covered grill. I like to smoke them for some time by the indirect method in a large grill—that is, have the coals and the wood chips on one side and the frog legs on the other, out of the direct heat. They can be fully cooked by this method. Of course, the water smoker-cookers will also do a good job if you follow the directions that came with the unit.

    frogs
    bacon drippings
    salt

Frogging Laws

Some years ago, during the great race for the moon—and back when the New York outdoor magazines were still publishing such useful information for the nation's outdoor sports—I did a nationwide survey of the game and fish laws for taking frogs. Some states had no laws at all, and others had some surprises. Louisiana, for example, one of the very best frogging states, did not allow the use of a gig or spear or anything that pierced or punctured the skin or discolored the meat. They did allow some sort of mechanical frog grabbers!

So . . . check your laws carefully. Some states have frogs that are now on the endangered list, and of course it is illegal to take them. In some states, you'll need a hunting license; in others, a fishing license. And in a few states whether you'll need a hunting license or a fishing license, or both, depends on how you go after the frogs.

I've even got an old news release from Land Between the Lakes that states that gigging is not permitted after midnight! Some rules allow the use of firearms, blowguns, nets, bow and arrows, clubs, and fishhooks. In short, frogs can provide some mighty good eating, but check local laws before catching or taking them by any means.

Aztec Fare

Tadpoles were eaten by the Aztecs and have no doubt been eaten by other people—including the author of this book. That's right. I have cooked bullfrog tadpoles once or twice, not because I was hungry but as a matter of research. They resemble fried okra in texture and taste. Perhaps I should point out that a bullfrog tadpole can grow as much as 4 inches long, making a good bite, and some species get even larger. Believe it or not, a 2½-inch South American frog produces a tadpole that reaches 10 inches in length!

Build a charcoal fire in your smoker, and have hickory chips (or other wood) ready. Soak the dressed frogs in bacon drippings while the smoker gets hot.

Salt the legs, then put them on a greased rack in the smoker. Add the hickory chips, cover, and smoke at about 200 degrees for 30 minutes or so. Baste from time to time with bacon drippings.

Grilled Frogs

Frogs tend to dry out quickly, so don't grill them too long over high heat. Frequent basting will also help.

I like to grill frog legs on my stove-top electric grill, but, of course, they can also be grilled over charcoal or gas heat.

Here's all you need:

frogs
butter
lemon juice, freshly squeezed
salt

Heat the grill. Grease the racks. Salt the frogs and put them on the rack. Cook them for a few minutes, then baste frequently with a mixture of butter and lemon juice. Cook until frog legs have a golden brown color and are tender. Exact cooking times vary, depending on the size of the frogs, the heat, and so on. Try not to overcook.

Variations: It's easy to modify this recipe. The last time I cooked it, I basted with a mixture of melted butter and pomegranate syrup, a Middle Eastern ingredient—and it was delicious.

Frog Leg Omelet

Here's a good recipe when you want something quite unusual but have only a few frogs. I got the idea from an article by Marjorie Latham Masselin in the July 1968 edition of *Virginia Wildlife:*

frog legs
chicken eggs
green onions
butter
salt and pepper

The article said of frog leg omelets: "To make one you need at least 2 pair of frog legs per person. Skin and bone them and cut them in small pieces. Beat up 1 egg for each pair with a not-too-full teaspoon of water for each egg. For every 4 legs (2 pair) mince the white part

Dressing Frogs

Frogs are easy to dress. If you want to keep only the hind legs, make a cut across the top of the lower part of the back. Loosen the skin a bit and grasp it, using pliers or your fingers. Pull the skin off. Cut off the hind legs at the joint (I prefer to separate them.) The feet can be trimmed, or you can leave them on.

If you want to dress out the whole frog, make your initial cut on the back just behind the head. Skin the frog as described above. Remove the innards and cut off the head. Cut off the two hind legs, then cut the back just behind the two front legs. This method will give you four pieces: two hind legs, one segment of back, and one piece containing both front legs.

Skinning a frog for only the legs.

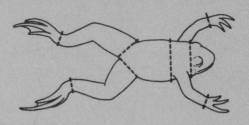

Cutting up a frog for the hind legs, a segment of back, and the front legs in one piece.

of a spring onion (green onion). Heat plenty of butter in a heavy skillet and sauté the onion and cut-up frog legs for five to ten minutes, depending on how tender the frogs were and how full the pan is. Sprinkle on a little salt and pepper and pour on the eggs.

"Reduce the heat and let this cook gently, lifting it from time to time with a spatula so that the uncooked part runs underneath and keeps the part that is cooked first from getting overly dry. Turn one half over the other and slip it onto a hot platter."

12

TURTLES AND GATORS

I must have eaten as many kinds of turtles, cooked in as many different ways, as any man alive. In addition to sea turtle steaks (which are no longer legal in most places), I have eaten alligator snapping turtles, ordinary snappers, terrapins, Suwannee terrapins, several kinds of softshell turtle, and the delicious dryland gopher tortoise. All of them were very good, and I could fill up a whole book about turtles and ways to cook them. (I have, for example, dressed out "roasts" from the hind part of large Florida softshells, some of which weigh as much as 40 pounds.) But, unfortunately, there isn't enough room in a book like this, covering a large number of edible wild creatures, to do full justice to the turtle.

I must point out, however, that modern cookbooks do a great injustice by either ignoring the turtle or implying that it is a meat of the past. Yes, it's true that sea turtles are highly protected in this country. Also, the gopher tortoise—true gourmet fare—is now protected throughout most of its range. Sadly, disrupted habitat and automobiles have greatly decreased its numbers. I can remember when, only a few years ago, "gophers," as they are called, were quite plentiful in rolling sandy scrub-lands of Florida and south Alabama, and I ate quite a few back when they were still called Hoover Hens, a term they acquired during the bad years of the Great Depression. At one time, believe it or not, there were commercial gopher men who "pulled" gophers for the market. That is, they rigged a dull hook onto the end of a grapevine. The hook was worked down into a gopher hole, which went into the dirt at a precise angle. Upon contact, the puller could feel the gopher's shell. He would work the hook around until it took hold between the upper and lower shells, then pull the gopher out.

Since they were not injured, the gophers could be kept in a pen until they were ready for the table or for the market.

In spite of the troubles of the sea turtle and the land tortoise, I must point out that, in terms of pounds of meat available, outdoorsmen in most parts of the country never had it so good. Snappers and soft-shelled turtles are available in greatly increased numbers, owing mostly to increased habitat provided by the large impoundments, recreational lakes, and thousands upon thousands of farm ponds.

Freshwater alligators are also on the rise, because of increased habitat and management techniques. I didn't know whether to cover the alligator in the fish section of this book or in the game section. I put it here because it comes from the water, or from water's edge, and because I have caught more than I've shot. That's right. I have caught them with topwater plugs attached with a wire leader to 50-pound Dacron line! Also, some people catch them with baited shark hooks suspended just above the water from tree limbs.

But I suspect that most of the alligators are shot, and limited hunting is now available in several states. In fact, I helped eat one that my brother got with the aid of a slingshot loaded

Doing Good

Of the 22 species of alligators, crocodiles, caymans, and gharials that once thrived in the tropical and subtropical areas of the world, 19 species are now either threatened or endangered. Most of the problems have been caused by man, partly because of reduction of suitable habitat and partly because of a great demand for the hides of these reptiles, which are used in luxury leather products.

Surprisingly, the American alligator *(Alligator mississippiensis)* is doing very well in modern times. Not many years ago, there was cause for concern for its future. But proper management techniques and rigid game protection laws helped the species rebound, and now it is present in such numbers that legal hunting is permitted in some states. Also, the large impoundments that have been built in the southeast and in Texas have increased the alligator's habitat, as have the warm water discharges from some nuclear electric plants along the larger rivers. Alligators are also raised on farms for hides and meat.

Alligator meat is very good table fare (or can be if it is properly prepared), and is now available commercially in some fish or meat markets. It is also served in restaurants, and many alligator tail steaks are grilled at tailgate parties prior to the annual football game between the Georgia Bulldogs and the Florida Gators. At least from a culinary standpoint, the Georgia fans seem to have the best of this event. (The Chinese, however, might argue that the bulldog is the better table fare, and that our informal word for "chow" came from you know what.)

—*Edible Plants and Animals*

with a hunk of lead. I told him that he couldn't kill a gator with a slingshot. He said that he knew it didn't *kill* the gator; he shot the thing right between the eyes and just *stunned* it.

"And what if it had come to while you were dressing it out?" I asked.

"Well," he said, "I reckon it would have been me and the gator."

Anyhow, if you are lucky enough to live in an area where gators are legal game, try the following recipes. Note also that gator meat (as well as freshwater turtle meat) can be purchased by mail order and perhaps in some seafood markets, fresh or frozen.

I suppose that the popular term *alligator's tail*, like frog's legs, leaves the impression that the rest of the gator is no good. This is not the case, and I have eaten the whole thing.

Fried Gator Fingers

If I had to choose one wild meat over all the others, I think I would take a yearling gator 4 to 5 feet long. And I would cook it as follows:

gator meat fingers, ½ inch wide
buttermilk
flour
peanut oil
salt and pepper

Soak the gator fingers in buttermilk for several hours. Drain the meat, then sprinkle with salt and pepper. Heat ¾ inch or so of peanut oil in a skillet. Shake the gator fingers in the flour, then fry them on medium high heat for several minutes, turning, until all sides are browned.

Gator Ribs

A friend of mine who worked with a civil engineering firm had his survey party sloshing around amongst the alligators in a Florida swamp. Deciding to take one for tail steaks, they tied a shark hook on a rope, baited up, and secured it to a tree limb. After catching a good-sized gator, they shot it, sawed off its tail section, and quickly buried the rest before the game warden came. Word got out, and the next day a Florida cracker came to dig up the rest of the gator, saying that he wanted the ribs.

"How do you cook gator ribs?" my friend asked.

"There ain't but one way to cook ribs," the Florida Cracker said, "and you cook gator ribs that way."

Alligator Sauce Piquante

This is a sort of traditional recipe from down in Louisiana, and it is indeed a very good way to cook gator. It calls for cubed gator meat, which can be from the tail, front legs, or anywhere you can get it.

The Meat
2 pounds cubed gator, cut about 1 inch square
2 cups dry white wine
salt and pepper

The Sauce

2 cups chopped onions
½ cup cooking oil
16 ounces canned tomato sauce
8 ounces fresh mushrooms, sliced
1 can Rotel (10-ounce size)
½ large bell pepper, chopped
1 rib celery, chopped
2 tablespoons Worcestershire sauce
¼ teaspoon oregano
¼ teaspoon basil
1 bay leaf

Dressing a Gator

Alligators of reasonable size aren't too difficult to dress out. Start by cutting the hide under the bottom from the throat to the tail. Next, cut from the bottom side of all the legs out to the paws. Then pull and work the skin back any way you can manage, using pliers and a skinning knife if you have them on hand.

After you have skinned the gator, you can fillet the meat off the tail or cut the tail, across the grain, into steaks. Also, the tail can be boned, then sliced into steaks. The rest of the gator meat can be cut off the bone and cubed. Just don't throw any of it away!

Note: If your primary purpose in skinning the gator is to get the hide for sale, be sure to check for instructions with market hunters or with dealers who traffic in such things. Also check the local game laws before taking an alligator for hide or meat.

Late Additions

½ cup chopped green onions with tops
¼ cup chopped fresh parsley
salt and pepper
rice (cooked separately)

Cube the gator meat, then salt and pepper it. Put the meat into a glass container, pour the wine over it, cover, and refrigerate for 1 hour or longer.

Heat the oil, then sauté the onion until it is golden. Add the bell pepper and celery and cook until tender. Stir in the tomato sauce and Rotel. Add the basil, bay leaf, Worcestershire sauce, and oregano. Bring to boil, cover, reduce heat to very low, and simmer for 10 minutes. Drain the gator meat, then add it and the mushrooms to the sauce. Cover and cook for 1 hour, or until the gator is tender. Then add the parsley and green onions. Stirring, add salt and pepper to taste. Simmer uncovered for 10 minutes. Spoon the meat and sauce over rice. Feeds 4 to 6.

Broiled Gator Tail Steaks

Alligator tail steak can be excellent when it is broiled. All manner of fancy marinades and basting sauces are used, as well as barbecue sauce. But I like the following simple recipe, with more emphasis on technique than on ingredients.

gator tail steaks (or fillets) about ½ inch
    thick
Zesty Italian dressing (store bought)
salt and pepper
paprika

Put the steaks in a nonmetallic container, pour some Zesty Italian dressing over them, and put them into the refrigerator for several hours. When you're ready to cook, drain the steaks but do not wash them. Sprinkle with salt and pepper. Turn the broiler on and arrange a rack so that the steaks will be very close to the heat source—about 3 inches or so. At the last minute, sprinkle one side of the steaks with paprika. Put them on the rack, paprika side up, and broil for 3 or 4 minutes. Turn the steaks over, sprinkle the other side with paprika, and broil 3 or 4 minutes, or until done.

Note: Exact cooking times will depend on the heat source, thickness of the meat, and so on. Just remember that the meat will be tough if it is overcooked. Usually, gator meat is best when cooked very quickly at high heat—or for a long time at low heat. Avoid anything between these extremes. An old Florida cracker told me this years ago, and my experience confirms his advice.

Variations: The above recipe can also be used for cooking on an outdoor grill. For best results, put the rack close to the fire—and watch the meat closely. If you are using a smoker-cooker, reverse your thinking. Use the same marinade and so on, but put the rack a good ways above the heat (using coals for low heat), add some green hardwood chips, and cook the meat for about 3 hours.

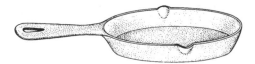

Fried Soft-Shelled Turtle

A fried soft-shelled turtle of reasonable age is about as tasty as meat can get. I somehow have the impression that very old turtles may be tough, but on the other hand, I have fried soft-shells up to 30 pounds (Florida soft-shells, which grow larger than other kinds of soft-shells) and found them to be quite good. The best ones, however, are not much larger than a dinner plate, cooked as follows:

    turtle, cut into serving pieces
    peanut oil
    salt and pepper
    flour

Heat at least ¾ inch of peanut oil in a skillet. Salt and pepper turtle pieces, then shake them in flour, put them into the hot oil, and fry until golden brown. The oil should be very hot, and for this reason, I prefer peanut oil, which has a high smoking point. Turn the heat on high, then reduce it to medium high after the meat starts cooking. If you've got lots of turtle, cook it in several batches.

Ground Turtle Spaghetti

This dish is one of my favorite ways to cook turtle and other game. The recipe below calls for half turtle and half pork or armadillo, but any reasonable mix will work, provided that the meat is good and properly ground. I like a medium ground meat (made with a ⅜-inch blade) for this dish.

Dressing a Turtle

I'll be honest about it. I've never found a good way to skin and dress a turtle, and I don't believe that anyone else has. I've tried various "easy" directions that I've found in magazines and books, but they simply don't work for me. Many of these involve dipping the whole turtle into boiling water, which is said to make the skin easier to get off. Then, after you've got the skin off, you've got to disjoint the limbs, somehow. In my opinion, however, it is best to dress the turtle without half cooking it.

The first step is to behead the turtle and give the muscles an hour or so to quit moving. When you get ready to dress the turtle, turn it upside down and try to fix the shell so that it doesn't move about. Pushing the turtle partly into sand or dirt might help to hold it still. Then cut through the flat bottom shell on either side, close to where it joins the rounded top shell. But of course, cutting through the shell is easier said than done. Believe it or not, a snapper is much easier than a soft-shell to dress, and upper and lower shells can be disconnected with a heavy knife.

A large soft-shell, however, is another matter, and an ordinary knife is not satisfactory. At one time or another, I have tried a meat cleaver, a hatchet, an ax, and a chisel. But the best thing I've found to get through a turtle shell is a portable electric circular saw. I have one with an old, dull blade, and this is what is needed simply because a shell is not wood and a large turtle will ruin a good blade. Adjust your blade so that it makes shallow cuts, and be very, very careful while using a saw in this manner.

After I cut through the shell, I cut the

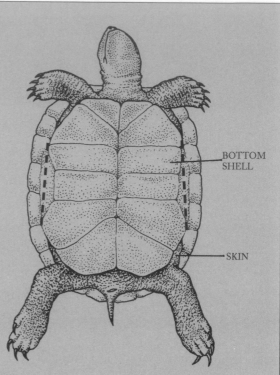

Bottom view of turtle, showing where cut should be made through flat bottom shell on both sides.

skin away from the bottom shell and work it toward the outer rim of the top shell. After the two shells are separated, I cut the bottom shell free with a sharp fillet knife. This leaves all the meat and innards exposed. Next, I remove the liver, which is very good. Then I twist and turn the legs until I can determine where to start cutting. The two front quarters can be removed separately, but I usually take the hind part out in one piece. In fact, I often trim off the small part of the legs, then make a roast of the hind quarter.

Turtle joints have a physical layout all their own, and by much twisting and turning and a little slicing, you can usually get them apart without using the saw again.

1 pound ground turtle
1 pound ground pork or armadillo
16-ounce package spaghetti (cooked
    separately)
2 cans tomatoes (16-ounce size)
1 can tomato paste (6-ounce size)
2 ribs celery, chopped with tops
8 ounces fresh mushrooms, sliced
1 large onion, chopped
4 cloves garlic, minced
½ large green bell pepper, diced
½ large red bell pepper, diced
1 tablespoon chopped fresh parsley or
    cilantro
½ tablespoon oregano
2 tablespoons peanut oil or armadillo fat
salt and pepper
3 bay leaves
freshly grated Parmesan cheese (optional)

Heat the oil in a skillet, brown the meat lightly, then add the onions, garlic, celery, mushrooms, peppers, parsley, oregano, and bay leaves. Sauté for 5 minutes, stirring as you go. Add the tomato paste and tomatoes, along with the juice from the can. Add a little salt and pepper, stir, and simmer for 10 minutes. Cook the spaghetti in a pot, following the directions on the package. Drain the spaghetti, put a serving on each plate with tongs, and top with the sauce. Grate some Parmesan cheese over each serving. Serve with tossed salad and hot bread. Feeds 6 to 8.

A. D.'s Turtleburger Steak

This recipe should be cooked in a large skillet or, much better, on a griddle.

1½ pounds ground turtle meat
½ pound fresh ground pork
1 tablespoon butter
onion
fresh mushrooms
salt and pepper
½ cup water
flour

Dice an onion. Slice a few mushrooms. Draw ½ cup of water; set aside, handy to your

Ground Turtle Meat

Some of the best spaghetti sauce I've ever eaten was made with ground turtle meat, with a little pork mixed in. Ground turtle can be used to advantage in meatloaf, chili, and so on—and in my turtleburger steak. It's best to bone the meat and cut it into chunks about 1 inch square. Put the chunks into the freezer until they are almost frozen, then grind them with a regular meat grinder. For most purposes, I like a ⅜-inch blade. Being low in fat, ground turtle freezes nicely for future use. I like to have it in 1-pound packages put up in small plastic containers or flat in Ziplock bags. Be sure to cook the recipes in this chapter, but also try ground turtle in any recipe that calls for ground beef. You can mix ground turtle with other ground meats such as beef, armadillo, or bear. Any reasonable mix made from properly dressed turtle and game is better and lower in fat than supermarket hamburger. It's also safer these days.

grill. Heat the grill. Combine the ground meats well, then shape the batch into a "steak" about 1 inch thick. Melt the butter on the griddle, then cook steak on high heat for 5 minutes. Turn carefully and cook for 4 minutes. With a spatula, divide steak into quarters (if you are serving 4 people). Check the center for doneness. Do not overcook, but the steak should be done.

Separate the steak quarters to gain working room, and pour a little water onto the griddle. Add the onions and mushrooms. Salt and pepper steak to taste while the onions and mushrooms cook. Add a little more water, then add a pinch or two of flour, stirring, until you have a gravy. Put the steak quarters on plates and top with gravy.

Add to or reduce the measures as required.

Allow ½ pound of meat per person—or more for big eaters.

Shankle's Turtle Stew

Here's a recipe from Terry Shankle, Division of Conservation Education, North Carolina Wildlife Resources Commission:

> 5 pounds of turtle meat
> 2 or 3 pounds chicken
> 1 pound pork chops
> 1 pound stew meat or venison
> 1 pound onions
> 1 large can tomato juice
> ½ gallon milk
> 2 tablespoons ground red pepper
> 1 small bottle A-1 steak sauce
> salt and pepper
> water

Put all of the meat into a pot, cover it with water, bring to a boil, reduce the heat to very low, cover, and simmer until tender. Then pick the meat off the bones. Put the meat back into the pot, along with all of the other ingredients. Simmer for at least 2 hours before eating. Serves 18 or 20.

Variations: This recipe makes a very good game stew if you use bear, javelina, or armadillo instead of pork chops, and rabbit, pheasant, or wild turkey instead of chicken.

13

COOKING FISH ON THE PATIO

A culinary sport by the name of Dan Webster changed my mind on two counts. I was brought up to believe that (1) fish ought to be cooked either in the house or along the water's edge, and (2) the saltwater amberjack isn't fit to eat. I was therefore surprised to learn that Dan proposed to cook an amberjack outside the house. He invited me to try it. So, I did—and now I know beyond a shadow of a doubt that accomplished outdoor cooks can work piscatory wonders over wood coals or charcoal.

Moreover, patio cooking gets easier and easier as better and more convenient equipment is developed. The newer gas or electric grills with reusable lava rock give us better control of heat, and packaged wood chips are now available in a variety of interesting flavors, from mesquite to sassafras. Even Jack Daniel whiskey barrel chips are on the market.

Dan Webster's Electric Grill Amberjack

Dan says to allow 4 ounces of amberjack per person. I don't want to argue with him, but I advise him to serve me a little more than that.

The Marinade
    2 tablespoons Worcestershire sauce
    1 tablespoon lemon juice
    1 clove garlic, minced
The Fish
    amberjack steak or fillets
    melted butter
    lemon-pepper seasoning
    salt

Mix the marinade. Put the amberjack into a nonmetallic container, pour the marinade over it, and let it sit for 15 or 20 minutes. Heat the electric grill. Brush the amberjack on both sides with melted butter. Sprinkle with lemon-pepper and salt. Grill for 3 or 4 minutes. Turn and grill the other side for 3 or 4 minutes, or until the meat flakes easily when tested with a fork. Serve hot with vinegar coleslaw, corn on the cob, and garlic bread.

Grilled Fish with Caper Sauce

Here's a dish that I got from California. The original recipe specified catfish, but I've cooked it with fillets from other fish and found them to be very good. The dish has a fine flavor, and the color is good, too. Make the sauce first.

The Sauce
  ½ cup cooking oil
  ⅓ cup lemon juice
  ¼ cup finely chopped onion
  2 cloves garlic, finely chopped
  2 tablespoons catsup
  2 tablespoons capers (and juice)
  1 tablespoon salt
  2 teaspoons sugar
  2 teaspoons Worcestershire sauce
  ¼ teaspoon pepper
  4 bay leaves, crushed
The Fish
  2 pounds fish fillets, skinned
  paprika

Mix all sauce ingredients, then let stand for 1 hour. Put the fillets in a suitable container, pour the sauce over them, and let stand for 30 minutes or longer, turning at least once.

Fire up the outdoor grill with charcoal, and grease your hinged wire rack. Arrange the fish

Lake Trout

The lake trout, a large char, is oily and does not fry very well. But it can be very good when cooked on a grill or under smoke. It can also be broiled and baked successfully. In any case, lake trout should be dressed quickly and refrigerated.

fillets in the hinged wire rack. Sprinkle the fish with paprika, then place them about 4 inches from the coals. Cook for 7 or 8 minutes. Turn. Baste with sauce. Sprinkle with paprika. Cook for another 7 to 10 minutes, or until the fish flakes easily when tested with a fork. Feeds 4 to 6.

Note: I like to sprinkle on extra paprika toward the end of the cooking time, giving this dish a deep reddish color.

Grilled Mullet Fillets

Here's a great recipe for grilling rather fatty fish such as mullet, mackerel, or bluefish.

  2 pounds mullet fillets
  ¼ cup bottled French dressing
  1 tablespoon grated onion
  juice of 1 lemon
  salt and pepper

Prepare the grill for hot coals. In a pan, mix the French dressing, onion, lemon juice, salt, and pepper. Dip the fish fillets in the sauce, then put them in a hinged wire grill. Cook 4 inches above the coals for 5 to 7 minutes.

Baste, turn, and cook for another 5 to 7 minutes, or until the fish flakes easily when tested with a fork. Feeds 4 to 6.

Lemon Rice Haddock

This recipe came to me from the Nova Scotia Department of Fisheries. At first, I had doubts about cooking a stuffed fish over the coals. But I tried it, following the instructions carefully, and I'm happy to report it's a winner. The recipe calls for haddock, but bass, lake trout, or other fish of suitable size can also be used.

        1 whole haddock
        1 cup sliced celery
        1 medium onion, chopped
        6 ounces sliced mushrooms
        1 small grapefruit, thinly sliced
        ¼ cup lemon juice
        2 teaspoons lemon zest
        butter
        2½ cups water
        1¼ cup long-grain white rice
        1 teaspoon salt
        ⅛ teaspoon pepper
        ¼ teaspoon basil

Scale the fish and clean it, leaving it whole and head-on. Melt 3 tablespoons of butter in a saucepan. Sauté the onion and celery until tender. Add the basil, lemon zest, lemon juice, and water. Bring to a boil and add the rice. Bring to a boil again, reduce heat, cover tightly, and cook for 20 minutes.

Outside, start the coals burning in the grill so that you'll be ready to cook. Inside, melt another 3 tablespoons of butter in a small skillet. Add the mushrooms and cook until tender.

Combine with the rice mixture. Add some salt and pepper. Stuff the fish.

Grease your hinged fish rack. Place half the grapefruit slices onto the rack, stringing them out to approximate the shape of the fish. Then put the fish on top. Put the other half of the grapefruit slices on the fish.

Cook over the coals until the fish flakes easily when tested with a fork; 10 minutes for each inch of thickness will be about right. Turn several times and baste with melted butter. Feeds 4 to 6.

Grilled Striper or Hybrid Bass

        4-pound striper or hybrid bass, dressed
            whole
        ½ cup oil
        ½ cup lemon juice
        1 tablespoon lemon zest
        3 teaspoons garlic salt
        1 teaspoon pepper

Scale the fish, dress it, and remove the head. Score both sides with slashes about ½ inch deep. In a bowl, mix the garlic salt, lemon zest, and pepper. Rub the fish with this mixture, put it on a platter, and refrigerate for 8 hours or longer.

When you are ready to cook, prepare a medium hot fire in the grill. Mix the oil and lemon juice. Place the fish over medium coals, cover, and cook for 15 minutes, basting several times with oil mixture. Turn the fish carefully and cook for another 15 minutes, basting several times, or until fish flakes easily when tested with a fork. (Test the thickest part of the fish.) Feeds 4 or 5.

Barbecued Pike Steaks

This recipe works well with northern pike, lake trout, or other fish in the 10- or 12-pound class. It's best to cut the fish into 1-inch steaks.

pike, about 12 pounds, steaked
½ cup soy sauce
½ cup orange juice
¼ cup olive oil
¼ cup catsup
¼ cup chopped parsley
juice of 1 large lemon
2 cloves garlic, minced
2 teaspoons salt
1 teaspoon pepper

Mix the soy sauce, orange juice, olive oil, catsup, parsley, lemon juice, garlic, salt, and pepper. Put the fish steaks into a nonmetallic container, pour the sauce over it, and marinate for several hours under refrigeration. Turn once or twice. When you remove the fish, bring the leftover marinade to a boil, remove it from the heat, and save it for a basting sauce.

Bring the coals to heat in the outdoor grill. Grease the hinged racks. Arrange the fish steaks in the racks. Cover and cook for about

10 minutes on each side over medium hot coals, turning once and basting with the sauce. The fish is done when it flakes easily when tested with a fork. Feeds 8 to 10.

Grilled Crappie

Being soft and tender, crappie are not normally recommended for cooking over charcoal. But here's a recipe that works nicely if you have a hinged wire grill.

3 pounds pan-dressed crappie (dressed weight)
sliced bacon
1 stick butter
1 envelope onion soup mix
¼ teaspoon pepper
salt to taste

Dress the fish and heat up the grill. Pulverize the soup mix in a food processor or with a mortar and pestle. Make a basting sauce by melting the butter and stirring in the soup mix, pepper, and salt. Baste fish inside and out. Wrap a strip of bacon around each crappie. Grease a hinged grill and arrange the fish in it. Cook over moderate coals 5 or 6 minutes. Baste, flip grill over, and cook the other side of the fish for another 5 or 6 minutes, or until the bacon is crisp and the fish flakes easily when tested with a fork. Feeds 4 to 6.

Oysters, Clams, or Mussels over the Coals

Such shellfish as oysters, clams, and mussels can be cooked, or "roasted," over the coals for a

The Great Cajun Pot Plot

Ever since the Cajuns were booted out of Nova Scotia by the British, they've been trying to get even with the rest of the world. Take, for example, their plot to corner the market on cast-iron skillets.

Recently I was shopping for a Dutch oven and discovered a set of cast-iron cookware in a large department store. The box containing the utensils was labeled "Cajun Cookware."

It struck me as odd that a skillet could be Acadian. Those who have fended for themselves for very long know what cast-iron does for fried chicken, pork chops, and beans, but that saucy foods are better relegated to stainless-steel. What were those Cajuns up to? I bought the pots anyway and took them home—that's when I discovered the scheme.

Inside the skillet was a recipe for blackened redfish.

It all started to click. I recalled that last year [1986], offshore of Louisiana, millions of spawning size redfish were caught by a small fleet of purse-seiners, who then were able to sell the fish to a market hungry for the main ingredient to chef Paul Prudhomme's gastronomical creation. . . . Then chef Prudhomme told the media that the big specimens such as were being netted aren't fit to be blackened. About that time, cooks started blackening everything they could find—catfish, flounder, prime rib—possibly even ducks. . . .

Blackening calls for an almost white-hot skillet, and nothing but cast-iron will do. All of a sudden, people were thronging in stores to buy vessels in which they could blacken things. I have no proof that the redfish rhubarb was the result of marketing genius by Cajun members of the pot-and-pan industry, but it's almost for certain that the skillet-makers are in the black.

—Larry Teague, *Southern Outdoors*

few minutes until they pop open. (They can also be cooked in this manner in an oven, but this can be a messy business and is best handled outside.) As soon as the shells open, grasp them in a heavily gloved hand and "cut" with a suitable knife held in the other hand. Shellfish cooked in this manner are ideal for serving and eating while cooking red meat (or smoking fish) for a longer period of time. The idea is to stand around the grill on a cool night and wait for an oyster or clam to pop open, then remove it and replace it with another. It's fun—and it's good.

Note: Shellfish eaten in this manner must be suitable for eating raw and should therefore be taken from clean waters.

I often purchase fresh Apalachicola oysters by the burlap bagful, and I've eaten thousands of them without ill effect. But unless I know exactly where oysters, clams, or mussels are coming from, I always fry them or cook them in chowder.

In any case, "roasted" oysters are usually eaten with some sort of sauce, and I recommend one that I got from the Nova Scotia Department of Fisheries.

½ cup melted butter
juice of 1 lemon
1 teaspoon dill seed
½ teaspoon sweet basil
½ teaspoon salt
¼ teaspoon cayenne

Mix all ingredients and refrigerate for several hours. Before serving, melt the sauce and keep it warm near the roasted shellfish.

Mother Hubbard's Secret

I'll have to admit that the 1978 Edition of the California Department of Fish and Game's *Catfish Manual and Cookbook* took me by surprise. Before then I had considered the catfish to be a southern specialty, but I had to admit that at least some of those California folks know what they are doing. They've got recipes called "Southern Rap-scallion," "The Colonel's Favorite," "Doyle's Dixieland Delight," "Calhoun's Sauté, Meunière" (named, I'm sure, for Calhoun, Georgia—Bert Lance's stomping grounds), "General Longstreet's Victory Dinner," "Pat's Plantation Party," and "Chicamauga Hush Puppies." But whether you live in the North, South, East, or West, be sure to try this recipe:

3 pounds catfish fillets, skinned
1 gallon water
1 cup salt
½ cup beer or ale
½ cup prepared mustard
½ cup sesame seeds, toasted (divided)
¼ cup Louisiana hot sauce (or Tabasco sauce)
2 cloves garlic, finely minced
2 tablespoons chopped fresh parsley
½ teaspoon Worcestershire sauce
paprika

Dissolve the salt in water. Put the fish into nonmetallic container, pour the salted water over them, and let stand for 30 minutes. Drain. Mix the beer, mustard, garlic, Worcestershire sauce, Louisiana hot sauce, ¼ cup of the sesame seeds, and parsley.

Heat up the grill, rigging for indirect grilling. If you have a large grill, build the fire on one side, leaving the other side for the fish. Dip the fillets into the mustard sauce, then sprinkle with the remaining sesame seeds. Put fillets on well-greased rack in the grill. Close the hood and cook for 1 hour, or until the fish flakes easily when tested with a fork. (Try to keep the temperature at about 250 degrees.) Feeds 5 or 6.

Pompano and Permit

The pompano is high in oil and should not be fried. It is usually baked or broiled, but it can also be cooked on a charcoal grill or smoked. The meat is firm and rich. For maximum enjoyment, catch a pompano in the surf with a live sand flea for bait, dress it, and grill it over charcoal on the beach.

The permit, cousin to the pompano, is medium high in oil content and should be smoked, grilled, broiled, or baked. The smaller permit are better, as a rule, than the larger specimens.

Smoked Fish with Hot Sauce

This recipe is often used in Florida and around the Gulf Coast to prepare mullet. It can also be used with most any other fish, but the sauce seems to go better with the fatty species, such as mullet or Spanish mackerel.

The Fish
    6 whole fish, about 1 pound each
    1 gallon water
    1 cup salt
    ¼ cup cooking oil
The Hot Sauce
    ½ cup honey
    ½ cup apple cider vinegar
    ½ cup prepared mustard
    ¼ cup Worcestershire sauce
    1 tablespoon chopped fresh parsley
    2 teaspoons Louisiana hot sauce (or Tabasco sauce)
    1 teaspoon salt

Do not scale the fish. Remove the head just below the collarbone, then cut along the backbone almost to the tail—but do not cut through the belly. The fish should fold out flat, in one piece. Dissolve the salt in the water, then pour the brine over the fish, in a suitable container, and refrigerate for 30 minutes. Take the fish out of the brine, rinse in cold water, and dry.

While the fish is soaking in the brine, ready a charcoal fire in the smoker or on one side of a large barrel or covered wagon grill (or heat up the gas or electric smoker). Close the hood and let the coals burn down until they are covered by white ash. Then cover the coals with wet (soaked) hickory chips or fresh hardwood (without any bark). I prefer fresh wood.

Grease the grill and place the fish on it, skin side down. Close the smoker, let cook awhile, then baste with oil. Do not turn the fish. Baste often. Cook for about 1½ hours, or until the fish flakes easily. Add more wood if needed to keep the smoke coming.

Make a sauce while the fish is smoking. In a small pan, blend the honey, mustard, and vinegar. Stir in the other ingredients, bring to boil, then cool a bit.

Serve fish whole, skin side down, on individual plates with hot sauce. Pull the meat off the skin with a fork. Feeds 6.

Smoked Fish with Wild Rice

Fish that are flaky and low in oil content, such as cod, tend to dry out during the hot-smoking process. But here's a recipe that I highly recommend.

The Fish
    1 whole fish, about 4 pounds (dressed weight)
    12 slices of bacon
    ½ cup sliced green onions with part of tops
    salt and pepper
Wild Rice Stuffing
    4 ounces uncooked wild rice
    bacon drippings
    ½ cup chopped onion
    ½ cup chopped celery
    ½ cup chopped mushrooms
    ¼ cup chopped parsley
    salt and pepper

Rig for hot smoking at about 200 degrees. On the kitchen or camp stove, fry half of the bacon. Retain the drippings. To make a stuffing, cook the wild rice according to the directions on the package. Sauté the onions, celery, and mushrooms in bacon drippings until they are tender. Add the crumbled bacon, parsley, cooked wild rice, salt, and pepper. Set aside.

Sprinkle the fish inside and out with salt and pepper. Stuff the fish, then close the openings with toothpicks or skewers. Place the uncooked bacon on top of each fish, then sprinkle with the chopped green onion. Put the fish on a well-greased grill in the smoker. Cook for about 1½ hours at about 200 degrees, then test for doneness. If the fish flakes easily with a fork, it's ready. Be sure to test the larger portion of the fish. Feeds 7 or 8.

Catfish and Bullheads

All of the freshwater catfish and bullheads are good to eat, but of course some are better than others. In my opinion, a good deal depends on the water they come from. These fish are of medium oil content and can be cooked by most any method. Generally, the catfish (channel, blue, flathead, yellow, white, and so on) are better than the bullheads (yellow, spotted, speckled, brown, black, and so on). The bullhead, however, can be very good table fare if it is dressed quickly and eaten fresh. Some bullheads do not freeze well. With the catfish, I much prefer the smaller size.

In salt water, the gafftopsail catfish is very similar to the better freshwater cats of similar size. The sea catfish, on the other hand, is not quite so good, though it is edible.

Small Fish Smoke

Smoking small fish, such as stunted bluegill and three-finger crappie and cigar-size smelt, can be done easily by putting them between hardware cloth. You need two sheets of hardware cloth of the same size, and some wire to sew the edges of the sheets together. Merely put the fish on one sheet, cover with the second sheet, baste, put on the grill, and turn the sheets over instead of trying to flip individual little fish. It's faster and doesn't tear up the fish as badly. This method works best when you've got a rather large covered grill, such as one made from a 55-gallon drum. Of course, any good covered grill will work, but remember that small fish take lots of room; consequently, not many can be cooked at one time in a very small unit.

> panfish, dressed
> 1 stick margarine or butter
> juice of 1 large lemon
> ½ teaspoon garlic juice
> salt and pepper

Melt the butter in a saucepan, heat, and add the lemon juice, garlic juice, salt, and pepper. Ready a slow fire in your smoker and let coals form a white ash. Salt and pepper the fish inside and out, arrange them on the hardware cloth, secure, and put over slow coals. Baste lightly, then add green (or wet) hickory chips or other good wood to the coals or heat. (I use green pecan without any bark.) Lower the hood and cook for 30 minutes or so, until fish flakes easily when tested with a fork. Turn and baste the fish every 10 minutes or so.

Note: The measures for the basting sauce should be increased if you've got a large batch of fish to cook. But I highly recommend that you cook a moderate batch first, simply because no recipe can pin down exact cooking and smoking periods for fish. Too much depends on who is doing it on what and to which kind and size of fish.

Smoke-Barbecued Arctic Grayling

Here's a recipe I adapted from an article by Nelson R. Lewis in *Outdoor Canada.* The original called for two arctic grayling and chopped alder. I tested it with two redeye bass and South Alabama pecan wood. If I thought grayling and alder would taste much better, I would head for Canada posthaste.

2 grayling, about 1 pound each, split but not skinned
1 tablespoon coarse salt
2 tablespoons brown sugar
1 clove garlic, finely chopped
1 teaspoon Dijon mustard
1 to 2 teaspoons maple syrup
1 teaspoon sweet basil
1 teaspoon chopped fresh parsley
1 lemon, sliced thinly

Split the fish down the back and remove innards. Do not scale. Open the fish, butterfly fashion, and place them, scales down, on a rack and sprinkle with coarse salt. After 2 hours, rinse the fish with cold water. Pat dry with absorbent paper. Put the fish back on the rack, skin side down.

Mix the garlic, maple syrup, mustard, brown sugar, basil, and parsley. Coat the fish with this mixture, then place the lemon slices on top. Put the rack over a shallow pan and let sit for 2 hours. (Retain the drippings in the pan.)

Build a small fire with charcoal (or hardwood) and let it burn down to hot coals. Add a handful of chopped green alder, pecan, or other good hardwood. When the smoke builds up, place the rack over fire, a good distance from the heat, and cover it with a large piece of heavy-duty aluminum foil. Smoke and cook for about 1 hour, basting several times with the sauce from the pan. Tend the fire from time to time, adding more wood chips if needed to keep the smoke coming.

After cooking for an hour, turn the fish over and cook 4 inches from the fire for 10 minutes. Serve the fish scale side down. Eat with forks if you've got them. Allow 1 fish per person.

Note: If you prefer, fillet the fish instead of butterflying it. This makes it easier to eat with a fork because it eliminates the backbone.

Skewered Sailfish Oriental

Usually, soft fish such as crappie, smallmouth bass, or walleye won't stay on a skewer. But some fish, such as sailfish, have tougher flesh and stay on much better. Moreover, they are delicious if they are prepared as follows:

The Marinade
  1/2 cup soy sauce
  1/4 cup pineapple juice
  1/4 cup sake or dry vermouth
  2 tablespoons brown sugar
  1 teaspoon ground ginger
  1 teaspoon dry mustard
  2 cloves garlic, minced
For Skewers
  2 pounds firm fish
  1 can pineapple chunks (16-ounce size)
  1 green bell pepper, cut into 1-inch squares
  1 red bell pepper, cut into 1-inch squares

Cut fish into 1-inch chunks and put into a glass or ceramic container. Mix all the marinade ingredients, pour over the fish, and refrigerate for at least 4 hours. After marinating the fish, put the liquid into a saucepan, bring to a boil, turn off the heat, and retain for use as a basting sauce.

Rig for grilling kabobs. String up fish, pepper squares, and pineapple chunks on skewers (preferably bamboo, for an oriental touch). Grill 4 inches above very hot coals for 5 or 6 minutes. Baste. Turn. Baste. Cook the other side for 5 or 6 minutes, or until fish flakes when tested with a fork. Feeds 4 or 5.

Variations: Add cherry tomatoes, mushroom caps, or onion wedges if you prefer more vegetables or if you have lots of people to feed on a small shark.

This dish can also be broiled in an oven or cooked with the aid of a rotisserie.

Flounder with Crab Stuffing

At first I called this recipe Taxpayer's Flounder because I got it from a booklet called *Fish and Shellfish over the Coals,* which I ordered from the Superintendent of Documents. The U.S. Government Printing Office in Washington published it. But looking further, I'm not quite sure who footed the bill for the thing. I found that it was "issued" by the National Marine Fisheries Service as a part of its continuing Consumer Educational Program in cooperation with the commercial fishing industry, and it was "developed" at the National Marketing Services Office in Chicago. In short, I don't know exactly who should get credit for the recipe, but I think it is pretty safe to say that, ultimately, the bill was footed, at least once, by "We the People." So, here's *your* recipe:

The Fish
  6 flounder, about ¾ pound each
  ¾ cup butter or margarine, melted
  ⅓ cup fresh lemon juice
  2 teaspoons salt
  paprika
The Stuffing
  1 pound crabmeat
  2 cups soft bread crumbs
  ½ cup chopped onion
  ½ cup chopped celery
  ⅓ cup chopped green pepper
  ⅓ cup cooking oil
  3 chicken eggs, beaten
  2 cloves garlic, minced
  1 tablespoon chopped parsley
  2 teaspoons salt
  ½ teaspoon pepper

Make the stuffing first. In a large skillet, heat the oil. Sauté the onion, celery, green pepper, and garlic for a few minutes. Mix in bread crumbs, eggs, parsley, salt, pepper, and crabmeat. Set aside.

Dress the flounder, leaving the head on. As the booklet explained: "To make a pocket for the stuffing, lay the fish flat on a cutting board, light side down. With a sharp knife cut down the center of the fish along the backbone from the tail to about 1 inch from the head end. Turn the knife flat and cut the flesh along both sides of the backbone to the tail, allowing the knife to run over the rib bones."

Rig for grilling. Then stuff the fish. Note that the stuffing will be exposed, and can be piled up a little above the fish. Mix the melted butter, lemon juice, and salt. Cut and grease an 18-by-18-inch sheet of heavy-duty aluminum foil for each fish. Place 2 tablespoons of this mixture on each piece of foil and smear it out, flounder-shape. Place a fish atop the sauce,

It's Good for You

Not only is fish a delicacy to savor, but it's also a healthy choice. Ideally, we should eat fish once or, when possible, twice a week. Fish is naturally low in cholesterol and saturated fat. A 4-ounce serving of fish provides about one-third the recommended daily amount of protein, yet does so with fewer calories than red meat. Fish is low in sodium and is a good source of minerals and vitamins A, D, B-6, and B-12.

The scientific community became interested in fish as something more than food when observations showed that Greenland Eskimos, who eat a diet rich in fish, have a low incidence of heart disease. The most significant benefit of fish in the diet is omega-3. Fish are the primary source of omega-3, a fatty acid believed to reduce heart disease and circulatory problems.

According to nutritionist Dianna Colson, studies have shown that omega-3 may cause blood cholesterol levels to drop. Research suggests that the ratio of low-density lipoproteins (LDL) to high-density lipoproteins (HDL) improves with the consumption of omega-3 fatty acid. Omega-3 is also believed to lower triglycerides and thin the blood, both of which reduce the risk of clogged blood vessels.

Long thought of as a brain food, fish can now be labeled heart food as well. Sometimes I wonder whether it's the consumption of the fish that benefits our brains and hearts, or maybe it's the act of fishing itself. A quiet fishing trip at sunrise may not boost your omega-3, but it will surely help your heart. Stress seems to melt away while watching a new day dawn, bringing with it new beginnings. And you probably won't find a better way to help your brain than to spend a couple of hours listening to nature's song without the distractions of a ringing phone or fax machine.

—Adapted from an article by
Johnnie F. Davis in *Kentucky Afield*
March–April 1995

---

then top the fish and stuffing with 1 tablespoon of sauce. Sprinkle the fish lightly with paprika. Bring the foil over the fish and seal all edges tightly with double folds.

Place each package of fish on your grill, which should be about 6 inches from the coals. Cook for 25 to 30 minutes. Feeds 6.

Variations: Crabmeat makes an excellent stuffing, but it can get expensive if you buy canned or frozen meat, and it can be time-consuming if you catch and dress your own. You can substitute fish flakes for crabmeat, or try diced shrimp or crawfish if you've got them.

Sea Island Snapper

Here's a recipe that I sort of put together from a booklet called *How to Catch Your Fish and Eat It Too*, which was handed out many years ago by the Georgia Department of Industry and Trade.

The Fish
    2 pounds fish fillets
    cooking oil
    salt and pepper

The Marinade
1 cup white wine vinegar
2 bay leaves
½ teaspoon thyme

To make the marinade, heat the wine vinegar, add the bay leaves and thyme, simmer for a few minutes, and let cool. Put the fish fillets into a nonmetallic container, pour the marinade over them, toss to coat all sides, cover, and let stand for at least 30 minutes.

Prepare a charcoal fire. Drain the fillets, sprinkle with salt and pepper, then brush them with cooking oil. Place the fillets on a well-greased grill positioned 4 inches above the coals. Cook for 7 minutes, then turn and cook for 5 minutes on the other side. The fish is done when it flakes easily when tested with a fork. Feeds 4.

Note: Flaky fish, such as largemouth bass, will be easier to turn if you put them in a hinged grilling rack or basket.

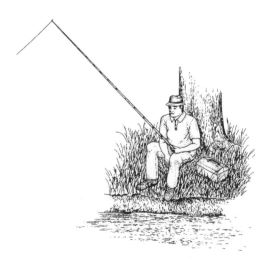

Two-Fish Kabobs

For the sake of comparison, conversation, and color variation, try combining different kinds of fish. If possible, use fish of different colors. Haddock and salmon are specified below, but try shark, tuna, and other fish, including 1-inch segments of fresh eels.

½ pound haddock fillets
½ pound salmon fillets
¼ cup soy sauce
¼ cup vegetable oil
2 tablespoons sake or vermouth
1 tablespoon brown sugar
1 clove garlic, crushed
¼ teaspoon ground ginger
1½ teaspoons orange zest

Cut the fillets into kabob-size cubes. Mix all the other ingredients, pour over the fish in a nonmetallic container, and marinate for 3 hours in the refrigerator, or at room temperature for 1 hour. Bring the leftover marinade to a boil in a saucepan, then take it off the heat and retain it for basting.

Rig for grilling. Thread the fish chunks, alternating the types, onto well-greased skewers. Place the skewers about 4 inches above hot coals. Grill for 4 minutes, baste, and turn. Basting several times, cook the kabobs until fish flakes easily. Do not overcook. Feeds 2 to 3.

Grilled Salmon Steaks

Fresh or fresh-frozen salmon steaks, cut about 1 inch thick, can be very good when cooked correctly over coals.

2 pounds salmon steaks
1 cup dry vermouth
¾ cup cooking oil
⅓ cup lemon juice (freshly squeezed)
2 tablespoons chopped chives
1 clove garlic, minced
2 teaspoons salt
¼ teaspoon pepper
¼ teaspoon marjoram
¼ teaspoon thyme
⅛ teaspoon sage
⅛ teaspoon Tabasco

If the steaks are frozen, thaw them out very slowly. Put the steaks into a glass container. Mix the remaining ingredients to make a marinade, pour over the fish, then refrigerate for at least 4 hours. After marinating, put the liquid into a saucepan, bring to a boil, remove from the heat, and retain for basting.

Rig for grilling. Place fish on a well-greased rack 4 inches over the hot coals. Cook for about 7 minutes. Baste with marinade liquid. Turn and cook on the other side until fish flakes easily when tested with a fork. This should take 6 or 7 minutes. Baste several times. Feeds 4 or 5.

Variations: I have also cooked slabs of salmon fillets by this recipe. Also try the recipe with large lake trout. If you plan to cook in camp and don't want to pack in all the ingredients, use a commercial teriyaki sauce for the marinade and basting sauce.

14

COOKING FISH IN CAMP

Some of the best fish I've ever eaten were cooked on a portable two-burner gas stove in the wilds of the Wacissa River in Florida, near where some of the Tarzan movies were made, and over oak fires on the banks of the Choctawhatchee River in Alabama. But the cooking process was exactly the same as was described in the first recipe in this book. Note carefully, however, that *frying* fish, or anything else, is more difficult in camp than in a kitchen, primarily because of limited equipment and problems with temperature control. Nonetheless, most of the recipes in this book can be cooked in camp, if you've got the equipment and ingredients. In this chapter, I will concentrate on a few recipes that I consider to be especially appropriate for the fisherman—who will have enough trouble taking all his angling gear along, let alone elaborate cooking gear.

See also chapter 44, about cooking game in camp, along with some tips on campfires and cooking techniques.

Bacon and Whatever You Catch

This recipe, or method, is a great way to prepare a few fish along a stream or in camp. Note that it does not require a lot of stuff to be packed along. Also, the bacon can be eaten without any fish—just in case you don't catch any. Make up the seasoning mix at home, and take it along in a small bottle or plastic container.

fish fillets
bacon
white fine-ground cornmeal
seasoning mix

Prepare the seasoning mix with 1 tablespoon salt, 1 teaspoon black pepper, and 2 teaspoons dried and crumbled oregano (or thyme). Put it into a small container. Pack the container with your tackle or gear, along with bacon slices wrapped in aluminum foil, and some cornmeal. (Make sure that grease won't leak out of the bacon package.)

If you don't catch fish, mix some cornmeal and some seasoning mix in water. You'll need a rather mushy texture. (It is at the right consistency when you put a spoonful of "mush" into the hot skillet and it flattens out into a patty.) Fry the bacon in a skillet and set aside. Cook the corn bread in hot bacon drippings. If you don't have fish, eat the corn bread with the bacon.

If you've got fish, dress them, then roll them in cornmeal to which you have added the seasoning mix. Fry quickly in bacon drippings. Eat with corn bread and bacon. If you see any watercress along the way, get some for salad.

Note: You can sauté trout and other fish in a pat of butter or a small amount of oil. Flour or meal is not essential. A little salt helps, but it isn't necessary. Small fish, such as brook trout, can be cooked whole, but larger fish will be easier to sauté if they are filleted or cut into small pieces. A large or heavy skillet is not necessary to sauté fish. Many memorable meals have been cooked up with nothing more elaborate than a mess kit! But a thin skillet will quickly burn your fish, so you'll need to keep a constant eye on what you are doing.

Wader's Fish Lunch

If you wade a stream all day, as, for example, between two bridges, you may not want to lug around a skillet. Even if you are in a canoe, a skillet, cooking oil, and so on is a bit much. Take along a few squares of heavy aluminum foil, folded compactly and stuck into your pocket or tackle box. Also, take along a few tiny packs of salt and pepper, which can be folded up into the aluminum foil—along with a sealed pat or two of butter. Ironically, these fast-food conveniences are quite helpful for wilderness hikes!

An hour or so before eating time, keep a sharp eye out for a good supply of dry wood. If you are knowledgeable about natural foods and have already caught a fish for your meal, also keep a sharp eye out for cattails, edible mushrooms, arrowwood, watercress, and so on. Build a good fire, then let it burn down to coals before cooking. While the fire is burning down, dress your fish.

When the coals are ready, open up a square of aluminum foil and carefully press it flat. With the pat of butter, grease part of the foil that will be in contact with the fish. Salt and

Crappie

Both the white crappie and the black crappie are very good table fare, low in oil, and can be prepared by a variety of ways. To me, their flesh is a little on the soft side. For best results, dress the fish quickly and keep them on ice or under refrigeration. Crappie fillets freeze well in water. Crappie have a number of local names, including "white perch" and "sacalait."

Flatfish

There are hundreds of flatfish, similar to flounder, that make very good eating. These range in size from panfish to huge halibut. Most of these fish have low oil content and good white, flaky flesh, regardless of size.

Each year sportsmen take many thousands of flukes and other flatfish by hook and line by day and by spear at night. Some of the common coastal flounders move into shallow water after dark, and they usually prefer a sand bottom to mud. Thus, they can be spotted with a strong light and speared.

pepper the fish, then place it (either whole or filleted) in the center of the greased portion of the foil. Seal the fish, folding seam and ends of the aluminum foil tightly. Rake out a small bed of coals and lay the aluminum foil on top. Leave small fish in the coals for 10 minutes. Large fish require more time.

Fish and Shucks

I've read a dozen tips on how to wrap fish in green corn shucks and cook them in a campfire. I've always wanted to try it, but somehow I have never had fish, campfire, and green corn shucks all at the same time.

If you've got the makings, however, here's an excellent way to cook a wonderful camp meal. If you don't have fresh corn, take along some dried shucks and then soak them in water before cooking. The method is from an old scrapbook about General. Wade Hampton, as quoted in *The Progressive Farmer* years ago. Hampton was a Civil War general, a U.S. senator, and a noted bear hunter.

"The general is spending the summer in Sapphire, N.C. He is a good fisherman and knows how to cook fish. Here is the way, says a friend:

"The instant the fish was landed, it was dressed, and a chunk of sweet fresh butter, a pinch of salt, a shower of pepper, and a diminutive rasher of breakfast bacon were placed inside. A fresh shuck, out of which the roasting ear had just been taken, was procured, and the trout, thus prepared, put in place of the ear. The shuck was smoothed down and tied at the silk end. Then this shuck with its precious cargo was put in the embers and covered with live coals until the fish was done to an exact turn; the roasting ear was toasted before the fire, and corn hoecake was brought into requisition. The fish must swim in the water before he is caught, and again in butter after he is roasted."

Fish and Elder Bloom Fritters

Here's a recipe that I prefer to prepare in camp by lake or stream when the elder is in bloom. But I've eaten it more than several times in a house, and it's good there, too. Once we lived on an island in a Florida lake, and the elders around our house bloomed all year! It was a nice spot, but I had to leave it because of lack of willpower. I worked at home, or was supposed to, and had my office in the boathouse. What angler can concentrate on office work while lunker bass slosh around after frogs in the boat slip? Anyhow, be sure to try this recipe. In flavor, it hints slightly of fried oysters, which I love. Here's what you need:

    2 cups cooked fish flakes
    2 cups elder blooms
    2 chicken eggs
    ⅓ cup flour
    ⅓ cup fine-ground white cornmeal
    ¼ cup milk
    cooking oil
    salt and pepper to taste

Mix the milk, flour, and cornmeal. Add the mixture to fish flakes. Gently stir in the eggs, elder blooms, salt, and pepper. Form the mixture into patties. Fry in medium hot cooking oil until the fritters are brown on both sides. Be warned that fritters burn easily, so keep an eye on what you are doing. Eat while hot. Feeds 4.

Planked Fish

I have seen recipes for placing fish on a plank and then putting the whole thing into a kitchen oven. I see no point in this unless you don't have any baking pans or broiling racks. Nor do I see any need for, or advantage to, using a plank in camp if you have other cooking aids. I do admit that planked fish can be very tasty, but note that too often the fish ends up dropping off the plank and into the fire, coals, or dirt. Then what do you do?

I concede that, on first thought, planked fish might be a good way to cook fish in camp or in an emergency situation. Of course, finding a suitable driftwood plank is entirely possible along ocean beaches, lakeshores, and even streambanks. But finding such a plank in the deep woods often presents problems. Some people, writing for Boy Scouts and such, recommend that a log be split. But splitting a log is easier said than done. If you've got an ax, your best bet would be to heat the blade in your fire and cook the fish on it instead of trying to split a log.

Even if you get a plank or a log, attaching the fish to it is not always easy. Most people recommend nails, but often nails are not readily available. If you've got a knife, try cutting pegs and boring suitable holes into the plank—a time-consuming task.

Many people recommend that the plank, with the fish attached to it, be put on one side of the fire and a reflector oven, or some such aid, on the other. The reflector can be a piece of aluminum foil—but note that if you have aluminum foil, it might be better to wrap the fish in it and put it under a few coals for cooking.

But, nonetheless, planks can be used to cook great fish. It's best to butterfly the fish, that is, cut the fish down the back and almost through the bottom, then spread the fish open, using the belly skin as a hinge. Nail or otherwise secure the fish to the plank skin side down. Note that it is not necessary, or desirable, to scale or skin the fish. Eat it off the plank, pulling the meat from the skin with fork or fingers. Salt and pepper helps, and a little butter or

Shad

The bony American shad is highly touted as table fare in some quarters. The hickory shad is also edible, but it is best when smoked. Threadfin shad and gizzard shad are seldom eaten. Shad roe is very good.

bacon swabbed onto the fish from time to time works wonders.

Notes: Planks from pine trees and other conifers may impart an unpleasant taste to the fish, and may even ooze a tarlike substance. Also, using a boat paddle to plank fish may seem to be a good idea, but think twice about using one if it has any sort of varnish on it.

Country-Boy Treat

Here's a method of cooking fish that almost every outdoorsman has heard about but not enough of us have actually tried. The following quote from an *Outdoor Life* column by C. B. Colby gives some good directions: "Have you ever tried trout cooked in clay packs? If not, you've missed a real country-boy treat. Dig under the gravel of a stream bed and you'll find clay. Clean your fish, and enclose it, head and all, in an envelope of clay. Some folks like to salt and pepper the cavity and put in a slice of onion. Put the clay-covered trout into a

Flat Rock Fish?

It is entirely possible to cook fish on a flat rock that has been heated in or over a fire. But be careful—rocks that contain moisture may pop or explode. A number of other flat surfaces can be used in a pinch. The blades of axes, hoes, and machetes come readily to mind. In fact, the term "hoecake" for a certain kind of bread might have arisen from the practice of cooking hand-size pones of corn bread on a hoe handle.

bed of coals, and dig them out 45 minutes later if the fish are small or an hour later if they're large.

"If you can't find clay, use mud. If you do, however, first wrap the fish in green corn husks, which will protect the meat from the mud. Clay bakes hard and so doesn't dirty the fish."

Camp Grilled Fish

Split unscaled fish from throat to tail, working from the top. Cut so that only the belly skin holds the two halves together. (Cut out the backbone, if you want to do so.) Salt to taste. Put the fish skin side down on a rack or screen and place over hot coals. Baste with a little oil, if available. For more smoke flavor, reduce the coals and add green hardwood chips such as oak, hickory, or mesquite. To get more smoke flavor, make a tent over the fish with aluminum foil. Cook until the fish flakes easily. Put the fish flat on a plate or other surface, and eat it with a fork, pulling the meat off the skin side. Remember that the fish has not been scaled.

Note that some fish, such as catfish and eels, can also be cooked in this manner without skinning them. In fact, some people prefer to leave the skin on them so that the meat won't dry out. Note further that the skin on small fish of this sort can be eaten without having to pull it off after cooking. The Indians of the Northeast, I understand, were especially fond of unskinned eels cooked over the coals.

Easy Bacon 'n' Fish

Here's a good recipe for the campfire, and it works nicely on canoe float trips where exten-

Smelt on Ice

A spring tradition along the Chicago-Waukegan lakefront, the smelt season annually attracts thousands of urban anglers who use dip nets and throw nets to take the tiny silver-sided fish. Many smelt fishermen set up small charcoal grills or camp stoves and cook their catch on the spot.
—*Outdoor Highlights*
Illinois Department of Conservation

sive cooking gear usually isn't feasible. All you need are a folding wire broiler, fish, and a few strips of bacon wrapped in foil or plastic. Clean the fish, wrap them with bacon, and put them into a folding wire basket, which will facilitate turning without tearing up the fish. Cook over wood coals until the bacon is crispy.

Sumac Trout

Here's a recipe, reprinted from my *Trout Cookbook*, that I devised to use whenever I have fresh sumac berries growing along a stream. That's right. Sumac. The berries are covered with hairs, which in turn are coated with a substance called malic acid, which has a pleasing tart flavor. Similar berries are used in the Middle East, and recipes from Apicus (the ancient Roman culinary sport) call for Syrian sumac. All the American sumacs with red berries (genus *Rhus*) can be used. In fact, a pleasing drink, sometimes called Indian lemonade, can be made from the berries and a little sugar. Also, the early settlers used a sumac infu-

sion as a substitute for lemon juice. Usually, the drink is made by sloshing some berries around in cold water. The berries don't have to be crushed, since most of the flavor is on the tiny hairs that grow on the surface. The liquid is then strained through a double thickness of cloth to get rid of the spent berries and the fine hairs that come off. (Note that washing the berries in the stream will rob them of flavor; note also that a strong rain can wash the flavor off the berries, so it's best to get them during dry weather.) For the recipe below, boil some of the juice until it is greatly reduced and tastes as strong as lemon juice.

1 or 2 small trout, less than 1 pound
2 or 3 tablespoons butter
flour
sumac concentrate
watercress
salt to taste

Dress the trout with or without head, depending on the relative size of your skillet, and sprinkle it inside and out with salt. Dust the trout lightly with flour. Rake a few coals away from the fire and melt the butter in the skillet. Sauté the trout until done on both sides, turning once. Remove the trout to drain. Add a little sumac concentrate to the skillet, stirring and shaking the pan for a few minutes. Taste and add more sumac if needed. Pour the sauce over the trout and eat.

Note: Sumac berries grow in bunches and are very easy to gather. They can be stored in a dry place for winter use, or you can freeze the juice. Make a little extrastrong juice by boiling as directed above, and try it in recipes that call for lemon juice. Then you can smile the next time you price a lemon at the supermarket. Green or unripened grapes (sour grapes) also can often be gathered along a stream or lake during fishing season. Juice from these (called *verjuice*) was a popular cooking ingredient during the Middle Ages, and was used in Egypt especially on fish. Sour grape juice is still used as a seasoning in the Caucasus, where it is called *abgora*. You can use it too in camp or at home. You may even like it better than lemon juice.

Blue Trout

Here's a dish that's ideal for cooking beside a stream, especially if you don't want to eat butter or oil. My mother-in-law, I might add, would never be able to prepare this dish properly because she would wash it too much. She'll scrub the flavor out of anything wild. I'm serious. The blue color is caused by the slime on the skin.

The fish should be freshly caught and kept alive up until the last minute. The measures below can be increased if you've got more than one trout. If you're working with a small pan, it would be better to repeat the entire process for each fish.

1 small trout
1 quart water
1 cup vinegar
1 tablespoon salt
salt and pepper
lemon (garnish)
butter (optional)

Heat the water to a boil, then add the vinegar and 1 tablespoon salt. Quickly gut the fish and put it into the boiling water. Simmer for 10 minutes. The skin will turn blue, hence the name. Serve with lemon juice, salt, and pepper. I like some butter on mine.

15

CRAWFISH, GARFISH, PEA CRABS, AND MORE

Once I drove through Louisiana while headed for Texas. Feeling hunger pains, I stopped in a small café in a small town and took a seat at an old wooden table. There were some fellows sitting at stools along what looked like an oyster bar—but they were eating crawfish. There wasn't a printed menu at the table, so I ordered some sort of crawfish dish from a chalkboard menu on the wall. It was delicious. On toward Texas I drove—but I kept thinking about the crawfish. Finally, I turned around and headed back for another helping!

Nevertheless, I have a problem with the Cajun method of cooking crawfish, at least as published in most books about cooking. They usually call for boiling the crawfish in highly spiced water for a few minutes. The crawfish are then peeled and eaten, or used for cooking other dishes, such as crawfish etouffée. (Note that many of the market crawfish, and some frozen crawfish, have already been boiled.) Although I enjoy these, I prefer to boil them for a few minutes without all the spice, as indicated in the recipe below. Further, if the crawfish are to be cooked by some method other than boiling, I prefer to omit the boiling and go directly to the recipe. The main advantage of boiling the crawfish first is that it makes the tails easier to peel. It also makes the meat easier to keep. Also, the fat in the head of the crawfish is a major ingredient in some dishes. Nevertheless, some of the very best crawfish are not boiled at all, although the Cajuns and the French might argue the point.

There are dozens of kinds of crawfish in North America, available in just about all streams, lakes, and ponds, and all of 'em are good to eat. Because crawfish are so much better to eat if they are kept alive until the last moment, it makes sense for the sportsman to catch his own.

In addition to crawfish, this chapter also offers a few recipes for shrimp, crabs, and some other shellfish. Moreover, I have included recipes and advice for cooking such fish as carp that are widely available and frequently caught, along with saltwater skates and rays. A number of people are reconsidering the term "game fish," and this statement applies to the table as well to stream, lake, or ocean. I hope the recipes in this chapter will help fill a real need in this area.

Boiled Crawfish

All you'll need are live crawfish, water, salt, and a pot large enough to hold at least a gallon of water. If you don't have enough water for the number of crawfish, the technique and timing won't work. Of course, the size of the crawfish will have a bearing on the amount of water needed. The larger Louisiana reds will require more water per crawfish if you are going to cook the whole batch at one time. The idea is to have enough hot water to cook the crawfish without drastically reducing the temperature. To cool the pot much below the boiling point won't do.

80 or 90 creek crawfish, live
seawater
1 cup butter
juice of 1 lemon
1 clove garlic, crushed

Prepare a sauce by melting the butter and stirring in the lemon juice and garlic. Let this steep in a saucepan. Keep the sauce warm but not hot. Put the water into a large boiler or stock pot. Use seawater if you have it. If not, stir in 1 cup of sea salt (kosher salt) per gallon of water. Bring the water to a rapid boil on high heat. Add the live crawfish and cook them for 2 or 3 minutes, depending on their size. Remove from heat. Strain the crawfish and serve hot, letting each guest peel his or her own. This is a finger-licking food, so normal table manners don't apply.

To peel a crawfish, hold it between the thumb and forefinger of each hand. Wiggle the tail section back and forth, then break it apart from the body. The idea is to loosen up some of the fat so that it will come off with the tail. (Good ol' boys in Louisiana will suck the rest of the fat out of the shell, but you may not want to go that far if you are courting.) Peel the shell off, working carefully back to the flippers. Break off the two outside flippers, then gently twist and pull the center flipper. If all goes according to plan, the vein, as it is called, will pull out intact. If not, you'll have to decide whether to devein the meat or eat it as is. Whenever we serve these at my house, I don't worry about the vein. If I did, my boys would eat up the crawfish before I got enough. If you aren't too picky about the vein, you can leave the tail flippers on and use them as a handle. In any case, dip the meat into the butter sauce and then eat it. The crawfish can be served hot or chilled, but they are much better hot. In the rare event of leftovers, chill the crawfish and make a cocktail for lunch.

For a complete meal of boiled crawfish, serve them with plenty of hot French bread and a huge tossed salad.

Some people, especially in Louisiana, some of whom are in the Crab Boil or spice business, will advise you to put all manner of spices into the water before boiling. Don't do it. Crawfish are much better without all this stuff. If you do choose to use the spice, get the crawfish out of the liquid after 2 or 3 minutes not only to prevent overcooking, but also to prevent the crawfish from absorbing too much of the spice flavor. Lots of salt is essential, however, and I also like to put a pod or two of hot pepper into the water.

If you want a lot of spice, don't put it into the water. First boil the crawfish in salt water and then drain them. While they are still steaming, sprinkle on some powdered spices (including some cayenne) and toss the crawfish about to coat them. When you peel the crawfish, the spice will get onto your fingers and onto the peeled meat.

Sautéed or Fried Crawfish Tails

Crawfish tails are just as good if you call them crayfish or crawdads. The problem is not in cooking these but in having the patience to catch and clean enough to feed everybody.

If you've got only a few crawfish tails, just for yourself or maybe one other person, try sautéing them in butter. Peel the tails off the meat, sprinkle them with a little salt and pepper, and cook them in hot butter for 3 or 4 minutes, or a little longer for large tails. Sprinkle the meat with a very small amount of lemon juice, if you've got it at hand.

If you've got a big batch of crawfish, you might want to dress them all, salt and pepper them to taste, shake them in flour, and fry them quickly in hot oil. Don't cook them too long.

Crawfish and Eggs

If you've got only a few crawfish, try this recipe for breakfast or brunch.

  crawfish tails
  chicken eggs
  butter
  green onions
  salt and pepper

Peel the crawfish tails, then dice the meat finely. Mince a couple of green onions, including part of the tops, and sauté them in butter in a skillet. Add the crawfish tails and cook them for 3 minutes. Break the eggs into a bowl and whisk them for scrambling. Pour the eggs into the skillet and stir until they are ready to eat. Salt and pepper to taste. Serve with toast.

Crawfish Salad

Crawfish tails can be used in almost any salad that calls for boiled shrimp or lobster. If you don't have a favorite recipe, try this:

  1 pound crawfish tails (about 4 pounds
    whole crawfish)
  4 bay leaves
  juice of 1 lemon
  1½ tablespoons mayonnaise
  1½ tablespoons sour cream
  3 stalks celery, sliced crosswise
  ½ cup finely chopped onion
  1 teaspoon celery seeds
  1 tablespoon dry dill weed, crushed
  salt and white pepper
  paprika
  lettuce leaves
  2 cups cooked macaroni

Bring water to boil in a large pot with bay leaves. Boil crawfish for about 6 minutes, more or less, depending on the size. Discard the water and bay leaves. Let crawfish cool, then shell and devein the meat. Sprinkle with lemon juice, toss, and refrigerate until you are ready to proceed.

In a large bowl, mix crawfish tails with mayonnaise, sour cream, macaroni, onion, celery, celery seed, dill weed, salt, and white pepper. Fix individual servings on lettuce leaves and sprinkle lightly with paprika. Eat with crackers. Serves 4 for a light lunch.

Pea Crabs

You may find more inside an oyster shell than just the oyster. Many oysters serve as host for the tiny pea crab, or oyster crab. The small crabs take up residence as larvae. The females live permanently with their host, but the males are free-moving. At maturity, the females are pink, one inch in diameter, and soft-shelled. They neither hurt nor help their host, the oyster, but merely share its food.

Fishermen have long recognized the pea crab as a seafood delicacy. Many a fisherman will demonstrate his or her fondness for the tiny crabs by consuming them alive. Others eat the crab steamed along with their oysters or sautéed in butter.

—*Coastal Carolina Cooking*

Crawfish Bisque

Here's a dish—often made with shrimp, crabmeat, or lobster—that can be purely excellent when prepared with freshwater crawfish. The natural fat from the crawfish adds a little something extra to a bisque.

4 pounds whole crawfish
4 bay leaves
2 tablespoons butter (divided)
1½ tablespoons crawfish fat (see text below)
¼ cup finely chopped green onions
1 tablespoon minced fresh parsley
2 tablespoons flour
2 cups whole milk
¼ cup heavy whipping cream
salt and white pepper
¼ cup sherry

Boil the crawfish tails in water with bay leaves for 4 to 7 minutes, depending on size. Discard water and bay leaves.

Peel the crawfish. Devein the tails and cut into ½-inch pieces. Remove 1½ tablespoons of fat from the heads. (When you remove the tails from the heads, look at one and you'll see the fat inside. Scoop it out with a teaspoon or baby spoon, depending on the size of the crawfish.)

In a small saucepan, melt ½ tablespoon of the butter and add the crawfish fat to it. Sauté the green onions and parsley until the onions are clear. Stir in salt and white pepper. Set aside.

In a pot of suitable size, melt 1½ tablespoons butter and stir the flour into it. Heat and stir for about 5 minutes, then add the milk, whisking briskly while you pour slowly.

Allow the mixture to heat up, but do not boil. Add crawfish and cook for 2 minutes. Do not boil. Reduce heat and stir in the cream. Add onions and parsley from the saucepan and stir in the sherry. Eat the bisque with toast. Serves 4 or 5.

Short Measure Gumbo

Here's a dish designed to feed lots of people on a small amount of shrimp, crawfish tails, crabs, or lobster. You can use any combination of these shellfish, and fill in with fish flakes if you like. I always try to cook a batch of this gumbo a day or two following a shrimp or crab boil, thereby using up leftovers.

1 pound shrimp or crab, cooked and peeled
2 cups okra, sliced crosswise
2 cups beef bouillon (can be made from
    cubes)
5 medium tomatoes, peeled and chopped
½ cup cooking oil
½ cup chopped celery
½ cup chopped onion
½ cup chopped green bell pepper
½ cup chopped red bell pepper
2 cloves garlic, minced
2 teaspoons salt
¼ teaspoon pepper
¼ teaspoon thyme
1 bay leaf
⅛ teaspoon Tabasco sauce
rice (cooked separately)
filé (optional)

Heat the oil in a large skillet or Dutch oven, then sauté the onion, garlic, celery, and peppers. Add the beef bouillon, okra, tomatoes, salt, pepper, thyme, bay leaf, and hot sauce. Cover and simmer for 30 minutes. Add the shellfish meats. Cover and simmer for 10 to 15 minutes. Put about a cup of rice into each soup bowl, then fill with hot gumbo.

Have some filé on hand in case anyone wants to thicken his or her gumbo a bit—but don't put filé into the main pot unless you want to risk having a sticky mess. (Also, gumbo with filé in it shouldn't be reheated later.) Feeds 7 or 8.

Boiling Shrimp, Crabs, and Lobster

Whenever I head through Florida, I'll drive a hundred miles out of my way to eat at a little café at Salt Springs, in the Big Scrub or Ocala National Forest. There is a special blue crab that grows there—many miles from the ocean—but I think the real secret is that the people in the Scrub know how to cook them! And it's easy. Very easy. Too easy, perhaps. Nonetheless, it is the best way to cook any kind of crab from any part of the country.

Boil the crabs for 10 minutes. If you want to get fancy, add salt to the boiling water. (Add 1 cup of salt per gallon of water; better, use seawater if you've got it nearby.) Pile the crabs onto a platter in the middle of the table. Get the meat out the best way you can. Dip the meat in a mixture of half melted butter and half lemon juice.

Of course, when boiling, you can add all manner of Cajun spices to the crabs (or shrimp), or you can buy a commercial crab boil mix, which usually comes packaged in easy-to-use cloth bags. But I prefer mine simple, as indicated in the crawfish recipe above. Note that no matter how much spice you put in them, crabs will not be good if you boil them too long. Of course, my "10-minute" rule of thumb will have to be modified for cooking very large crabs or stone crab claws. For best results, there should be lots of water in the pot in relation to the number of crabs. If you add too many crabs, the water will cool and cease to boil, making a guessing game out of cooking crabs. Note also that some adjustment will have to be made at high elevations. If in doubt, remember that the crab is done when the "apron" starts to rise.

For shrimp in the shell, use the method set forth above, but boil normal shrimp for only 5 minutes. And don't put too many into the pot. Jumbo shrimp may take a little longer. The shells will turn pink when they are ready to eat. If in doubt, try one.

Personally, I prefer to boil the whole shrimp and clean them at the table, as they are eaten. I also like them with the head removed but with the shell still on. Again, I prefer mine cooked plain, with a little salt in the boiling water, and with a dipping sauce made of half melted butter and half lemon juice. Leftovers (if any) can be refrigerated and eaten cold, possibly with a little red cocktail sauce. It's best to shuck and devein the shrimp when eating them cold.

Lobsters and "saltwater crawfish" can be boiled by the same method described above. Just use more water and increase the cooking time. A lobster of regular size requires about 15 minutes, but of course a huge 30-pound granddaddy will take longer. In any case, the lobster will turn red when it is ready.

Many recipes for shrimp, crab, and lobster salad and so on call for boiled meat. All these recipes will be better if you do not cook the shellfish too long.

Deep-Fried Crab Patties

This is a very tasty dish that can be prepared with pure crabmeat or with a combination of crabmeat and fish flakes or finely diced shrimp. It should, however, contain at least half crabmeat.

    ½ pound cooked crabmeat
    oil for deep frying
    ½ cup dry Italian bread crumbs
    2 tablespoons finely diced onions
    2 tablespoons mayonnaise
    ½ teaspoon dry mustard
    ½ teaspoon white wine Worcestershire
        sauce
    salt and pepper

Drain the crabmeat well, then mix it with bread crumbs, onions, mayonnaise, mustard, salt, pepper, and Worcestershire sauce. Shape it into patties ½ and ¾ inch thick. Heat the oil for deep frying. Cook the patties until they are golden brown. Feeds 2 or 3.

Fried Eel

Although frying is not the best way to cook eels, most Americans are going to fry them anyhow. To be honest, I've eaten some fried eel that was good and some that wasn't. It is best to have small or medium-size eels, no heavier than 1 pound each. Skin the eels, bone them, and cut them into 4-inch pieces. Salt and pepper the pieces, shake them in cornmeal, and pan-fry each piece in very hot oil until it is brown on both sides. Always eat eel shortly after it has been caught—and eat it hot. I can't recommend that you warm up leftover fried eel.

Smoked Eels

Many people regard hot smoking as the very best way to prepare eels, and of course there are dozens of variations. Here's a basic recipe that I adapted from the *Home Book of Smoke-Cooking Meat, Fish & Game* by Jack Sleight and Raymond Hull. First, prepare a brine with the following:

> 4 gallons water
> 8 cups salt
> 1 pound dark brown sugar
> 1½ cups lemon juice
> 2 tablespoons liquid garlic
> 2 tablespoons liquid onion

Dissolve the salt in the water, then mix in the other ingredients. (Reduce the above measures proportionally if you don't have many eels to smoke.) Skin and gut the eels while they are very fresh. Soak them in the brine for 1 hour. Rinse.

Have a pot of boiling water ready. Dip the eels for a few seconds in the boiling water. Then smoke the eels over your favorite green hardwood at 140 degrees. Small eels will be ready to eat in 2 hours, but large eels may take up to 4 hours. Delicious.

Baked Eels

Here's an interesting recipe from the Maine Department of Marine Resources. Clean and skin the eels, then cut them into 3-inch pieces without splitting them open. Twist out intestines with a knife, fork, or piece of wood. Preheat the oven to 350 degrees. Lay pieces of fat salt pork in a baking pan, then add the pieces

---

Eels and Lampreys

The culinary history of eels and lampreys goes back thousands of years. Over the centuries they have been held in high regard in France and England. It was the annual custom for the City of Gloucester to present a lamprey pie to the British monarch. The importance of the eel to an Englishman has been such that even when England and Holland were at war the eel trade carried on uninterrupted, and the Dutch eel barges, holds bulging with the slithering live fish, ploughed up the Thames to the London markets.
> —Frances MacIlquham
> *Fish Cookery of North America*

---

of eel. Bake for about 25 minutes, or until the eel is done.

Eel Quiche

Here's one of the best ways to prepare an eel for people who think they don't like it.

> ½ pound dressed eel
> pie shell, unbaked (9-inch)
> 6 ounces Swiss cheese, grated
> 1 cup light cream or half and half
> 2 chicken eggs
> 1 tablespoon flour
> salt and pepper
> water

Preheat the oven to 450 degrees. Heat some water in a pan, then poach the eel for 20 minutes. Use a fork to pull the meat off the bones, then salt and pepper it to taste. Prick pie shell with a fork, then bake for 10 minutes, until browned slightly. Combine the flaked eel and cheese, then spread the mixture evenly in pie shell. Mix the eggs, cream, and flour, then pour them over the eel mixture. Place the pie in an oven, reduce the heat to 325 degrees, and bake for 1 hour. Feeds 4.

Florida Indian use of Garfish

The various kind of fish and amphibious animals that inhabit these inland lakes and waters may be mentioned here, as many of them here assembled, pass and repass in the lucid grotto: first the crocodile alligator: the great brown spotted garr, accoutered in an impenetrable coat of mail: this admirable animal may be termed a cannibal amongst fish, as fish are his prey; when fully grown he is from 5 to 6 feet in length, and of proportionable thickness, of a dusky brown color, spotted with black. The Indians use their sharp teeth to scratch or bleed themselves with, and their pointed scales to arm their arrows. This fish is sometimes eaten, and, to prepare them for food, they cover them whole in hot embers, where they bake them; the skin with the scales easily peels off, leaving the meat white and tender.

—*Travels of William Bartram*

Carp for a King?

In some lands, such as China, the carp is highly regarded as table fare and as a wary gamefish. Yet, I've never felt quite right about eating carp at my home. The foreign masters of carp cookery, I understand, keep these bottom feeders in special tanks for several days before cooking them. I could catch carp and get them home alive, but I have no carp holding tank on my premises, and I haven't yet figured out a good way to keep them. My wife raised hell about two dozen little shiners that I kept in the bathtub for a day or two, and I'm not going to test our bonds with a couple of 5-pound carp nosing about in the tub!

But . . . the following recipe is a good one when cooked with or without the aid of a carp holding tank. If you don't have a tank, it's best to dress the carp soon after catching it, then ice it down as soon as possible. Skinning the fish helps, and it's also best to remove the strip of dark meat that runs down the lateral line just under the skin.

2 pounds carp fillets, skinned and boneless
1 large onion, chopped
1 cup dry bread crumbs
6 tablespoons fresh lemon juice (divided)
1 tablespoon chopped fresh parsley
1 teaspoon salt
¼ teaspoon pepper
½ teaspoon paprika
⅛ teaspoon dried thyme
⅛ teaspoon celery salt
1 bay leaf, powdered
butter
water

Preheat the oven to 300 degrees. Butter an oblong baking dish of suitable size, then sprinkle the onions on the bottom. Arrange the carp fillets over the onions. Mix the bread crumbs, salt, pepper, paprika, thyme, celery salt, powered bay leaf, and parsley. Sprinkle this mixture over the fillets, then dot with pieces of butter. Next, mix 3 tablespoons of lemon juice with ½ cup of water, then sprinkle it evenly over the fish. Bake for 15 minutes. Mix the remaining 3 tablespoons of lemon juice with ½ cup of water and sprinkle it evenly over the fish. Bake for another 15 minutes, or until the bread crumbs are browned. Remove the baking pan from the oven. Let the fillets sit in the juice for a few minutes before serving. Feeds 4 to 6.

Frying a Carp

Here's a method that I got from Euell Gibbons, and I've seen variations of it printed in other sources: Get a very fresh carp. Skin it, then, using your fingers and thumb, tear pieces of flesh from the backbone. Sprinkle these pieces with salt, then fry them in very hot peanut oil for a few minutes. That's right—use nothing but salt on the fish. Eat while quite hot. Too easy? Try it. We've got lots of carp in our waters that need catching and eating!

Gar Balls Toogoodoo

This recipe has been adapted from the *The South Carolina Wildlife Cookbook*, to which it was submitted by James M. Bishop of Charleston.

2 pounds garfish meat, flaked
1 pound potatoes
2 large onions, chopped fine
1 cup (or more) mixed parsley, green
   onions, and celery tops, chopped
½ cup prepared yellow mustard
½ cup vinegar
flour
cooking oil

Peel the potatoes, cut them into pieces, boil them in water until tender, then mash them. Rig for deep frying. Mix a sauce of yellow mustard and vinegar. Then mix the fish, potatoes, onions, and vegetables. Shape fish mixture into balls about 1½ inches in diameter. Roll these balls in mustard sauce, then in flour, and deep-fry. Feeds 6 or 7.

Fried Bowfin or Mudfish

The bowfin fights harder than anything that swims, and it terrorizes bass anglers in the South and up the Mississippi drainage system. It covers mid-America and is as game as a fish can be. It's also known as the mudfish, grindle, cypress trout, blackfish, and so on. In any case, the bowfin is eaten in some areas. As soon as the fish is caught, bleed it by making a cut on both sides just above the tail. Skin the fish and fillet it. Sprinkle with salt and pepper, shake in flour, and fry quickly in very hot peanut oil. *Eat the fish very hot.* If it cools, the flesh becomes spongy, like cotton. Note that the end of the fillet toward the tail is better than the other end.

This method can also be used to fry other fish that are not noted for taste and texture.

A Better Scallop

You can usually catch a better scallop than you can buy. In the past, some of the "scallops" on the market, and in restaurants, were actually meat punched from rays, sharks, and other fish. Often market scallops are soaked in water, which makes them bigger and improves the color—but at the expense of flavor.

Sautéed Bay Scallops

If you see people wading about with a long-handled dip net in a shallow saltwater bay, they may be after scallops, especially if there is some eelgrass growing in the area. Unlike the oyster, the adult scallop constantly moves about in the water by opening and closing its shell. In so doing, it develops a muscle, and this is what we normally eat. When you shuck a scallop, cut the muscle on both ends very close to the shell.

The small bay scallop makes better table fare than the other species, and it is the one more often taken by sportsmen.

The flavor is quite delicate, and I cook it delicately.

fresh scallops, dressed
butter
salt

Heat some butter in a skillet and add a little salt. Sauté the scallops for a few minutes, until they start to brown. Do not overcook. Drain on absorbent paper, but don't let them get cold.

The Squid and The Octopus

If you tie into a squid or octopus, remember that they can be cooked in a number of ways. The body as well as the tentacles are eaten. Sometimes the body is stuffed, but more often the meat is cut into thin strips and pounded to tenderize it. The larger specimens are especially tough. Use any good deep-frying recipe for squid or octopus.

The orientals hold the octopus in high esteem as table fare, and the peoples around the Mediterranean region consider the squid to be a delicacy. Some of the French even stuff squid bodies with chopped tentacles and spinach!

Clam Fritters

I love clams on the half shell, but I am very uncomfortable about eating them these days because of water pollution. I therefore recommend that they be cooked in a good chowder recipe, or as follows:

2 cups chopped clams
clam juice
1 chicken egg, beaten
¼ cup flour
¼ cup white cornmeal
¼ cup diced green onions with part of tops
salt and pepper
cooking oil

Mix the flour, cornmeal, egg, clams, green onions, salt, and pepper. Add a little clam juice, mixing with your hands, until you get the right consistency for fritters. Heat a little oil in a skillet or on a griddle. Test one spoonful of the fritter mixture. If it doesn't hold together well when you turn it with a spatula, add a little more flour to the mixture. If the texture is right, continue to cook the patties on both sides until they are golden brown. Feeds 4 or 5.

Fried Oysters

Fried oysters happen to be one of my very favorite foods, and I've tried all manner of egg dips and batters. I much prefer to have them freshly shucked than in a bucket. Fresh oysters have more taste, and, if they are taken on low tide in the fall, they require no seasoning. If I've got fresh oysters and shuck them myself, here's all I want:

> oysters
> saltine crackers
> oil

Crush some fresh crackers quite finely with a rolling pin. Heat at least ½ inch of oil in a skillet. Shuck the oysters—but do not wash or drain them. Drop the oysters one by one into the cracker crumbs, then roll or shake. Fry the oysters in hot oil for 3 or 4 minutes, or until browned.

Note: If you cook many oysters by this method, you'll need to change the oil and clean the burnt cracker crumbs from the bottom of your skillet from time to time. Have two skillets ready if you've got lots of folks to feed.

Steamed Periwinkles

Periwinkles are small, snail-like mollusks that cling to rocks and pilings and other structures in and around saltwater. There are over a hundred species—all good to eat. Steam them over boiling water for 10 minutes, or until their "caps" can be lifted. Stick the steamed periwinkle with a toothpick and pull it out of the shell, dip it into a bowl of melted, lightly salted butter, and eat.

Conch, Whelk, and Abalone

There are several kinds of conchs and whelks, all of which are marine snails. I don't have any sort of scientific breakdown, but my rule of thumb to separate them from the periwinkle is size. Conchs and whelks are big enough to be taken more seriously. They are all edible saltwater mollusks—and are all tough.

There are several ways to remove the meat from the shell, but the most widely used method is to boil the whole thing for about 15 minutes, then pull the meat from the shell. Generally, only the muscular foot part is used, which must be cut away from the rest. Often, the meat is pounded with a meat mallet, chopped up finely, ground up, or steamed in a pressure cooker before it is used in recipes. It can be made into fritters, or sliced thinly and fried. Usually, however, the meat is used in a chowder. (See the recipe in chapter 7.)

Abalone is a sort of large California version of conch, and it is also tough. The meat (or foot) can be tenderized by pounding it with the edge of a plate or with a meat mallet. The meat is usually cooked in a chowder, but it can also be cooked in other ways, including baking. Try cutting it into thin strips (about ⅛ inch thick), salting and peppering to taste, shaking in flour, and frying in butter. Abalone does not keep well and should be eaten right away or kept quite cold.

Skates & Rays

In case you tangle with a big skate or ray, here's some good information from UNC Sea Grant's brochure *Skates and Rays:* "Unfrozen or uncooked skate and ray meat will not keep as long as bony fish. Once a skate dies it spoils rapidly because it contains urea. This fluid is broken down quickly by surface bacteria, forming ammonia which gives the meat a strong odor and bitter taste. The animal must be dressed within 15 to 20 minutes after it is caught. The most usable portion of the skate or ray is the wings, although roasts from the back section can be obtained from large rays. After you're pulled in your catch, cut off the pectoral fin (wings) on each side of the fish, and rinse thoroughly to remove any excess blood. . . . Discard the head and body. If the fish is large, wings can be skinned, but this is difficult and not necessary. To skin a skate or ray, peel away the hide. Make a cut under the skin to get a skin flap big enough to grip. Grip the skin with one hand, then use the other to cut back with a sharp fillet knife. It will be easier and quicker to leave about one-fourth of an inch of meat attached to the skin. Skinned meat can be cut into chunks and sautéed or pan fried. If you choose not to skin them, skates and rays can be cooked or frozen with the skin on. The skin is easily removed after poaching.

"Before cooking or freezing, it is important to soak the fish in a brine or acidic solution to remove any excess urea. Salt, vinegar, milk or lemon juice can be used for this. A standard salt or vinegar solution is one cup of salt or half cup of white vinegar to one gallon of water. Since the meat becomes firmer in vinegar than in salt, it is recommended that the fish be placed in a cool area (refrigerator) for four to eight hours in brine and four hours in vinegar. Skates and rays can be left in lemon juice or milk for up to 24 hours. Milk soaking is often used when the skate will be deep fried, while lemon soaking is recommended for broiling recipes. After brining, the skin should be scraped with a knife and rinsed.

"Skates and rays become very dry if overcooked. They can be prepared by steaming, broiling, baking, boiling, or barbecuing. Frying is probably the most difficult method, because skate meat contains a lot of moisture that causes the grease or oil to splatter. Cooked fish flakes when brushed with a fork. The cooking period is short: five to eight minutes for steaming, 10 minutes for broiling, and 10 to 20 minutes for baking."

16

RAW, SMOKED, AND PRESERVED FISH

A few years ago, Lew Childre, who developed Lew's Speed Spool and other fine fishing tackle, landed a rather large airplane near my hometown. On it were a bunch of people connected in some way or another to the fishing tackle trade. I never did know exactly why they came here, but at the time I was publishing *Bass Fishing News* and Lew was trying to get me to edit a magazine for a bass tournament organization they were planning. He also wanted to see the little Stump Knocker boat that my nephew, David Livingston, was making in his shop on the outskirts of town. David had joined us for lunch at the local café, Edd's Place, home of what was billed as the World's Best hot dog. After we were all seated, Lew walked over to the oyster bar and came back smiling. Since he imported most of the oyster knives used in this part of the country, I thought he was checking on business. But it

was the oysters that interested him. "Boys," he said, "they've got Apalachicola oysters!"

Among Lew's company was a very important fishing tackle fellow from Japan, the vice president of a large company that manufactured, among other products, fishing reels. Also with Lew was a guy from Arkansas who made his way in the world by selling fishing tackle to underdeveloped countries, and he had some good stories about unloading half a million dollars worth of leadhead jigs to Saudi Arabia. This fellow became interested in the World's Best hot dog, eating enough of them to kill a normal man. Maybe he was thinking of getting the franchise for Iceland or somewhere.

But it was the Japanese businessman who really stole the show and became the talk of our town. He ate only oysters. Oysters. No crackers. No sauce. He would lean over the tray, holding his tie with his left hand, pick up an

California Yellowtail

The California yellowtail is an ocean fish that is quite popular in California and Baja California waters. This fish is high in oil content, and it is best when grilled, broiled, or smoked. It also may be canned. Some anglers rate it highly as a food fish.

oyster with his right hand, raise it to his mouth without spilling the juice, and slurp the morsel down, swallowing it without chewing. After the rest of us had filled up and were smoking and talking good fishing, this guy kept eating those Apalachicola oysters. It was unbelievable, what with him being so little. More than once the waitress had to clean the shells off the table. Recalling the event later, David said it was probably the only home-cooked meal the guy had eaten since he left Japan!

I too am fond of raw Apalachicola oysters, and I also enjoy other dishes made with raw meat and fowl. But I am uncomfortable about eating them these days. I still eat the oysters if I know the dealer, and I do sometimes eat raw fish if I have caught them myself. The main risks involve various kinds of food poisoning and such diseases as hepatitis, as well as anisakis worms. I don't know whether the hazard is greater these days or whether we merely have more knowledge and better communications. In any case, I really can't advise anyone to eat raw fish or shellfish these days.

If you are going to eat them, however, I do advise you to catch your own from clean water, take good care of them, and prepare them properly. In this chapter I include sections on

seviche (made from raw fish) and on smoked, canned, salted, and pickled fish. Note that some salted and cold-smoked fish aren't really cooked.

SEVICHE

This dish, popular in Mexico and other parts of Latin America, is usually served as an appetizer. I also like it as a light lunch, often made with bass or other low-fat fish that I catch. The Mexicans, however, often use fatty fish and, in fact, other seafood, such as conch, clams, oysters, and scallops. In any case, seviche must be made several days ahead of time. I have prepared seviche by several recipes, all of which depend on lemon or lime juice and a tomato-based topping; in recent years, I have leaned more and more toward a simple method made with the aid of prepared chunky salsa, either canned or fresh.

A. D.'s Easy Seviche

Any good fish can be used for this recipe, and I often use fillets from 1-pound largemouth bass. The main requirement is that the fish and lemon juice be very fresh. Salsa is available in mild, medium, or hot, as well as in a variety of textures. I prefer it medium and chunky.

½ pound fish fillets (very fresh)
juice of 3 or 4 large lemons
prepared salsa
salt to taste

Cut the fillets into 1-inch chunks, put these in a nonmetallic container, and pour the lemon juice over them. Refrigerate for at least 24 hours. Remove the fish chunks, drain, and top generously with salsa and, if needed, some salt. Eat on crackers.

Long-List Seviche

If the recipe above isn't sophisticated enough to suit you, try this one, which, I admit, will be much more interesting to your guests.

1 pound fish fillets
5 limes
1 lemon
1 large onion, finely chopped
5 finely chopped green onions with part of
 tops
3 tomatoes, peeled and chopped
1 can tomato sauce (8-ounce size)
¼ red bell pepper, finely chopped
2 green chili peppers, seeded and chopped
2 tablespoons capers
2 tablespoons finely chopped fresh cilantro
1 teaspoon Tabasco sauce (or to taste)
1 teaspoon oregano
1 teaspoon sweet basil
olive oil
dry white wine

Dice the fish, then put it into a nonmetallic container. Pour the lemon and lime juice over the fish pieces, add enough wine to barely cover, and refrigerate for at least 24 hours, stirring a time or two with your finger.

After 24 hours, drain the fish, then add the chopped onion, green onions, tomatoes, tomato sauce, capers, bell pepper, hot pepper, oregano, basil, cilantro, and Tabasco. Stir and refrigerate for a few hours. When you are ready to eat, serve the seviche in individual bowls and top each serving with ½ teaspoon of olive oil. Crisp wheat crackers go nicely with seviche. The measures above will serve 4 or 5 for a light lunch. If well refrigerated, leftover seviche will keep for 2 or 3 days, but it is better when freshly mixed.

SALT-CURED FISH

Traditionally, fish are salted and stored in a wooden barrel or box. Other containers can be used, but it's best to avoid any container that contains metal. Some practitioners even caution one to avoid stirring the fish (in a brine) with a metallic spoon. Any kind of salt can be used. Purchase it in 50- or 100-pound bags if you plan to salt down many fish or other meat.

There are several ways to salt-cure fish, but I recommend that you fillet the fish, or at least cut them in half lengthwise. Do not skin or scale the fish.

Sprinkle a thick layer of salt into your container, then put down a layer of fish skin side down. Cover with salt, then add another layer of fish, skin side down.

Repeat until all the fish are gone, placing the last layer skin side up and covering with plenty of salt.

Cover the container and leave in a cool place for a week. As the salt draws the moisture out of the fish, a brine will form. The fish in turn shrink and the flesh becomes firmer. After a week, pour off the brine, remove the fish, and prepare a fresh brine by first boiling some water and then dissolving salt until the brine will float an egg. Make enough of this brine to half fill the container. Put the fish back into the container. Pour the brine over them, and add some crushed peppercorns. Weight with a block of wood or other nonmetallic object to make sure that the fish stay completely covered with brine.

Cover with a cloth, and leave in a cool place for 2 weeks.

The fish are now ready to eat, or they can be stored for a longer period in the brine. Or, better, the fish can be packaged and frozen. It can be eaten raw, preferably thinly sliced. Also, the fish can be rinsed, air-dried, and cold-smoked.

Oyette Taylor's Salt Crappie

Here's a good recipe from my hometown barber, who salts down crappie and then freezes them. Before cooking, put the salt-cured crappie into a nonmetallic container with cool fresh water. Soak the fish overnight, changing water several times. When you are ready to cook, wash the fish with a pressure hose, which should knock off the scales; if not, help it along with a spoon or fish scaler. Dry the fish, shake them in cornmeal, and fry in hot peanut oil until nicely browned.

Oyette says that salting the crappie firms up the flesh without making it strong, resulting in a good-tasting fish that is like no other.

Salt Fish Balls

1 cup salt fish, finely diced
3 medium potatoes, diced
1 chicken egg, separated
2 tablespoons butter
flour
cooking oil
⅛ teaspoon pepper

Put the diced fish and potatoes into a small saucepan, cover with hot water, and simmer until the potatoes are tender. Drain, let cool, and put into a blender. Add the butter, pepper, and egg yolk. Blend on high speed for 30 seconds. Beat the egg white lightly by hand, then add to the mixture. Blend on medium speed for 30 seconds.

Cool the mixture in the refrigerator for 1 hour or so, then shape it into balls (golf-ball size) and roll in flour. Heat the cooking oil in a deep fryer to at least 375 degrees. Fry the fish balls a few at a time until golden brown. Drain on brown paper. Feeds 4 or 5.

Note: If you want patties instead of balls, flatten the balls and sauté them in a little butter on a griddle.

Gulf Coast Breakfast

During the Great Depression, most of the southern towns had electricity, but many of the houses in rural sections did not. The folks who peopled these areas relied partly on salt fish, trucked up from the Gulf of Mexico in barrels or wooden boxes, as a sort of staple food. The markets in every country town, and every crossroads store, as well as all the rolling stores, had at least one barrel of fish delivered weekly. These were sold by the pound. These days, the widespread availability of electricity and ready refrigeration has all but eliminated the barrels and wooden boxes, but salt fish, wrapped in plastic now and refrigerated, are still available in some markets.

Anyhow, here's the way my father and grandfather ate, and enjoyed, mullet for breakfast:

2 pounds salt mullet
cooking oil
fine white stone-ground cornmeal
grits
biscuits from scratch
butter
pepper
cane syrup

Soak the mullet overnight in cold water, changing the water a time or two if convenient. An hour before dawn, get up and build a fire in the wood stove. Draw a bucket of water from the well. Put on the coffee and heat up the oven for cooking biscuits. Prepare dough, roll it, and cut out the biscuits. Put the biscuits into the oven. Put the grits into a boiler with a little water. Drain the fish. Heat the oil in a skillet. Shake the fish in a bag with cornmeal, then fry them in the hot oil until nicely browned on both sides.

With luck, everything will be ready at the same time. Dish out and butter the grits. Pepper to taste. Butter the biscuits. Each person can break up his fish and stir each bite into the grits.

Note that hard or lumpy grits "ain't fit to eat" and grits that are too soupy are difficult to eat with a fork. The biscuits are saved for last, then used to sop up the cane syrup. The procedure is made easier by placing both elbows firmly on the table and lowering the head directly over the plate.

Salt fish are quite filling, and 2 pounds will feed 5 or 6 modern people for breakfast. If you have to plow a mule until noonday, however, you might eat an extra biscuit or two.

Cod Cakes Nova Scotia

I must have caught, or snatched, a ton of codfish somewhere north of Halifax, using some sort of heavy jig that I bought from an enterprising Eskimo.

The cod is a fine fish and is often salted, just as mullet are salted around the Gulf Coast. This recipe came from the Home Economist section of the Nova Scotia Department of Fisheries.

1 pound salt cod or other salt fish
2 cups cooked mashed potatoes
¼ cup finely chopped onion
¼ cup finely chopped fresh parsley
¼ cup grated cheddar cheese
dry bread crumbs
cooking oil
1 teaspoon black pepper

Soak the fish overnight in cold water, changing once or twice if convenient. Simmer the fish for 10 or 15 minutes, or until it flakes easily when tested with a fork. Drain the fish and flake it, being careful to remove all the bones. Mix the flaked fish, mashed potatoes, onion, parsley, cheese, and pepper. Form the mixture into patties, like small pancakes. Roll in bread crumbs, coating lightly. Heat a little oil in a skillet or griddle, then fry the cakes for 2 or 3 minutes on each side, or until golden brown.

Note: The last time I saw a cod-snatching jig was in Columbus, Mississippi, home of an Air Force SAC base. It's a weird-looking thing, about 5 inches long, made of solid lead, and it weighs at least a pound. The thing curves around a little, like a flat banana, and has a large hook sticking out the end. The jig is lowered to the bottom in deep water, then snatched up for 1 or 2 feet. The shape of the jig causes it to arc up so that the hook point sticks low-lying cod in the belly. In a good spot, you could hook one on almost every third snatch. Anyhow, I saw one of these jigs in a tackle shop in Columbus, Mississippi. It no doubt came from one of the Air Force boys who had spent some time in Tuhle and had hung it in the shop as a conversation piece. I asked the guy at the cash register how much it cost. He laughed and asked what in the world I would do with it. To his surprise, I told him that I was going cod snatching in the Tombigbee River!

SMOKED FISH

Smoking can be an aid in preserving fish, but modern refrigeration and freezers have practically eliminated the need. Modern cooks usually smoke fish primarily for flavor. Most of the patio "smoking" these days is really cooking, with a little smoke generated for flavor. The two basic kinds of smoking are defined below—and be warned that confusing the two can be dangerous.

Hot smoking is accomplished during cooking, often slow cooking, and is usually done in a covered patio grill or a silo-shaped smoker-cooker. Hot smoking is usually accomplished—or should be accomplished—at temperatures higher than 140 degrees. Otherwise, the meat won't really be cooked, and bacteria can not only survive but also multiply to dangerous levels. This method of smoke-flavoring fish and meats while cooking is covered more fully in the chapter on patio cooking.

Cold smoking is accomplished at temperatures below 100 degrees, and preferably at 80 degrees or cooler. It does not cook the meat or fish, but it does help preserve it. Most cold smoking is accomplished in a large smokehouse, or in a smaller smoke box with the heat some distance away, as shown in one of the drawings. Dozens of smoker designs have been set forth in books and magazine articles. Just remember that the smoke chamber must not get very hot.

Before fish is cold-smoked, or before it can be safely cooked in some patio smokers, it should first be cured with salt and perhaps some sugar and spices. The salt will impede the growth of bacteria. Here's a basic brine that I recommend:

1 gallon good water
lots of salt
¼ cup brown sugar or molasses
1 tablespoon peppercorns

Mix the salt into the water until the solution will float a raw egg. Then stir in the brown sugar and pepper.

After soaking the fish in brine, it should be hung in a cool, airy place for an hour or so, or until a pellicle forms. Then the fish can be cold-smoked for a few hours—or for a few days or weeks. As a rule, the color of the smoked fish—a deep mahogany—is the best guide to knowing when to quit smoking it.

THREE BASIC SMOKERS

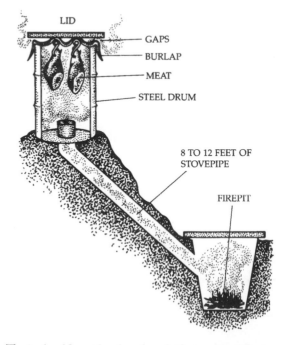

Typical cold smoker handmade from a steel drum and stovepipe.

In any case, both hot and cold smoking add flavor to fish, and often the smoked fish are used in recipes. Here are some of my favorites:

Smoked Fish Patties

This recipe can be prepared with either hot- or cold-smoked fish. Hot-smoked fish, or leftovers, can usually be flaked with a fork, but it's best to minced most cold-smoked fish with a knife.

2 cups smoked fish
2 cups mashed potatoes
½ cup bread crumbs
½ cup finely chopped onions
½ cup parsley flakes
2 chicken eggs
cooking oil
salt and pepper
lemon (garnish)

Sauté the onion in a little cooking oil in a skillet. Whisk the eggs. Then mix the onion, eggs, and all the other ingredients except for the lemon. Shape the mixture into patties. Brown the patties on both sides in the skillet,

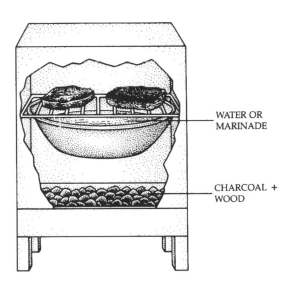

Commercial hot smoker.

WATER OR MARINADE

CHARCOAL + WOOD

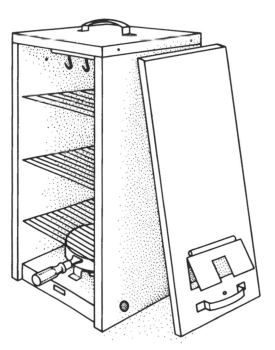

Commercial portable (hot) smoker.

Rainbow Trout

Although it is medium to high in oil content, the rainbow trout fries well and can be cooked by any other method. As a rule, fish from free-flowing streams are better than commercially raised trout.

turning carefully with the aid of two spatulas. Drain the patties on brown bags or other absorbent paper before placing them on a serving platter or plates. Garnish with lemon wedges or slices.

Potato Salad with Smoked Fish

This dish is very good when made with cold-smoked fish that has been steamed or poached to cook it.

    1 pound flaked smoked fish (cooked)
    2 cups diced potatoes (cooked)
    1 rib celery, chopped
    1 medium onion, chopped
    ¼ red bell pepper, chopped
    ¼ green bell pepper, chopped
    ¼ cup sliced olives
    ¼ cup mayonnaise
    juice of ½ lemon
    1 tablespoon chopped fresh parsley
    1 tablespoon prepared mustard
    1 teaspoon wine vinegar
    ¼ teaspoon celery seed
    salt and pepper to taste

Trim and flake the fish, then toss with the potatoes, celery, onion, peppers, olives, and parsley. In a separate bowl, mix the mayonnaise, mustard, vinegar, lemon juice, and celery seed. Mix with the fish and vegetables, adding salt and pepper to taste. Chill for 1 hour or so before serving.

Smoked Fish Quiche

Since this dish is fully cooked, it can be made with either cold- or hot-smoked fish. The recipe below calls for a 9-inch pie shell, which can be purchased at the supermarket. If you want to make your own pastry, fine.

    1 cup flaked smoked fish
    1 cup shredded Swiss cheese
    1 pie shell (9-inch)
    4 chicken eggs
    2 cups cream
    2 tablespoons chopped parsley
    ½ teaspoon salt
    ⅛ teaspoon white pepper

Preheat the oven to 425 degrees. Mix the fish and cheese, then sprinkle the mixture evenly into the pie shell. Mix the other ingredients and spoon over the fish mixture. Bake in the center of the oven for 10 minutes; reduce the heat to 300 degrees, then bake for 40 minutes, or until done. To test for doneness, insert a knife blade into the center of the quiche; if the blade comes out clean, the dish is done. Let cool a few minutes, cut into wedges, and serve.

CANNING FISH

One of my favorite lunches during a day-long fishing trip is a can of sardines, salmon, or tuna eaten on crackers, along with a little red-rind hoop cheese and a big cola drink. Often I have thought about canning fish myself to eat on such trips, but I never do it. The art of home canning has been on the decline for a number of years, mostly because of the advent of the home freezer.

One excellent reason for canning some fish is that the process softens the bones.

I have canned fish, but I usually cook it thoroughly before eating it, and *the instructions given here apply only to fish that is intended to be boiled or recooked thoroughly after it is removed from the jars.* Note that you will need a pressure cooker, along with some good canning jars with proper seals.

Skin the fish, gut it, and cut it into chunks or fingers. If you have large fish, fillet them before cutting them into chunks. Smaller fish can be cut into pieces, or even canned whole. Put the fish into a brine solution made with 1 cup of salt per gallon of water for 1 hour. Rinse the fish well.

Pack the fish into hot widemouthed jars,

leaving 1 inch of space at the top. (Do not use jars that have cracked or nicked rims.) If you have cut the fish into fingers, stand them so that the skin side is against the glass. Add 1/4 teaspoon of salt to pint jars, or 1/2 teaspoon to quart jars. Do not add oil or liquid.

Put the lids on the jars. Most lids are made in two pieces: a screw band and a flat sealing element with a gasket-type sealing compound. (The sealing element should not be reused for canning purposes, and may not be interchangeable with all brands of screw bands. To be certain, buy new lids and follow the manufacturer's instructions.) Tighten the lids, place the jars into a pressure cooker, and process at 10 pounds for 100 minutes. (If you live at high altitude, you'll have to adjust the pressure. Use 15 pounds above 2,000 feet.) Follow the directions that came with your pressure cooker—and be careful.

Store the jars in a dark place. Before eating or even tasting the contents, simmer or steam the fish for 10 minutes per inch of thickness.

These canned fish can be used in any recipe that calls for flaked fish and that is fully cooked.

Smoke Big Minnows

The northern squawfish, a true minnow, often weighs 10 pounds, and a related fish, the Colorado squawfish, can grow up to 80 pounds! The fish are bony, but they can be quite tasty when smoked properly. Other methods of preparing the squawfish are not highly recommended.

PICKLED FISH

Pickled fish is one of my favorite snacks, and I am especially fond of fish that is pickled by a cold method—in other words, the fish is uncooked and is eaten raw. But most of the recipes below are cooked and can be enjoyed even by squeamish folks.

Pickled Bullheads

After running across this recipe in Illinois' *Outdoor Highlights,* I tried it with bullheads out of the Chattahoochee River, and I can recommend it highly for that species, provided that they are fresh, not frozen. The recipe is quite heavy on the bay leaf, so cut down a little on the measure if you don't care for the flavor or aroma. The mixed pickling spices are available at most spice markets.

Ciguatoxin

Some tropical and subtropical reef fish can carry ciguatoxin, which is produced by microalgae and can accumulate in the flesh of fish that eat it. It can accumulate to dangerous levels in predator fish, such as the barracuda, amberjack, and jack crevalle. Although ciguatoxin can be deadly, the chances of fish from American waters having dangerous amounts are slim. The danger is limited to waters around deep reefs, and usually involves the larger fish. Small barracuda and jacks from coastal flats are usually safe to eat.

1 to 2 pounds skinless bullhead fillets
4 medium onions, sliced
4 or 5 bay leaves
1½ cups water
1½ cups white vinegar
1 tablespoon mixed pickling spices
1 tablespoon salt
⅛ teaspoon pepper

Layer the onions in the bottom of a large boiler. Add the bay leaves and pickling spices. Place the bullhead fillets on top. In a separate container, mix the vinegar, water, salt, and pepper. Cover the fish with this mixture. Bring to a boil, cover, reduce the heat, and simmer for 8 to 10 minutes, or until the fish are done. Let the fish cool in the pan. Refrigerate and serve cold. I like to cut the fish into chunks and eat them on crackers. I also like to eat the onion slices.

Pickled Pickerel

Small pikes and pickerels are good eating, but the fillets have too many troublesome bones. Here's a recipe that softens the bones. It can also be made with other bony fish, such as suckers.

2 pounds pickerel fillets, skinless
1 medium onion, sliced
1 lemon, sliced
2 tablespoons pickling spices
vinegar
water
½ teaspoon black pepper

Cut the fillets into 1-inch chunks, put them into a suitable nonmetallic container, and cover

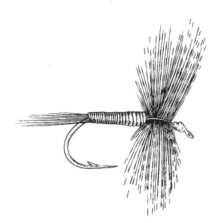

them with a mixture of ½ vinegar and ½ water. Refrigerate for 24 hours.

Drain the fish. In a pan of suitable size, prepare a solution of 3 cups of vinegar and 1 cup of water. Add the pickling spices, pepper, and sliced lemon. Bring to a boil. Put about half of the pickerel chunks into the boiling mixture and simmer for 10 minutes, or until the fish is done. Put the chunks into a sterilized widemouthed jar and add a layer of sliced onions. Simmer the rest of the pickerel chunks for 10 minutes, or until done. Add the chunks to the jar, then cover with another layer of sliced onion. Bring the liquid in the pan to a rolling boil, then fill the jar with the liquid. Seal. Refrigerate. Serve cold fish pickles with crackers and beer. Eat within a week or so.

Gourmet Pickles

I don't know what this recipe should be called. I got it from the late Euell Gibbons, who developed it for bluegill fillets. Since I refuse to fillet bluegills, however, I have cooked it only with fillets from other species. Because the pickling softens the bones, I usually make the pickles with fillets of sucker or pickerel. The recipe calls for a bag of crab boil. This handy item, a Cajun product, is available commercially at supermarkets or sometimes at seafood markets. The Cajuns use it for boiling shrimp and crawfish as well as crabs. It is, essentially, a mixture of pickling spices packaged in a cloth bag, making it easy to use without getting bits of spice all over the food.

I like to make the pickles in small chunks, sized just right for sitting atop a cracker. Soak the fish chunks in a brine made with 1 cup of salt per ½ gallon of water for 2 days. Wash and drain the fish chunks.

Put the spice bag into the bottom of a 1-quart widemouthed glass jar. Cover the bag with thinly sliced onion. Top the onions with a layer of fish. Alternate onions and fish until the jar is full, being sure to top off with a layer of onions. Make a mixture of ½ water and ½ red wine vinegar, then pour it into the jar, filling all the way to the top. Let it settle, tapping the jar all around to dislodge any air bubbles. Cover and refrigerate for 3 weeks before eating.

Pickled Herrings

The recipe below comes from Scotland, where herrings have been traditional fare for a good many years. The recipe can be used for other small fish, such as 8- or 9-inch brook trout or hornyheads. I've even used it for small channel catfish.

8 small herrings or other small fish
½ cup white vinegar
½ cup water
1 medium onion, diced
4 bay leaves
1 teaspoon peppercorns
½ teaspoon pickling spices
salt and pepper

Preheat the oven to 325 degrees. Fillet the fish. Sprinkle with salt and pepper, then roll the fillets, working from the tail toward the head. Crush the bay leaves and sprinkle the pieces on the bottom of a baking dish of suitable size.

Place the rolled fillets on top of the bay leaves, packing them rather tightly so that they won't unroll. Crush the peppercorns and sprinkle them over the fillets, along with the diced onion and pickling spices. Mix the water and vinegar and pour over the fillets. Cover with foil and bake for 40 minutes. Let the fish cool in the liquid. Save the liquid, strain it, and pour a little of it over each fish fillet just before serving.

17

FISH SAUCES

I caught a nice bass, 7 or 8 pounds, from Elk River back when I lived on a farm near Fayetteville, Tennessee. Actually, I lived on Pea Ridge, near Skin 'um, home of the Big Mac Chicken Coop Factory. A local chamber of commerce changed the name of Pea Ridge to Highland Rim, but the folks around Skin 'um weren't too hot for that idea.

Anyhow, I set out to cook this Elk River bass by a fancy French recipe, which, I figured, would interest the somewhat sophisticated guests that I had invited. One of them came from England, one from Germany, one from Japan, and one from Indianapolis. Highland Rim folks, for sure. They all worked in America's space program in Huntsville, Alabama, located on red clay lands just across the state line off the south slope of Pea Ridge.

The big cookbook that I was trying to use, a sort of encyclopedia that had been translated from the French, must have weighed 10 pounds

more than the bass. I had to clear all my jig-tying stuff off the kitchen table just to spread the thing open.

I found an interesting recipe but was referred right off to a section on court bouil-lons. At that entry, I read that I needed some fumets in order to make court bouillon. So I turned to fumets, where I found out that I had to have the bass head, fins, skin, and bones—all of which I had already buried out beside my tomato plant. But I had put these French ingredients into a plastic bag for convenience of handling, and when I dug them up I found them to be in good shape and not yet fuming too badly. I decided that I could indeed handle both the fumets and the court bouillon.

Back to the main recipe, which called for Hollandaise sauce. Well, the book contained entries for several hundred sauces, and there were no less than three recipes for Hollandaise. The first one called for a bain-marie, or double

Eulachon: The Candlefish

The importance of the eulachon to the economy of the Indians of the northwest coast of North America goes far back, with great value placed on the little fish as food, a source of cooking oil, of light, and as a medium of barter.

The eulachon is a very oily fish, and when dried and fitted with a wick from the inner bark of the cedar, burns like a candle. Hence, the name "candlefish."

. . . A very perishable little fish, eulachon is superb when broiled fresh from the water, over hot coals. It is highly esteemed by Indians from California to Alaska.

—Frances MacIlquham
Fish Cookery of North America

boiler. I couldn't find the top half of my bain-marie, so I went on to the second Hollandaise sauce. This recipe called for Isigny butter. While trying to find out what Isigny butter is, I got interested in the Izard, a wild goat of the Pyrenees. Not finding any Izard recipes that I thought would do justice to Henry (a rogue goat who lived on Pea Ridge and always seemed to show up when I had invited guests who sported cars with tasty vinyl tops), I went on to Hollandaise number three.

It called for 2 tablespoons of Allemande sauce. Four kinds of Allemande sauce were listed, and I started on the first one, which called for another bain-marie. I found the missing part of my double boiler and proceeded. The recipe required 2½ cups of Velouté sauce. (Remember that I needed only 2 tablespoons of Allemande sauce in the first place.) So, I looked up Velouté sauce and found out that I needed ½ cup of Allemande in order to make it. In other words, I needed ½ cup of Allemande in order to make 2 tablespoons of Allemande! At first I jumped to the conclusion that some French writer or fancy chef was pulling my leg, but then I decided that it was merely a typographical mistake or an error of literary translation instead of intercontinental hanky-panky.

By now, I had forgotten the name of the fish recipe that I had set out to prepare in the first place, and I couldn't find my way back to it. So I said to hell with it and buried the fumets again under Henry's watchful eye.

The sun was already setting over Pea Ridge, and I didn't have time now to prepare a fancy dish, so I filleted the bass closely and cut it into fingers about the size of New Hampshire brook trout. Out came the old cast-iron skillet, peanut oil, water-ground white south Alabama cornmeal, and catsup.

In short, I fried the damned fish and served it up on ordinary brown grocery bags along with catsup, lemon wedges, and hush puppies. I also had a pile of bluegills and their roe from the farm pond. Of course, I couldn't put a bottle of catsup before such guests, so I put the bottle in the top part of my bain marie to heat the catsup enough to shake it out. I served the catsup in a puddle on a little platter. Any robust red sauce like my Highlander's Rimpearidge Rouge, I told my guests, should be served at room temperature in order to bring forth its full flavor. Ordinary sauces, like Allemande or Velouté, are, of course, a different ball game, I claimed.

They all loved it, they all agreed that the sauce made the fish, and they all wanted recipes.

The inspiration for this quaint dish, I said,

pushing my luck, came upon me while I was camped out in the Appalachians, where I was at the time hunting for the azard, a rare wild goat of the region, the ancestral home of Henry. More Highlander's Rimpearidge Rouge sauce, anyone?

If so, see my catsup recipe below. If not, maybe one of the other sauce recipes will fill the bill. In any case, I use the above story to illustrate a point: Far too many cookbooks have far too many references in them, so that it's just too hard to use them. Perhaps I have erred in the other direction, in that most of the recipes in this book are pretty much self-contained. But I believe that a chapter on sauces will be helpful here, simple because most people want, for example, tartar sauce even with fried fish. If you are one of these, you should know that you can usually make a better sauce than you can buy.

Lemon Butter Sauce

I prefer this sauce for dipping boiled shrimp, and we usually use the Easy Method to prepare it. When the sauce is to be poured over poached or broiled fish, try the Fancy Method.

Easy Method
    ½ cup melted butter
    ½ cup lemon juice, freshly squeezed
Fancy Method
    ½ cup melted butter
    ½ cup lemon juice, freshly squeezed
    1 tablespoon white wine Worcestershire
        sauce
    1 tablespoon minced fresh parsley
    ⅛ teaspoon salt
    ⅛ teaspoon white pepper
    ⅛ teaspoon mild paprika

Mix everything in a suitable bowl shortly before dinner. Do not refrigerate. Serve at room temperature.

Cocktail Sauce

Many people like some sort of cocktail sauce for dipping shrimp, fish fingers, and so on. For hot shrimp, I prefer the simple Lemon Butter Sauce above, but for cold shrimp or cold poached fish, this red sauce is hard to beat.

    1 cup catsup
    juice of 1 large lemon
    2 tablespoons red wine
    1 teaspoon olive oil
    1 large clove garlic
    1 teaspoon grated fresh horseradish
    ¼ teaspoon Tabasco sauce
    ⅛ teaspoon salt

Crush the garlic clove and let it steep in the olive oil for several days. Then drain the oil into a small mixing bowl, discarding the garlic pulp. Stir in the catsup, lemon juice, wine, horseradish, Tabasco sauce, and salt. Chill until time to serve.

Walleye

The popular walleye is one of the best fish that swims, and they can be cooked in any way. They are medium low in oil content, and their flesh is firm, white, and flaky. Walleye are also called "jack salmon," "pike," "doré," and "opal eye."

Billfish

Billfish are large, big-game ocean fish, including sailfish, swordfish, and spearfish. All of these are high in oil content, but they are quite tasty if properly handled and appropriately cooked. The term "billfish" is quite broad, however, and includes dozens of different fish. The black marlin, for example, is of moderate oil content, whereas the blue marlin is rich in oil.

The marlins and swordfish are especially good when grilled or broiled, and they are often eaten raw in sashimi dishes. The sailfish and spearfish tend to be a little tough and they are often smoked or cooked over charcoal. Frying is not normally recommended for billfish.

Billfish for the table should be dressed out and iced down as soon as they are caught. Saving the fish for dockside snapshots is a waste of good meat.

Hot Egg Sauce

2 hard-boiled chicken eggs, sliced
4 tablespoons butter
2 tablespoons flour
1 cup boiling water
salt and pepper to taste

Melt the butter in a saucepan, then slowly mix in the flour, stirring as you go. Stir in the boiling water a little at a time. Simmer until the mixture thickens. Salt and pepper to taste. Add the sliced eggs. Serve hot over baked, poached, or broiled fish.

Catsup

If the truth be known, more Americans dunk more pounds of fish into more gallons of catsup than all other sauces combined. I too could be a catsup man, but for two reasons. First, I don't have the patience to shake the bottle to get out a sufficient amount. Second, I don't like the feeling of being ripped off by the catsup bottlers. They keep coming out with various kinds of squirt bottles, but none of these work any better. After studying this situation for a number of years, my conclusion is that they don't want a better bottle. Why? Because they want you to throw away 10 or 20 percent of the catsup so that you'll buy more. But I know how to package catsup—thick catsup. Put it into widemouthed jars like mayonnaise. Then you can get out all you want with a spoon, and you can even clean off the sides of the jar with a long spoon, wasting very little. So, if you want to try this recipe, be sure to have some widemouthed jars on hand. I prefer 1-pint size.

2 gallons vine-ripened tomatoes
5 large onions
2 cups white vinegar
½ cup sugar
2 or 3 hot peppers
2 tablespoons dry mustard
2 tablespoons salt
black pepper

Quarter the tomatoes, putting them into a large pot on high heat. Peel the onions, quarter them, and add them to the pot. Reduce the heat and simmer for an hour, mashing from time to time with a potato masher. Strain out the tomato and onion pulp. Return the liquid to the pot. Add the hot peppers (whole), mustard, vinegar, sugar, salt, and pepper. Bring to a boil, reduce the heat, and cook at a low boil until the sauce thickens. (This will take some time because the liquid must be reduced by half, more or less, depending on how thick you want the catsup.) Stir from time to time.

Take the pot off the heat and discard the hot peppers. Using a ladle, spoon the catsup into sterilized widemouthed jars. Refrigerate.

Fish-Finger Dip

I seldom use anything on fried fish, except perhaps a little lemon juice, but I do enjoy tartar sauce and such when it is available. If you have guests to feed but don't have any sauce on hand, it's really easy to whip up something for the occasion. Here's one that I like for both flavor and color:

1 cup sour cream
¼ cup catsup
1 tablespoon white wine Worcestershire sauce
2 tablespoons grated onion
juice of ½ lemon
1 clove garlic, grated
1 teaspoon Tabasco sauce
⅛ teaspoon pepper

Mix all the ingredients. Chill for several hours before serving.

Easy Tartar Sauce

Some cookbook authors tend to make fun of tartar sauce, but it would not be so popular if it were not easy to make—and good. Here's all you need:

1 cup good mayonnaise
2 tablespoons sweet pickle relish
2 tablespoons minced green onions with part of tops
1 teaspoon prepared mustard

Mix all the ingredients in a suitable bowl, then put it into the refrigerator for at least 1 hour before serving.

Redfish

Blackened or not, the redfish is one of the more popular sport fish along the Gulf of Mexico and other coastal areas. Owing partly to the market demand created by the blackened redfish craze, size limits have been imposed in some areas. Size limits or not, the best ones for frying or baking are on the small side. The large ones tend to be coarse and are best used in chowders. There is a considerable range of opinion on exactly how small redfish should be for table fare. Some say 15 pounds. Others say 10. In any case, these fish are also known as red drum and channel bass. The smaller fish are also sometimes called "puppy drum."

Sauce Tartare

If you want a more sophisticated sauce than the one above, change the name from tartar sauce to Sauce Tartare and add more ingredients.

1½ cups good mayonnaise
½ cup cream
4 green onions, minced with part of tops
⅓ cup finely chopped dill pickle
1 tablespoon chopped fresh parsley
1 tablespoon chopped capers
1 tablespoon chopped fresh tarragon
1 tablespoon chopped fresh chervil
juice of ½ lemon
juice from 2 cloves garlic
2 teaspoons anchovy paste
1 teaspoon dry mustard
salt and white pepper
fresh parsley (garnish)

Mix the mayonnaise and anchovy paste. Stir in the green onions, pickle, capers, parsley, tarragon, chervil, and mustard. Then stir in the cream, lemon juice, and garlic juice. Taste. Add salt and white pepper, stirring and tasting as you go. Refrigerate until ready to serve. Spoon the sauce into individual serving bowls. Garnish with a sprig or two of parsley.

Molbo Cru

Here's an excellent sauce from Angola. Serve it over poached fish fillets or other seafood. Also try it as a dip for fried fish fingers.

1 cup diced green onions with part of tops
½ cup chopped parsley
½ cup vinegar
½ cup water
3 cloves garlic, minced
2 tablespoons freshly ground cumin
½ teaspoon salt

Mix all the ingredients in a good processor or blender, then zap it until it forms a smooth paste. Refrigerate or put on ice before serving.

18

FISH SALADS

At one time, I toyed with the notion of putting a fish salad chapter in the front of this book, just to whet the reader's appetite. Then I remembered our son Bill's reaction to a salad bar at a seafood restaurant that our family went to. We had driven some distance to the place, and, getting hungrier and hungrier by the mile, Bill no doubt had visions of red lobsters and piles of pink shrimp and platters of golden brown hush puppies and so on. Before ordering, we all went over to a salad bar, which was quite long and might well have been the most complete selection that I had ever seen in one place. Bill wasn't much more than waist high when he walked down the spread, craning his neck to look at the lettuce and tomatoes and so forth. He took nothing. Looking up at me with a long face, he suddenly broke into tears. This, he thought, was it!

Bill is taller now than I am, and maybe even he will read on.

Bluegill-Stuffed Tomatoes

Few foods are better in hot weather than chilled tomatoes, and when they are in season I tend to eat far too many of them. Also during the same season, fish are quite plentiful, because this is the season when bluegills hit topwater bugs and flies with abandon. Any good fish can be used in this recipe, but bluegill is highly recommended. First scale the bluegill with a spoon, then gut it. Poach the fish until the flesh flakes off easily. Drain and cool. Scrape the skin off the bluegills, then flake off the meat with a fork.

2 cups bluegill flakes
4 large tomatoes, chilled
2 slices bacon
½ cup good mayonnaise
1 medium onion, grated
½ rib celery, finely sliced

161

salt and pepper to taste
grated cheese

To make a stuffing, mix all the ingredients except the tomatoes, bacon, and cheese. (Add salt to the stuffing; a little more will be sprinkled on the tomatoes.) Chill the stuffing. Fry the bacon until crisp, crumble it, and set it aside. Peel the tomatoes, cut off the top part, and scoop out the core and seeds. Sprinkle a little salt on the inside of the tomato. Spoon the stuffing into the tomatoes, sprinkle lightly with cheese and crumbled bacon, and serve on lettuce leaves. Serve a tomato to each person for a light lunch, or perhaps as a side dish to a larger meal.

Hot Stuffed Tomatoes

1½ cups cooked fish flakes
4 large tomatoes
4 strips bacon
1 tablespoon chopped fresh parsley
1 tablespoon melted butter
½ tablespoon lemon juice
salt and pepper to taste

Preheat the oven to 350 degrees. Mix the fish flakes, melted butter, parsley, lemon juice, salt, and pepper. Cut off the stem ends of the tomatoes, then scoop out the centers with a spoon. Stuff the tomatoes with the fish mixture, place them in a suitable pan, and bake for 20 minutes. While the tomatoes are in the oven, fry the bacon until it is crisp, drain, and crumble. Sprinkle the bacon bits over the stuffed tomatoes. For lunch, we like hot stuffed tomatoes served with hot cheese toast. Feeds 4 for a light lunch.

Fish Flake Salad

Here's a recipe that my mother used for canned tuna. I fix it with any good flaked fish.

1 cup cooked fish flakes
½ cup finely chopped celery
juice of 1 lemon
2 tablespoons olive oil
1 tablespoon chopped fresh parsley

Mix all the ingredients. Chill. This salad can be served on lettuce, but I confess that I spread it on bread just as often, or scoop it up on crackers. As a salad, the recipe makes about 4 servings.

Marinated Fish Salad

This salad can be made with leftover baked fish, but it's better to start with freshly poached fish. If you have a choice, use a fish that tends to flake off in chunks, such as large bass.

Salad
2 cups cooked fish flakes
2 hard-boiled chicken eggs, diced
½ cup mayonnaise
½ cup thinly sliced celery
¼ cup diced green bell pepper
¼ cup diced red bell pepper
salt and pepper
Marinade
½ cup olive oil
juice of 1 lemon
chopped onion

Squeeze some chopped onion in a garlic press until you have about 1 teaspoon of juice.

Mix with the olive oil and lemon juice. Pour this mixture over the fish flakes, toss lightly, and refrigerate for 2 hours. Then combine the fish flakes with the bell peppers, celery, and mayonnaise. Mix in the eggs, along with some salt and pepper to taste. Makes 6 to 8 servings.

Ring-Mold Salad

If you want a pretty salad on your table, as well as a tasty one, try this recipe.

    2 cups cooked fish flakes
    3 large tomatoes, quartered
    2 hard-boiled chicken eggs, chopped
    1 cup mayonnaise
    1 cup sour cream
    ½ cup almond slivers, toasted
    ½ cup ripe black olives, chopped
    ½ cup chopped fresh parsley
    ¼ cup chopped green bell pepper
    ¼ cup chopped purple onions
    2 tablespoons fresh lemon juice
    1 tablespoon grated onion
    1 tablespoon unflavored gelatin
    salt
    water
    more mayonnaise

Mix the fish flakes, olives, and almonds in a large bowl. Set aside. In the top part of a double boiler, put the gelatin in ¼ cup of cold water. Soak for 5 minutes, then heat some water to a boil in the bottom part of the double boiler, put the top in place, and stir the gelatin until it dissolves. Add the sour cream, 1 cup mayonnaise, grated onion, salt, lemon juice, and parsley. Combine this mixture with the fish, stir, and transfer to a ring mold. Chill until

Bluegill and Other Bream

A number of panfish similar to the bluegill make purely excellent eating. These include the redbreast and the pumpkinseed. Most of these fish, except for the redear or shellcracker, can be taken readily on flies, bugs, or tiny spinners, as well as on worms, crickets, and other natural bait. All of these fish have delicate white flesh, of low oil content, and are very good when fried. They can be poached, flaked, and used in various salads, or they can be fried or grilled.

firm. Shortly before serving time, unmold the salad, then fill the center with tomatoes, green pepper, chopped eggs, and purple onion. Top with mayonnaise. Makes 8 to 10 servings.

Molded Fish Salad

    2 cups cooked fish flakes
    2 envelopes gelatin, unflavored
    1 cup cold water
    1 cup sour cream
    ½ cup finely chopped celery
    ¼ cup finely chopped bell pepper
    ¼ cup sliced black olives
    ¼ cup finely chopped cucumber
    ¼ cup French dressing
    ¼ cup white wine
    2 hard-boiled chicken eggs, chopped
    ¼ teaspoon dry mustard
    salt and pepper
    lettuce or watercress (garnish)

Put the water into a saucepan, add the gelatin, and let sit for 5 minutes. Heat the water, then stir until the gelatin dissolves. Pour into a large mixing bowl and let cool. Then stir in the wine, French dressing, sour cream, and mustard.

Next, stir in the celery, bell pepper, olives, cucumber, fish flakes, and eggs, along with some salt and pepper. Grease a salad mold, preferably fish-shaped, and place the mixture into it.

Chill until the salad is firm. Serve with lettuce or watercress.

Makes 6 to 8 servings.

Cold Potato Salad with Fish Flakes

1 cup cooked fish flakes
1½ cups diced cooked potatoes
2 strips bacon
¼ cup chopped onion
1 rib celery, chopped
¼ green bell pepper, finely chopped
2 tablespoons mayonnaise
salt and pepper to taste
paprika

Cook and crumble the bacon. Mix all the ingredients except the paprika. Put the mixture into a serving bowl, sprinkle lightly with paprika, and chill until you are ready to eat. Makes 4 or 5 servings.

Hawaiian Fish Salad

This dish can be made with any good fish, but it works best with firm, white flesh that doesn't flake apart too easily.

2 pounds boneless fish fillets
1 can pineapple chunks (20-ounce size)
1 small can water chestnuts, sliced
1 rib celery, diced
1 cup mayonnaise
½ cup toasted sliced almonds
¼ green bell pepper, diced
¼ red bell pepper, diced
¼ cup shredded coconut
1 teaspoon curry powder
salt and white pepper to taste

Poach the fillets gently for about 10 minutes, or until done. Chill, then cut into 1-inch chunks. In a large bowl, mix the mayonnaise, water chestnuts, celery, bell peppers, pineapple, almonds, curry powder, salt, and pepper. Gently mix in the fish chunks. Sprinkle the top with coconut. Chill. Serves 4 to 6 for lunch.

Stuffed Eggs

8 large chicken eggs
½ cup cooked fish flakes
¼ cup mayonnaise
juice of 1 lemon
1 tablespoon white wine Worcestershire
   sauce
¼ teaspoon salt
⅛ teaspoon pepper
mild paprika

Hard-boil the eggs, cool, peel, and carefully cut in half lengthwise. Scoop out the yolks, place them in a small bowl, and mash with a fork, along with the mayonnaise and fish flakes. Add the lemon juice, white wine Worcestershire, salt, and pepper. Mix well, then spoon the mixture into the egg whites. Refrigerate. Sprinkle lightly with paprika before serving.

Bass-Flake Salad

This dish makes a good snack on crackers, or it can be served as a light lunch.

2 cups cooked bass flakes
1 medium onion, chopped
1 hard-boiled chicken egg, chopped
1 rib celery, chopped
2 tablespoons finely chopped pickles
juice of ½ lemon
1½ tablespoons mayonnaise
1 tablespoon chopped fresh parsley
1 tablespoon finely chopped red bell pepper
salt and pepper to taste

Mix the mayonnaise, lemon juice, onion, celery, pickles, parsley, and bell pepper, along with salt and pepper to taste. Gently mix in the bass flakes and chopped egg. Chill before serving. As a salad served on lettuce leaves, this recipe makes 6 to 8 servings. Eat leftovers on crackers.

Fish Coleslaw

Here's a dish that is not only good but also pretty, what with the red cabbage and yellow lemon wedges. Use any mild, white fish for this recipe.

2 pounds boneless fish fillets
1 quart water
2 cups shredded red cabbage
1 medium onion, chopped
¼ cup mayonnaise or salad dressing
2 tablespoons pickle relish
1 tablespoon pickling spice mix
juice of 1 lemon
salt and pepper to taste
lettuce leaves
lemon wedges

Bring the water to a boil, add the pickling spices, and simmer for a few minutes to bring out the flavor. Add the fish fillets, then poach for about 10 minutes, or until the fish flakes easily when tested with a fork. Drain the fish, chill, and cut into 1-inch chunks. Refrigerate.

In a large salad bowl, combine the mayonnaise, onion, lemon juice, pickle relish, salt, and pepper. Pour this mixture over the fish, then chill for several hours. Shortly before you are ready to eat, add the shredded cabbage and toss. Serve over lettuce leaves. Garnish with lemon wedges.

Note: It is a mistake to add the cabbage too soon, as it tends to make too much juice.

Eat More Fish

The American Heart Association recommends two meals of fish per week for preventive measures against heart disease. Two recent studies reported in the *New England Journal of Medicine* show that the polyunsaturated fatty acids have metabolic effects that differ substantially from other polyunsaturated fatty acids and may reduce the incidence of coronary heart disease. Oily fish such as bonito have higher levels of polyunsaturated fatty acids than leaner fish such as flounder and grouper.

—*Atlantic Bonito,* UNC Sea Grant

Hot Potato Salad with Fish Chunks

If you are a potato salad fan, be sure to try this German-style dish made with chunks of fish. Any good fish with mild, white flesh will do.

1 pound boneless fish fillets
3 cups diced cooked potatoes
6 strips bacon
½ cup diced onion
½ cup chopped celery
½ cup white wine vinegar
1 cup water
3 tablespoons sugar
1 tablespoon flour
½ teaspoon paprika
¼ teaspoon celery seed
salt and pepper to taste
chopped fresh parsley

Fry the bacon until crisp, crumble, and set aside. In the bacon drippings, sauté the onion and celery for 5 or 6 minutes, then drain off the excess bacon grease. In a small bowl, mix the sugar, flour, paprika, salt, pepper, and celery seed; stir this mixture into the sautéed onions and celery. Mix the vinegar and water, then slowly add the liquid to the onion mixture. Bring to heat and simmer, stirring constantly

with a wooden spoon, until the mixture thickens. Cut the fish fillets into 1-inch chunks, then add them to the skillet. Add the crumbled bacon and potatoes. Cover the skillet and cook on low heat for 10 to 12 minutes, or until the fish flakes easily when tested with a fork. Sprinkle with parsley and serve hot. Feeds 4 or 5.

Ambrosia with Fish Chunks

Ambrosia was one of my mother's favorite dishes, and I have eaten enough of it to establish criteria. The flavor is almost always good with any reasonable recipe, but it's the texture that really distinguishes one batch from another. A good deal depends on the oranges and on how they are handled. For the fish, select a low-fat fish such as flounder.

1 pound fish fillets
1 or 2 large navel oranges
juice of 1 lemon
1 rib celery, thinly sliced
½ cup mayonnaise
½ cup chopped green onions with part of tops
¼ cup sliced green olives
¼ cup shredded coconut
2 teaspoons sugar
1 bay leaf
water

Boil the bay leaf in water for a few minutes, then simmer the fish fillets for 10 minutes, or until they flake easily when tested with a fork. Drain the fillets, chill, and cut into 1-inch chunks. Grate the zest from 1 large navel orange, avoiding the bitter inner pulp, and set aside. Section the orange, then peel the sections. (This last step is important.) Then cut

Cutthroat Trout

The cutthroat is an excellent fish of fine flavor and medium oil content. The color of its flesh ranges from white to red. It can be cooked by any method.

the sections into 1-inch chunks. You should have at least a cup of cut-up orange chunks. Measure, adding more if necessary.

Make a sauce by mixing the mayonnaise, lemon juice, orange zest, and sugar. Set aside. In a large bowl, mix the chilled fish, orange chunks, celery, olives, green onions, and coconut. Add the sauce. Toss carefully. Serve chilled on lettuce leaves. Makes 4 to 6 servings.

Avocado Stuffed with Fish

I've saved the best for last. It's best to use a large, very ripe avocado.

1 cup cooked fish flakes
1 large avocado
1 lemon, cut into quarters
mayonnaise
salt and pepper to taste
lettuce leaves (optional)

Cut the avocado in half lengthwise and remove the pit. Smear a little mayonnaise into each cavity. Stuff with the fish flakes. Squeeze 1 lemon quarter over each stuffed avocado half. Salt and pepper to taste, then top with mayonnaise. Serve each avocado half with a lemon quarter and a lettuce leaf. Serves 2 for a light lunch.

19

DRESSING FISH

Before you start dressing your fish, give some thought to how you are going to cook and eat them. Then proceed with the easiest way to get what you want. In my opinion, it's best to keep the fish whole, if it is practical to do so, until you are ready to cook. This will give you the options of cooking it whole, filleting it, pan dressing it, and so on. At the end of the chapter, I'll have some tips on freezing fish and caring for your catch.

Not long ago, I read a magazine article, an excerpt from a book published by a leading outdoor publishing house, that described dressing fish from a small pond the author and her husband had built. On the day of reckoning, they caught a few small catfish and some bluegills to eat. The bluegill presented a problem, she said, because they couldn't find any fish scalers for sale where they lived. So, presumably unable to figure out a way to get the scales off, they *skinned* the bluegills. Then they

filleted them. What a waste of time—and good eating. Anyone who fillets small fish is not only a glutton for punishment but is also quite wasteful. I have therefore decided to explain how to *eat* fish, and how to use the whole thing, before getting into filleting, steaking, and so on.

THE LIVINGSTON EDGE

For several years my family lived on an island in Florida's Lake Weir. Just about every Saturday night, and sometimes during the week, we fried up forty or fifty hand-sized bluegills. I enjoyed catching them on a fly rod, but I didn't enjoy filleting them and flatly refused to do so, even for guests. It's better, I say, to teach them how to eat the fish. Once, for example, we had an assorted crowd that included a brain cell specialist from England, a schoolteacher from Scotland, and a Ph.D. of some sort. Before the fish ran out, they were eating bream like old-time Florida crackers!

There is a method for eating whole fried fish. First, forget about a knife and fork and pick up the whole fish, working on it with your fingers and teeth as directed in the sidebar on page 170. My older brother Jim and his son David, as well as my son Bill, a true Livingston, are past masters of this method of eating hand-shaped fish; consequently, they will clean up a whole platter of bluegills, shellcrackers, stump-knockers, and other bream, as well as small crappie, while an unsuspecting guest nibbles and picks at one little fish or rib cage.

My wife's people, the Nortons, also know how to eat fish, and I always cheat a little when I eat those delicious little Long Branch bream at their table. My strategy is to clean the back-bone of each fish pretty well, but I don't bother with the rib cages until all the fish are gone from the serving platter. Of course, if the Norton fish are small enough, as they often are, and are fried properly, as they usually are, I eat the rib cage bones and all. That way I have only a few bones on my plate, making it look as though I haven't had my fair share.

If fried crisply, really small fish can be eaten bones and all. As saltwater gourmets know, fried whitebait (about an inch long) are always eaten whole. And I mean *whole*. Bones, head, scales, guts, and all. I have also eaten small cigar-shaped fish bones and all, but there is a limit to this. A good deal depends on how hot the grease is and on how crisply the fish are fried, but the limit (for me) is about 3 fingers for bluegills and 5 or 6 inches for cigar-shaped fish.

Although bony fish may slow down your guests and may turn some of them off, they are really safer than you might think. I've eaten lots of fish during my lifetime, and the only two times that I know of people getting into serious problems with bones occurred when the fish were believed to be boneless and were wolfed down. On one such occasion, a good ol' boy had to be taken to the emergency room. On the other occasion, my nephew had to get a bone out of his daughter's throat with needle-nosed pliers. Over the years, the use of pliers has added to the story considerably. They were used because they were handy, and any suitable set of forceps or long tweezers would have been just as good.

I have eaten fish that seemed to be boneless in restaurants, but which nonetheless had a bone here and there. In general, your best bet is to assume that the fish have bones. If you dress your own fish, a knowledge of the physical layout of each species will help a lot in producing fillets or steaks that are truly boneless. I might add that the small intermuscular bones in some species, such as suckers, are more of a nuisance than a threat to your health.

SCALING FISH

I've used all manner of devices to scale fish, including ordinary knives, electric knives, store-bought scalers with alligator teeth, knives with sawtooth scalers on one side of the blade, scalers made at home by nailing bottle caps to wooden handles, and so on. But the scaler that I use more often than any other is an ordinary

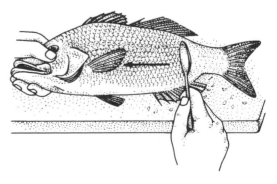

Scaling a fish with a spoon.

Eating Small Fish

Small fish may not bend the rod or stand out in photographs, but they can change your mind about what's really good eating. Moreover, these small fish are often quite prolific, so catching a lot of them for the frying pan won't hurt a thing—and may even improve the fishing in some waters. Almost all farm ponds are overpopulated with 2- and 3-finger panfish. I especially like bluegill, pumpkinseed, and other little sports that can be taken in large numbers on a fly or tiny bug as well as with bait.

The usual complaint is that small fish are too bony. The bones that cause most of the problems, however, are not skeletal; that is, they are not connected to the backbone.

They are attached to the fins. The key to eating these small fish is to realize that each spine of the fin that sticks up has a bone that extends deep into the body of the fish. If you pull out all of these bones along with the fins, you can eat the rest of the fish pretty much like corn on the cob.

Start by holding the fish with your left hand, then carefully pull out the top fins as a unit by grasping them firmly between the thumb and forefinger of the right hand and pulling forward so that the rear pulls out first. When the fins pull free, look at them. Any spine that sticks up should have a bone of similar shape sticking down. If you see a gap in the pattern, you'll know before biting into the fish that you missed a bone.) Next, turn the fish over and pull out the anal fins in the same

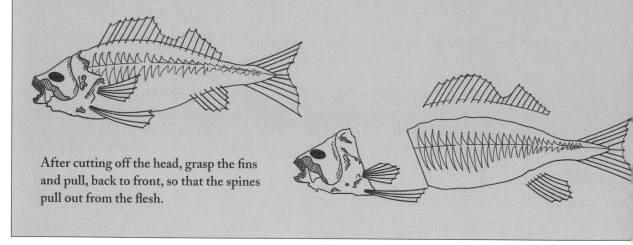

After cutting off the head, grasp the fins and pull, back to front, so that the spines pull out from the flesh.

large kitchen spoon. It's true that one spoon is not necessarily as good as another, but most of them are satisfactory. I suppose I use spoons for two reasons. First, they do a good job. Second, I can usually find one in my kitchen, whereas other scalers tend to get away from me. Once I

had a knife, made by Case, I believe, that had a spoon scaler on one end, and this design worked very well. I don't know what happened to it.

The scaling process should start at the tail of the fish and move toward the head. Small fish

manner. Removing the fins and bones can be done before the fish is fried, but you'll have to cut into the meat on either side of the fins with the point of a very sharp knife. Then you can lift out the whole fin assembly intact. Never cut off the fins with scissors or kitchen shears, as has been suggested by some writers.

After removing the fins, hold the fish by both ends and take your first bite gently from the top, pulling off the meat just above the rib cage. Take similar bites all the way down to the tail. Bite off the crispy part of the tail if you want it, then turn the fish over and work from the rear up toward the rib cage. You'll now have most of the meat, but you can enjoy the rib cages if you are a nibbler. With small fish that have been crisply fried, I normally break the slab of ribs from either side of the backbone and eat them whole, bones and all.

While writing the procedure above, I have assumed that you will cut off the head when you clean the fish. (Removing the head may be optional on some cigar-shaped fish.) With bluegill and similar hand-shaped fish, I always remove the head just behind the gill flap, cutting on a slight diagonal so that both the pectoral and pelvic fins (and associated bones) come off with the head.

difficult to scale than wet fish. Although soaking dry fish in water will help, it's best to scale the fish before it becomes dry. In fact, the best place to scale and clean fish is at the stream or lake, not at home. There are other opinions on this matter, but I always felt that the turtles and crawfish appreciate whatever is left of the fish if you throw it back into the water. I don't, however, recommend that you clean the fish at a crowded public boat ramp. In any case, the sooner the fish are dressed and scaled, the better—and the easier. I must admit, however, that I sometimes break all the rules, and I plead guilty of freezing bass whole—scales, head, guts, and all. I always, however, keep the fish alive until shortly before freezing. I'll discuss this later in the chapter, and I hereby deny charges that I am just too lazy or too tired to scale and clean the fish when I come in from the lake.

There is often a question of whether to scale or skin certain fish. A lot of books and magazines published in New York City say that skinning a bass keeps it from tasting muddy. This statement has been repeated so many times by people in high places that it has even been picked up by writers who probably know better, but who add the advice just in case Yankee bass really *do* taste muddy. In almost all cases, leaving the skin on fish helps hold in the juices during cooking and often helps hold the fish together. Besides, the skin tastes good and often adds to the flavor and certainly to the color.

A few fish, including trout, have tiny scales that can be eaten along with the skin. Some other fish, such as some catfish or eels, should usually be skinned, unless they are small, in which case it's all right and much easier to eat them skin and all.

are usually easier to scale than large fish of the same species. It is with the large fish that special scalers become more useful. I heard of one woman who lived along the Outer Banks of North Carolina who would use a garden hoe to scale large drum! Also, dry fish are much more

SKINNING FISH

One of the New York editors who said that bass should be skinned to get rid of the muddy taste also had some words to say about skinning catfish. The best method, he said, was to scald the catfish in boiling water and then scrape the skin off. I simply can't imagine that anyone would do this, or would think that skinning was so difficult that scalding and scraping would be the easier course. The thing is simply flabbergasting, leaving me speechless for words fit for publication in a book of this sort.

In addition to the large catfish, eels, and bullheads, some other fish should be skinned because the skin is thick and tough.

I always use special fish skinning pliers for this job, if I have them at hand. These are

SKINNING A FISH

1. With a sharp knife, make a shallow cut on both sides above the gills. Loosen enough skin to grasp with pliers.

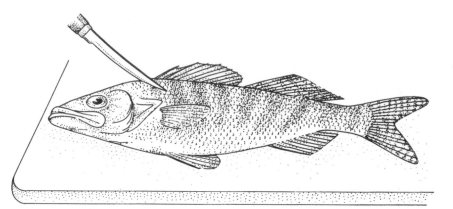

2. Often the skin will pull off evenly until it splits about halfway down the head; then it will taper off, leaving a triangle of skin on the belly, just under the gills. Grasp the end with pliers and pull it toward the tail.

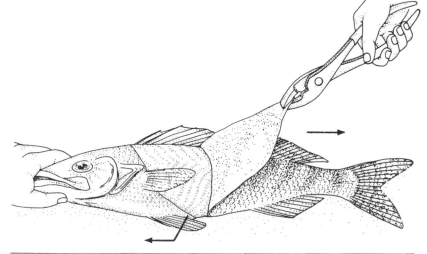

good for skinning because they don't become clogged up with skin and slime, which can quickly become a problem with regular pliers. There are several brands of fish pliers on the market, and usually the more expensive kind, sometimes called commercial grade, are better than cheaper ones. For best results, the two halves should meet up properly and fit tightly. I have also skinned catfish and eels by grasping the skin between my thumb and knife blade, but it's better to use skinning pliers.

Before trying to skin the fish, make a cut behind the head. Then loosen the skin a bit with the knife blade, just to get it started and provide a grip for the pliers. Next, grasp the head of the fish with the left hand. (If you are skinning catfish, be careful to hold the head in such a way that the spines on either side of the head can't stick into you; these can be painful, and some are even poisonous and may cause a serious reaction. If in doubt, hold the fish by the upper lip with regular pliers, or else nail the head to a piece of wood or suspend it from a tree limb with a fish stringer. Eels can be dealt with in the same manner.) After you have secured the fish's head, grasp the loose skin with the pliers and pull down toward the tail. If you have a good grip, the skin comes off easily. On the way down, the skin will probably tear and split, so you will have to take a new grip from time to time. Work both sides all the way to the tail. This method will leave a triangular patch of skin under the throat, which you can pull back toward the head without much effort.

There are other methods of skinning a catfish, sometimes billed as being quick. One such method, mentioned earlier, requires that the fish be scalded in boiling water. Another requires that the fish be put into a hot, dry

An Ice-Fishing Problem

Ice fishermen sometimes have a problem with their catch freezing before they are ready to dress the fish. If this happens, it's best to leave the fish frozen, transfer them whole to a suitable bag or box, and put them into your freezer without ever letting them thaw out. When you are ready to cook, thaw the fish and dress them as usual.

skillet; then, when the fish is picked up, the skin will stick to the skillet and pull off. Well, hell, it's easier to skin a catfish than to clean a skillet. In any case, I recommend the method above, especially if you've got skinning pliers, for use on catfish, bullheads, eels, and frogs, and sometimes for other kinds of fish that need to be skinned for one reason or another.

Some fish that are to be filleted, however, don't have to be skinned whole. You first fillet the fish, leaving part of the skin attached at the tail end, flop the fish over, and work your fillet knife between the flesh and skin, producing a skinless fillet. (Filleting is discussed later in this chapter.)

BEHEADING FISH

After you have skinned or scaled the fish, the next step is to behead it, if you are going to do so. The object here is to remove the forward fins and gills along with the head, while at the same time saving as much meat as possible. This usually requires a slightly diagonal cut, as shown in the drawings.

Normally, I lay the fish flat and make a cut

BEHEADING A FISH

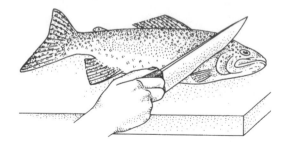

1. Make a diagonal cut to the backbone on both sides of the fish.

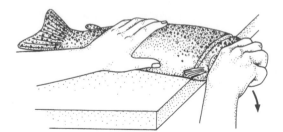

2. Snap the backbone off the side of the table.

with a sharp knife, going down the backbone. To make the cut, I snug the knife blade at an angle against the base of the fin, then cut in and forward to the backbone. Then I flip the fish over and make a similar cut on the other side. Next, I cut from the top down to the backbone. After that cut, the backbone can usually be snapped with a slight bending pressure from the hands, holding the fish head in one hand and the body of the fish in the other. Thus, you can behead the fish without actually having to cut through the backbone. If the fish is large, place it at the edge of a table or counter with the head sticking out; then press down on the head, snapping the backbone. With very small fish such as bluegill, you can merely cut the head off without having to break the bones with your hands. The larger fish, however, may require some hacking with a large knife or a cleaver.

Note that when cutting a fish head off by the method described above, you will leave a piece of meat called the throat attached to the head. This piece can be cut out and eaten. Since it is a very good piece of meat, it is worth getting from some fish such as bass, snapper, and grouper. Snapper throats are served in some restaurants. The throat does have some odd bones in it, so be careful the first time or two that you eat one.

If you fillet the fish and don't want to keep the meat on the backbone, there is no need to remove the head. Also, many people prefer to cook fish with the heads on. I normally remove the head of fish that are pan-dressed and leave the head on those to be baked, poached, or fried whole, if the fish fits nicely into the cooking utensil. The head of the fish helps hold the rest together during the cooking process, and, in addition, it contains some very good eating. On the other hand, some people don't want a fish head on the table. Suit yourself—and consider your guests.

GUTTING FISH

After you have either skinned or scaled the fish (if necessary) and have removed the head (if desirable to do so), the next step is to remove the innards. This is easily accomplished by making a cut at the vent, inserting a knife point, and cutting toward the head. It's best to run the point of the blade just under the skin, facing up, so that the innards won't be slit open.

GUTTING A FISH

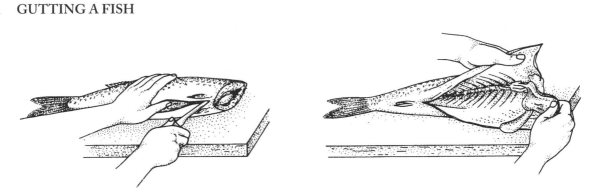

After beheading the fish, insert knife point into the vent and make a shallow cut forward. Remove the entrails.

After you have made the cut, remove the innards with your hand. If the fish has roe, be very careful not to cut the sac. The liver can be removed from the pile if you want it. If you have left the head on, you'll have to cut the tube that attaches the innards. Then you should wash out the fish. I usually scrape away the bloody masses attached to the underside of the backbone, but this may not be necessary. Some people prefer to remove the gills from fish that are dressed with the head on, but I leave them in. Suit yourself.

If you plan to fillet the fish, there's not much point in gutting it, unless you want to keep some of the innards.

MAKING FISH STEAKS

Some people call a fillet a steak. What I mean by fish steak, however, is a cross section of the fish that contains a segment of the backbone. Fish steaks are usually made from fairly large fish of about 10 pounds or so. Steaks are traditional cuts for broiling and grilling, partly because they hold together better than fillets.

Although you can steak fish with a knife, getting through the backbone is sometimes a problem, and making steaks of uniform thickness can be difficult. A butcher's saw will help, but your best bet is to find a good commercial butcher who will steak the fish for you with an electric meat saw.

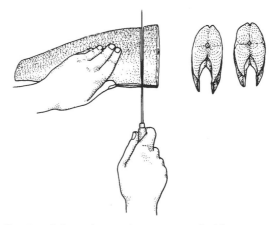

Cutting fish steaks requires a strong knife or a cleaver. Usual thickness is about 1 inch.

FILLETING FISH

There are several ways to fillet a fish. Many of my friends use an electric fillet knife, and others use a thin knife. I use a regular knife with a 7-inch blade. A good deal depends on how you go about the job, the size of the fish, and so on. In all cases, filleting is going to leave some meat on the backbone and rib section. As a rule, the smaller the fish, the greater the percentage of meat that is lost. It seems to me that filleting a small bluegill results in a loss of 50 percent, but a large catfish, in only 5 percent. If course, you can also cook the backbone section, but most practitioners throw it out.

In any case, here are some popular approaches to filleting:

Method I

Start with a whole fish, not gutted, scaled, or skinned. With the fish on its side, start with a crosscut behind the head, then cut along the backbone toward the tail, cutting right through the rib bones. Cut all the way to the tail, but do not go all the way through the skin. Flop the fillet over, hinged by the skin, and start a

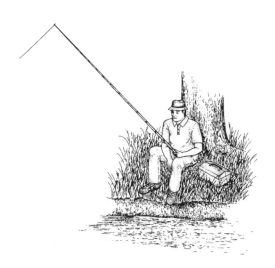

cut between the meat and the skin. Work the knife toward the rib cage and on out the big end. Then turn the fish over and fillet the other side in the same way. Thus, you end up with two skinless fillets, with the rest of the fish attached.

The rib bones will still be attached to the fillet. They can be removed, but most people leave them in when using this method. An electric fillet knife is at its best when using this method.

Method II

Most people, including me, start filleting a fish at the tail, then cut along the backbone up through the rib cage and out at the head. Then the other side is done the same way. Usually, this method is used when the fish has been scaled but not skinned. Also, as a rule, the fish has been beheaded and drawn before filleting. The rib cage is sometimes left in the fillet, or it is removed entirely, without attempting to debone it.

Method III

This method is used to produce a boneless and skinless fillet. It works best with larger fish, and it saves the boneless flesh between the rib bones and skin. Start by cutting behind the head and toward the tail, working the knife down along the backbone and along the edge of the rib cage. The idea is to cut all the meat off the rib cage as well as the backbone. After you've cleared the rib cage, it's easy to work on back toward the tail, working all the way to the bottom.

I dislike this method, except perhaps for large fish. With smaller fish, it works better in magazine articles and books than in practice. Some writers take this a step further, showing

FILLETING (I)

1. Lay fish flat and make a
diagonal cut close to the fins
and gills. Cut down to, but
not through, the backbone.

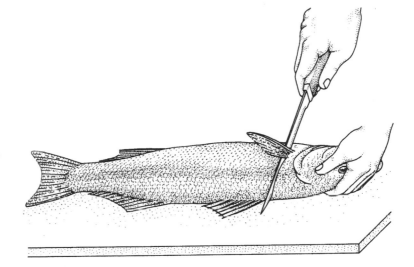

2. Work toward the tail,
keeping the blade close to the
backbone.

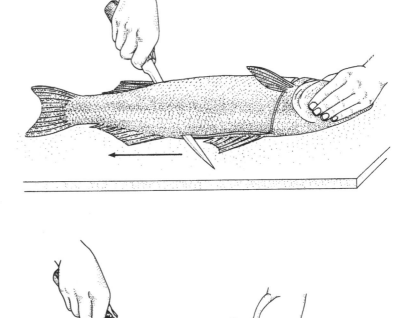

3. Turn the fillet over and cut
carefully through the thin
layer of meat down to the
skin; then cut the fillet from
the skin. Cut the other fillet
in the same way.

FILLETING (II)

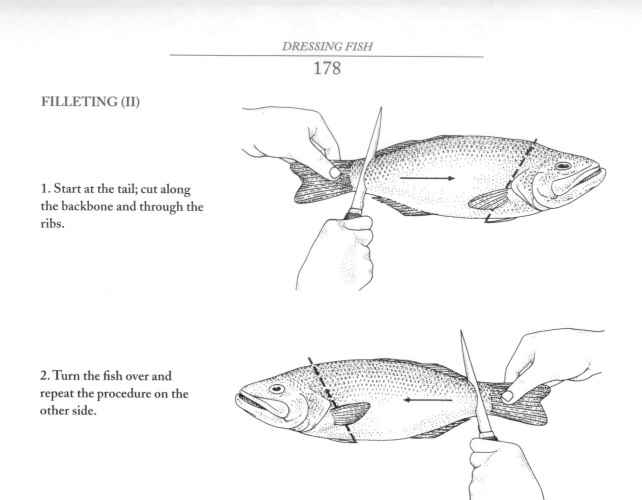

1. Start at the tail; cut along the backbone and through the ribs.

2. Turn the fish over and repeat the procedure on the other side.

FILLETING (III)

Start behind the head and cut toward the tail, taking all the meat off the rib cage as well as the backbone.

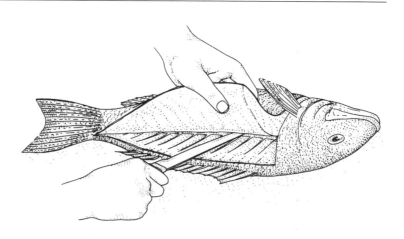

how to flop the fillet over and run the knife between the skin and the meat. In my experience, the meat cut off the rib bone is very sparse—and separating the skin from the meat is impossible, except perhaps on larger fish. It would be easier to merely cut around the rib cage, leaving both meat and skin intact.

FISH FINGERS

Fish fingers are nothing more than strips of fish flesh about 1 inch thick and 1 inch wide, more or less, depending on the size of the fish and how the fingers will be used. Usually, fingers are cut from the fillets of large fish, such as 100-pound jewfish. But the lower part of most fillets can be cut crosswise into nice fingers. I also get fingers from the backbone of medium-size fish by making my "family" cut, as described later in this chapter. Fish fingers are usually boneless and skinless, and are excellent for deep frying. Children love this cut.

PAN-DRESSING FISH

This term is rather vague, but in general it means getting fish ready for the skillet. A small bluegill that has been scaled, beheaded, and gutted is considered to be pan-dressed. On the other hand, a very large bluegill, weighing 2 pounds, should be halved lengthwise and might even be reduced to quarters, depending on individual taste and the size of the skillet.

A 1-pound bullhead or similar fish might be pan-dressed by first cutting it in half, then cutting each strip into two pieces, as shown in the illustration. Note from the illustration that I recommend leaving the tail and fins on the fish. If you do remove the fins, be sure to get all the associated bones from the flesh. The bones from some soft-rayed fish will not cause a problem, but those from some spiny-rayed fish can be real trouble.

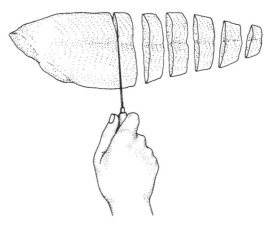

Cutting fish fingers from a fillet.

The Livingston Pan-Dressing Method

Larger fish, such as a 3-pound bass, can of course be filleted, but I like to use all the fish. At the same time, I realize that many families who have small children may want to have some boneless pieces. Thus, I have developed a method of obtaining a maximum of boneless pieces while minimizing waste. The method works nicely for fish in the 3- or 4-pound class or larger, but I also use it for 1-pound fish if I've got children or guests to feed. Of course, it's up to the cook to keep the boneless pieces separate from the rest.

Dotted lines in the illustrations indicate that the fillets from the small end of the fish can be cut in half lengthwise. Usually, fillets from fish of 2 or 3 pounds can be so divided. Larger fish can be divided into smaller pieces or cut into fingers.

Also, the two pieces of boneless fish that I get from the thicker part of the fish, right behind the head, can also be cut into strips. I normally dress out the throat from fish that are 1 pound or larger.

PAN-DRESSING SMALL FISH

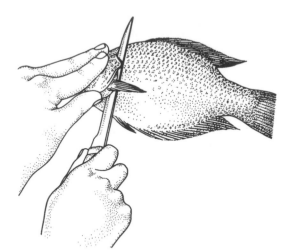 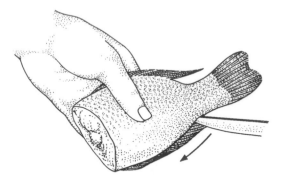

1. Remove head with a diagonal cut just behind the gill.

2. Cut from vent forward and remove entrails to make ready for pan.

PAN-DRESSING A ONE-POUND FISH

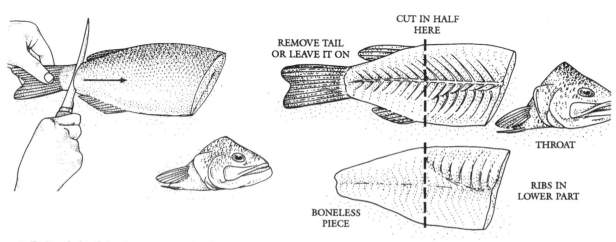

CUT IN HALF HERE

REMOVE TAIL OR LEAVE IT ON

THROAT

RIBS IN LOWER PART

BONELESS PIECE

1. Behead the fish; then cut it in half starting at the tail.

2. Cut both parts of the fish in half again.

NO-WASTE METHOD

Fillet the fish, then cut each fillet in half. Remove tail and cut remaining piece in half as shown. This produces six boneless pieces and four pieces with bones. Note also that the throat can be cut off and eaten.

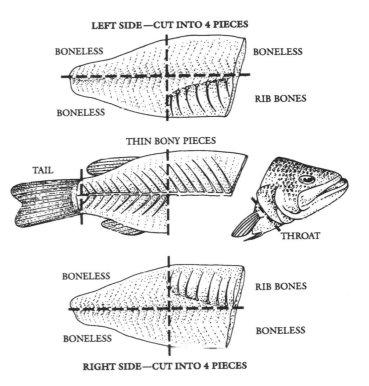

LEFT SIDE—CUT INTO 4 PIECES

BONELESS   BONELESS

BONELESS   RIB BONES

THIN BONY PIECES

TAIL   THROAT

BONELESS   RIB BONES

BONELESS   BONELESS

RIGHT SIDE—CUT INTO 4 PIECES

BONING FISH

A few recipes call for boned fish, but I don't recommend the method. I like some of the recipes—but I'll let somebody else do the boning. Once I read a magazine article that called for boned fish. It said the process was easy, and recommended that you ask your butcher to bone the fish for you. Well, one day I told the meat man at my local Piggly Wiggly store that I wanted six boned mullet. He didn't know what I was talking about. When I explained to him how to do it, he didn't even answer me. Maybe he thought I was joking.

If you want to give it a try, start with a scaled fish that weighs at least 5 or 6 pounds. Some smaller fish can be boned, but they are more difficult. Start by cutting out the top fin and associated bones. Insert a very sharp, small knife blade into the fish on the side of the dorsal fin, then make a shallow gash the entire length of the fin. Then make a similar cut on the other side. Pull out the fin. If it won't come out easily, you haven't cut the gashes quite deep enough. After removing the fin, extend a single gash to the head and another one back to the tail. Carefully work the knife down to the backbone, then cut down on either side of the backbone, working all the way from the head back to the tail. At the head end, you'll have to work the knife along over the rib cage, being careful not to cut through the skin. Cut all the way to the bottom on either side, but do not cut through the belly skin. Then cut through the backbone at the head, and again at the tail. At

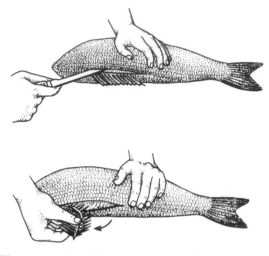

To remove dorsal fin, make two shallow cuts on either side and pull it out.

the head end, you'll also have to cut the tubes. (On most spiny-rayed fish, you'll have to cut around the fins on the bottom, removing them entirely.) If everything has gone according to plan, you can then lift the backbone, rib cage, and innards out the top. Thus, you'll have a whole fish with a slit in the top. Such a boned fish is usually stuffed.

REFRIGERATING FISH

I don't like to keep fish in the refrigerator or on ice longer than 3 days after they are caught. But I have kept them longer, and a good deal depends on what has or has not been done to the fish between catching and refrigerating. Of course, it's best to dress the fish, or at least gut it, before putting it into the refrigerator.

In any case, it's best to put the fish into a suitable container, or on a platter, and cover with plastic wrap. Do not wrap each individual fish. Keep the fish in the coldest part of the refrigerator.

FREEZING FISH

By far the most satisfactory way to freeze fish with ordinary home equipment is to cover them completely with water. In other words, freeze them in a block of ice. I like to fillet or pan-dress the fish, put the pieces into plastic milk cartons or similar containers, cover the meat with water, and freeze the whole thing. But suitable containers are not always on hand, in which case I wrap the fish in plastic wrap and then in freezer paper.

Unless I've got plenty of freezer space, I usually reduce large fish to fillets or other pieces, then freeze them in water. Large fish can, of course, be frozen whole, if you've got the freezer space. Many experts recommend that you first dip the fish in icy water, then freeze it. After it is frozen, dip it again in icy water, then quickly freeze it again. If it is properly glazed, such a fish doesn't have to be wrapped. I seldom use this method, but I see nothing wrong with it, technically. If you are going to freeze a whole fish, glazed or not, it's best to leave the skin and scales on it. If the fish is very fresh, I also leave the innards in— but I have learned not tell my guests of this practice during a fish fry, and I am reluctant to advise the widespread use of this method. Still, I've got three largemouth bass in my freezer at the time of this writing. All were put on ice immediately after catching, and were then wrapped with two coats of plastic wrap and frozen within 2 hours. Freezing the fish whole by this method gives me several options. I can fillet it, or I can use it whole, either scaled or skinned, depending on the recipe.

If you've got a lot of fish to freeze and not much space in the freezer, it may be best to poach the fish for 10 minutes, flake off the meat, and freeze it in 1-cup packages. I like the little rectangular freezer containers, and I always put a little water (or, better, broth from the poaching pan) in with the fish flakes. You can also freeze the fish flakes in Ziplock bags, along with a little water.

Some fish don't keep very well when frozen. Usually, lean fish keep better than fatty fish. Also, there is much variation among different types of fish. Channel catfish from running water, for example, freeze much better than bullheads.

As a rule, I don't freeze fatty fish unless I have to. Some people recommend that fatty fish be soaked for a few minutes in a solution of water and ascorbic acid, mixed in the proportions of 1 teaspoon of acid to 1 cup of water. Also, I believe that frozen fish with white flesh keep longer than those with darker or reddish flesh. In spite of what other writers say, I have kept small largemouth frozen in water for over a year, and found them quite tasty and almost as good as fresh. But I emphasize that these were very fresh when frozen, and were in a block of ice.

Thawing Out Frozen Fish

According to the experts, fish should be thawed by taking them out of the freezer and putting them into the refrigerator. I seldom do this simply because it takes too long. I usually thaw mine at room temperature, putting them out a few hours before time to cook. As often as not, I'll end up running cool tap water over them to help them along. Personally, I've never had a problem with fish thawed in this manner, and I'll put more stock in having fresh and properly frozen fish than in how they are thawed. Hell, I've even thawed fish in a microwave. But slow thawing is probably better.

I'll also admit that I have cooked fish that weren't thawed out entirely—and the results were still very good. I don't make a habit of this, and I've never attempted to cook a large fish while it was frozen. But partly frozen panfish, dropped into a deep fryer, are delicious.

Once a fish has been thawed, do not refreeze it—unless it has first been cooked. Leftovers can be refrozen if necessary. If I have to thaw

Dealing with Longnose Gar

The longnose garfish *(Lepisoteus osseus)* is a common denizen of the state's coastal waters and an unused resource. Commonly considered trash fish, there is no commercial market for this species. When properly prepared, however, the flesh is mild, boneless, and can be obtained in large quantities for social gatherings. Gar are the bane of shad fishermen, who are more than happy to pass these net tanglers on to anyone willing to accept them.

Cleaning garfish involves some effort, but this lessens with experience. Beginning at the head, split the shell (armored scales) open down the back with a hatchet or suitable instrument. Remove head and tail, separate shell from meat along sides with a knife. Scrape exposed meat from carcass with a large spoon, fork, or serrated fish scaler. Gar meat is permeated with tendons and fascia, and this procedure leaves most of the gristle behind. Grind the meat if necessary.

—*South Carolina Wildlife Cookbook*

out more fish than I need, as sometimes happens when I have put fish into large packages, I usually poach the surplus, flake off the meat, and refreeze it in 1-pound packages.

CARING FOR THE CATCH
With rare exceptions, the best course is to dress your fish as soon as they are caught, then eat them on the spot. (I have read that some trout, caught from waters with a very high algae content, are better when they are aged for a few days before eating—but I have never encountered this condition, and I don't yet subscribe to it fully.) The next best bet is to keep the fish alive after they have been caught, then dress them shortly before cooking. The Chinese, I understand, keep carp alive in holding tanks until the last instant. Eels and hatchery trout are also kept in holding tanks. The third best bet is to dress the fish and put them on ice (or freeze them) immediately after catching them. The fourth best bet is to put the undressed fish in an ice chest immediately after catching them.

All of the above choices are usually better than putting the fish on a stringer, into a creel, or into an overcrowded live well with insuffi-cient oxygen in the water. I'm not one to talk, however, since I've strung up several thousand fish during my lifetime. Sometimes a stringer seems necessary, as when you are wading a stream, a lake, or salt flats. My brother came up with a solution to part of the problem. Once he was wade-fishing Lake Okeechobee, in south Florida, catching bluegills on a fly rod and stringing them up behind him, when he discovered that a large cottonmouth was tugging on the other end of the stringer. That's when he invented the Okeechobee Jig, he said. After that, he started pulling a little plastic boat behind him. The craft—a toy, I suppose—was about 2½ feet long—and just big enough to hold a small ice chest, a little spare tackle, and a .410 scattergun pistol for snakes! I've never seen another miniature boat quite like it, but I have noted that some flounder giggers and frog giggers, as well as people after bay scallops, sometimes pull a small washtub behind them.

In any case, putting fish on a stringer is one of the worst things to do. If you do use a stringer, invest in a good one with snaps so that individual fish can be held through the lips instead of stringing them all together through the gills.

PART TWO

BIRDS

20

DOVES AND PIGEONS

One of my sons took a summer position with a large timber company to help fill the infinite gap between high school graduation and college. At about the same time, a pretty young thing of good upbringing caught his eye. The shift foreman put the boy in the yard stacking lumber, and I told him that a little hard work would be good for him. The girl was more sympathetic, however, and to give him daily strength she started bringing a hot lunch to him at noonday. Her chicken and dumplings quickly made him the envy of the lumberjacks, all of whom said they wished they had a woman like that.

"Boy," I told him, "as much as you like to fish and hunt you've got to look beyond chicken and dumplings. Bring the girl a dozen doves and see what she can do."

Much cooing could be heard across the land during the days of summer, but slowly the nights began to cool off and the doves quit their nests and began to flock together. The early part of the split dove season opened in September. Shortly thereafter, the romance began to wane and the boy started moping about. Perhaps my advice had been too pointed, the test too hard. In spite of a temporary feeling of guilt, however, I have no permanent misgivings about offering him those words of fatherly wisdom. The plain truth is that tough, chewy doves simply don't make for culinary bliss, and the fact is that almost all women tend to cook all game much too done simply because it is wild. When overcooked, the dove is difficult to swallow. When cooked to perfection, however, the breast of dove—dark and firm and juicy with just a hint of the wild—is the best of all meats. It's my favorite, although good wild ducks come close. And the dove legs and the back and the giblets are simply too good to throw away, as some of the recipes in this chapter show.

To be sure, doves can be cooked for a long time on low heat with good results. What usually ruins them is frying, grilling, baking, or broiling them too long under or over dry heat. How much is too long is impossible to define and depends on the intensity of the heat and the distance of the bird from the heat. When done to perfection, the inside of the bird should be moist and medium rare, and the outside nicely browned. Many patio chefs have learned that wrapping a dove's breast in half a strip of bacon before grilling it over hot coals makes the process almost foolproof, and the same trick works nicely for broiling doves in the kitchen oven. For either grilling or broiling doves, all one really needs is celery salt, pepper, and the strip of bacon. For frying them, salt, pepper, flour, and cooking oil will do.

But there can be more. For all newlyweds, I hereby offer a recipe that my father enjoyed. I don't know whether he taught my mother how to make it or whether it came from her side of the family. In any case, I highly recommend the following:

Daddy's Smother-Fried Doves

Pluck and draw the birds. Separate the breasts from the bony pieces. Then cut the backs in half lengthwise, so that you have 2 leg pieces. It's best to cook this recipe in a large skillet that has a lid or in a stove-top Dutch oven. Although some books recommend one bird per serving, I always wonder how many "servings" it will take to satisfy each of the people I'm feeding. At least 2 doves per person are usually required, and I need 3 or 4.

8 to 10 doves
½ cup bacon drippings or cooking oil
1 medium onion, chopped
8 ounces fresh mushrooms
1 can cream of celery soup (10¾-ounce size)
½ soup can water
1 tablespoon chopped parsley
flour
salt and pepper
rice (cooked separately)

Heat the bacon drippings or oil and sauté the onions and mushrooms in the skillet for 5 or 6 minutes, then remove them from the skillet with a slotted spoon. Drain on a brown bag. Salt and pepper the bird pieces, then shake them in flour. Increase the heat and brown the bird pieces on all sides. Put the onions and mushrooms back into the skillet (or Dutch oven) with the birds. Add the cream of celery soup, water, and parsley. Turn the heat down, cover the skillet, and simmer for 1 hour. Serve the birds with rice, vegetables, bread, and good red wine.

It's true that some women and even some

How Many?

Regardless of what other fish and game cookbooks say, allow at least 2 mourning doves per adult. I want 3—and 4 aren't too many for me if doves are the only meat served during the meal. But on the other hand, I am inordinately fond of doves. I like their mild, dark meat with just a hint of the wild. It's the perfect game, at least for my taste.

I suspect that some of the contributors to other cookbooks confused doves with pigeons, and that this confusion was compounded by having multiple authors or con tributors. One cookbook, for example, has a tabular guide to bird servings and allows 1 to 1½ doves per person. Yet, a few pages later, the author says that he has gone hungry at "boards" where the cook served up only 1 dove per hunter.

Moreover, another cookbook, in a table of approximate weights, lists the dove as weighing ¾ pound (12 ounces) and the quail as weighing 6 ounces. Thus, they are telling the world that the dove is twice as big as the quail. Well, in my part of the country, adult bobwhites are quite a bit larger than any adult doves that can be legally hunted. Of course, there are several kinds of quail and several kinds of doves, and there are some size variations—but none that will put the largest quail only half the size of the largest dove. I'm talking about game doves with legal hunting seasons, not fat Central Park pigeons.

In the Far West, there is a limited amount of hunting for band-tailed pigeons, but these are usually called pigeons, not doves. These birds range from British Columbia south to Panama, and their size, according to one fish and game cookbook, is about twice that of a mourning dove; yet another book says that 12 pigeons feed 4 people—the same number listed for the dove recipes.

In any case, only the mourning dove is widely hunted in the United States, although the whitewing is hunted in limited ares of the Southwest. Another dove species, which I call the ground dove, is quite small and is not hunted legally in most states. In any case, the recipes for doves can be used with either mourning dove or whitewings. Pigeons can be used, in reduced numbers, in any recipe that requires long, slow cooking. A couple of pigeon recipes are also included at the end of this chapter. I have no experience with cooking band-tailed pigeons, but one authority says those that have fed mostly on acorns tend to be on the bitter side. The same authority, however, says that the mourning dove feeds mostly early in the morning and at dusk—which is not the case, as they head for the watering hole shortly before sundown and then head for the roost at dusk. The same expert talked about the high speed of the dove, and its evasive tactics, upon being *flushed*. Apparently this fellow has never been on a dove shoot.

Finally, a note of warning about using dove and pigeon recipes from other countries. There are about three hundred species of these birds, which vary widely in size. Technically, there is no difference between doves and pigeons, but generally the doves are the smaller birds. Many of the doves and pigeons are hunted and eaten in other lands, and some are also raised for food. The largest one grows wild in New Zealand, where it is hunted for both food and sport. This is the crowned pigeon, which grows as large as a chicken.

hunters have no practice at, or patience for, picking the meat from dove backs and legs. Give 'em the breasts and dig into the bony pieces yourself. I usually gnaw around the legs and then chew up the back section, bones and all.

The recipe above will also work with quail, served, of course, with a white wine instead of red. As a rule, quail are more tender than doves and require only about 30 minutes of simmering.

Smother-Fried Late-Season Doves

Here's a recipe that I like to cook whenever my state has a late dove season, when the wild onions are ready for pulling in my neck of the woods. It can also be used to cook snipe or woodcock. The technique is similar to Daddy's method, only the birds are sautéed instead of being outright fried.

    doves, plucked and halved
    wild onions with part of tops, chopped
    butter
    all-purpose flour
    salt and pepper
    water

Heat some butter in a skillet, then sauté a few of the wild onions. Remove the onions with a slotted spoon and set aside. Salt and pepper the dove halves, then shake them in a bag of flour. Brown the birds on both sides over medium low heat, then set aside. Quickly add some flour to a little water, making a thin paste. Add the paste to the butter in the skillet (adding more butter if needed) and stir about

with a wooden spoon until you have a thin gravy. Return the birds and onions to the skillet, cover tightly, and simmer for 30 minutes or longer, adding a little water if needed. Serve the birds along with vegetables of your choice, spooning the gravy over mashed potatoes or fluffy white rice.

Fried Early-Season Doves

In the early dove season, which often opens in September in some states, a goodly number of the birds are young and tender. These can be fried to perfection if the cook knows his stuff.

    doves or dove breasts
    oil
    all-purpose flour
    salt and pepper

Heat at least ½ inch of oil in a skillet, or more if you have a skillet with good deep sides. Deep frying works best, but this method isn't always practical for cooking only a few birds. So, use a skillet for 5 or 6 birds, and a larger pan or deep fryer for a large dove supper. Salt and pepper the birds, then shake them in a bag of flour. Fry in oil at medium high heat until browned.

Be warned that fried doves will be dry and tough if they are cooked too long—and they usually are.

Texas Doves

I got onto this recipe out at Choctawhatchee Lodge, to which it was brought by a fellow from Eufaula, Alabama, who in turn says that his son got it from a rich, young Texan at Tulane University in New Orleans. In any case, it's a good way to grill doves. The bacon keeps the breast from drying out and the jalapeño lends a distinctive flavor. Be warned, however, that some jalapeño peppers are hot to the extreme. Bite into one at your peril. Here's what you'll need:

doves
1 fresh jalapeño for each bird
bacon
salt

Pluck the birds and draw from the rear, making only a small opening. Build a good charcoal fire in the grill or, better, a wood fire of hickory or mesquite. When the coals are ready for cooking, lightly salt each bird inside and out, stuff with a jalapeño, wrap with half a strip of bacon, and secure with a round toothpick. Grill over medium coals for about 20 minutes. The exact time will vary with the heat and the distance from the grill to the coals. As a rule, the birds will be done when the bacon looks ready to eat. But if they are cooked too close to very hot coals, the birds will burn on the outside before they are done inside.

Quail can also be cooked by this recipe, but they are a little larger than doves and will require a longer cooking time.

Variations: There are a thousand variations of grilled birds wrapped in bacon. Most of the good ol' boys of my acquaintance breast the birds and wrap them in bacon before grilling. Often they marinate them first in Zesty Italian salad dressing. One tasty variation, which I picked up in Leary, Georgia, is to tuck a thin slice of lemon under the bacon.

Bill Ard's Breakfast

Rumors sometimes get started in unfounded ways. Take the case of Bill Ard, a local banker and sport of good name and character. After the S&L scandal broke and the Federal Bank Examiners started buzzing around like bees, Bill's attitude turned sour, and even those of us who knew him best figured that his bank had fallen on hard times or at least was under scrutiny. Little did we know what business matters bore on the man's mind. More than half of his customers (good friends and neighbors, mostly) had overdrawn their checking accounts, and some of his large loans were secured by family farms. Surely, anyone who has tried to do business off the dash of a pickup truck while the Federal Bank Examiners looked over his shoulder will understand Bill's problems.

The notion that Bill had himself fallen on hard times was encouraged by something that happened at a big dove shoot on a local peanut farm. While most of the hunters merely breasted their birds, Bill was caught in the act of plucking the whole dove, saving the legs and back for table fare. Not knowing Bill's secret, the members of the club figured that anyone who would gnaw on dove crags was hungry and hard put.

My own suspicions were set to rest when I caught him eating a dove crag breakfast about noon one Saturday. Seeing that I wouldn't leave without hard information, he smiled knowingly and gave me a dove crag or two along with a biscuit half with gravy piled on it. One bite was enough said, and I wouldn't leave without the recipe.

"Well," Bill said, "you save the breasts for Sunday dinner or company and you eat the rest

Russian Birds

In one of his books, Bradford Angier suggests coating a bird with clay and roasting it in hot coals without removing either feathers or entrails. The insides shrink up and harden, making them easy to deal with, and of course, the feathers come off with the clay. The moisture in the insides helps steam the birds. The innards shrink up and are easily discarded, or consumed in one bite if you are so inclined. Don't shudder. The French and some other Europeans have, in times past, relished bird entrails and even the innards of some fish, such as the mullet, which they named the Woodcock of the Sea. (The mullet has a large gizzardlike organ that is eaten in some quarters.) Anyhow, this practice is very old, but it seems to be on the wane these days. If you want to try the innards, it's best to cook them with a little seasoning. The ancient Roman culinary sport Marcus Gabius Apicus, who gave us a cook-

book called *Cooking and Dining in Imperial Rome,* discovered that herbs and spices could be stuffed down the bird's throat before cooking. I don't want to corrupt this simple technique with a long list of ingredients, but I might suggest that liquid seasonings are easier to administer than dry stuff, simply by using an eyedropper or syringe, or perhaps a straw. Try gin, which is flavored with juniper berries, a popular spice for game birds of all sorts.

In rural Russia, a slightly different method is used, one that may be more appealing to modern tastes. The bird is drawn, but not plucked, and a pat of butter is placed inside the cavity, along with a little salt and pepper. The head and feet are snipped off, the bird is encased with clay, and the ball is covered with hot coals. When the clay hardens and cracks, the bird is done to perfection. Try this method with doves, quail, snipe, or woodcock—and you may never tote another skillet to camp.

yourself. Split the back right down the middle. Salt and pepper the pieces, then shake them in flour. Use lots of pepper. Black pepper. Heat some peanut oil right hot in a skillet. Fry the birds right crisp so that you can eat bones and all, like you do those three-finger bream out of the Choctawhatchee. Drain the birds on a brown bag and pour off most of the grease from the skillet. Add some flour to the skillet and brown it a little, as when making a coonass roux. Pour in a little hot water or black coffee and some pepper, and stir. Pour and stir, pour and stir, until you have the gravy just the way

you want it. Then add some pepper. Quite a bit of pepper. Eat the birds bones and all, and pour the gravy over biscuit halves. It's the best breakfast that any man can enjoy, rich or poor."

When I tried the recipe in my own kitchen, I was a little apprehensive at first about chewing up the bones. But it worked fine and I had no trouble with the back parts. (I still tend to pull the meat off the legs with my teeth, but that's no problem once you get the hang of it.) After trying Bill's recipe several times, I read in a book of Middle Eastern cooking that the

Egyptians eat pigeons in this manner, claiming that the birds have soft bones.

In any case, I realized at our late Saturday breakfast that Bill Ard wasn't saving the bony parts of the doves because he had come upon hard times. He was after the best part of the bird for culinary purposes.

Dove Pie

I cook this dish in a Dutch oven, first heated on a stove top, then transferred to a preheated oven.

    8 doves
    8 slices bacon
    4 medium potatoes, diced
    4 carrots, sliced
    8 green onions with part of tops, cut into
        1-inch segments
    1 cup sherry
    pie pastry or refrigerated biscuit dough
    2 bay leaves
    salt and pepper
    water

Cook the bacon in a large skillet with an ovenproof handle. Remove the cooked bacon and drain. In the bacon drippings, brown the doves all around. Return the bacon to the skillet. Sprinkle with salt and pepper. Cover with water, add the bay leaves, and bring to heat. Cover tightly, reduce the heat to low, and simmer for 1 hour. Add the carrots, potatoes, and green onions. Add the sherry and enough water to almost cover the vegetables and birds, but not quite. Cover and simmer for 30 minutes.

Preheat the oven to 400 degrees. Sprinkle some flour on a flat surface and make a batch of pastry, using a recipe of your choice, or pop open a can of refrigerated biscuits, mix them up, and roll flat. Cut the pastry into strips about ½ inch wide and crisscross them on top of the dove and vegetable mixture. Put the skillet into the preheated oven and bake for 20 minutes, or until the pastry is browned. Feeds 4.

Variations: Put some pastry strips down in the pie to make dumplings. You can also roll out two rounds of dough, using one for a bottom crust, in which case you will have to use a second skillet or a pie pan of suitable size.

Zesty Broiled Doves

Doves can be broiled to perfection, but be warned once more that they should not be cooked too long lest they wind up dry and tough.

    8 or 10 doves, halved lengthwise
    2 tablespoons bacon drippings
    2 tablespoons Worcestershire sauce
    1 teaspoon fresh lemon juice
    salt and pepper

Preheat the broiler. Salt and pepper the birds on both sides. Heat the bacon drippings in a saucepan, then mix in the Worcestershire sauce and lemon juice. Dip the birds in the sauce, then arrange them, breast up, on a rack. Arrange the rack so that the birds are about 3 inches from the heat. Broil for 3 minutes, then baste, turn, and broil for another 3 minutes. Turn again, baste, and broil for 5 more minutes, flipping the birds every minute or so until done. Feeds from 3 to 5 if you've got plenty of vegetables, rice, and a little bread. A rice pilaf goes nicely with this dish.

Doves in Easy Gravy

8 to 10 doves, dressed whole
4 to 5 strips bacon
1 can beef gravy (10½-ounce size)
4 ounces fresh mushrooms, sliced
½ cup good red wine
2 green onions
1 tablespoon cooking oil
salt and pepper

Salt and pepper the birds. Cut the bacon strips in half, wrap each piece around a dove, and pin with a round toothpick. (This works best if the bacon is at room temperature.) Heat the oil in a skillet with deep sides, then brown the birds and set them aside. Chop the green onions, including part of the tops. Sauté the green onions and mushrooms in the pan drippings, then stir in the gravy. Add the doves, cover, and simmer for 30 minutes. Add the wine and simmer for another 15 minutes. Have ready some rice, mashed potatoes, or biscuit halves to top with the gravy, and serve with steamed vegetables or a green salad. Feeds 3 or 4.

Doves Wyatt Earp

According to George Leonard Herter, Charles Shibell of Tombstone once questioned Earp about his best shot. Without hesitation, Wyatt answered, "The time I killed nine mourning doves out of a flock coming into a water hole with one shot." That's a pretty good shot all right, and it certainly beats the time I dropped seven doves with two shots at a watering hole. Herter says that Earp was fond of cooking game and fowl and that in parts of the West, Earp's cooking methods will be remembered long after his deeds with a gun are forgotten.

(Herter said the same thing about Bat Masterson, but I was disappointed in the recipe called Prairie Dogs Bat Masterson, which was merely a recipe for hot dogs, maybe from Coney Island.) In any case, I do recommend that you try the following recipe, to which I have added some salt and pepper, the next time you get lucky at a watering hole.

10 doves
2 tablespoons butter
2 tablespoons beef suet
1 medium head cabbage
6 carrots
1 cup cooked lima beans
1 cup cooked macaroni
1 large onion, diced
1 teaspoon sage leaves
salt and pepper
water

Pluck and draw the birds, then separate the back and leg sections from the breast. (I think it is better to cut the birds in half lengthwise, but suit yourself.) Heat the butter and suet in a skillet, then quickly brown the bird pieces. Drain the pieces. Put the carrots into a large pot or stove-top Dutch oven. Cut the cabbage into 8 wedges, and add them to the pot along with the lima beans, diced onion, sage leaves, salt, and pepper. Add the browned dove pieces last, then cover everything with about 2 inches of water. Also add the dredgings from the skillet. Bring to heat, cover the pot tightly, and simmer for 1½ hours. Serve the dove pieces with potatoes or brown rice. Remove the carrots and cabbage, serving them up as vegetables.

Add 1 cup of cooked macaroni to the pot liquor (Herter advises), making a soup to be served with buttered hot bread.

Baked Doves

If I had to choose one method of cooking doves, I'd have to consider this recipe carefully. It has a certain flavor that complements the taste of wild dove—and the gravy is superb!

8 to 10 doves
1 can chicken broth (10¾-ounce size)
½ stick butter or margarine
1 tablespoon Worcestershire sauce
1 teaspoon onion juice
¼ teaspoon garlic juice
all-purpose flour
salt and pepper
1 cup cold water

Pluck the birds and dress them whole. Preheat the oven to 350 degrees. Salt and pepper the doves inside and out, then shake them in a bag with 1 cup or so of flour. Heat the butter or margarine in a skillet and brown the birds. Remove the birds and set aside. Stir 1 tablespoon of flour into the water and add to the pan drippings, stirring as you go. Mix thoroughly and increase the heat. When the gravy starts to bubble, add the chicken broth and Worcestershire sauce. Stir in the onion and garlic juices. Simmer for a few minutes. Arrange the doves, breast up, in a baking pan or casserole dish. Pour the gravy over the birds and bake for 30 minutes, basting the bird breasts several times with the liquid from the casserole dish. Feeds 3 or 4. The gravy goes nicely with rice, served along with asparagus or other vegetables.

Crockpot Dove

Although this dish is quite tasty if prepared with the whole dove, the legs and wings tend to come apart during long cooking, filling the pot with bones. I therefore recommend that you use only dove breasts, saving the rest of the birds for other recipes in this chapter.

20 dove breasts
1 can condensed cream of celery soup
   (10¾-ounce size)
4 medium potatoes, sliced
2 medium onions, sliced
2 carrots, sliced
4 cloves garlic, sliced or minced
cooking oil
salt and pepper
all purpose flour
1 teaspoon oregano

Salt and pepper the dove breasts, then shake them in a bag with a little flour. Heat the cooking oil in a skillet. Brown the bird breasts and put them into the crockpot along with the potatoes, onions, oregano, carrots, garlic, and celery soup. Turn the crockpot to low and cook

Good News for Hunters

The mourning dove is as good in the pan as it is sporting in the field. These darting little game birds are equally adaptable to today's world. They flourish in spite of all we do to destroy game bird habitat. In fact, the mourning dove population in the United States is increasing because the birds are able to select excellent nesting sites in our expanding suburbs.
   —Sylvia Bashline
   The Bounty of the Earth Cookbook

for 9 hours. During the last hour, add a little salt and pepper if needed to suit your taste. This dish makes a complete meal if you cook some rice to go with the gravy, or serve it with biscuit halves.

Feeds 7 or 8.

Deer 'n' Doves

I got the idea for this dish from *Cooking the Sportsman's Harvest,* published by the South Dakota Department of Game, Fish, and Parks. But I changed the recipe considerably and bear the responsibility for the changes. Try it the first time you've got leftover venison roast and a mess of doves.

12 doves
2 cups leftover venison, diced
6 strips bacon
1 can cream of mushroom soup
   (10¾-ounce size)
1 cup sour cream
½ cup water
1 tablespoon bacon drippings
1 teaspoon garlic juice
salt and pepper

Preheat the oven to 350 degrees. Select a casserole dish of suitable size and shape for holding 12 doves. Grease the casserole dish with a mixture of bacon drippings and garlic juice. Spread the diced venison on bottom. Wrap each dove in half a strip of bacon and arrange them on top of the venison. Sprinkle with salt and pepper. Mix the mushroom soup, water, and sour cream; spread the mixture evenly over the birds. Bake for 3 hours in the center of the oven.

Feeds 4 to 6.

What Mattie Cobb Missed

Whenever I cook this dish, I think of my mother. I also remember, with mixed feelings, a little redheaded lady named Miss Mattie Cobb, who, in spite of chronic neuralgia in her arm, tried hard to teach me Latin in high school. No doubt she was among the last of the small-school Latin teachers, having been retained by a staunch principal named Mr. J. J. Yarborough, who suffered no neuralgia in his arm. For some reason that I never did understand, Mother invited Miss Cobb over to our house for a bird supper. I had bagged lots of doves, quail, and a few snipe during the holidays, and, since we had plenty, and had company to feed, my mother cooked only the breasts. She also starched my shirt so stiff that the collar made my neck sore.

In spite of the neuralgia in her arm, Miss Cobb consumed, with tiny bites, about 10 bird breasts—10 times what I had figured her for. Even so, her feast didn't pull up my Latin grade *quid pro quo.*

Looking back, I think that Mother invited Miss Cobb to the wrong meal. Although the bird breasts were mighty good, served with grapes and all, the real finger-licking, table-hunkering feast was yet to come.

When dressing the birds for this recipe, save the hearts, livers, and gizzards, along with the legs, backs, wings, and necks. It's all right to leave the feet on the birds. Set the livers aside. Boil the bony parts of the birds, along with the livers and hearts, in a small amount of water for about 1 hour. Save the broth for the recipe. Take a fork and pull the meat from the bones. Mince the hearts and gizzards. Chop up any bird breasts left over from the main meal and add to the giblets. Add the livers. Proceed as follows.

2 cups of bird giblets and pickings
1½ cups bird broth from above
⅓ cup all purpose flour
1 medium onion (tennis-ball size), minced
2 chicken eggs, hard-boiled and sliced
butter
salt and pepper to taste
corn pone

In a cast-iron skillet, sauté the onions in a little butter. Add the stock to the skillet and heat quickly. Reduce the heat and add the flour slowly, stirring constantly, whisking with a fork. (There is an easier way to do this by first mixing the flour with a little water, but much whisking helps the flavor of the gravy and cures neuralgia.) When all the lumps are gone, stir in the giblets and onion. Salt and pepper to taste, stirring again. Add the eggs—but don't stir. Heat almost to a boil, then quickly reduce the heat and simmer for 30 minutes.

Serve with hot corn pone. Be sure to have enough corn pone to feed everybody, then let the gravy stretch as far as it needs to go. Then it's every man for himself. So . . . if you don't know how to sop gravy with corn pone, just skip this one and wait until Miss Mattie Cobb comes for more proper fare.

Grilled Band-Tailed Pigeons

Young band-tailed pigeons, which are larger than mourning doves, can be split in half and either grilled or broiled. For best results, pluck the birds instead of skinning them. Allow at least 3 halves per person.

    young band-tailed pigeons
    bacon drippings
    lemon-pepper seasoning salt

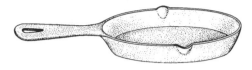

Build a good charcoal fire and grill the birds about 4 inches above the coals. Baste with bacon drippings and sprinkle lightly with lemon-pepper seasoning salt after each baste. Do not overcook.

Smother-Fried Band-Tailed Pigeons

Young pigeons can be cut in half, sprinkled with salt and pepper, dusted with flour, and fried like quail. Older birds, however, tend to be tough and require long simmering.

    pigeons, cut in half
    flour
    salt and pepper
    cooking oil
    water

Pluck the birds, cut them in half lengthwise, sprinkle them with salt and pepper, and dust them with flour. Heat about ½ inch of cooking oil in a large skillet. Brown the birds on both sides and drain them. Pour off most of the grease, then brown a little flour and stir in some water, making lots of thin gravy. Put the birds back into the skillet, bring to a simmer, cover, reduce heat, and simmer for 1 hour or so, or until all the birds are tender. Serve with vegetables, rice, and gravy from the skillet.

Note: The first recipe in this chapter, called Daddy's Smother-Fried Doves, can also be used for cooking older band-tailed pigeons.

Chinese Pigeons

I don't know the history of this recipe, but I found it in *A General's Diary of Treasured Recipes,* by Brigadier General Frank Dorn. Because Dorn allows 3 pigeons per person, I assume that the birds are on the small side. Band-tails work fine, if the birds are young and tender.

3 young pigeons
½ cup sugar
⅓ cup melted butter
⅓ cup rice wine or sherry
2 tablespoons soy sauce
1 teaspoon minced candied ginger
½ teaspoon dry mustard

In a small saucepan, mix the melted butter, soy sauce, wine, mustard, sugar, and ginger. Bring to a boil, reduce heat, and simmer for 2 minutes. Set aside but keep warm.

Pluck and draw the pigeons, then split them in half, or cut them down the center and open them "spread-eagle." Preheat the broiler, adjusting the rack so that the birds will be 3 inches below the heat. Place the birds in a broiling pan, pour the sauce over them, and broil for 8 to 10 minutes, or until nicely browned on both sides. Baste the birds several times with the sauce and pan drippings. Do not overcook.

21

QUAIL

Never go quail hunting with a long-legged barber. He'll walk you to death, unless you've got a horse or jeep. The reason, I figure, is that most barbers stand up all day long, with their movement being confined to short steps in a circle around the swivel chair. When they get afield, however, they break the circle and head on out, straight as a tangent. Sometimes even a pointer has trouble keeping up with them during a day's hunt.

Oyette Taylor is one such barber in my hometown of Headland, Alabama, in the heart of the Wiregrass area. It's quail country, and Taylor's Barber Shop, just off the town square, is a sort of headquarters for local outdoor news. As indicated in Oyette's recipe for salt fish elsewhere in this book, the Taylors will tell you not only where the fish were biting yesterday, but also exactly how to get there, exactly how to dress the fish, and exactly how to cook them. But Oyette doesn't talk too much these days about his favorite quail-hunting spots. I think I know why. You'll know, too, when you try this recipe.

Quail Oyette Taylor

Allow 3 birds and 2 biscuits per person, or 2 birds and 3 biscuits.

> quail
> buttermilk
> peanut oil
> flour
> fresh mushrooms, sliced
> salt and pepper
> buttermilk biscuits from scratch (cooked separately)

Pluck the birds, dress them whole, and remove the shot, if any. Put the birds into a glass

199

container, cover them with buttermilk, and refrigerate for several hours. Drain. Salt and pepper the birds, then dust them with flour. Heat about ¾ inch of peanut oil in a skillet. Brown the birds on all sides, then remove them to drain.

Sauté the mushrooms for 5 or 6 minutes, pour off most of the oil, and scrape up the pan drippings with a wooden spatula. Add a little water to the pan, then increase the heat. Pour in a little buttermilk, stir, and return the birds to the pan. Cover and simmer for 30 minutes. Serve hot, spooning the gravy over biscuit halves.

Polynesian Quail

Here's a dish that is best cooked in a large skillet that has a lid. An electric skillet will do nicely. I allow at least 2 birds per person.

8 quail, dressed whole
1 can tomato sauce (8-ounce size)
1 cup brown sugar
1 cup dark soy sauce
¼ cup sake, dry vermouth, or sherry
½ stick margarine or butter
rice (cooked separately)

Melt the margarine or butter in a large skillet. Cook the quail on medium heat for 10 minutes, turning once. Mix the soy sauce, sake, and tomato sauce in a saucepan. Heat, add the sugar, and stir until the sugar is melted. Pour the sauce over the birds in the skillet, cover tightly, and cook over low heat for 15 minutes. Put the quail on a bed of rice, then spoon the sauce over them. Serve with vegetables cooked as follows.

1 bell pepper, cut into chunks
1 can pineapple chunks (15⅓-ounce size)
1 can water chestnuts (8-ounce size)
1 can bamboo shoots (8-ounce size)
½ cup liquid from the quail dish
2 tablespoons margarine or butter

Heat the margarine in a skillet or wok. Stir in the bell pepper. Drain the pineapple, saving the liquid from the can. Brown the pineapple chunks in the skillet. Add ½ cup pineapple juice together with ½ cup of liquid from the quail dish. Add the water chestnuts and bamboo shoots. Simmer for about 5 minutes. Serve with quail and rice.

Fried Garlic Quail

This recipe can be used with whole quail or quail breasts. If using whole birds, I usually cut them in half lengthwise.

quail
cooking oil
flour
garlic powder
salt and pepper

Heat about ¾ inch of cooking oil in a skillet. Sprinkle the birds with salt, pepper, and garlic powder. Shake or roll the birds in flour, then fry them until golden brown on both sides. Allow 2 birds per person.

Golden Quail

The recipe for Daddy's doves (one of my favorites) requires that the birds first be fried, then simmered in gravy. The Chinese sometimes do things backward, or sideways, and in this recipe the birds are first simmered in sauce and then deep-fried in hot peanut oil.

    4 to 8 quail
    peanut oil
    2 cups chicken stock (see below)
    1 cup soy sauce
    ½ cup rice wine or sherry
    3 slices fresh ginger root
    pepper to taste

Pluck the birds, draw, and cut them in half lengthwise. (Save the giblets, wings, and feet for another day.) In a pot, mix the chicken stock, wine, soy sauce, ginger, and pepper. (A "slice" of ginger is ⅛ inch thick, made from a root of about 1 inch in diameter. The chicken stock used here can be homemade, or you can use a 16-ounce can of store-bought chicken broth.) Bring the sauce to a boil and simmer for a while. Increase the heat and simmer the quail for 5 or 6 minutes. While the quail simmer, rig for deep frying at 375 degrees. Remove the birds from the sauce and dry them quickly with paper towels. Immediately put the birds into the hot oil and fry for 3 or 4 minutes, until the birds are golden. Do not overcook. This recipe works best in a large deep fryer with at least 1 quart of oil. It can also be cooked in a skillet, but you may have to fry the birds in more than one batch.

If you like this recipe, save the stock in which the birds were simmered. If refrigerated, it can be used several times during the quail season.

Lemon Broiled Quail

Broiled quail are delicious. It's best to pluck the birds, then cut them in half lengthwise.

    8 quail, halved
    juice of 2 lemons
    ¼ cup butter
    ½ cup white wine Worcestershire sauce
    salt and pepper

Melt the butter in a saucepan, then stir in the white wine Worcestershire sauce, lemon juice, salt, and pepper. Preheat the broiler. Grease a broiling rack, then position it about 4 inches under the heat. Place the birds on the rack, baste heavily, and broil for about 5 or 6 minutes on each side, basting several times, until nicely browned and done. Allow 2 birds per person.

Variation: Baste with ½ cup of melted butter mixed with ½ cup of pomegranate sauce, available in specialty food shops that traffic in Middle Eastern fare. Good stuff.

Quail Fricassee

It's true that some recipes work best with quail breasts, leaving a lot of backs, wings, and legs. Although many people throw these parts away, I highly recommend that they be used to make some sort of pie or a quail fricassee. Of course, the recipe below is so good that you will find yourself making fricassee of the whole birds! If so, figure 1 bird for 1 cup of chopped meat.

    quail parts for 2 cups meat
    ¾ cup diced onion
    ¾ cup sliced mushrooms
    1 tablespoon butter
    salt and pepper to taste
    flour or cornstarch (optional)

Boil the quail parts in a little warm water until the meat pulls away from the bones easily. Strain the pot liquid and reserve it. Drain the bird parts and pull the meat with a fork. (If you use whole birds, chop the breasts.) Heat the butter in a skillet, then sauté the onion and mushrooms. Add the quail meat. Cover with some of the reserved broth. Salt and pepper to taste. (I prefer to go a little heavy on the pepper for this dish.) Bring to a quick boil, then reduce heat. Cover and simmer for 1 hour. Add a little flour or cornstarch to thicken the gravy, if desired. (It's best to stir the flour or cornstarch into a little water, then slowly add the liquid, stirring as you go until the gravy comes.) Serve the fricassee over rice. Feeds 3 or 4.

Greek Quail

The Greeks and other peoples of the Middle East enjoy grilling birds over charcoal. Recipes are numerous, and I have held the one below to the essentials. Olive oil is the key for cooking Greek.

    quail, plucked and halved
    virgin olive oil
    freshly squeezed lemon juice
    salt and pepper

While the charcoal gets hot, mix a basting sauce with ½ olive oil and ½ fresh lemon juice. Marinate the birds in the sauce for a few minutes. When the coals are hot, salt and pepper each bird half and grill over the hot coals. Cook for about 15 minutes, or until done, turning from time to time and basting a time or two. (Much depends, of course, on how hot your fire is and on the distance from the birds to the coals.)

Note: This is also a good camp recipe, using wood coals instead of charcoal.

Egyptian Quail

Reportedly, large numbers of migrating quail are netted each year on the beaches near Alexandria—and are cooked over fires built in the sand. (This tradition goes back to biblical times, when quail, exhausted from the flight across the Mediterranean, were captured with a weighted blanket.) I've never had the good fortune to feast on migrating quail, but I have tried the Egyptian recipe on wild American bobwhites, as well as on pen-raised quail that I buy freshly dressed from a local farmer or frozen from my grocer.

The onion juice and other ingredients in the marinade sauce in this recipe are just right. The measures below provide plenty of marinade for

8 quail. (The butter is my own addition and was not in the original.) If this dish is to be served as an entree, you'll need at least 2 birds per person. I'll take a few more, if available. In any case, this recipe has been adapted from the one that appears in my book *Grilling, Smoking, and Barbecuing*.

8 quail
1 large onion
2 tablespoons finely chopped fresh parsley
¼ cup olive oil
1 teaspoon ground cumin
1 teaspoon ground coriander
salt and cayenne pepper to taste
butter (optional)

When dressing the quail for this recipe, I pluck them, remove the innards, and cut them in half. Usually, wild meat is better after it has seasoned for a few days in the refrigerator, but quail really doesn't require this curing. I often eat birds that have been frozen, and I much prefer that quail, doves, and similar birds be frozen in water in a milk carton.

When your birds are ready, peel the onion, quarter it, and squeeze out the juice with a garlic press. Mix onion juice, oil, parsley, cumin, coriander, salt, and cayenne pepper. (Remember that cayenne is really hot stuff.) After the mixture has steeped for a while, rub the birds with it inside and out. Then place the birds in a suitable glass container and pour the sauce over them. Marinate for 1 to 2 hours, turning once or twice. Build a hot fire with the grill about 4 inches from the heat. Grill the bird halves for 5 or 6 minutes on each side, or until done. I usually baste mine with hot melted butter when they are almost ready to take up, then I grill them for a minute or so more on each side.

Mesquite Quail

Here's an easy quail recipe that can be prepared in the oven. The mesquite barbecue

---

Scaled Quail of the Desert

Often called blue quail, this game bird measures about 11 inches long and weighs an average of 6½ ounces. Scaled quail are easily identified by their overall bluish cast above and light gray to whitish coloring below. Feathers of the breast, neck, and upper back have dark margins, giving the birds a scaled appearance. These birds also sport a short, white tuff of feathers atop their heads.

Scaled quail are typically desert or semi-arid species which reside in the southwest United States and northern Mexico. In Oklahoma, they occur in rugged terrain featuring sand, sagebrush, mesquite, juniper, and cactus cover.

In winter, the birds gather into coveys that average 30 birds but sometimes exceed 100. . . . Unlike bobwhites, they are more apt to run into dense cover than suddenly take wing when alarmed. While scaled quail will fly for short distances, their advantage clearly lies in their running ability as they can outdistance a sprinting man.

—Oklahoma Wildlife News Service

Fat and Protein in Birds
(Based on 100-gram edible portions)

Bird	Calories	Protein	Fat
chicken	124	18.6 grams	4.9 grams
wild duck	233	21.1	15.8
pheasant	151	24.3	5.2
quail	168	25.0	6.8

Note: This table was made up from data published in *The South Carolina Wildlife Cookbook,* which in turn credited the Georgia Extension Service.

sauce can be found in most supermarkets. Allow 2 birds per person, but be warned that whole birds are difficult to eat with a thick sauce on them.

This is really a finger-licking recipe, so choose your guests accordingly.

   8 quail
   1 bottle mesquite barbecue sauce (19-ounce size)
   salt and pepper

Preheat the oven to 400 degrees. Salt and pepper the birds inside and out, then put them into a well-greased baking dish. Pour the barbecue sauce over them, then bake for about 30 minutes.

Baste several times with the pan sauce while cooking.

Variation: If you prefer, try my homemade barbecue sauce instead of the commercial mesquite sauce.

   ¼ pound bacon
   1 cup catsup
   ½ cup minced onion
   1 clove garlic, minced
   2 tablespoons red wine vinegar
   2 tablespoons brown sugar
   1 teaspoon salt
   ½ teaspoon pepper

Cook the bacon in a skillet until well done, crumble, and set aside. Sauté the onion and garlic for a few minutes in the bacon drippings. Add the wine vinegar, catsup, salt, pepper, brown sugar, and bacon bits. Simmer for 10 minutes, then pour over the quail and bake as directed above.

Honey Quail

The firm of Lea and Perrins sent me a booklet called *Light & Elegant,* which contained a recipe for chicken wings. After sneaking a little butter and salt into the ingredients, I tried it on quail with great results.

The Marinade
   1 cup white wine Worcestershire sauce
   ¼ cup honey
   ¼ cup pineapple juice
   ¼ cup soy sauce
The Birds
   8 to 10 quail
   salt and pepper
The Basting Sauce
   ¼ cup melted butter
   ¼ cup marinade sauce, from above

In a large nonmetallic bowl, mix the white wine Worcestershire sauce, honey, pineapple juice, and soy sauce. Cut the quail in half lengthwise, put them into the bowl, coating all sides with the marinade, and cover. Refrigerate for 6 hours, or overnight, turning several times.

Preheat the oven to 350 degrees. Drain the quail. Retain ½ cup of the marinade sauce, mix it with the butter, bring to a boil, and set aside as a basting sauce. Place the quail in a well-greased baking pan, baste with the sauce, and bake for 35 to 40 minutes, or until the birds are done. Baste several times while cooking, turning once. Feeds 4 to 8.

Good Ol' Boy Quail

Build a good charcoal fire. Breast the birds, then wrap each breast with half a strip of bacon, pinning it with a round toothpick. Put the bird breasts over the coals, close the hood, and cook until the bacon looks ready to eat, turning with tongs and basting from time to time.

Country Breakfast Quail

Here's a good dish to serve anywhere, anytime, but it is especially good for breakfast. It's best to cut the birds in half lengthwise.

    quail
    cooking oil
    minced green onions with part of tops
    salt and pepper
    flour
    water
    toast

Heat about ¾ inch of cooking oil in a skillet. Salt and pepper the quail halves, then dust them with flour. Fry on medium heat until nicely browned on both sides. (If you've got many birds, you'll have to cook them in several batches, perhaps adding a little more oil as needed.) Put the quail on a brown bag. Pour off most of the oil, then sauté the green onions for 3 or 4 minutes. Stir in some flour with a wooden spoon, then slowly add a little water, stirring constantly until you have a thin gravy. Put the birds back into the skillet, coating them on all sides with gravy. Cover, reduce the heat, and simmer for 20 to 30 minutes. Serve on toast with gravy.

Quail Giblet Breakfast

Now is the time to thaw out all your bird giblets, wings, and feet. For the measures below, you'll need 2 cups of giblets, more or less, in addition to the feet and wings.

    2 cups bird giblets
    bird wings and feet
    2 cups broth (see below)
    2 hard-boiled chicken eggs, sliced
    8 or 10 green onions with part of tops
    ¾ cup flour
    ½ cup butter or margarine
    2 bay leaves
    salt and pepper
    biscuits (cooked separately)

Put the gizzards, hearts, feet, and wings into a pot and barely cover them with water. Add the bay leaves along with a little salt and pepper. Bring to a boil, cover, reduce heat, and simmer for 1 hour. Using a slotted spoon, remove the bird parts and measure out 2 cups of the broth. (Add a little more if necessary.) Throw away the feet, wings, and bay leaves. Dust the bird gizzards, hearts, and livers with flour. Save the remaining flour. Melt the butter in a large skillet and quickly brown the hearts, gizzards, and livers on medium high heat. Chop the onions, including about half the green tops, and add them to the skillet. (If you don't have green onions on hand, chop a regular onion of medium size and add 1 tablespoon of chopped chives.) Reduce the heat and simmer for about 5 minutes. Pour in the reserved broth, bring to a boil, and reduce heat. Mix the remaining flour with a little water, and slowly stir this paste into the contents of the skillet, which will now quickly become gravy. Simmer for about 30 minutes. Stir from time to time, adding a little water if needed. After about 25 minutes, mix in the egg slices and simmer for another 5 minutes. Serve the gravy over open biscuit halves.

Although I prefer this gravy for breakfast, I ought to point out that it also beats chicken and dumplings for a hot lunch. It can also be used to advantage with rice or dressing at a big family feed, such as Thanksgiving dinner. Anyone who is still courting, or who otherwise feels the need for a candlelight and red wine dinner, may need more fancy fare. I would then suggest using quail eggs instead of ordinary chicken eggs, and I hereby recommend French bread instead of biscuits for formal sopping.

22

WILD TURKEY

Seldom do I look forward to a dinner of domestic turkey. The way most people cook it, the meat is far too dry to suit me. The meat goes down better as leftovers, sliced thinly against the grain and made into white-bread sandwiches, spread with plenty of good mayonnaise to lead the way.

The wild turkey, on the other hand, is a good deal moister. It is a shade darker meat, which suits me fine. But, unfortunately, the whole turkey is likely to be cooked far too long in most kitchens. For one thing, a wild turkey is usually much smaller than a domestic market bird, which means that cooking times for whole-bird recipes should be reduced drastically. For another thing, many people cook wild meat much too long merely because it is wild. Also, the tricks for testing the doneness of domestic birds don't always work with wild turkey. The leg doesn't move as easily when it is done, and

the meat does not feel as soft when poked with the finger.

The best bet for baking a turkey is to use what I call the hunter's best friend: a meat thermometer. This instrument can be inserted into the breast or into the thickest part of the thigh—but not touching bone—and left there during the cooking process. I prefer my birds to be cooked to no more than 150 degrees, but I must point out that the current recommendation from the Department of Agriculture is 180 degrees. In either case, turkey to be roasted should not be stuffed until shortly before it is placed into the oven.

At the risk of being un-American, I must say that baking in general is not the best way to cook a wild turkey, and the recipes in this chapter include some alternatives to baking. Of course, I also include some recipes for cooking the whole bird in case the hunter of the family wants to show it off. For a really pretty bird, you might consider frying it whole, as detailed in this chapter.

Fried Turkey Fingers

Anyone who likes southern fried chicken will really like this recipe. Note that the turkey fingers are merely dusted lightly with flour instead of coated with a thick batter. Although a thick batter may be tasty and crunchy, it also soaks up lots of grease, which is a concern for some of us these health-conscious days.

To make turkey fingers, cut the fillets from either side of the breast, getting as much meat as possible. Then cut the fillets lengthwise into long fingers about 1 inch thick. Save the rest of the turkey for other recipes.

> turkey fingers
> cooking oil
> milk or buttermilk
> flour
> salt and pepper

Put the turkey fingers into a nonmetallic container, cover with fresh milk or buttermilk, and marinate in the refrigerator for several hours or at room temperature for 2 hours. When you are ready to cook, heat about ½ inch of cooking oil in a skillet on medium high. Salt and pepper the turkey fingers, then shake them in a small bag of flour. Shake off the excess flour and fry the pieces until nicely browned on both sides, turning once. Do not overcook. Drain on a brown bag. Pour most of the grease out of the skillet and scrape up any pan dredgings. Stir in a little flour, as when making a roux. (Go easy on the flour unless you want a gooey mess.) Add water a little at a time, stir-

---

Wild Turkey

There's a saying in Virginia, "Just get a husband who can kill a wild turkey." This sage further advises to catch both man and turkey in their youth, as both are easier to handle while young.
—*Progressive Farmer's Southern Cookbook*

---

ring as you go, until you have a gravy just as thick as you want it. Serve the fried turkey fingers with bread and vegetables of your choice, along with mashed potatoes topped with the turkey gravy.

Note: If you are cooking lots of turkey for a crowd, consider using a deep fryer instead of a skillet.

Save-the-Day Fried Turkey Fingers

Old birds don't fry up too successfully, unless you like to chew. My father was fond of what he called "smother frying," used whenever I brought home tough squirrels, and this technique can also be used to advantage on old turkey toms and even barnyard roosters.

Quickly fry the fingers as directed in the recipe above. The fingers should be nicely browned but don't have to be done inside. Remove the fingers, setting them on a warm plate. Make a thin gravy, then return the turkey fingers to the skillet. Cover tightly, turn the heat down to low, and simmer until the fingers are tender enough to be cut with a fork. Add a little more water from time to time if needed, along with some salt and pepper. The longer this dish cooks (within reason), the better it smells—and the hungrier you become. When you can stand it no longer, serve it up, spooning the gravy over biscuit halves, rice, or mashed potatoes.

Sessions Whole-Fried Turkey

Frying a whole turkey is not usually very practical, but it can be done with excellent results. I say it's not practical simply because the method requires about 4 gallons or more of cooking oil and a large pot. On the other hand, some cooking oils (I recommend peanut oil) can be used over and over and have a very long shelf life; also, more and more patio cookers are becoming available for frying fish, boiling shrimp, and so on. Some of these are heavy enough to hold a large pot and several gallons of oil. If you ever have occasion to cook several turkeys for a large game supper or some such event, frying may well be the way to go. Once you get rigged up and the oil is hot, you can fry any number of birds one at a time without the expense of buying more oil.

I got the recipe below from Sessions peanut oil company. It was intended for domestic turkey, but the technique is the same with wild turkey, and I used it (and this text) in my *Wild Turkey Cookbook.* It is important that you have lots of oil when using this recipe, so that when you add the turkey, the temperature won't drop too low. It is also important that the bird be completely covered in oil. Obviously, the first step should be to determine whether you have a large-enough pot and a means of heating it. (The oil should reach 375 degrees, and some small burners simply won't provide enough heat.) Before starting to cook, it's best to test the size of your pot by pouring 4 gallons of cold water into the pot and immersing the turkey in it, just to make sure that it fits and won't cause the oil to overflow.

Remember that hot oil is very dangerous. Make sure your cooking rig is steady. Plan a way to get the turkey into and out of the pot safely. Sessions recommends tying a cord through the turkey by which to lower and lift it. In any case, be very careful not to drop the bird into the hot oil. A splash can cause burns and create a fire hazard.

1 wild turkey, plucked
about 4 gallons peanut oil
paprika
salt and pepper

Heat the oil to 375 degrees. Sprinkle the bird inside and out with salt, pepper, and paprika. Tie the wings and legs of the turkey with cotton cord. Also tie the cord through the turkey if you plan to lower and raise it by this method. When you lower the bird into the pot, make sure that it doesn't become wedged. Fry it for 3 or 4 minutes per pound, moving it about from time to time. The turkey is done when it floats to the top. If you don't overcook the bird, it will be golden brown and succulent.

Note: I don't recommend that you fry a stuffed bird. Leaving the body cavity open helps it cook through.

Charcoal Grilled Turkey Fingers

Although this recipe is set up for grilling over charcoal on the patio, it is also a good one for cooking over wood coals in camp. Of course, gas or electric grills can also be used.

turkey fingers
½ cup melted butter
juice of 1 lemon
salt and pepper to taste

Build a hot fire. Mix and warm the melted butter, lemon juice, salt, and pepper. Put the turkey fingers onto a greased grill positioned about 6 inches over hot coals. Grill for 5 or 6 minutes on each side, basting from time to time.

Variations: In camp, you may want to forget the butter and use bacon drippings left over from breakfast. Also try lemon-pepper seasoning salt instead of lemon juice, salt, and pepper, but do not mix a sauce. Merely baste the turkey fingers with the bacon drippings or melted butter, then sprinkle on a little lemon-pepper right out of the shaker bottle. With these variations, you won't have to tote in lots of ingredients. Turkey fingers are ideal for camp because you won't need a knife and fork.

Note: There's one cardinal rule. Grilling or broiling wild turkey fingers too long is a culinary sin. Beyond the point of medium rare, the longer you cook turkey breast by direct heat (without water), the tougher and dryer it becomes. On the other hand, most of us want to get it nicely done. Accomplished patio chefs won't have a problem, but most of us should cut into a turkey finger at the widest part to check for doneness before serving. If the meat is just right, it will be opaque but moist throughout; if too done, it will be opaque and dry throughout; if partly raw, it will be translucent or even reddish in the center.

Broiled Turkey Teriyaki

In grilling, the meat is placed directly over the heat. In broiling, it is placed directly under the heat. The same basting recipes and techniques

How Safe Is It?

Years hence, in the annals of culinary history, the 1990s will be dubbed the decade of salmonella of the supermarket strain—a time in which cooks deem it necessary to cook poultry well done in order to kill all the bugs. Indeed, TV commercials of this era show countertops being sprayed with Lysol to kill all the bacteria, which supposedly infects everything it touches. Since the Department of Agriculture has been hard put to protect even meat stamped "U.S. choice," it has started issuing booklets on controlling salmonella in the kitchen—and has even set up a 1-800 hotline. One woman on TV, who worked for the Department of Agriculture, advised cooks and meat handlers to wash their hands for 30 minutes after handling meat. Of course, she intended to say 30 seconds, which is considerably shorter, but which is still a very long time for a cook to wash his or her hands.

I was setting forth these sentiments one day in the presence of a female banker who "hated" game, including wild turkey. After considerable banter, I told her, in short, that wild turkey was not only better than it's domestic cousins but also safer, simply because it hasn't been run through a salmonella bath. She informed me that she liked salmonella in her poultry!

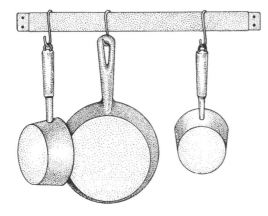

can be used, and the meat should be about the same distance from the heat. With an electric broiler, I like to leave the thermostat at the highest setting and broil the turkey fingers on a rack or broiling pan about 4 or 5 inches under the heat. For true broiling, leave the oven door open. If you close it, you'll be combining baking and broiling. The marinade and basting sauce in the recipe below will be enough for 1 to 2 pounds of turkey fingers. If you want to cook a larger batch, simply make more sauce.

1 to 2 pounds of tender turkey fingers
½ cup soy sauce
¼ cup sake, dry vermouth, or sherry
2 tablespoons brown sugar
1 tablespoon finely grated fresh ginger root
2 cloves garlic, finely grated
pepper to taste (optional)
rice (cooked separately)

Mix the soy sauce, sake, brown sugar, ginger root, and garlic. (I add some pepper, but this is not really a conventional teriyaki ingredient. Salt is not needed because the soy sauce is quite salty.) Put the turkey fingers into a nonmetallic container and pour the marinade over them. Stir the fingers about to coat all sides, then marinate for 1 to 2 hours. When you are ready

to cook, preheat the broiler. Place the turkey fingers on a rack or on a broiling pan with a rack, adjusting the height so that the turkey is 4 to 5 inches from the heat. Broil for about 5 minutes on each side, basting 2 or 3 times with the leftover marinade. Test for doneness. Serve with precooked rice and stir-fried oriental vegetables.

Wild Turkey, Country Dressing, and Giblet Gravy

Giblet gravy and either dressing or stuffing can tilt the scales in favor of roasting a wild turkey. By stuffing, I mean just that—a bread mixture, chestnuts, or what have you, with which the turkey is stuffed. By dressing, I mean a mixture, usually made with a breadstuff for a base, that is cooked separately and served with the meat. Dressing doesn't complicate the cooking as much as stuffing. Also, dressing usually has a better color for the table. Both should be served with sliced turkey and giblet gravy.

The Bird
1 tender wild turkey, plucked and dressed
bacon drippings
salt and pepper
water
The Dressing
6 cups crumbled corn bread
2 cups dry biscuit crumbs
2 medium onions, chopped
2 ribs celery with tops, chopped
3 hard-boiled chicken eggs, chopped
4 raw chicken eggs
1 teaspoon salt
¼ teaspoon pepper
water (if needed)

The Gravy
 turkey neck
 turkey head (if you want to clean it)
 turkey liver
 turkey gizzard, diced
 turkey feet
 2 ribs celery with tops, chopped
 2 hard-boiled chicken eggs, sliced
 2 bay leaves
 water
 flour
 salt and pepper to taste

Preheat the oven to 325 degrees. Pluck and dress the turkey, saving all the giblets, including the neck, head, and feet. Baste the turkey inside and out with bacon drippings, then sprinkle it inside and out with a little salt and pepper.

Place the turkey on a rack in a suitable roasting pan, insert a meat thermometer into the breast or the thickest part of the thigh, and cover the bird with aluminum foil, leaving an opening for the meat thermometer. Put a little water into the roasting pan, cover the pan, and put it into the oven. It's best to center the turkey in the middle of the oven as best you can. Mark the time.

As the turkey bakes, make the gravy. Put all the giblets into a pot and add enough water to almost cover them. (Because the gizzard takes longer to cook, it's best to dice it before putting it into the pot.) Add the bay leaves and celery. (The bay leaves are mostly for the cook, as they add a pleasing aroma to the kitchen as the giblets boil.) Bring to a hard boil, reduce heat, cover, and cook until the giblets are tender, about 1½ hours. When the parts are tender, pull the meat off the head, then whop it with a large kitchen spoon and dig out the brains. Pull the meat off the neck. Chop the meat along with the gizzard and liver. Discard the feet and bones. Boil the broth left in the pot until it is reduced by about half. Discard the bay leaves. Add the chopped giblets and thicken with a little flour paste. When the gravy is almost as thick as you like it, stir in some salt and pepper to taste. Carefully add the eggs. Keep the gravy warm.

Mix all the dressing ingredients, using a little water if needed to make a soft dressing. (The texture will depend largely on the consistency of your corn bread. A soft bread made with fine, stone-ground meal will not require as much water as most breads made with gritty off-the-shelf meal.) Set aside.

After the turkey has baked for 2½ to 3 hours, remove the pan from the oven and increase the temperature to 375 degrees. Remove the aluminum foil. Put the dressing mixture into the pan around the turkey, letting it mix with the pan juices, and baste the turkey with bacon drippings. Put the pan back into the oven and bake the turkey until it is a golden brown, or until the thermometer reads 180 degrees. If the thermometer reaches 180 degrees first, turn on the broiler to quickly brown the bird's breast. Do not overcook. (In fact, your bird will be better eating if you cook it to 160 degrees or less; the 180 degrees comes from the USDA and is recommended for safety's sake. Personally, I feel that the wild turkey will be safe to eat on the rare side—unless you contaminate it with salmonella-infected meat from the supermarket.) Carefully place the cooked bird on a large platter and slice one side of the breast. Put the platter onto the dinner table, along with the giblet gravy, cranberry sauce, vegetables, breads, and other festive victuals.

Roast Wild Turkey à la Seminole

I don't know how authentic this recipe really is, historically speaking, but I have adapted it from a real booklet called *Seminole Indian Recipes*. Some of the ingredients, of course, would be available only to modern Seminoles.

1 wild turkey, 8 to 10 pounds
6 to 8 slices smoked bacon
2 small apples, quartered
2 stalks celery, chopped
1 medium onion, chopped
1 teaspoon sage
salt and pepper
cheesecloth soaked in bacon drippings

Pluck and dress the turkey, making only a small opening. Preheat the oven to 325 degrees. Sprinkle salt and pepper on the turkey, inside and out. Put the chopped apples, celery, sage, and onions into the cavity. Pull the turkey's legs upward and in, and tie them with cotton string.

Talking Turkey

Each turkey has a different voice. They all sound different and other turkeys know who is calling. When I go into the woods, I try to be a turkey. I want to be a bird the other birds don't know, and I want them to be curious enough to come check me out.

—Ray Eye, quoted by Gary Thomas in Illinois' *Outdoor Highlights*

Turn the wings under the bird's back and pin with skewers or round toothpicks. Put the bird, breast up, on a rack in a roasting pan. Cover the breast with bacon strips and with a cheesecloth that has been soaked in bacon drippings. Bake for 20 to 25 minutes per pound of bird. (You can also use a meat thermometer, as described in the previous recipe.) Baste several times with pan juices. If you are eating Seminole, slice the turkey and serve it with swamp cabbage (heart of palm) or young cattail shoots, boiled squash, fried green tomatoes, and corn bread.

Turkey with Chestnuts

I read not too long ago that spiders will avoid chestnut wood. It may be true. For several years I lived in a house in Tennessee that had been built from wild chestnut wood before a blight wiped the trees off the face of that countryside. I don't know whether or not the statement is true, but I never saw a spider or spiderweb inside the house. In any case, here's a good recipe that calls for chestnuts. I got it from a column by C. B. Colby in the July 1967 issue of *Outdoor Life* magazine—a year during which I lived in the chestnut wood house!

"Use about 3 cups of good, sound chestnuts. Peel the shells from the nuts with a knife, or cut a hole in the shell and soak them overnight to soften and separate the shell from the meat. If you use a knife, cut from side to side over top of nut and peel down and away from cut.

"Boil peeled chestnuts in water until nut meats are tender. Then put meats through a colander or a meat grinder. Add 2 tablespoons butter, and salt and pepper to taste. Other seasoning may be added as desired.

"Into this stuffing base, mix 1 cup of finely

crushed cracker crumbs. Moisten the mixture with sweet cream, adding a little at a time until the desired consistency is reached.

"When the chestnut stuffing is ready, fill the bird, packing the stuffing into every part of the cavity. Just before closing the opening, place the pieces of turkey liver with the stuffing. Thrust skewers through the bird's flesh on both sides and across the opening. Lace stout twine about both ends of skewers and draw the opening closed.

"Cook the bird in an oven at about 450 degrees, and baste frequently with pan liquid. You may want to add water to the liquid to keep meat moist during cooking. Some cooks baste with butter and add strips of bacon across the breast of the bird to add moisture and help brown the skin. It will take about 2 hours for the turkey to cook properly, depending upon its size. Test about every 30 minutes with a fork. If flesh is too dry, add water to liquid, baste, and turn off oven. If skin is not brown, baste with butter or fat for last few minutes."

Pork Skin Turkey

Anyone who believes that roast turkey is too dry should try the following cooking method from the National Wild Turkey Federation.

1 wild turkey, 10 to 12 pounds
2 pounds pork spare ribs or skin from pork
    shoulder ham
3 ribs celery with tops, chopped
1 large onion, quartered
2 bay leaves
salt and pepper
garlic powder

Wash and dry the turkey, rub inside the cavity and outside with salt, pepper, and garlic powder, then place the onion, celery, and bay leaves in the cavity. Place the bird on rack in roaster, breast side up. Cover with spare ribs or pork skin, which can be ordered from your meat merchant. When meat is done, the pork skin will be crisp, and the cracklings can be used in corn bread. If spare ribs are used, you will have a delicious second dish. Roast the turkey at 325 degrees for 3 or 4 hours. Remove the pork skin or ribs during the last half hour of cooking to allow turkey to brown.

Wild Turkey Roll

Here's an interesting recipe from Brian Hyder of the North Carolina Wildlife Resources Commission, as published in a booklet (now out of print) called *Wild Game Recipes*. I have added a little salt and pepper.

8 pieces of turkey breast (about 6 ounces
    each)
8 slices bacon
3-ounce package pressed beef
½ pint sour cream
1 can cream of mushroom soup (10¾-
    ounce size)
salt and pepper

Wrap a piece of bacon around each piece of breast, then lay the breast on 2 slices of pressed beef. Sprinkle with salt and pepper. Bring the edges of the beef around the turkey breast and pin with toothpicks. Place the breasts into a well greased 9-by-13-inch pan. Mix the sour cream and soup, then pour it over the turkey rolls. Bake uncovered for 2 hours. Serve with wild rice and vegetables. Feeds 8 with a serving each. If you've got heavy eaters at the table, cook lots of rice.

Giblets on Toast

I'm fond of any good giblet gravy, which you should make whenever you bake a whole turkey, and serve it on sliced turkey and on the stuffing or dressing. If you choose to use the breast and other parts of the turkey for frying or soup, you can still make very good use of the giblets, as follows.

turkey neck, head, wings, liver, and gizzard
2 strips bacon
2 hard-boiled chicken eggs, chopped
1 medium onion, finely diced
2 bay leaves
salt and pepper
flour
water
toast or biscuits

Put the turkey neck, head, wings, liver, and gizzard into a pot and almost cover them with water. Add the bay leaves, bring to a boil, reduce the heat, and simmer for 30 minutes. Remove the liver and set aside. Boil the rest of the giblets for 1 hour or so, until the gizzard is tender. Remove the giblets. Pull the meat from the bones and chop it. Crack the head with the back of a large spoon and remove the brains. Chop the meat, brains, liver, and gizzard. Discard the bay leaves and add a little salt and pepper to the stock. Fry the bacon in a small skillet until crisp. Crumble the bacon and put it into the stock. Add the chopped giblets. Sauté the chopped onion in the bacon drippings for 5 minutes, then add to the stock. Bring to a new boil, reduce heat, and simmer for a few min-

utes. Mix a little flour and water, then pour the paste into the gravy, stirring as you go, until it thickens. Simmer a while longer until you have a thick gravy. Stir in the chopped eggs. Serve over well-browned toast or biscuit halves.

Turkey Casserole

Here is a good recipe to use for leftover turkey. It makes a lot of casserole, but it can be frozen.

Fresh Cranberry Sauce

Any reasonable cranberry sauce, canned or otherwise, adds something rather festive to a turkey dinner, and is also good with venison, bear, and other wild game. If you've got access to a cranberry bog, or if you can purchase fresh or frozen cranberries, you may want to try this easy sauce recipe:

1 pound fresh or frozen cranberries
1¼ cups sugar
1¼ cups water

Dissolve the sugar in the water and bring to a boil. Add the cranberries and bring to a second boil. Reduce the heat and simmer for 10 minutes, stirring as you go. Let cool. Pour into a serving dish (or dishes) and refrigerate until you are ready to eat. Leftover sauce can be kept for several days in the refrigerator.

If you want an American Indian sauce, use maple sugar.

3 cups cooked wild turkey, diced
2 cups crushed potato chips
2 hard-boiled chicken eggs, chopped
1 cup chopped onions
1 cup chopped celery
1 cup mayonnaise
1 can chicken and rice soup (10¾-ounce size)
½ cup slivered almonds
½ tablespoon white wine Worcestershire sauce
½ teaspoon salt
¼ teaspoon pepper
juice of ½ lemon

Preheat the oven to 375 degrees. In a large bowl, mix the turkey, soup, onion, celery, almonds, salt, pepper, white wine Worcestershire sauce, and lemon juice. Stir in the mayonnaise, then carefully toss in the chopped eggs. Put the mixture into a well-greased casserole dish, then sprinkle the crushed potato chips over the top. Bake for 30 minutes. Serve with vegetables and hot bread. Feeds 6 to 8.

Wild Turkey Gumbo

A gumbo is hard to beat as a dish to use up leftover turkey, and it is especially good when made with smoked turkey. Gumbo recipes vary quite a bit from one book to another, and from one cook to another; but to be a real gumbo, it must contain okra, since the name of the dish comes from an African word for okra. The okra pods give the stew a characteristic mucilaginous consistency. Some Cajuns might argue this, saying that filé (dried and powdered leaves from the sassafras tree, long used in stews by the Choctaw Indians) is better than okra for making a gumbo with the

right texture. Suit yourself. The quart of stock in the recipe can be made by boiling the bony parts of the turkey, or you can use chicken stock or stock made from chicken bouillon cubes.

2 cups chopped cooked turkey meat
1 quart turkey or chicken stock
4 strips smoked bacon
2 cups fresh or canned tomatoes
2 stalks celery with tops, sliced
1 cup fresh or frozen okra, sliced
1 medium onion, diced
½ green bell pepper, diced
½ red bell pepper, diced
2 tablespoons chopped fresh parsley
1¼ cups uncooked long-grain rice
salt and pepper

Fry the bacon in a skillet and set it aside. In the bacon drippings, sauté the okra for 10 minutes, then add the celery, onion, and bell peppers and sauté for another 5 minutes or so. Transfer the sautéed vegetables to a suitable pot or stove-top Dutch oven, then add the crumbled bacon, diced turkey meat, and parsley. Add the tomatoes (and juice from the can), stock, uncooked rice, salt, and pepper. Bring to a boil, reduce the heat, cover, and simmer for 45 minutes. Feeds 6 to 8.

Filé Variation: Cook the above with only 2 cups of stock, and do not add the rice to the main pot, but cook it separately. When you are ready to serve, ladle some of the gumbo mixture into individual bowls while it is very hot and stir in filé powder, a little at a time, until the gumbo consistency comes. Then add a few spoons of rice to each bowl. This method gives each diner the opportunity to use filé to taste— and precludes the possibility of ruining the whole batch with too much filé. In any case, it's

Cook Appropriately

An old bird, whether it be a pheasant or a chicken or a turkey, is simply not tender. As a rule, however, an old hen is not as tough as an old tom or rooster. With turkey, the jakes and first-year hens usually make the best eating. These can be cooked by any method and are delicious when fried. Older birds should be stewed or steamed. (I consider a bird that is wrapped tightly in foil, or put into a baking bag, and cooked in the oven or indirectly on a grill to be partly steamed instead of merely roasted or grilled.) As a rule, the longer a tough bird is stewed or steamed, the more succulent it will be, but the inverse is true with any dry method of cooking—true baking, broiling, or grilling. If you've got a really tough bird, remember that the crockpot is about as foolproof as any method of cooking can be.

Also, choose a method of cooking to suit the occasion. While I was putting the finishing touches on this book, for example, our grown boys and son-in-law all gathered for the Christmas holidays, and I considered various ways of cooking. It was a special time for us, and we also had a crowd from my wife's side of the family coming in. In short, I figured we would need lots of meat and lots of trimmings. I decided to cook the meat out in the yard and let my wife have the kitchen. The weather turned too cold for comfortable patio cooking, so I decided that a bonfire and a cooking pit would be in order. The day before Christmas, the boys dug the hole enthusiastically, making it a little larger than my specifications, and gathered plenty of good oak wood. At first dark we lit the fire. It was nice for us to stand around the pit, warming first one side and then the other, and tell stories of times gone by. We even rigged a grill across one end of the hole and roasted fresh oysters. At about midnight, when the fire had burned down to a bed of glowing coals, I wrapped a whole turkey and a 10-pound sirloin tip in heavy aluminum foil, lowered them into the pit, and covered them up with the dirt that came out of the hole.

The next morning, about an hour before noon, we dug the meat out and brought it in for the womenfolks to finish. I would be less than honest if I didn't say here that the primary method of cooking didn't work as planned and the meat wasn't done. My good wife came to the rescue, zapping the meat in a microwave oven. Of course, the boys had a belly laugh at the old man's expense. I told 'em, hell, I didn't dig the hole. But it all turned out to be a wonderful meal, with plenty of meat and good cheer. I wouldn't want to change it.

—Livingston's *Wild Turkey Cookbook*

not a good idea to boil the gumbo mix after the filé has been added.

Oyster Variation: If you have access to fresh oysters, or have plenty of money to buy them at market, shuck out a pint (saving part of the juice) and add them to the gumbo during the last 20 minutes of simmering.

If you do use the oysters, my recommendation is to cook the rice separately, as in the filé variation.

Wild Turkey Salad

My wife likes chicken salad made with diced apples, and I asked her to come up with a recipe for wild turkey. The sour cream is an interesting variation on the mayonnaise that is called for in most recipes of this sort. Also try it with plain yogurt instead of the sour cream.

> 3 cups diced cooked turkey
> 2 hard-boiled chicken eggs, sliced
> 1 large apple
> 1 medium onion, diced
> lemon juice
> ½ cup walnut or pecan pieces
> 4 tablespoons sour cream
> 2 tablespoons pickle relish
> 1 teaspoon prepared mustard
> salt and pepper to taste

Dice the turkey meat, sprinkle it with freshly squeezed lemon juice, and refrigerate. Peel, core, and chop the apple. After the turkey has chilled, put it into a glass bowl. Add the chopped apple and onion, then mix in the sour cream, mustard, pickle relish, and nuts. Gently stir in the sliced eggs, along with a little more sour cream if needed. Chill. Serve cold on lettuce leaves.

Feeds 5 or 6 for lunch.

Cold Turkey Sandwiches

The best part of the traditional Thanksgiving or Christmas turkey, apart from the giblet gravy, comes several days after the main event. I'm talking about cold turkey sandwiches.

> cold turkey leftovers
> good mayonnaise
> soft white bread
> salt and pepper

There are tricks to making a good turkey sandwich: Slice meat thinly against the grain, then put several slices on very fresh white bread that has been spread generously, top and bottom, with good high-fat mayonnaise. Salt and pepper to taste. For some reason, turkey sandwiches go down better if you cut them in half diagonally.

Azerbaidzhanic Pheasant and Walnut Stew

Any culinary adventurer setting out in search of the world's best kabobs might save some time by starting in the Caucasus, focusing on Azerbaidzhan. In the past, great bird hunting was available to the sporting men in this area, and from the Caspian Sea across the plains or steppes to the Far East, falconers took pheasants and great bustards and bitterns and other good birds in large numbers. Nomadic cooking on the steppes was probably on the primitive side—that is, sticking a bird onto the tip of a sword and roasting it over a campfire—but around the Caspian grew a variety of fruits and vegetables, allowing a great cuisine to develop. Here is a recipe from that heritage.

In addition to lots of walnuts, this recipe calls for pomegranate juice, an ingredient that may be difficult to locate in some areas. As it happens, five pomegranate trees grew on the farm where I was born, and once I wrote a poem about them bursting open in autumn and laughing with rows of bright red teeth. It's an image that I was saving for posterity, and I was rather shocked to learn recently that a Turkish poet had beaten me to the punch line a millennium or so ago. In any case, the best fruits are indeed allowed to ripen on the tree, and I urge anyone who is interested in this recipe to find some pomegranate trees or to plant some in his private orchard, as King Solomon did.

Anyhow, after you obtain a couple of large, ripe pomegranates, simply peel the fruit, shell out the translucent red seeds, and discard the bitter pith. Then press the juice from the seeds. (Be warned that pomegranate juice will stain your shirt.) If you can't find any fresh pomegranates, you may be able to purchase some juice in ethnic grocery outlets that specialize in Middle Eastern fare. You can also buy concentrated pomegranate syrup. (The last bottle I found, from Lebanon, was called "pomegranate molasses.")

2 pheasants
1 medium onion, minced
¼ cup kyurdyuk or butter (see text below)
2 cups chicken or pheasant broth
2 cups English walnuts (see text below)
1 cup fresh pomegranate juice
juice of 2 lemons
salt and pepper to taste
½ teaspoon cinnamon

Grind the walnuts coarsely in a meat grinder or zap them in a food processor. Pluck the birds and cut them into pieces—breast halves, drumsticks, thighs, and bony parts. Wash, drain, and sprinkle with salt and pepper. In a heavy skillet, heat the kyurdyuk or butter. (Kyurdyuk is a cooking fat obtained from the tail of a sheep that has been bred over the centuries—reported even by Herodotus—and called, most appropriately, fat-tailed sheep.) Sauté the pheasant pieces on both sides until lightly browned. Drain the pieces on a brown bag. Next, sauté the chopped onion for 3 or 4 minutes. Then stir in the ground walnuts. Add the chicken broth, pomegranate juice, lemon juice, cinnamon, and a little salt and pepper. Bring the mixture to a boil, stirring as you go. Reduce the heat, simmer, and stir for 10 minutes. Add the pheasant pieces to the skillet, making sure that all of them are coated with sauce, cover, and simmer on very low heat for 40 minutes or longer, until the pheasant is ten-

23

PHEASANT

Both in the field and on the table, the ring-necked pheasant is surely one of the most popular game birds in its range. In the field, the size and the brilliant plumage of the cock no doubt account for much of the birds's appeal. As table fare, the white, mild-flavored meat can easily be compared with chicken, and it therefore makes an excellent bird with which to introduce people to wild game and fowl. But the bird can be disappointing if it isn't properly cooked. The meat is quite lean and tends to be dry, and the old cocks can be on the tough side. Unless you've got young, tender birds, it is best to be careful with the recipes that are fried, baked, broiled, or grilled.

Pheasant Teriyaki

If this dish sounds foreign, remember that the pheasant was originally an Asian bird. I suppose that the real teriyaki ought to be cooked on a cast-iron hibachi by somebody wearing a kimono, but I won't go that far and I allow any charcoal-burning grill. The last batch that I cooked up was on an electric Jenn-Air stovetop grill. It wasn't bad, although I think that charcoal works better. Here's all you need:

1 or 2 pounds pheasant breast fingers
½ cup soy sauce
½ cup sake
½ tablespoon grated fresh ginger root

Fillet and skin the pheasant breasts, then cut them, with the grain, into long fingers. Mix the soy sauce, sake, and grated ginger root in a nonmetallic container. Add the meat fingers, tossing to coat all sides. Marinate for about 4 hours at room temperature, or longer under refrigeration. When you are ready to cook, build a good charcoal fire and let it burn down to coals. Grill the strips about 6 inches over medium heat, turning and basting with the leftover marinade. Do not overcook.

If you are inexperienced at grilling and want to cheat a little, add the leftover marinade to some melted butter or bacon drippings. This will make a basting sauce, which, if used frequently, will help keep pheasant breast from drying out quite so quickly. Be warned that dry pheasant meat tends to be dry indeed and is difficult to swallow. If done to perfection, however, the meat is well worth the effort.

The above recipe can also be cooked on skewers. The trick here is to cut thinner strips and thread them ribbon fashion onto bamboo or other skewers. (Bamboo sticks should be soaked in water.) The thinner strips require even less cooking. I have also used the same simple recipe for cooking what I call quail nuggets. These are made by filleting quail breasts, getting a "nugget" off either side of the breastbone. Delicious.

Either pheasant or quail teriyaki goes well with rice and steamed vegetables.

Pheasant Kiev

A Russian dish, chicken Kiev is a purely excellent way to prepare pheasant. The dish is a treat in our family, and it is surely one of my favorites. But be careful with cooking times, as discussed at the end of the recipe.

> 2 pheasant breasts (4 fillets)
> ½ stick chilled butter
> 1 chicken egg, lightly beaten
> peanut oil for deep frying
> flour
> ½ tablespoon minced green onions
> ½ tablespoon minced fresh parsley
> 1 tablespoon water
> fried bread crumbs
> salt and pepper

Skin the pheasant breasts, then carefully cut out the fillets. Place each fillet, skin side down, between 2 sheets of waxed paper. With a smooth meat mallet, pound each fillets, starting at the center and working out. Continue to pound until the fillets are a uniform ¼ inch thick.

Remove the top sheets of waxed paper. Sprinkle the fillets with salt and a little pepper. Divide the minced onion and parsley into 4 equal portions, then sprinkle ¼ on each fillet. Cut the butter lengthwise into 4 strips, placing a strip on the wider end of each fillet. Roll each fillet around the piece of butter; do this neatly, tucking in the sides a bit to hold in the butter. Coat each fillet with flour. Mix the beaten egg with the water. Dip each fillet into the egg mixture, then roll it in the bread crumbs. Chill for at least 1 hour.

Rig for deep frying, heating the oil to 375 degrees. Fry the fillet rolls for about 5 minutes,

or until golden brown. Eat while hot. Serve 2 fillets per person.

Wooster Pheasant Breast

Regular Worcestershire sauce is a rich, dark brew more suited for a venison meatloaf than for a pure white meat like breast of pheasant. A relatively new product marketed by the venerable firm of Lea and Perrins has changed all that, however, with a formula called white wine Worcestershire sauce. Shake a little on your finger, taste it, and then try this recipe:

> 2 young pheasant breasts (4 fillets)
> ½ cup white wine Worcestershire sauce
> ½ cup butter
> 1 medium onion, finely diced
> 1 tablespoon fresh parsley, finely diced
> crushed sea salt and white pepper
> Hungarian paprika

Pluck the birds and fillet out the breasts, working a sharp knife carefully down either side of the breast bone. Then divide each fillet into 2 pieces so that the meat will cook through. Sprinkle the pieces with a little salt and white pepper. In a large skillet, heat the butter and sauté the pheasant breasts on each side until they are nicely browned and done. Do not overcook.

Put the bird pieces onto a heated serving platter, stacking them up like stove wood so that they will stay hot and continue to cook through.

Quickly, put the onions and parsley into the skillet with what's left of the butter. Sauté for a couple of minutes, stirring as you go, and then pour in the white wine Worcestershire

sauce. Add a little salt and white pepper to taste. Simmer and stir until a white sauce comes. Note that no flour or cornstarch or tapioca is required to thicken it. Pour the hot sauce over the bird pieces, sprinkle nicely with Hungarian paprika (mild) for color, and serve hot. I like this dish with steamed asparagus, French bread, and dry white wine. But it's also good with stir-fried oriental vegetables, perhaps cooked with a little of the white sauce. Wild foods enthusiasts will want to try sautéed wild radish seedpods in season, mushrooms, fiddleheads, and Jerusalem artichokes.

Plan B: When writing this recipe I had assumed that tender young pheasants are available. If you're dealing with a tough old rooster you'll have to resort to Plan B. Proceed as directed above until the bird pieces are browned slightly. Then put the pieces aside and prepare the sauce. Put the bird pieces back in the sauce, cover tightly, and simmer for 30 minutes or until the meat is tender. Add a little water from time to time if necessary, and turn the pieces over. Do not boil. Call this gravy and serve the dish over fluffy rice or mashed potatoes.

der. Move the pieces about and turn them over from time to time. Serve hot over fluffy rice.

The walnuts called for in this recipe are what Americans call English walnuts, not black walnuts, and which the English call Persian walnuts. In any case, the nut is now cultivated in California and can be found in the wild from Europe to the Himalayas. Although the walnut has never been more than noshing fare in America, it was once an important part of French and European cuisine. In times of famine, the European peasants even ground walnut shells together with acorns to make their daily bread.

Although the recipe above is for pheasant, a similar dish made with duck, walnuts, and pomegranate juice is said to be one of the national dishes of Iran, where it is called *fesenjan*. So, if you want to eat Iranian instead of Azerbaidzhani, use mallard instead of pheasant. Season with a pinch or two of cardamom and sprinkle additional ground walnuts atop the dish before serving it forth. Eat *fesenjan* with rice cooked exactly as directed by my good wife, who has hands-on experience with Iranian and regional Kurdish foods. Use 2 level cups of water for every level cup of rice. Bring the water to a rapid boil in a suitable pot with a tight lid. Add the rice and a little salt, bring to a new boil, reduce heat, cover, and simmer for exactly 20 minutes without removing the lid under any circumstances whatsoever.

When you open the lid at the end of the 20-minute countdown, you'll find (if all goes according to plan) a white, fluffy rice with each grain having its own perfect being. If you have a goo, however, you can always accuse some innocent person of violating the 20-minute no-peek rule. If you get a strong whiff of a burned smell when you take off the lid, squeal with joy and retell the story about how knowledgeable Kurds and pre-Khomeini Iranian epicures delighted in having a well-browned crust on the bottom of their rice. This crust is, the woman says, reserved for the elder men of the house or for the guest of honor. I've heard it all before.

Cock Pheasant Pilau

This country recipe for barnyard rooster is suitable for a tough old cock pheasant. Pilau can be served as a side dish, or you can serve it in bowls. I can make a complete meal of it, especially if I've got a can of tomatoes to dump on top.

cock pheasant
2 cups long-grain rice
water
½ teaspoon red pepper flakes
salt and black pepper

Dress the pheasant and cut it up, being sure to save the giblets. Put the pieces into a pot of suitable size and cover with water, bring to a boil, reduce heat, add the red pepper flakes, cover tightly, and simmer until the bird is tender. (The time will vary, depending on how tough the bird is.) Remove the pieces and drain. Pull the meat from the bones and chop it; set aside. Measure out 6 cups of the broth; if there isn't that much left in the pot, add enough water to make 6 cups. Add the measured broth back to the pot, then add the chopped meat, salt, and black pepper. Bring to a boil. Add the rice, bring to a new boil, reduce the heat, and simmer for 20 minutes. This will yield a somewhat thin pilau suitable for serving in a bowl. If you want pilau to serve as a side dish, simmer without a lid until it thickens—or reduce the amount of broth used. I think it is better on the thin side, but modern restaurants seem to think that pilau is a pile of seasoned rice.

Feeds 6 or 8.

Variations: Add some chopped onion or chopped tomatoes to the dish. If you've got mild onions, you can add them after the pilau has been cooked. See also Big Scrub Purloo.

Zesty Pheasant Fingers

Here is a tasty dish to use when you are bagging lots of pheasants. It works best with breast, but be sure to save the rest of the pheasant for a casserole, salad, fricassee, or soup.

Allow $\frac{1}{3}$ to $\frac{1}{2}$ pound of meat per person.

pheasant breasts
Zesty Italian salad dressing
butter

Fillet the breasts and cut them lengthwise into strips about $\frac{1}{2}$ inch wide. Put the meat into a nonmetallic container, pour in some Zesty Italian salad dressing, and marinate for several hours in the refrigerator. (Tough birds should be marinated overnight.) Drain the meat. Melt some butter in a skillet and cook the pheasant strips a few at a time, stirring with a wooden spoon, on medium high heat for 4 or 5 minutes, or until slightly browned. Serve hot with steamed vegetables and garlic bread.

Note: You can also broil the fingers or cook them over charcoal. In either case, do not overcook.

Roast Pheasant

Some people cook any wild game too long, and pheasant tends to be too dry to start with. The result is a culinary disaster. One way to keep the bird moist is to cook it in a bag along with a little suitable liquid, so that the bird is partly steamed instead of dry-cooked. Here's such a recipe that I got from the American Rifle Association. It calls for a plastic baking bag, which are widely available in supermarkets.

1 pheasant
$\frac{1}{2}$ cup apple cider
$\frac{1}{2}$ apple or orange
1 tablespoon melted butter
1 tablespoon flour
favorite seasoning (see below)
salt and pepper

This recipe almost got by me because the "favorite seasoning" ingredient put me off. But my wife came to the rescue with 1 teaspoon garlic juice, 2 teaspoons prepared mustard, and $\frac{1}{8}$ teaspoon Tabasco sauce. Her thinking was that this batch of seasoning could be mixed in with the melted butter. It worked nicely.

Preheat the oven to 350 degrees. Shake the flour in a small 10-by-16-inch oven cooking bag. Place the bag into a 2-inch-deep roasting pan. Pour the cider into the bag, then stir the flour into the cider with a wooden spoon until it is smooth. Melt the butter and mix in the "favorite seasonings." Brush the pheasant inside and out with the butter and seasoning mix. Sprinkle the bird inside and out with salt and pepper. Place $\frac{1}{2}$ apple or $\frac{1}{2}$ orange (I prefer the apple) inside the body cavity, then place the pheasant inside the bag. Tie off the bag and make 5 or 6 $\frac{1}{2}$-inch slits in the top. Bake for

1½ hours. If the pheasant isn't nicely brown, slit the top of the bag, increase the oven temperature to 400, and cook for an additional 15 minutes, or until the pheasant is browned. Put the pheasant onto a serving platter and spoon the gravy from the bag over it.

Pheasant Salad

Most recipes for chicken salad also work for pheasants. If you don't have a favorite, try this one. Leftover pheasant can be used, or better, you can simmer a bird in water, along with a bay leaf or two and a rib of chopped celery, until tender; then cool the meat and bone and dice out 2 cups. Use the rest of the meat, and the broth, for making pheasant soup.

2 cups diced cooked pheasant
8 ounces sour cream
1 medium small apple, diced
1 rib celery, diced
juice of ½ lemon
2 hard-boiled chicken eggs, chopped
½ cup chopped pecans
1 tablespoon capers
butter
salt and pepper to taste

In a suitable bowl, combine diced pheasant meat, apple, celery, and lemon juice. Chill. Sauté the pecans in a little butter; these scorch easily, so go slowly on low heat and watch your business. Salt the pecans lightly, then mix them in with the meat, along with the sour cream, capers, salt, and pepper. Toss in the chopped eggs last. Serve cold on lettuce leaves. Feeds 4 to 6 for a light lunch. This salad can also be used as a sandwich spread.

Pheasant Castillane

This old Spanish-Mexican dish is an excellent way to cook pheasant. It makes an attractive dish and is quite tasty. The last time my wife cooked it, she asked me to help chop the vegetables. While I worked away with my chef's knife, a female guest told me that I should put all that stuff into an electric food chopper. Well, it wouldn't be the same, and I like to chop stuff the way I want it.

1 large pheasant or 2 smaller ones
3 cups water
1 cup white wine
3 medium tomatoes, peeled and cut into 1-inch chunks
1 medium onion, diced
2 cloves garlic, minced
½ green bell pepper, diced
½ red bell pepper, diced
½ yellow bell pepper, diced
¼ cup seedless raisins, chopped
¼ cup chopped fresh parsley or cilantro
2 bay leaves
2 tablespoon butter
1 teaspoon salt
½ teaspoon pepper
3 cups fluffy cooked rice (cooked separately)

Dress the pheasant and cut it into pieces, retaining the good giblets. (Be sure to dress the gizzard properly.) Put the pheasant and giblets into a boiler, along with the water and bay leaves, salt, and pepper. Bring to a boil, reduce heat, cover tightly, and simmer for 1 hour, or until the pheasant is tender to the fork. Tough birds will take longer. Remove and drain the pheasant pieces and giblets, discard the bay leaves, and retain the stock. When the pheasant is cool, pull the meat from the bones and chop it, along with the giblets, into bite-size pieces.

Melt the butter in a large skillet. Sauté the onion, garlic, and bell peppers for 5 minutes or so. Add 2 cups of the stock from the pot, along with the chopped meat, parsley, tomatoes, raisins, and wine. Bring to a boil, reduce heat, cover, and simmer for 15 minutes. Spread the rice onto a platter, making a hollow in the center, and pour the pheasant mixture in it. Eat while hot. Feeds 4 people.

Note: If you've got fresh mushrooms, add a few when you sauté the onion, garlic, and peppers.

Patio Pheasant and Portabella Mushrooms

For grilling over direct heat, it's best to cut the bird in half or reduce it to breast halves and leg quarters. I recommend quarters. In either case, it's best to pluck the bird so that the skin will help hold in the moisture. Large portabella mushrooms grill nicely and work best when they are cut into ½-inch slices.

1 pheasant halved or quartered
portabella mushrooms, sliced
1 cup olive oil
1 cup sauterne
½ teaspoon freshly ground black pepper
salt

Mix the olive oil, sauterne, and pepper; set aside ¼ cup of this mixture as a basting sauce, and use the rest as a marinade. Put the pheasant and sliced mushrooms into a nonmetallic container, then pour the marinade over them, tossing to coat all sides. Refrigerate for several hours.

When you are ready to cook, build a charcoal fire and adjust the rack about 6 inches over the coals. Drain the pheasant pieces and grill them over the coals, basting from time to time with the reserved marinade mixture. When the pheasant is almost done, add the mushrooms to the grill. Salt the pheasant and mushrooms to taste. Feeds 2.

Roast Pheasant with Applejack

The basics of this recipe came from the *Ducks Unlimited Cookbook,* to which it was submitted by David Lee Wells of North Kansas City, Missouri. Be careful with the applejack.

The Meat
2 pheasants
4 slices bacon, cut in half
½ cup chicken stock
½ cup applejack (divided)
¼ cup heavy cream
2 tablespoons melted butter
salt and pepper
The Stuffing
2 pheasant livers, chopped
1½ cups cubed day-old bread
½ cup chopped apple (peeled)
¼ cup finely chopped onion
4 tablespoons butter (divided)
1 tablespoon parsley
salt and pepper to taste

To make the stuffing, first sauté the onion and livers for 4 or 5 minutes in 2 tablespoons of butter in a skillet, stirring with a wooden spoon. Spoon the skillet contents into a large mixing bowl. Using the same skillet, add the rest of the butter, bring to medium high heat, and cook the bread cubes for 3 or 4 minutes. Add the bread to the liver mixture, along with the apple, parsley, salt, and pepper. Mix well.

Preheat the oven to 375 degrees. Rub the pheasants with 2 tablespoons of melted butter, then sprinkle them inside and out with salt and pepper. Spoon the stuffing mixture into the cavities. Truss. Carefully arrange the bacon pieces over the breasts and legs. Place the birds breast side up on a rack in a baking pan. Bake for 30 minutes in the center of the oven.

Heat ¼ cup of the applejack in a small saucepan. Then light a long match, flame the applejack, and pour it, burning, over the pheasants. Bake for another 15 minutes, or until the pheasant is brown, the bacon crisp. Place the pheasant onto a heated serving platter.

Quickly dump the contents of the baking pan into a skillet, scraping up the pan dredgings with a wooden spoon or spatula. Add the chicken stock and ¼ cup of applejack. Bring to a simmer for 3 minutes. Add the cream, bring to a light boil, quickly reduce the heat, and simmer for 3 or 4 minutes. Pour this sauce over the pheasant. Serve hot. Feeds 4.

Creamed Pheasant with Biscuits

Although pheasant tends to be a little dry, this recipe will work wonders for even tough old cocks. You can also make this dish with leftover pheasant or turkey.

> pheasant
> 1 cup light cream
> ½ cup butter
> ½ cup flour
> 1 can condensed mushroom soup (10¾-ounce size)
> 1 small to medium onion, finely chopped
> 1 red bell pepper, cored and finely chopped
> bay leaf
> water
> salt and pepper to taste
> biscuit dough or 1 package ready-to-cook refrigerated biscuits

Simmer the pheasant in water with a bay leaf until tender. Remove the bird, drain, and let cool. Reserve 2 cups of the broth. When the bird cools down a bit, bone and dice the meat. Measure out 2 cups, saving the rest of the meat for sandwiches or salads. Preheat the oven to 450 degrees. Mix the butter and flour, then shape it into small balls. Heat the 2 cups of stock in a pan, then stir in the flour balls. Cook, stirring constantly, until the mixture thickens. Stir in the cream. Add the chopped pheasant, mushroom soup, bell pepper, onion, salt, and pepper. Turn the mixture into a greased baking dish, about 9 by 12 inches, and cover with uncooked biscuits spaced about 1 inch apart. Bake for 10 to 15 minutes, or until the biscuits are browned. Feeds 4 to 6.

Oven-Fried Pheasant

I'm not too happy with the title of this recipe, or with the idea of "frying" a bird in the oven, but I really can't argue with the results.

1 fryer pheasant
1 stick butter
jalapeño potato chips, crumbled
flour
salt and pepper

Cut the pheasant into serving-size pieces—that is, drumsticks, thighs, breast halves, and back. Preheat the oven to 400 degrees. Salt and pepper the pheasant pieces, then roll or shake them in a bag with flour. Select a baking pan of suitable size to hold the bird in a single layer, line it with aluminum foil, and grease the foil with part of the butter. Melt the rest of the butter. Dip and roll each piece of pheasant into the butter, roll it in the crumbled potato chips, and fit it into the pan.

When all the pieces are finished and fitted into the pan, drizzle the remaining butter over them. Cover the pan with aluminum foil, then bake for 45 minutes in the center of the oven. Remove the aluminum foil and bake until the top of the pheasant pieces are nicely browned.

Feeds 2.

Pheasant Giblet Pâté

The following recipe can be used with giblets from doves, quail, turkey, duck, and other game birds, as well as pheasant. If you don't have 2 cups of wild bird giblets, fill in with chicken parts or adjust the measures in the recipe to fit what you do have.

2 cups (about 1 pound) bird livers, gizzards, and hearts
2 hard-boiled chicken eggs, sliced
½ cup finely diced onion
¼ cup soft butter
1 tablespoon rosé wine
1 bay leaf
salt and pepper

Put the bird gizzards and hearts into a pot, along with the bay leaf, cover with water, bring to a boil, and simmer until tender. (Make sure that the gizzards are dressed properly—that is, spilt open, turned, and "peeled.") Remove and discard the bay leaf. Add the livers, then simmer for another 20 minutes. Put all the bird parts, eggs, onions, and butter into a blender, processing until smooth and creamy. Add the salt and pepper to taste. Mix in the wine. Shape the mixture into a loaf on an oblong serving dish, cover, and refrigerate. Serve on crackers or use for sandwiches.

24

PARTRIDGE, GROUSE, AND SIMILAR BIRDS

Once I puzzled over a recipe from the Corn Belt that called for a 4-pound partridge. What the author had in mind was a pheasant, not a partridge or grouse. In another recipe, this one from Alabama, the author advised cooks to allow 2 or 3 partridges per person. He had bobwhite quail in mind. To avoid further confusion, let me say that the game birds in this chapter include grouse, ruffed grouse, sage grouse, sage hen, partridge, chukar partridge, chukar, ptarmigan, prairie chicken, willow ptarmigan, white-tailed ptarmigan, rock ptarmigan, spruce grouse, sharp-tailed grouse, gray partridge, Hungarian partridge, and so on.

All of these birds have been grouped together here because they are of a similar size, with an average weight (undressed) of about 2 pounds and with a range of about 1½ to 2½ pounds. It's true that there is some difference in flavor, but this can also be said of any family of birds; for example, wild turkeys that have fed exten-sively on acorns in a hammock in Florida will have a different flavor than turkeys that have fed on the edge of cornfields in Indiana. In spite of variations, all the birds of the partridge or grouse family are good eating. But, for the most part, they don't taste as mild as chicken or quail. If you object to a gamey flavor, a marinade will be in order. I prefer ordinary milk; soak the birds under refrigeration for several hours, preferably overnight. The flesh of these birds is low in fat and will be too dry if you cook it too long by direct heat.

Baked Ruffed Grouse with Wine

I usually cook this dish with the aid of Gallo Livingston Cellars burgundy, available at a local supermarket for $2.99 the bottle, but other dry red wines can be used in the recipe—

and I won't say a word if you use a dry white wine.

> 4 grouse
> 6 ounces large portabella mushrooms
> 1 cup dry red wine
> 1 cup half and half
> 1 cup olive oil
> flour
> salt and pepper
> 1 teaspoon minced fresh tarragon

Pluck the grouse, then cut them into quarters. Salt and pepper each quarter, then dust them with flour. Heat about ½ inch of olive oil in a skillet. Brown the bird quarters quickly, a few pieces at a time. Preheat the oven to 350 degrees. Grease an ovenproof baking dish of suitable size. Slice enough mushrooms to line the bottom of the pan, making the slices about ½ inch thick. Arrange the browned grouse quarters over the mushrooms. Then finely chop the rest of the mushrooms.

Pour most of the olive oil out of the skillet, scraping up any pan dredgings with a wooden spatula. Add the wine, half and half, chopped mushrooms, and tarragon to the skillet. Bring the mixture to a boil, then reduce the heat and simmer for a few minutes, stirring and shaking the skillet as you go to make a smooth sauce. Pour the sauce over the birds, then bake in the center of the oven for 1 hour. Serve the birds hot with the gravy, rice, steamed vegetables, hot French bread, and the rest of the red wine. Feeds 4.

Chatfield Grouse

This recipe came from Chuck Dixon of the Wildlife Branch of Manitoba Natural Re-

sources. It is heavy on the brandy, but the results are good and I enjoy it (the soused grouse, that is) on a cold winter's night. The recipe calls for grouse fillets.

> 6 ruffed grouse breasts (12 fillets)
> 1 can cream of mushroom soup (10¾-ounce size)
> ½ cup good brandy or cognac
> ¼ cup dry white wine
> ⅓ cup flour
> ¼ cup butter
> 1 medium onion, diced
> 4 cloves garlic, minced
> 1 teaspoon white pepper
> ½ teaspoon salt
> ⅛ teaspoon Tabasco sauce

Heat the butter in a skillet. Mix the flour, salt, and pepper. Roll the fillets in the flour mixture, then brown them in the butter. Add

the onion and garlic, cook for 1 or 2 minutes, and stir in the mushroom soup, wine, brandy, and Tabasco. Reduce the heat, cover, and simmer for 30 minutes. Test for doneness. Add more salt if needed.

Feeds 4 to 6.

Variations: If available, use wild mushrooms along with ½ pint of whipping cream instead of the canned soup. Also, try this recipe with breast fillets of wild ducks.

Creamed Grouse on Toast

You can use leftovers for this dish, but these days, with relatively few grouse and reduced bag limits, most of us don't have leftovers. In fact, a lot of us have a practical need for a 1-bird recipe.

    1 grouse
    ½ cup heavy cream
    ½ cup finely chopped onion
    ½ cup finely chopped mushrooms
    ½ cup dry white wine
    2 tablespoons butter
    juice of 1 lemon
    1 bay leaf
    salt and pepper
    toast

Pluck, draw, and disjoint the grouse, saving the giblets. Put the parts into a boiler of suitable size, cover with water, and add the bay leaf. Bring to a boil, then reduce the heat, cover, and simmer for 1 hour, or until tender. Remove the bird, saving ½ cup of stock from the boiler. Pull the meat off the bones and chop it along with the giblets. In a skillet, melt the butter, then sauté the onions and mushrooms for 5 minutes. Add the chopped grouse,

> ## Oklahoma Prairie Chickens
>
> Prairie chickens feed mostly on sorghum crops such as milo and maize after a killing frost in the fall, so pass-shooting over feed fields is one of the most popular methods of hunting them. Hunting grasslands over bird dogs is also popular.
> —Oklahoma Wildlife News Service

reserved ½ cup stock (use ½ cup chicken stock, if you are using leftovers), and lemon juice. Heat. Stir. Add salt and pepper to taste. Simmer for 20 minutes, add the wine, and simmer for another 20 minutes. Remove from the heat. Stir in the cream. Serve hot over toast.

This dish makes a nice lunch, and I'll want 2 pieces of toast topped by plenty of creamed grouse. I also like lots of pepper on this dish, which should be freshly ground from a mill on the table.

Sharon McPhee's Partridge

Here's a good, easy dish from *The Maine Way*, to which it was contributed by Sharon McPhee of Eagle Lake:

"Cut partridge breast into slices. Soak all day in refrigerator in milk and beaten egg batter. Before frying, coat slices with cracker crumbs. Fry in deep fat (375 degrees) until golden brown."

This is, I might add, an excellent way to fry pheasant breast fillets.

Dr. Tom's 40 Garlic Chukar—Microwaved

A memorable story always makes a good recipe better, in my opinion. I'll never cook this dish without thinking of Dr. Tom, although I personally love lots of garlic. In any case, the recipe and the story came from Paula J. Del Giudice's *Microwave Game & Fish Cookbook.*

4 chukars
40 garlic cloves (about 4 heads)
½ onion, cut in half lengthwise and
    separated into sections
⅔ cup olive oil
3 tablespoons water
4 whole bay leaves
1 crumbled bay leaf
1 teaspoon dried parsley
1 teaspoon dried thyme
1 teaspoon ground sage
1 teaspoon dried rosemary
salt and pepper

"Separate the onion sections. Keep the four smallest ones. In each of the four sections, sprinkle ¼ teaspoon parsley, ¼ teaspoon thyme, and 1 whole bay leaf. Set aside.

"In a heavy stove-top skillet, heat olive oil.

Add crumbled bay leaf, sage, rosemary, and dried thyme (remaining ¾ teaspoon) to oil. Add chukars. Brown chukars on all sides in oil. Remove from oil and dust with salt and pepper.

"Stuff an onion section into each body cavity. Tie legs together with string to hold onion in place. Place small pieces of aluminum foil around ends of legs to keep legs from overcooking. Make sure pieces of foil do not touch each other and are at least 1 inch from oven walls. Place birds in an 8-inch square glass dish. Add garlic cloves around birds. Add water to bottom of dish.

"Cover tightly. Microwave on 60 percent or bake for 18–19 minutes. Remove from the oven. Cover with aluminum foil, shiny side down, for at least 5 minutes before serving.

"Note: Dr. Tom Gallager was my childhood dentist and longtime family friend. He can't stand garlic, but he has had to tolerate its notorious odor for many, many years as an innocent bystander—a hazard of his profession. He is also an avid shotgunner and hunter. I raided his freezer to test some of the recipes for this cookbook, including this one for 40 Garlic Chukar.

"Just for you, Tom, the garlic won't be missed too much if you leave it out of the recipe.

"Traditionally, the garlic cloves are served with the birds. The creamy cooked cloves are pressed out and spread on pieces of toast. In the traditional recipe, chicken is cooked instead of chukars. But the spices in the recipe work great with chukars.

"In a regular oven, the cloves become browned. This won't happen in a microwave, but for those who like garlic, serve it with pieces of toast anyway. The cooked cloves taste completely different than you would imagine."

Capercaillie

The bones of the capercaillie—a grouse that may weigh up to 12 pounds—have been found in kitchen middens of Denmark and other places. By modern standards, this large game bird is perhaps the best tasting of all the grouse, and maybe of all the European game birds. Its delicate meat is whiter than pheasant. The bird can be found, here and there, from Lapland to Turkestan, and south to the northern edges of Spain. The bird always lives in or near pine forests, which provide its food in winter.

In Scotland, the bird is hunted with the aid of beaters, who frighten the birds out of the forest and across the moors, where hunters are waiting. In other parts of Europe, the birds are sometimes taken by stalk hunting during the courtship season. Usually, the male capercaillie has a sharp eye and is difficult to stalk, but when courting it has a habit of sitting in the very top of a tree, stretching its neck up, and emitting a loud mating call. During this call, it closes its eyes. Thus, the hunter can advance by starts and stops until he gets within easy shooting range.

—Adapted from *Edible Plants and Animals*

Sage Grouse for Two

Here's a dish that my wife and I like to serve over rice. Be sure to try it, using sage grouse, partridge, ptarmigan, or similar birds.

2 sage grouse
4 ounces fresh mushrooms, sliced
juice of 1 lemon
2 tablespoons butter
1 tablespoon finely chopped onion
1 tablespoon white wine Worcestershire
    sauce
1 bay leaf
water
salt and pepper
rice (cooked separately)

Put the birds into a suitable pot, barely cover with water, bring to a broil, reduce heat, add the bay leaf, and simmer until the meat is very tender. Remove the birds to cool. Retain the stock from the pot. Pull the meat from the bones, chop it, and put it into a bowl. Sprinkle the meat with the lemon juice, then toss to mix. Cover the bowl and refrigerate for 1 hour or longer.

In a small skillet, heat the butter. Sauté the mushrooms and onions for 5 minutes. Add the chopped meat and white wine Worcestershire sauce. Stir in ¼ cup of the reserved stock. Add salt and pepper to taste. Bring to heat, cover, and simmer on very low heat for about 1 hour. Add a little more stock as needed. Serve piping hot over rice, along with vegetables and hot French bread. Feeds 2.

Heald Pond Road Partridge

From *The Maine Way* comes a rather curious recipe that was contributed by Mrs. Douglas C. Miner of Hampden. Before writing this book, I never thought I would find myself beating cabbage with a wooden spoon, but I did it and I can highly recommend the results. "Chop equal parts of onion and crisp cabbage, then beat them with a wooden spoon and blend the two until each attains some of the virtue and flavor of the other. To this, add 1 lightly beaten egg, salt, pepper, a few bread crumbs, and enough evaporated milk to make a wet dressing. Fill the small orifices of partridge with the mixture, sew up neatly, then cover the birds with strips of bacon. Roast in a 400 degree oven until tender—about 40 minutes. Remove bacon for last 15 minutes, if breast is not browning. The dressing becomes hot and the steam permeates the flesh of the birds; as a result, the meat is juicy and tender, full of rich flavor."

Camp Partridge

If you're going to camp out during a hunt, take along a few basic ingredients so that you can cook this recipe.

young partridge or grouse
bacon
lemon
salt and pepper

Clean and quarter the birds. Soak them for 2 hours in water with a little salt. Build a good keyhole fire so that you'll have coals that can be raked away from the blaze. Dry the birds. Sprinkle with salt and pepper. Take a piece of bacon and grease a grill. Wrap the partridge quarters (especially the breasts) with bacon. Put them on the grill about 4 inches from the coals. While cooking, squeeze a little lemon juice on the birds 2 or 3 times. Cook until the bacon is ready to eat.

Partridge . . . in a Pear Tree

As a New Englander, when I learned that the bird which I had trustingly called a partridge to the end of my adolescence was an impostor whose real name was the "ruffed grouse," the disillusionment was comparable to that of a child when he discovers that there is no Santa Claus.
—Waverley Root, *Food*

Note: Bacon grease dripping into hot coals tends to start a fire; use a large grill so that the birds can be moved easily, or have long tongs at hand for moving the meat around as needed.

Wyoming Sage Hens

This recipe is from *Cooking in Wyoming*, to which it was submitted by Mrs. John C. Pickett of Cheyenne:

"The following method is one I use for either sage hens or pheasants. Soak in cold, salted water for several hours. Dry thoroughly. Dip the pieces of meat in a batter of 2 beaten eggs to which has been added a tablespoon of cold water. Remove and roll the pieces in flour to which salt and pepper have been added. Dip again in crumbs. Allow to stand for an hour or so in refrigerator, if possible.

"Brown pieces in hot fat, then place in roaster. Pour rich milk over it and allow to steam in covered roaster for an hour or more at 325 degrees, or until tender. Add more milk if necessary to keep meat moist during the baking."

25

WOODCOCK AND SNIPE

These two birds do resemble each other and the recipes are pretty much interchangeable, but on average the woodcock is a little larger than the snipe. The long bill, built for feeding in soft ground, is what links the birds in the mind's eye. This image is further enforced by an old French and English practice of leaving the heads on the birds when they are cooked, and then tying the long bills to the legs. Some people even hang the birds for a week or longer, until they are high. Even the entrails (or "trail") have been cooked and eaten in some quarters. Most red-blooded, weak-stomached Americans can get by without the entrails. Culinary sports can go directly to the last recipe in this chapter.

Camp Woodcock

This dish is good anywhere, but I designed it to be used in camp where staples must make up the diet and where fried foods tend to get old. Apart from the birds, which I assume you will bag on the trip, the ingredients are easy to tote in and won't spoil. This recipe can also be used for quail and other small birds.

4 woodcock
½ cup Coffee-Mate
2 tablespoons cooking oil or butter
2 chicken bouillon cubes
hot water
flour
salt and pepper
1 cup rice (cooked separately)

Pluck and draw the birds, salt and pepper them inside and out, and then shake them in a bag with flour. Heat the cooking oil in a skillet or Dutch oven. Brown the birds. Carefully pour off most of the oil. Mix the Coffee-Mate in 1 cup of hot water, then pour over the birds.

The Taste of Woodcock

Never cook woodcock with any other bird unless you want the others to have the flavor of woodcock.

—*The Maine Way*

Cover and simmer for 1 hour. Remove the birds, let them cool a little, and pull the meat from the bones with fork and fingers. Add a little water to the skillet, then stir in the bouillon cubes. Simmer and stir. Add the bird meat, then simmer for 20 minutes, adding a little more water if needed. Serve over rice. Feeds 2 to 4.

To cook the rice, heat 2 cups of water to a boil in a pan with a lid. Add the rice along with a little salt. Bring to a new boil, reduce the heat to low, cover tightly, and simmer for exactly 20 minutes. Do not remove the lid while the rice cooks.

Fried Buttermilk Woodcock

Buttermilk makes an excellent marinade for game birds, and also causes the skin to pick up more flour, making a thicker coating.

8 woodcock
½ cup buttermilk
cooking oil
flour
salt and pepper

Pluck the birds, draw them, and cut them in half lengthwise. Put the halves into a non-metallic container, cover them with buttermilk, and refrigerate for several hours or overnight.

Drain the birds but do not wash or dry. Quickly sprinkle them inside and out with salt and pepper, then shake them in a bag with flour. Heat ¾ inch of cooking oil in a skillet, then cook the birds on medium high heat until nicely browned. Do not overcook. Allow at least 2 birds per person. If you want gravy, pour off part of the grease, scrape up the pan dredgings with a wooden spoon or spatula, add a little flour and water paste, and simmer, stirring as you go, until you have a smooth gravy. Serve the gravy over rice, mashed potatoes, or biscuit halves.

Variation: For a different marinade, try 1 cup of red wine vinegar mixed with 1 cup of water.

Crockpot Snipe

For this dish, I always breast the birds, simply because long cooking will cause the meat to come off the bones easily. The rest of the birds are cooked in a separate pot, boned, and added to the crockpot for flavor and texture. This dish can also be cooked with other small birds, such as doves or even blackbirds.

20 snipe breasts
1 can cream of chicken soup (10¾-ounce size)
1 can cream of celery soup (10¾-ounce size)
2 medium onions, diced
½ cup green onion tops, finely diced
fresh mushrooms
1 tablespoon fresh parsley, chopped
¼ cup red wine
cooking oil
flour
salt and pepper
rice (cooked separately)

Clean and draw the snipe. Detach the breasts and set them aside. Put the rest of the birds into a boiler, cover with water, and simmer for 1 hour, or until the meat can be pulled from the bones easily. Chop the meat and put it into a crockpot, along with the chicken and celery soups, onions, parsley, wine, salt, and pepper. Cover the crockpot. Turn the heat to low.

Salt and pepper the snipe breasts, then shake them in flour. Heat some oil in a skillet, brown the snipe breasts a few at a time, and then add them to the crockpot. Add a double handful of fresh mushrooms, or fill the crockpot to the rim with them. Cook on low heat for 8 hours. Cook plenty of fluffy rice to go with this dish. Leftovers can be heated up and served over toast for lunch.

Woodcock in Sour Cream

4 woodcock
2 slices smoked bacon
½ cup peanut oil
½ cup beef stock (or bouillon made with a
  cube)
½ cup sour cream
flour
salt and pepper

Preheat the oven to 350 degrees. Salt and pepper the birds inside and out, and shake them in a bag with flour. Heat the peanut oil in a skillet; quickly brown the birds on high heat. Drain the birds. Grease a casserole dish or baking pan with the bacon strips, then place the bacon in the bottom. Place the browned birds over the bacon. Pour the beef stock over the birds, cover, and bake for 1 hour. Reduce the heat to 200 degrees. Pour the sour cream over the birds, cover, and bake for 10 minutes. Feeds 2.

Woodcock in a Bag

Remember the Maine partridge recipe (page 233) that called for beating cabbage with a wooden spoon? Well, here's another rather curious recipe from that state, submitted to *The Maine Way* by Gennie Peppard of East Holden. You'll have to try it.

"Put several birds (number needed) into a Brown and Bake bag. Add about a quarter of a fruit juice glass of wine and 2 packages of onion gravy mixture. Seal bag. Put a small amount of water in an electric fry pan, then put in bag which has been punctured with several fork holes. Cover and simmer about 65 minutes. Add water as needed to fry pan. When tender remove woodcock from bag; pour juices into fry pan and thicken the gravy."

Why the Woodcock Is Crazy

The American woodcock truly is a wonder of nature as a shorebird that has evolved to live in the woods. To adapt to wooded habitat, the woodcock's eyes have "migrated" far back in its head, enabling it to see a full 360 degrees. In the process, the bird's brain flip-flopped to an upside-down position. The bird also evolved short, rounded wings enabling it to fly through dense cover.

—Illinois Department of Conservation
Outdoor Highlights

Woodcock with Grapes

4 woodcock
1 cup white grapes, whole
½ cup fresh orange juice
¼ cup dry red wine
¼ cup butter
¼ cup water
1 teaspoon orange zest
salt and pepper

Preheat the oven to 350 degrees. Pluck and draw the woodcock, salt and pepper them inside and out, and arrange them in a well-greased casserole dish or baking pan. In a small saucepan, heat the butter, water, orange juice, orange zest, wine, and grapes. Pour the sauce over the birds and bake for 50 minutes, basting several times with pan juices. Feeds 2.

Sautéed Birds with Sherry

Here's an excellent skillet dish from Louisiana. It is especially good with snipe or woodcock, both of which are sometimes available in great plenty in that state. The recipe also works with doves.

8 to 10 snipe or woodcock
1 cup sherry
½ cup chopped green onions with part of
  tops
¼ cup chopped fresh parsley
½ cup butter
juice of 1 lemon
salt and pepper

Pluck and draw the birds, then sprinkle them inside and out with salt and pepper. Melt the butter in a large skillet. Brown the birds, then add the onions and parsley for a couple of minutes. Add the sherry and lemon juice. Reduce the heat, cover, and simmer on very low heat for 20 minutes. Serve hot, spooning the pan juices over the birds.

Rare Roasted Timberdoodle

Here's a very good recipe that I have adapted from Sylvia Bashline's *Bounty of the Earth Cookbook.*

8 woodcock
1 cooking apple
½ cup port
3 tablespoons butter

Preheat the oven to 450 degrees. Cut the apple lengthwise into 8 wedges, then put a piece into the cavity of each bird. Rub the birds with butter, then place them breast up into a greased roasting pan of suitable size. Heat the port in a saucepan, then pour a little over each bird. Place the pan in the center of the oven for 25 minutes, basting a time or two with pan juices. Feeds 4.

Brazilian Snipe

Brazilian cooks like to grill small birds such as snipe, seasoning them with salt and herbs put into the body cavity, and basting them with a mixture of orange juice and Madeira. Grill these over charcoal or wood coals—and do not overcook.

Gutsy Woodcock or Snipe

As pointed out in the text for Russian birds on page 192, peoples in times past have cooked birds whole, innards and all, by one means or another. In some quarters, especially France, the "trail" was eaten along with the liver, heart, and gizzard.

According to *Larousse Gastronomique,* you chop the intestines together with "an equal quantity of *foie gras* or fresh grated bacon fat, season with salt and pepper and add a pinch of grated nutmeg and a dash of brandy. Spread this mixture on pieces of bread, either fried or cooked in the dripping pan."

If you don't want to go quite that far, you might at least try this recipe from Bradford Angier's *Gourmet Cooking for Free:*

"Another way to cook woodcock without drawing them is by dry-plucking birds shot that day, rubbing them with salt and freshly ground black pepper and perhaps a bit of tarragon, and lowering them carefully into a pot of deep oil that is seething at about 365 degrees. After they have tossed and bobbed for 6 minutes, the viscera will have tightened into

a clean hard ball that can be discarded, along with the well-picked bones, while heart, liver, and perfectly cooked meat are enjoyed to the utmost."

I note with considerable interest that Angier specifies birds that have been recently shot (that day, in fact) and not "hung" for a week or so!

Wines for Woodcock

The woodcock calls for the richest and most powerful-tasting red wines that could ever be enjoyed with game. To their everlasting credit, no sauce or extra ingredient will ever completely hide the earthy aroma and taste of woodcock. Eating a brace of woodcock with a chunk of hard bread and a bottle of robust Bordeaux red, or claret, as the British choose to call it, is a rare taste sensation.

—Sylvia Bashline
The Bounty of the Earth Cookbook

26

DUCKS AND GEESE

I've never eaten a duck that I didn't like, and I feel that most people who object to the so-called wild or gamey flavor of ducks and geese simply don't like the flavor of the meat. Period. But it's true that ducks that have been eating grain are better, on the average, than those that have been eating water-borne fare. Usually, grain-fed ducks should be plucked so that they will be moister and more succulent after cooking. With stronger ducks, consider skinning and preparing them by a wet-cooking method instead of baking or cooking them by any dry heat method. It also helps to field-dress ducks as soon as possible after they have been killed. A duck is well insulated because of its feathers, and the body heat simply can't escape quickly. Plucking the birds right away isn't always feasible, but they should at least be drawn. This will remove a good part of the body heat, contained by the innards, and open up a cavity for air circulation. It's best to age ducks and

geese in the refrigerator for 3 or 4 days before cooking them. This is best accomplished with drawn but unplucked or unskinned birds.

In the following recipes, I have tried to follow a somewhat tempered approach to duck cookery. Many hunters and epicures prefer their duck to be very rare. That's fine with me and I want mine on the rare side—but not dripping blood. Suit yourself. Newcomers to duck cookery might do well to stay away from the recipes for roasting whole birds, first acquiring a taste for the meat with some wet-cooking method. In fact, a crockpot is hard to beat for cooking ducks, and the first few recipes below reflect this thinking.

Duck Soup, Crockpot-Style

Duck soup with lots of barley is very, very good. I also like to use lots of celery with the

240

green tops. For the measures below, the exact amount of duck meat isn't critical, but 2 mallards are about right.

2 mallard-size wild ducks
4 cups water
½ cup red wine
1 cup pearl barley
3 large ribs celery with tops, finely chopped
1 medium onion, chopped
3 cloves garlic, minced
1 tablespoon chopped chives
½ teaspoon pepper
salt to taste
3 bay leaves

Skin the ducks. Fillet out each side of the breasts and set aside. Disjoint the rest of the ducks, put the pieces into a stove-top pot, cover with water, add the bay leaves, cover, and simmer slowly for 1 hour, or until the meat is tender. While the bony pieces simmer, cut the breast pieces into chunks and put them into the crockpot. Add the water, pepper, chives, celery, onion, salt, and garlic. (It's best to scrape the stalks of celery, then cut the stalks into several strips lengthwise before chopping, making for smaller-than-usual pieces.) Turn the crockpot to low.

When the duck in the pot is tender, take it out and bone the meat. Chop the meat and giblets, adding them to the crockpot. Add 2 cups of the duck broth and discard the rest. Stir in 1 cup of pearl barley. Add ½ cup red wine. Cover and heat on low for 6 or 7 hours. Serve in bowls and eat hot with a good bread.

Warning: Make sure that you don't add more than 1 cup of pearl barley. This stuff soaks up lots of water and expands greatly. It may even push the top off the crockpot. After the barley has cooked for 1 hour or so, check the liquid in the pot. Add a little very hot water if needed.

Cheek's Camp Ducks

If your cabin or camp (or RV) has electric power, consider the crockpot as a possible cooking aid. I got this idea from a book called *Answering the Call to Duck Cookery,* by Chandler S. Cheek, who said, "When at camp, use duck taken the previous day; brown ducks and cut up vegetables the evening before so you can quickly put this together and turn on the pot before you head out the door in the morning. A mouth watering, ready to serve treat will be ready when you return from the hunt in the evening." Here's what you'll need:

2 ducks, skinned
4 or more small potatoes, peeled
2 onions, quartered
2 ribs celery, chopped
2 carrots
½ cup cooking oil
½ cup sauterne
oregano
garlic salt
lemon-pepper seasoning

Trim the fat from the ducks. Heat the cooking oil in a skillet, then quickly brown the ducks on high heat. Dust the birds with oregano, garlic salt, and lemon-pepper inside and out. Cut 2 carrots to fit into the bottom of the crockpot to serve as a rack. Stuff the birds with the onions and celery, then fit the birds into the pot. Top with potatoes. Pour in the wine, cover, and cook on low heat for 8 hours. Discard the stuffing and carrot rack. Serve the ducks with potatoes.

Duck Gumbo, Crockpot-Style

Ducks of any size can be cooked to advantage by this method. Just increase the number of birds.

For best results, it's best to fill the crockpot almost to the top, or to the top. I usually make adjustments in the quantity of mushrooms, which are added last.

    4 mallard-size wild ducks
    1 cup duck stock (see below)
    4 strips bacon
    1 can tomatoes (16-ounce size)
    1 can tomato paste (6-ounce size)
    2 cups sliced okra wheels
    8 ounces fresh mushrooms
    2 ribs of celery, diced
    2 medium onions, diced
    ½ large green bell pepper, diced
    ½ large red bell pepper, diced
    1 tablespoon parsley
    1 tablespoon freeze-dried chopped chives
    4 small bay leaves
    salt and pepper
    rice (cooked separately)
    filé (optional)

Skin and disjoint the duck. Separate the legs into drumsticks and thighs. Fillet the meat off both sides of the breast. Put the breasts, thighs, and drumsticks into the crockpot.

Put the bony pieces into a large pot, barely cover with water, and simmer for 1 hour, or until the meat is very tender.

Meanwhile, fry the bacon in a skillet until it is crisp and set aside. Sauté the onions, peppers, and celery for 10 minutes in bacon drippings. Remove, drain, and set aside. Sauté the okra for 10 minutes in the bacon drippings (add more drippings if needed). Put the sautéed vegetables and crumbled bacon into the crockpot along with the duck pieces. Add tomatoes, tomato paste, mushrooms, chives, bay leaves, parsley, salt, and pepper. Turn the crockpot to low.

After the duck bones have simmered for 30 minutes or longer, add 1 cup of broth to the crockpot. Remove the bones and pull the meat from them. Chop the meat along with the giblets and put it into the crockpot. Cook on low heat for 10 hours or so.

Prepare the rice. Ladle the gumbo into individual bowls, and, if you wish, thicken with a pinch or two of filé. (Proceed carefully with the filé.) Add the rice last, spooning some into the center of each bowl of gumbo. Feeds 6 to 8.

Slow-Grilled Duck

For grilling, young grain-fed birds work best, plucked instead of skinned, and require no marinade.

    2 or 3 wild ducks, plucked
    ½ cup melted butter
    ½ cup lemon juice
    ½ cup red wine vinegar
    1 teaspoon garlic juice
    salt and pepper

Fire up the charcoal grill, or heat the gas or electric grill for cooking on medium heat. Mix a basting sauce with the melted butter, lemon juice, garlic juice, and red wine vinegar. Cut the ducks in half lengthwise, and season both sides with salt and pepper. Grill over slow heat, or until the skin is crisp and brown, basting from time to time. Do not overcook.

Governor's Duck

The following recipe was submitted to *Cooking in Wyoming*, by Mrs. Joe Hickey, whose husband was governor from 1959 until 1961. I have reworked the format of the recipe. It's best to use large wild ducks.

The Meat
   2 wild ducks
   6 slices bacon
The Stuffing
   6 cups soft bread crumbs
   1 cup chopped celery
   1 cup chopped onion
   1 cup seedless raisins
   1 cup chopped pecans
   ½ cup milk
   2 chicken eggs
   ½ teaspoon salt
Basting Sauce
   1 cup catsup
   ½ cup Worcestershire sauce
   ½ cup A-1 sauce
   ½ cup chili sauce
The Garnish
   orange slices
   candied cranberries

Pluck the ducks, dress for stuffing, weigh the birds together, and record the weight. Mix all the ingredients listed under basting sauce. Set aside. Heat the milk. Whisk the eggs. Combine the milk and eggs with the bread crumbs, celery, onions, raisins, pecans, and salt. Preheat the oven to 350 degrees. Fill the ducks with the stuffing and close, then place the ducks in an uncovered roasting pan, cover each duck with 3 strips of bacon, and baste heavily with the sauce. Roast for 15 to 20 minutes per pound of duck, basting twice.

Serve the duck with orange slices and candied cranberries. For best results, peel the orange and slice it crosswise. Then pile the cranberries onto each slice. Feeds 2 to 4.

Camp-Fried Duck

I'll have to be honest. Some of the best duck I've ever eaten was nothing fancy. We had pitched tents somewhere between the Choctawhatchee and Pea rivers in southeast Alabama, and we were after turkey. We got two. We also got some unexpected ducks, and a fellow with us cooked them in a skillet on coals from our campfire. Although the list of ingredients is short, the fellow went about the cooking quite meticulously.

   duck breasts, skinned and filleted
   cooking oil
   flour
   empty wine bottle
   salt and pepper

Salt and pepper the fillets, then roll them in flour, and beat each one thoroughly with the mouth of an empty wine bottle. That's right. Each time you pound the meat, you leave a ring impression in it. If you pound long enough, you'll overlap the rings several times. The more the better, provided that the fillets hold together. (If you prefer, you can use a meat mallet or the edge of a plate, or perhaps a Coke bottle, but I'm not going to guarantee the results.) Heat about ½ inch of oil in a skillet. Salt and pepper the fillets again, roll in flour, and fry for 2 or 3 minutes on each side. In skillets of normal size, it's best to cook only 3 fillets at a time, and the oil should be quite hot. Do not overcook.

Honey Duck

Here's an interesting dish that I have adapted from Sam Goolsby's *The Great Southern Wild Game Cookbook*. Use wild honey for this recipe, and inform your guests accordingly. If you don't have wild honey, lie about it.

2 mallard-size wild ducks
2 cups wild honey
½ cup butter
2 oranges (unpeeled)
6 tablespoons orange juice
2 teaspoons orange zest
4 teaspoons lemon juice
4 teaspoons salt
2 teaspoons ground basil
2 teaspoons ground ginger
1 teaspoon pepper
¼ teaspoon dry mustard
paste of cornstarch and water

Preheat the oven to 350 degrees. Pluck and draw the ducks for stuffing. Cut the unpeeled orange into ½-inch slices. Mix the salt, basil, ginger, and pepper. Rub half of this mixture inside the ducks. Set the other half aside. Heat the butter in a saucepan, then stir in the honey, mustard, orange juice, lemon juice, and orange zest.

Rub 2 tablespoons of this mixture inside each duck; set the rest of the mixture aside. Stuff the ducks with the orange slices, then pour 2 tablespoons of the honey mixture inside each duck. Truss the ducks. Rub the rest of the salt mixture onto the outside of the ducks.

Place the ducks on a rack in a roasting pan, pour the rest of the honey mixture over them, cover, and bake in the center of the oven for 2 hours. Uncover, baste, and bake for about 20 minutes, or until the birds are nicely browned. Place the birds onto a heated serving platter. Thicken the pan liquid with a small amount of paste made of cornstarch and water, then pour the gravy over the ducks. Serve hot.

Teal Stuffed with Rice

Here's a very good recipe that can be used with any duck but was designed for use with early-season teal.

The Birds
4 teal or 2 mallards
bacon drippings
salt and pepper
The Stuffing
1 cup cooked rice
6 ounces fresh mushrooms, sliced
1 tablespoon chopped fresh parsley
2 slices bacon
The Sauce
1 cup fresh orange juice
½ cup butter
½ cup red wine

To make a stuffing, fry the bacon, crumble it, and mix it with the rice, mushrooms, and parsley. Set aside. Preheat the oven to 350 degrees. Rub the ducks inside and out with bacon drippings, then sprinkle them with salt and pepper. Stuff the birds, then put them into a baking pan, breast side down. Melt the butter in a saucepan, then add the wine and orange juice. Pour about half of this sauce over the ducks.

Cook the ducks for 30 minutes in the center of the oven, basting several times with the remaining sauce. Turn the ducks breast side up and continue to bake until they are nicely browned, depending on the size of the birds. If in doubt, cut into one of the breasts before serving. When done, the breast should be nicely pink but should not run blood. Place the ducks onto a serving platter and pour the pan drippings over them. Servings? I like at least 2 teal or 1 mallard, but I can make do with less.

Caddo Wild Duck

I got the name for this slow-bake recipe from *Southern Living* magazine, where I was, surprisingly, once an editor. I don't know where they got it, but I suspect that it came from Caddo Lake in East Texas.

The Birds
    2 wild ducks, plucked and drawn
    bacon
    lemon
    salt and pepper
The Stuffing
    1 apple, chopped
    1 medium onion, chopped
    1 rib celery, chopped
    2 teaspoons Worcestershire sauce
    1 teaspoon salt
    $\frac{1}{8}$ teaspoon black pepper
    $\frac{1}{8}$ teaspoon cayenne pepper

Preheat the oven to 325 degrees. Mix the stuffing, then spoon it into the duck cavities, pinning with round toothpicks or small skewers. Heat the oil in a large skillet and quickly brown the ducks. Wrap each duck with bacon and pin it with round toothpicks. Place the ducks close together, breast up, on a rack in a roasting pan of suitable size. Bake for about 2 hours in the center of the oven, or until the birds are done to your liking.

Easy Way to Age Your Ducks and Geese

Waterfowl should be drawn as quickly as possible. In ideal conditions (at home) you should age your field-dressed ducks, with feathers on, in the refrigerator. A normal refrigerator temperature of 38 to 40 degrees, for 3 or 4 days, is all that is necessary.

Hunting camp is another story. First, you do not generally have the facilities that you do at home. Second, you may not be in camp for 4 straight days. In my hunting camp I just reverse the process. I completely clean my field-dressed ducks, put them in heavy freezer bags, and freeze them in containers of water. In thawing the ducks prior to a big dinner, I'll be sure to age them in the fridge for 3 or 4 days.

—Billy Joe Cross, *Ducks Unlimited*

Smothered Duck

Here's an easy recipe that works for wild ducks of any size. Cut the birds into breast halves, drumsticks, and thighs, saving the rest for soup, stock, or stews.

> duck pieces
> 1 cup half and half
> butter
> flour
> salt and pepper

Salt and pepper the duck pieces to taste, then shake them in a bag with flour. Heat the butter in a skillet. Brown the duck pieces. Reduce the heat and cook for a little longer, then add the half and half, cover, and simmer slowly for 1 hour.

Duck with Orange Sauce

Here's a winning dish, adapted from Betty Melville's *The Hunter's Cookbook,* for people who think they don't like duck.

> 4 large or 8 small wild ducks
> 2 cans cream of chicken soup (10½-ounce size)
> 2 apples, peeled and quartered
> 2 cloves garlic, minced
> 2 tablespoons orange juice
> ½ teaspoon grated orange rind (zest)
> salt and pepper
> water

Dress and disjoint the ducks, then put the pieces into a large pot along with the apples and garlic. Cover with water, bring to a boil, reduce the heat, and simmer until the meat is very tender. Remove the duck pieces, discard the apple, and simmer the broth, uncovered, until it is reduced to 1 cup, skimming from time to time to remove the scum. As the broth is cooking down, bone the duck pieces, placing all the meat onto a chafing dish or in a shallow serving dish suitable for heating on the stove.

In a bowl, mix the chicken soup, 1 cup duck broth, orange juice, and grated orange rind, along with salt and pepper. Pour this mixture over the duck, then heat to a simmer for 10 minutes. Serve hot with rice and steamed vegetables. Feeds 4 to 6.

Twice-Stuffed Gadwalls

Here's a Louisiana recipe for gadwalls, or gray ducks, which are called "canard gris" in that state. The ingredients call for pecans, which are popular for cooking purposes in that part of the South.

> gadwalls, plucked and cleaned
> lemon juice
> onions, chopped
> celery, chopped
> red wine
> half and half
> bacon drippings
> orange segments
> pecan halves
> chicken stock
> salt and pepper

After plucking and cleaning the birds, rub their insides with lemon juice and stuff them with chopped onion and celery. Place the birds in the refrigerator overnight, then remove and discard the stuffing. Preheat the oven to 400 degrees. Mix a little lemon juice, red wine, and half and half, then pour the mixture into the cavities. Rub the ducks with bacon drippings, then sprinkle lightly inside and out with salt and pepper. Stuff with orange segments and pecan halves. Bake in the preheated oven for 2 hours, basting from time to time with chicken stock. Serve up the ducks whole, garnished with sliced oranges.

Sauerkraut Duck

Sauerkraut lends a wonderful flavor to wild ducks, as well as to doves. In this recipe, the sauerkraut more or less cooks away, however, leaving only the flavor. It's best to cook this recipe in a cast-iron Dutch oven inside the oven of a kitchen stove. The recipe can also be cooked to advantage in camp.

      2 mallard-size ducks
      1 can sauerkraut (20-ounce size)
      1 small can frozen orange juice concentrate
         (6-ounce size)
      2 stalks celery with green tops, chopped
      1 medium onion, chopped
      salt and pepper

Preheat the oven to 450 degrees. Salt and pepper the ducks inside and out, then fit them into a Dutch oven or other suitable baking dish with a tight-fitting lid. Mix the sauerkraut, orange juice, celery, and onion. Pour the mixture over the ducks evenly. Put the ducks into the center of the oven for 30 minutes. Reduce the heat to 325 and bake for about 3 hours. After the birds have cooked for 2 hours, check them every 30 minutes or so and baste them with pan liquid. Add a little water if needed.

For camp cooking, dig a 3-foot-deep hole large enough for the Dutch oven. Build a good fire and fill the hole with 10 inches of red-hot coals. When putting the ducks and other ingredients into the Dutch oven, add 1 cup of water. Put the Dutch oven into the hole, leaving the bail sticking up. Cover the Dutch oven with more hot coals, then cover the whole thing with the dirt that came out of the hole. The ducks should be done in about 6 hours. It is important that you have a tight-fitting lid and add the cup of water to the ingredients. You may even want to build a rack in the bottom with carrots and add more water. You can help seal the lid of the Dutch oven by smearing flour paste around the rim of the lid.

Roast Teal

The recipe below calls for 4 birds, but the measures can be increased as needed. You'll need at least 1 teal per person; I want 2 if they are available.

      4 teal, dressed whole
      3 Granny Smith apples, chopped
      4 slices bacon
      bacon drippings
      salt and pepper

Preheat the oven to 450 degrees. Rub the ducks with bacon drippings, and sprinkle them inside and out with salt and pepper. Stuff the birds loosely with chopped apples, then place them, breast up, on a rack in a roasting pan. Cut the bacon strips in half and place a piece on each side of the duck breasts. Roast in the center of the oven for 15 minutes, then baste with the pan drippings. Roast for 5 or 6 more minutes and baste again. Keep this up until the bacon is ready to eat.

Wild Duck Purloo

This variation of pilaf is a standard dish in some rural areas, and it can be cooked with squirrel, rabbit, chicken, or what have you. The amount of meat isn't critical, and the dish is often served on the side of a major meat dish.

1 wild duck
6 cups water
1 cup long-grain rice
salt and black pepper
2 bay leaves
dried red pepper pod

Skin and draw the bird, reduce it to pieces, and put it, along with the giblets, into a pot. Add the water, bay leaves, salt, pepper, and pepper pod. Bring to a boil, cover, reduce the heat, and simmer until the duck is tender. Add the rice, bring to a boil, reduce the heat, and simmer for at least 25 minutes. This dish will be on the soupy side. If you want it more solid, simmer it uncovered until the water evaporates, or reduce the water added to the duck pieces at the outset. This is a good, substantial dish to cook in camp. I like to eat it from bowls along with soda crackers.

Stir-Fried Duck

I confess that I really don't follow a recipe for stir-fried duck. Although I have cooked the dish a dozen times, the ingredients often depend on what I have on hand. I might use a little hoisin sauce, for example, if I've got some handy. Any good stir-fry cook can easily come up with ingredients. Of course, the basic technique is pretty much the same. First heat the oil, then add the oil flavoring (such as ginger root or garlic). Next, cook the meat and vegetables. Then add sauce ingredients and, sometimes, a sauce thickener, and cover the wok or skillet for 1 minute or so. With duck, it's best to use only the breast fillets, which should be sliced thinly across the grain.

In any case, here's a very easy stir-fry dish that will work even with tough ducks. It calls for kiwi fruit, which is a natural tenderizer. The celery tops are optional, but they are often used in oriental cookery, although they are usually thrown out in America. I like to make use of them. Of course, you can also chop and stir-fry some of the celery stalks to serve with the duck, if you like.

duck breasts
peanut oil
kiwi fruit
celery tops, chopped (optional)
salt and pepper

Cut the breast fillets crosswise into strips about ⅛ inch thick. (Partly frozen meat is easier to slice.) Put the meat into a nonmetallic container. After peeling the kiwi, mash or puree it. (Use ½ kiwi for each duck.) Add the fruit pulp to the duck, tossing to coat all sides of the meat. Let stand for 30 minutes to let the enzymes work. Heat the oil. Sprinkle the meat with salt and pepper, then stir-fry with celery tops for 2 or 3 minutes, just until the meat is medium rare. Do not overcook. Serve with steamed or stir-fried vegetables and rice.

Note: This is a good recipe for camp cooking. The kiwi keeps well and is easy to transport, and the tenderizing enzymes can work wonders on tough birds. This technique can also be used with wild goose.

Duck or Goose Jerky

Duck or goose breast can be used to make jerky, and any good recipe for beef jerky will work. I like to keep mine simple. Skin the breast, trim off all fat, and slice the meat with the grain into pieces no thicker than ¼ inch. The slicing is easier if the fillets are partly frozen. Put the duck into a nonmetallic container, cover with soy sauce, and add some crushed garlic. Marinate overnight in the refrigerator. Pat the duck pieces dry, then place them across the racks in your oven. Turn the oven to the lowest setting and leave them for 3 hours or longer, depending largely on the temperature of the oven. It's best to leave the oven door ajar, which will help keep the temperature low. Check the jerky from time to time, and take it out of the oven when the pieces are dry.

If you live in a dry climate without many bugs, you may choose to make jerky the old-fashioned way. Simply hang the strips of meat out on the clothesline during the day. Bring it into the house at night, then hang again the next day. This slow-drying process makes better jerky, in my opinion. Other people will want to speed up the process, using even a microwave oven to make jerky.

In any case, jerky that isn't eaten right away can be put into airtight jars and stored until needed. Refrigeration isn't necessary. After being prepared, the jerky can be gnawed or soaked in water for use in soups and stews.

Grilled Duck

Here's a recipe that I use with 2 mallard-size ducks, but it can also be used with smaller birds. No marinade is required if the ducks are young and haven't been feeding extensively on fish. Overcooking the birds, however, will make them tough and unpalatable.

2 mallards or several smaller ducks
1 cup cooking oil
½ cup red wine vinegar
¼ cup soy sauce
¼ cup chopped celery tops or cilantro
4 cloves garlic, crushed
salt and pepper to taste

Rig for grilling. In a saucepan, mix the oil, vinegar, soy sauce, celery tops, garlic, salt, and pepper. Bring to heat and simmer for about 10 minutes. Keep warm. Grease the rack and grill the ducks close to the heat, turning once, until they are medium rare. Baste with the mixture several times while grilling.

Good Ol' Boy Ducks

Over the years, I've seen many recipes for wrapping bird breasts and chunks of venison

Watch for Wood Ducks

One of the most beautiful of American birds, the wood duck is also a great success story. It was almost extinct in 1915, according to the *Louisiana Conservationist,* but today it is the number one duck taken by hunters in the Atlantic Flyway—and number two by hunters in the Mississippi Flyway!

with bacon, then grilling them over coals. The technique makes for good eating—and is about as foolproof as grilling can get. Basically, the meat is done when the bacon looks ready to eat. Of course, the bacon also keeps the meat from drying out too much.

> duck breast fillets
> bacon at room temperature
> lemon-pepper seasoning
> paprika
> wood chips

Build a hot fire in a covered grill, or heat up the gas grill. Sprinkle each duck breast with lemon-pepper seasoning, then wrap it with a strip of bacon, and secure at each end with round toothpicks or skewers. Sprinkle again with lemon-pepper seasoning and paprika. Add some green or soaked wood chips to the edge of the coals, then cook breasts under closed hood for about 10 minutes on each side. Raise the hood, sprinkle again with lemon-pepper seasoning and paprika, and grill until the bacon is ready to eat. If in doubt, cut into a fillet at the thickest point before serving. The meat should be juicy but not running red.

Variations: Cut the meat into chunks and wrap each with ½ strip of bacon. You can string bacon-wrapped chunks on skewers, kabob fashion.

Duck Giblet Delight

Traditionally, giblet gravy is served on dressing along with a turkey or other fowl. Duck makes very good giblet gravy, but the meat in main-dish duck is so rich that dressing and gravy really aren't called for. The best bet is to save the giblets for a next-day treat. Modify the term "giblets" in the recipe to include not only necks, hearts, liver, and gizzards, but also any leftover bony duck meat, including the goodies from inside the back cavity. If the neck or other parts are included, they should be boiled until tender, boned, and used to help make up the 3 cups of giblets. If necessary, add chicken or pheasant giblets.

> 3 cups duck giblets
> 2 cups duck (or chicken) broth (divided)
> 1 medium to large onion, diced
> 3 hard-boiled chicken eggs, sliced
> ¼ cup flour
> salt and pepper
> rice or biscuits (cooked separately)

In a saucepan, boil the gizzards for 1 hour or so, or until they are quite tender. Add the rest of the giblets, and cook for about 20 minutes or until tender. Chop all the giblets and drain. In a large skillet, heat ¼ cup of broth, slowly stir in the flour, and reduce the heat. Add the rest of the broth, along with some salt and pepper. Mix in the onion, eggs, and diced giblets. Bring to a bubble, reduce the heat to very low, and simmer for 20 minutes, stirring a time or two. Serve over rice or biscuit halves.

Stir-Fried Snow Goose

If you've got geese and a wok, you may want to try this stir-fry recipe, which I have adapted from a booklet *Wild Game Recipes* from the North Carolina Wildlife Resources Commission. It was submitted to that publication by Dorothy Donnelly, who apparently used an electric wok. If you have a different sort of wok, use it instead, provided that it is a heavy-duty

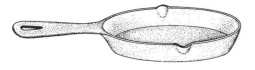

job designed to cook with very hot oil, which may damage some of the thin teflon-coated models. You can also use a cast-iron skillet. The recipe calls for breast fillets, but be sure to save the rest of the bird for gumbo or soup. In the ingredients list, I have doubled the amount of mushrooms. Cut them back to 4 ounces if you so desire.

4 goose breast fillets
8 ounces fresh broccoli
8 ounces water chestnuts
8 ounces fresh mushrooms
3 green onions with part of tops
2 tablespoons peanut oil
1 tablespoon sherry (or sake)
1 tablespoon soy sauce
1 tablespoon cornstarch
rice (cooked separately)

For stir-frying, it's best to get everything ready to cook before you heat the oil. Slice the goose breast fillets, onions, mushrooms, and water chestnuts into thin strips. Cut the broccoli into 3-inch lengths. Blend the soy sauce, sherry, and cornstarch together until smooth. Set the wok to 420 degrees. Heat 1 tablespoon of the oil, then quickly stir-fry the goose breast strips for 2 or 3 minutes. Quickly drain and set these on a heated platter. Add the remaining peanut oil to the wok. Stir-fry the broccoli for 2 minutes. Add the onions, mushrooms, and water chestnuts, stirring and cooking for another 2 minutes. Stir in the goose breast strips. Add the sauce and lower the heat, stirring and cooking all ingredients together until

the sauce thickens. Serve hot with wild grain and brown rice. Feeds 4 to 6, depending on appetite and rice.

Apricot Goose

Here's an excellent recipe for wild goose. I don't know its origin, but I got it from a lady in Florida. After plucking and drawing the goose, record its dressed weight.

1 wild goose
6 slices smoked bacon
bacon drippings
liquid smoke (optional)
3 cups soft bread crumbs
1 cup boiling water
1 cup dried apricots, chopped
1 tart apple, peeled, cored, and diced
1 medium onion, chopped
juice of 1 lemon
salt and pepper

Pluck and draw the goose for stuffing. Put it onto a flat surface, then sprinkle it inside and out with lemon juice, salt, and pepper. Preheat the oven to 325 degrees. To make the stuffing, add a small amount of bacon drippings to a large skillet. Sauté the onion for 5 or 6 minutes. Stir in the apple, apricots, bread crumbs, salt, and pepper. Stuff the goose with this mixture, then close the opening with round toothpicks or skewers.

Soak a piece of cheesecloth (enough to wrap the goose with a double thickness) in some bacon drippings. Drape bacon strips over the breast of the goose.

Place the goose, breast up, on a rack in a suitable baking pan, then put it into the oven. Mix a basting sauce with 1 part bacon grease and 1 part liquid smoke. Roast the bird for 20 minutes per pound of dressed weight, basting several times. At the end of the calculated cooking period, pour 1 cup of boiling water into the pan, cover, and cook for 30 more minutes. Feeds 3 or 4.

Baked Goose Breast

Here's a recipe that I made up one day from scratch, based on the fact that I had some sliced portabella mushrooms and a goose breast that needed to be cooked.

> 2 goose breast fillets
> 6 ounces sliced portabella mushrooms
> onion slices
> 1 strip thin bacon
> 1 cup red wine
> salt and freshly ground black pepper
> 2 bay leaves
> water as needed

Grease a small casserole dish that has a lid. I use a 7-by-7-inch Corning Ware dish. Preheat the oven to 325 degrees. Place the sliced onion and the bay leaves on the bottom of the dish. Arrange the goose breasts over the onions and bay leaves, skin side up. Place ½ strip of bacon on each breast. Arrange the mushrooms on and around the duck breasts. Sprinkle with salt and pepper, then pour in the wine and a little water. Put the dish into the center of the oven and bake for 1½ hours. Remove the breasts and slice them across the grain. Return to the dish, add a little water if needed, cover, and bake for 30 minutes. Serve the sliced goose breast and gravy with rice or mashed potatoes, steamed vegetables, and hot sourdough bread.

Note: If desired, thicken the gravy with a little paste made with water and cornstarch, stirred in very slowly until the gravy thickens to suit your taste.

Goose Breast with Orange Marmalade

For this recipe, thank Art Boebinger and the Kentucky Department of Fish and Wildlife's magazine, *Happy Hunting Ground.*

> 1 large goose breast
> 1 package brown gravy mix
> 1 can frozen orange juice concentrate (6-ounce size)
> 2 tablespoons orange marmalade
> ¼ cup flour
> salt and pepper
> orange slices (for garnish)

Preheat the oven to 375 degrees. Combine all the ingredients except the goose breast in roasting pan or ovenproof dish of suitable size. Place the goose breast in the pan, then turn it to wet all sides. Cover the pan with aluminum foil. Bake in the center of the oven for 1½ to 2 hours, or until the meat is tender. Slice the meat, placing it on a platter. Scrape the pan with a wooden spatula, stir up the pan juices, and pour over the sliced goose meat. Serve hot. Garnish with orange slices.

Native American Stuffed Goose

Here's an interesting recipe that I have adapted from *Native Harvests,* by Barrie Kavasch. The ingredients call for 1 teaspoon of leaves from the spicebush. This is a native American plant that was widely used by the Indians and early settlers—but usually it's the dried berries that are used. The original recipe also calls for dill-weed, which I doubt was a native American ingredient. Moreover, it calls for 1 tablespoon of dillweed, which is enough, I think, to over-power the spicebush. I don't think that dillweed and cranberries go together too nicely, but I'll have to admit, my Indian lineage (25 percent) goes back to the Cherokee, not to the northern tribes that would have had cranberries in great plenty. So, I have omitted the dillweed. Add it if you are so inclined.

The Bird
   1 wild goose
   2 cups apple cider
The Stuffing
   goose giblets
   2 cups cranberries, chopped
   2 cups fine white cornmeal
   4 ounces chopped fresh mushrooms
   1 tablespoon honey
   1 teaspoon chopped fresh spicebush leaves
   water

Simmer the goose giblets in boiling water for 40 minutes. Drain and chop the giblets. Measure out 1½ cups of the broth, return it to the pot, and add the chopped giblets. (If you don't have 1½ cups of broth, add some water.) Thoroughly mix in the rest of the stuffing ingredients.

Preheat the oven to 350 degrees. Stuff and truss the goose, place it breast side up in a roasting pan, and roast it uncovered in the oven for 4 hours, basting from time to time with apple cider and pan drippings.

Remove the goose, placing it onto a serving platter. Scrape the pan with a wooden spatula, mixing the pan dredgings with the drippings. Place the pan over a stove burner, tilting it a little to one end to concentrate the liquid. Slowly add a little paste made with cornstarch and water, heating and stirring until you have a smooth gravy. Serve the goose hot, along with the gravy, wild rice, stuffing, and good American vegetables such as beans, corn, squash, potatoes, and Jerusalem artichokes.

27

BLACKBIRDS, MARSH BIRDS, AND OTHERS

Always rather frisky from a culinary viewpoint, the French people have made good use of various birds in their cuisine. Although the woodcock has always been high on the gourmet's list of game birds, a surprisingly large number of other birds were once eaten in France. I'm talking birds, not necessarily game birds. That's right—sparrows and songbirds and wading birds. Anyone who doubts this should browse through an old edition of *Larousse Gastronomique*. Under thrush we find thirteen recipes. Of course, one thrush is not as good, gastronomically speaking, as another; the song thrush, for example, is more highly regarded whenever it has grown fat on grapes. The ancient Romans fattened thrushes for their private tables and even for the market, feeding them a mixture of millet, crushed figs, and flour.

Larks? *Larousse* lists nine recipes. The ortolan (also nine recipes) was especially esteemed as

table fare, partly because it contains lots of tasty fat, making it ideal for grilling on a spit. Among the wading birds, plovers were highly regarded and were cooked undrawn, as were doves and larks. So many small birds were eaten that the French had a catchall culinary term for them: *petits-pieds.*

Of course, birds were also eaten in other European countries, and eastward into the steppes of Asia. The taste for birds was also brought to America, where the immigrants found plenty of carrier pigeons and other tasty fare. Some of the settlers ate just about everything that flew. There are old recipes even for birds of prey, and I have known people during my lifetime who maintained that owls were the best of all birds for the table. My uncle Alec Stinson, when disputing the high reputation of robins, once told me that the brown thrasher is one of the best eating birds, closely

Marsh Hens

Hunting for the long, skinny marsh hen (clapper rail or *Rallus longirostris waynei*) requires stamina and good eyesight. The thin, grayish brown bird with a needle-like beak will scurry through the marshes, duck underwater, and even hold itself under by a weed to avoid hunters. Its slow, low flight has prompted a regulation against the use of a motor in the marsh. But those who cherish the delectable meat in brown gravy with onions will paddle and brave the cold autumn winds at high tide to bring home a clapper rail.

—*The South Carolina Wildlife Cookbook*

followed by the yellowhammer (the state bird of Alabama). The early settlers of Georgia and Florida were especially fond of the limpkin, a marsh bird that is now highly protected. In fact, it is important to check the law these days before eating any bird in the United States and elsewhere. Last fall during dove season, for example, I saw a several ground doves piled up in the bed of a pickup truck parked outside a Beer, Bait, and Baloney store down in Sopchoppy, Florida; apparently the two fellows in the truck didn't realize that even ground doves are now protected in some areas.

In any case, just about all the world's twelve thousand species of birds are edible and have been eaten at one place or another. For sheer numbers, the auks and other seabirds that nest on islands or along the northern coasts of the Atlantic would probably take the prize. (One of these, the flightless great auk, now extinct, was herded and forced to board ships via the gang-plank.) Some of the seabirds have been exploited commercially; the short-tailed shearwater, for example, also known as the mutton bird, has even been canned extensively in Tasmania. Also, eggs of seabirds have been used in large numbers by American bakeries; during the nineteenth century, for example, eggs of the sooty tern were taken from Dry Tortugas and sold to bakers not by the dozen but by the gallon.

For culinary variety, however, the Indians and early settlers of the Amazon basin and the savannas of Brazil had the best of it. This vast region is blessed with an outstanding variety of toothsome birds. The most highly prized of these might well be the macuca (a species of tinamou), which grows almost as large as a wild turkey and has bluish flesh, sweetened by its diet of wild fruits and seeds. It is sometimes stuffed with Brazil nuts and stewed until tender, then served with a gravy made by thickening the pan liquid and adding the juice of a sour orange (similar to the Seville orange).

There are several species of trumpeters in Brazil, and some of these get as large as barnyard chickens. In fact, some of the trumpeters resemble the guinea fowl of West Africa, a bird that was brought to South America and that now grows in the wild. Even the parrots, macaws, and parakeets make good eating, although some of these grow to be old and tough and, I say, downright quarrelsome. The Brazilians also enjoyed various sorts of quail, doves and pigeons, larks, and even mockingbirds.

In any case, modern Americans are more restricted in that many of our birds are protected by law. Even so, most of us don't take advantage of legal shooting and fine eating provided by some of our birds. Some suggestions follow.

Marinated Clapper Rails

Clapper rails or marsh hens can be very good, but it is usually better to marinate them before cooking for company of unknown tastes. This recipe should suit everybody.

The Birds
 8 or 10 clapper rails
 cooking oil
 salt and pepper
 flour
 water
The Marinade
 ¾ cup white wine Worcestershire sauce
 ¼ cup white wine vinegar

Dress the birds, cut them in half length-wise, and put them into a nonmetallic container. Mix the marinade, pour it over the birds, cover, and refrigerate overnight, turning several times.

Drain the birds, salt and pepper them, and shake them in a bag with flour. Heat ½ inch of cooking oil in a large skillet or stove-top Dutch oven, then brown the bird halves a few at a time on medium high heat. Pour off most of the oil, then fit the birds into the skillet. Add

1 cup of water, bring to a boil, then reduce the heat, cover the pan, and simmer for 30 minutes, or until the birds are very tender. Add a little water from time to time if needed, and turn the birds so that the bottoms won't burn. Serve with French bread and steamed carrots or other vegetables. Feeds 3 to 6.

Sautéed Sora Rails

Here's a good, simple recipe from Don Maris as published in *The Maine Way:*

"Pluck rails after cutting off head, feet, and wings. Split up back and clean. Open ('flatten') and sauté in butter, bacon fat, or a little oil. Sprinkle with onion salt or garlic salt if desired. Cook 10 to 15 minutes, splash with white wine or good hard cider, cook a couple more minutes, and serve with remaining liquid. Good with dark rice and currant jelly."

Pat's Pan-Fried Rail in Giblet Gravy

I found this recipe in an article by Vin Venters in the September 1993 issue of *Wildlife in North Carolina.* Interestingly, he included a cast-iron skillet in the list of ingredients—and only partly in jest. Many people believe that cast iron imparts a distinct flavor to food, and some even say that food cooked in cast iron is healthier for you. Although the article listed the skillet in the ingredients, I have finagled with it a little because of format problems. Here, however, is exactly what was said about this ingredient: "1 large well-seasoned (blackened) cast-iron skillet with lid. (Warning: do not try this recipe with European cookware or anything Teflon. A seasoned iron fry skillet is essential, your grandma's is preferable.)" Here's what else you'll need:

4 to 6 young marsh hens
1 cup flour
1 pound bacon, fried, and reserve the grease
1 large onion, finely diced
bay leaves
salt and pepper
dash of Worcestershire sauce
various spices to taste (a little sherry and garlic are okay if desired, but in excess verges on foppery)
rice (cooked separately)

"Separate young birds from older birds. Young birds generally are smaller, lack full plumage, and have lighter gray colored legs. Young birds are tender and should be cooked together.

"Skin and clean birds by splitting down the back with poultry shears. Breasts are thin and legs have the most meat. Save neck, gizzards, livers, and heart. Clean, skin, and mince gizzards, adding them with necks and hearts to a pan of water. Season with spices to taste, bring to boil, and simmer 30 minutes or so. Scrape meat from neck bones and mince giblets when tender.

"In the meantime, brown onion in bacon grease. Remove onion and add to giblet sauce.

"Lightly flour birds inside and out, adding salt and pepper as desired. Butterfly birds to open chest cavity. Brown in bacon fat in the skillet over medium/low heat, turning birds often to prevent burning. Remove marsh hens to a warm plate. Pour off most of the bacon grease and add giblets and liquid to skillet. Reduce liquid to gravy and add cornstarch to thicken, if needed. The well-seasoned pan gives your gravy that dark, rich flavor.

"Serve marsh hens with gravy, over rice, with buttermilk biscuits. Crumble cooked bacon over the top, and leave plenty of elbow room!

"Older marsh hens can be cooked in a similar fashion, but must be parboiled after browning. Add giblets and enough chicken stock or water to cover browned birds and simmer with lid on skillet until they are tender. Older birds are tougher, says Pat, but 'they make better gravy.'"

Fricassee of Marsh Bird

Some marsh birds tend to have a rather strong flavor, at least as compared with quail. The baking soda and lemon juice in this recipe will help cut any undesirable flavor or odor. This basic recipe can be used with rails, gallinules, fish-fed ducks, or coot.

marsh birds for approximately 2 cups chopped meat
1 quart water
¾ cup minced onion
¾ cup minced fresh mushrooms
2 tablespoons butter
1 tablespoon baking soda
juice of 1 lemon
chicken broth
salt and pepper
1 bay leaf
rice (cooked separately)

Skin and draw the birds, put them into a nonmetallic container, and marinate overnight with a solution of 1 quart water and 1 tablespoon baking soda. Drain and rinse the birds, put them into a pot, and simmer them in a little water, with the bay leaf, until they are tender. Drain the birds, cool, and pull the meat off the bones with a fork. (If you use whole birds, the breast should be chopped.) Sprinkle the bird meat with lemon juice and refrigerate for several hours.

Heat the butter in a skillet, then sauté the onion and mushrooms for 3 or 4 minutes. Add the marsh bird meat, salt, and pepper. Barely cover with chicken broth. Bring to a quick boil, reduce the heat to very low, and simmer for 1 hour, stirring from time to time and adding a little more chicken broth if needed. Spoon the mixture over rice. Feeds 4.

Purple Gallinule & Fresh Mushrooms

This recipe makes a tasty gravy, which I like to spoon over, or sop with, French bread.

    8 purple gallinules
    1 can cream of mushroom soup (10¾-
        ounce size)
    12 ounces fresh mushrooms
    1 cup red wine vinegar
    1 medium to large onion, chopped
    salt and pepper
    water

Place the birds in a nonmetallic container. Mix vinegar and 1 cup water, pour over the birds, and refrigerate overnight. When you are ready to cook, rinse the birds and put them into a stove-top Dutch oven or other suitable container. Add the mushrooms, onion, salt, and pepper. Mix the mushroom soup with 1 can of water, and add to the pot. Bring to a light boil, reduce the heat to very low, cover tightly, and

simmer for about 4 hours. Add a little water if needed. Add the red wine for the last few minutes of cooking. Feeds 3 to 6.

Chinese Crane with Parsley Rice

Here's an excellent dish that I adapted from *Sportsman's Gourmet Guide,* by Henrietta Goplen.

    1 sandhill crane, breast and thighs
    1 cup chopped celery with tops
    water
    3 tablespoons cooking oil
    3 tablespoons flour
    2 tablespoons soy sauce
    2 tablespoons dried parsley
    1⅓ cups dry rice

To cook the rice, heat 2⅔ cups water, add the rice and parsley, bring to a boil, reduce the heat, cover tightly, and simmer for 20 minutes without peeking. Slice the meat thinly. (If the sandhill has been frozen, slice it before it completely thaws out.) Heat the cooking oil in large skillet. Dredge the meat in flour, then brown on high heat. Add ½ cup water and soy sauce. Bring to a quick boil, reduce the heat, and simmer for 15 minutes. Add the celery, cover, and simmer for another 10 minutes. Spoon the rice into serving bowls, then top with the meat and gravy. Feeds 4.

Sandhill Stir-Fry

This recipe works best with breast fingers, prepared as directed in the previous recipe. The sesame oil used in this recipe is the Chinese type, which is used mostly for flavoring instead of cooking. The sesame cooking oil doesn't have the same burnt flavor.

1 pound sandhill crane breast fingers
½ cup soy sauce
½ cup sake, dry vermouth, or sherry
peanut oil
1 teaspoon sesame oil (Chinese-style)
2 slices fresh ginger root
pepper
stir-fry vegetables
rice (cooked separately)

Put the meat fingers into a nonmetallic container, then mix in the soy sauce, sesame oil, wine, and ginger. Marinate for several hours. Drain the meat, retaining the marinade. Heat some peanut oil in a wok or cast-iron skillet, fry the ginger root for several minutes, then quickly stir-fry the meat fingers for about 2 minutes. Remove the meat, then stir-fry the vegetables for a few minutes. Put the meat back into the wok, pour in the reserved marinade, cover, and steam until the vegetables are tender. Discard the ginger root. Serve with rice.

Sandhill Fingers

Here's a delightful way to prepare crane breasts, and they can be served as a main course or as an appetizer or side dish. Be sure to save the rest of the bird for a gumbo or fricassee recipe.

crane breast
butter
lemon juice
flour
salt and pepper

Sandhill Crane

Today, large numbers of sandhill cranes wing over the prairies from Canada into Mexico. Along the way, several states offer hunting seasons for the bird. If you hunt the sandhill, watch out for your eyes when you go after wounded birds. They can stand tall, having both long legs and long necks. Adults are gray with black wing tips. Young birds are somewhat brownish.

The sandhill feeds mostly on grain, and its mild meat can be excellent table fare. An adult bird, well fed, weighs about 4 to 4½ pounds when dressed. The sandhill's wide wings contain very little meat, and the long legs are full of tendons. It's best to fillet out the breast and perhaps the thighs, then save the rest for stewing.

Skin and fillet the breast meat, then cut it into fingers, lengthwise, about ¾ inch thick. Put the fingers into a nonmetallic bowl, sprinkle them with lemon juice, and refrigerate for several hours. Drain the fingers, sprinkle them with salt and pepper, and shake them in a bag with flour. Heat the butter in a skillet, then sauté the fingers on medium high heat until they are browned. Do not overcook.

Dr. Frye's Favorite Coot

Some years ago, I got hold of an interesting news release from the state of Florida. They've got a lot of coots down there, and maybe they

Coot Liver and Gizzard Pilau

A coot liver and gizzard pilau is made simply by cooking available coot livers and gizzards with enough rice to feed as many people as need feeding!

—Marjorie Kinnan Rawlings
Cross Creek Cookery

wanted them thinned out for one reason or another. This recipe no doubt helped! It was billed as Dr. O. E. Frye's favorite hunting camp recipe for coot. Head of the Fresh Water Fish and Game Commission at that time, Dr. Frye said, "It is indeed unfortunate that more sportsmen don't add a few coots to their waterfowl bag. The daily bag limit is a generous 15 per day (check the current bag limits) and the coot may be found throughout Florida. Bagging a coot is not much of a challenge to the average gunner and this, perhaps, may be one reason sportsmen tend to overlook the bird." The news release made it clear that the secret to the coot recipe is in skinning the bird and removing all the fat.

coot breasts (skinned) and giblets
cooking oil
flour
vinegar
water
salt and pepper

Skin the birds and remove the meat from either side of the breast bone with a fillet knife. Save the liver and gizzard. Split the gizzard, turn it inside out, and clean. Make a solution with water, vinegar, and salt in a glass or crockery container (see note below). Put the coot breasts into a nonmetallic container, pour the solution over them, and marinate overnight. Keep the gizzards and livers in a refrigerator or ice chest.

When you are ready to cook, boil the livers for a few minutes and set aside. Boil the gizzards for 1 hour and set aside. Salt and pepper the coot breasts, roll them in flour, and fry them in hot cooking oil. Drain. Dice the livers and gizzards, then add to the skillet, stirring about with a wooden spoon or spatula. Add a little water, bring to a boil, and thicken with a thick paste made with flour and water, stirring all the while until you have a smooth gravy. Serve the coot breasts and gravy with biscuits and hot coffee.

Variations: Dr. Frye's recipe is very good, but in my opinion it will be improved by adding a handful of minced fresh onion to the skillet with the coot breasts and gizzards. And, if you've got it to spare, a little red wine won't hurt a thing.

Note: The Florida recipe didn't say how much vinegar to add to the marinade. I suggest 1 tablespoon salt and 1 cup vinegar per quart of water. If you plan to cook this recipe in camp but don't want to lug a jug of vinegar along, pack a box of ordinary baking soda and use 1 tablespoon salt and 1 tablespoon soda per quart. (The next recipe recommends only 1 teaspoon of soda per quart of water, however.)

New England Coot Stew

Here's a recipe from Colton H. Bridges of Grafton, Massachusetts, which I have adapted from the Ducks Unlimited *After the Hunt Cookbook.*

4 or 5 coot breasts
5 medium onions, chopped
4 cups chopped tomatoes
½ cup butter
¼ cup red wine
¼ cup cider vinegar
2 or 3 beef bouillon cubes
1 tablespoon salt
1 teaspoon baking soda
¼ teaspoon pepper
⅛ teaspoon marjoram
flour
2 bay leaves
water

Mix the baking soda into 1 quart of water. Skin the coot breasts, trim off any fat, and cut them into bite-size pieces; put the pieces into a nonmetallic container, cover with the soda solution, and marinate overnight in the refrigerator. Rinse and drain the coot breast pieces, and shake them in a bag with flour seasoned with a little salt and pepper.

Heat the butter in a cast-iron pot or Dutch oven, then brown the coot pieces. Add 1 quart of water and the bay leaves. Bring to a boil. Stir in the bouillon cubes. Add the onions, tomatoes, salt, pepper, marjoram, wine, and cider vinegar. Cover and simmer for 2 hours. Feeds 4 or 5.

Ocala Coot

My sister once sent me a little recipe book, full of advertisements, from Ocala, Florida. I've fished the flats of Orange Lake, just north of Ocala, a number of times, as well as Lake Weir, south of Ocala, and in the Big Scrub to the east of town. Thus I can verify that there is no shortage of coots in that part of Florida. In fact,

I even caught a coot on Lake Weir with hook and line while fishing for bream!

The Meat
  2 coots
  salt and pepper
The Marinade
  ¾ cup fresh lemon or lime juice
  ¾ cup chicken stock
  1 medium to large onion, sliced
  1 stalk celery with tops, sliced
  1 tablespoon chopped fresh parsley
  1 bay leaf
The Sauce
  1 small to medium onion, chopped
  ¾ cup tomato juice
  ¼ cup catsup
  ¼ cup butter or margarine
  salt and pepper

Combine all the marinade ingredients. Skin the coots, draw them, and sprinkle salt and pepper inside and out. Put the coots into a nonmetallic container, pour the marinade over them, cover, and refrigerate for 2 days, turning occasionally.

When you're ready to cook, preheat the oven to 350 degrees. Combine the sauce ingredients. Remove the coots from the marinade, pat them dry with paper towels, and dip them into the sauce. Arrange the coots in a suitable baking pan or casserole dish. Pour the rest of the sauce over them, cover, and bake for 1 hour, basting several times with the pan liquid. Feeds 2.

Crow Bradford Angier

Here's a crow recipe and considerable opinion from Bradford Angier's *Gourmet Cooking for Free.*

Hunting Crow

Hunters should read their state game laws carefully, looking for off-beat and off-season action. In Missouri, for example, the crow season is open until the first week in March (at the time of this writing), providing some late-season shooting and, hopefully, some bonus fare for the table.

Anyone who has ever tried to stalk a crow knows that these wary creatures are difficult to bag. The successful hunter will usually depend on the skillful use of crow calls and decoys. Often, owl decoys will work better than crow decoys simply because they are natural enemies. But check your game laws before resorting to electronic crow calls or live owl decoys.

"Tasting like chicken with savory overtones of duck, the dark meat of the crow is well worth eating. If you've too many for deep freeze and friends, even when proffered under the more alluring name of rook, why not feast on the breasts?

"Sprinkle with salt and freshly ground black pepper. Melt a liberal amount of butter in a preferably heavy iron frypan and heat it as much as possible without scorching. Put in the breasts and cover. Lower the heat to moderate and cook about 7 minutes until brown on one side. Then turn and bronze the other.

"Add a cup of sherry, re-cover, and simmer until the meat is tender, adding more wine if necessary. Then move the breasts to a warm place. Spoon off all possible fat. Bring the wine and juice to a bubble, stirring and scraping, and add a tablespoon of heavy cream to bind and thicken. Pour over the meat and serve. By this time the air will be permeated with the fragrant promise of wonderfully good things to eat."

Crow Hash

Here's a recipe that may change your mind about "eating crow."

> 4 or 5 crows
> 1 can chicken broth (10 ¾-ounce size)
> 8 to 12 ounces fresh mushrooms, sliced
> 1 large onion, sliced
> ¼ cup butter
> juice of ½ lemon
> flour
> salt and pepper
> bay leaf
> water
> milk
> toast or rice (cooked separately)

Skin and draw the crows, trim away any fat, and cut them into quarters. Put the pieces into a nonmetallic container, cover with milk, and refrigerate for 12 hours. Drain the birds, cover with fresh milk, and refrigerate for another 12 hours. Drain and rinse the bird quarters, put them into a suitable pot, cover with water, add a bay leaf, bring to a boil, reduce heat, cover, and simmer until the birds are tender. Drain the birds, then remove the meat from the bones using fork and fingers. Slice the meat against the grain.

In a large skillet, heat the butter. Sauté the mushrooms and onions for 5 minutes. Add the crow meat, chicken broth, and lemon juice, along with some salt and pepper. Simmer for 20 minutes. Thicken with a paste made with a little flour and water, stirring it in a little at a time. Serve over rice or crisp toast. Feeds 4.

Fried Crow Breast

 6 crow breasts (12 fillets)
 1 medium to large onion, chopped
 flour
 peanut oil
 ginger root
 salt and pepper

Skin the birds and fillet out the breasts, saving the rest of the birds for a fricassee or stew. Heat ½ inch of oil in a large skillet. Add 3 or 4 slices of ginger root, cooking on low for 10 minutes. Discard the ginger and increase the heat to medium high. Salt and pepper the crow breasts to taste, shake in a bag of flour, and quickly brown in hot oil. Drain the crow breasts. Brown and drain the onion. Pour off most of the oil, then add 1 tablespoon of flour to the skillet, stirring with a wooden spoon or spatula. Pour in a little water, stirring as you go, until you have a thin gravy. Put crow breasts and onion back into the skillet, cover, and simmer for 1 hour. Serve hot, spooning the gravy over rice or biscuit halves. Feeds 2 or 3.

Blackbird Pie

Actually, any small bird can be used in this recipe. Before gathering ingredients for this recipe, however, be warned that red-wing blackbirds and other species may be protected by law in some areas. On the other hand, some other blackbirds, or ricebirds, can be taken legally and in large numbers with no closed season. You may be surprised. Often, shooting ricebirds will be a help to farmers, and these off-season birds may open up a whole new ball game for you.

In any case, this pie recipe is one of my favorites. My mother cooked it for me years ago whenever the blackbirds or ricebirds started flocking on our farm. Often a single shot from a 12-gauge would drop enough birds for a pie. I don't know the proper way to clean these birds, but I merely pull back the skin, lift the breast plate with my finger, and cut the wings off with kitchen shears. No knife is required.

The recipe below calls for 24 small black-

Four and Twenty Blackbirds

In America, large flocks of blackbirds of one sort or another sometimes do considerable damage to the yield of grain fields, and often cause problems when large numbers roost in town squares. All of these birds can provide good eating. The Fish and Game Departments of some states have very liberal laws concerning these birds and have encouraged hunters to go after them—but with little success.

In Corsica, the blackbird feeds heavily on berries that grow on the lower slopes of the mountains. These plump blackbirds have a very good reputation as food, and they are the main ingredient in a Corsican specialty, *pâté de mereles*. The dish is prepared with juniper berries and a local spirit flavored with myrtle.

 —Adapted from
 Edible Plants and Animals

birds. If you've got larger birds, such as crows, skin them, fillet out each side of the breast, and cut them into 24 thumb-size pieces.

24 blackbirds, breasted
8 slices of bacon
4 medium potatoes
4 medium carrots
10 green onions with part of tops
8 ounces fresh mushrooms
flour
water
1 cup sherry
3 hard-boiled chicken eggs
salt and pepper
pie pastry

Fry the bacon in a stove-top Dutch oven until crisp. Remove the bacon and set aside on paper towels. Salt and pepper the bird breasts and shake them in a bag with flour. In the bacon drippings, stir-fry the birds for 5 or 6 minutes on high heat. (Do not overcook.) Put the bacon back into the pot and barely cover the meat with water. Cover, reduce the heat, and simmer for 1 hour. While waiting, peel the potatoes and cut them into slices ¼ inch thick. Scrape the carrots and cut them into ¼-inch wheels. Peel the green onions and cut them into 1-inch lengths, along with about half of the green tops. (If you don't have green onions, try a medium onion diced and a few sprigs of green stuff, such as parsley.) Slice the mushrooms.

After the birds have simmered for 1 hour or so, mix in all the vegetables and the sherry. Add enough water to almost cover the mixture. Bring to a boil, reduce heat, cover, and simmer for 30 minutes. While waiting, preheat the oven to 400 degrees. After simmering the pot for 30 minutes, carefully slice the boiled eggs and add the slices to the pot, making a layer. Cut the pie

pastry into strips. Crisscross the strips on top, leaving some diamond-shaped holes. Then bake the pie, uncovered, for 20 minutes, or until the top of the pastry is nicely browned. Delicious.

Variation: Try using halves of refrigerated biscuits instead of pie pastry. Ready-made, frozen pie crusts can also be purchased at the supermarket.

This bird pie can also be made in camp using an old fashioned camp Dutch oven with a flanged lid designed for holding hot coals on top. Instead of browning the pie pastry in an oven, cover the pot with the flanged lid and pile red-hot coals on top. (It helps to start with a preheated lid.) When the coals burn down, the pastry should be nicely browned. If it isn't, stir the strips into the mixture—and call the recipe "birds and dumplings."

Ricebird Fricassee

Ricebirds, or small blackbirds, are easy to dress if you pull the skin off the breast and pull or cut out the meat. It's possible to dress out the whole bird, but the breasts on some species aren't much bigger than your thumb, and the thighs and wings simply aren't worth the trouble. Anyhow, for the recipe below, I figure at least 5 or 6 small birds per person. Or more, if I've got them.

20 to 30 ricebird breasts
1 cup sliced fresh mushrooms
1 cup diced onion
½ cup chicken broth
½ cup red wine
water
2 tablespoons butter
salt and pepper
rice (cooked separately)

Heat the butter in a skillet. Sauté the onions, mushrooms, and bird breasts for 5 or 6 minutes, stirring with a wooden spoon. Add some salt and pepper, then pour in the chicken broth and enough water to almost cover the bird breasts. Bring to a quick boil, reduce the heat to very low, cover, and simmer for 45 minutes. Add the red wine and simmer for another 15 minutes. Serve over rice. Feeds 4.

Bird Giblet Breakfast

Now is the time to thaw out all your bird giblets, wings, backs, and feet. For the measures below, you'll need 2 cups of giblets, more or less, in addition to the feet and wings.

Blackbird Stew

Letha learned to cook by watching her mother, grandmothers, and occasionally her father. She tells this story: "I remember when I was a small child, and my mother was sick during a snow so my father cooked. He was a good cook. He killed some birds, cleaned them, and put them in a big iron frying pan with water. He put some sides of hog meat in with the birds. The meat had only been salted one or two days. We called it corned. Anyway, he made some dumplings and cooked the stew down to a slow gravy. We children thought it was the best stew we had ever eaten. My father called it blackbird stew."

—*Coastal Carolina Cooking*

---

2 cups bird giblets
bird wings and feet
2 hard-boiled chicken eggs, sliced
8 or 10 green onions with part of tops
¾ cup flour
½ cup butter or margarine
2 bay leaves
salt and pepper
biscuits (cooked separately)

Put the gizzards, hearts, feet, and wings into a pot and barely cover them with water. Add the bay leaves along with a little salt and pepper. Bring to a boil, cover, reduce heat, and simmer for 1 hour. Remove the bird parts with a slotted spoon, and measure out 2 cups of the broth. (Add a little more if necessary.) Throw away the feet, wings, and bay leaves. Dust the bird gizzards, hearts, and livers with flour. Save the remaining flour. Melt the butter in a large skillet and quickly brown the hearts, gizzards, and livers on medium high heat. Chop the onions, including about half the green tops, and add them to the skillet. (If you don't have green onions on hand, chop a regular onion of medium size and add 1 tablespoon of chopped chives.) Reduce the heat and simmer for about 5 minutes. Pour in the 2 cups of bird broth, bring to a boil, and reduce the heat. Mix the remaining flour with a little water and slowly stir this paste into the contents of the skillet, which will now quickly become gravy. Simmer for about 30 minutes. Stir from time to time, adding a little water if needed. After about 25 minutes, mix in the egg slices and simmer for another 5 minutes. Serve the gravy over open biscuit halves.

Although I prefer this gravy for breakfast, I ought to point out that it also beats chicken and dumplings for a hot lunch. It can also be used to advantage with rice or dressing at a big family feed, such as Thanksgiving dinner.

28

DRESSING BIRDS

Birds, like other game, should be field-dressed, or drawn, as soon as possible after they are killed, and should certainly not be carried around all day in a game bag or compartment in the back of a hunting jacket. This is especially true in warm weather—and I have hunted early-season birds many times in a short-sleeved shirt. In such weather, the birds really should be put on ice, and taking a light Styrofoam ice chest to a dove field or an early-season teal blind may be a good idea.

Some culinary sports hang birds in a cool, airy place for several days, and longer, until the meat becomes "high." I agree that aging the meat in a cold, dry environment for a few days, after the innards have been removed, certainly won't hurt the flavor. But too many people have gotten sick from eating tainted meat that has been hung too long, and I can't recommend the practice from a safety viewpoint. If you do hang

birds for culinary reasons, I recommend that you take the innards out and leave the feathers on. Some people argue for hanging the birds by the head (even until they drop by their own weight) and others insist on hanging them by the feet.

I don't see that it matters, and in fact, the whole hanging concept is suspect. I feel that most modern hunters, especially those who live in the city or suburbs, don't hold with the hanging theory. Their wives don't, either, and only the neighborhood cats will be enthusiastic about the project.

In my opinion, game birds can be improved by refrigerating the meat for a few days before eating it. The larger the bird, the more important this becomes. But curing is not necessary for mild birds such as pheasant or quail. Stronger meat, such as coot, is usually marinated before cooking.

THE EASIEST WAY TO DRESS WHOLE BIRDS

It may be difficult to take time away from your hunting, but usually it's best to dress birds in the field. Plucking the bird first will make the drawing process easier, and certainly less messy. Pull the feathers in the direction from which they grow. Usually, leaving the feathers in the field or woods won't hurt a thing, and it's better to leave them there than in your kitchen after dark. Also, note that most birds are easier to pluck when they are fresh and still warm. (Plucking will be covered in more detail later.)

To draw the bird, most people make a cut near the anus and remove the innards. Then they remove the crop, or otherwise get the undigested grain or food from under the skin of the crop.

With small birds, the field dressing can be accomplished without the aid of a knife. Pluck the bird (or skin it if you must). Then hold the bird by the head and whirl the bird's body around. This will wring off the head. Then hold the bird in your right hand and insert your left fingers into the tender spot about midway between the end of the breastbone and the tail, pushing up slightly on the end of the breastbone. After opening the bird, remove the innards as carefully as possible. (I usually save the liver and the gizzard, and the liver must be removed without breaking the gallbladder. In any case, put all the innards into a plastic bag, then dress out livers and gizzards later.) Next, break the skin into the crop area and clean it out. I leave the feet and wingtips on the birds, or I might cut them off if I've got a knife handy.

Most hunters cut birds in one way or another before drawing them, and many people cut them up the back from the vent to the neck.

Usually, a bird cut in this manner will eventually be halved or flattened. Before you make an opening to draw the bird, consider the possibility that you may want to stuff the birds later on. The smaller the opening, the easier it is to close after the bird is stuffed.

Some birds have an oil sac on the rump, just atop the tail, that contains a substance with which the birds waterproof their feathers. I usually ignore this, but some people may want it out. It can be removed with a knife just after the bird has been plucked or skinned, but it is probably best to cut off the entire tail rather than cutting the sac out.

If you want to save only the breasts of the birds, your field dressing will be even easier (at the expense of your good eating). Either skin or pluck the breast clean, then cut it off, starting just behind the breastbone and working toward the crop. Put the breast into a plastic bag and throw the rest away.

Location of oil sac. If desired, remove with a knife after bird has been plucked and skinned.

BREASTING A BIRD

1. Insert fingers into tender spot below breastbone and pull breast upward. Remove innards.

2. Cut breast free; then cut into crop and clean it thoroughly.

PLUCKING BIRDS

I almost always prefer to pluck my birds instead of skinning them simply because the skin helps keep the meat moist while cooking. But skinning can be much easier on some birds, such as quail, and I'll have to admit that I have eaten some skinned birds that were mighty fine indeed. Note that some recipes, such as a fricassee, are better than others for using skinned birds. Usually, birds to be fried or roasted should be plucked, not skinned. But some birds of strong flavor, such as the coot and fish-eating ducks, are probably better when they are skinned, regardless of the cooking method.

As stated earlier, I recommend that the birds be dry-plucked in the field while the birds are still warm. If you've got them in camp or at home, however, you may prefer to try wet plucking. This is accomplished by heating some plain water to between 150 and 190 degrees. While the water is heating, it's best to wet the birds down in water. Then carefully lower the wet bird into the hot water. But don't leave it too long; you don't want to start the cooking process and certainly don't want to heat up the innards. As soon as you remove the bird from the hot water, start pulling out the feathers, pulling in the direction of their growth. Pulling the opposite way may damage the skin, which is quite tender on most birds.

No matter how carefully you pluck your birds, or regardless of your method, you will find that some pinfeathers will remain embedded in the skin. There is no easy method of getting these out; I recommend using ordinary tweezers.

The Paraffin or Wax Method

Some birds, such as ducks, are harder to pluck than others, simply because they have more and thicker feathers. Many people prefer to pluck them by the paraffin method. Using low heat, melt some paraffin in a large pan. Fill a bucket with cold water. Pull out the bird's large wing feathers, or cut off the wings if you don't want to keep them. Dunk the bird into the melted paraffin, then quickly dip it into the cold water. The cold water, of course, will harden the melted paraffin. Then you can pull the paraffin off in chunks, along with the feathers.

This method takes quite a bit of paraffin, but you can use it over again if you reheat the chunks, melting the paraffin, and strain it through cheesecloth or fine-mesh screen to remove the feathers.

In a similar method, you add paraffin to a pot of hot water (about 180 degrees), then dip the birds into the pot. The paraffin will float on top of the water, so dipping the bird into the pot a time or two will usually coat the feathers with a thin layer of paraffin. This method requires less paraffin. Try 1 cake per quart of water.

Singeing

I singe some birds, but not all. Some doves, for example, seem to need it and others don't. This may be a function of temperature or climate, but I'm not sure. In any case, the down and hair on ducks and other birds can be singed off with a flame. But it is best to avoid very hot flames, although some of the hand-held torches are very convenient. I recommend that you use newspaper sheets that have been rolled up loosely. Holding the paper downward at a slight angle will produce more flame, and holding it up will produce less flame. Be careful, and be sure to have a good place to drop the burning paper if necessary.

Singeing should be held to a minimum, and I seldom singe birds such as doves these days. Burning the feathers and feather roots (which stay in the skin) can give an unpleasant taste

Wet plucking a bird.

to the meat. Singe, yes, if necessary—but don't overdo it.

FREEZING BIRDS

Small birds, such as doves, quail, and snipe, can be dressed and frozen in water like fish, and this is by far the best way to go, because the water prevents freezer burn. Freeze the birds in convenient units so that you can take out, thaw, and cook exactly what you need. I find that a 1-quart milk carton is just right for small birds. Freezing the birds in large blocks of ice takes longer to thaw. I heard of a hunting club in Georgia that froze a 55-gallon drum full of doves and quail, all covered with water. While getting ready to cook, the birds dropped out of the block of ice for 2 days.

Even larger birds can be frozen by this method, if you've got enough room in your home freezer or have access to a commercial unit. Pheasants, ducks, and so on can be wrapped tightly in freezer paper or put into zip freezer bags. In either case, it's best to get as much of the air out of the package as possible, and, in this regard, the new vacuum-pack systems work best, especially if the birds are to be frozen for any length of time.

If you have very fresh birds, you might consider freezing them whole, feathers, guts, and all. When you get ready to eat the birds, thaw, pluck, draw, and cook as usual. I feel a little guilty about bringing up this method, but, on the other hand, I have used it to freeze birds satisfactorily for several months. The feathers and skin, as well as the wrapping, protect the outside from freezer burn, and the innards keep the inside from filling up with air. I wrap each bird, label it, and put it into a bag or box of similar birds. Then I can get out exactly what I need without having to thaw the whole batch.

SAVE THE GIBLETS

As a few of the recipes in this book indicate, some of the best eating from the bird comes from the giblets. If I am going to freeze giblets, I normally put them in a small container and cover them with water. I find that plastic spice containers work well for this purpose. Be sure to label each container. This method allows me to thaw and cook the giblets without having to thaw out the whole bird, which I couldn't do if I were to freeze the giblets inside the bird cavity. The first step, however, it is to dress the giblets properly.

Liver. Handle carefully. Cut away the gallbladder, being careful not to cut or puncture it. If you do cut into it, quickly cut away that part of the liver discolored by the gall. If the contamination is bad, throw out the whole liver.

Heart. Trim the tubes away. It may be best to split the heart, although I usually eat them whole.

Gizzard. Cut this organ across the top, but not all the way through. Turn the gizzard inside out, then peel away the inner skin and contents.

Neck. The neck contains some good meat, although it is difficult to bone, that will add flavor to stock and giblet gravy. It should be either skinned or plucked along with the rest of the bird, then cut off close to the body.

Head. This part of the bird isn't often saved these days, but anyone who has ever had the pleasure of eating chicken heads will consider trying a pheasant head. This part can be fried or boiled, and it should be eaten by hand. Gnaw around it, then crack it with a spoon so that you can get the brains out. If you are making giblet gravy, just put the head in with the rest, then fish it out for yourself, your lady love, or your guest of honor. In any case, it can be skinned or plucked with the rest of the bird. Cut out the beak and remove the eyeballs if you or your guests are squeamish.

REMOVING SHOT

It's best, although not always practical, to remove all the shot from the birds. This step should be performed after you have plucked or skinned the bird. Simply look for holes in the flesh or skin at the point of entry, which will often be darker than the surrounding flesh and will sometimes have parts of feathers in it. Remove the shot with tweezers or with a pointed knife. In some cases, the shot will have gone on through the bird or have been removed when the bird was drawn. Anyone who eats a lot of game birds bagged with a shotgun will get a shot from time to time, a fact that shouldn't bother people who are enthusiastic about eating game in the first place. But minimizing the problem will make your bird supper more pleasant.

REMOVING THE TENDONS

Some running birds, such as the cock pheasant and the wild turkey, have tendons in the legs that make them difficult to carve at the table. Once you cut the legs off, it will be almost impossible to remove these tendons. If they bother you, your best bet is to freeze the birds without disjointing them and without removing the feet. When you remove the bird from the freezer for thawing, cut around each leg just above the knee joint, then break the bone by applying pressure the opposite way from the natural bend in the knee. Then, grasp the drumstick in one hand and the scaled part of the leg (or the feet) in the other hand. Pull apart, and the tendons will usually pull out—but not always. Frankly, I don't bother about the tendons, especially when the bird is to be simmered in a stew or gumbo.

DRESSING THE WILD TURKEY

Some people believe that the turkey should be bled before it is dressed. I don't think that bleeding will do much good, but it is usually accomplished by slitting the underside of the neck, then holding the turkey up by the legs. I

PULLING OUT THE TENDONS

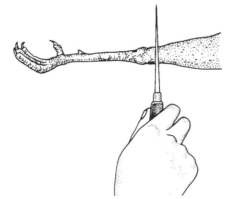

1. Cut around each leg above the knee joint and break the bone.

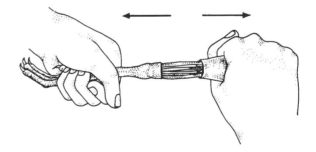

2. Pull on leg to remove tendons.

feel that normal field dressing, if performed soon after the kill, will bleed the bird better than slitting the neck.

To begin field-dressing, place the bird on its back. Quickly pluck a row of feathers from the vent up to the breastbone. With your knife, make a slit from the vent to the breastbone, being careful not to puncture any of the innards. (To make the cut, insert the point of the knife, then cut forward with the blade pointed up.) Reach into the cavity with your hand. Get out the intestines, heart, and liver. Reach up and partly remove the lungs, then reach in toward the neck and sever the windpipe. Put all the innards aside.

Pluck the bird. Then make a slit at the neck just above the breastbone. Carefully remove the contents of the crop. If your turkey is to be stuffed, keep the slit as narrow as possible and do not tear the skin.

Your turkey contains quite a bit of meat and body heat. Part of the heat is removed with the innards, but the rest of the carcass should be cooled down as soon as possible, especially in warm weather. If possible, refrigerate the carcass. In camp, it helps to hang the dressed bird by the feet from a tree limb, then prop open the body cavity with a stick to aid ventilation.

Plucking your turkey can be something of a job. Using the hot water method will be a little easier, if you have enough water. A washtub, 5-gallon lard can, or some such container is needed. Dry plucking is often easier than trying to find a large container.

DRESSING DUCKS AND GEESE

In theory, ducks and geese should be plucked and drawn as soon as possible after they are brought down. The feathers and down hold in the body heat, so the larger the bird and the warmer the weather, the more important this becomes.

In practice, a good compromise is to pluck the feathers away from the breast area, thereby helping the heat to escape from the thickest part of the body.

If you are plucking ducks at home or in camp, I recommend that you use either the wet method or the paraffin method, as discussed earlier.

CARVING GAME BIRDS

Pheasant and turkey can be carved like domestic chickens and turkey, and should present few problems at the table provided that the host knows what to do. If not, it might be best to partly carve the birds in the kitchen, cutting off enough meat to at least get everybody started.

Ducks and geese are different and a little more difficult to carve and disjoint, however, because the legs are attached in a different location, which is what causes the ducks or geese to waddle when they walk.

Some people use poultry shears to disjoint a bird, but a knife does a good job if the cuts are made in the joints. Thus, you can cut off the wings and leg quarters, and separate the drumstick from the thigh, without having to cut through a bone.

PART THREE

GAME

29

SQUIRREL

My father left me a 12-gauge double-barreled shotgun, which had belonged to my grandfather before him. It was—or is—a LeFever, and, if I remember correctly, my father said it was the first double in our part of the country without rabbit ears. It has a 32-inch barrel, full on the left and modified on the right. The left barrel has worn somewhat, but in better days its pattern of 6s was well nigh perfect, its range quite long. It was in fact considered (by some people) to be the best turkey and squirrel gun in Henry Country. I retired it years ago when I switched to a rifle and scope for squirrels, but I still like to shoulder the long gun from time to time and think back on different times.

Back then, following the bad Depression years, we ate the whole squirrel, from head to tail. I mean we actually skinned out the head, fried it, and ate it at the table. A fried squirrel head contains some good gnawing all around,

and there is a tasty chunk on each cheek. The brain, however, is the real prize. To get at it, hold the head firmly in the left hand, then grasp a tablespoon in your right hand and whop the head hard enough to crack the skull open so that you can get to the good part. With spoon in hand, I once set forth a rather graphic description of this process to a company of hunters at Choctawhatchee Lodge, which seemed to have diminished their interest in my duck soup. The subject may sound unappetizing to some people, but the plain truth is that the head of a squirrel is far better than a chicken head. If you don't believe it, be sure to try Buck Chauncey's Squirrel Head Stew later in this chapter.

Anyhow, before trying the following recipes, please note that there is a very big difference between tender young squirrels and tough old squirrels. In short, a young squirrel, properly handled and cooked, is one of the best kind of game; an old squirrel, improperly handled and cooked, is sorry fare. For this reason, it is important to read the recipes below carefully and choose one to suit the squirrels on hand. As a rule, it is not a good idea to cook both young squirrels and old squirrels by the same recipe for the same meal, but there are exceptions, as when a young hunter brings home a mixed bag and wants to feed the whole family. The young hunter, in his enthusiasm, can probably eat most anything that he brings home, but note that old squirrels fried by ordinary methods are just too tough for most people, and old squirrels cooked for a long time over charcoal are virtually impossible to eat.

Most cookbook writers don't distinguish among the different kinds of squirrels, but this information has a bearing on how they are cooked. There are at least 267 species of squirrels scattered around the world. All of these are edible, but some are too small to be of much interest to hunters. In America, the most popular are the gray squirrel *(Sciurus carolinensis)* and the fox squirrel *(Sciurus niger)*. These may be called by different names in different parts of the country. The fox squirrel is the larger of the two.

Brunswick Stew

The original Brunswick is a native American dish, and was first made with small game. The following recipe can be made with young squirrels or old, or a mix of the two. If you have more than enough squirrels to make the dish, use old ones and save the young ones for frying. This recipe is also good when made with squirrels mixed with rabbits and other game. Also try a tough pheasant along with a squirrel or two.

In my opinion, Brunswick stew is best when made with fresh or fresh-frozen vegetables, but canned vegetables can also be used, especially in camp.

5 to 7 gray squirrels (or 3 fox squirrels)
½ pound bacon or (better) salt pork
2 cups baby lima beans (or butter beans)
2 cups corn (whole kernel)
8 medium potatoes, diced
4 cups tomatoes, chopped
2 medium onions, chopped
2 tablespoons sugar
½ cup butter or margarine
4 tablespoons flour
3 bay leaves
salt and pepper
water

Dress the squirrels, cut them up, and put the pieces into a large pot containing about 1 gallon of water and the bay leaves. A cast-iron pot seems to work best. Bring the water to a light boil, reduce the heat to very low, and simmer for 1 hour or longer, until tender, skimming off any scum that might accumulate on top. If you have a mix of old and young squirrels, you may want to boil the old ones for 1 hour, then add the young ones until tender. Otherwise, the tender young squirrels might cook apart before the old ones are tender. Remove and discard the bay leaves. Remove and drain the squirrel pieces. When cool enough to handle, pull the meat from the bones with fork and finger. Chop the meat into chunks and put it back into the pot.

Cut the bacon into 1-inch strips and add them to the pot. (If you are using salt pork instead of bacon, dice it into cubes of about ½ inch.) Add the onion. Simmer for 20 minutes. Add the lima beans, corn, potatoes, tomatoes, and sugar. Simmer for about 30 minutes, stirring from time to time. Mix the butter and flour into paste balls. Bring the stew to a light boil, add the paste balls, reduce the heat, and stir for 10 minutes. Add a little salt and pepper to taste if needed.

Brunswick stew should be served hot. But it may be even better when heated the next day.

Belgian Squirrel

With slight variations, I've seen this good recipe in several places and, frankly, I don't know the origin of it. In his *Bull Cook and Authentic Historical Recipes and Practices,* George Leonard Herter said that the recipe was originally used in the Ardennes to cook rabbit, but that the Belgian immigrants to the United States used it to cook squirrel as well as rabbit. In any case, I was skeptical about the recipe owing to my lack of enthusiasm for prunes—until I cooked it.

> 3 gray squirrels (or 2 fox squirrels)
> 1 stick butter or margarine
> 18 prunes
> 2 medium onions, thinly sliced
> 3 tablespoons wine vinegar
> 1½ tablespoons flour
> ⅛ teaspoon dried thyme
> salt and pepper
> water

Cut the squirrels into serving pieces. Preheat the oven to 350 degrees. Melt the butter in a skillet, then quickly brown the squirrel pieces. Place the pieces in a well-greased baking dish that has a cover and is suitable for cooking on a stove burner as well as in the oven. (A cast-iron Dutch oven is fine.) Brown

the onions in the skillet, then reduce the heat and stir in the salt, pepper, thyme, and wine vinegar. Pour this mixture over the squirrel pieces and put the container into the center of the oven. Bake for 1 hour. Add the prunes, placing them one at a time between the pieces of squirrel and poking them under the liquid. Reduce the heat to 250 degrees and cook for 1 more hour.

Mix the flour into 1 cup of water, stirring until no lumps are present. Remove the squirrel dish from the oven, pour in the flour mixture, and simmer over low heat for about 15 minutes, or until the gravy thickens to the desired consistency.

All of the recipes that I have seen for this dish recommend that the gravy be served over potatoes or on toast. I submit that it's also very good over rice. Feeds 2 to 4.

Fox Squirrels and Dumplings

Here's a dish that's hard to beat in camp or at home. It is quite filling, and hits the spot on a cold night.

> 3 fox squirrels (or 5 gray squirrels)
> 1 hard-boiled chicken egg, sliced
> flour
> salt and black pepper
> ¼ teaspoon red pepper flakes
> 2 bay leaves
> water

Clean the squirrels, cut them into serving-size pieces, and put them into a pot along with the bay leaves and red pepper flakes. Cover with water and bring to a boil. Reduce the heat, cover, and simmer for 1 or 2 hours, or until tender. Remove the squirrel pieces, retaining the broth. Pull the meat from the bones, return it to the broth, and add some salt and pepper to taste. Simmer.

To make the dumplings, put 1 cup of water into a bowl and mix in flour until you have a stiff dough. Knead. Dust a suitable surface with flour, then roll out the dough. Make it thin—about ⅛ inch. Cut the dough into strips. Bring the squirrel broth to a light boil, then drop the strips into it. Add the egg slices. Simmer for about 5 minutes. Serve hot. Feeds 4 to 6.

Variation: To make cornmeal dumplings, or corn dodgers, mix ½ cup of water with ½ cup of broth from the squirrel pot. Stir in a little meal and salt until you have thick batter (as when making hush puppies). Form the batter into small balls or patties, and carefully place them in the liquid around the edge of the squirrel pot. Or drop them in gently from a spoon. Simmer for 10 minutes or so.

Fried Squirrel

Once I shot a big gray boar squirrel off an ear of corn in a field that bordered a wooded creek. I don't know how old he was, but he certainly had some credentials of maturity. I gave him to the fellow who farmed the corn, who later told me that the meat was so tough he couldn't stick a fork into its gravy! He had, of course, fried it. Although he spoke in jest, there is more than a grain of truth in what he was saying. An old squirrel should not be fried as usual. On the other hand, tender young squirrels are delicious when fried. Here's all I use:

    young squirrels
    peanut oil
    flour
    salt and pepper

Skin the squirrels, cut them into pieces, sprinkle with salt and pepper, and shake them in a bag of flour. Heat from ½ to ¾ inch of peanut oil in a large skillet, then fry the squirrels for a few minutes, until nicely browned on both sides. Do not overcook. To make gravy, pour off the excess oil from the skillet, scrape up the dredgings with a wooden spoon, slowly add a little paste made with water and flour, stirring as you go, and cook until you have a smooth gravy. Serve the gravy over rice, noodles, biscuit halves, or mashed potatoes.

Note: Young squirrels can also be deep-fried successfully if you've got a big batch to cook. For the best gravy, however, stick with the skillet.

Skillet-to-Crockpot Squirrel

I've eaten my share of squirrel, cooked in a number of ways, and one of my all-time favorites for cooking a mixed bag of young and old squirrels came from a fellow by the name of Floyd "Jake" Kringer. I don't know him, but he was more or less featured in an article on

Lots of Squirrels

The Illinois Department of Conservation, in a publication called *Outdoor Highlights,* says that 150,000 hunting Illini will bag an average of at least 10 squirrels each per year. They set the annual estimate at 1.5 to 2 million in the state. If other states average the same numbers, we bag some 85,000,000 squirrels per year in the United States. Most of 'em are fried.

squirrel cookery in *Outdoor Highlights,* published by the Illinois Department of Conservation. The article was somewhat vague about exactly how much of what to add, and my guess is that Kringer wasn't too eager to talk. But here's what I use, and my boys don't argue with the results:

7 or 8 gray squirrels (or 5 fox squirrels)
8 ounces fresh mushrooms, sliced
2 cans creamy chicken mushroom soup
    (10¾-ounce size)
2 cups sour cream
1 medium to large onion, chopped
cooking oil
flour
salt and pepper

Dress the squirrels and cut them into pieces. Salt and pepper each piece, then roll in flour. Heat some cooking oil in a skillet. Quickly brown the pieces on both sides, putting them into the crockpot as you go. Add the onions, mushrooms, and soup. Cover. Turn the crockpot to high and cook for 1 hour. Then turn the heat to low, add the sour cream, and cook for at least 6 more hours. Feeds 8 to 10.

"And the gravy from this recipe over baked potatoes is superb," Kringer said. Indeed it is. But also try it over rice or biscuit halves. The gravy can be thinned with water or thickened with flour, as needed. As I write this recipe down, the squirrels around my place are feeling good and frisky. They had better watch out.

Squirrel Cacciatore

Cacciatore is a chicken dish of Italian origin. But it has a tomato base—and the tomato is American. Who can say that the original recipe

wasn't in fact made with tomatoes and squirrels? In any case, the following recipe works best with tender young squirrels, but a mixed bag can also be used, as discussed below.

5 gray squirrels (or 3 fox squirrels)
2 pounds fresh tomatoes, peeled and
    chopped
1 can tomato sauce (8-ounce size)
6 ounces fresh mushrooms, sliced
1 large onion, sliced
2 cloves garlic, minced
½ bell pepper, diced
½ cup wine
⅓ cup olive oil
2 bay leaves
1 teaspoon salt
¾ teaspoon dried oregano
¼ teaspoon dried thyme
¼ teaspoon pepper
flour

If any of the squirrels are old and tough, simmer them in water until tender. Cut all the squirrels into serving pieces. In a skillet, heat a little of the olive oil, then sauté the onion, bell pepper, mushrooms, and garlic for about 10 minutes, stirring with a wooden spoon. Remove these with a slotted spoon, putting them into a stove-top Dutch oven or other suitable pot. Put some flour into a bag, then shake the squirrel pieces in it. Put the rest of the olive oil into the skillet, heat, and fry the squirrel pieces, turning once, until they are golden brown on both sides. Add the squirrel pieces to the pot. Then add the tomatoes, tomato sauce, salt, pepper, thyme, bay leaves, and oregano. Bring to a bubble, reduce heat, cover tightly, and simmer for 40 minutes, turning the squirrel pieces several times so that the bottom won't burn. Add the wine and remove the bay leaves. Simmer for another 15 minutes. Eat while hot with rice or baked potatoes and steamed vegetables, or maybe fried eggplant. Feeds 6 or 7.

Squirrel Salad

Young squirrels make a good meat salad, and any good recipe for chicken salad will work, provided that the squirrel meat is tender. If you don't have a favorite chicken salad recipe, try the following.

> 3 gray squirrels (or 2 fox squirrels)
> 3 stalks celery, diced
> juice of 1 large lemon
> 2 tablespoons capers
> 2 bay leaves
> mayonnaise
> 1 teaspoon onion juice
> salt and pepper
> Tabasco sauce (optional)
> Hungarian paprika
> lettuce leaves

Simmer the squirrels in water, along with the bay leaves, until the meat is tender. Remove the squirrels, cool, and bone. Chop the meat, then put it into a large glass bowl. Squeeze the lemon juice over the meat, toss, cover, and refrigerate overnight.

Mix the meat, celery, 1 cup of mayonnaise, and capers. Add the onion juice, salt, and pepper, along with a little Tabasco sauce to taste. Serve atop leaves of lettuce, along with crackers. Top with mayonnaise, then sprinkle lightly with paprika.

This salad can also be used as a sandwich spread.

Big Scrub Purloo

Here's a dish from the Big Scrub area of central Florida, now called the Ocala National Forest, where sharpshooters and their families have been eating purloo for a long time. Naturalist William Bartram partook of the dish during his travels into the Scrub, calling it *pillo.* In her book *Cross Creek Cookery,* Marjorie Kinnan Rawlings called the dish *pilau.* But most of the rural folks call it *purloo.* Here's all you need:

> 2 squirrels
> 1 cup long-grain rice
> water
> bay leaves
> salt and pepper
> dried red pepper pod

Skin and disjoint the squirrels, saving the giblets. Put all the meat pieces and giblets into a pot and almost cover them with water. Add 1 or 2 bay leaves and a pod of dried red pepper. Bring the water to a boil, reduce heat, cover tightly, and simmer for 1 or 2 hours, or until the meat is tender. Remove the meat pieces from the pot. Throw away the bay leaves and

red pepper pod. Retain 3 cups of the broth and discard the rest; add a little water if you don't have 3 full cups. Put the meat back into the pot along with the retained broth. Add the rice, salt, and pepper. Bring to a boil, reduce the heat, cover with a lid, and simmer for 30 minutes. If the purloo contains too much moisture at this point, you can simmer it for a few minutes longer without the lid. If you want soupy purloo, as for serving from bowls with soda crackers, reduce the simmering time or stir in a little water if needed. Serve while hot. Fill up—and enjoy.

Buck Chauncey's Squirrel Head Stew

Here's another unusual Florida recipe that I have adapted from the *Apalachicola Cookbook*. Be sure to try it the next time you have enough squirrel heads. Anytime you get only 2 or 3 squirrels, freeze the heads and save them until you have enough for this feast. Of course, the head should be skinned.

10 to 20 squirrel heads
2 or 3 potatoes, diced
1 medium onion, chopped
1 clove garlic, minced
¼ teaspoon celery seed
¼ teaspoon filé powder
salt to taste
Louisiana hot sauce or Tabasco
1 tablespoon chopped fresh parsley

Put the squirrel heads into a stove-top Dutch oven or other suitable pot. Cover with water, add the salt, and bring to a boil. Cover, reduce heat, and simmer for 2 hours or longer. The heads should be very tender for easy pickings. Add the potatoes, onion, garlic, parsley, celery seed, and hot sauce. Simmer until the potatoes are done, about 15 minutes. Turn off the heat and stir in the filé powder. Do not boil after the filé has been added.

30

RABBIT

Shortly after the first edition of this book came out a few years ago, a college professor by the name of Frank Lynn Payne called me long-distance concerning my recipe for Pea Ridge rabbit. He said he raised New Zealand whites, belonged to the Oklahoma Commercial Rabbit Growers' Association, taught music at a major university, and published books on fiddle music and such topics.

He didn't say so but I quickly surmised that he was also an astute student of southern geography.

"Are you certain that Pea Ridge is near Fayetteville, Tennessee?" he asked.

"Well . . . yes," I said, somewhat taken aback.

"There is a Pea Ridge in Alabama," Payne said. "You *are* from Alabama, are you not?"

"Yes. No. Look, I *came* from Alabama. I mean I came to Pea Ridge, Tennessee, from Alabama, or went to that place from Alabama."

"I can't find a Pea Ridge on any map of Tennessee," he said. "You said in the book, page one fifty-four, that it was near a place called Skin 'um?"

"That's right," I said. "I think the name came from skinning all those Pea Ridge rabbits."

"I can't find Skin 'um on the map either," he said.

"Well, maybe it's too small to be on the map," I allowed. "I don't remember ever putting my finger on it, but it was there, sir, I assure you. Skin 'um, Tennessee. Home of the Big Mac Chicken Coop Factory."

"I have eliminated Fayetteville, Georgia, Fayetteville, West Virginia, and Fayetteville, North Carolina," Payne went on, nothing daunted, "but there is a Pea Ridge near Fayetteville, Arkansas. In fact, it's the site of a well-marked Civil War battleground. Do you suppose that you could have somehow confused the states of Tennessee and Arkansas?"

"Well, maybe I did," I said, somewhat defensively now. "Look, mister, I lived there for only three or four years. All I remember for certain is that it was called Pea Ridge and that it had lots of cottontail rabbits and that it was pretty close to a Jack Daniels distillery."

Payne said that he was a scotch man himself, but fortunately he decided that he would nevertheless share a rabbit recipe with me and my sour-mash readers.

Frank Lynn Payne's Thumper Nuggets

Payne didn't specify New Zealand whites in his list of ingredients, and I suspect that the recipe below would be fine for ordinary domestic rabbits as well as for various sorts of wild rabbits. Or maybe even Tasmanian devils or Australian hoppers. I cook it with swamp rabbits and marsh rabbits as well as with cottontails. Other rabbits and hares will work just fine if the meat is tender. In all cases, young rabbits or hares work better in this recipe than older ones, and this is especially true of scrawny west Texas jackrabbits—which are really hares.

    1 fryer rabbit, boned
    1 chicken egg
    ⅓ cup flour
    ⅓ cup water
    ½ teaspoon salt
    2 teaspoons sesame seeds
    cooking oil

Cut the meat into ½- or ¾-inch chunks or pieces. Rig for deep frying. Break the chicken egg into a bowl and whisk in the water. Add flour, salt, and sesame seeds to make a runny batter. Dip the rabbit pieces into the batter, stirring well to coat the meat.

America's Favorite Small Game

My guess is that the rabbit (including cottontails, snowshoes, hares, jackrabbits, and the others) are by far America's favorite small game. If they aren't, they ought to be. They can be found in deep woods, hedge-rowed farmlands, suburban yards, unkempt pastures, piny woods, hardwood forests, prairies, and even swamps. From coast to coast, from Mexico to the Arctic, rabbits are plentiful. They are easy to find. Easy to bag. Easy to dress. Easy to cook. And easy to eat. It's good meat and healthy too, being low in calories and very high in protein.

Moreover, most states have long seasons and very liberal bag limits. No special equipment is needed to hunt rabbits successfully. Many have been taken with bow and arrow, and even with a slingshot. Either a .22 rifle or a shotgun will do fine. But the rabbit gun, in my opinion, is an over-and-under combo with a .22 rifle on top and a 20-gauge shotgun on the bottom.

In hot oil, fry the rabbit pieces until they are golden brown, about 4 or 5 minutes. Remove the pieces and drain on a paper towel. Either of the following dips is good with the nuggets:

Creamy Dill Sauce
Mix ½ cup sour cream, ½ cup mayonnaise, and 1 teaspoon dill weed. Let the mixture stand for 1 hour. Serve at room temperature.

Nippy Pineapple Sauce

In a saucepan of suitable size, mix ½ cup of pineapple preserves, 2 tablespoons of prepared mustard, and 2 tablespoons of prepared horse-radish. Stir on low heat. Keep warm until ready to serve.

Brunswick Stew

A number of good stews are made with rabbits, and I recommend long-simmering recipes for cooking up tough old rabbits. There's little doubt in my mind that this recipe is based on American Indian fare, and that it was made with rabbit or squirrel instead of with chicken. I might add that it also has in it some basic American vegetables: corn, tomatoes, beans, potatoes, and red peppers. (The American Indians didn't eat Worcestershire sauce.) There is, however, some question about where the name came from. I feel that it originated somewhere near the Atlantic seaboard, possibly in or near Brunswick, Georgia; Brunswick County, North Carolina; Brunswick County, Virginia; Brunswick, Maryland; or Brunswick, Maine. But I'm not sure, and, since I'm a stickler for facts, I checked with Professor Frank Lynn Payne over

the telephone. He said none of the above. It is, he felt, a recipe from mid-America, and that his first geographical choice is Brunswick, Ohio, and his second Brunswick, Missouri.

In any case, the stew works best if you use fresh vegetables in the recipe. If fresh ones aren't available, try fresh-frozen lima beans and corn, along with canned tomatoes. In camp, it's okay to use canned vegetables. Here's what else you'll need:

2 tough old rabbits
½ pound salt pork, diced
4 cups diced potatoes
4 cups diced tomatoes
2 cups diced onions
2 cups baby lima beans or butter beans
2 cups whole-kernel corn
2 cups sliced mushrooms (optional)
3 bay leaves or wax myrtle leaves
salt to taste
½ teaspoon red pepper flakes
½ cup white stone-ground cornmeal or
    flour

Tell your wife to save the giblets, especially the liver, when she dresses the rabbits. Cut the rabbits into pieces and put them into a stove-top Dutch oven. Barely cover the meat with water. Add the bay leaves, bring to a boil, reduce heat, cover tightly, and simmer for 1 hour, or until the meat is fork-tender. Take out the rabbit pieces and drain. Discard the bay leaves but retain the broth. Pull the meat from the bones and chop it. Put the chopped meat, salt pork, and all the vegetables into the Dutch oven. Add 2 or 3 cups of water, salt, and red pepper flakes. Bring to a boil, stir in a little cornmeal, reduce heat, cover tightly, and simmer for 2 hours. Stir from time to time, adding a little cornmeal as you go. Add a little salt to taste and a little water if necessary to adjust the texture. I like my Brunswick Stew to be just a little thin, to be eaten from a bowl. Others will want it thicker, maybe to put on a barbecue plate.

Note: See also the recipe for squirrel Brunswick Stew in the previous chapter.

Pueblo Jackrabbit Stew

Jackrabbits were once plentiful in the Southwest, and the American Indians made good use of them—and still do in some areas. Here's a good recipe adapted from *Pueblo Indian Cookbook.* The ingredients set forth in this work call for cooked lime hominy. I'm not quite sure what this is, but I am very fond of an old-timey dish that many southerners call lye hominy, made with the aid of lye leached from oak fires used for heating iron washpots. Modern cooks will probably want to use canned whole hominy, available in either white or yellow corn. It's even better, in my opinion, to use dried hominy (posole) if you can find it. Soak dried hominy in water before use. In any case, hominy is made from whole corn kernels and should not be confused with grits. The measures below call for 2 cups. Using 1 cup of white hominy and 1 of yellow makes a more attractive stew.

1 jackrabbit
2 quarts water
6 large carrots, scraped and halved
2 bell peppers, halved and seeded
2 large onions, whole
1 large onion, chopped
2 cups hominy
¾ cup melted lard or cooking oil
flour for dredging
⅔ tablespoon chili powder
4 teaspoons salt

Cut the rabbit into pieces, sprinkle with salt, and dredge with flour. Heat the oil in a large pot or stove-top Dutch oven. Brown the rabbit pieces and pour off the excess oil. Add the water, bring to a boil, cover, reduce the heat, and simmer for 2 hours. Add all the other ingredients and simmer until the carrots are tender. Serve hot.

Note: Also see the next recipe, another Pueblo rabbit stew dish, also adapted from *Pueblo Indian Cookbook.*

Taos Rabbit

The old Indian secret of making good stews is in long, slow simmering instead of boiling. Since the ingredients in this dish are not browned or sautéed before stewing, it's an ideal recipe for cooking in a crockpot. (Cook on low for 8 or 9 hours.) Instead of red chili powder, you may want to try a little cayenne or red pepper flakes (my favorite), seasoning to taste as the dish cooks.

1 rabbit
½ gallon water
1 cup vinegar
1 large onion
2 or 3 teaspoons red chili powder
1 teaspoon salt
sunflower seeds

Cut the rabbit into serving pieces. Dice the onion. Put all the ingredients except the sunflower seeds into a large pot or crockpot. Bring to a bubble, reduce heat, cover tightly, and simmer without hard boiling for 8 or 9 hours. While the dish cooks, grind a few sunflower seeds in a mortar and pestle. Thicken the stew with the sunflower meal.

Variation: If you don't have sunflower seeds, try thickening the stew with ground walnuts, hickory nuts, pine nuts, or even sweet acorns.

Wiregrass Rabbit

I was raised on a farm in the wiregrass area of southeast Alabama, and this is the way my mother fried rabbits. It is very good—especially if your rabbit is tender. Older rabbits cooked by this method tend to be on the tough side. Usually, the back section is more tender than the legs.

1 or more young rabbits, pan-dressed
peanut oil
flour
salt and pepper

Heat about ¾ inch of peanut oil in a large skillet. Salt and pepper the rabbit pieces, then shake them in a bag with flour. Fry the pieces over medium heat until they are browned on both sides. Do not overcook. I don't remember how my mother determined when the rabbits were sufficiently done, but my wife goes by the sound of the grease. In fact, she can watch TV in the den and tell you when the rabbit (or chicken) is done in the kitchen. Apparently, the meat doesn't pop and crackle as much when it gets done, but I always have to look at mine. And sometimes at hers. Anyhow, when the rabbit pieces are done, drain them on a brown bag before serving.

Tasty Onion Rabbit

Although I don't like to use the term "oven fried" because the meat isn't really fried, I do recommend that you try the following dish for flavor and crunch.

1 or 2 rabbits
buttermilk
1 package onion soup mix (2.6-ounce size)
1 cup dry bread crumbs, fine
butter
salt and pepper to taste
paprika

If your rabbit is young and tender, cut it up and soak it in buttermilk for 20 minutes or longer. If it is old and tough, marinate the pieces in buttermilk for 12 hours or longer in the refrigerator, using a glass or other non-metallic container.

When you are ready to cook, preheat the oven to 375 degrees. Put the onion soup mix into a mortar and pestle, a little at a time, and grind it to a powder. Also mash the bread crumbs a little. Then mix them together, along with the paprika, salt, and pepper. Put this mix-

Rabbit Fever Phobia

Not long ago, I read that rabbits should not be hunted until 2 or 3 weeks after a heavy frost, and that rabbit hunters should carry with them a pair of gloves and a can of Lysol. The gloves, the author said, were for wearing when you handle or clean a rabbit, and the Lysol was for spraying on your hands when you finished the job.

The author, from New York City, was, of course, setting forth precautions against the disease tularemia, or "rabbit fever," which can be transmitted to humans. The disease causes a lymphatic inflammation, along with chills, headaches, and fever. Tularemia can be fatal to humans and it should be properly treated.

But the odds against a particular rabbit having tularemia are quite long. Even if a rabbit has the disease, it can be dressed, cooked, and eaten without a problem. The disease is caused by a microorganism that can be transmitted from rabbit flesh (or from other infected rodents) to an open wound or sore on the human skin. Thus, it is not a good idea to dress rabbits when you have a cut, scratch, or sore on your hands.

The disease can also be present in beavers and muskrats, both water rodents, and waterborne epidemics of tularemia have been documented in Russia and Turkey. But probably most of the cases of tularemia in this country are caused by bites from the deer fly and ticks.

So . . . if you have rabbit fever phobia, take mosquito netting and tick repellent along with rubber gloves and Lysol when you go hunting. And stay out of the water. Avoid Russia and Turkey.

Should you really wait 2 or 3 weeks after first frost to go rabbit hunting? I don't think so. Although I don't have extensive data, my feeling is that most cases of tularemia are caught in warm weather, from flies, ticks, and mosquitoes, not from dressing rabbits. The best time to hunt (and eat) rabbits is whenever the season is open in your state. True, you can catch tularemia while rabbit hunting on warm days. But you can also catch Legionnaires' disease while sitting at home under your air conditioner.

ture into a small bag. Remove the rabbit pieces from the buttermilk, drain, and lightly pat dry with paper towels. Shake the pieces in the bag, then arrange them in a well-greased baking pan of suitable size. Place a small piece of butter atop each piece. Bake for 1 hour, then baste the rabbit with pan drippings, sprinkle lightly with paprika, and bake for another 10 minutes. Serve hot.

Rabbit Sauce Piquant

I have eaten this dish two or three times made with Florida marsh rabbits and once, in Louisiana, made with what I now believe to have been 2 muskrats. In any case, be sure to try the recipe with cottontails or the small marsh rabbits.

2 wild rabbits
8 ounces mushrooms, sliced
1 cup cooking oil
1 can tomato juice (12-ounce size)
1 can tomatoes (16-ounce size)
1 cup diced celery (with part of green tops)
1 cup diced onions
½ cup diced green onion tops
½ cup diced green bell pepper
½ cup diced red bell pepper
3 cloves garlic, minced
juice of 1 lemon
1 tablespoon parsley
salt
½ to 1 teaspoon red pepper flakes
butter
flour
water
rice (cooked separately)

Cut the rabbit into pieces and sprinkle with salt. Heat the cooking oil in a stove-top Dutch oven. Brown the rabbit pieces in 2 or more batches on medium high heat. Set the rabbit pieces aside. Pour off about half of the oil, then stir in about 1 tablespoon of flour, stirring until it browns. Add 1 cup of water and the red pepper flakes, stir, and return the rabbit to the Dutch oven. Cover tightly and simmer for 30 minutes.

Heat a little butter in a skillet, then sauté the onions, celery, garlic, and bell peppers. Add the tomato juice and tomatoes, cover, and simmer for 30 minutes. Then add the contents of the skillet to the rabbit in the Dutch oven. Stir in the mushrooms, green onion tops, lemon juice, and parsley. Cover and simmer for 30 minutes. Serve over rice. Feeds 5 or 6, or maybe 7 or 8 if you cook lots of rice.

Peppers Stuffed with Rabbit

The meat for this dish can be from leftover rabbit, or you can boil a fresh rabbit, or parts of rabbit, until tender. I normally let mine simmer for about 1 hour on low heat. Bone and chop the meat. Chilled meat is easier to chop, making a neater dice, if that matters.

2 cups diced cooked rabbit
1 cup cooked rice
½ cup grated Parmesan cheese
4 medium to large bell peppers
¼ cup finely chopped onion
2 tablespoons finely chopped mushrooms
1 can Rotel (10-ounce size) or Mexican-
   style stewed tomatoes
1 tablespoon butter
1 tablespoon Worcestershire sauce
salt and pepper

Cut the tops off the green peppers, remove the seeds, and simmer the shells in slightly

North Country Eating

Trappers commonly eat muskrat and beaver meat and some gourmets eat blackbirds.

Perhaps the best of all small game animals in Manitoba is the snowshoe hare or bush rabbit. They make excellent sport and eating. Cottontails are good to eat but are much less common in Manitoba. Jack rabbits, more common than cottontails, are also delicious in stews and sausage.

—*Field Handling of Game and Fish*
Manitoba Natural Resources

salted water for 10 minutes. Drain the peppers while you prepare the stuffing. Also, preheat the oven to 350 degrees.

Heat the butter in a large skillet. Sauté the onion and mushrooms for 4 or 5 minutes. Add the rabbit meat, rice, salt, pepper, Rotel, cheese, and Worcestershire sauce. Mix well. Spoon this stuffing into the peppers, then stand them upright in a baking dish. Bake for 30 minutes. Feeds 4 as a side dish—but I'll need 2 peppers for a main course.

Pea Ridge Buttermilk Rabbit

Once I knew a somewhat chubby poker player who kept a pack of beagle hounds. If there was anything he liked better than country-fried rabbit, it was rabbit gravy served over biscuit halves. At the time, I lived on Pea Ridge, near Fayetteville, Tennessee, where I played a little poker and cooked this dish from time to time. It can be made with older rabbits as well as young ones.

> rabbits, cut up
> buttermilk
> cooking oil
> flour
> salt and pepper
> water

Put the pieces of rabbit into a crockery or other nonmetallic container, cover with buttermilk, and marinate in the refrigerator for 12 hours or longer, depending somewhat on the age of the rabbits.

Heat about ½ inch of oil in a cast-iron skillet. Drain the rabbit pieces, sprinkle them with salt and pepper, and shake them in a bag with some flour. Fry the pieces at medium high heat

Rabbits and Hares

Altogether, some 44 species of rabbits and hares live in many parts of the world. Often, however, it's difficult to tell which is which. The well known long-eared black-tailed jackrabbit of the American west, for example, is really a hare. Even more confusion arises by calling other animals rabbits or hares; for example, the Patagonia hare is really an agouti, which is also edible.

Both rabbits and hares were eaten by primitive man, and their bones have been found in ancient kitchen middens. Strangely, the Greeks shunned rabbit, believing that eating them would cause insomnia. The ancient Romans, on the other hand, more or less domesticated rabbits and raised them in enclosed areas called *leporaria*. They considered roast rabbit to be good eating; but the real delicacy was the unborn or newly born rabbit fetus.

—Adapted from
Edible Plants and Animals

until browned on both sides. Remove the pieces. Pour off most of the oil. Stir a little flour into some water, making a paste. Pour the paste slowly into the remaining oil in the skillet, stirring as you go with a wooden spoon, scraping up any bits that might have stuck to the bottom. Slowly add about 2 cups of water. Cook and stir until you have a thin gravy. Put the rabbit pieces into the gravy, cover tightly, and simmer for 1 hour, turning a time or two and adding a little more water if needed.

Serve the rabbit pieces separately, and spoon the gravy over biscuit halves. I like to grind some black pepper on top before eating.

Rabbit Salad

Here's an excellent dish for a hot summer day. Take a rabbit from the freezer, let it thaw out, and then simmer it until the meat is done and tender. Bone the meat and put it in the refrigerator for a while before dicing it.

The Salad
2 cups cooked rabbit meat, diced
1 cup diced celery
1 cup mayonnaise
2 hard-boiled chicken eggs, sliced
¼ cup almond slivers
butter
juice of 1 lemon
salt and pepper to taste
The Garnish
lettuce leaves
1 tablespoon capers
1 hard-boiled chicken egg, sliced
1 tablespoon mayonnaise
paprika

Sauté the almond slivers in a little butter. Mix the rabbit meat, celery, and lemon juice. Chill. Shortly before serving, add 1 cup mayonnaise, slices from 2 hard-boiled eggs, almond slivers, salt, and pepper. Line a bowl with lettuce, then fill with the rabbit salad. Arrange slices of the third hard-boiled egg on top, then put capers onto the eggs. Top with 1 tablespoon mayonnaise, then sprinkle with a little paprika. Serves 6 or more as a salad, or feeds 3 or 4 for a light lunch.

Note: Rabbit salad makes an excellent sandwich. First, trim the brown crust from the slices of white sandwich bread; next, if you aren't on a diet, spread the slices with lots of mayonnaise, then spread thickly with the rabbit salad.

Rabbit à la King

If I had to choose a recipe for introducing wild game dishes to people of squeamish nature, this one might be it. It's also a good recipe for using up leftovers.

2 cups rabbit meat, cooked and diced
1½ cups cream
8 ounces mushrooms, finely chopped
1 onion, golf-ball size, finely chopped
juice of ½ large lemon
½ green bell pepper, finely chopped
½ red bell pepper, finely chopped
3 tablespoons butter (divided)
1½ tablespoons flour
2 chicken egg yolks
1 bay leaf
salt and pepper to taste
crisp toast, cooked separately

Dress the rabbit, put it into a suitable pan, cover the meat with water, and add a little salt and the bay leaf. Bring to a boil, then reduce heat to very low, cover tightly, and simmer for 1½ hours or longer, until the meat is very tender. Remove the rabbit, let it cool, and bone the meat.

Heat 1½ cups of cream in a double boiler. In a small container, blend the flour and 2 tablespoons of butter, then stir it into the heated cream. Melt 1 tablespoon of butter in a skillet. Add the red and green peppers, mushrooms, and onions. Simmer for a few minutes. While waiting, beat the egg yolks in a small container and stir in a little of the heated cream. Add the egg yolks to the rest of the cream, then stir it into the mixture in the skillet. Stir in the lemon juice, salt, and pepper. Then add the diced meat. Bring to heat but do not boil. Serve over crisp toast. This dish makes a terrific lunch, and will feed 4 to 6.

Germantown Rabbit Stew

Here's a German dish that was published by Art Boebinger in Kentucky's *Happy Hunting Ground*. As Boebinger explained, "Many German and French immigrants settled in the Ohio River Valley between Louisville and Cincinnati, Ohio, about the time of the Civil War. These people had a tradition of hunting in their native countries and they soon adapted older recipes to the native game animals. Here is a rabbit stew with just a little continental flavor."

1 rabbit
¼ pound bacon, diced
½ pound sliced mushrooms
1 cup beef stock
1 cup red wine
8 small white onions
2 tablespoons flour
2 carrots, sliced
1 tablespoon butter
1 tablespoon minced parsley
1 bay leaf
salt and pepper to taste

In a stove-top Dutch oven or similar heavy pot of suitable size, fry the bacon in butter until brown. Brown all the rabbit pieces and remove them to drain. Sauté the onions and mushrooms. Add the flour, blending it into the mixture. Add the beef stock, wine, parsley, carrots, bay leaf, salt, pepper, and browned rabbit pieces. Bring to a light boil, cover, reduce the heat to very low, and simmer for 2 hours, or until the rabbit is tender. Boebinger says he likes to serve this stew with American corn bread and a salad. Feeds 2 or 3.

Note: Also see the German recipe below.

Hasenpfeffer

This German dish has been around for centuries simply because it is so good! There are dozens of variations. The one I normally use

---

Swamper Tricks

Swamp rabbits are worthy of a few special comments, simply because they're much more difficult to bag than cottontails. The same techniques are used to hunt them, but keep in mind they're twice as big as cottontails, leading dogs on much longer chases. They're much less numerous, too. It takes a lot more work to bag them. When pursued, they'll often take to the water, float a safe distance downstream, then exit the water and head for thick cover. In slow-moving water, they'll dive and hide nose-up under shoreline vegetation. Such strategies evade even the best dogs, and a disappearing swamper is by no means a strain on a beagle pack's reputation. Instead, it speaks for this rabbit's amazing adaptability.
—Keith Sutton, *Arkansas Game and Fish*

was adapted some years ago from an early edition of *The Good Housekeeping Cookbook*.

The Meat and the Marinade
    3 to 4 pounds of rabbit or hare, cut up
    2 medium onions, sliced
    2 cups red wine
    1 cup water
    1 tablespoon mixed pickling spice
    2 bay leaves
    ½ teaspoon dried thyme
    2 teaspoons salt
    ½ teaspoon pepper
Other Ingredients
    10 slices bacon
    ¾ cup flour
    1 teaspoon sugar

Put the rabbit pieces into a large nonmetallic bowl, then pour in the wine and water. Add the onions, pickling spice, thyme, salt, pepper, and bay leaves. Cover the bowl and refrigerate overnight.

When you are ready to cook, fry the bacon in a large skillet until it is quite crisp. Drain the bacon, crumble it, and set it aside. Retain the bacon drippings. Remove the rabbit from the marinade and pat the pieces dry with paper towels. (Retain the marinade liquid.) Shake the rabbit pieces in a bag with flour, then brown them a few pieces at a time in the bacon drippings. When all the pieces have been browned, put them into a stove-top Dutch oven or in a large skillet that will hold everything. Sprinkle the crumbled bacon over the rabbit pieces. Strain the marinade mixture, discarding the seasonings, and stir in the sugar. Pour the liquid over the rabbit, bring to a quick boil, reduce heat to very low, cover, and simmer for 2 hours.

Oven Barbecued Rabbit

Some people will say that real barbecue has to be cooked on a grill; others will say that the secret lies in the sauce. In any case, be sure to try this recipe—then call it what you like.

The Meat
    2 cottontails, cut into pieces
    juice of 1 lemon
    salt and pepper
The Sauce
    ½ cup vinegar
    ½ cup catsup
    ½ cup Worcestershire sauce
    ½ cup water
    1 can V-8 juice (12-ounce size)
    2 medium onions, diced
    2 cloves garlic, minced
    2 medium green peppers, diced
    2 tablespoons butter
    1 teaspoon salt
    ½ teaspoon pepper

Preheat the oven to 350 degrees. Salt and pepper the rabbit pieces, then place them in a single layer in a well-greased baking pan. Squeeze the lemon juice on top. Bake for 30 minutes.

As the rabbit bakes, combine all the sauce ingredients in a pan and bring to a quick boil.

Reduce the heat and simmer for 30 minutes, stirring from time to time. Pour the sauce over the rabbit, reduce the oven heat to 250 degrees, and bake for 3 hours, turning the pieces a time or two. Serve hot with rice and vegetables. Feeds 4 or 5.

Irish Rabbit

One of my favorite rabbit recipes is Irish fare, and the book that I got it from *(Traditional Irish Recipes,* by George L. Thomson) had some strange measures in it, such as "1 dsstsp." This turns out to be a "dessertspoon," which is equal to 2 Irish teaspoons. An Irish tablespoon, by comparison, is equal to 3 Irish teaspoons. Further, the book went on, a standard teaspoon in Irish measure is a little larger than the American. Thus, I have translated the measures into "heaping teaspoons" and "heaping tablespoons" in the recipe.

Any tender rabbit can be used for this dish; I usually cook it with cottontail. The rabbit is skinned and cut into serving pieces, which include 2 hindquarters, the saddle, and 2 shoulders.

1 rabbit
4 slices cooked bacon
2 medium onions, chopped
1 heaping tablespoon flour
2 heaping teaspoons chopped parsley
2 ounces melted butter
½ pint scalded milk
salt and pepper
vinegar and water

Put the rabbit pieces into a glass container and cover with a mixture of vinegar and water, mixed in more or less equal volume. Marinate for at least 2 hours. When you are ready to cook, preheat the oven to 375 degrees. Then drain the meat and sprinkle each piece lightly with salt and pepper. Dredge in flour. Heat the butter in a skillet and brown the pieces. Place the rabbit in an ovenproof baking dish. Crumble the bacon and sprinkle it over the rabbit, along with the chopped onions and parsley. Pour the scalded milk over the meat, cover tightly, and bake for 1 hour.

Serve this stew for supper on a cold night, along with boiled Irish potatoes and vegetables of your choice.

After eating, pour yourself a sip of good Irish whiskey (not scotch whisky, which is spelled without the *e*), retire to your easy chair beside the hearth, poke up the wood fire, pat your dog on the head, and pick up your favorite cookbook by A. D. Livingston.

31

CLASSIC RECIPES FOR BIG GAME

One of the worst ways to introduce people to the joys of venison and other big game is to bake a whole roast too long. Venison is much more lean than feed-lot beef, and baking it in an oven is likely to make it too dry. More-over, this problem is compounded because far too many people tend to cook wild meat longer than they cook supermarket meat.

One of the best ways to introduce people to the joys of wild game, or to convert skeptics, is to prepare a stew-type dish with which they are already familiar. Thus, they will be starting off with a familiar classic flavor, and if you prepare the dish with tender loving care, they will be more likely to come back for seconds. Here are some old favorites for stews and boiled meats—many of which were first developed with venison, bear, or other wild game:

Venison

The term "venison" comes from the Latin term *venatus* which means "to hunt." The latter probably is akin to the Sanskrit term *venati*, which means "he desires, attacks, gains." Originally, the word veni-son applied to the flesh of any beast or bird of the chase, but has now come to apply only to flesh of deer and deer kind.

—Frank G. Ashbrook, *Butchering, Processing and Preservation of Meat*

Big-Game Stroganoff

Traditionally, stroganoff is made with beef, but its classic flavor goes with the better cuts of deer, elk, moose, caribou, and similar wild game. This recipe can easily be cut in half or otherwise modified. If the full measures are used, the volume will be too much for a single skillet of ordinary size. Consequently, I use a skillet together with a stove-top Dutch oven.

2 pounds venison tenderloin or tender steak
16 ounces sour cream
15 ounces medium egg noodles
8 ounces fresh mushrooms, sliced
1 cup chopped onion
2 cloves garlic, minced
2 cans condensed beef broth (10½-ounce size)
¼ cup red wine
2 tablespoons tomato paste
flour
butter or margarine
salt and pepper

The success of this stroganoff recipe depends in part on having thin strips of tender meat. The first step, therefore, is to get the meat ready to cook. Cut the meat against the grain into ¼-inch slices; then cut the slices into ½-inch strips. The meat is much easier to slice if it is partly frozen.

Heat about ¼ cup of butter in a skillet, then sauté the onions, garlic, and mushrooms for 5 minutes, stirring with a wooden spoon. Put these ingredients into a stove-top Dutch oven or similar pot, together with about ½ can of the beef broth. Put the pot on low heat.

Salt and pepper the meat, then shake it in a bag with a little flour. Add 2 tablespoons butter to the skillet. Sauté about half of the meat for 5 or 6 minutes, stirring it about with a wooden spoon; transfer the browned meat to the Dutch oven. Add a little more butter to the skillet, brown the rest of the meat, and add it to the Dutch oven.

Add ⅓ cup of flour to the skillet, stirring it in with the pan drippings and cooking it on very low heat for 5 minutes or longer. Slowly stir in a little of the beef broth and the tomato paste. Cook and stir over low heat until bubbly, adding either flour or beef broth until you have a nice gravy.

Add the gravy to the Dutch oven, then stir in the wine and sour cream. Reduce the heat to very low so that the sour cream will not curdle. Do not allow the mixture to boil, or you'll have an unappetizing mess.

While the stroganoff sits on very low heat, bring 1 gallon of water to a roiling boil in a suitable pot. Add the noodles slowly. Salt to taste and cook uncovered for 12 minutes, stirring several times. Drain the noodles in a colander, top them with 1 teaspoon of butter, and stir.

Serve the hot stroganoff over the noodles, along with plenty of hot sourdough bread and vegetables. I like to use frozen mixed vegetables, especially the San Francisco blend. Feeds 6.

Variations: Stroganoff can be served over rice or mashed potatoes instead of noodles.

Note: The above recipe is based on tenderloin or other choice cuts of tender meat. Lesser cuts can also be used, but the meat should first be tenderized by marinating it, by sprinkling it with commercial meat tenderizer, by beating it, or by simmering it for a longer time. I recommend the following: Cut the meat as directed in the recipe—with emphasis on thin cuts—and brown it in the skillet. Add 1 cup of water, cover the skillet, and simmer the meat for 1 hour or longer. Then proceed with the recipe.

Leftover meat from such dishes as venison roasts can be sliced up, or even cubed, for use in stroganoff recipes. Stroganoff is a good recipe for using up any leftover meat that tended to be on the dry side after the original cooking. Even ground meat, made into small balls or patties, can be used in stroganoff.

Stroganoff freezes well and uneaten portions can be kept for quite some time. Also, try any leftover gravy on French-cut green beans

All in all, stroganoff is a tasty, versatile dish that every cook should know. Any hunter needing (or wanting) a new .30-06 for birthday or holiday should drop the hint after serving up venison stroganoff at a family dinner!

Game Hungarian Goulash

This dish is very old and, of course, there are many variations. Here is my favorite version for use with big-game meat:

> 2 pounds game meat
> 3 tomatoes, chopped
> 1 medium to large onion, chopped
> 2 cloves garlic, minced
> 2 tablespoons minced fresh parsley
> 1 can beef broth (10½-ounce size)
> cooking oil
> flour
> 2 bay leaves
> 2 teaspoons caraway seeds
> ½ teaspoon Hungarian paprika
> salt and pepper to taste

Cut the meat into 1-inch cubes, season with salt and pepper, then sprinkle with flour. Heat 2 tablespoons of cooking oil in a skillet, then sauté the onion and garlic for 5 minutes or so. Transfer these to a stove-top Dutch oven or other suitable pot. Add a little more oil to the skillet and brown about half of the meat; then brown the rest. Transfer all the meat to the Dutch oven. Add the beef broth to the Dutch

Stewing Perfectly

Some modern cooks know that the crockpot makes wonderful venison stew, but they may not realize exactly why. It's the low temperature and the long cooking time. The same effect is sometimes difficult to achieve on the stove top simply because the lowest heat is not always low enough. (Stoves vary widely in this regard.) In this case, the cook can help matters by using a large, heavy pot. In other words, a cast-iron Dutch oven on a small stove burner will simmer a better stew than a small aluminum pan on a large burner.

In any case, stewing venison and other game at a hard boil will make the meat tougher and drier. A slow simmer is much better.

oven, bring to a simmer, and reduce the heat to low. Add the bay leaves, caraway seeds, paprika, parsley, and tomatoes. Cover and simmer on very low heat for 3 hours. About 30 minutes before serving, season the goulash to taste with salt and pepper. Serve with egg noodles. Feeds 4 or 5.

Sauerbraten

This old German dish is an ideal way to serve up a good-size chunk of elk, deer, moose, or other red meat to guests who might be a bit squeamish about even a hint of gamey flavor. I have even made it successfully with a hindquarter of beaver.

The Marinade

    2 medium onions, sliced

    1 lemon, sliced

    12 cloves garlic

    1 tablespoon sugar

    1 tablespoon salt

    3 cups water

    2 cups red wine vinegar

    10 peppercorns

    8 bay leaves

    1/4 teaspoon dry ground ginger

The Meat

    4- or 5-pound game roast

    strained marinade from above

The Sauce

    1 cup crumbled gingersnaps

    pan juices from the meat

    1/2 cup water

Put the roast into a large crock or other non-metallic container. Mix the water, wine vinegar, and other marinade ingredients. Pour over the roast and refrigerate for 24 to 48 hours. Turn the meat every 8 hours or so.

When you are ready to cook, remove the meat and pat it dry with paper towels. Strain the marinade and retain the liquid. In a stove-top Dutch oven, heat the oil and brown the meat. Add the strained marinade. Cover tightly and simmer for 2 hours. (Do not boil.) Put the meat on a serving dish. To make gravy, retain 2 cups of the liquid in the Dutch oven. Add 1/2 cup of water and the cup of crumbled gingersnaps. Simmer and stir until the gravy bubbles and thickens. Slice the meat and serve the gravy over individual servings. Feeds 8 to 10.

Variations: Try an apple cider marinade. Substitute 3 cups of cider for the red wine vinegar. Also, use 2 tablespoons of brown sugar instead of 1 tablespoon regular sugar.

Note: Sauerbraten doesn't freeze well, so plan to eat the roast within a few days. Refrigerated sauerbraten slices nicely, and I highly recommend it in white-bread sandwiches. The trick is to slice it thinly, then use several slices per sandwich. My oldest son, Jarrod, likes 3 or 4 sauerbraten and lettuce sandwiches together with a couple of packs of potato chips and a jar or two of kosher dill pickles. For lunch. Then he asks, "What's for supper?"

New England Boiled Dinner with Venison

If there's anything better than corned beef, it's corned venison. And if there's anything better than corned venison with cabbage, it's a full-fledged New England boiled dinner. Be sure to try this recipe. Any good piece of venison can be corned, but I prefer to use the segments of the rear leg or perhaps a boned shoulder. There are many recipes for corning the venison, some calling for such chemicals as sodium nitrite and sodium nitrate, or perhaps a commercial mix such as Morton's Tender Quick. (Look for the curing salts in the canning section of your local supermarket.) The main advantage of using these chemicals is that they give the meat a red color.

I prefer to keep the process simple, however, using only sea salt and good water. Sea salt contains lots of good minerals that help preserve meat, and it has a good flavor. Although it is too expensive for large-scale corning operations, I don't mind a little extra expense for corning a roast or two. Usually, I corn 2 or 3 pounds as needed for the recipe below, but larger amounts can be corned and frozen. Having good water is essential to really good corned meats. Avoid water that tastes of sulfur or chlorine. Often well water or spring water will be

Hunt or Harvest?

Year by year, more and more property owners believe that they own any deer or other game found on their land. This is understandable, and pay-to-hunt or lease deals for game are becoming more and more important to land management and farming. I have no quarrel with the pay-to-hunt ethic, although I do have mixed feelings about participating in some of the hunts, and I see here a trend toward game for the rich.

In order to maximize the profits, more and more of these private hunting lands are being managed on a professional basis. In balance, this is to the good, I suppose, because it increases the numbers of game animals, some of which don't honor man's boundaries. The practice begins to break down, however, when the landowners and the managers start planting pen-raised birds and animals to be flushed and shot.

Further, the "college degree" game-management mentality shifts the emphasis from hunting game to harvesting game. Of course, this use of the word *harvest* has been around for a long time and has grown steadily in game-management circles and in both state and federal agencies. Thus, a report from a state wildlife department will say that so many thousand white-tailed deer were *harvested* during a particular year. It won't say the deer were shot or bagged. The subtle implication, of course, is *not* that the state's skilled hunters successfully bagged *x* number of deer, but that the bureaucracy successfully raised and *permitted* the harvest of *x* number of deer. This same mentality filters down to the populace through a constant flow of news releases to magazines, newspapers, and TV shows and is also reflected in the various state-published fish and game brochures, magazines, and other publications.

Regardless of their good intentions, many of the people who manage the wildlife areas drift into the habit of putting more importance on hunter success in mere numbers, tending to neglect the *quality* of the hunting. I won't go into the reasons for this, but it has to do with job security and with the empire-building tendency that is common to bureaucracies. The trend toward easy hunting in order to ensure a higher statistical success will also become more and more evident on leased private lands as well as on booked hunts. We'll be planting and fertilizing more and more fodder to attract and hold deer. The more productive the land, the larger the harvest and the greater the profits. If we don't watch out, we'll end up with hybrid or selectively bred deer. They'll have big racks and will be easy to "harvest."

Of course, no one can question the success of the American white-tailed deer and wild turkey restoration programs. But let's not overmanage a good thing.

better than local tap water, although health officials might argue this point.

Corned Venison
  2- or 3-pound venison roast
  3 cups sea salt
  1 gallon water

Dissolve the salt in the water. Wash the roast and trim off all the fat and sinew. Put the roast into a nonmetallic container and cover with brine solution.

Place a plate or heavy saucer atop the roast to keep it submerged. The roast must be submerged at all times. (If you don't have enough brine, mix some more.) Place the container in the refrigerator, or in a cool place below 38 degrees, for at least 2 weeks. I turn the roast after a week or so, mostly, I suppose, because I want to look at it. After 2 weeks, the roast will be ready for cooking or freezing.

New England Boiled Dinner
  2 or 3 pounds corned venison
  6 or 8 small onions, golf-ball size
  4 medium potatoes
  4 medium carrots
  1 medium head cabbage
  1 can sliced beets (optional)
  2 bay leaves
  2 cloves
  1 teaspoon dried basil leaves
  ½ teaspoon pepper
  water

Rinse the brine off the venison roast and put it into a large stove-top Dutch oven or pot. Cover the meat with water, bring it to a boil, and simmer for a few minutes. Pour off the water, cover with new water, and bring to a new boil. Add the bay leaves, onions, pepper, cloves, and basil. Simmer—do not boil—over very low heat for 5 or 6 hours. (If you cook it too fast, the meat will be tough.) Add the potatoes and carrots; cook until they are almost done. Cut the cabbage into quarters, add to the pot, and increase the heat a little. (The cabbage does not have to be covered with water, as steam will do the cooking.) Cover the pot and simmer for 12 minutes. If you use the beets, which I highly recommend because they add color to the dish, heat them in a separate boiler. When you are ready to serve, place the venison roast on a large platter and arrange the vegetables around it. Serve with corn bread. Feeds 4 to 6.

Variations: A number of recipes for New England boiled dinner call for different vegetables. Try turnips, parsnips, rutabagas (peeled and cubed), and whole mushrooms if you've got them on hand. This is a very old New England dish, and the original called for salt pork boiled along with the corned meat. I like to include the salt pork, and serve it along with the venison, but the trend these days is to cut back on animal fat—which is one very good reason for using venison instead of modern feed-lot beef in the first place.

Moussaka

This classic favorite of the Greeks and Turks is a wonderful dish to serve whenever you have lots of folks to feed on a minimum amount of meat.

The Meat
- 1 pound ground venison or other ground game
- 3 medium eggplants
- 1 medium to large onion, chopped
- 1 medium tomato, peeled and chopped
- ¼ cup chopped fresh parsley
- 1 can tomato sauce (8-ounce size)
- 1 cup bread crumbs (divided)
- ½ cup grated American cheese
- ½ cup grated Parmesan cheese
- ¼ cup red wine
- 2 chicken eggs
- cooking oil
- butter or margarine
- cinnamon
- salt and pepper

Topping Sauce
- 3 tablespoons butter
- 3 tablespoons flour
- milk
- nutmeg
- 1 chicken egg
- salt and pepper to taste

Peel the eggplants and cut them into ½-inch slices. Spread the slices out, well spaced, on absorbent paper, and sprinkle them with salt. (This will require lots of space, so clean off a counter or table.) Let stand for 1 hour or so. While the salt is drawing the bitter juices from the eggplant, sauté the chopped onions in a little butter or margarine in a skillet. Add the ground venison and cook it for a few minutes, until browned. Stir in the tomato sauce, chopped tomato, parsley, and wine. Salt and pepper to taste. Simmer on low heat until most of the liquid has been absorbed. Remove the skillet from the heat and let cool.

Rinse the eggplant slices under cold water and pat dry. Heat a little oil in another skillet or griddle (or remove the meat mixture to a bowl) and brown the eggplant a few slices at a time. Drain the slices on absorbent paper.

Preheat the oven to 350 degrees. Now prepare the topping in a saucepan. Melt the butter, and slowly stir in the flour. Add salt, pepper, and a little nutmeg. Pour in the milk, a little at a time, stirring until the sauce bubbles and thickens. In a small bowl, whisk 1 egg with a little of the sauce, then add to the sauce mixture and simmer over very low heat for about 2 minutes. Remove from the heat.

Back to the meat mixture, which should have cooled down by now. Whisk 2 eggs and stir them into the meat, along with half of the bread crumbs, a little cinnamon, and the American cheese. Grease a 12-by-8-by-2-inch dish, and sprinkle the remaining bread crumbs onto the bottom. Add a layer of eggplant, then crisscross another layer, using up about half the slices. Spoon on the meat mixture, spreading it evenly. Add the rest of the eggplant slices in even layers. Pour the sauce over the top and spread. Sprinkle with Parmesan cheese. Place the dish into the center of the preheated oven and bake for about 45 minutes, or until a crust has formed on top. Serve hot with lots of green salad and Greek bread. Feeds 6 to 8.

Variations: Try moussaka cooked and served in small individual dishes. Also, try the dish topped with a layer of mashed potatoes or sautéed sliced potatoes. With sliced potatoes, retain the sauce detailed above. With either sliced or mashed potatoes, sprinkle with Parmesan before baking. Try the Greek Kephalotyri cheese instead of Parmesan if you can get it.

Don't tell my son Bill, who is always on guard for "ucky" stuff, but add some zucchini if you have some that needs to be used up; it can be sliced and added along with the eggplant. Also, try using thin eggplant slices with the peel still on. The peel adds an unusual flavor and provides color contrast.

Venison Lasagna

There are a number of excellent lasagna recipes that work with ground venison. I would like to say that my favorite and heretofore secret recipe came from my Aunt Anna or somebody from the Old Country—but the plain truth is that I modified it from a recipe that came in the

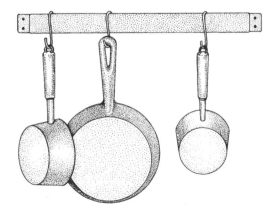

instruction booklet for a small auxiliary oven that I recently purchased. Good stuff. Try it.

1½ pounds ground venison
½ pound uncooked lasagna noodles
2 cups cottage cheese
2 cups shredded mozzarella cheese
½ cup grated Parmesan cheese (divided)
1 can tomatoes (16-ounce size)
1 can tomato sauce (15-ounce size)
1 medium to large onion, diced
1 clove garlic, minced
3 tablespoons dried parsley (divided)
2 tablespoons olive oil
1½ teaspoons dried oregano
1 teaspoon dried basil
1 teaspoon sugar
salt

Heat the olive oil in a large skillet, sauté the onions and garlic for 5 minutes, and brown the ground meat. Add the tomatoes and the liquid from the can, tomato sauce, 2 tablespoons parsley, sugar, basil, and about ½ teaspoon salt. Bring to a bubble, stirring constantly. Reduce the heat and simmer for 1 hour. Then preheat the oven to 350 degrees.

In a large boiler, cook the noodles according to the directions on the package. (If you make your own noodles, you're ahead of me and probably know what to do.) Take ½ cup of the meat sauce from the skillet and set it aside. Into the rest of the meat sauce, mix the cottage cheese, ¼ cup Parmesan, 1 tablespoon parsley, about 1 teaspoon salt, and the oregano.

Grease a 9-by-13-inch baking pan, then make three layers in the following order: ⅓ of the cooked noodles, ⅓ of the meat sauce, ⅓ of the mozzarella, and ⅓ of the cottage cheese mixture. Repeat the layers. Repeat again. Spoon on the ½ cup of reserved meat sauce, then sprinkle with ¼ cup Parmesan. Bake in the 350-degree oven for 45 minutes. Remove from the oven and let cool for 15 minutes. Serve with hot Italian, French, or Greek bread and lots of good tossed salad. Feeds 4 or 5.

Variations: Although venison is specified, almost any game meat can be used with this recipe. Be sure to try it with ground turtle or turkey. Or rabbit. Or bear.

Venison Swiss

Here's a good recipe that can be used with most cuts of steak from deer, elk, or moose. Unless you are using tenderloin or perhaps loin, the meat should be tenderized before cooking. I usually pound it with the edge of a plate, first one way and then crosswise. Others prefer a meat mallet. Suit yourself.

The Meat
 2 pounds good venison steak
 ½ cup flour
 2 or 3 tablespoons cooking oil
 1 tablespoon dry mustard
 salt and pepper to taste
The Trimmings
 1 cup diced carrots
 1 cup sliced onions
 1 can stewed tomatoes (14-ounce size)
 1 tablespoon brown sugar

Preheat the oven to 325 degrees. Mix the flour, mustard, salt, and pepper. Sprinkle a little of this mixture over the steaks. Pound the steaks thoroughly, working in more of the flour mixture as you go. Then dredge the steak with what's left of the flour mixture. Heat the cooking oil in a skillet and brown the steaks on both

sides. Grease a pan or casserole dish of suitable size and place the steaks into it, preferably in a single layer. Mix the carrots, onions, tomatoes, and brown sugar. Pour this mixture over the steaks. Cover and bake for 2 hours. Serve with vegetables and bread for a main meal. Feeds 5 or 6.

Venison Pepper Steak, Chinese Style

There are at least two kinds of "pepper steak." The dish covered here is cooked with green peppers and other vegetables and Chinese ingredients. It should be served with or over rice. The other is prepared by pounding freshly ground black pepper into the meat, then pan-broiling it for a short time over high heat. A recipe for this French dish, called Steak au Poivre, follows this one.

 1½ pounds venison steak, 1 inch thick
 meat tenderizer (if needed)
 2 medium tomatoes
 1 red bell pepper
 1 green bell pepper
 1 clove garlic, minced
 1 cup beef broth
 ⅓ cup peanut oil
 2 tablespoons soy sauce
 1 tablespoon cornstarch
 2 teaspoons sugar
 1 teaspoon grated fresh ginger
 salt and pepper to taste
 rice (cooked separately)

Sprinkle the steaks with meat tenderizer, if needed. Pound with the edge of a plate or with a meat mallet. If possible, place the steaks in a freezer until partially frozen, or refrigerate for 1 hour. (This will make the meat easier to slice uniformly.) Cut the steaks into strips about 2 inches long and ¼ inch wide.

Prepare the vegetables. Cut the onions and peppers into strips lengthwise, about ½ inch wide in the middle. Cut each tomato lengthwise into 8 pieces.

Heat the peanut oil very hot in a large skillet or wok. Add the venison strips, stirring constantly with a wooden spoon for 5 minutes. Stir in the beef broth, onion, garlic, and ginger. Simmer for 15 minutes. Add the peppers, then simmer for another 5 minutes. Quickly prepare the sauce by blending in a saucepan the soy sauce, cornstarch, sugar, salt, and pepper. Stir this mixture into the meat mixture. Bring to a boil and cook for 2 or 3 minutes. Reduce heat. Put the tomatoes on top of the mixture, cover, and cook on low heat for 4 minutes. Feeds 4 or 5, if you've got lots of rice.

Venison Steak au Poivre

Here's a French way of preparing beefsteak. It will work nicely with very tender venison steaks or cutlets. It's best to use the loin, which can be cut into 2-inch segments and then butterflied, making a hinged steak 1 inch thick. Beseeching the reader to use tender meat for this recipe is tempting, but perhaps the better advice is not to overcook the meat. If you do, it will be tough.

For this dish, I insist on having real butter. To clarify it, heat it in a small pan and then carefully pour it into another container, leaving the sediments in the bottom. Clarified butter can be heated to a high temperature without burning.

2 pounds tender venison steaks
2 tablespoons clarified butter
2 jiggers cognac
salt
freshly crushed black pepper (rather coarse)

I prefer to crush some peppercorns in a mortar and pestle, or put them between sheets of waxed paper and crush them with the smooth side of a meat mallet. A pepper mill can be used, but you'll need a coarse grind. You can also buy a bottle of coarse pepper at the supermarket, but freshly crushed is better. Sprinkle the steaks lightly with salt, and then press some pepper into both sides of the meat. The recipe works best if you use lots of pepper, but taste and experience are your best guides.

Heat a serving platter on the side. Heat the clarified butter in a cast-iron skillet almost to the smoking point. Quickly sear the steaks in the skillet on both sides, then sauté the meat for about 3 minutes on each side, until it is rare or medium rare, as you prefer. Quickly put the steaks onto the heated serving platter. Using a wooden spoon, dislodge any bits of meat that may have stuck to the bottom of the skillet. Pour the cognac into the skillet, shake it around for several minutes, then pour it over the meat and serve. Eat while hot. Although steak au poivre is a French dish, it goes nicely with an ordinary baked Idaho potato and tossed salad. Do use the chewy French bread, however, and some good red wine.

Venison Kabobs

Russians, Turks, Azerbaijanis, and others all claim to have invented this great dish. In all probability, it originated on the steppes of Asia, but the basic technique of sticking meat on a stick probably goes back to the caveman. Although we now consider lamb to be traditional kabob meat, beef and other good meats, including venison, bear, and other wild game, can also be used. Venison might well have been the original meat. Any good cut of venison can be used, but I prefer boned shoulder, well marinated as in the recipe below.

2 pounds good venison
2 medium onions, grated
2 medium onions, quartered
juice of 1 lemon
½ cup fresh parsley, chopped
¼ cup melted butter
¼ cup olive oil
¼ cup red wine vinegar
salt and pepper
rice (cooked separately)
2 or 3 green onions with tops, chopped
    (garnish)
home-grown tomatoes (garnish)

Grate 2 of the onions, zap them in a food processor, or quarter them and squeeze out the juice with the aid of a garlic press. While you're crying, quarter the other 2 onions and set them aside for later use. Mix the grated onions, salt, pepper, parsley, lemon juice, and vinegar in a nonmetallic container. Cube the meat into kabob-size pieces and toss them in the container with the onion mix. Put the container in a cool place and marinate for several hours, tossing from time to time to make sure all sides of the meat are covered. A large plastic Ziploc bag makes everything easier.

When you're ready to cook, build a good charcoal fire: mix the butter and olive oil, warming it as the coals heat. Thread the meat onto skewers, alternating each piece with a segment of the onion quarters. Grill about 4 inches from hot coals on an uncovered grill for 4 or 5 minutes on each side, basting several times. Do not overcook. Serve medium rare over rice. Garnish with chopped green onions and tomato slices.

32

VENISON

All of the world's thirty-six species of deer are good eating if they are handled and cooked properly. In Europe and parts of Asia, the relatively small roe deer gets high marks as table fare, although the much larger red deer is more highly regarded for the chase. The smallest deer, the southern pudu, an endangered species that lives in the foothills of the Andes, weighs only about 17 pounds. The largest deer, the moose (which is called elk in Europe), weighs in at 1,750 pounds or so. In America, the white-tailed deer is very popular with both hunters and meat eaters.

At one time, the whitetail had disappeared from a good part of its range because of over-hunting and other problems. But thanks to modern game-management techniques, it has been restored to most of its former range. In fact, the deer are now considered to be pests in many agricultural areas and in some suburbs, where they eat gardens and potted plants and may be traffic hazards.

Some of the deer have been domesticated, and many others are managed to such an extent in parks and preserves that they may well be somewhere between wild and domesticated. In any case, the meat of all deer is often known as venison, and it is very good eating if it has been wisely selected and properly handled before and

A Success Story

In 1900, there were only about 350,000 white-tailed deer in the entire United States. Thanks to ever-improving game-management programs, today we have more than 14,000,000!

during cooking. Unlike modern beef, venison has very little fat marble in the tissue.

In this chapter, however, venison refers only to the meat of the American deer, such as the white-tailed and mule deer. Elk, moose, and others are covered in separate chapters.

Fried Venison

One day I was talking to a hefty local farmer who operated a small pork sausage-making operation on the side. He enjoyed a local reputation for his sausage, and also for his deer-hunting skill, but he was pretty tight-lipped about both subjects. Carefully, I worked the conversation into the culinary aspects of the hunt, and he told me that he and his family hung their deer for ten days in the sausage cooler. When I asked him flat out how he cooked the deer, a puzzled look crossed his face. "Why, we fry 'em," he said, almost as if it had not occurred to him that there might be another way. He did add that he cuts the better parts into steaks, then grinds the rest for "hamburger" or sausage meat. He wouldn't give me his family sausage secrets, but here's his fried steak recipe:

venison steaks, ½ inch thick
meat tenderizer
peanut oil
flour
garlic salt
pepper
milk
water

Treat the steaks with the meat tenderizer (following the directions on the package), then sprinkle them with garlic salt and pepper. Pound the steaks with a meat mallet. Sprinkle flour lightly over one side of the steaks, then pound them again. Turn the steaks over, sprinkle with flour, and pound again. After pounding, sprinkle both sides with flour or dredge in flour. Heat ½ inch of peanut oil in a skillet, then fry the steaks until nicely browned on both sides, turning once. Remove the steaks from the skillet and set aside to drain. Pour off most of the oil, then scrape up any bits of crust that may have stuck to the skillet. Put 2 tablespoons of flour into the skillet; cook and stir for a few minutes, shaking the skillet the whole time. Slowly add 1 cup of water and 1 cup of milk, in that order, cooking and stirring as you go. Put the steaks back into the gravy, cover, and simmer for 1 hour, or until the steak can be cut with a fork. Add more water as needed. Have ready a pan of hot biscuits for the gravy.

Primitive Deer

Bones found in kitchen middens indicate that deer of one sort or another was one of ancient man's favorite foods. Further, the many cave paintings of deer that have been discovered, some dating back 14,000 years, suggest that deer had importance beyond mere food. Many of these deer paintings indicate a hunt, and it is quite possible that deer hunting was a sport even back then. In any case, we know that deer have been very popular with hunters throughout man's recorded history.

5 till 9 Roast

Here's a good venison roast dish that can be put on at 5 o'clock in the morning (before you go hunting) and taken out at night (when you get back). If you don't want to get up that early, or don't want to wait that long before eating, cut back the cooking time to 8 or 9 hours. In either case, you'll need a crockpot.

  1 venison roast, 5 or 6 pounds
  3 strips smoked bacon
  1 package onion soup mix (1.2-ounce size)
  vegetables (optional)
  water
  salt and pepper

Put the whole roast into your crockpot. (The roast can be frozen, but, if so, do not force-fit it, lest you crack your crockpot; also, cook for at least 9 hours if the roast is frozen.) Add ¼ cup water. Sprinkle the onion soup mix, salt, and pepper over the roast, then drape the bacon over it. Put the crockpot on low heat and leave it there all day.

If you choose to cook potatoes, mushrooms, carrots, and other vegetables along with the roast, simply add to the crockpot. If you cook the dish longer than 8 hours, the vegetables may start to cook apart, but the gravy will be very good.

Backcountry Venison

I designed this recipe for Dutch-oven cooking in remote camps, where a wide variety of ingredients would not be available and where perishable ingredients would not be practical. Dried apples can even be carried in your pocket.

  3 pounds venison stew meat
  4 ounces dried apples
  1 tablespoon brown sugar
  1 cup water
  salt and pepper

To cook at home, dump everything into a crockpot and cook on low heat for 8 or 9 hours. The dried apples will cook away, almost, leaving a thick gravy of very nice flavor that goes with venison. If you've got apple cider on hand, use it instead of water.

In camp, dig a hole in the ground (about 2 feet deep and 2 feet wide) and build a good fire in it and on the side. When you have plenty of coals, dump all the ingredients into a Dutch oven, cover it, and put it in the hole atop the coals. Cover the Dutch oven first with coals and then with dirt. Leave it for 8 or 9 hours. (Camp cookery is covered more fully in chapter 44.)

Pan-Fried Venison Parmesan

This tasty dish should be cooked only with fairly tender steaks or chops, cut about ¼ inch thick or a tad thicker. Loins and tenderloins work fine, either sliced or butterflied.

  2 pounds small steaks or chops
  1 cup cooking oil
  ½ cup freshly grated Parmesan cheese
  ½ cup fine cracker crumbs
  2 chicken eggs
  ½ teaspoon garlic juice
  salt and pepper

Mix the cooking oil and garlic juice in a suitable nonmetallic container. Add the steaks, toss to coat all sides, and marinate for several hours. Pour the marinade liquid into a skillet and heat. Add a little more oil if needed (depending in part on the diameter of the skillet). Salt and pepper the steaks. Whisk the eggs. Mix the grated Parmesan and cracker crumbs. Dip the steaks in the egg, roll in the crumbs, and fry on medium high heat until golden brown on both sides, turning once. Eat while hot. Feeds 4 or 5.

Note: I often keep garlic oil on hand for cooking. To make it, I fill a jar with garlic cloves and cover them with olive oil. After a month or so, the oil has a wonderful flavor and the cloves can be used for cooking purposes. This mix works better and has a better flavor than the oil and garlic juice. In my part of the country, I often find lots of wild garlic and use this method partly to preserve the garlic cloves and partly to make the garlic oil. Try it. Olive oil is best for this purpose, but peanut oil will also work.

Barbecued Tough–Buck Ribs

Here's a recipe that makes tough ribs tender, moist, and tasty. If you are in doubt about the quality of the ribs you are about to cook, then you should try this recipe. Change the measures to suit your needs. I figure at least 1 pound of ribs for each person. If you've got lots of ribs you might consider boning them after simmering. Your guests will eat more and keep cleaner hands. But if you're running short of meat, reduce the simmering time recommended below, leave the meat on the bones, and make 'em gnaw. The sauce for the ribs is very thick and somewhat sticky, so put a bowl of water and a roll of paper towels or napkins within easy reach.

The Meat
  4 pounds ribs
  water
  salt
  2 bay leaves

The Sauce
  2 cups catsup
  2 cups water
  1 medium onion, finely chopped
  1 rib celery, finely chopped
  juice of 1 lemon
  ½ cup vinegar
  ½ cup Worcestershire sauce
  2 tablespoons butter or margarine
  2 tablespoons brown sugar
  2 tablespoons blackstrap molasses
  1 teaspoon pepper
  1 teaspoon chili powder

Put the ribs into a large pot and cover them with water. Bring to a boil, add the bay leaves, reduce the heat, cover tightly, and simmer on very low heat for about 2 hours. Do not boil.

While simmering the ribs, prepare the sauce. Heat the butter in a skillet. Sauté the onions and celery. Add water, catsup, lemon juice, vinegar, Worcestershire sauce, brown sugar, molasses, chili powder, and pepper. Stir. Simmer the sauce while the ribs are parboiling.

Preheat the oven to 250 degrees. Remove the ribs from the water and drain. Salt the ribs, then arrange them in a well-greased baking pan of suitable size. Pour the sauce over the ribs and place the pan into the oven. Bake for 2 hours.

Either baste the ribs or turn them 2 or 3 times. Broiling the ribs for a few minutes before serving will thicken the sauce, if needed. Feeds 4 to 6.

Venison Shank Montana

Here's a helpful recipe that I have adapted from E. N. and Edith Sturdivant's *Game Cookery*, which explained: "Most hunters cut the meat off the shank and either grind it or use it as stew meat. But contrary to what many of them suppose, the meat is tender and has a rich, nutty flavor. Here is a different method of cooking the shank, which we like very much. We use the shank of the deer or antelope for this dish, serving one shank per person."

4 deer shanks
1 large onion, chopped
1 small can tomato sauce (8-ounce size)
2 tablespoons bacon fat or cooking oil
1 cup water
½ cup cooking sherry
¼ cup brown sugar
¼ teaspoon crushed rosemary
¼ teaspoon thyme
flour
salt and pepper

Salt and pepper the shanks, then dredge them with flour. Heat the bacon fat or cooking oil in a skillet or stove-top Dutch oven. Lightly brown the shanks. In another container, mix the onion, tomato sauce, water, sherry, brown sugar, rosemary, and thyme. After the shanks have browned, pour the sauce over them. If the sauce does not completely cover the shanks, add enough water to do so. Cover the Dutch oven tightly and simmer for 1½ to 2 hours, or until the shanks are tender. The Sturdivants recommend serving the shanks with rice or mashed potatoes, spinach, and spiced figs. I don't know about the spiced figs, but I'll certainly go along with the rest. Feeds 4.

Easy Swiss Venison Steak

This easy dish makes lots of good gravy, which my boys like poured over homemade biscuits. For breakfast.

2 pounds venison steak
3 medium onions, sliced
1 clove garlic, minced
1 can tomato soup (10¾-ounce size)
1 soup can water
4 tablespoons cooking oil (divided)
flour
garlic powder
salt and pepper

Cut the steak into serving-size pieces. Season them with salt, pepper, and garlic powder, then sprinkle with flour. Pound the steaks with the edge of a plate or with a meat mallet. Turn the steaks over, sprinkle with flour, and pound again. Repeat. Then dredge the steaks in flour. Heat 2 tablespoons of oil in a large skillet or stove-top Dutch oven. Sauté the onions and garlic for a few minutes, then remove and set aside. Brown some of the steaks on both sides. Add another 2 tablespoons of cooking oil if needed and brown the rest of the steaks. Arrange the steaks and sautéed onions in a Dutch oven, then add the tomato soup and water. Bring to a boil, reduce the heat, cover tightly, and simmer for 3 hours. Turn the steaks once or twice so that they will not scorch. Feeds 4.

Alaskan Barbecued Venison

Here's a very good dish—one of my favorites—that apparently originated in Alaska. Be sure to try it.

2 pounds venison shoulder meat
½ pound bacon
1 medium to large onion, chopped
2 cloves garlic, minced
1 cup catsup
½ cup red wine vinegar
¼ cup Worcestershire sauce
¼ cup brown sugar
milk
salt and pepper
water
rice (cooked separately)

Trim the venison and cut it into bite-size pieces. Put the meat into a nonmetallic container, cover it with whole milk, and refrigerate for at least 8 hours before cooking. When you are ready to cook, fry the bacon in a large skillet. Set the bacon aside to drain. In a bowl, mix the onions, garlic, catsup, vinegar, Worcestershire sauce, brown sugar, salt, and pepper. Drain the venison and brown it lightly in the bacon drippings. Pour off most of the liquid from the skillet. Add the onion mixture and crumbled bacon. Stir well. Bring to a bubble, cover tightly, and simmer (do not boil) for 1 hour, or until the venison is very tender. Stir occasionally and add a little water if needed. Serve over rice. Feeds 4 to 6.

Venison Steak Rolls

Here's a recipe that was sent to me by Tammy Ryan of the Montana Fish, Wildlife, and Parks Department. Before cooking, the steak is pounded and cut into serving size pieces.

2 pounds venison steak
4 slices bacon
2 cups bread crumbs
½ cup cracker crumbs
½ cup butter
½ cup finely chopped onion
¼ cup finely chopped celery
1 chicken egg, well beaten
1 teaspoon sage
salt and pepper
sliced Swiss cheese

Fry the bacon until crisp, remove from skillet, and crumble. Add the onion and celery and sauté. Add the bacon, bread crumbs, egg, sage, salt, and pepper. Spoon about 3 tablespoons of the mixture onto each piece of venison (the exact amount will depend on the size of the venison pieces). Top with cheese and roll up. Secure with toothpicks. Roll each roll in cracker crumbs and fry in butter. Turn often. For tough venison, use a lid and very low heat, then remove the lid for crustiness.

Hot Crockpot Stew

Because of the Rotel, which is a canned mixture of tomatoes and hot chili peppers, this delicious dish has a hint of old Mexico in its

Crockpot Flavors

Meat cooked on low heat for a long period of time, under cover, tends to absorb more flavor from herbs and spices. You might therefore consider cutting back on measures when cooking recipes that were not designed especially for crockpots.

flavor. If you don't like hot stuff, reduce the Rotel or use regular canned stewed tomatoes.

2½ pounds venison, cubed
2 cans Rotel (10-ounce size)
2 bell peppers, sliced
1 large onion, sliced
½ cup flour
1 tablespoon Worcestershire sauce
1 teaspoon Tabasco sauce (or to taste)
salt and pepper

Mix the flour, salt, and pepper in a paper bag. Shake the meat in the bag and dump it into a crockpot. Also include all the flour from the bag. Add the Rotel, onion, peppers, Tabasco sauce, and Worcestershire sauce. Cover the crockpot and cook on low for 8 or 9 hours. Feeds 5 or 6.

This dish makes a gravy that is just right for eating with lots of white-meal corn bread. Don't sop it. The procedure is to break up the corn bread on a plate and spoon gravy onto it. Then mash it all up with a fork.

Crockpot Pepper Steak

Here's one of my favorite crockpot dishes, this one with an oriental theme:

2 pounds steak from deer or elk
1 can tomatoes (16-ounce size)
1 green bell pepper, sliced lengthwise
1 red bell pepper, sliced lengthwise
8 ounces fresh mushrooms, sliced
½ cup flour
3 tablespoons blackstrap molasses
3 tablespoons soy sauce
salt and pepper
rice (cooked separately)

Cut the steaks into strips or fingers. Mix the flour, salt, and pepper in a bag. Shake the steak fingers in the bag, then put them into a crockpot. Add the remaining flour mixture and all the other ingredients. Cover and turn the crockpot to low for 8 or 9 hours. Serve with rice.

Tough-Buck Roast

Here's another easy crockpot recipe similar to the 5 till 9 Roast earlier in this chapter. If I seem to lean toward the crockpot for cooking venison, it's because the results are so good and so dependable.

1 venison roast, 4 or 5 pounds
1 can mushroom soup (10¾-ounce size)
1 package onion soup mix (1.2-ounce size)
fresh mushrooms
salt and pepper

Salt and pepper the roast, sprinkle it with the onion soup mix, and put it into a crockpot. Fill the pot with fresh mushrooms. Add the mushroom soup, cover, and cook on low for 8 or 9 hours.

Note: If you don't have a crockpot, wrap the roast and other ingredients tightly in wide, heavy-duty foil, sealing the edges with double folds. Put the package into a roasting pan and cook in a 250-degree oven for 4 or 5 hours.

Grilled Tenderloin Barbecue

The tenderloin is usually removed (or should be) when the deer is field-dressed. It requires no aging and can be cooked right away. Any good baste or barbecue sauce will work if the broiling technique is right. It's best to cook the meat quickly. If it's overcooked it will no longer be a *tender*loin. I cook this recipe (and variations) on my stove-top grill.

venison or other big-game tenderloin
melted butter or bacon drippings
barbecue sauce
salt and pepper

Preheat the stove-top grill. (If you don't have a kitchen grill, read the note below.) Slice the tenderloin across the grain into 2-inch pieces. Then slice each piece almost through. Fold out into a butterfly. Salt and pepper each piece to taste. Melt the butter and dip the steaks into it. Place the steaks on the grill and broil uncovered for 3 or 4 minutes. Turn the steaks, baste the top side with barbecue sauce, and grill the

About Beef Suet

After I published a magazine article long ago about adding beef suet to ground venison, a doctor from Tallahassee, Florida, wrote me that this stuff is poison. He may be right, but, nevertheless, most books on game cookery stick with the notion of adding either beef suet or hog fat to ground venison, no doubt trying to make it more like ordinary hamburger. In my experience, commercial meat processors who custom cut venison add far too much fat to gameburger and sausage. I suggest other ways to go in chapter 34.

Also, the old books (and most modern works) on game cookery suggest that beef suet or strips of fatback be put into venison roasts and other cuts of meat. Essentially, this adds fat to lean meat. Special larding needles are sometimes used for this purpose, or, more often, the meat is slit with a knife and the suet is poked in. Also, the suet is sometimes placed atop the meat during cooking, and liquid fat can be pumped into the meat with a special syringe.

In any case, beef suet is no longer used in everyday cookery and is therefore not widely available in supermarkets these days. In fact, a clerk in my local supermarket didn't even know what the term meant. A good butcher or a specialized meat market can, of course, provide beef suet. Loosely, it is merely beef fat. More specifically, it is the firm, white fat found in the kidney and loin sections of beef. Purists won't agree, but in my opinion it is permissible to substitute a strip of bacon for beef suet. Calorie counters and modern fat-conscious cooks may want to omit the fat entirely and may indeed have been drawn to venison in the first place because it is low in fat.

My wife says that a Greek family living in California taught her that garlic cloves stuck into slits in lean meat will keep it from being too dry and tough after cooking. I don't know what the garlic does, if anything—but I don't argue with the results, for she serves up a succulent roast every time.

In my opinion, cooking venison properly is more important than the use of suet or hog fat. Modern kitchen ovens have thermostatic controls, and modern meat thermometers help the cook get the meat done to perfection without overcooking it.

underside for 3 or 4 minutes. Again turn and baste with barbecue sauce. Turn once more and grill for another minute or so. Cut into a steak to test for doneness. Rare or medium rare is best. Do not overcook.

Note: These steaks can also be broiled in the kitchen oven. Cook close to the heat, leaving the oven door open. If you want to grill the steaks on the patio, build a hot charcoal or wood fire and let it burn down to hot coals, or heat the gas or electric grill. Adjust the rack to 3 or 4 inches above the coals and grill quickly on both sides, basting as directed above.

Easy Venison Steak

Here's an easy dish that I like to cook in the oven, working with a round steak about 2 inches thick.

venison steak
large onion
milk
bacon drippings
Worcestershire sauce
salt and pepper

Marinate the steak overnight in milk. When you are ready to cook, preheat the oven to 300 degrees. Dry the steak and brush it lightly with bacon drippings, then sprinkle it on both sides with salt and pepper. Center the steak on a sheet of heavy-duty aluminum foil. Douse the top generously with Worcestershire sauce, then cover with thin slices of onion. Cover the steak with another sheet of foil, bring the ends together, and make a 1-inch fold. Then make a ½-inch fold in the first fold to seal the package; sealing is important so that the steam will ten-

derize the steak. Place the package in a shallow baking pan and place it in the center of the oven. Cook for 4 hours.

Venison Steaks Teriyaki

This tasty dish has a thousand variations, all of which must contain soy sauce to be valid. My favorite also calls for freshly grated ginger root and sake, both of which are available in most large supermarkets these days. Although this dish is suited for the patio grill, I also like to cook it in the kitchen on a stove-top grill, such as the Jenn-Air. Any good venison steak can be used, but I recommend that you keep them on the thin side (about ¼ inch thick) and cook them quickly on a preheated grill. I like to prepare venison tenderloin by this method, cutting the pieces into ½-inch segments and then cutting almost through each segment and opening it like a butterfly. Note that the meat slices much more easily when it is partly frozen.

2 pounds venison steaks, ¼ inch thick
1 cup soy sauce (divided)
1 cup sake or dry vermouth (divided)
½ cup peanut oil
1 tablespoon grated ginger
1 tablespoon brown sugar
1 medium onion, chopped
3 cloves garlic, minced
pepper

First, mix a basting sauce with ½ cup soy sauce, ½ cup sake, peanut oil, pepper, and brown sugar; set this aside. Next, mix a marinade with the rest of the soy sauce, sake, grated ginger, onion, and garlic. Put the meat into a nonmetallic container and pour the marinade over it, tossing to coat all sides. Marinate at room temperature for 2 hours, or longer in the refrigerator.

Preheat the stove-top grill and grease it. Drain the meat and discard the marinade. Then toss the meat in the basting sauce. Grill the pieces for about 2 minutes on each side. Using tongs, dip each piece into the basting sauce, turn, and grill the other side for 2 minutes. Cut into a piece to test for doneness. I like mine medium rare—that is, pink and juicy in the middle. Do not overcook.

Note: It is customary in some quarters to cook teriyaki in thin strips, threaded onto a bamboo skewer, ribbon fashion. The strips should be about 1 inch wide, ¼ inch thick, and 6 inches long. When using beef, the strips are often cut from sirloin that is 1 inch thick. Try strips from similar cuts of buffalo or elk.

Venison Steak, Ranch Style

I've always enjoyed reading recipes written by people of firm opinion, and usually I can't argue with the results. Here's one from Mrs. Wm. C. Lindmier, Sr., as published in *Cooking in Wyoming.* Said she, "We have used the venison steak recipe for years, feeding hunters from Louisiana, Wisconsin, Minnesota, Iowa, and Michigan, and they really go for it cooked this way.

"When you have your venison processed, insist that the butcher cut your steaks and chops at least 1 inch thick, and 1½ inches is even better, since venison is a naturally dry meat, and this will allow the natural juices to remain in the meat, rather than be cooked out.

"If your animal is young, marinate the steaks or chops ½ hour to 1 hour in plain cold water. If

Advice on Venison from South Dakota

Tender cuts (loins and ribs) can be broiled or roasted. Round steaks, the meat from the leg, and less tender cuts should be cooked with moist heat (stewed, pot roast, or braised). To tenderize the meat, let it stand in an acid marinade—vinegar, tomato paste, French dressing—for 24 hours. Also remember that venison is sweeter than beef, so cut down on the sugar used in beef recipes.
  —*Cooking the Sportsman's Harvest*

the animals is older, or of an indeterminate age, then it is best to marinate for at least 1½ hours. Be sure all hairs are removed.

"For 4 servings, you will need 2 venison rounds, enough seasoned flour (flour with salt and pepper added) to dredge the steaks, and about ½ cup bacon drippings or shortening.

"Remove the steaks from the water, remove all fat, fell the thin, bluish outer layer of tissue around the edges of the rounds, and the bones, and the fat around the bones. Pound each serving, and dredge in the prepared flour.

"Meanwhile, heat fat in a heavy skillet. I use cast aluminum, but cast iron or an electric skillet will do as well. Have the fat smoking hot. Place pieces in hot fat. Allow to brown well on one side, turn, and brown on the other. Do not crowd the meat in the skillet. It may be necessary to reduce the heat once the meat has browned on one side, to prevent burning. It must be watched carefully during the cooking time. It may also be necessary to turn it once more if the animal is very old, or thin, but for an animal in good condition, once is enough. It will be very slightly rare. This preserves the juices and the flavor. Remember, overcooking can ruin otherwise excellent venison."

As I indicated at the outset, I can't argue with the results—but I'll have to point out that Mrs. Lindmier says that she uses an aluminum skillet. Being a cast-iron man, I really can't go that far!

Big-Game Soup

I've always appreciated the term "soup bonc"—especially in relation to venison and other big game. First, the idea of making a soup with the bone and some trimmings permits me to be a little careless when boning out a shoulder or other piece of meat. Second, big-game bone, with a little meat on it, can be the makings of a truly wonderful soup. Here's what I recommend, provided that some meat is left on the bone:

> venison bones from a hindquarter or 2 shoulders
> 2 cans stewed tomatoes (14½-ounce size)
> 16 ounces fresh-frozen soup vegetables
> 2 bay leaves
> salt and pepper

Crack the bones or saw them in half. Put them into a pot of suitable size and cover with water. Add the bay leaves, bring to a boil, cover, and simmer for 2 to 3 hours, or until the meat is very tender. Remove the bones and chop the meat. Discard the bones and bay leaves. Put the meat back in the pot, along with the tomatoes, vegetables, salt, and pepper.

Simmer for 30 minutes, or until all the vegetables are tender. Add more water if needed. Serve in soup bowls with lots of hot sourdough bread.

Variations: Add up to ½ pound or so of fresh mushrooms if you have them on hand. Also, ¼ cup of quick-cooking barley will make the soup more filling. Or soak regular barley or hard wheat germ overnight, then cook ¼ cup with the soup. In a pinch, a little long-grain rice will do.

Venison Pot Roast

I'll have to admit that I seldom follow the recipe below exactly, adding fresh mushrooms and celery and other ingredients if I have them at hand. I also cook it using 2 16-ounce packages of frozen stew vegetables and a can of tomatoes. So take some leeway if you choose. Just be sure to have the potatoes, onions, carrots, and bell pepper. Any good cut of venison can be used, and I am especially fond of a boned shoulder roast.

> 3- to 5-pound venison roast
> 5 medium potatoes, cut in quarters
> 8 onions (golf-ball size)
> 6 carrots, cut into chunks
> 2 tomatoes, cut into chunks
> 1 bell pepper, cut lengthwise into ½-inch strips
> 3 cloves garlic, minced
> oil
> flour
> 2 bay leaves
> ½ teaspoon thyme
> salt and pepper
> water

Season the roast with salt and pepper, then dredge it in flour. Heat a little oil in a stove-top Dutch oven or other suitable pot and brown the roast (on high heat) on all sides to sear it. Reduce the heat and add 1 cup of water and the bay leaves to the pot. Cover tightly and simmer (do not boil) for 3 hours, or until the meat is very tender. Turn the roast from time to time and add a little more water if needed. Add the rest of the ingredients and season to taste with salt and pepper. Cover and cook for 20 minutes. Throw out the bay leaves and serve hot. Feeds 6 to 8.

Venison Crust Pie

Here's a tasty dish adapted from the South Dakota Department of Game, Fish, and Park's *Cooking the Sportsman's Harvest:*

The Crust
    1 pound ground venison
    ½ cup dry bread crumbs
    ½ cup tomato sauce
    ¼ cup finely chopped onion
    ¼ cup finely chopped green pepper
    1½ teaspoons salt
    ⅛ teaspoon pepper
    ⅛ teaspoon oregano
The Filling
    ½ cup uncooked long-grain rice
    ½ cup water
    ½ cup tomato sauce
    ¼ cup grated sharp cheddar cheese
    ½ teaspoon salt
Late Addition
    ¾ cup grated sharp cheddar cheese

Preheat the oven to 350 degrees. Grease a deep 9-inch pie pan. Thoroughly mix all the crust ingredients. Pat the mixture into the bottom of the pie pan, then pinch 1-inch flutings around the edge. Put the crust into the preheated oven for 15 minutes.

While the crust cooks, mix all the filling ingredients. Remove the crust from the oven and spoon in the filling, spreading it evenly. Cover with aluminum foil and bake at 350 for 25 minutes. At the end of this period, the filling should have the texture of a soupy pudding. Top the filling with ¾ cup of grated sharp cheddar cheese, then bake, uncovered, for 15 more minutes. Makes 6 servings.

Note: This dish can be a little tricky. Follow the directions closely.

Pemmican

The American Indians made a high-energy trail food from meat that had been dried (as in making jerky), ground, and mixed with bear fat and dried berries. Blueberries, buffalo berries, and a good many others were used, depending on location and availability. The mix was carried afield on hunting trips in leather pouches, and it was also stored and eaten during the winter months when other food might be scarce.

To make pemmican, first make some jerky and pulverize it so that it can be mixed well with fat. I use a mortar and pestle for pulverizing the jerky, and the process isn't difficult if you make the jerky from meat that has been cut across the grain. Mix equal parts (by weight) of ground meat, fat, and dried berries. Any good fat that doesn't require refrigeration can be used. Try Crisco. Shape the mixture into thumb-size pieces. Modern Indians can wrap each piece in plastic wrap. For long storage without refrigeration, it's best to dip the pieces in melted paraffin and keep them in a cool place.

The American settlers picked up the pemmican idea from the Indians and no doubt added other ingredients to the mix, and the mix itself became more widely used in recipes. In fact, it could be argued that the American version of mincemeat pie developed from pemmican, since most of the recipes call for ground meat (venison or beef), fat, and various fruits. (See also the recipe for mincemeat pie on page 318. The information on pemmican and mincemeat pie has been adapted from my *Venison Cookbook.*)

A. D.'s Jerky

The American Plains Indians made jerky from buffalo—and they didn't use any Worcestershire sauce or other ingredients. All they did was hang the meat out in the sun to dry, perhaps taking it into the tepee during a rain. I like the method, but I do add a little salt, which does three things: It helps draw the moisture out of the meat, it helps preserve the meat, and it lends a wonderful flavor to the jerky. I also prefer to use natural sea salt. To try my method, dissolve 1 cup of sea salt in ½ gallon of water in a nonmetallic container. (Use clean, good-tasting water. If your tap doesn't put out good water, head for a natural spring or buy some bottled water.) Cut the venison into strips about ¼ inch thick, 1 inch wide, and 8 inches long. Place the strips in the brine, stir with a wooden spoon, and marinate overnight. (Use ½ gallon of brine for each 2 pounds or so of venison.) Dry the strips and place them on the racks of your oven. Place a pan at the bottom to catch the drippings. Leaving the oven door ajar, cook at 150 degrees for 10 to 12 hours, or until dry. Store the jerky in air tight containers. I normally use quart fruit jars.

Alaskan Jerky

Here's a good jerky recipe that I adapted from an article by Karen Cantillion in *Alaska Fish & Game.* Cut the venison into strips about 1 inch wide and ¼ inch thick. For a crisp texture, cut the meat across the grain; for a chewy texture, cut it with the grain. I normally use the muscles from the hind leg for jerky. The meat should be fat free and well trimmed.

> 3 pounds venison strips
> ½ cup Worcestershire sauce
> ½ cup soy sauce
> 1 tablespoon liquid smoke
> 1 tablespoon onion powder
> 1 tablespoon garlic powder
> 1 tablespoon black pepper
> red pepper flakes
> Tabasco sauce

Mix all the ingredients except the venison strips. Then put the meat into a nonmetallic container and pour the marinade over it, tossing well to cover all surfaces. Marinate in the refrigerator for 8 to 12 hours. Drain the meat and put it on the racks in your oven, placing a shallow baking pan at the bottom to catch any drippings. Cook at 150 degrees for 10 to 12 hours, or until the meat is dry. Leave the oven door ajar so that the moisture can escape. Store the jerky in tightly covered containers. Refrigeration isn't necessary.

Mincemeat Pie

Mincemeat pie is an old English dish dating back to the Middle Ages. According to *Larousse Gastronomique,* it is made without meat in England but in America it is made with either beef or venison. I believe that the American version is a combination of the British mince pie and the American Indian pemmican, which contains ground venison, animal fat, and dried berries. In any case, mincemeat pie is a festive dish often associated with Christmas. Like eggnog, it is sometimes considerably spiked with spirits. I suspect that applejack is often used, but most recipes list brandy or cognac, or even rum and Madeira. Most recipes are for large batches, and mincemeat is usually put up in sterilized jars. The recipe below, which I have rather freely adapted from *Larousse Gastronomique,* is for a relatively small batch, and I recommend it highly. Be warned, however, that it does contain lots of good cheer.

The Mincemeat
    1 pound boiled venison
    1 pound beef suet
    1 pound minced raisins
    1 pound currants
    1 pound tart apples, peeled and chopped
    5 ounces candied citron, finely diced
    3½ ounces candied orange peel, chopped
    juice and chopped rind of an orange
    1 pound light brown sugar
    1 ounce mixed spices (cinnamon, mace, cloves, nutmeg)
    2½ teaspoons salt
    1 pint brandy
    ½ cup rum
    ½ cup Madeira

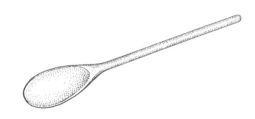

Grind the cooked venison, beef suet, and apples in meat grinder with a coarse blade. Put all the ingredients into a large bowl and mix everything thoroughly. Cover the bowl and refrigerate for 1 month, stirring the mixture every 8 days.

(*Note:* The recipe above is not cooked, except for the boiled venison. Most American texts call for cooking the mixture. Also note that the measures given will fill more than 1 pie of ordinary size.)

The Pie
    pastry for a 9-inch double crust
    2 cups venison mincemeat
    juice and zest of 1 lemon

Preheat the oven to 450 degrees. Line a 9-inch pie plate with pastry. Add the lemon zest and juice to the mincemeat. Fill the pie crust with the mincemeat. Cover with the upper crust.

Punch holes in the upper crust with a fork, put the pie into the center of the oven, and bake for about 30 minutes, or until the crust is properly browned.

If you make your own pastry and are good at baking, you might prefer to make small individual pies, or maybe tarts. The famous Banbury tarts of England are filled with a mixture quite similar to mincemeat.

33

FANCY AND UNUSUAL VENISON DISHES

I've always been fond of trying new dishes, new tastes, or new ways of cooking an old dish. The recipes for cooking such dishes need not be long, complicated, or difficult, although one or two of the recipes in this chapter are not short. Also, some of the recipes depend on an unusual ingredient, such as green tomatoes, acorns, coffee, or kiwi.

Seminole Venison Stew

It's not often that you find a recipe calling for green tomatoes, which happen to be one of my favorite vegetables, in season. Moreover, I am including this recipe because I am certain it was originally cooked with unpeeled potatoes. Permit me to explain. While serving a hitch in the navy, I peeled no less than 67,000 pounds of potatoes during a 3-month period. I don't peel them anymore, and I welcome the follow-

ing recipe on the grounds that no self-respecting Seminole would waste time peeling spuds. Anyhow, here's what you'll need:

3 or 4 pounds venison
4 medium to large potatoes, sliced
4 ribs celery with green tops, chopped
4 medium onions, chopped (divided)
3 large green tomatoes, chopped
¼ cup cooking oil
salt
red pepper flakes
water

In a crockery or other nonmetallic container, mix 2 tablespoons of salt into 5 cups of water. Chop a medium onion and add it to the mixture. Trim the venison and cut it into 2-inch chunks. Put the chunks into the salt solution, cover, and marinate overnight, or at least 10 hours.

319

When you are ready to cook, drain the meat. In a large pot or Dutch oven, heat the cooking oil and ¼ cup of water. Add the meat and vegetables, along with some salt and red pepper flakes. (If you aren't familiar with the impact of red pepper flakes, start with only ⅛ teaspoon or less; this is hot stuff indeed.) Bring the mixture to a simmer, reduce the heat to very low, cover, and simmer—do not boil—for 2 to 3 hours, adding more water if needed. Feeds 6 to 8.

Note: All of the ingredients above, except possibly for the celery, were available in the New World before the Europeans came. For cooking, the Indians used an oil made from the sweet acorns of the live oak as well as oil from the bear and the manatee. See the next recipe for more on acorn cookery.

Indian Venison Stew with Acorn Gravy

I'm told that I am part Cherokee, which might explain why my favorite venison stew is thickened with the sweet meal made from live oak acorns of the Southeast. (Anyone who thinks that all acorns are bitter with tannin is simply misinformed and is not widely tasted; some acorns can be eaten out of hand, or roasted in a campfire like chestnuts, and some were even used by the Indians as well as the early settlers for making a mild cooking oil, as noted in the previous recipe.) Even bitter acorns can be used if they are crushed and soaked in two or more changes of water, and any modern-day venison chef should take the trouble to gather a supply. The acorns can be ground into meal with a simple mortar and pestle, and acorn meal keeps almost indefinitely in a sealed container. I also keep it in the freezer.

In any case, the following basic recipe was widely used all across North America. Of course, chestnuts, hickory nuts, and so on were also used in stews. (The Seneca even pulverized butternut kernels with venison and used this as baby food.) But use sweet acorns in the following recipe if you've got them.

2 pounds cubed venison
water to cover
1 cup sweet acorn meal
crushed juniper berries
salt

Put the cubed meat into a pot, cover it with water, and add the juniper berries. Simmer on very low heat—do not boil—for 6 or 7 hours, or until the meat is very tender. Stir and add a little water from time to time. (If you've got a crockpot, use it and cook for 8 or 9 hours. No stirring is necessary with most crockpots.) About 1 hour before eating, stir in the acorn meal and a little salt. Add more water if needed. You should have a very thick, nourishing gravy to eat along with the meat.

Note: Juniper berries are often used in game recipes. You can pick your own or purchase them at some spice markets. You can substitute a few crushed hackberries, dried spicebush berries, or commercial allspice—another American ingredient—or omit the berries entirely.

Rock Salt Venison

Here's a very old recipe that probably originated in England. I have cooked it several times for guests, who find it interesting as well as tasty. The version below, making good use of marinated pears and brandy, has been adapted from a book called *Dress 'em Out,* by Captain James A. Smith. For best results, you'll need a venison roast that is well rounded and not flat. The rump section works nicely for this recipe. I have, however, cooked it successfully with other cuts and with other meats—including breast of wild turkey.

The Meat
    venison roast, about 3 pounds
    3 strips bacon, halved
    5 or 6 pounds rock salt
    pepper
    garlic (optional)
Late Additions
    apple slices
    fresh parsley
    marinated pears, sliced
    good brandy

Preheat the oven to 500 degrees so that it will be very hot. Weigh the roast and note the figure. Sprinkle the roast with pepper. Spread about 1 inch of rock salt in the bottom of a roasting pan and place the roast on top of it. Carefully pile rock salt around the roast, building a mound that completely covers the meat. Use a little hot water here and there if needed to help hold the salt. Place the roasting pan into the center of the oven. Reduce the heat to 450 degrees. Cook for 14 minutes per pound of roast.

Sip on the brandy while waiting for and worrying about your roast. That's all you can do. At the end of the calculated time, remove the roast from the oven and call in your guests. Crack the mound of salt, using a hammer and chisel if necessary. Once cracked, the pieces of salt crust should lift off easily. When the salt crust has been removed, lift the roast out of the pan and brush off the excess salt. Put the meat onto a heated serving platter. With toothpicks, quickly stick apple and pear slices and sprigs of parsley onto the roast. Quickly heat ¼ to ½ cup of brandy in a small pan, then, at the table, under dim light, pour it over the roast and ignite it. Slice the meat. Feeds 4 to 6.

West African Stew

If I were attempting to write a complete history of American game cookery, I suppose I would start with Central Europe, take a quick look at the American Indians from the Incas and Aztecs to the Eskimos, and finally bog down somewhere in the continent of Africa. Indeed, I have dipped into some modern African cookbooks, but they were, for the most part, written for American kitchens. After all, how many kitchens in Duluth, Minnesota, or Pascagoula, Mississippi, have fresh tenderloin of wildebeest? Or monkey? Anyhow, some of the best of American cookery owes a lot to the early African-Americans.

Since my name is Livingston, I suppose I could claim roots to the great explorer, Dr. David Livingstone, who recorded the recipe below somewhere in the big bend of the Niger, between Timbuktu and Gao. In truth, I got the recipe from a booklet about cooking with peanuts, to which it was submitted by one Myron Boutwell, of Slocomb, Alabama. The peanut connection is for real, since many of the recipes from western Africa do indeed call for "groundnuts." Many of the people in my neck of the woods call the peanut "ground peas." It's not a bad name, really, since they are legumes rather than nuts. Anyhow, . . . here's my version of Myron Boutwell's West African South Alabama stew:

> 1 pound venison, diced
> 1 medium onion, sliced with the grain
> 1 large ripe tomato, diced
> ¼ cup peanut oil
> ¼ cup peanut butter
> 1 tablespoon cornstarch
> ½ teaspoon red pepper flakes
> salt to taste
> water

In a large skillet, heat the peanut oil and quickly brown the cubed venison. Add 1 cup of water, cover, and simmer—but do not boil—for 1 to 2 hours, or until the meat is tender. Add another cup of water, bring to heat, and stir in the peanut butter. Add the tomato, onion, salt, and pepper.

Bring to a quick boil, reduce the heat, and simmer, stirring as you go, for 15 minutes. Mix the cornstarch into 2 tablespoons of water. Increase the heat and slowly stir the starch paste into the stew; stir and cook until the gravy is creamy.

Remove from the heat and serve hot, along with vegetables and rice.

Feeds 3 or 4, if there's plenty of rice.

Note: All connoisseurs of gravy must try this dish. It's hot but smooth. In taste, texture, and color, it is like no other. My wife likes it, saying that it doesn't seem as greasy as other heavy gravies.

The recipe is a little on the hot side, and anyone who prefers bland food will be tempted to leave out the red pepper flakes, and others may be inclined to substitute a little black pepper. Do so at your culinary peril. The red pepper flakes add to the dish visually.

Venison Coffee Roast

One of my favorite ways to cook venison roasts was adapted from *Southern Family Recipes,* by Geddings de M. Cushman and Ora Lou O'Hara Cushman, who cooked it with roast beef. If you are fond of coffee, as I am, be sure to try this unusual recipe. Its flavor is an experience that should not be missed; and for hours, during cooking, it gives off a tempting aroma. I use very strong coffee for this dish, actually brewed with part coffee and part chicory. The coffee makes for a very good, dark gravy. You can freeze leftover breakfast coffee and save it for cooking this dish.

> 4- to 5-pound venison roast
> 2 cups black coffee
> 1 cup apple cider vinegar
> ¼ cup cooking oil
> 1 medium onion
> 2 cloves garlic
> water
> salt and pepper

With a long, thin knife cut 6 or 8 narrow, well-spaced slits deep into the roast. Sliver the onion and garlic, then poke the pieces into the slits. Put the roast into a suitable bowl and pour the vinegar over it. Refrigerate for 24 hours, turning the roast every 2 hours or so if convenient. After marinating, discard the vinegar.

Heat the oil in a stove-top Dutch oven. Sear the roast on all sides, heating it almost to the burning point. Pour the coffee over the roast, then add enough water (if needed) to barely cover the meat. Bring almost to a boil, reduce the heat, cover tightly, and simmer for 6 to 8 hours, turning the meat every 2 or 3 hours.

About ½ hour before eating time, season the roast with salt and pepper.

Slice the roast. Serve with vegetables and rice. Spoon the gravy over the roast and rice. Feeds 8.

Variation: After searing the roast, put it into a crockpot, then add the coffee, salt, and pepper. Hold the water. Cook on low for 8 or 9 hours.

Golden Venison Steaks

Seasoning steaks with marigold (yes, the flower) dates back to medieval times and probably earlier. Like saffron, marigold imparts a golden yellow color to foods. My recipe has been adapted from *The Forgotten Art of Flower Cookery*, by Leona Woodring Smith. To prepare the marigold flowers, pull the petals from the stem. Hold the stem end of each petal (or a group of petals) between thumb and forefinger of one hand, then cut off the white or pale greenish heels with scissors. Wash and drain the trimmed petals.

1½ to 2 pounds venison steak, 1 inch thick
1 cup marigold petals
1 cup tomato paste
1 cup chopped onion
½ cup chopped carrot
½ cup chopped celery
¾ cup red wine
½ cup flour
¼ pound butter
2½ tablespoons Worcestershire sauce
salt and pepper to taste

Preheat the oven to 325 degrees. Melt the butter in a large skillet with an ovenproof handle. Brown the steaks, then set them aside. Stir the flour into the melted butter. Cook and stir with a wooden spoon until you have a brown roux. Stir in the wine, tomato paste, onion, carrot, celery, Worcestershire sauce, salt, and pepper. Simmer for a few minutes, then put the venison steaks into the sauce, coating all sides. Cover the skillet and bake in the oven for 1½ hours, or until the steak is very tender. Then stir in the marigold petals, cover, and simmer for 5 minutes. Serve hot with rice and vegetables.

Boiled Venison with Caper Sauce

The recipe below was sent to me from the University of Florida, but the amounts of the ingredients were not included. I sneaked in some red pepper flakes and worked out the following measures:

The Meat
3 to 4-pound shoulder of venison
1 medium onion, diced
½ cup chopped fresh celery tops
¼ cup chopped fresh parsley
juice of ½ lemon
3 bay leaves
2 teaspoons salt
½ teaspoon red pepper
water

The Sauce
stock from venison (above)
1 cup cold milk
3 tablespoons flour
3 tablespoons capers
1 tablespoon orange juice
juice of ½ lemon

1890

In the not-too-distant past we have further evidence of the decrease in meat consumption by reading a menu of the 1890's, when game was a food for epicures. Imagine sitting down to an elaborate and sophisticated dinner where the course of soup and fish were followed by "relieves," six or more in number, among them turkey *à la Toulouse*, saddle of venison with currant jelly, and stewed terrapin *à la Maryland*. And after that came a number of cold, ornamented dishes; then the entrees and hors d'oeuvres.

The second main course offered canvasback ducks, pheasants, partridges, and grouse, with ten vegetables. And finally came 15 desserts and coffee. Such was the culinary tradition of the inns, taverns, and hotels of our larger cities during the nineteenth century.

—Frank F. Ashbrook, *Butchering, Processing and Preservation of Meat*

Place the venison shoulder, whole, into a large pot. Cover it with water, then add the bay leaves, onion, parsley, celery, lemon juice, salt, and red pepper. Bring to a boil, reduce the heat, cover tightly, and simmer for 3 hours.

To make the sauce, dip out 2 cups of the venison stock and heat it in a saucepan. Mix the flour with the milk, then stir into the hot stock, simmering until it thickens. Add the lemon juice, orange juice, and capers. Simmer for a few minutes. Slice the venison thinly and serve with the sauce, along with rice and vegetables. A 3- to 4-pound roast will feed 6 to 8, or more.

Kiwi Pepper Tenderloin

Some time ago, the kiwi gained culinary kudos. I like the fruit very much, eating one occasionally. I also cook with the fruit, partly because it tenderizes meat, making it ideal for venison. Here's one of my creations:

tenderloin of venison
kiwi fruit
salt and freshly ground black pepper

Peel the kiwi, then slice it crosswise. Cut the tenderloin into slices about ¾ inch thick. Lay a piece of plastic wrap flat on a countertop. Make a loaf on the plastic wrap by alternating slices of kiwi and tenderloin. Wrap the plastic around the loaf, then put the works into the refrigerator for several hours.

Preheat a broiler. Adjust the rack so that it is very close to the heat source; the meat should be about 2 inches from the heat. Unwrap the loaf, removing the tenderloin slices. Also retain the kiwi slices, handling them carefully. Sprinkle the tenderloin slices with salt. Then sprinkle each piece on both sides with coarsely ground black pepper, mashing the pepper into the meat. Put the meat on a rack and broil for 3 or 4 minutes on each side, or until medium rare. Add a kiwi slice to each piece of tenderloin, then broil for another 2 minutes. Serve hot.

Carpetbag Steak

The Australians invented a recipe for combining the oyster and the beef steak. It can also be used to advantage with other tender cuts of meat, such as backstrap of venison or kangaroo. Since the size of the venison backstrap will be much smaller than most beefsteaks, I recommend the use of small oysters. For the best flavor, the oysters ought to be right from the shell and *not* washed in fresh water. This unusual recipe was also used in my *Venison Cookbook* in slightly modified form.

boneless venison chops or tender cutlets,
    1½ inches thick
small oysters
melted butter
salt and pepper
fresh parsley, chopped

With a sharp fillet knife, cut a pocket into each venison chop, working from the side. Work a little salt and pepper inside the pocket, then insert an oyster. The pocket should be large enough, or the oyster small enough, to permit the slit to be completely closed. Skewer shut with a couple of round toothpicks inserted at such an angle as to permit the steaks to lie flat. Prepare as many of these chops or cutlets as you need to feed everybody.

In a skillet, heat a little butter and quickly cook the chops for 4 or 5 minutes on each side, turning once.

Put the chops onto a heated serving platter and sprinkle them with parsley, salt, and pepper. Scrape the pan with a wooden spatula and pour the drippings over the steaks. Eat immediately.

Note: In one of his books, James Beard suggested putting a small ice cube inside hamburger patties before they are grilled or broiled, saying that the ice will melt and keep the inside of the burger moist. It's a great idea for ground venison, which tends to run dry, and I hereby suggest that an oyster has almost as much moisture as an ice cube and a whole lot more personality and flavor.

Galantine of Venison and Pork

This recipe is based on a very old Scottish dish. It takes a little doing, but I can highly recommend it. You'll need some venison bones, so save a few the next time you bag a buck and bone out the hams or shoulders, leaving a little meat on them. The bones, which should be cracked, broken, or cut in half, can be frozen until you are ready to cook.

3-pound venison roast, boned
venison bones
1 pound pork sausage
½ pound ham
3 hard-boiled chicken eggs, halved
    lengthwise
3 cloves garlic, minced
6 peppercorns
½ teaspoon chopped fresh thyme
½ teaspoon chopped fresh marjoram
salt and pepper
8 cups water
flour

Put the venison bones into a large pot. Add the water along with the peppercorns, thyme, and marjoram. Bring to a boil, reduce the heat, cover tightly, and simmer.

Cube the ham, then mix it and the minced garlic into the sausage. Place the boned roast onto a flat surface. Sprinkle it well with salt and pepper, then spread on about half of the sausage mixture. Cover the mixture with the egg halves. Then cover the eggs with the rest of the sausage mixture. Roll up the roast as best you can, then carefully wrap it in a cloth that has been dusted with flour. Tie both ends.

Remove the bones from the pot and put the

roast into the liquid. Cover and simmer for 4 hours. Let the roast remain in the stock while cooling. When cool, take the roast out of the pot, remove the cloth, and place the roast into a dish. If possible, the roast should fit snugly into the dish. Cover the roast with foil, then put a weight (such as a large bag of rice) on top of it. Chill overnight. Slice and serve.

Venison Fondue

A good friend of mine once said that, shoot, he didn't jog. He ran. He also said that when he ate, he ate instead of messing around with fondue. I tend to agree on both counts, but I'll have to admit that fondue can be great fun on occasion. And venison fondue can be something to talk about. So try it if you've got a fondue pot, a tenderloin of venison, and good company.

> venison tenderloin
> peanut oil
> milk
> salt and pepper
> Worcestershire sauce
> lemon juice

Cut the venison into thin strips and marinate for 8 hours in milk. When you are ready to fondue, set up the pot and heat the oil. Mix a sauce in the proportions of 1 tablespoon Worcestershire sauce to the juice of ½ lemon; warm the sauce in individual bowls. Dry the venison, then salt and pepper it to taste. At this point, each guest sticks a strip of venison with a fondue fork and dips it into the hot oil for a minute, dips it into the sauce, and eats it directly.

Variations: Any good meat sauce can be used instead of Worcestershire and lemon juice. If you like thick sauces, try Chinese duck or plum sauce, or oyster sauce.

Big Horn Venison Birds with Wild Rice

For this recipe I am indebted to Mrs. Robert E. Helvey, of Big Horn. It was published in the book called *Cooking in Wyoming,* and I have adapted it from there. The original called for a small can of mushrooms, but I have specified fresh mushrooms as they are readily available these days in most supermarkets.

> 3 venison round steaks, sliced thin
> 1 cup uncooked wild rice
> 1 carrot, sliced
> 1 medium onion, chopped
> 2 cloves garlic, minced
> 6 ounces fresh mushrooms, sliced
> ½ pint sour cream
> 3 tablespoons red currant jelly
> 1 bay leaf
> butter
> flour
> salt and pepper
> water

Bring 2½ cups of water to a boil, then add the wild rice and 1 teaspoon salt. When a new boil is reached, reduce the heat. Simmer for 1 hour.

While waiting, trim the venison steaks well. Rub both sides with salt, pepper, and flour. Pound well with the edge of a plate or a meat mallet. Cut the steaks into quarters. Heat ¼ cup of butter in a stove-top Dutch oven, then sauté the onions, carrots, mushrooms, and garlic for 5 or 6 minutes; remove these, putting them on a plate or bowl. When the rice is done, place 1 heaping tablespoon of this mixture onto each steak. (There will be quite a bit of rice left over, to be served separately.) Fold the steaks in half, then secure with toothpicks or skewers. Brown the steaks on both sides, adding a little more butter to the Dutch oven if needed. Add the onions, carrots, mushrooms, and garlic to the pot, along with the bay leaf and ½ cup of water. Cover tightly and simmer very, very slowly for 40 minutes.

Place the venison birds on a serving platter. Stir the red currant jelly into the pot with a wooden spoon. Stir in the sour cream, salt, and pepper, along with a little water if needed. Cook and stir until the sauce is smooth and bubbly. Spoon the sauce over the venison birds and the remaining wild rice. Serve immediately. Feeds 3 or 4.

Backstrap Wellington

Over a period of years, I eyed a number of Wellington recipes, but they all seemed too complicated for me. Essentially, the Wellington recipe is for a loin or tenderloin, which, together with a liver pâté, is encased in a pastry and baked. All this takes some doing, but what really bothered me was the cooking time. The recipes say to cook the dish until the crust is brown, but that the meat should be pink and not overdone. Well, what if you can't get it both ways? It seems to me that it's a matter of proportion and exact timing at the right temperature. But, regardless of my fears, I finally hauled off and cooked the dish. I hit the jackpot the first try, and I can highly recommend that any hunter take the gamble.

Actually, the recipe that I follow came from an article in *Sports Afield* (October 1967) by Jack Denton Scott who said: "How should you serve what most of us consider the best piece of venison, the filet, that tender muscle that can almost be cut with a sharp glance? Although the English have the reputation of being unimaginative cooks, I believe they have a method of serving that prized filet that leads all others—even the French. It passes the test of all superior dishes, is dramatically presented, appeals to the eye, and is so tasty that once eaten it is never forgotten. I had it in the home of a baronet in Kent who stalked his meal on ancestral acres in Scotland. It was the filet from a royal stag, well hung, and it easily served eight drooling guests. I watched his cook, a gentle and skillful Irish woman, prepare it."

Well, when I tried the dish I wasn't in Kent with an Irish cook and a royal well hung stag from Scotland, and I don't really know whether the "filet" in Scott's recipe was a true tenderloin or a loin or backstrap. In any case, the dish fed, Scott said, eight drooling guests. My assumption is that the meat weighed about 4 pounds. This rules out a tenderloin from an ordinary American white-tailed deer. Therefore, I recommend that the recipe be cooked with a loin of a whitetail or with the tenderloin from an elk or moose. Any very tender, loaf-shaped piece of red meat in the neighborhood of 4 pounds will be satisfactory. I might add that I have changed Scott's recipe somewhat, and, if the results be suspect, blame me, not Scott.

The Pastry
   4 cups flour
   ½ cup butter
   ½ cup lard
   1 large chicken egg, beaten
   1 teaspoon salt
   water (about ½ cup)

In a bowl, thoroughly mix the flour, butter, salt, and lard. Whisk in the beaten egg. Slowly, blend in just enough water to make a dough. Put the dough in a bowl and refrigerate. Proceed with the pâté.

The Liver Pâté
¾ pound chicken livers, minced
5 tablespoons butter
4 green onions, finely chopped
3 tablespoons Madeira
salt and pepper to taste

Melt the butter in a skillet, then sauté the green onions for 3 or 4 minutes. Add the minced livers, and cook until they turn pink. Mix in the Madeira, salt, and pepper. Set aside while you prepare the meat.

The Meat
1 whole tenderloin or backstrap, about 4 pounds
¼ cup butter
2 chicken eggs, well beaten
1 teaspoon dry mustard
salt and pepper

Melt the butter in a large skillet, then brown the meat on all sides over high heat, cooking no longer than 10 minutes. Salt and pepper the meat, remove from the skillet, then sprinkle on all sides with the dry mustard. Allow the meat to cool, then spread the pâté on top of it. Preheat the oven to 425 degrees.

Take the dough from the refrigerator and put it onto a smooth surface at least 2 feet square. Roll the dough into a rectangle roughly 12 by 20 inches. It should be ¼ inch thick. Carefully place the meat on one end of the dough. Then lift the other end of the dough and fold it over the top of the meat and under the bottom.

To seal, cut off the excess dough at both ends of the roll, brush the bottom well with part of the beaten egg, and fold the dough. Brush the seams well with the beaten egg.

Place the roll seam side down on a baking sheet. Then brush the entire roll with the rest of the beaten egg. Place the roll in the center of the preheated oven for 30 minutes. When done, the pastry will be crisp and golden. With luck, the meat will be pink and just right. Overcooking the meat a tad is not disastrous because the jacket of dough helps seal in the moisture. But medium rare is best.

Serve with good red wine, hearty bread and butter, and vegetables of your choice. Feeds 6 to 8 royally.

Note: In recent years I have become a devoted fan of the meat thermometer. If you want to take some of the luck out of the Backstrap Wellington recipe above, insert a meat thermometer into the center of the meat, then pinch in the dough around it and brush with the beaten egg. When the thermometer reads 140 degrees, turn off the oven heat and let the Wellington coast a while.

It will then be done to perfection.

34

GROUND GAME MEAT

Venison and other game can be ground into "hamburger" meat successfully, but most game does not contain as much fat as beef, so the ground meat will be different. It's better, in my opinion, and certainly better for you. It can also be fresher than supermarket meat, or at least you will know how fresh it is if you grind your own. If the ground venison or game is to be used in spaghetti sauce, casseroles, and so on, it can be used as is, but for meatballs and patties, and especially for grilled burgers, the meat may require a couple of beaten eggs, or some such binding, to hold it together during the cooking process.

Most books and articles on game cookery recommend that ground venison or other wild meat be mixed with beef fat (suet) or ground pork. If you grind up a large batch of venison burger at one time (as many people do), you may want to include up to 25 percent beef suet, which you can obtain from your meat processor.

While one could do a good deal worse than making up a large batch of venison burger, I really can't recommend the practice and therefore offer no fixed recommendation for mixing in fat, simply because lean meat is better for you. In my opinion, it is best to grind all lean meat and freeze it in 1-pound packages; then, if necessary, you can always add some beef fat or ground pork. A few of the recipes in this chapter do call for a mixture of meats or ground venison and fat.

It's even better, or more versatile, to cut the venison into stew meat, then freeze this in 1-pound packages. Then you can use it in stew recipes or chili, or grind it for burger meat. If you go this route, you will have to grind your own instead of having it done at a meat processor. This method will be a little more trouble, but it will give you the best and freshest ground meat. Since meat should be cut into chunks before it is ground and since meat grinds easier if it is partially frozen, it's really not difficult to grind 1 or 2 pounds as needed.

Creole-Style Game Loaf

I've always been a meatloaf man, and here's one of my favorite recipes for this dish.

The Loaf
   1 pound ground venison
   1 pound lean pork, bear, or armadillo
   ½ medium onion, grated
   ¼ green bell pepper, grated
   ¼ red bell pepper, grated
   2 chicken eggs, beaten
   1 cup milk
   1 cup toast crumbs
   1 tablespoon Worcestershire sauce
   ¼ teaspoon Tabasco or similar hot pepper
      sauce
   ½ teaspoon salt
   ⅛ teaspoon black pepper
The Sauce
   2 cups diced fresh tomatoes
   1 cup milk
   ¼ green bell pepper, minced
   ¼ red bell pepper, minced
   ½ medium onion, minced
   2 cloves garlic, minced
   2 tablespoons cooking oil
   2 tablespoons flour
   1 tablespoon Worcestershire sauce
   ½ teaspoon salt
   ⅛ teaspoon black pepper

Preheat the oven to 350 degrees, then make the Creole sauce as follows: Heat the oil in a skillet, then stir in the flour. Cook on low heat until a nice brown color develops, stirring continuously with a wooden spoon. Add the minced onion, garlic, bell peppers, and tomatoes. Simmer for 5 minutes. Stir in the milk. Add the Worcestershire sauce, salt, and pepper. Bring almost to a boil, reduce the heat, and simmer for 5 minutes.

While the sauce cooks, mix the 2 meats thoroughly. (If you grind your own from cubed meat, mix the meats before grinding.) Mix in the toast crumbs and the rest of the loaf ingredients. Shape the mixture into a loaf and put it into a greased baking pan of suitable size and shape. Top with the Creole sauce. Bake for 1 hour in the center of the oven.

Feeds 5 or 6.

Zesty Gameburger Steaks

Here's a good, quick recipe for the skillet. The gameburger steaks can be eaten between buns or served as the meat during a regular meal.

   2 pounds ground game meat
   1 chicken egg, beaten
   ½ cup tomato puree
   ¼ cup fine Italian bread crumbs
   Zesty Italian salad dressing
   olive oil
   salt and pepper

Mix the tomato puree, beaten egg, bread crumbs, salt, and pepper. Add this mixture to the meat and form serving-size patties. Heat a little olive oil in your skillet and brown the patties on both sides. (You'll need a large skillet to hold all the patties.) Shake a bottle of Zesty Italian salad dressing and pour some over the burger steaks, getting a little on each patty and a little on the bottom of the skillet. Cover the skillet, reduce the heat, and cook for 10 minutes. Feeds 4 to 6.

Venison Macaroni

Here's a good recipe that I adapted from *Cooking the Sportsman's Harvest,* published by the South Dakota Department of Game, Fish, and Parks:

    1 pound ground venison
    1 can cream of celery soup (10¾-ounce size)
    1 cup sliced fresh mushrooms
    1 cup crushed potato chips
    4 ounces dry elbow macaroni
    ¾ cup catsup
    ½ cup milk
    ½ cup grated cheddar cheese
    ⅓ cup chopped green bell pepper
    1 small onion, chopped
    1 tablespoon cooking oil
    1 teaspoon salt

Cook the macaroni according to the directions on the package. Drain. Turn the oven to 350 degrees. In a skillet, lightly sauté the onion and green pepper in the oil. Add the meat and brown it, stirring from time to time. Mix in the cooked macaroni and all of the rest of the ingredients, except for the potato chips. Put the mixture into a well-greased 2-quart casserole dish. Bake for 45 minutes. Sprinkle the top of the mixture with potato chips. Bake for another 5 minutes. Feeds 4 to 6.

Poyha for Bill

At age 8 or 9, one of my sons was the best fish-bait digger that I've ever seen. So I can't say, categorically, that he is lazy. But I do know that he doesn't clean up a tasty quail, leaving meat on the bones, and, more than once, he has requested "corn off the cob." In short, he likes

Game Meat Chili

When first planning this book, I thought I would include several recipes for chili in this chapter. But things don't always go as planned, and I ended up with a whole chapter on the subject. Chili is just too good when made with game, and there are too many matters of opinion to cover the subject with only a recipe or two. Besides, who says that chili ought to go into a ground meat chapter anyhow? Some people hold that it ought to be made with chunks of meat before it can be called chili. So . . . see chapter 35.

his food easy to eat, and the following recipe is just right for him. I got it from *Cy Littlebee's Guide to Cooking Fish & Game,* as compiled by Werner O. Nagel and published by the Missouri Department of Conservation. Nagel said that he heard the recipe read over the radio, but other than that, he doesn't know exactly where it came from. In any case, I tried *poyha,* a sort of Cherokee meat loaf, and can highly recommend it for those who prefer corn off the cob.

In the recipe that follows, I have changed only the format, not the ingredients or the proportions.

    1 pound ground venison
    1 can whole kernel corn (17-ounce size)
    1 small onion, chopped
    2 chicken eggs
    ½ cup water-ground cornmeal
    salt to taste
    cooking fat
    (absolutely no pepper, Nagel says)

Preheat the oven to 350 degrees. Brown the venison in a little fat. Drain the corn and add it to the venison. Add the onion and cook for 10 minutes. Stir in the eggs, salt, and cornmeal. Cook for another 15 minutes, then put the mixture into a well-greased meatloaf pan. Bake for 30 to 45 degrees. Slice the meatloaf and serve it with gravy. Feeds 4 to 6.

Tough Meat Stew

Here's a recipe that takes a lot of attention—but it makes good eating from the worst cuts of the oldest, toughest game. It's so good, in fact, that once you cook and eat it you'll be tempted to run a whole bull moose through the meat grinder.

Meatballs
  2 pounds ground game meat
  ½ cup cooking oil
  8 small green onions (save tops)
  2 cloves garlic, minced
  3 cups soft bread crumbs
  2 chicken eggs
  1 tablespoon Worcestershire sauce
  1 teaspoon salt
  ½ teaspoon black pepper
  ½ teaspoon cayenne pepper
  ¼ cup cold water

The Gravy
  pan drippings from above
  ¼ cup cooking oil
  cold water (about 3 cups)
  2 cans beef broth (10½-ounce size)
  1½ cups flour
  ½ teaspoon salt
  ¼ teaspoon black pepper

Late Additions
  green onion tops from above
  ½ cup minced parsley

Chop the green onions, setting the tops aside, and mix with the meat, garlic, bread crumbs, eggs, salt, black pepper, cayenne, Worcestershire sauce, and water. Form meatballs about 1 inch across, place them on a tray, and refrigerate for 30 minutes.

In a skillet, heat the cooking oil almost to the smoking point and quickly brown a batch of the meatballs. Then place the meatballs into a stove-top Dutch oven over low heat. Brown the rest of the meatballs and transfer them to the Dutch oven.

To make gravy, add ¼ cup of oil to the drippings in the skillet, heat on medium, and

Easy Breakfast Sausage

Everybody has a favorite recipe for sausage, and some people even go to the trouble to obtain natural casings for them. I enjoy any good sausage, but as often as not I take the easy way out—especially early in the morning when I have a taste for sausage patties.

  1 pound ground venison
  1 pound of your favorite pork sausage

Mix thoroughly, shape into patties, heat your griddle, and fry on medium heat until done. In my part of the country, I can purchase sausage made by small local producers, and it's available in hot, medium, and mild. For the mix above, hot is my favorite.

slowly mix in the flour, stirring as you go with a wooden spoon. Cook and stir for 15 minutes, adding a little water all along. Keep stirring. Add the beef broth, salt, and pepper. When ready, the gravy should be light brown and thick.

Add the meatballs to the gravy, cover, and simmer—do not boil—for 45 minutes, stirring gently 2 or 3 times to prevent sticking. Chop the green onion tops and add them to the pot, along with the parsley. Simmer for another 20 minutes.

Serve over a bed of rice, or if you don't have fancy company at the table, try sopping the gravy with bread or biscuits. In any case, this dish has thick gravy and should be served hot. Feeds 4 to 6.

Note: This dish is even better, I think, if you use wild onions instead of green onions. Since these are usually on the strong side, you may want to leave out the garlic.

Easy Venisonburger Pie

Here's a dish that is very easy to make. It can even be made from ground leftover meat, and it freezes nicely.

   1 pound ground venison
   1½ cups mild cheddar, shredded
   ¾ cup milk
   ½ cup mayonnaise
   ½ cup chopped onion
   3 chicken eggs
   2 store-bought frozen pie crusts (9-inch size)
   2 tablespoons cornstarch
   1 tablespoon bacon fat
   salt and pepper to taste

Preheat the oven to 350 degrees. In a skillet, brown the venison and onions in the bacon fat. Salt and pepper to taste. In a bowl, thoroughly mix the milk, chicken eggs, mayonnaise, and cornstarch. Add this mixture to the ground venison. Add the cheese. Stir well, then spoon the mixture into the pie crusts. Bake for 40 minutes. Feeds 4.

Southwestern Game Loaf

Here's a recipe to try if you like the flavor of Mexican or Southwestern dishes but want it on the mild side. If you prefer hot stuff, add some red chili pepper sauce.

The Meat Loaf
   2 pounds ground venison
   2 strips bacon, minced
   1 medium onion, chopped
   ½ green bell pepper, chopped
   ½ red bell pepper, chopped
   1 small can tomato sauce (8-ounce size)
   2 slices white bread soaked in milk
   1 chicken egg
   1½ teaspoons sugar
   1 teaspoon salt
   ½ teaspoon black pepper
The Sauce
   1 cup catsup
   ¼ cup dark brown sugar
   ¼ teaspoon dry mustard
   ¼ teaspoon nutmeg

Preheat the oven to 350 degrees. Whisk the egg, shred the bread, and mix both with the meat, bacon, onion, bell peppers, tomato sauce, sugar, salt, and pepper. Shape the mixture into a loaf and put it into a well-greased dish or loaf pan. Bake for 1 hour. As the loaf cooks, make the sauce by mixing the brown sugar, dry mustard, and nutmeg; then mix in the catsup. When the meatloaf is almost done, cover it with sauce and return it to the oven for a few minutes. Serve hot. Feeds 4 to 6.

Get a Meat Grinder

If you cook a lot of game, you really need a good portable meat grinder. There are several manual and electric models on the market that are fine for most family use, but of course some are better than others. I recommend that you invest in the old-fashioned kind that you turn with a handle. Before buying, however, be certain that you can mount the unit in your kitchen or wherever you intend to grind the meat. Some models require bolts and are difficult to use on kitchen counters. Some clamp on, but again will not work on countertops. We have an old wooden table in our kitchen—a table that my wife's father built when he got married—and this works nicely with a clamp-on grinder. Probably the best grinders are those that are made primarily for that purpose (as opposed to multipurpose food processors) and have attachments that offer a choice of texture. Some have a funnel attachment to use for stuffing sausage casings.

If you plan to grind meat in small batches, as I do, then you should consider a grinder that is easy to clean and store.

Deerburgers

This unusual dish comes from C. V. Gaugler, of Joplin, Missouri, and the recipe was published by the Missouri Department of Conservation in *Cy Littlebee's Guide to Cooking Fish & Game:*

"Many cuts of venison are best ground into a deerburger without adding any other kind of meat. Before grinding the different cuts, I cut off all the fat, then cook the deerburger in a small amount of bacon grease. After the deerburger is cooked, break an egg into the skillet, then press the deerburger down on the egg hard enough to break the yolk. After the egg is cooked, salt and pepper the burger and serve while hot. The egg will moisten the deerburger."

Seminole Deerburger

The recipe I found for this dish called for ground beef. Since opening large bingo gambling houses and theme parks, some Seminoles can indeed afford to eat beef if they want it, and I suppose that any Seminole can make a raid on the large cattle ranches just north of Lake Okeechobee, where, I understand, rustling is more of a problem than it is in Texas. But I feel that honest Seminoles would rather have venison, and I have modified the recipe accordingly.

By the way, the pumpkin was very important in the diet of some of the American Indians, partly because it is so easy to keep without canning or deep freezing. It can also be dried for future use, and both the seeds and blossoms are edible. Modern Seminoles can use canned pumpkin pulp from the supermarket.

These burgers, I might add, are very easy to hold and eat, and children love them.

2 pounds ground venison
2 cups cooked pumpkin, mashed like
    potatoes
2½ cups self-rising flour
½ cup chopped onion
salt and pepper
water to make dough
cooking oil or fat

Mix the ground venison, onion, salt, and pepper. Set aside. Mix the pumpkin, flour, and enough water to make a soft dough. Knead the dough for a few minutes, then separate it into 3-inch balls. Knead and pull each ball of dough until it is rather elastic, then flatten it out like a pancake, about ¼ inch thick. Shape the meat into patties, then put each patty onto a piece of dough. Fold the dough up and seal it into itself. Heat the oil on medium high and fry the patties until they are brown on each side. Eat while hot. Feeds 6.

Note: Cook one patty at a time, and test it for doneness. The first one that I cooked was a little rare because the meat was too thick and the bread browned before the patty cooked through. If you have a problem, try cooking the patties on a lower heat. Rare or medium rare meat will probably be all right if you are using good venison that you butchered and cared for—but I can't recommend it for supermarket meats these days.

Venison Sloppy Joes

Here's a favorite dish around my house, especially when we have a bunch of hungry boys to feed. The measures below work nicely in a skillet. If you want to cook a larger batch, you may need a larger skillet or a stove-top Dutch oven.

1½ pounds ground venison
1 can tomatoes (16-ounce size)
1 can tomato sauce (15-ounce size)
1 medium onion, diced
1 clove garlic, minced
2 tablespoons chopped parsley
2 tablespoons margarine
1 teaspoon salt
½ teaspoon pepper
½ teaspoon chili powder

Put the margarine in a skillet, then brown the onion and garlic. Add the ground meat and brown it. Add the tomatoes and the liquid from the can, along with the tomato sauce, parsley, salt, pepper, and chili powder. Bring to a quick boil, stirring well. Reduce the heat, cover, and simmer for 1 hour. Serve over open hamburger buns. Feeds 4 or 5.

Antelope Sausage

The following recipe was given to me by Michael E. Sievering, who is a wildlife biologist at the Oakmulgee Wildlife Management Area in Brent, Alabama. He is also a wildlife artist. If you like sausage, be sure to try this one.

9 pounds antelope meat (boned)
2 pounds pork fat or 3 pounds hog jowls
3 tablespoons sage
3 tablespoons thyme
3 tablespoons pepper
3 tablespoons marjoram
salt

Bone the antelope meat and grind it with pork fat. Mix in the spices, then make the mixture into patties for the skillet or for freezing. (If you prefer, it can be frozen in bulk and then made into patties after thawing.)

Variations: Use meat from deer, elk, or other game instead of the antelope.

Game-Stuffed Peppers

This is one of my favorite dishes, and I especially like it with ground game meat. Here's what you need to feed 3 or 4 people, assuming that 1 or 2 will want more than 1 pepper:

6 large green bell peppers
3 cups ground game meat
1 medium to large onion, finely chopped
2 cloves garlic, minced
2 cups soft bread crumbs
1/2 cup melted butter (divided)
grated cheese
salt and black pepper to taste
water

Melt 1/4 cup of the butter in a skillet and sauté the onions and garlic for 5 minutes or so. Set aside. Brown the ground meat and keep it warm. Cut the tops off the bell peppers and remove the seeds and inner pith. Boil some water with a little salt in it, add the peppers, and cook for 8 minutes. Drain.

Preheat the oven to 375 degrees. Place the peppers in a baking pan of suitable size and set aside.

Mix the meat, bread crumbs, salt, black pepper, sautéed onions, and garlic. Toss, adding the rest of the melted butter. Stuff the bell peppers loosely with this mixture, then sprinkle with grated cheese. Pour 1/2 cup of water into the bottom of the baking pan. Bake the peppers for 20 minutes, or until the cheese is ready.

Note: Some stuffed peppers are too bland for my taste, and I sometimes add a little Tabasco sauce to the meat mixture for individual servings as I stuff the peppers. Thus I can make some hot, some not.

Grilled Meatballs

Although the Turkish shish kabob is popular in the Middle East and other parts of the world, the Arabs as well as the Iranians have another interesting way of grilling meat. Instead of stringing up chunks of lamb or camel or other good meat on a skewer, they shape ground meat around a skewer and grill it over hot coals. Usually, this skewer has a flat, sword-shaped blade, so that the meat stays on it better. Both ends of the skewer rest across the coals, with no support in the middle. In other words, no grid is used. To accomplish this at home, I use two bricks with the coals between them, and a third

Jackass Stew

There are some wild, or feral, donkeys, burros, or jackasses around the world, and, believe it or not, they make good eating. Before shooting one, however, check the game laws in the area where you are hunting—or take one for survival food if you need to. According to the big French culinary tome, *Larousse Gastronomique,* donkey meat has been eaten for a long time in some quarters, and in the Orient wild donkey was at one time considered to be choice "venison."

brick in the rear. The trouble with using a rack is that the meat tends to stick to it and tear off the skewer.

The Arabs prefer a finely ground meat. More often than not, lamb is specified in the recipes. Game meat can also be used, and it should be ground rather fine; try running it through your grinder twice. I suspect that any combination of good meat can be used, such as turtle and camel. I like to use this method for cooking what I consider to be inferior cuts. In other words, I use the recipe below for the tougher cut and reserve the tenderloin for shish kabob. I also like this method because it allows me to mix the spices into the meat rather than simply swabbing them onto the surface.

> 2 pounds of finely ground game meat
> 1 chicken egg
> 2 medium onions, chopped
> 1 tablespoon fresh parsley, chopped
> ½ teaspoon dried thyme
> ½ teaspoon ground coriander
> ½ teaspoon ground cumin
> 1 teaspoon salt
> ⅛ teaspoon cayenne

Mix all the ingredients well and put the mixture into the refrigerator for 1 hour or longer. Build a fire and rig for grilling. When the coals are ready, shape the meat mixture around a skewer into balls, about 1½ inches in diameter. Fill up the skewer, but don't pack the balls together. Put the skewers across the coals and grill until done, turning frequently. I prefer mine to be cooked for 10 minutes about 4 inches from hot coals, but cooking times will vary, depending on your fire and your rig. In any case, the inside of the balls should be done but quite moist.

Serve the meat over a bed of rice, along with steamed, boiled, or grilled vegetables. Note that the vegetables can also be cooked kabob fashion.

Variation: The Arabs cook a similar dish by shaping the ground meat onto the skewer in a long sausage shape instead of balls. Suit yourself. In Iran, my wife informs me, they use sword-shaped skewers and shape the ground meat around it, then they pull it off with the aid of a flat, pliable bread not unlike the Mexican tortilla. Sometimes they eat the meat in the bread, and sometimes they eat it separately. Pita bread from the supermarket will work.

Note: This recipe has been adapted from my book *Grilling, Smoking, and Barbecuing*.

Spaghetti Sauce

I've always been fond of spaghetti, and I like a sauce that has been simmered for a long time—and venison is perfect for long, slow cooking. Note that this recipe, one of my favorites, is made mostly with fresh vegetables instead of canned.

> 2 pounds ground venison
> ½ pound ground fresh pork
> 1 can beef broth (10¾-ounce size)
> 10 medium vine-ripened tomatoes
> 8 to 12 ounces fresh mushrooms, sliced
> 2 medium onions, diced
> 2 cloves garlic, minced
> ½ green bell pepper, diced
> ½ red bell pepper, diced
> 2 cups water
> ¼ cup Worcestershire sauce
> ½ teaspoon red pepper flakes
> salt and black pepper to taste
> 2 small bay leaves
> olive oil

Heat a little olive oil in a large skillet and brown the meats. Stir in the red pepper flakes, beef broth, and 2 cups of water. Cover tightly, reduce the heat to very low, and simmer for 6 hours.

Heat some water to a rapid boil in a large pot. Put the tomatoes into the pot for a minute or two, until the skin starts to peel. Cool the tomatoes, peel them, cut out the stem end, and quarter. (Do this over a bowl to catch any juice that comes out.) Pour the water out of the pot and put the tomatoes and their juice back into it; simmer for 1 hour, then break up the tomatoes and dump them into the skillet with the meat.

Heat a little olive oil in a small skillet or saucepan, then sauté the onions, garlic, mushrooms, and peppers. Add these to the meat sauce, along with salt and black pepper. Add the bay leaves and Worcestershire sauce. Bring to a boil, reduce the heat to low, cover, and simmer for 1 hour. If the sauce needs to be thickened, simmer it for part of the hour without the cover.

Fish out the bay leaves and ladle the sauce over hot freshly cooked spaghetti. Serve with garlic bread and lots of tossed salad dressed with olive oil and vinegar. Feeds 6 to 8.

Venison Meatballs Hawaiian

Here's a dish that can be served as an appetizer, or as a main course along with rice and steamed vegetables.

The Meatballs

2 pounds ground venison
1 cup oatmeal
½ cup minced onion
¼ cup milk
1 teaspoon salt
¼ teaspoon pepper
½ teaspoon garlic powder
oil for frying

Thoroughly mix the venison, oatmeal, onion, milk, salt, pepper, and garlic powder. Shape the mixture into small balls. Heat ½ inch of oil in the skillet and cook the meatballs, stirring from time to time with a wooden spoon, until they are done and nicely browned. Do not overcook. Keep warm while making the sauce.

The Sauce

1 can crushed pineapple (15 ¼-ounce size)
1 can sliced water chestnuts (8-ounce size)
¼ cup chopped green bell pepper
¼ cup chopped red bell pepper
½ cup brown sugar
⅓ cup white vinegar
2 tablespoons cornstarch
1 tablespoon soy sauce
1 cup water

Mix all the sauce ingredients except the pineapple in a small pan and heat, stirring as you go, until the mixture thickens. Add the pineapple and the juice from the can. Pour the sauce over the meatballs and bring to heat. Serve while hot. Feeds 4 to 6.

35

CHILI

A number of connoisseurs, as well as many of the jackleg chefs who frequent the various cook-offs around the country from Arizona to Minnesota, insist that chili be made with chunks instead of with ground meat—and with no beans whatsoever. Others, especially those of Texas bent, allow genuine pinto beans, but not red kidney beans or other legumes. Still others allow all of the above, along with tomatoes or tomato pastes, such as catsup, as well as various spices, so that the list of ingredients becomes longer and longer year by year, including even fire ants. I like most of the recipes that I have tried, but from time to time I enjoy going back to basics with the following recipe:

A.D.'s Chili Con Carne

I won't say flat out that tough meat makes better chili, but I do believe that long cooking improves a batch. Some meats, such as fat Angus steers, well marbled with fat, tend to cook apart after several hours, but venison tends to hold its own after long cooking. Venison may in fact be the perfect meat for chili, and, of course, the tougher cuts and scraps can be used. But most any good meat, including one of my favorites—turtle—can be used for chili. Even old Texas longhorn range cows. A friend of mine cooks what he calls a zoo chili, containing everything from squirrel to shark. A mix of this sort makes for good conversation, but really, simple venison from the whitetail is hard to beat for texture and flavor.

4 pounds tough venison
water to cover the meat
dried hot chili peppers

That's all. Chili con carne means simply peppers with meat, and those are really the only ingredients needed, along with a little water, to make a tasty dish. Cut the meat into chunks, put it into a heavy pot of suitable size, cover it with water, and turn up the heat. Crush the red peppers and add them to the meat. (Be careful. Some of these things are too hot to handle.) If you don't have whole peppers, try 1 teaspoon of crushed red pepper flakes, which are available in the spice section of the supermarket. (Black pepper or white pepper or paprika won't do.) Bring everything to a hard boil, reduce the heat, cover tightly, and simmer for 3 to 4 hours, or until the meat is tender.

This recipe is a good one to cook in camp, mainly because it doesn't require lots of ingredients to tote in. Most modern chili recipes, however, have a taste and aroma that go beyond the simple ingredients listed above. This special flavor is made by cumin seeds, which are used in all commercial blends of chili powder, and are so universal here and abroad that they may now be necessary for making what is accepted as "genuine" chili. So add 1 tablespoon

---

The Right Stuff

There isn't space enough here for me to list all the reasons why most of the alterations to chili are phony, so please take my word that tomatoes, paprika, sour cream, lime juice, catsup, red wine, Tabasco sauce, soy sauce, butter, or beans of any kind, but especially kidney beans, have no place whatever in chili con carne.

—Mel Marshall
Complete Book of Outdoor Cookery

---

of crushed cumin seeds to the recipe if you feel so inclined. Ground cumin is readily available, but the crushed seeds are better in flavor and aroma. I crush them with a mortar and pestle. I also like to add a little crushed salt to my chili.

Indian Chili

After working with the recipe above for a number of years, I found out that some of the Indians of the American Southwest did things a little differently. First, they boiled the meat (no doubt venison or jackrabbit) until tender and then took it out of the broth. Next, they sprinkled a chili powder over the broth, added a little garlic juice, and stirred the mixture over medium heat until it thickened slightly. Then they added the meat back into the broth until it heated through.

To make the chili powder, they dried red chili peppers on a string, or *ristra,* as often shown in modern cowboy movies set in the north of Mexico. Next, they broke open the chilies and took out the seeds and pith, which are the hottest parts. They put the deseeded peppers into a skillet or onto a flat rock and roasted them until they were browned. Then they cooled the toasted chilis and ground them into a powder. Because this method removes the hot seeds, the resulting powder will have more flavor of the chili pepper without too much heat. If you want to try the method, grow your own chili peppers or purchase them from a source of hot stuff. Save the seeds. As the Indians knew, they can be burned as a fumigant to get rid of bedbugs.

Also, the American Indians might have argued amongst themselves about whether or not "real chili" had beans in it. The Zuñi Indians were fond of cooking pinto beans or red kidney beans along with the meat, then seasoning the works with salt and chili powder.

Venison Chili and Corn Tortillas

Normally ½ pound of meat, on the average, will feed 1 person, but it's best to allow a little more of this dish because it is so good. I sometimes make my own tortillas from very fine stone-ground cornmeal (also called water-ground style meal), but most experts recommend *masa harina,* which is available from Mexican food stores. Ready-made corn tortillas are also available at supermarkets, and these should be steamed slightly before serving. I sometimes serve this chili atop a thin "hoecake" made to plate size and shape on a round griddle. This bread is made with only white cornmeal (fine is necessary) and water. No salt or other ingredients. The resulting flat taste of the bread goes just right with the chili.

3 pounds venison cut into ½-inch cubes
½ pound salt pork
2 cups water
1 large onion, diced
1 can tomato paste (6-ounce size)
3 tablespoons chili powder
1 tablespoon mild paprika
½ tablespoon cumin seeds
1 teaspoon salt (or more, to taste)
1 small dried chili pepper, crushed
tortillas (prepared separately)

Dice the salt pork and heat it in a Dutch oven or in other suitable pot until some grease

fries out and the pieces brown. Add the venison and onions, stirring for 4 or 5 minutes. Add the water and increase the heat. Stir in the tomato paste, chili powder, paprika, and salt. Crush the cumin seeds with your mortar and pestle and add them to the pot. Next, crush the dried chili pepper in the mortar and pestle and add it to the pot. (If you aren't sure of the strength of the pepper, add only ½ of the pepper at this time.) Taste the chili after about 30 minutes of cooking, then add a little more chili pepper if needed. (Keep the crushed chili pepper off your hands; it can burn your eyes and private parts.) Bring the chili to a boil, reduce heat, cover, and simmer for 3 hours.

Stir from time to time, and add a little water all along if needed, but keep in mind that this chili should be quite thick so that it can be rolled in tortillas. (You can also serve it in bowls, in which case you should add more water.)

I like the tortilla chili topped with a little sour cream and chopped onions.

A. D.'s Chili with Pinto Beans

Most cookbook writers and TV chefs recommend that dry beans be soaked overnight in water so that they can be cooked quickly. Soaking does indeed cut down on cooking time, but in my opinion it also cuts down on flavor. Pinto beans, and some others, profit from long, slow simmering. Since I also believe in simmering venison for a long time, the two come together nicely in this pot of chili. I like to use neck or shoulder meat along with shanks and other parts with both meat and bones. The bones are part of the recipe.

3 pounds venison meat
bones from above
12 ounces dry pinto beans
3 tablespoons chili powder
1 can tomatoes (16-ounce size)
1 huge onion, chopped
3 cups water
salt and red pepper flakes (if needed)

Before starting, bone the meat pretty well. Put the pinto beans into an iron pot and add the water. Crack or saw the bones and put them into the pot. Bring to a boil, cover, reduce heat, and simmer. If you want the chili with chunks, cut the meat into chunks and add to the pot. If you prefer ground meat, run the meat through the coarse plate of a sausage grinder or otherwise reduce it. (Personally, I prefer ground venison in most chili recipes that call for beans. But suit yourself.) Add the onions, tomatoes, juice from the tomato can, chili powder, red pepper, and salt. Simmer for several hours, or at least until the pinto beans are tender. Be warned that the pinto beans will absorb water as they swell up. Check the liquid in the pot from time to time, and stir. Add more water if necessary to prevent burning on the bottom or to adjust the consistency of the chili to suit your taste. I like it pretty thick, but my boys like to dump a handful of crumbled crackers into the bowl, and this works better with a rather liquid chili.

Crockpot Chili

Because I like chili simmered for long hours, it shouldn't be surprising that a crockpot is one of my favorite ways to cook it. Almost all chili recipes can be adapted to the simple crockpot technique, in which all the ingredients are dumped in, covered, and cooked on low all day long, while you are at work or on the hunt. The thousands of recipes calling for canned beans, however, may work better if the beans are held back and not cooked so long, lest they come apart and make a gob of mush. Also, a pot containing dried beans should not be left all day unless you are sure that they have enough liquid.

I make one of my favorite crockpot recipes whenever I have too many red ripe tomatoes in the garden and too much venison in the freezer. I merely put about 3 pounds of venison (chunks or ground, or a combination of both) into the crockpot, add 1 tablespoon of chili powder for each pound of meat, and fill the crockpot up with fresh peeled tomatoes. I usually add a little salt at this time, then adjust the seasonings after the chili has cooked for 6 or 7 hours. I sometimes add fresh peppers to the pot if

I have a surplus. These might be mild green bell peppers or hot chilies or fresh jalapeños or even banana peppers. In any case, let the chili simmer for 9 or 10 hours. Stirring isn't necessary, but, nevertheless, I like to stir mine every hour or so and taste it. If you stir it too frequently, however, you'll lose too much heat from the pot.

Dr. S. N. Hodges's Buzzard Breath Chili

Here's a chili, adapted from *Ducks Unlimited Cookbook*, that's not quite as foul as its name might indicate:

    2 cups ground deerburger
    2 cups chopped onions
    1½ cups chopped green pepper
    2 cans tomatoes
    2 cans tomato sauce
    2 cans kidney beans
    2 cans mushrooms
    2 to 2½ teaspoons salt
    2 tablespoons chili powder
    1 or 2 cayenne peppers

In a stove-top Dutch oven or large skillet, sauté the ground meat, onions, and green peppers until the meat is browned. Mix in the tomatoes, tomato sauce, kidney beans, salt, chili powder, cayenne peppers, and mushrooms. Bring to a boil, reduce heat, and simmer for 1 hour. Feeds 8 to 10.

Opposite-Sex Guest Chili

I don't care what you call this dish. It looks like chili, but its good clean flavor and mild consequence, so to speak, are quite different. Carefully note that it contains no beans.

    4 pounds ground moose or other suitable
        game meat
    2 cans Rotel (Mexican-style stewed
        tomatoes)
    2 teaspoons salt
    1 teaspoon dried parsley
    1 teaspoon garlic powder
    1 teaspoon basil
    1 teaspoon oregano
    chopped onions to taste

Put the ground meat into a crockpot, then add the Rotel and all the other ingredients except the onions. Cook on low heat for 8 hours or more. (I have cooked it as long as 24 hours.) Serve in bowls and top with chopped onions. We like to eat this chili with Wheatsworth crackers. Feeds 6 to 8.

Note: This dish can also be cooked in a Dutch oven. Just reduce the cooking time to 2 hours or so.

Variation: If you've got vine-ripened tomatoes, chill and dice one. Serve it atop the chili, with or without the onions. Also try the chili served in taco shells, with shredded lettuce, cheese, taco sauce, plenty of onions, and tomatoes.

Bedfellow Variation. Once the Broad Street boys gathered at our house to discuss a major event. It seems that an out-of-town girlfriend would be staying the night at the home of a 14-year-old. The several boys who were discussing this possibility were all about 11 or 12 years old at the time, except for our son Jeff, who was only 7 or 8. I overheard part of the conversation, which went pretty much as follows:

"Reckon where she's going to sleep?" one of the boys asked.

"With him, I reckon," said another.

"I wish I was him," said a third.

"Man yeah!" another said.

"Shoot," Jeff said, "I sure wouldn't want to sleep with no *girl*. Why, you couldn't even fart. You could lie there all night long and couldn't even fart."

Well . . . under such circumstances, try the above recipe without the garlic powder or onions. Add beans at your social peril.

Texas Good Ol' Boy Chili

I realize that the short list of ingredients in most of the recipes in this chapter might be something of a cultural shock to some Americans. For some time now the trend has been to add more and more stuff to a pot of chili, and this tendency has been carried to the extreme by the good ol' boy chefs and Texas sports who participate in cook-offs, usually with a can of beer in one hand and a jar of pepper in the other. What I consider to be a typical recipe of this sort, prepared, of course, without store-bought chili powder, was published a few years back in *The Only Texas Cookbook.* I am listing below only the ingredients, not the arguments and the how-to instructions, under the assumption that nobody in Ohio is going to be able to get all the stuff anyhow and, even if he could, would add some poisonous buckeyes or something to the pot.

Here's the list: 3 pounds lean stew meat—beef, venison, or other dark red meat (elk? bear? moose?), ground coarse or in ½-inch cubes; 1 pound pork loin, ground coarse or cubed; 2 tablespoons pure lard or shortening; 3 large yellow onions, chopped fine; 2 teaspoons cumin seeds; 1 teaspoon ground cumin; 7 cloves garlic; 1 tablespoon ground *chiles pasillas;* 1 teaspoon crushed *chiles quebrados* (pequins); 1 teaspoon Tabasco sauce; 2 teaspoons salt; 5 jalapeños, fresh, seeded; 1 pound tomatoes, dead-ripe (or canned if you must); 7 dried *chiles anchos* (big black ones); 1 dried chili New Mexico (big red one); 2 dried Jap chilies (little skinny red ones); 1 teaspoon sugar; 1 can Tecate beer; 1 ounce unsweetened chocolate; 1 quart water; and ½ cup *masa harina.*

Well, I'll allow that all the above sounds good, but I think it could be simplified somewhat by omitting the sugar and substituting sweetened chocolate for unsweetened. The Tecate beer, however, is said to have no equivalent. It is brewed in Mexico. In Texas it is drunk, as often as not, with a little lime juice and a grain or two of salt.

Osmose Zoo Chili

Here's a good large-batch recipe from a culinary sport by the name of Greg Rane, who said it was used in the Southeast Regional contest of the International Chili Society's cook-offs.

Group One
 5 pounds lean hamburger meat
 1 pound deer tenderloin, cubed small
 1 pound mild pan sausage
 6 ounces rabbit (lean)
 6 ounces squirrel (lean)
 10 ounces shark (preferably from just
  behind dorsal fin)
 10 ounces chicken (white meat, finely
  chopped)

Group Two
 3 large onions, chopped
 2 large green peppers, chopped
 1 jar pepperoncini peppers, chopped
 2 large jalapeño peppers, chopped
 4 chili peppers, punctured several times
  with a fork

Group Three
 1 large can chili powder (add to taste)
 3 to 5 teaspoons cumin powder (add to
  taste)
 1 teaspoon MSG (monosodium glutamate)
 2 teaspoons salt
 black pepper to taste (approximately 1
  tablespoon)
 3 tablespoons sugar

Group Four
 2 large cans tomatoes
 3 cans tomato puree (10-ounce size)
 1 can tomato paste (10-ounce size)
 1 lemon
 ½ stick butter
 1 small jar lemon-pepper seasoning salt
 2 cans Budweiser beer

"Pour tomato products from group 4 into a large pot (approximately 3- or 4-gallon). Be sure to squash tomatoes with your hands. Cook on low heat for 1 hour, stirring frequently and making sure not to burn. Add ingredients from group 3. Stir in and mix. Cover and simmer.

"Lightly sauté onions and green peppers in a skillet. Add to pot. Brown hamburger and sausage in the skillet. Drain off, add to pot, and stir in. Sauté cubed deer tenderloin and add to pot. Stir in. Chop rabbit, squirrel, and chicken. Sauté and add to pot. Stir in.

"Melt butter in the skillet, then add lemon pepper and lemon juice. Sauté shark. When it is cooked, flake it and stir into the pot.

"Add last 3 items in group 2. Stir in. Cook on low slowly for at least 2 hours, stirring frequently.

"As chili cooks down and consistency thickens NEVER ADD WATER! Add beer as needed to suit thickness. The longer this chili cooks, the better it gets. Enjoy."

My Version of Ed's Hot Dog Chili

Ed's place, a café in my hometown, claims to have the world's best hot dogs, and Ed advertises accordingly. And they are very good. I even published an article about them in an airline magazine.

Of course, everyone wants to know his recipe, but this is Ed's secret. All he'll say for sure is that the chili makes the hot dog. Into more detail he won't go. But my notes on the delivery traffic from a local meat market indicate that Ed's chili contains about 2 parts beef and 1 part pork, both finely ground. Adjusting a little for venison, I've come up with the following recipe.

Fat and Protein in Meat
(Based on 100-gram edible portions)

Meat	Water	Calories	Protein	Fat
beef	56.7 percent	301	17.4 grams	25.1 grams
beaver	56.2	248	29.2	13.7
opossum	57.3	221	30.2	10.2*
rabbit	73.0	135	21.0	5.0
raccoon	54.8	255	29.2	14.5
venison	74.0	126	21.0	4.0

*This figure might seem low to some people who hold the possum to be downright greasy, but most of the fat on a possum is layered between the hide and the meat.

Note: This table was made up from data published in *The South Carolina Wildlife Cookbook,* which in turn credited the Georgia Extension Service.

1 pound fine-ground venison
1 pound fine-ground pork
½ cup finely chopped onion
1 clove garlic, minced
1 cup water
peanut oil
3 tablespoons chili powder
1 tablespoon brown sugar
1 teaspoon salt
1 teaspoon pepper

Heat a little peanut oil in a skillet, then brown the ground venison and pork. Add the other ingredients, cover, and simmer for 6 to 8 hours. Spoon the chili on regular hot dogs, or make chili dogs without the wiener.

Ed won't say so, but in my opinion the one key to good hot dog chili is to use fine-ground meat and to cook it down. After cooking, dip it with a strainer so that there won't be enough liquid to make the bun soggy. For the best results, steam the buns until they are warm and soft. Any sort of steamer can be used, but don't get the buns too soggy.

Pedernales River Chili

Some years ago, the Alabama CowBelles published their *Beef Cookbook,* and the recipe from Mrs. Lyndon Baines Johnson has become one of my favorite chili-type dishes. Lyndon might roll over and bellow from the grave, or otherwise discharge, but I have taken license to change the ingredients from beef to venison with beef suet and have otherwise finagled with the recipe here and there.

The Chili
4 pounds venison
½ pound beef suet
1 large onion, chopped
2 cloves garlic, minced
1 can tomatoes (16-ounce size)
1 tablespoon oil
6 teaspoons chili powder
1 teaspoon ground oregano
1 teaspoon cumin seeds
½ teaspoon (or more) red hot pepper sauce
salt
2 cups hot water

Noche Specials
corn tortillas
cooking oil
grated cheese
jalapeño pepper

Cut the venison and beef suet into chunks, mix it well, and grind it in a sausage mill. Heat a little oil in a Dutch oven, then sauté the onion and garlic for about 5 minutes. Then brown all the ground meat a little at a time. Stir in the oregano, cumin seeds, chili powder, tomatoes, hot sauce, salt, and water. Bring to a light boil, reduce the heat to very low, and simmer for 1 to 2 hours, or longer. Serve with the Noche Specials, prepared from above ingredients as follows:

Preheat the oven to 400 degrees. Heat at least 1 inch of oil in a large skillet. Cut the tortillas into quarters and fry until brown and crisp. Drain the tortillas on absorbent paper. Put 1 teaspoon of grated cheese (I use sharp cheddar) and a slice of jalapeño pepper on each piece of tortilla. Place on a flat baking sheet and put it into the oven until the cheese starts to melt. Serve hot with chili. Cool off with ice-cold cola, iced tea, or Mexican beer. Feeds 10 to 12.

Easy Chili with Beans

2 pounds ground venison
4 strips bacon
1 can stewed tomatoes (14½-ounce size)
1 can kidney beans (16-ounce size)
1 cup catsup
1 medium onion, chopped
2 cloves garlic, minced
3 tablespoons chili powder
½ teaspoon salt
¼ teaspoon black pepper
water

Cook the bacon in a large skillet, crumble, and set aside. Quickly brown the venison in the bacon drippings. Stir in the onion, garlic, bacon bits, and chili powder; simmer for a few minutes. Add the tomatoes, catsup, beans, salt, pepper, and a little water. Bring to a light boil, reduce the heat, cover, and simmer for 3 hours. Stir from time to time, adding a little water if needed. Feeds 4 to 6.

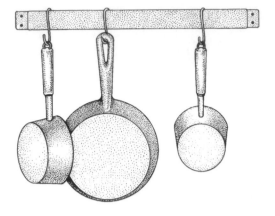

Easy No-Bean Chili

2 pounds ground venison
2 cans stewed tomatoes (14½-ounce size)
2 packs chili mix (1¾-ounce size)
1 tablespoon cooking oil
salt

Heat the oil in a large skillet, then brown the venison. Stir in the chili mix, salt, and tomatoes. Simmer for 1 hour, adding a little water if needed. Serve hot in individual bowls, topped with oyster crackers. Feeds 4 to 6.

36

BEAR

At its best, bear, wild or domestic, is one of the best meats available to man. At its worst, it is bad indeed. Because of its thick hair, a bear should be field-dressed and skinned as soon as possible. Aging or hanging the meat for long periods of time before cooking is not necessary, but leaving it under refrigeration for a day or two is recommended. Diet and mating seasons no doubt have some influence on the quality of the meat, but I suspect that most of the really bad meat is caused by chasing the bear all over the country with dogs before killing it. Even a prime domestic hog wouldn't be very good after such a chase. I am not expressing an opinion on the sport and excitement of the chase. I'm merely saying that hunting with dogs is not the best way to get prime meat.

Be warned that all bears, like all domestic and wild hogs (including the javelina), can carry the trichinosis parasite. The only safeguard is to make sure that the meat is done. Avoid rare steaks and rare roasts, no matter how tempting they might be. Even so, bear can be cooked in a number of ways, as shown in the recipes that follow.

Bigos

This old Polish dish was originally a hunter's stew, traditionally served after a bear hunt. It contained bear and other available game. The measures below make a rather large dish, which serves about 10 people, and a stove-top Dutch oven or some such pot will be required to cook it. I also use an auxiliary skillet. All of the meat should be cut into bite-size cubes.

The Best Bears

A male bear in the mating season, like a boar hog, is not fit to eat. A female nursing bear not only has tough and stringy meat, but for humanitarian reasons should never be destroyed. A young male bear in the off-season provides meat better than the best beef.

—Marjorie Kinnan Rawlings
Cross Creek Cookery

Many hunters prefer the meat of a bear killed just after hibernation in the spring, when most of the animal's fat has been lost and its muscles are soft from inactivity. Others say that the meat of a bear that's been eating berries is best, regardless of the time of year.

This, too, is a matter of opinion and probably depends upon where you are lucky enough to bag a black bear in the first place.

—C. B. Colby, *Outdoor Life*

The flavor of grizzly meat is more pronounced [than that of the black bear] and slightly coarser in texture but no less tender or edible. Grizzly meat does not freeze well. Three months is maximum. However, black bear freezes much better, very similar to pork.

—*Yukon Bear, Bacon,
and Boot Grease Recipes*

Do not eat bear liver or feed it to your pets. Bears sometimes secrete Vitamin A in their livers in amounts that can be toxic to humans and dogs or cats. Discard the liver with the intestines.

—Mel Marshall
Complete Book of Outdoor Cookery

1 pound bear meat, cubed
1 pound venison, cubed
½ pound Polish sausage, sliced
½ pound smoked bacon, cut into 1-inch pieces
8 ounces fresh mushrooms, sliced
2 medium to large onions, chopped
2 cans sauerkraut (16-ounce size)
2 cups beef broth
½ cup dry white wine
2 bay leaves
1 teaspoon paprika
½ teaspoon pepper
salt

Fry the bacon in a skillet, then drain it on a brown bag. Sauté the onions and mushrooms in the bacon drippings for 5 or 6 minutes. Remove the onions, then brown the bear meat and the venison. Transfer the meat to a Dutch oven or suitable pot. Add the beef broth, onions, mushrooms, bacon, sausage, paprika, salt, pepper, and bay leaves. Bring to a simmer, reduce heat to very low, and simmer for 2 hours. Stir in the wine, and simmer for 15 minutes. Just before serving, drain the sauerkraut, then stir it into the meat. Serve hot.

Variations: Substitute any good game meat for the venison. The bacon can be omitted if you use cooking oil to brown the meat, onions, and mushrooms.

Barbecued Bear

Here's a good recipe from Mike Stephens of the North Carolina Wildlife Resources Commission. It was published by the commission in a booklet (currently out of print) about cooking wild game.

The Meat
    bear roast, 3 or 4 pounds
    water
    salt and pepper
The Sauce
    ½ cup catsup or chili sauce
    ½ cup water
    3 tablespoons Worcestershire sauce
    2 tablespoons barbecue sauce
    1 medium to large onion, chopped
    1 clove garlic, minced

Preheat the oven to 350 degrees. Salt and pepper the roast, then put it on a rack in a baking pan that has a lid. Cover and bake in the center of the oven for 2 hours. Add ½ cup of water to the pan, cover, turn off the oven heat, and let the meat steam until the oven cools down. While waiting, heat the skillet, add ½ cup water, catsup, barbecue sauce, Worcestershire sauce, onion, and garlic. Simmer. When the roast is cool enough to handle, slice it thinly against the grain. Serve with the sauce. Allow ½ pound of meat per person. Leftovers can be reheated or used in sandwiches.

Crockpot Bear

This dish has an intriguing hint of sweet and sour in the taste of the gravy. If I had to pick a single recipe for cooking wild game of any sort, this one would certainly be in the final few. A roast of any reasonable size and shape can be used, provided that it fits nicely into your crockpot, leaving enough room for the rest of the dish. Add the mushrooms last. If they won't all fit, try again after the roast has cooked for a few hours.

    bear roast, 4 or 5 pounds
    2 medium potatoes, quartered
    2 medium tomatoes, quartered
    2 medium onions, quartered
    1 green bell pepper, sliced
    1 red bell pepper, sliced
    8 to 10 mushrooms (or more)
    1 cup water
    1 cup brown sugar
    ½ cup prepared mustard
    ¼ cup Worcestershire sauce
    1 tablespoon prepared horseradish
    1 beef bouillon cube
    2 bay leaves
    garlic powder
    onion powder
    salt and pepper

Mix the salt, pepper, onion powder, and garlic powder. Sprinkle the seasonings over the bear roast, then rub them in a little. Fit the roast into the crockpot. Add the potatoes, onions, and bell peppers, in that order. Top with mushrooms, filling the pot. (More mushrooms can be added after the dish has cooked for a while.) Heat the water, dissolve the bouillon cube, and stir in the brown sugar, mustard, horseradish, and bay leaves; pour the mixture into the crockpot. Cook on low heat for 8 or 9 hours. Turn to high and cook for 1 hour. Have plenty of biscuits for the gravy, or serve the gravy over rice. Allow ½ pound of meat per person. Leftovers are great when chopped, warmed up, and served over rice.

Appalachian Bear Roast

Here's a good dish from *Wildlife Chef,* published by the Oklahoma Wildlife Federation:

"Trim excess fat from roast. Parboil in water with 4 apples added to each quart of water. When apples start to fall apart remove meat. Salt and pepper meat, and bake it in a roaster in 350 degree oven until tender.

"Be sure meat is well done. Even when cooked it may have a pinkish tinge which will darken on contact with air."

Bear Loaf

If you like meatloaf, be sure to try this recipe the next time you bag a bear.

  1½ pounds ground bear meat
  8 slices American cheese
  2 stalks celery with tops, diced
  1 medium to large onion, diced
  ½ red bell pepper, diced
  1 tablespoon chopped fresh parsley
  1 can tomato paste (6-ounce size)
  1 cup cracker crumbs
  1 chicken egg
  1 tablespoon Worcestershire sauce
  ½ cup hot water
  1 beef bouillon cube
  1 teaspoon salt
  ¼ teaspoon pepper

Preheat the oven to 350 degrees. Dice 4 slices of the cheese, then mix it with the ground bear and the rest of the ingredients except for the 4 remaining slices of cheese, water, and bouillon cube. Form the mixture into a loaf and put it into a well-greased baking dish of suitable size and shape. Dissolve the bouillon cube in hot water, then pour it over the loaf. Place the remaining cheese slices on top. Bake for 45 minutes. Feeds 4.

Simmered Bear

Any good cut of bear meat can be used in this recipe. Try a rump roast or perhaps a rolled shoulder roast. I wanted to call this recipe "boiled bear," but actually it should not be boiled. Long, slow simmering is much better, resulting in a moister, more tender meat.

The Meat
  1 bear roast
  cooking oil
  salt and pepper
The Marinade
  1 cup vinegar
  1 cup water
  1 can tomato paste (6-ounce size)
  1 tablespoon Worcestershire sauce
  1 stalk celery with tops, minced
  1 large onion, minced
  1 clove garlic, minced
  1 teaspoon celery salt
  1 teaspoon dry mustard
  ½ teaspoon rosemary
  ½ teaspoon crushed bay leaves

Trim the roast, weigh it, and place it into a nonmetallic container. Mix all the marinade ingredients, pour over the roast, and marinate it in the refrigerator for 2 days, turning from time to time. When you are ready to cook, heat about ¼ inch of oil in a skillet. Remove the roast from the marinade, pat it dry, salt and pepper it, and brown it on all sides in the skillet. Put the roast into a stove-top Dutch oven or other suitable pot. Pour the marinade over the roast, bring to a simmer, cover tightly, reduce heat, and simmer for 45 minutes for each pound of meat. Turn the roast several times, adding more water if needed. At the end of the cooking time, you should have a nice thick gravy. If not, thicken the pot liquid with a little cornstarch and water solution. Serve with rice and vegetables. I allow ½ pound of roast per person.

Barbecued Bear Loin

Here's a neat, time-efficient recipe that I got from a booklet called *Black Bear, Nature's Forgotten Delicacy,* published by the Ontario Federation of Anglers and Hunters.

2 or 3 pounds bear tenderloin
¾ cup catsup
¾ cup vinegar
1 cup water
3 tablespoons brown sugar
1 tablespoon Worcestershire sauce
1 medium to large onion, chopped
1 clove garlic, minced
2 teaspoons salt
1 teaspoon dry mustard
¼ teaspoon pepper
¼ teaspoon Tabasco sauce

Preheat the oven to 350 degrees. Cut the meat crosswise into ½-inch slices. Put the slices into a greased oblong baking dish, then bake it in the center of the oven for 30 minutes. While the meat cooks, mix the other ingredients. After the meat has cooked for 30 minutes, pour the sauce over it, then bake it for 1 hour. Allow ½ pound of meat per person.

The Practical Domestic Uses of Bear Grease

Tanya Chasse of Yukon Renewable Resources was kind enough to send me a copy of a booklet called *Yukon Bear, Bacon, and Boot Grease Recipes,* which unfortunately is now out of print. From this booklet I learned that caked bear lard, at room temperature, makes good boot grease and softens leather. I also learned that it makes hair soft and shiny, but my wife still insists on paying good money to a cosmetologist.

Big Scrub Bear Roast

Not too long ago, black bear was plentiful in the Big Scrub of central Florida, and this recipe is from that area. I cook the dish in a stove-top cast-iron Dutch oven, but an old-timey campfire Dutch oven can also be used. In fact, any large, heavy pot can be used if it has a tightly fitting lid that is "self-basting." The cast-iron lid, dome-shaped, has little titlike protuberances in it. When the steam rises from the bottom of the pot, it condenses on the dome-shaped lid. Water droplets form on the ends of the protuberances and drop down on top of the roast. That's what keeps it moist.

4-pound boneless bear roast
¼ cup butter
1 cup dry red wine
3 cloves garlic
½ tablespoon dried rosemary
salt and pepper
cornstarch or flour

Dead Bears Are Also Dangerous

There's no doubt that bears can be dangerous. Grizzlies, blacks, browns, and whites all have chewed hell out of numerous citizens.... But I have a hunch that more people have been hurt skinning dead bears than were ever injured by bears on the hoof. Reports of knife cuts, ax cuts, assorted hernias, and pratfalls while packing hides to camp are legion.

Even more serious are the home accidents cause by head-mounted rugs lying between the cocktail bar and the gun cabinet. The risk is about 100 to 1, compared to the relative safety of hunting the shaggy brutes across the ice, on the tundra, in the woodlands, and beside the glaciers.

—C. E. Gillham, *Field & Stream*, November 1968

Peel the garlic and cut each piece in half lengthwise. Using your fish fillet knife, make six slits into the roast, spaced out nicely. Insert each garlic half into the roast and press it down so that the opening of the slits close. Sprinkle the top and bottom of the roast with salt, pepper, and rosemary. Let the roast sit at room temperature for 1 hour or so.

When you are ready to cook, heat the butter in the Dutch oven. On high heat, brown the roast on all sides. Pour in the wine and scrape up any bits that might have stuck to the bottom of the pot while browning the meat. Bring the mixture to a light boil, reduce heat to low, cover tightly, and simmer for 2 hours. Turn the roast every ½ hour or so. Add a little water if needed, but if the lid fits tightly this shouldn't be necessary.

After 2 hours, remove the roast and check the consistency of the liquid to see whether it will do for gravy. If you want it thicker, increase the heat. Stir a little flour or cornstarch into some water. Add some of this mixture slowly to the gravy, stirring constantly.

Slice the roast thinly, allowing several slices per serving. Spoon some of the gravy over the slices, and put the rest in a bowl for eating with some fluffy rice. Serve the meat and rice with vegetables of your choice. I like bear roast with another Big Scrub favorite—swamp cabbage, which is merely the heart of a young palm tree, eaten raw or boiled a little as a vegetable. I have also purchased sections of palm trees in Florida. The last batch I saw was near Perry, stacked up beside a country store like firewood. If your country store doesn't carry swamp cabbage and you don't have a suitable palm tree that needs cutting, remember that the canned heart of palm or millionaire's salad sold in the gourmet sections of some supermarkets and fancy restaurants is nothing but ordinary swamp cabbage. These tins are usually imported from Brazil, but I have also seen some from Central America.

Bear Sobieski with Croissants

Be warned that this dish is very, very rich, partly because it calls for a whole quart of wine and another quart of meat stock. I have adapted the dish from *Joe's Book of Mushroom Cookery*, by Jack Czarnecki, who said that the dish is named for King Jan III Sobieski (1629–96), "the savior of Vienna and the greatest king in Poland's history." Czarnecki adds that croissants were invented to celebrate the stopping of the Ottoman Empire at Vienna in 1683, adding that they were used to "finish off the sauce of this dish." Do you suppose that King Sobieski was sopping? In any case, the original was no doubt cooked with European brown bear. American black bear will also work.

2 pounds bear meat, cubed
1 quart dry red wine
1 quart strong meat stock
1 cup honey
1½ cups sliced fresh mushrooms
½ ounce dried cèpes (mushrooms)
3 large onions, chopped
3 cloves garlic, chopped
3 tablespoons sifted flour
3 tablespoons butter
2 tablespoons soy sauce
1 tablespoon crushed cumin
2 teaspoons salt
croissants

Put the bear meat into a stove-top Dutch oven or suitable pot. Add the wine, meat stock, garlic, onions, honey, cèpes, and cumin. Bring to a boil, reduce heat to very low, cover tightly, and simmer for 1½ hours, or until the meat is tender.

Remove the meat. Strain the liquid, then cook it down to 3 cups. (If you have a pot with cup gradient markings, strain the liquid into it, then cook it down to measure. You can also pour 3 cups of water into a pot and measure it with a ruler. Then discard the water, put strained liquid into the pot, and cook until it is reduced to the proper 3-cup depth.) Anyhow, after the liquid has been reduced to 3 cups,

pour it back into the main pot. Mix the flour and butter in a skillet, cooking on low heat, stirring as you go with a wooden spoon, until you have a dark brown roux. Add the roux to the pot, along with the salt and soy sauce. Heat and stir until the mixture thickens. Add the bear meat and fresh mushrooms. Cook for 5 minutes. While waiting, warm the croissants.

Feeds 4 to 6 royally.

Bear Fricassee V-8

Once I needed a little water in a fricassee that I was cooking, and I happened to have a can of V-8 juice at hand. I poured part of it in—and both the meat and the gravy turned out just right. Try it.

2½ pounds bear stew meat
1 can V-8 juice (10-ounce size)
1 medium onion, diced
1 clove garlic, minced
2 tablespoons cooking oil
1 tablespoon Worcestershire sauce
1 teaspoon salt
½ teaspoon pepper
½ teaspoon dried thyme

Heat a little oil in a skillet, then sauté the onion and garlic. Add more oil and brown the bear meat in several batches. Transfer the meat, onion, and garlic to a stove-top Dutch oven or some such pot. Pour in the V-8 juice and add the rest of the ingredients. Bring to a quick boil, reduce the heat, cover, and simmer on very low for 3 hours or longer, adding a little water if needed. Serve with rice or noodles, along with steamed vegetables.

Feeds 5 to 7.

37

ELK AND MOOSE

Many people consider the elk to be the best eating of all big game. It resembles beef and has a texture that is a little coarser than deer meat. Moose is also very good; it is of similar texture and is usually not as dry as deer. Both moose and elk make good sausage and excellent gameburger.

The elk is usually taken in cool weather at high elevations, allowing for proper cooling of the meat, which in turn makes for better eating. On the other hand, elk are large and difficult to handle, facts that often delay dressing and transporting the meat. Also, the elk should be dropped on the first shot. A wounded elk tends to run much farther than a deer, and this of course hurts the quality of the meat. With moose, the big problem is in getting it dressed out quickly, especially if the animal was shot while it was wading in water.

Most of the recipes in the venison chapters can be used for moose or elk, or you may want to try these:

Moose Mozzarella

This dish works best with a fairly good cut of meat, sliced about ½ inch thick. Round steak will do just fine.

1½ pounds moose steak
1 can stewed tomatoes (15-ounce size)
6 ounces sliced mozzarella cheese
1 cup cooking oil
½ cup grated Parmesan cheese
½ cup cracker crumbs
½ cup chopped onion
¼ cup chopped red bell pepper
1 tablespoon chopped fresh parsley
3 cloves garlic, finely chopped

356

1 chicken egg
1 teaspoon oregano
½ teaspoon marjoram
salt and pepper

Pound the steak with a meat mallet or the edge of a heavy plate, then put it into a non-metallic container. Mix the oil and garlic, pour it over the steak, toss about to coat all sides, and marinate for at least 4 hours, turning the steak from time to time. Save the oil marinade.

Preheat the oven to 325 degrees. Heat about 1 tablespoon of the oil marinade in a suitable pan or skillet. Sauté the onion and pepper for 5 minutes. Stir in the tomatoes (and juice from the can), parsley, oregano, marjoram, salt, and pepper. Simmer. Put the rest of the marinade oil into a large skillet. Whisk the chicken egg. Mix the Parmesan cheese and cracker crumbs together. Dip the steaks into the egg, roll in the crumb mixture, and brown in the skillet. Put the browned steaks into a well-greased baking dish; ideally, the steaks should cover the bottom but should not overlap. Mix the tomato sauce and pan drippings, then pour the mixture over the steaks. Top with mozzarella cheese slices. Bake in the center of the oven for 40 to 50 minutes, or until the cheese is starting to brown

nicely. Watch closely toward the end of the cooking time to make sure the cheese does not burn. Feeds 5 or 6.

Moose Steaks Supreme

This recipe was designed for meat that is on the tough side. If you've got tender meat, so much the better. The steaks should be cut ¾ inch thick.

3 pounds round moose steak (or elk)
1 can cream of chicken soup (10¾-ounce size)
½ cup red wine vinegar
½ cup olive oil
¼ cup cooking oil
½ teaspoon garlic juice
salt and pepper
flour
water

Mix the olive oil and vinegar in a nonmetallic container, and marinate the steaks for several hours or overnight, turning the meat several times.

Drain the steaks, salt and pepper them, and sprinkle with garlic juice. Roll the steaks in flour, then beat them with a meat mallet or the edge of a plate. Roll again in flour. Heat the cooking oil in a large heavy-duty skillet. Brown the steaks on both sides. Add a little water to the skillet, cover, reduce heat, and simmer on very low heat for 1 hour, turning the steak a time or two and adding more water as needed. In a saucepan, heat the soup, stirring in 1 cup of water. Add the soup mixture to the meat, cover, and simmer for 15 minutes. Serve the gravy over mashed potatoes or rice. Feeds 6 to 8.

Big-Game Chow Mein

The following dish is a very good way to feed lots of folks on a little game. I've made it with several kinds of meat, but if you use elk or moose, I recommend round steak or some similar cut. Usually, the "instant" tenderization method recommended below will be sufficient for properly cured or frozen meat; if the meat is very tough, however, consider marinating it overnight or longer.

1½ pounds round steak
1 can bean sprouts (14-ounce size)
1 can bamboo shoots (8-ounce size)
1 can sliced water chestnuts (8-ounce size)
1 cup beef bouillon (made with bouillon cube)
½ cup soy sauce
3 ribs celery, sliced crosswise, with green tops
1 medium to large onion, sliced with the grain
6 ounces fresh mushrooms, sliced
1 red bell pepper, thinly sliced
2½ tablespoons cornstarch dissolved in ½ cup water
peanut oil
salt and pepper
meat tenderizer (if needed)
chow mein noodles

If the steak is tough, sprinkle it with instant meat tenderizer, then beat it with a meat mallet or the edge of a plate. Let the meat sit for a while under refrigeration, then cut it, against the grain, into thin strips.

In a large skillet, heat a little peanut oil. Stir-fry the meat, then put it into a larger pot (I use a Dutch oven). Quickly sauté the onions, mushrooms, celery, and bell pepper in the skillet, adding a little more peanut oil if needed. Combine the cornstarch mixture, beef bouillon, and soy sauce; stir the mixture into the sautéed vegetables. Put the vegetables into the pot with the meat. Drain the water from cans of water chestnuts and bamboo shoots, then add them to the pot. Bring to a boil, stir, salt and pepper to taste, reduce heat, cover tightly, and simmer on very low heat for 30 minutes. Drain the water from the bean sprouts, and add them to the pot. Simmer for 15 minutes. Serve with chow mein noodles. Feeds 4 or 5.

Moose Pie

Any cut of moose meat can be used in this recipe, but it should be on the tender side. Try shoulder meat or, perhaps, meat cut from around the neck bone. In any case, the meat should be cut into 1-inch pieces.

2 pounds moose meat
frozen pie crust (or other suitable pastry)
2 cups water
2 tablespoons cooking oil
1 medium onion, diced
1 tablespoon Worcestershire sauce
2 teaspoons flour
¼ teaspoon dried thyme
¼ teaspoon dried basil
⅛ teaspoon nutmeg
salt and pepper
Hungarian paprika

Heat the water to boiling in a saucepan. In a large skillet with a tight-fitting lid, lightly brown the meat in hot oil. Sprinkle the meat with salt and pepper, then add the boiling water, cover, reduce heat, and simmer for 45 minutes on very low heat. (If the meat is tough, simmer it until it is tender, adding more water if needed.) Add the onion, basil, nutmeg, and thyme. Mix the flour with a little water, stirring until you have a smooth paste, and stir it into the steak along with the Worcestershire sauce.

Preheat the oven to 400 degrees. Put the steak into a greased round casserole dish of suitable size. Cut the pie pastry into strips and crisscross it over the meat mixture. Sprinkle with paprika. Place the dish into the center of the oven and bake for 30 minutes, or until the pie crust is nicely browned. Feeds 4 to 6.

Elk with Flaming Bourbon

Most people enjoy a dish of this sort, made with flaming whiskey or brandy This one is easy, as well as good. Also try this dish with loin chops or butterflied tenderloin.

2 pounds tender elk steak, ½ inch thick
½ cup chicken broth
½ cup cream
⅓ cup butter
⅓ cup bourbon
salt and pepper

If your meat is not tender, either marinate it overnight or treat it with a commercial meat tenderizer before cooking it.

Warm the bourbon in a small saucepan. Melt the butter in a large skillet. On high heat, brown the steaks for 3 or 4 minutes on each side. Pour out the surplus butter. Reduce the heat. Pour in the warm bourbon, then ignite it with a long match. Shake the skillet while the bourbon burns off. Put the steaks onto a heated serving platter. To the skillet, add the chicken broth, salt, and pepper. Stir with a

wooden spoon or wooden spatula, scraping up any pan dredgings. Add the cream, stirring until the gravy thickens. Pour the gravy over the steaks. Eat while hot. Feeds 4 to 6.

Steak Diane (or Jutland Moose)

I adapted this recipe from an article by Jack Denton Scott, as published in the October 1967 *Sports Afield*. As Scott explained, "Diane is Goddess of the Hunt, and steaks cooked in her name could make hunting as popular as sex. I first had them in Copenhagen in the home of a Danish friend who was given a strip of sirloin, well aged, of what they call elk and we know as moose."

Wapiti

The name *wapiti*, derived from the Algonquin language, refers to a large deer, which is commonly called elk in America. It stands over 5 feet high at the shoulders, weighs up to 1,000 pounds, and has a large, impressive set of antlers. The wapiti makes very good venison and is highly regarded both for sport and for meat.

In addition to its range in northwestern North America, it also lives in parts of Asia. The wapiti is an important source of food in parts of Siberia, where a variety called *maral* is bred on farms.

—Adapted from
Edible Plants and Animals

2 pounds boned moose sirloins, ¾ inch
thick
8 tablespoons butter (divided)
1 tablespoon Worcestershire sauce
1 tablespoon minced fresh parsley
2 shallots, minced
1 clove garlic

Place each steak between sheets of waxed paper, then flatten it with the smooth side of a meat mallet or with the side of a heavy meat cleaver. Melt half of the butter in a large skillet. Sauté the flattened steaks for 20 seconds on each side. Melt the rest of the butter in a chafing dish, adding the Worcestershire sauce, parsley, shallots, and garlic; sauté and stir until the clove of garlic starts to brown. Discard the garlic. Continue to stir the sauce for a few more minutes. Add the steaks, then cook for 3 minutes, turning them in the sauce several times. Do not overcook; the steaks should be pink-rare on the inside. Serve hot on warmed plates, along with good red wine, French bread, and vegetables. Feeds 4 to 6.

Moose Ribs

If you've got 3 or 4 pounds of moose ribs and a pressure cooker, try this dish, adapted from Alaska Department of Fish and Game's *Wildlife Cookbook,* which is now out of print.

Preheat the oven to 350 degrees. Place the ribs in a pressure cooker. Lay strips of pork over the ribs. Add 2 or 3 sliced onions, then pour in ½ cup of water. Cook at medium pressure for ½ hour. Remove the ribs, placing them in a large cast-iron skillet with an oven-proof handle. Mix 1 tablespoon of brown sugar and a little dry mustard with the liquid from the pressure cooker. Pour this mixture over the ribs. Place the skillet into the oven for ½ hour, uncovered, or until the ribs are nicely browned on top, basting from time to time with the pan juices.

How many ribs to cook depends on how meaty they are—and how good they are. I allow at least 1 pound for each person.

Tenderloin of Elk with Mushrooms

This dish calls for elk, but it can be made from any tenderloin or other cut of good meat.

Meat and Marinade
2 pounds elk tenderloin cutlets, ½ inch
thick
½ cup butter
Worcestershire sauce
salt to taste
Mushrooms and Sauce
8 ounces fresh mushrooms
¼ cup butter
¼ cup chopped fresh parsley
juice of ½ lemon
1 teaspoon onion juice
½ teaspoon garlic juice
1 teaspoon Worcestershire sauce
½ teaspoon salt
Garnish
slices from ½ lemon
fresh parsley sprigs

Stick a fork several times into each piece of tenderloin, then put them into a suitable container, sprinkle with Worcestershire sauce, and marinate for several hours, turning from time to time.

To prepare the mushroom sauce, heat the butter in a skillet. Stir in the lemon, onion, and garlic juices. Add the mushrooms; sauté for a few minutes. Add the Worcestershire, salt, and parsley. Keep warm.

Heat another skillet. Drain and salt the tenderloin pieces. Melt the butter, then cook the tenderloin over high heat for 3 minutes on each side. Arrange the tenderloin cutlets on a serving platter, pour on the mushrooms with their sauce, and garnish with parsley and lemon slices. Serve hot with baked potatoes, tossed salad, bread, and red wine. Feeds 4 to 6.

Slow Oven–Barbecued Elk

Here's a good dish that takes about 12 hours to cook—but it's worth the wait, and makes a fun project for a cold day in the cabin.

The Meat
    elk roast, 5 to 7 pounds
    ¼ cup cooking oil
The Sauce
    2 medium onions, chopped
    2 cloves garlic, minced
    juice of 2 lemons
    1 can tomato sauce (12-ounce size)
    ½ cup water
    ¼ cup catsup
    ¼ cup vinegar
    2 tablespoons brown sugar
    1 tablespoon Worcestershire sauce
    1 tablespoon salt
    ½ teaspoon dry mustard
    ½ teaspoon paprika
    ½ teaspoon pepper
    ⅛ teaspoon Tabasco sauce

Preheat the oven to 200 degrees. Heat the cooking oil in a skillet, then brown the roast on all sides. Put the roast into a suitable bak-ing dish with a cover. Sauté the onion in the skillet, then add the rest of the sauce ingredients. Simmer for a few minutes, then pour the sauce over the roast, cover tightly, and cook for 12 hours. Turn from time to time, basting with the pot liquid. Add a little water, or whatever you're drinking, if needed. Feeds 10 to 12. Leftovers are great when sliced thinly and used in sandwiches, or when diced, heated in the sauce, and served over rice.

Cubed Elk Tenderloin over Rice

Here's a great little dish that is very easy to prepare. It works best with loin or tenderloin, but other meat can also be used.

The Biggest Game?

Hippopotamus meat is highly sought in some parts of Africa. Rhinoceros meat is edible and better than elephant, which is said to be tough and leathery (although elephant trunks and feet are delicacies).

Another large animal, the whale, has been hunted around the world and is still eaten by the Japanese and the Eskimos. According to *Larousse Gastronomique*, a French work, "Whale meat was not greatly esteemed by our grandfathers, but they did set some store by the tongue of the animal, usually salted, and Ambroise Pare says that 'it is tender and delicious.' They also much appreciated whale fat which they ate 'during Lent, with peas.'"

2 pounds elk
1 medium onion, diced
½ cup chili sauce
2 tablespoons cooking oil
2 tablespoons flour
1 cup hot water
½ cup cold water
rice (cooked separately)
salt and pepper

Cut the meat into 1-inch cubes. Heat the oil in a skillet, sauté the onions, and brown the meat. Add the hot water, cover, and simmer for 30 minutes. In a bowl, mix the cold water, chili sauce, salt, and pepper. Slowly stir in the flour. Add the sauce mix to the meat, stir, and bring to a boil. Then reduce heat, cover, and simmer for 30 minutes. Serve hot over rice. Feeds 4 to 6.

Variation: Serve over egg noodles cooked according to the directions on the package.

Easy Elk Bourguignon

2 pounds elk steak
1 can cream of mushroom soup (10¾-
　　ounce size)
8 ounces fresh mushrooms, sliced
¾ cup red wine
¼ cup bacon drippings or cooking oil
1 package onion soup mix (1¼-ounce size)
salt and pepper
¾ cup water
flour (if needed)
rice (cooked separately)

In a large skillet or stove-top Dutch oven, brown the meat in the bacon fat or cooking oil. Add the water. Stir in the mushroom soup, then the mushrooms, onion soup mix, wine,

salt, and pepper. Bring to a boil, reduce the heat to very low, cover, and simmer for 3 hours, or until the meat is tender. If the gravy isn't thick enough, stir in a little paste made with flour and water. Serve over rice. Feeds 4 to 6.

Stuffed Elk Steak

Here's a good recipe that was sent to me by the Alaska Department of Fish and Game in Juneau. The loin steaks should be 2 inches thick. It can also be made with steaks from the hind leg.

2 elk loin steaks
½ cup water
2 tablespoons butter
1½ slices day-old bread
1 tablespoon chopped green bell pepper
1 tablespoon chopped celery
1 tablespoon chopped onion
flour
salt and pepper

To make a stuffing, break the bread into small pieces. Mix in the salt, green pepper, onion, and celery. Set aside. Salt and pepper the steaks, then coat them with flour. With a sharp knife, cut a slit in the steak, forming a pocket. Stuff the steaks with the dressing. Heat the butter in the bottom of a pressure cooker. Brown the steaks. Add the water. Cook for 20 minutes at 10 pounds pressure.

Creamy Elk Casserole

Here's an easy dish to prepare. It's also quite tasty and filling.

2 pounds elk round steak
1 can cream of onion soup (10¾-ounce
   size)
1 can cream of nacho cheese soup (10¾-
   ounce size)
1 can cream of mushroom soup (10¾-
   ounce size)
4 ounces elbow macaroni
2 cups tortilla chips, crushed
butter
salt and pepper

Cook the macaroni according to the directions on the package. Drain. Preheat the oven to 350 degrees. Cut the steak into thin strips. Heat a little butter in a large skillet, then brown the steak strips lightly. Add all the soups, salt, pepper, and cooked macaroni. Pour the mixture into a greased casserole dish. Bake for 45 minutes. Sprinkle with crushed chips, then bake for another 5 minutes. Serve hot. Feeds 4 to 6. If you've got more people to feed, add more macaroni.

Elk Cutlets

The meat from this dish can be cut from the loin or tenderloin or, if your meat is tender, from one of the muscles of the hind leg.

2 pounds elk cutlets
juice of 1 large lemon
2 chicken eggs, whisked
dry bread crumbs
flour
cooking oil
1 cup water
1 tablespoon Worcestershire sauce
salt and pepper

Salt and pepper the cutlets, roll them in flour, dip them in egg, then roll them in bread crumbs. Heat some oil in a skillet. Brown the cutlets in batches, draining them on a brown bag. When all the cutlets have been browned, pour off the excess oil and scrape up the pan dredgings with a wooden spatula. Put the cutlets back in the skillet. Mix the water, lemon juice, and Worcestershire sauce, and pour over the cutlets. Cover and simmer for 2 hours. Serve hot, topped with gravy from the skillet. Feeds 4 to 6.

Maxwell House Moose

Round steak 1 inch thick works nicely with this recipe, but other cuts of meat can also be used.

2 pounds round steak
1 cup red wine vinegar
1 cup water
1 cup sour cream
½ cup strong black coffee
½ cup dry red wine
2 medium onions, diced
8 ounces fresh mushrooms, sliced
1 stick butter or margarine
salt and pepper to taste
flour

Cut the meat into 1-inch cubes, put it into a nonmetallic container, pour in the water and red wine vinegar, and marinate overnight. When you're ready to cook, preheat the oven to 300 degrees. Melt the butter in a skillet. Sauté the onions and mushrooms for 5 minutes, then drain. Roll the meat in the flour, then brown it in the skillet, adding more butter if needed. Put the meat, onions, mushrooms, salt, and pepper into a large greased casserole dish that has a cover. Pour in the red wine and black coffee. Bake for 3 hours. Stir in the sour cream. Put the dish back into the oven for a few minutes, but turn the heat off. Serve with steamed vegetables and rice or egg noodles.

Feeds 4 to 6.

38

CARIBOU AND ANTELOPE

As table fare, the pronghorn antelope is one of the very best game animals, and many people rate it above all others. The average pronghorn is only about half the weight of a fully grown white-tailed deer, and it doesn't present as many field-dressing and handling problems. This fact may help account for its popularity as table fare. As pointed out in the chapter on dressing game, however, a scent gland on the rump, which the antelope uses to signal danger, is quite powerful and should be avoided.

The caribou is considered by some hunters to be the best of all game meat. It is rather fine-grained in texture. These animals look quite large because of their antlers, but they are a good deal smaller than a moose or an elk. Students of Old World cookery should note that the caribou is the same animal as the European reindeer. Anyone interested in making a complete study of caribou cookery should look into the culture of the Lapps, a people who depend on the animal—and who use every part of it.

Most of the recipes set forth in the venison chapters will do nicely for either antelope or caribou. Or try one of the following:

Caribou Steak in Sour Cream

Here's a very good, easy dish that can be cooked with round steaks about ¾ inch thick. Loin chops can also be used.

2 pounds round steak from caribou
8 ounces fresh mushrooms, sliced
1 medium to large onion, diced
½ cup sour cream
½ cup peanut oil
flour
½ cup hot water
salt and pepper

Cut the steaks into 3-inch pieces, salt and pepper them, roll them in flour, beat them with a meat mallet or the edge of a plate, and set aside. Heat the peanut oil in a skillet, then sauté the onion and mushrooms for 5 minutes. Remove the onion and mushrooms with a slotted spoon. Brown the steaks on both sides, adding a little more oil if needed. After browning all the steaks, pour off most of the oil. Scrape up any pan dredgings with a wooden spoon or wooden spatula. Add the hot water, onions, mushrooms, and sour cream. Heat but do not boil. Add the browned steaks, cover tightly, and simmer for 2 to 3 hours, or until very tender. Stir from time to time, and add more water if needed. Be sure to have biscuits, mashed potatoes, or rice for the gravy. Feeds 4 to 6.

Easy Jalapeño Antelope

I once got on a jag of cooking various kinds of meats, especially venison, with red currant jelly, mayhaw jelly, and so on. From that period came one of my favorites of the "easy" dishes, made in a crockpot. The roast can be 2 boned shoulders rolled together or a boned hind leg, rolled and tied. The exact weight doesn't make much difference, except that the crockpot method works best with a pot that is full or almost full.

    antelope roast, 4 to 6 pounds
    ½ cup hot jalapeño jelly
    ½ cup water
    salt and pepper

Salt and pepper the roast, then put it into a crockpot. Dump the jelly on top of the roast, then pour in the water. Cook on low heat for 8 or 9 hours. Slice part of the roast. Serve with crockpot gravy, along with rice and vegetables. Feeds 8 to 12, allowing ½ pound of meat per person.

Note: The gravy can be thickened with a solution of cornstarch and water, stirred in sparingly until the pot liquor thickens.

Caribou Stew

    2 pounds stew meat
    2 cups chopped tomatoes
    1 cup sour cream
    1 large onion, diced
    ¼ cup butter
    salt and pepper
    mashed boiled potatoes or rice

Heat the butter in a large skillet or stove-top Dutch oven. Sauté the onions for 5 minutes, then add the meat and brown it. Add the tomatoes, salt, and pepper. Bring to a bubble, then add the sour cream. Reduce the heat to very low, cover tightly, and simmer for 3 hours. Stir and add a little water from time to time, if needed. Serve with rice or mashed potatoes. Feeds 4 to 6.

Variations: If you want a little zip in this stew, add 1 or 2 chopped green chili peppers. Be sure to remove the seeds and cores from the peppers, and wash your hands after seeding.

Antelope Ragout

Here's a delicious stew. I cook it in a stove-top Dutch oven. Any good cut of meat can be used, but I recommend shoulder, thereby saving the loin, tenderloin, and hind leg for other recipes.

3 pounds antelope, cut into 1½-inch cubes
½ pound bacon
8 ounces fresh mushrooms, sliced
3 medium onions, chopped
5 cloves garlic, minced
1½ quarts water
1 can cream of tomato soup (10¾-ounce size)
¼ cup beer
2 tablespoons bourbon or other whiskey
1 teaspoon curry powder
salt and pepper

Cook the bacon in a stove-top Dutch oven. Crumble and set aside. Brown the meat in the bacon drippings. Set aside. Pour off about half of the bacon drippings. Brown the onions and garlic, then add the water, tomato soup, beer, bourbon, salt, pepper, and curry powder. Bring to a boil, add the browned meat and bacon, reduce the heat to very low, cover, and simmer for 1 hour, or until the meat is tender. Add the mushrooms, then simmer for another 15 minutes. Serve hot. Feeds 6 to 8.

Easy Rotel Caribou

A commercial product named Rotel, a mixture of stewed tomatoes and hot chili peppers, has been a favorite ingredient of mine for a number of years. It's great stuff for camp and kitchen alike. These days, several kinds of seasoned tomatoes are on the market and may be substituted for the Rotel.

3- or 4-pound roast
1 can Rotel (10-ounce size)
chili powder
salt

Sprinkle the roast with salt and chili powder, fit it into a crockpot, and pour the Rotel and the juice from the can over it. Turn the heat to low, and cook for 8 or 9 hours. Serve the gravy over rice, mashed potatoes, or biscuit halves. Feeds 6 to 9.

Rock Springs Antelope Roast

I always appreciate a little story with my recipes, and sometimes my guests also find them amusing. Here's one of my favorites, freely adapted from *Cooking in Wyoming*, to which it was

Pass the Salt

In an article in *Field & Stream* some years ago, C. E. Gillham wrote about hunting antelope with a group of Indians on the Porcupine River in the Yukon Territory. The Indians cooked one on a sandbar, but their method and cut of meat didn't fulfill Gillham's vision of roast ribs and fillets. Instead, they suspended the head and neck from a pole tripod over a roaring fire. After an hour, the caribou's eyes "bugged out in the heat, giving the charred head an expression of great surprise. At last it was finished, and we fell to. The burned skin was scraped off. This was hard as a butcher's heart, but the meat beneath was tender and toothsome."

Since Gillham was the guest of honor, the Indians offered him one of the eyeballs. "It might have tasted all right," he said, "with a touch of salt."

submitted by Mrs. W. Robert DuBois of Cheyenne. She said that her husband, Rob, got the recipe from another hunter, who in turn got it from a chef in Rock Springs, who released the recipe only after being sufficiently plied with liquor.

The recipe calls for ¼ pound fat pork. I almost always use salt pork or fatback. The last time I cooked this recipe was with the aid of some home-cured fatback from a wild acorn-fed hog. It was delicious.

The Meat
    6- to 8-pound antelope roast
    1 large can tomatoes (29-ounce size)
    ¼ pound butter
    salt and pepper
    allspice
    bay leaf
The Sauce
    ¼ pound salt pork, diced
    8 ounces fresh mushrooms
    1 pint red wine
    1 cup chopped onion
    1 cup chopped green pepper
    1 cup chopped celery
    2 cloves garlic, minced
    ⅛ pound butter

Make the sauce first. In a large skillet, heat the butter and fry out the salt pork until the cracklings are crisp. Add the rest of the ingredients. Simmer uncovered on very low heat for 1½ hours. Add a little water if needed.

Preheat the oven to 300 degrees. Heat the butter in a stove-top Dutch oven, then brown the roast on all sides. Add the bay leaf, allspice, salt, pepper, and tomatoes. Bake in the center of the oven for 5 hours. After 1 hour, start basting with the sauce. Baste often, using all the sauce. Then start basting with the pan juices. Turn the roast after 3 hours. Feeds 12 to 16.

Antelope Chops

Here's a delicious dish to try whenever you are tired of the usual brown-and-simmer-until-tender method of cooking wild game. You guessed it: This recipe takes a simmer-and-brown approach. You can use loin chops or chops cut from the hind leg.

    6 chops, ½ inch thick
    3 tablespoons cooking oil
    flour
    garlic salt
    pepper
    water

Season the chops with pepper and garlic salt, then dust them heavily with flour. Heat the oil in a heavy skillet that has a cover. Put the chops into the skillet, reduce the heat to very low, cover, and simmer on very low heat for 1 hour, turning and adding a little water from time to time. When the meat is tender, remove the cover, increase the heat, and cook until the chops are browned. Allow ½ pound of meat per person.

Country Baked Antelope

Here's a wonderful dish that combines skillet and oven cooking. The gravy is outstanding. Shoulder meat works nicely for this recipe, but loin or hind leg can also be used.

Eskimo Dinner Party

The host's wife is busy boiling meat from the newly caught game over her blubber lamp, and when everybody has had enough of the dozen delicacies, they start in on the steaming walrus or seal meat. The polite guests fart and belch to show how well they are digesting the treats of the house. They continue eating until they are too gorged to get another bite down. If a guest gets tired, he will simply go to sleep where he sits and start in on the meal again when he wakes up. If it becomes apparent that the provisions of the house are about to give out, another hunter will stand up and ask to be allowed to show what his house has to offer. Thus the party goes from house to house, and the feast may last for days.
—Peter Freuchen, *Book of the Eskimo*

2 pounds antelope
about 3 cups water
¹/₂ cup catsup
¹/₄ cup cooking oil
2 medium onions, chopped
3 tablespoons flour
2 tablespoons brown sugar
1 tablespoon Worcestershire sauce
1¹/₂ teaspoons chili powder
1 teaspoon prepared mustard
salt and pepper

Cut the meat into 1-inch chunks. Heat the oil in a skillet. Brown the meat, then set aside. Sauté the onions for 5 minutes. Stir in the flour with a wooden spoon. Slowly stir in the water, stirring until you have a smooth gravy. Add the catsup, brown sugar, mustard, chili powder, and Worcestershire sauce. Salt and pepper to taste. Simmer for ¹/₂ hour.

Preheat the oven to 300 degrees. Put the meat into a greased baking dish, then pour the sauce over it. Cover and cook for 2 hours, or until the meat is tender. Add more water if needed. Serve with rice, biscuits, or mashed potatoes. Feeds 4.

Antelope Cutlets in Sherry

The meat for this recipe can be from the loin or one of the hind leg muscles, sliced across the grain.

2 pounds antelope cutlets, ¹/₂ inch thick
¹/₂ cup dry sherry
2 chicken eggs
juice of 1 lemon
dry bread crumbs
cooking oil
flour
salt and pepper

Whisk the chicken eggs. Heat a little cooking oil in a large skillet that has a lid. Salt and pepper the cutlets, dust them lightly with flour, dip them in the egg, roll them in flour, and brown them in the skillet. Add enough water to almost cover the cutlets. Add the lemon juice, cover tightly, and simmer for 2 hours, or until the meat is tender. Add the sherry. Simmer for another 10 minutes. If the gravy is too thin for your taste, thicken it with a little flour. Serve with rice and vegetables. Feeds 4 to 6.

39

SHEEP AND GOAT, BOAR AND JAVELINA

Bunching sheep, goat, boar, and javelina into a single chapter does great injustice to them. They can all be excellent table fare and therefore deserve their own chapters. But their range is limited, although some, like the javelina, can be quite plentiful in some areas. If you are lucky enough to have these animals to hunt, try the following:

Sheep Kabobs

Use a good cut of meat and don't overcook it. I specify loin in the recipe below, but the shoulder of a prime animal can also be used. You can put vegetables on the kabobs in the American patio manner, but also try this dish with meat only, cooking the vegetables on the side. The original kabobs were probably cooked with meat only—and were no doubt made with sheep or goat.

2 pounds sheep loin
2 cups olive oil
6 cloves garlic, crushed
salt and pepper

Cut the meat into kabob-size chunks. Crush the garlic, then put it into a glass container with the olive oil. Let this mixture steep for a while or, better, for several days. Place the meat into a nonmetallic container, then pour the garlic oil over it. Marinate for several hours.

It's best to build a hot fire from hardwood and let it burn down to coals, although you can use charcoal, gas, or electric heat if you must. Skewer the meat and broil very close to the heat for 4 or 5 minutes. Turn and broil the other side for a few minutes, or until the meat is medium rare. Sprinkle a little salt on the meat, then eat it hot, along with vegetables and rice.

Variation: Baste during cooking with a mixture of melted butter and lemon juice.

Rocky Mountain Bighorn Roast

I've always been fond of roast recipes that call for garlic stuck into the meat. Here's a good one from the book *Game Cookery*, by E. N. and Edith Sturdivant, who said, "Any sportsman who has eaten properly cared-for sheep will tell you that it tops everything for tastiness among large game animals. This is doubly true of the Rocky Mountain bighorn sheep. A chuck roast from the blade will do in the event that you have cut the loin into chops." Unfortunately, I've never encountered the Rocky Mountain bighorn, but I did try the recipe with lesser meat. It's good, it's easy, and it doesn't require a long list of ingredients.

    3- or 4-pound bighorn roast
    1 clove garlic
    flour
    salt and pepper

Preheat the oven to 400 degrees. Wipe the roast with a damp cloth. Insert the point of a thin fillet knife into the meat at 3 nicely spaced locations. Split the garlic clove into 3 pieces lengthwise, then insert the slivers into the meat. Salt and pepper the roast, then sprinkle it with flour. Put the meat into a roasting pan. Bake for 30 minutes, reduce the heat to 325, and bake for about 2½ hours, or until done— but not too done. Make gravy with the pan juices. The Sturdivants say to serve the roast with mint jelly, potatoes, a green vegetable, and a salad of lettuce wedges and your favorite dressing.

Note: It's a mistake to cook a roast too long. If in doubt, use a meat thermometer to guide you. Insert the thermometer into the thickest part of the roast, then bake until the thermometer reads 140 to 145 degrees for medium rare. After it reaches 140, take it out of the oven and let it coast for a while before slicing.

Leg of Sheep

Here's a good recipe that is cooked in the oven with the aid of aluminum foil. It can also be adapted for use in a large covered grill, using the indirect method.

The Meat
    leg of sheep, 4 to 6 pounds
    salt and pepper
The Marinade
    1 cup red wine
    ½ cup olive oil
    4 tablespoons vinegar
    4 cloves garlic, crushed
    1 teaspoon salt
    ½ teaspoon pepper
    ½ teaspoon thyme
Basting Sauce
    ½ cup melted butter
    juice of 1 lemon

Mix the marinade ingredients. Place the meat into a nonmetallic container, cover with the marinade, and refrigerate for at least 24 hours, turning several times.

Preheat the oven to 325 degrees. Place a long, wide sheet of heavy-duty aluminum foil into a large baking pan. Sprinkle the leg of sheep with salt and pepper, then place it onto the sheet of aluminum foil. Bend the foil up, making a boat, but do not let it touch the sides of the leg. Mix the basting sauce, then pour it over the meat. Bake for about 3 hours in the center of the oven, basting from time to time with the juices from the aluminum foil. For best results, use a meat thermometer, as discussed in the note to the previous recipe.

Kurdish Goat

Here's a dish that my wife has cooked for me a number of times. It probably originated in the rugged mountain range between Iran and Russia, or in other highlands inhabited by the Kurds. This is mountain goat country.

1 pound cubed goat meat
2 cups uncooked long-grain rice
½ pound fresh green snap beans
1 medium onion, chopped
1 clove garlic
1 can tomato paste (6-ounce size)
salt and pepper
⅛ teaspoon ground cinnamon
water
olive oil

Snap the beans into 1-inch segments. Pour a little olive oil into a skillet. Sauté the onion and garlic for a few minutes. Add the meat and green beans, stirring about until the meat is lightly browned. Stir in the tomato paste, cinnamon, salt, and pepper. Cover the skillet and simmer.

Put the rice into a large pot, then add enough water to cover the rice by ½ inch. Add 2 teaspoons salt. Bring to a boil, then pour it into a colander. Don't rinse the pot. Cover the bottom of the pot with olive oil, put on low heat, and spoon in a layer of rice. Heat until the oil bubbles through the rice, then add a layer of meat mixture from the skillet. Add another layer of rice and another layer of the meat.

Repeat the layers until rice and meat are gone, ending with a layer of rice. Toward the end of the layering, form the mixture into a mound. Take a long spoon and make a hole through the middle of the mound all the way down to the bottom of the pot. Make several similar holes spaced out between the center and the rim.

Cover the dish tightly and cook on very low heat for 30 minutes.

After 30 minutes, dip the pot for a few seconds into a larger container (or sinkful) of cold

America's First Big-Game Hunters

Many thousands of years ago, mammoth ranged the plains of North America, while mastodon browsed along the deciduous forest edges of the Southeast. On the trail of these and other game, hunters from the Old World made their way across the Bering Strait land bridge into Alaska. From there they followed interglacial corridors down into the New World, exploiting the rich environment so successfully that soon their presence was felt as far south as the tip of South America.

We know that these early Indians hunted mammoth because at places like the Blackwater Draw site in New Mexico, prehistoric spear points have been found among the bones of the mammoths they killed.

—Evan Peacock, *Mississippi Outdoors*

Bighorn Shank

The front shank of the bighorn sheep contains some excellent eating. Use the recipe for Venison Shank Montana on page 309.

water. Serve immediately. Feeds 4 to 6. If this dish works out to perfection, my wife says, the bottom layer will be somewhat crusty, and this crust is considered to be the best part.

Crockpot Goat with Beer

Meats that are slow-cooked in crockpots are usually very tender and full of flavor. It's an easy way to cook tough meat, and contrary to popular opinion, the meat doesn't have to be browned in oil. Any part of the goat can be used for this recipe, but I recommend shoulder or leg meat.

4 pounds goat meat
6 strips thick sliced bacon
1 can beer (12-ounce size)
12 small onions, peeled (golf-ball size)
16 ounces fresh mushrooms
½ cup flour
1 tablespoon salt
1 tablespoon vinegar
1 tablespoon paprika
½ tablespoon pepper
1 teaspoon sugar
½ teaspoon thyme
2 bay leaves

Cut the meat into 2-inch cubes. Put the flour, salt, pepper, and paprika into a bag, then shake the meat in it. Cut the bacon into 2-inch strips. Place the bacon, onions, and half of the mushrooms into the bottom of the crockpot. Add the meat, then the rest of the mushrooms. Mix the beer, vinegar, sugar, and thyme, then pour it into the crockpot. Add the bay leaves, cover the crockpot, turn the heat to low, and cook for 9 or 10 hours—while you're out hunting another goat. Feeds 8 to 10. Serve with rice or noodles and vegetables.

Goat Goulash

I prefer to make this dish with fresh, vine-ripened tomatoes, but canned tomatoes can also be used. To peel fresh tomatoes, bring a pot of water to a boil. Add the tomatoes one at a time for a minute or so. Remove, let cool a bit, and peel the skin off.

3 pounds goat stew meat
7 or 8 fresh tomatoes, peeled and quartered
2 medium onions, diced
1 bell pepper, diced
¾ to 1 cup fresh lemon juice
4 or 5 tablespoons mild paprika
1½ teaspoons salt
½ teaspoon black pepper
cooking oil
water

Put the goat meat into a nonmetallic container. Cover with water, then mix in the lemon juice. Cover the container, put it into the refrigerator, and marinate for 2 days, stirring from time to time.

When you're ready to cook, heat a little

cooking oil in a skillet. Brown and drain the meat. Sauté the onion and pepper for 5 minutes. Put the meat into a stove-top Dutch oven or other pot of suitable size. Add the tomatoes, onions, bell pepper, salt, black pepper, paprika, and 3 cups of water. Cover and simmer—do not boil—for 3 hours, stirring and adding a little water if needed from time to time. Feeds 6 to 8. Serve with rice or noodles, along with vegetables and hot bread.

Ancient Roman Wild Boar

An ancient Roman sport by the name of Apicius left us the oldest extant cookbook, called *Cookery and Dining in Imperial Rome*. Game was very important to the Roman diet, and Apicius set forth ten recipes for cooking it, some of which are for sauces. All of the recipes are on the cryptic side, at least by modern standards, and no measures were given. Also, some of the ingredients are in doubt, and the exact cooking techniques are not specified. Fortunately, here's a good recipe that can be cooked today—and one could do a great deal worse, as vinegar and mustard go nicely with fresh pork, wild or domestic. The sprigs of laurel listed in the recipe are no doubt bay leaves, an ingredient that I usually put into boiled or simmered meats. For best results, it is best to simmer the boar for a long time instead of cooking it at a hard boil. With this recipe you can cook the whole boar or any part of it.

> wild boar
> seawater
> sprigs of laurel (bay leaves)
> mustard
> salt
> vinegar

Bring a pot of seawater to a boil, add the sprigs of laurel, and cook the boar at a simmer until it is very tender. Remove the boar. When it cools a bit, remove the skin. Serve the meat with salt, mustard, and vinegar.

Apicius also set forth several recipes for sauces to be served with boiled boar, one of which he called "pepper, lovage, cumin, silphium, origany, nuts, figdates, mustard, vinegar, broth, and oil." Other similar sauces call for coriander (cilantro) seeds, dill seed, and celery seed, along with several other ingredients. The common elements in all these sauces seem to be (apart from mustard and various spices and seeds) oil and vinegar. It therefore seems to me that a Zesty Italian dressing would be pretty close to an ancient Roman sauce. A good sweet-and-sour sauce also goes well with boiled wild boar meat.

Wild Boar Chops

By "chops," I mean loin or tenderloin that has been taken in a strip from along the backbone and sliced into pieces, or perhaps butterflied. This is usually the tenderest part of the boar.

How Wild Is It?

Wild boar has the reputation of being quite strong, leading to long periods of marination in potent brews. It is generally agreed that the age of the boar has a lot to do with its toughness and strength, and one famous French authority, *Larousse Gastronomique*, says, "Only the *marcassins* [up to 6 months old] and the *betes rousses* [from 6 months to 1 year old] are used in their entirety in the kitchen. Every part of these creatures, leg, saddle, loin, shoulder, and back is excellent. In an old boar only the head is eatable, and even then it is necessary to add to it a great number of other ingredients, such as fine pork forcemeat, chicken meat, fresh pork tongue, fat bacon, truffles, and pistachios."

It's true that the age of a wild boar has a bearing on its edibility, but a clean kill and prompt field dressing are also important. Even a prime domestic boar would be tough and gamey if it were chased all over the country with hounds, or otherwise riled up, before butchering.

I might add in this regard that modern man might have become too used to relatively tasteless and tender supermarket meats. Reportedly, the ancient Romans, who loved wild boar and other game, were fond of the wild taste—and would intentionally rile up an animal before the slaughter.

If you've got an older hog, it's best to marinate the chops in cold water with a little baking soda for 24 hours before proceeding with this recipe. Exact measures aren't too important; use about 1 tablespoon of baking soda per quart of water.

2 pounds wild boar chops, ½ inch thick
peanut oil
8 ounces fresh mushrooms, sliced
5 or 6 green onions with tops
½ cup milk
1 chicken egg
2 beef bouillon cubes dissolved in 2 cups
    water
juice of ½ lemon
1 tablespoon chopped fresh parsley
salt and pepper
fine bread crumbs
flour and water paste (if needed)

Heat the peanut oil in a skillet. Whisk the egg and milk together. Salt and pepper the chops, dip them into the egg mixture, and flip them in bread crumbs that have been spread out on a plate. A few at a time, brown the breaded chops and transfer them to a stove-top Dutch oven.

After browning all the chops, mince the green onions, along with about half of the green tops, and sauté them in the skillet for about 5 minutes, along with the parsley and mushrooms. Add the bouillon solution, bring to a boil, reduce the heat, and simmer. Add the lemon juice, along with some salt and pepper. Stir for a few minutes, then pour the mixture over the chops in the Dutch oven. Bring to a light boil, reduce heat, cover tightly, and simmer for 1 hour, adding a little more water if needed. Remove the chops to a heated serving platter. Thicken the gravy, if it needs it, with a little flour and water paste. Feeds 4. Serve hot, along with rice or mashed potatoes and steamed or boiled vegetables.

Seminole "Wild Boar" Stew

This recipe has been adapted from a booklet called *Seminole Indian Recipes,* by Maria Polvay. It cooks up into a rather thin stew, almost a soup, with chunks of meat in it, a texture that is, I understand, characteristic of many Seminole dishes. The "wild boar" specified in the recipe is really not the European wild boar. It is a feral hog, many of which roam parts of Florida. They are especially plentiful in the panhandle in the vicinity of Sopchoppy, where my daughter and her husband live. The last time I checked, there were no game laws concerning these feral pigs, and the hunter was free to take one as needed, with permission of the landowner. I understand that feral hogs also roam parts of California in large numbers. Be warned that these hogs tend to revert to the wild state, and even grow long tusks. So don't assume that they are harmless. In any case, check the game laws in your state. You may have some good bonus hunting at hand —and some good eating. Some of the people around

Sopchoppy cure and smoke the hams and bacon, treating them just like domestic pigs. If handled properly, they can be very good eating.

My father called these wild pigs "piney wood rooters," and I have heard the term several times. But if the Seminoles, or the crackers around Sopchoppy, want to call 'em "wild boars," I'm not going to argue with them.

Any part of the hog can be used in the recipe below. I recommend shoulder meat.

3 or 4 pounds wild pig
2 medium onions, quartered
2 ribs celery, chopped into 1-inch pieces
2 carrots, cut into 1-inch pieces
2½ quarts water
2 or 3 tablespoons apple cider vinegar
3 tablespoons flour
3 tablespoons lard or shortening
2 teaspoons salt
ground pepper

Cut the meat into 2-inch cubes, then put it into a Dutch oven or other suitable pot. Add the water, vinegar, salt, and pepper; bring to a boil, reduce the heat, and simmer for 30 minutes, skimming off the foam from time to time. Add the onions, celery, and carrots. Bring to a new boil, reduce heat, cover tightly, and simmer on very low heat for 2 to 3 hours. Heat the lard in a skillet, stir in the flour, and cook until golden brown, stirring constantly with a wooden spoon. Add 1 or 2 cups of broth from the stew, stirring until the mixture is smooth, then stir the mixture into the stew. Simmer until the stew has thickened only slightly—it should be served on the thin side. Serve in bowls or soup plates. Feeds 6 to 8.

If you have leftovers, add a little more water, a can of tomatoes, and some rice. Simmer for 25 minutes, then serve hot.

Javelina Chops Parmesan

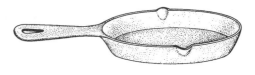

The top weight of a javelina is about 50 pounds, and the "pork chops" are therefore smaller than those from a mature domestic hog, so allow 3 or 4 chops per person.

12 javelina chops
1 can cream of celery soup (10¾-ounce
    size)
½ cup grated Parmesan cheese
⅓ cup Italian bread crumbs
peanut oil
juice of 1 lemon
salt and pepper

Squeeze the lemon juice over the chops in a nonmetallic container, then refrigerate for several hours. Preheat the oven to 350 degrees. Heat a little oil in a skillet. Salt and pepper the chops, brown them quickly on high heat, and transfer them to an ovenproof casserole dish or other suitable container. Cover the chops with celery soup, spreading it out smoothly. Sprinkle with bread crumbs, then with Parmesan cheese. Bake for 40 minutes. Feeds 3 or 4. Serve the gravy over rice or mashed potatoes.

Variation: You can also cook this dish with slices from a javelina hind leg, or ham. Before cooking, marinate the slices for 24 hours in milk. Use the juice of only ½ lemon, adding it to the celery soup.

Sweet-and-Sour Javelina

Loins or tenderloins can be used for this recipe, or try part of the shoulder or leg. The ingredients call for 1 cup of beef broth, for which you can substitute 1 beef bouillon cube dissolved in 1 cup water.

2 pounds javelina, cut into 1-inch cubes
1 cup beef broth
1 can pineapple chunks (8-ounce size)
1 medium onion, diced
½ red bell pepper, sliced
½ green bell pepper, sliced
juice of 1 small lemon
½ cup brown sugar
¼ cup apple cider vinegar
2 tablespoons soy sauce
2 tablespoons cornstarch
1 teaspoon dry mustard
cooking oil
salt and pepper
water
1 tablespoon baking soda
rice (cooked separately)

Trim and cut the meat into 1-inch cubes, and put it into a nonmetallic container. Mix the baking soda and vinegar into 1 quart of water. Pour the mixture over the meat, cover, and refrigerate overnight. Then drain the meat, pat it dry with paper towels, and sprinkle it with salt and pepper. Heat a little oil in a large skillet. Brown the meat on high heat, then pour the beef broth over it, cover, reduce the heat, and simmer until the meat is very tender, adding more water from time to time if needed.

Mix the cornstarch and brown sugar. In a separate bowl, combine the juice from the can of pineapple, lemon juice, soy sauce, and mustard; then stir in the cornstarch and brown sugar mixture. Pour the sauce over the meat a little at a time, stirring as you go. Add the pineapple chunks, diced onion, and sliced peppers. Simmer for a few minutes, then serve over rice. Feeds 4 to 6.

Javelina and Sauerkraut

I have adapted this recipe from *Dress 'em Out,* by Captain James A. Smith. It's best to use sauerkraut fresh from the crock, but canned will do. The recipe calls for chops. You can use loin or tenderloin rounds, preferably butterflied. Also try this recipe with wild boar, with or without a marinade, depending on the quality of the meat. In fact, I suspect that this recipe was originally used for wild boar in northern Europe.

2 pounds javelina chops
1 quart sauerkraut, drained
5 or 6 medium potatoes
cooking oil
salt and pepper

Preheat the oven to 325 degrees. Drain the meat, sprinkle with salt and pepper, and brown it a few pieces at a time in a little cooking oil in a skillet. Put all the browned meat into the Dutch oven or other suitable container, then dump the sauerkraut over it. Bake in the center of the oven for 1 hour.

Peel the potatoes, cut them in half, sprinkle them with salt and pepper, and arrange them atop the sauerkraut. Cover tightly and bake for 1 hour, or until the potatoes are done. Feeds 4 to 6.

40

BONUS EATING FROM THE TRAP LINE

The more or less nocturnal animals covered in this chapter are taken primarily by trapping. It's true that coon hunting is still fairly common, but for the most part the hunter is more interested in the performance of the dogs than in the meat that might result from the quest. At one time, possums were hunted quite often for meat in some parts of the country, but that sport has pretty much died out.

Just the other day, following the first nip of frost, I ran into a local lawyer at the post office. His box was under mine, and we often got each other's mail. "It's getting to be possum-hunting weather," I said, rubbing my hands together for warmth. The guy laughed a little, but I don't think he knew quite what I was talking about. Hell, he probably didn't even own a possum dog.

In any case, this chapter covers coons and possums, as well as muskrats and beavers. Even skunks get a few words.

OPOSSUM

The possum has rather light-colored, fine-grained meat that can be quite good. They are often very, very fat—and the fat isn't all on the surface; it is also distributed in the meat, which makes the possum more ideally suited for dry cooking than, say, lean squirrel.

During the bad Depression years of the 1930s, possums were hard to find in my part of the country because people hunted or trapped them for food. They were sometimes called "Hoover hens," but this name was also applied to the gopher tortoise, rabbit, and other critters that made a handy meal. Often the hunter or trapper penned up a possum for a week or so before dressing it for the table, and they had special cages for this purpose. The thought was that as the opossum is a scavenger, keeping it penned up would permit one to "clean it out." No doubt some people still hold to this belief and practice.

Today the possum is subjected to very liberal game laws in most states, and it is quite plentiful in the wild as well as in the suburbs. And in the inner cities. At one time, it was considered to be primarily a southern critter, but it has made its way north and into Canada. I don't have statistics, but in my experience it is more plentiful in towns and cities and suburbs than in the country. I've had quite a few around my house within the limits of a small town, and at least one family of possums lived in the walls of the house. These made noises at night, frightening our guests.

Several years ago, we had two possums that ate supper with our dog if we fed it after dark. They came right onto the back porch, and the three of them ate out of the same bowl. At first there was only one, and we named him Henry. Then another one got brave enough to climb the steps and waddle onto the porch, and we named him Henry II. The boys wanted to eat Henry II, but everyone agreed that we ought to keep Henry, since he was the first one to venture forth.

Possums will fool you. They look bigger than they are. Their hair is thick and coarse, and it tends to stick out every which way. Moreover, they often (but not always) have a very thick layer of fat under the skin. Thus, a big possum, when you hold him up by the tail under the spot of a flashlight, may look and feel as if it will feed 8 people. But when you skin it, remove the fat, and cook it down, you've got enough good meat for only 2 hungry boys.

A good many people say that a possum should not be skinned. Instead, they say, it should be scalded in boiling water and scraped like a hog or pulled (that is, you pull out the hair like feathers). According to the *Foxfire* books, the people in the southern Appalachians add ½ a cup of lime or ashes to the boiling water. I've tried scalding and scraping possums, but, in my opinion, it's best to skin them, because some of the fat comes off with the skin. I've never had a problem with the scent glands (under the forelegs), but some people advise removing them. Still other people say to singe off the hair in hot coals, then scrub the hide several times in water. That's not for me either, but suit yourself. In any case, here are a few recipes.

Fricassee of Possum

Most of the possums I have cooked by traditional recipes (usually baked) were far too greasy to suit me. Good, yes, but very greasy. I really prefer something a little lighter, as in the following recipe.

1 possum, skinned
2 cans beef broth (10¾-ounce size)
1 cup red wine vinegar
1 medium to large onion, finely chopped
3 bay leaves
½ teaspoon red pepper flakes
salt and pepper to taste
water

Skin the possum, trim off the fat, and put the lean meat into a pot. Cover it with water, and add the bay leaves, red pepper, and vinegar. Bring to a boil, reduce heat to very low, cover, and simmer for 30 minutes. Pour off the liquid. Add hot water, bring to a new boil, cover, reduce heat to very low, and simmer for another 30 minutes. Drain the possum, discard the water, and rinse any scum out of the pot. Bone the possum. Cut the larger chunks of meat across the grain into bite-size pieces. Put all of the meat into the pot. Add the beef broth and onions, bring to a boil, reduce heat to very low, cover, and simmer for 1 hour, stirring from time to time. Salt and pepper to taste, remove from the heat, and keep warm. Serve with rice, along with the pot gravy, vegetables, and bread. Baked sweet potatoes are traditionally served with possum.

Note: If this dish is simmered down properly, the gravy can be served as is. If not, you may have to thicken the gravy with a little flour and water paste or dilute it with water.

Skunk

When I was just a sprout, I recall a feller who worked for Uncle Ott say that of all wild meat, he figgered skunk had the sweetest taste. Now I was willing to take his word for it, without trying to prove it. But once you get past the idea of eating skunk, I reckon they ain't no reason why skunk meat shouldn't be as good as any. Ray Parker, from St. Louis, sent us a recipe that looks good enough to try, if any of you folks get the notion:

"Skin, clean, and remove the scent glands. Put in strong solution of salt water and parboil for 15 minutes. Drain off this water, add fresh water, season, and steam slowly for about 1 hour or until tender."

And if you do try it, let me know how it turns out!

—Cy Littlebee's
Guide to Cooking Game & Fish

Pea Ridge Possum with Chestnuts

Once I lived in a house (on Pea Ridge in Tennessee) that was made of chestnut wood. Years before, the hills had been covered with wild chestnut trees, but a blight killed them before my time. All of them. Only the house and outbuildings stood. A fellow who had been born and raised in the area gave me the following possum recipe, and it no doubt goes back to the days when the chestnut was plentiful. Today, market chestnuts can be used. The recipe might also work with chinquapins, a smaller cousin to the chestnut, but I've never tried it with these. The recipe also calls for sassafras roots. These are easily obtained in most parts of the country east of the Mississippi, and the tree has been transplanted in the West. It's the same stuff used for making sassafras tea and spring tonic. If you can't find the sassafras, substitute 2 bay leaves.

    1 possum
    water
    chestnuts
    applesauce
    bread crumbs
    sweet potatoes (with the skin on)
    juice of 3 lemons
    1 teaspoon baking soda
    pieces of sassafras root, about 1 cup
        (optional)
    salt and pepper

Skin and clean the possum, then trim off most of the fat. Bring 1 gallon of water to a boil, then add the possum, baking soda, and sassafras root. Bring to a new boil, reduce the heat, cover, and cook for 30 minutes. Drain and cool the possum, discarding the water.

Preheat the oven to 300 degrees. Sprinkle the possum inside and out with salt and pepper. Make a stuffing with equal proportions of shucked chestnuts, applesauce, and bread crumbs. Stuff the possum, fit it into a well-greased baking pan of suitable size, and surround it with sweet potatoes. Pour 1 cup of hot water into pan. Pour the lemon juice over the possum. Bake for 2 hours, basting from time to time with pan juices, or until the sweet potatoes are well done. Peel the sweet potatoes and serve them with the possum, along with plenty of bread and vegetables.

Variation: When baking the possum, sprinkle it with Chinese five-spice powder.

Skillet Possum

My father was fond of giving advice to my mother before she fried squirrels or possum. "Parboil it first," he would always say. It's good advice, especially for dealing with tough old critters. I also suggest that you try smothering the fried meat with a good barbecue sauce, or try the following recipe.

1 possum
2 cups catsup
1 medium to large onion, sliced
peanut oil
¼ cup Worcestershire sauce
salt and black pepper
1 teaspoon red pepper flakes
water
flour
1 tablespoon baking soda

Skin the possum, trim off the fat, and cut the lean meat into pieces. Mix the baking soda into 1 quart of water, then soak the possum pieces overnight under refrigeration. When you are ready to cook, drain the possum, put the pieces into a pan, cover with fresh water, and add the red pepper and onions. Bring to a boil, reduce the heat to very low, cover, and simmer for 1½ hours.

Heat some peanut oil in a large skillet. Salt and pepper the possum pieces, shake them in a bag with some flour, and then brown them quickly. Remove the pieces from the skillet. Pour off the excess oil. Stir in the catsup, Worcestershire sauce, and a little water. Put the possum pieces back into the skillet, bring almost to a boil, reduce heat, cover, and simmer for 30 minutes, turning the pieces from time to time and adding a little more water if needed. Serve hot, spooning the sauce over the meat and boiled rice or mashed potatoes.

RACCOON

Raccoon meat is on the dark side, but at its best it is rather mild and even sweetish. In my experience, many raccoons tend to be very fat, but, I might add, many of those I have eaten were taken from the edge of peanut fields, which the raccoons haunted after the harvest, gathering the thousands of nuts left on the ground by the mechanized harvesting techniques. Indeed, a trap set in any draw or gully leading from a swamp into a field was, and is, an excellent place to catch coons—if you can keep the possums away. These are, of course, fat and juicy. The fat isn't distributed throughout the meat, however, and most of it comes off with the skin. I never bother with the scent glands, but if you've got a big boar coon, you might want to remove the scent glands (bean shaped) from under the front legs and thighs. These may come off with the hide as you skin the animal.

Older raccoons should probably be marinated overnight before cooking, and any raccoon is better if the meat is refrigerated for 2 or 3 days, or frozen for several weeks, before it is cooked. In my opinion, any raccoon that has been chased and killed by dogs, or that stayed overnight in a steel trap, is not as good as one that has been cleanly killed.

Coon Casserole

This dish is best made with a young coon. It can also be made with a possum that isn't too fat, or with an armadillo.

The Meat
    1 young raccoon
    water
    juice of ½ lemon
    1 tablespoon salt
    2 bay leaves
The Filling
    4 cups dry bread crumbs
    2 cups mashed potatoes (hot)
    1 medium to large onion, chopped
    ½ rib celery with green tops, chopped
    2 cloves garlic, minced
    1 chicken egg, beaten
    1 tablespoon melted butter
    1 teaspoon salt
    ½ teaspoon pepper
    ½ teaspoon poultry seasoning
The Sauce
    1 cup hot raccoon stock
    2 tablespoons flour
    salt and pepper

Dress the coon, cut it into serving pieces, and put it into a pot. Cover with water and add salt and bay leaves. Bring to a boil, reduce the heat to very low, cover, and simmer for 1 hour, or until the meat is tender. Drain the meat (saving the stock), bone it with a fork, and dice it with a knife. Sprinkle the meat with lemon juice and refrigerate.

Make a gravy sauce by heating 1 cup of the broth left from boiling the coon. Slowly stir in the flour, salt, and pepper. Simmer until the sauce is thick and smooth, stirring as you go.

Preheat the oven to 350 degrees. Mix all the filling ingredients. Grease a casserole dish. Add a layer of filling to the bottom, then add a layer of coon meat and a layer of gravy. Repeat the layers until all the ingredients are used up, ending with gravy. Bake for 25 to 30 minutes, or until the casserole is nicely browned on top. Feeds 4 or 5.

Crispy Coon

Here's a recipe for cooking fat coons, and it isn't recommended for calorie counters. Skin the coon with the aid of a sharp knife, leaving a layer of fat on the meat. Preheat the oven to 300 degrees. Salt and pepper the coon inside and out. Wrap it in several layers of cheesecloth, then wet the cloth with 1 cup or so of water that has been boiled and steeped with several bay leaves. Put the coon into a suitable pan. Bake for 3 hours.

Remove the coon and unwrap the cheesecloth. Turn the oven to 400 degrees. Baste the coon with the pan drippings, then sprinkle it lightly with flour. Put the coon back into the oven. After 10 minutes, baste and sprinkle with flour. Baste and sprinkle once more after

Hard Times

With the stock market crash of 1929 and the depression of the 1930s, many Illinois residents again turned to the state's furbearer resource to provide basic necessities for their families, as had Illinois' native Americans for hundreds of years before. Wages of 50 cents per day were then all too common, and trapping and hunting provided the essential source of income and food that helped thousands of families survive the hard times.

—*Outdoor Highlights*
Illinois Department of Conservation

another 10-minute interval. Bake until the coon forms a crispy crust. Enjoy.

Fricasseed Coon

Here's a recipe for people who may think they don't like coon. Use leftover coon, or simmer the meat and 2 bay leaves for 1 hour in water. Bone and chop the meat.

3 cups diced cooked coon meat
¼ pound bacon
1 medium onion, diced
1 cup beef broth (or 1 cup water with bouillon cube)
juice of 1 lemon
flour
salt and pepper
rice (cooked separately)

In a skillet that has a lid, cook the bacon until it browns, then set it aside. Salt and pepper the coon meat, shake it in a small bag with flour, and brown the pieces in the bacon drippings. Holding back the meat with the lid, pour off any surplus bacon grease. Add the beef broth, onion, lemon juice, salt, pepper, and crumbled bacon. Bring almost to a boil, reduce heat, cover, and simmer for 2 hours, stirring from time to time and adding a little water if needed. Serve over steamed rice.

Barbecued Skillet Coon

I've eaten several messes of barbecued coon, some of which were cooked on a grill by a commercial establishment. Some of the best I've ever had, however, were cooked as follows. By "barbecue sauce," I mean a thick tomato-based sauce. Either use your own recipe or purchase some at the supermarket.

1 or more coons, cut into pieces
water
barbecue sauce of your choice
bacon drippings
2 bay leaves per coon
salt and pepper
rice (cooked separately)

Put the coon pieces into a pressure cooker, cover them with water, add the bay leaves, bring to heat, and cook at 15 pounds of pressure for 25 minutes.

Preheat the oven to 350 degrees. Drain the meat. Salt and pepper the pieces, then arrange them in a greased baking pan and brush with bacon drippings. Pour barbecue sauce over the meat, spreading evenly. Bake for 1 hour, basting with pan juices from time to time. Serve over rice.

BEAVER

For some reason, the beaver has never become as popular as it should have. The dark red meat, one of my favorites, is surprisingly moist, as compared with venison, and can be cooked by a variety of recipes. Also, it's clean meat, as the beaver is a vegetarian and spends most of its time in the water.

Fried Beaver

Beaver can be fried successfully, but I would recommend that only very young ones be cooked in this manner.

> young beaver
> water
> bacon drippings or cooking oil
> flour
> salt and pepper
> baking soda

Dress the beaver, cut it into serving-size pieces, and soak them for 2 days in a mixture

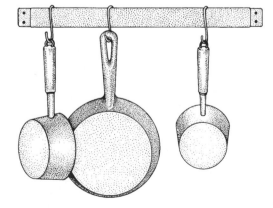

of water and baking soda (1 tablespoon per gallon), under refrigeration. Rinse the beaver pieces, put them into a pot, cover them with water, and simmer until tender. Drain. Salt and pepper the pieces, shake them in a bag of flour, and fry them in hot bacon drippings or cooking oil until nicely browned on both sides. Serve hot.

Barbara Bara's Beaver Stew

I have adapted this recipe from *The South Carolina Wildlife Cookbook,* to which it was submitted by Barbara Bara of Georgetown. It's a complete and very good meal for 6 or 7 people.

> 3 pounds boned beaver
> 3 potatoes, diced
> 3 carrots, diced
> 3 medium onions, chopped
> 3 turnip roots, chopped
> 1 cabbage, cut into wedges
> cooking oil or bacon fat
> flour
> water
> 2 bay leaves
> 1 teaspoon Worcestershire sauce
> salt and pepper

Trim all fat and tissue from the beaver, then cut it into bite-size cubes. Salt and pepper the cubes, shake them in a bag of flour, and brown the pieces in a little oil or bacon fat in a stovetop Dutch oven. Cover with water, then add the bay leaves and Worcestershire, salt, and pepper. Bring to a boil, reduce heat to very low, cover, and simmer until nearly tender. (The time will depend on the age and size of the animal.) Add the potatoes, carrots, onions, and turnips. Cover and simmer until the vegetables are tender. Add the cabbage. Simmer for about 10 minutes, or until the cabbage is tender. The pot liquor can be thickened into a gravy by stirring in a little flour and water paste. Serve hot.

Plum Good Beaver

The idea for this dish came from a recipe in *The Maine Way,* to which it was submitted by Kay Tukey of Milo, Maine. I have adapted it for cooking in a crockpot. If you don't have beach plum jelly and can't get it, use any tart jelly.

    7 pounds beaver meat, cut into chunks
    2 pounds onions, sliced
    1 cup beach plum jelly
    1 tablespoon salt
    1 teaspoon pepper

In a nonmetallic container, pack the beaver pieces with alternating layers of onion slices. Refrigerate overnight. Remove and rinse the meat. Discard the onions. In a crockpot, layer the meat with plum jelly, salt, and pepper. Cook on low heat for 9 or 10 hours. Serve hot, using the gravy over rice, mashed potatoes, or biscuit halves.

Suwannee River Beaver Roast

When I was a boy, the beaver was almost gone from Florida. Now, however, they are present in the northern parts of the state in large numbers. In any case, the following recipe is from Suwannee River country.

    1 young beaver
    1 pound sliced bacon
    6 carrots, cut into 2-inch segments and split
      in half
    4 medium onions, chopped
    2 ribs celery with leaves, chopped
    2 cloves garlic, minced
    4 small chili peppers, cored and chopped
    1 lemon, thinly sliced
    2 bay leaves or wax myrtle leaves
    1 teaspoon thyme
    1 teaspoon marjoram
    1 teaspoon basil
    salt and pepper
    2 quarts water
    4 beef bouillon cubes

Preheat the oven to 300 degrees. Heat the water and dissolve the bouillon cubes in it. Select a roasting pan with a cover and a rack to keep the beaver off the bottom. (If your pan isn't large enough to hold and cover the beaver, disjoint it.) Salt and pepper the beaver inside and out, then put it on the rack inside the baking pan. Cover it with bacon strips. Place lemon slices on top of the bacon. Pour the bouillon water into the pan. Scatter the chopped celery, carrots, onions, and garlic over and around the beaver. Add the bay leaves, chili peppers, thyme, marjoram, and basil. Cover and bake for 3 hours or longer, basting several times with pan liquid. Add more water if needed. Serve hot with heart of palm salad, plenty of bread, and boiled new potatoes.

Fried Beaver Tail

Skin the beaver tail. Put it into a pot of water, bring to a boil, add 2 bay leaves, and simmer until tender. Allow 1 hour for a young beaver, and 2 hours for an old fellow. Cool, cut into pieces, salt and pepper to taste, roll in flour, and fry in hot oil until golden brown. serve hot.

MUSKRAT

The muskrat is one of our better meats, but unfortunately most people can't get past the name or the ratlike tail. It is, however, surely one of the cleanest of all animals since it, like the beaver, stays in the water most of the time and eats only vegetation.

Oklahoma Special Muskrat

Here's a recipe that I adapted from the Oklahoma Wildlife Federation's book *Wildlife Chef*. I don't normally soak good game meat in salted water (unless I intend to pickle or corn it), but I did with this recipe, and the results were good. Since then, I have read several good muskrat recipes from Delaware, a good muskrat state, and all of them also recommend soaking the animals in salted water. Many recipes from another muskrat hot spot, Louisiana, also call for marinating in salt water.

> 2 muskrats
> 1 cup catsup
> ½ cup peanut oil
> 1 medium onion, sliced
> ½ tablespoon Worcestershire sauce
> salt
> ⅛ teaspoon pepper
> water

Soak the muskrats overnight in salted water, in the proportions of 1 tablespoon salt per quart of water. Drain the muskrats, then cut them into pieces. Place the pieces in a deep pot, and add 1 quart of water, 1 teaspoon salt, the pepper, and onion. Bring to a boil, reduce the heat, cover, and simmer for 1 hour. Drain the muskrat. Heat the oil in a skillet, then fry the muskrat pieces until browned on the bottom. Turn the pieces, then immediately pour the catsup and Worcestershire sauce over all. Add 1 cup of water, cover, and simmer for 30 minutes, or until the gravy is thick.

Fried Muskrat

A young muskrat can be fried, using your favorite recipe for fried chicken. I prefer a simple preparation, without thick batters and secret spices.

> young muskrats
> peanut oil
> flour
> salt and pepper
> water

Clean the muskrats, cut them into serving pieces, and let them sit for several hours in cold water. When you are ready to cook, drain the meat, salt and pepper each piece, and shake them in a bag with flour. Heat about 1 inch of peanut oil in a skillet. Fry the pieces on medium high heat until golden brown, turning once.

If you've got a lot of people to feed and not enough meat, you can make biscuits and gravy to go with the meat. To make the gravy, pour off most of the peanut oil left after frying. Leave about 2 tablespoons of oil in the skillet. Scrap up any dredgings that may have stuck to the pan. Add some flour, stirring with a wooden spoon, and cook until it starts to turn brown. Add some finely chopped onion, then cook for 3 or 4 minutes. Slowly pour in some water, stirring as you go, until you have a gravy of the consistency you like. Serve hot.

Muskrat in Cream

Here's a mild dish that's just the ticket for introducing slightly squeamish people to muskrat.

  2 young muskrats
  ½ pint cream or half and half
  cooking oil
  flour
  juice of 2 lemons
  salt and pepper

Cut the dressed muskrats into serving-size pieces. Arrange the pieces in a nonmetallic container, sprinkle them with lemon juice, and toss about to coat all sides. Refrigerate overnight.

Preheat the oven to 425 degrees. Rinse the muskrat pieces, drain, and sprinkle with salt and pepper. Heat some oil in a skillet. Shake the muskrat pieces in a bag with some flour, then brown them in the hot oil on medium high heat. Arrange the pieces in a well-greased casserole dish, pour the cream over all, and bake for 25 minutes.

Stuffed Muskrat

If you are feeding culinary sports who aren't put off by the name muskrat or the shape of whole critters, here's a recipe for you, adapted from Jack Ubaldi's *Meat Book*. Ubaldi used it for squirrels, but muskrats may be better.

The Meat and Marinade
  2 muskrats
  6 or 8 strips bacon
  ½ cup peanut oil
  ½ cup white wine
  juice of 3 lemons
  1 tablespoon grated lemon rind
  12 juniper berries, crushed
  salt and pepper
  water
  baking soda
The Stuffing
  12 ounces fresh mushrooms
  1 medium onion, chopped
  1 clove garlic, chopped
  1½ cups bread soaked in milk
  1 medium chicken egg, whisked
  2 tablespoons peanut oil
  salt and pepper
The Gravy
  ½ cup beef stock or bouillon
  2 tablespoons red currant jelly
  1 tablespoon softened butter
  1 tablespoon flour

Marsh Rabbits

Some people are not fond of the word "rat" and cannot imagine eating one. This is perhaps why muskrats are sometimes called "marsh rabbits" when marketed commercially. Muskrat is one of the most tender and flavorful of all wild meats and should never be wasted. It can be cooked without special preparation, though some cooks soak it overnight in a solution of 1 tablespoon salt and 1 cup vinegar in 1 quart water. Cook by most recipes calling for chicken.

Skin and draw the muskrats, leaving them whole for stuffing, then put them into a non-metallic container. Cover them with a solution in the proportions of 1 tablespoon baking soda per quart of water. Pour this mixture over the muskrats, cover, and refrigerate for several hours or overnight. Then rinse and drain the muskrats.

Mix ½ cup of peanut oil, crushed juniper berries, lemon juice, and lemon rind. (When grating the lemon rind, use only the outer part, avoiding the bitter white inner part.) Pour this mixture over the muskrat, then marinate for 2 or 3 hours under refrigeration, turning occasionally.

Preheat the oven to 350 degrees. Mix together the stuffing ingredients, then stuff the muskrats loosely, closing the openings with skewers or round toothpicks. Grease a baking dish of suitable size for a tight fit. Put the muskrats in the dish, sprinkle with salt and pepper, and cover them with strips of bacon. Bake in the center of the oven for 1½ hours, turning from time to time and basting with white wine. Toward the end, check often to see that the bacon doesn't burn; if it tends to do so, cover with aluminum foil.

Carefully put the muskrats onto a heated serving platter. Pour most of the bacon grease out of the baking pan. Pour in the beef stock, then scrape up the dredgings. Pour the contents of the baking dish into a saucepan. Mix the flour and butter, then heat with the liquid from the baking pan, stirring as you go with a wooden spoon. When the mixture thickens, stir in the red currant jelly. Spoon the gravy over the muskrats. Serve hot with rice, vegetables, salad, and bread.

Muskrat Stew

Here's a dish that came my way from Louisiana, a state noted for its muskrat population. It's very good.

5 muskrats
3 pounds fresh tomatoes, peeled and
  chopped
2 pounds fresh onions, peeled and chopped
1 whole bulb fresh garlic, peeled and
  chopped
2 cups cooking oil
2 cups flour
salt
black pepper
1 teaspoon sugar
¼ teaspoon red pepper flakes
rice (cooked separately)

Skin, draw, and disjoint the muskrats. Salt and pepper the pieces, then shake them in a bag with the flour. Heat the oil in a large cast-iron stove-top Dutch oven. Brown the muskrat pieces and set them aside to drain. Add flour from the bag to the oil in the Dutch oven, stirring as you go with a wooden spoon, and cook until the flour darkens. Add the onions and garlic and cook for 5 minutes, then stir in the tomatoes, 1 tablespoon salt, 1 teaspoon black pepper, red pepper flakes, and sugar. Mix in the muskrat pieces. Cover the ingredients with water, bring to a boil, reduce heat, cover tightly, and simmer—do not boil—for 4 to 5 hours. Stir from time to time so that the bottom won't burn, adding more water as needed.

Serve hot along with the pot gravy, rice, and vegetables.

41

RATTLESNAKES, ARMADILLOS, AND VARMINTS

Once I faced the problem of moving lock, stock, and barrel to another part of the country. Among other tasks, I had to clean out a large home freezer. The logical solution, of course, was to eat it out. After 2 or 3 weeks, all I had left in the way of meat was a large diamondback rattlesnake and an armadillo. If I had it all to do over again, I might well start on these first!

In any case, if you are lucky enough to have rattlesnakes or other offbeat fare, or have a chance to get any, here are some recipes you may want to try.

Fried Armadillo and Gravy

The armadillo is delicious when fried pretty much like chicken. Or at least, the way I fry chicken—without lots of batter. It's best to marinate the meat, as indicated below, but this step can be omitted if necessary.

1 armadillo
cooking oil
flour
milk
salt and pepper

Dress and cut the armadillo into serving pieces. Put the pieces into a nonmetallic container, cover with milk, and refrigerate overnight. Drain, pat dry with paper towels, sprinkle with salt and pepper, and shake in a bag with flour. Heat about ¾ inch of cooking oil in a skillet. On medium high heat, fry the armadillo a few pieces at a time until golden brown on both sides, turning once. Drain the pieces on a brown bag. Pour off most of the cooking oil, then scrape up the pan dredgings with a wooden spoon or spatula. Add a little flour, stirring it until it begins to brown. Add milk

Armadillo Country

In Brazil, the armadillo *(tatú)* has as many quaint legends and fancies woven around it as has the possum in our own South, for this curiously armored animal, with its comical head and rattling, plated tail, has the ability to roll into an impenetrable ball, dig itself into the earth so rapidly that no man with a shovel can keep up with it, and do other quaint tricks that no other animal is equipped to perform. When cooked, the armadillo tastes rich and porky, more like the possum than any other game. It is so easily captured and so universally liked that almost everybody from Mexico to Argentine eats armadillo, and down in Texas during the Depression it was popularized under the apt name of "Hoover hog."

Brazil has three varieties, and any cook will explain that it is not the rank-flavored kind, which lives in abandoned cemeteries, nor the giant kind, which is tough, but only the sweet, white-fleshed little *tatú mirim* that is fit for the table. After being dressed and the glands removed, the most frequent mode of preparation is to leave all the meat in the armored shell and bake it as is, merely with seasonings and a dash of minced parsley. Many delicatessen shops sell them already baked in this fashion, just as they do boiled lobsters.

—*The South American Cookbook*

slowly, stirring as you go, until you have a smooth gravy. Salt and pepper the gravy to taste. I like to go a little heavy on the black pepper, freshly ground.

Serve the armadillo hot, spooning the gravy over biscuit halves.

Grilled and Barbecued Armadillo

Armadillo is very good when cooked over open coals. Salt and pepper are all you need, but a basting sauce helps. Use any good barbecue sauce, or make do with the ingredients listed below.

Generally, cooking times and techniques are about the same as for pork.

1 armadillo, dressed and cut into pieces
1 cup butter
½ cup catsup
½ cup grated onion
2 tablespoons prepared mustard
Tabasco to taste
bacon drippings

Rig for grilling, preferably over a charcoal fire, with or without smoke chips. To make a basting sauce, melt the butter in a saucepan, then stir in the catsup, onion, mustard, and Tabasco. Simmer for a few minutes. When the coals are ready, brush the armadillo pieces with bacon drippings, then place them on a greased rack 6 to 8 inches over the heat. Grill for about 5 minutes, turn, and brush again with bacon drippings. Continue until the pieces are almost done. Then start basting heavily with the sauce, grilling until the pieces are done.

Armadillo Meatballs

This dish can be made with leftovers, but it's really better to start from scratch with fresh meat.

> 1 pound armadillo meat
> 1 chicken egg, whisked
> 2 tablespoons minced celery
> 2 tablespoons minced onion
> 1 tablespoon minced parsley
> 1 teaspoon salt
> ½ teaspoon pepper
> flour
> cooking oil
> water

Cut the meat into 1-inch chunks, then simmer it for about 30 minutes in enough water to cover. Chill the meat, then grind it in a sausage mill or mince it with a chef's knife. Mix the meat, chicken egg, celery, onion, parsley, salt, and pepper. Form the mixture into 1-inch balls and refrigerate for 30 minutes or longer. When you are ready to cook, heat ¾ inch of oil in a skillet. Roll the meatballs in flour, then fry them until golden brown. Serve hot. Feeds 2 or 3. Increase measures as required.

Brazilian Variation: As indicated in the sidebar on page 391, the armadillo is popular fare in Brazil, where it is often marinated and fried. Dress the armadillo, cut it into pieces, and marinate it for 6 hours in a mixture of the juice of 1 lime, 1 chopped tomato, 1 sliced onion, 1 teaspoon minced parsley, and 3 or 4 crushed peppercorns. This mixture should be thoroughly

mashed, or zapped in a food processor, before being used as a marinade. You might also try this marinade on rabbit that is to be fried.

Ray Lemelin's Barbecued Porcupine

Here's one from Ray Lemelin of Embden, Maine, as published in *The Maine Way:*

Possum on the Half Shell

The armadillo, formerly a critter of South and Central America, has been in Texas for many years, and it has now made its way through Louisiana, Mississippi, Alabama, Georgia, and Florida. Armadillos are very plentiful in all the Gulf Coast regions, and throughout Florida. I don't know exactly how far they have extended their range, but my guess is that they'll continue north and west.

In any case, they are neither wary nor fleet of foot, and therefore are not much sport for the hunter. But they do provide some very good eating. I've heard them called "possum on the half shell," and there is some similarity. Both meats tend to be rather fatty, and both are tender. In short, an armadillo can be eaten right out of the shell and requires no marinade or aging. Hence, it is an excellent meat for camp cooking. Also, the meat, like pork, can be ground up and used along with venison in game sausage, burgers, and so on.

"Skin one porcupine. The trick in skinning is to roll the quills under until you loosen the hide. Cut meat in serving pieces. Place in fry pan and brown on all sides. Remove to roasting pan and place in the oven, preheated to 325 degrees. Add 2 cups of your favorite barbecue sauce and cover pan. Baste often. Cook until well done, as for pork, about 2 hours. Vegetables may be added to pan during last hour. Porcupine are at their best when taken in the fall when they have been feeding on acorns and beech nuts."

Jim Babb's Twice-Baked Woodchuck

Here's a recipe from Jim Babb, editor, hunter, fisher, culinary sport, and Tennessean who now lives in Maine. I telephoned him for help with the woodchuck, or groundhog, and a week or so later I was delighted to receive not only a recipe, but also some advice and commentary about this delicious varmint. Some of his comments have been highlighted in a sidebar in this chapter (see page 394). Others of his comments were set forth in the list of ingredients, a stylistic Babbism that doesn't quite work with the format of the rest of this book. Under the wine entry, for example, he specified "½ cup full-bodied white wine; I like a dry French vermouth." I had to shorten this to "½ cup French vermouth," knowing that his full comment would be reflected in this preamble. In another of his ingredients-list comments, in which he specified white bread crumbs, he said, "preferably from French bread; Kleenex bread from the supermarket won't work." I was especially happy to see this comment from an editor. In the first edition of this work, a New York editor

informed me, when marking up my manuscript, that bread crumbs aren't made from bread.

Anyhow, here's Babb's recipe, a somewhat elaborate preparation that involves partly cooking marinated chuck parts, then browning them in a delectable crumb-and-mustard crust.

The Meat and Marinade
   3- to 4-pound woodchuck, cut into serving
      pieces
   ½ cup French vermouth
   ¼ cup olive oil
   2 large cloves garlic, minced
   1 teaspoon dried thyme
   ½ teaspoon minced lemon peel
   salt and pepper
The Crust
   1½ cups fresh white bread crumbs
   ⅔ cup Dijon mustard
   3 tablespoons melted butter or olive oil
   2 teaspoons mixed fresh green herbs (parsley, rosemary, etc.)

Mix the marinade ingredients in a plastic bag, add the woodchuck pieces, seal, and refrigerate overnight, turning the bag several times to ensure that the pieces are evenly exposed. About 2 hours before you plan to eat, preheat the oven to 325 degrees, wipe off the marinade, and bake the pieces slowly on a rack in a covered roaster until about half done; the legs and thighs should still be springy and quite rare, but some of the fat should have rendered out of the meat. (You can also use a microwave; make a rack from crisscrossed carrots and celery stalks to keep the chuck parts out of the liquid and to add flavor. This is a good trick to speed up cooking when charcoal-grilling a woodchuck—or anything else.)

In Praise of Groundhogs

Woodchucks, groundhogs, call them what you will, across much of the country they're the farmer's sworn enemy and the favorite target of long-range varmint hunters. Yet, for all the vast numbers on the receiving end of .52-grain boattails each year, few find their way onto tables, despite their being excellent eating. Young ones taste like good wild turkey, and even tough older chucks, if cooked properly, can hold their own against anything from the super-market freezer. Perhaps hunters pass by this excellent-tasting animal because they're classified as "varmints," which derives from vermin: "any of a number of small animals with filthy, destructive, troublesome habits, as flies, lice, bedbugs, mice, rats," and, guilty by association, woodchucks. Yet, compared with the diets of chickens, for instance, the woodchuck is a fastidious epicure, dining delicately on tender young alfalfa and—too often—a freshly planted row of broccoli seedlings.

As with any animal headed for the table, proper care in the field is essential. Wood-chucks should be skinned and drawn promptly, then put on ice. (If you tie flies, salt and save the skin for dry-fly tailing and Chuck Caddis wings.) You'll find scent sacs under each arm and four spaced along the backbone; cut these out carefully and dis-card. Large, older chucks should be soaked overnight in salt water. To my palate these old chucks taste best fricasseed in a pressure cooker. Young chucks can be treated just like turkey—stuffed and roasted whole, or cut up and cooked by any number of ways.

—James R. Babb

Let the chuck pieces cool for ½ hour while the oven preheats to 425 degrees. Mix the chopped fresh herbs with the bread crumbs. Coat the chuck pieces with mustard, roll in the herbed bread crumbs, arrange in a baking pan, and drizzle with melted butter or olive oil. Roast the pieces in the lower third of the oven until brown, about ½ hour. Serve with a giant grated potato pancake, a green salad, and a good young red wine, like a zinfandel or a pinot noir, Babb says. After partaking of this dish, he goes on, you'll never think of woodchucks as vermin again, and you could find yourself shop-ping for a .257 Roberts to keep the pantry filled with these delectable vegetarians.

Simmered Woodchuck

This recipe works best with woodchucks that are from ½ to ¾ grown, but old animals can also be used. Just increase the simmering time.

1 woodchuck
water
½ cup red wine vinegar
1 tablespoon Worcestershire sauce
1 teaspoon baking soda
flour
cooking oil
garlic powder
salt and pepper

Cut the chuck into serving-size pieces, put into a nonmetallic container, and cover with a solution of 1 quart of water, the vinegar, and baking soda. Marinate in the refrigerator for 12 hours or longer. Drain the pieces, pat them dry with paper towels, sprinkle with salt, pepper, and garlic powder, then shake in a bag with flour. Heat about ¾ inch of oil in a large skillet. Brown the pieces on both sides. Put the meat into a stove-top Dutch oven that has a tight-fitting lid. Add about 1 cup of water, cover, and simmer for 1 hour, or until tender. Add the Worcestershire sauce during the last 15 minutes of cooking.

Prairie Dogs

Originally called anything but "dog," prairie dogs would doubtless have regularly appeared on pioneer bills-of-fare. Certainly they are as clean feeders as any of the native rabbits or hares, or the woodchucks that many present-day varmint hunters shoot for meat. Even so, when other meat was in short supply, pioneers didn't gag on prairie dogs. Plainsmen, trappers, and soldiers followed suit, especially when they didn't want to attract the attention of hostile Indians.

Kit Carson, the great plainsman and Indian fighter, feasted on prairie dog, cooking the meat by broiling it on a stick after skinning and splitting the carcass.
—*The Varmint and Crow Hunter's Bible*

Randy Wilson's Whistle Pig Delight

This recipe comes from a booklet called *Wild Game Recipes*. Published by the North Carolina Wildlife Resources Commission, it was a collection of favorite "family" recipes from employees. Now out of print, the booklet contained the following groundhog or woodchuck recipe from Randy Wilson.

> 1 young groundhog
> 3 apples, halved
> 1 can sliced pineapple
> salt and pepper

"Clean groundhog thoroughly, leaving whole. Parboil until meat is beginning to get tender. Remove and stuff with apples. Garnish with salt and pepper. Toothpick the pineapple rings all over the groundhog and then place in brown-in bag. Cook at 300 degrees until 'whistler' is browned."

Hopi Prairie Dog

Here's a recipe that I found in Juanita Tiger Kavena's book *Hopi Cookery*, which stated, "When prairie dogs are in season and are prepared correctly, they are considered a delicacy. Fat prairie dogs have a milder flavor than lean ones." The nanakopsie and tuitsma listed in the ingredients are local plants that are used as seasonings by the Hopi. Substitute fresh thyme and other herbs if necessary.

1 fresh-killed prairie dog per person
pepper
salt
nanakopsie, tuitsma, or other herb
    seasoning

"1. Kill the prairie dogs and immediately singe the fur completely, to get rid of fleas. Scrape the carcass to remove any fur or ash and wash it well with clear water. Dress as you would a rabbit and leave whole.

Wildcats

In America, the meat of the bobcat was highly esteemed by the Indians and some of the pioneers. A few writers on the subject even proclaimed it to be the best of all wild game. Most modern hunters, however, hold rather strong opposing sentiments. A firsthand account was given by the late Euell Gibbons, who killed and ate a bobcat in the American Southwest. The "bob" part was quite good, he said, but the "cat" part was difficult to swallow. The lynx was also widely eaten in the northern parts of the New World, and might be a little easier for modern man to swallow. The lynx is still greatly valued as table fare in parts of Canada and Alaska, perhaps because the name is easier to swallow.

    Both lions and tigers have been eaten in various parts of the world, as have the cougar or mountain lion (also called painter, Florida panther, and so on).
        —Adapted from
        Edible Plants and Animals

"2. Stuff body cavity with seasonings and salt and pepper.

"3. Bake in a 350 degree oven for 3 hours, or until tender."

Clyde's Bobcat in White Wine

Recipes for bobcat are hard to come by, and I was fortunate enough to find this one in *The Maine Way,* published by the Maine Department of Inland Fisheries and Wildlife. It was contributed to that publication by Clyde Noyes of Dennysville, Maine. Here's what he recommends:

    2 pounds bobcat meat
    ½ cup white cooking wine
    ½ cup chicken bouillon
    ¼ cup butter
    1 teaspoon chopped parsley
    salt and pepper
    thyme

"Remove all fat from 2 pounds of bobcat meat. Slice ¼ inch thick and lightly season with salt and pepper. Heat butter in a skillet and brown meat on both sides. Transfer to casserole dish. Combine a pinch of thyme, chopped parsley, chicken bouillon, and cooking wine. Pour this sauce over meat, cover casserole, and bake at 350 degrees approximately 45 minutes."

Note: This recipe can also be used with lynx.

Cougar Bradford Angier

Cougar are legal game in some remote areas, but they are now highly protected in most states. I've never seen one in my home state of

Alabama, but I have heard, and continue to hear, tales about "black panthers." The only cougar I have ever eaten was purchased from an exotic meat supply house, and I cooked it according to a recipe by Bradford Angier, as published in his book *Gourmet Cooking for Free.* I can highly recommend the recipe, quoted here.

"Among many of the Indians who relied on wild meat, cougar was preferred to all other game including venison. Like lynx, it has no game taste whatsoever.

"If you ever have the chance to try some, a good way to start is with a heavy frypan with a lid. Sauté 2 medium-size diced onions in ½ stick of butter until they begin to tan. Then add about 2 pounds of cougar, cut into ½-inch cubes. Stirring, cook this, too, until it takes on a light bronze. Add salt and freshly ground black pepper to taste, a cup of dry vermouth, and enough boiling water to cover. Simmer, with the lid on over low heat for an hour.

"In a separate pan, smoothly blend 3 tablespoons flour with 2 tablespoons butter. Add a cup of chicken bouillon, made with a cube if no stock is at hand, stirring to prevent lumping. Chop a tablespoon of parsley and add that to the sauce, along with an equal amount of chopped chives. If you have any, ½ teaspoon of chopped chervil leaves will add an elusive flavor. Simmer all this for 6 minutes. Then add a cup of light cream and bring again to a bubble.

"Stir this gradually into the meat mixture, bring back to a simmer, mix in a tablespoon of fresh lemon juice, correct the salt and pepper if necessary, and serve over thick slices of French or sourdough bread which you have just turned into hot garlic toast. And don't be too surprised if someone exclaims this is the best meal he has ever eaten."

Fried Rattlesnake and Ham Gravy

There is a problem with fried rattlesnake. Some of the meat is along a backbone and some of it is along rib structures, which run almost the entire length of the snake. Merely cutting the snake into segments results in both types on each piece. If you fry the pieces long enough to cook around the backbone, the rib part is going to be cooked too much, making the meat tough and chewy. This problem is compounded because people tend to cook rattlesnake too much anyhow, and I confess that I certainly want mine well done, especially up around the head. But most people who try it are going to fry it anyhow, so here's how:

Skin and draw the snake, then cut it into pieces 3 or 4 inches long. Soak the pieces in cold water and a little baking soda for 2 days. Drain. Salt and pepper the pieces, then shake in a bag with a little flour. Heat about ¾ inch of oil in a skillet, then fry the pieces over medium high heat until nicely browned and done. Drain.

Pour off most of the grease, then fry some sliced ham in the skillet, browning it on both sides. Drain the ham alongside the pieces of snake. With a wooden spatula, scrape up any pan dredgings. Stir in a little flour, then slowly pour in some hot black coffee, stirring continuously until you have a smooth gravy. Add some salt and freshly ground black pepper to the gravy, which should be served over biscuit halves.

Note: This recipe, or combination of meats, is one that I hit on when I had 2 large snakes to cook and several high school boys wanted to try the meat. I cooked quite a lot of ham, just in case they chickened out on the snake. Well, they ate everything—and the snake-and-ham gravy was a big hit.

Snake Patties

I've never eaten a water snake, but I've seen some cottonmouths big enough to tempt me. If hungry, I wouldn't hesitate to eat any sort of American snake except the coral snake. But I don't think I would fry them in pieces. I would use the recipe below, which I developed with freezer-burned rattlesnake.

snake
water
bay leaves
flour
peanut oil
lemon juice
chicken eggs
dry bread crumbs
salt and pepper

Skin, draw, and behead the snake (or snakes), then cut into 4-inch segments. Place the pieces in a pan, cover with water, and add 2 or 3 bay leaves. Bring to a boil, reduce heat, cover, and simmer for 1 hour, or until tender. Drain and cool the pieces, then pull the meat off the bones with a fork. Chop and sprinkle the meat with a little lemon juice, then refrigerate for 30 minutes or so. When you are ready to cook, whisk an egg and mix it in with the snake meat and some bread crumbs along with a little salt and pepper.

Noshing Fare?

The diamond-backed rattlesnake was another favorite with Florida crackers, Georgia good ol' boys, and Texas cowboys, but these days some environmental groups frown on eating them. I understand that some of the rattlesnake roundups, which are annual events in some sections of the country, have stopped serving rattlesnake meat to the spectators. In my opinion, there's not much point in having a rattlesnake roundup if you're not going to eat them. Yet I once saw a spokesperson from the annual rattlesnake roundup in Opp, Alabama, who claimed on TV that all the snakes brought in for the event were released alive at selected sites. Does anybody believe that? I'm all for the environment, but I'll have to say that anyone who advocates turning rattlesnakes loose and hopes to sway popular opinion accordingly has got a steep hill to climb.

(You may need more than 1 egg if you have lots of meat.) Shape the meat into patties. Dredge each patty with flour. Heat about ½ inch of oil in a skillet, then fry the patties a few at a time for several minutes on medium high heat, until nicely browned on both sides. Serve hot.

42

VARIETY MEATS FROM GAME

Anyone who likes heart, liver, tongue, and such parts from domestic animals will probably like similar parts from wild game. These people really won't need an introduction to this chapter and will dig right in. Anyone who doesn't like variety meats won't need an introduction either. They'll simply move on to another chapter, no matter what I say here. Still, I'll have to point out that too many American hunters throw away some very good and highly nutritious eating, and I hope that the recipes in this chapter will be of help.

Some of the variety meats should be put on ice and eaten right away, and, for this reason, they are traditional fare for hunting camps. Venison liver is also a traditional feast in deer camp, as covered in chapter 44. Some of the recipes presented here can also be used in camp.

Sautéed Liver with Onions and Mushrooms

Although I've cooked this dish a dozen times or more, I've never written down exact measurements for the ingredients. Any reasonable measures will work, but remember that a little liver goes a long way. I allow ¼ pound per person as compared with ½ pound for most other meats.

  liver
  butter
  onion, sliced lengthwise and separated
  mushrooms, sliced
  flour
  salt and pepper

Getting Liver Ready to Cook

Mrs. Wilson Bell of Big Piney, in preparing liver for frying, and especially the liver from game, soaks the thinly sliced liver in a solution of warm water to which 2 or 3 tablespoons of vinegar have been added. This treatment was told to her by Rives Holcomb, a cowboy from Virginia, who was a cook on a destroyer during WWI. My mother rolled thinly sliced liver in ⅔ cup cornmeal to ⅓ cup flour before cooking it in bacon drippings. This makes liver crisp and delightful.

—Mrs. Mae E. Mickelson in *Cooking in Wyoming*

Slice the liver into fingers, salt and pepper them, and coat them lightly with flour. Heat a little butter in a skillet. Sauté the liver slices for a few minutes, then set them aside. Sauté the onion and mushrooms for 10 minutes or so, being sure to brown the onion slightly. Add the liver back to the skillet, stir about, and add more salt and pepper if needed. Serve hot with rice and steamed vegetables.

If you want some gravy, add a little paste made from flour and water and stir with a wooden spoon until the gravy thickens.

Skoog's Leverpostej

Here's a recipe from Denmark, from the Alaska Department of Game and Fish's *Wildlife Cookbook,* which is now out of print. The recipe was contributed by Ronald O. Skoog, who was a game and fish commissioner when the book was published.

1 pound caribou or deer liver
½ pound bacon or pork fatback
1 large onion, peeled and quartered
3 or 4 anchovies (optional)
1½ cups milk
½ cup flour
¼ cup butter
2 chicken eggs, whisked
1 teaspoon ground allspice
1 teaspoon salt
¼ teaspoon pepper

Preheat the oven to 350 degrees. Trim the sinews from the liver, then cut it into strips. Rig the sausage grinder with a fine wheel. Grind the liver, bacon, onion, and anchovies 3 times, mixing well. In a skillet, heat the butter and slowly stir in the flour with a wooden spoon for 3 or 4 minutes. Stir in the milk, bring to heat, and simmer—but do not boil—for a few minutes. Add the ground liver mixture, eggs, allspice, salt, and pepper.

Pour the mixture into a well-greased oblong baking pan. Cover the pan with aluminum foil and bake for 45 to 60 minutes.

Fried Venison Liver

Venison liver is good either sautéed with onions and mushrooms or chicken-fried in a skillet, using about ½ inch of oil. My favorite method uses only flour as a coating, but use a thicker batter if you want more crunch and more grease. Rabbit and pheasant livers are also very good when cooked by this recipe.

venison liver
cooking oil
flour
salt and pepper

Slice the liver ½ inch thick. Salt and pepper each piece, then shake them in a bag with some flour. Heat the oil to medium high, then cook the liver slices for about 5 minutes on each side, or until done. Cut into a piece to be sure that its center doesn't run red. Do not overcook.

Pour off some of the pan drippings, add some flour, cook until browned, stir in some water, cooking and stirring until you have a nice gravy. Serve the fried liver and gravy with rice or mashed potatoes, steamed vegetables, a salad, and hot biscuits.

Game Liver Casserole

This dish can be made with any kind of good liver, from eelpout to elk. It is highly recommend for liver from deer, antelope, or other big game.

2 pounds liver
½ pound bacon
2 cups chopped onions
2 cups cracker crumbs
3 chicken eggs, beaten
1 cup half and half
¼ teaspoon thyme
salt and pepper
water

Preheat the oven to 325 degrees. Simmer the liver for 10 minutes in a little water. Let it cool, then slice it thinly. Set 4 slices of bacon

aside and cook the rest in a skillet until it is crisp. Crumble the cooked bacon and mix it into the onions. Place about ⅓ of the onion and bacon mixture into a greased casserole dish, topping with a layer of ½ of the sliced liver and ½ of the cracker crumbs. Add another ⅓ of the onion mixture, then the rest of the sliced liver. Top with the rest of the onion mixture and ½ of the cracker crumbs. Mix the eggs with the half and half. Sprinkle the dish with thyme, salt, and pepper, then pour the egg mixture over

Porcupine Liver

Porcupine liver is the sweetest of all the wild-game livers I have tried. This sweetness is due to the animal's diet, which consists almost exclusively of the cambium layer of bark, plus buds, leaves, and even blossoms of deciduous trees. The porcupine also has an overpowering yen for anything salty, as witnessed by the many ax and paddle handles he ruins.

Preparation of porcupine livers is simple. Just trim off any fat or tissue, and slice in desired thickness. Dust the slices with flour, season with a bit of salt and pepper, and fry as you would calf's liver.

Porcupine livers are particularly delicious when fried with bacon for breakfast. Fry until the slices are fully cooked and uniform in color throughout.

Small pieces of porcupine meat and bits of the liver can be used with bacon, tomatoes, and mushrooms to make an unusual and highly delicious shish kebab.

—C. B. Colby, *Outdoor Life*

Liver and Port

W. G. Howe, from La Grange, Missouri, was quoted in *Cy Littlebee's Guide to Cooking Fish & Game* on the subject of cooking deer in camp. "Pour a little port wine over the liver while it's frying," says Mr. Howe. "It not only improves the taste, but the smell is sure to bring in any lost hunters that might be near-by and down-wind."

—Missouri Department of Conservation

all. Place the 4 reserved strips of bacon on top. Bake for 1 hour.

Tasty Tongue

Moose and elk have tongues large enough to feed 4 people. Tongue from smaller animals, such as the white-tailed deer, won't go as far, but is still worth having. One of the most popular methods of serving tongue is as an appetizer or snack, in which case the size (or number of servings) isn't of great consequence. In any event, the recipe below will work with either large or small tongues.

1 or more big-game tongues
1 medium onion, diced
3 bay leaves
3 cloves
1 tablespoon salt
½ teaspoon red pepper flakes
water (about 2 quarts)

Place the tongue into a suitable pan, cover it with water, and bring to a simmer. Add the onion, bay leaves, cloves, salt, and red pepper. Reduce the heat, cover the pan, and simmer until the tongue is tender. (Allow 2 hours for large tongues.) When the tongue is done, remove the skin.

The tongue can be served hot or cold. Slice it against the grain and serve on crackers or thin pieces of rye. Either mustard or prepared horseradish goes well with boiled tongue. I am fond of eating tongue on crackers with a little of the brownish Creole-style mustard.

Crockpot Elk Tongue

The crockpot is ideal for cooking large game tongue, if you've got the time.

1 elk tongue
1½ cups water
juice of 2 lemons
6 peppercorns
6 allspice berries
1 tablespoon salt
½ teaspoon pepper
1 bay leaf

Venison Tongue Sandwich Spread

Cut a cooked tongue into pieces, chill, and run it through a meat grinder. Mix in some chopped onion to taste and mayonnaise for texture. Spread on white bread with the crust removed.

Big Heart

Pound for pound, wild animals usually have larger hearts than their domestic counterparts. Apparently this is because wild animals run more, thereby pumping more blood and giving the heart (a muscle) more exercise. The antelope has a very large heart for its size.

Put the tongue into the crockpot with the water. Add the rest of the ingredients, turn the heat to low, cover, and cook for 9 or 10 hours. Peel the tongue, slice it, and serve it hot or cold, or use it for sandwiches or salad.

Tongue Salad

Some people are squeamish about eating tongue. The shape of the tongue has got a lot to do with it, and sometimes merely slicing it into cross sections isn't enough to disguise it. If you've got such people to feed, chop up the tongue and use it in the following:

1 cup finely chopped boiled tongue
½ finely chopped red bell pepper
2 tablespoons finely chopped onion
2 tablespoons chopped nuts
2 tablespoons pickle relish
creamy salad dressing

Mix the tongue, onions, pickle relish, bell pepper, and nuts. Slowly stir in the creamy salad dressing until you have the consistency you want. Serve on lettuce leaves for a light lunch, or eat with crackers.

Stuffed Venison Heart with Brandy Gravy

The heart of big game can be very good and is often stuffed and baked, as in this recipe. The heart of a white-tailed deer will feed 2 people of modest appetite.

heart of deer or antelope
½ cup beef broth (or bouillon in water)
½ cup water
¼ cup brandy
¼ cup bread crumbs
¼ cup chopped celery
¼ cup chopped onions
milk
1 teaspoon melted butter
⅛ teaspoon ground sage
bacon (maybe)
salt and pepper
saltwater marinade (1 tablespoon salt per quart)

Put the heart into a nonmetallic container, cover it with saltwater marinade, and refrigerate overnight. When you're ready to cook, preheat the oven to 350 degrees. For a stuffing, mix the bread crumbs, celery, onions, sage, and butter. Add salt and pepper to taste, and a little milk to bind and moisten the stuffing. Stuff the heart, then close the opening with skewers. (If you have any stuffing left over, and you probably will, wrap it with bacon and bake it along with the heart.) Put the heart and leftover stuffing into an ovenproof dish of suitable size, then pour in the water, beef broth, and brandy. Cover the dish and bake for 2 hours, or until the heart is tender.

Remove the heart from the dish and slice it carefully. Arrange the slices on a serving platter along with the stuffing. Quickly pour the juice from the dish into a small saucepan, bring to a boil, and simmer for a few minutes. Pour over the sliced heart. Serve hot.

Marinated Heart

Properly marinated deer heart can be cooked by several methods, as indicated below.

> deer or game heart
> ½ cup olive oil
> ¼ cup Worcestershire sauce
> ¼ cup grated onions
> 3 cloves garlic, minced
> salt and pepper

Trim the fat and tubes from the heart, then cut it into ½-inch strips. For a marinade, mix the oil, Worcestershire sauce, onions, and garlic. Put the heart into a plastic Ziploc bag, then pour in the marinade. Refrigerate overnight, turning the bag several times. Shortly before cooking, remove the meat from the marinade. Put the leftover marinade into a saucepan, bring to a boil, then remove from the heat, and keep warm for a basting sauce or cooking liquid. Cook the heart by one of the following methods.

1. *Broil.* Preheat the broiler, placing the strips on a rack about 4 inches from the heat source. Cook for about 5 minutes on each side, basting 3 or 4 times with marinade. Do not overcook.

Lights

The lungs of various animals are eaten in some areas, often under the name of "lights." I've eaten them myself, cooked together with liver, under the name of Liver 'n' Lights, but frankly, I have never cared for them and I therefore don't have much personal experience to offer the cook. Perhaps the lights that I have eaten were not prepared correctly or were not beaten adequately. In short, they were too "light" for me, owing, I suppose, to the air inside the tissue. By way of explanation, here's a quote from the great French work, *Larousse Gastronomique,* concerning calf's lights.

"Calf's lights contain little nourishment and are rarely sold in the U.S.A. It is recommended, before preparing them in one form or another, to beat them thoroughly to expel the air contained in them.

"Then immediately cut them into uniform pieces and prepare according to the recipe chosen. They are usually prepared in a ragout and always accompanied by a plentiful garnish."

Larousse sets forth several recipes for calf's lights as well as pig's lights, but nothing specifically for deer or other venison. Nonetheless, lights of deer have been eaten in various countries at times past. Anyone who wants to try them may proceed without fear of dire consequences, provided that the lights are removed during the field-dressing operation and kept cool. I would suggest that the lights be beaten and cut into pieces for use in a stew, along with other meat.

—adapted from *Venison Cookbook*

2. *Grill.* Build a hot charcoal fire or heat the gas or electric grill. Put the strips on racks about 4 inches over the heat. Grill for about 5 minutes on each side, basting 3 or 4 times with marinade. Do not overcook.

3. *Stir Fry.* Heat a little oil in a wok or skillet. Stir-fry the strips for about 5 minutes; then pour a little of the marinade into the wok and cook for 3 or 4 more minutes.

4. *Fry and Simmer.* Heat some oil in a skillet and quickly fry the heart strips until browned; then pour some marinade into the skillet and bring to a boil, reduce the heat, cover, and simmer for 2 hours.

Deer Heart Sandwiches

Although heart often tends to be on the tough side, it does make very good sandwich meat if it is cooked until tender. Poaching is my favorite method.

> deer heart
> 3 cups water
> 2 bay leaves
> 1 teaspoon salt
> ½ teaspoon red pepper flakes
> ½ teaspoon marjoram

In a suitable pot, bring the water to a boil. Add the salt, red pepper flakes, marjoram, and bay leaves. Cut the heart in half lengthwise. Put both halves into the pot, bring to a boil, reduce heat to very low, cover, and simmer for 1½ hours.

Turn off the heat and let the heart steep in the liquid as it cools. Put the heart into a suitable dish, cover with part of the liquid, and refrigerate. Slice across the grain as needed for sandwich meat. Thin slices work best. Also

Bone Marrow

I've always enjoyed bone marrow whenever I happen to come upon it while eating meat, such as the small bit left in a T-bone, a turkey neck, or a backbone cooked in greens for seasoning. I've never cracked any elk or moose bones open to get at the marrow, buy I wouldn't hesitate to do so. Some people do take the trouble to get at bone marrow—and eat it raw. In the Arctic Circle, bone marrow is sometimes called "Eskimo butter."

try thin slices atop thin crackers along with a little Creole or Dijon mustard.

Stuffed Heart

The measures below will make enough stuffing for a large heart from elk or moose. The recipe can be reduced for hearts from animals the size of deer or antelope.

The Meat
> 1 large heart
> 4 slices bacon
> salt and pepper

The Stuffing
> ½ cup mild sausage
> 4 slices bacon, chopped
> 1 cup chopped fresh mushrooms
> ½ cup chopped onions
> 2 slices bread, soaked in milk and squeezed
> 1 tablespoon chopped fresh parsley
> 1 large chicken egg, whisked
> salt and pepper

Kidney

Kidney from the deer carcass may be prepared as from any domestic animal. Kidneys from young animals should be cooked very briefly while larger ones may be chunked or sliced, browned, and added to a stew.

—*Cooking the Sportsman's Harvest*

Preheat the oven to 350 degrees. Trim the fat and sinew from the heart, remove the tubes, and cut an opening for the stuffing. Sprinkle inside and out with salt and pepper.

To make the stuffing, brown the chopped bacon, sausage, and onion in a skillet. Add the mushrooms and cook on low for another 4 or 5 minutes. Season with salt and pepper, then put the mixture into a bowl. Add the milk-soaked bread, egg, and parsley, mixing well.

Spoon the stuffing into the heart, then close with strips of bacon secured with skewers or round toothpicks. Place the stuffed heart into a pan and add the water.

Bake for 1½ hours for large hearts (elk or moose) or 1 hour for smaller hearts (deer or antelope). To serve, carefully slice the heart and spoon a little of the pan drippings atop the slices and stuffing.

Moose Kidneys in Tomato Sauce

Here's an excellent recipe that I have adapted from *Alaska Magazine's Cabin Cookbook*, which advised, "Remember, though, that kidneys toughen if cooked too long."

1 set moose kidneys (or elk kidneys)
2 cups fresh green peas
1 cup sliced puffballs or other mushrooms
¼ cup dry white wine
6 green onions, chopped
¾ cup tomato sauce
3 tablespoons olive oil
3 tablespoons butter
1 tablespoon minced fresh parsley
sea salt and pepper
rice (cooked separately)

Remove the skin and trim the fat from the kidneys, then slice them thinly. Heat the olive oil in a skillet. Sauté the green onions for 10 minutes. Add the tomato sauce, mushrooms, and green peas, along with a little salt and pepper. Simmer for about 10 minutes, then add the butter and increase the heat to medium high. Add the kidney slices. Cook for 2 minutes. Add the white wine, parsley, and if needed, a little more salt and pepper. Cook for another 2 minutes, or until the kidneys are tender. Serve with rice.

Ginnie Peppard's Venison Kidney

Recipes for venison kidney are hard to come by, and most hunters don't save these parts when field-dressing the deer. Although small, they make some of the best eating on the animal. Here's an excellent recipe from *The Maine Way*:

"Melt butter in an iron fry pan. Slice the kidney into ¼ inch thick slices and add to melted butter. Just a spoonful of water helps to simmer them slowly and keep them from becoming crusty before cooked. Don't cook them so slowly that they stew along. At the same time, don't cook from the inside out. Be sure to scrape the pan for the crispy pieces left behind. These with baked beans are favorite fare for all."

Menudo

Anyone who is fond of tripe will already have a favorite recipe or two. Those who think they don't like it should try *menudo*. This is a simple Mexican dish, and the recipe below was adapted from *Game Care & Cookery*, by Sam Fadala. Tripe is, of course, the stomach lining that is found in ruminants, or cud-chewing animals, such as elk, antelopes, goats, cows, giraffes, and so on. I confess that I have never been too fond of tripe, but I do like this recipe.

Stomach

It may not sound too good, but the stomach of grazing animals contains some good meat and salad. That's right. Salad. Some primitive peoples remove the contents of the first stomach and eat it. Reportedly, it tastes pretty much like salad greens sprinkled with a little vinegar. If you don't develop a taste for the contents, remember that the stomach itself makes some good eating, and is often called tripe. Also, the whole stomach is sometimes stuffed and eaten, as in the haggis. Further, the American Indians, the ancient Scythians, and other peoples used the stomach as a cooking pot—and then ate it.

—*Venison Cookbook*

Fadala said that some of his Mexican friends from across the border credit the dish with medicinal and even supernatural powers. I wouldn't go that far, but it *is* good.

2 pounds tripe from elk or other ruminant
2 cans yellow hominy (15 ½-ounce size)
1 medium onion, diced
2 cloves garlic, crushed
2 tablespoons chili powder
salt and pepper
water

Wash the tripe and cut it into 1-inch squares. Put the tripe into a stove-top Dutch oven or suitable pot. Add enough water to cover the tripe by 2 inches. Add the chili powder, onion, and garlic. Bring to a boil, reduce the heat to very low, cover tightly, and simmer for 1½ hours.

Drain the hominy, add it to the pot, and mix well, adding in some salt and pepper to taste. Let the pot simmer for a few more minutes, adding a little more water if needed. Serve the *menudo* in bowls. Fadala recommends that *menudo* be combined with freshly made, thick corn tortillas. I also like it with baked corn pone or fried corn bread. Or, even better, with crackling bread. Feeds 6 people.

Note: For more Mexican tripe recipes, see *The Complete Book of Mexican Cooking*, by Elisabeth Lambert Ortiz. I am especially fond of the Mexican recipe for tripe and garbanzo beans (chick-peas).

Fried Brains

If you like pork, calf's, or lamb's brains, be sure to try those from deer and other wild game. Fried brains are quite filling; ¼ to ⅓ pound will usually be enough to feed anyone of normal appetite.

brains
vinegar
2 chicken egg yolks, whisked
cooking oil
flour
cracker crumbs
salt and pepper
lemons
water

Put the brains into a nonmetallic container, then cover them with a solution of 1 quart water, 2 teaspoons vinegar, and the juice of ½ lemon. Marinate for several hours in a cool place, preferably in the refrigerator. Bring another quart of water to a rolling boil, adding 1 teaspoon of vinegar. Put the brains into the boiling water for 4 minutes. Remove the brains, drain, and cut into 1-inch cubes.

Heat at least 1 inch of cooking oil in a skil-

Mattak

We were invited to Uvdluriak's and there for the first time I tasted rotten *mattak*. This dish, which is a great delicacy for the Eskimos, consists of huge flakes of narwhale skin that have been in meat caches for several years. In the low temperature they do not become rancid, they just ferment, so that the skin tastes very much like walnuts while the blubber, turned quite green, tastes sharp—almost like roquefort cheese.

—Peter Freuchen's *Book of the Eskimos*

let. Salt and pepper the brain cubes, then roll them in flour, dip them in beaten egg yolk, roll in bread crumbs, and fry in the hot oil until nicely browned. Drain. Serve hot with lemon wedges.

Brains 'n Eggs

My favorite way to cook brains is to scramble them with eggs. Many people bake brains and eggs, but in my experience it is easier, and much better, to scramble them in a skillet. Exact measures aren't too important, but I usually have about half brains and half eggs.

brains
chicken eggs
butter
green onions with part of tops
salt and pepper

Chop up a green onion or two along with the lower half of the green tops. Heat a little butter in a skillet, and sauté the onions for a few minutes. Add the brains, scrambling and stirring for 2 minutes. Quickly whisk the eggs, add them to the skillet, along with some salt and pepper, and scramble, stirring constantly, until they set. Serve hot with toast, sliced tomatoes, and crisp bacon.

Fried Animelles

In France, *animelles* is the culinary word for testicles. Call this dish whatever you choose. Moose *animelles* have a good reputation in some parts, and I have heard of folks eating testicles from boar hogs and bulls, and sheep fries are highly regarded by some. Anyhow, here's a

French recipe that I adapted from *Larousse Gastronomique*. Try it with deer, elk, or moose. Usually, however, dishes of this sort are served along with plenty of more ordinary fare.

> testicles
> cooking oil
> flour
> 1 medium onion, sliced
> juice of ½ lemon
> 2 teaspoons tarragon vinegar
> 1 bay leaf
> ⅛ teaspoon thyme
> salt and pepper
> water

Scald the testicles in boiling hot water, skin them, and slice them into bite-size pieces. Soak the pieces in cold water with a bay leaf for several hours, then drain and cover them with a marinade made of the tarragon vinegar, 2 teaspoons oil, thyme, sliced onion, and juice of ½ lemon. Marinate for 1 hour. When you are ready to cook, drain the testicle slices, salt and pepper them, shake them in a bag with flour, and fry in oil over medium heat until golden brown. Serve hot.

Cooking Walrus

Walrus is just like other meat, except it has blubber instead of fat. Fry or boil as you would beef. The blubber tastes odd until you get used to it. The liver is extra good. The tongue is tough, so you had better pickle it.

—*Alaska Magazine's Cabin Cookbook*

Sautéed Animelles with Mushrooms

Scald the *animelles* (see text of previous recipe), skin them, and slice. Marinate in 1 pint of cold water with the juice of ½ lemon for 3 hours or longer. Drain. Sauté in butter for a few minutes. Remove and drain. Sauté chopped onion and sliced mushrooms for 5 minutes. Add the sliced *animelles*, salt and pepper to taste, and sauté for 1 minute.

Garnish this dish with fresh parsley sprigs, and serve hot.

43

COOKING GAME ON THE PATIO

A fellow called me from Atlanta not too long ago, saying that he was putting together a book about cooking on a barbecue, and that he would like to have a good recipe from me on cooking venison. He would, he said, give me full credit for the material. Well, I hemmed and hawed. Too much depends on the condition of the venison when the hunter gets it, on the kind of grill, the heat, the skill of the cook—and comparatively little on the recipe. And that's the plain truth. A skilled cook can consistently grill better venison without any other ingredients than a jackleg can cook with fancy marinades, basting sauces, and mesquite chips. I went into some detail on all this, but he didn't want to hear it, and finally he told me to forget it and hung up.

I suppose that the reader of this book doesn't want to hear it either. Still, I'll have to say that most game meat is easier to cook in the kitchen. On the other hand, some of the best game meat that I have ever tasted was done on a grill over wood coals and charcoal. But I guarantee nothing. Except for the following recipe, provided that you've got good venison to start with.

As You Go Barbecue

This recipe was designed to make a believer of anyone who doubts that game meat is good, and who has little confidence in cooking it on a grill. It is, however, really a combination indoor-outdoor recipe. The recipe works best with those grills that have a gas stove burner on one side to accommodate a skillet and a pot or Dutch oven.

The Meat
   4- or 5-pound venison roast, leg quarter,
      etc.
   bacon drippings
   salt and pepper

The Sauce
> ½ pound bacon
> 1 medium to large onion, minced
> 3 cloves garlic, minced
> 1 cup catsup
> 1 cup red wine vinegar
> ½ cup Worcestershire sauce
> ½ cup dark brown sugar

Build a hot charcoal fire in the grill, or heat up the lava rocks in a gas grill. On the stove burner (or perhaps on the kitchen range), fry the bacon in a large skillet or stove-top Dutch oven. Remove the bacon and pour off most of the drippings, saving them for basting. Sauté the onion and garlic in a little of the bacon grease. Mix in the catsup, vinegar, Worcestershire sauce, and brown sugar. Heat and stir. Crumble the bacon and put it into the sauce. Keep the sauce hot and ready.

When the coals are hot, salt and pepper the venison, then baste it with the bacon drippings. Put the meat onto the grill, very close to the hot coals, and put the container of sauce nearby, preferably on an auxiliary stove burner if available; the sauce should not boil, but it should stay very hot. Grill the meat, basting with bacon drippings, until part of the outside looks ready to eat. Slice the crust off in strips about ½ inch thick; for best results, the strips should be nicely done on one side and medium rare on the other. Add the strips to the pot of sauce. Baste the meat again (or the cutaway part) with bacon drippings and sprinkle again with salt and pepper. Cook until the outside of the meat is done, then slice it off and put it into the pot with the sauce. Repeat the process until all the meat is done. After you have sliced and put all the meat into the pot, stir it up and serve over hamburger bun halves, serving 2 halves per plate, along with chips or beans. I

allow at least ½ pound of meat per person. Leftovers can be heated the next day and served with rice and vegetables.

The amount of sauce specified above is for a roast of about 5 pounds. Larger chunks of meat, or a whole deer, can be cooked successfully by this method. It's just a matter of watching your business and slicing off the meat as it cooks.

Rabbit over Coals

Young rabbits are very good when cooked over coals. Most recipes and techniques for grilled chicken will work, except that rabbit is better. Ingredients for the marinade and basting sauce in this recipe will be enough for 2 rabbits. Increase the measures as needed. I allow at least ½ rabbit (cottontail size) per person.

The Meat
> 4 rabbit halves
> bacon drippings
> salt and pepper

The Marinade and Basting Sauce
> ½ cup red wine vinegar
> ½ cup fresh orange juice
> 1 medium to large onion, grated
> 1 green bell pepper, grated
> 1 red bell pepper, grated
> 2 cloves garlic, grated
> juice of 1 lemon
> 2 tablespoons olive oil
> 1 tablespoon orange marmalade

Skin and dress the rabbits, cutting them in half lengthwise. Put the halves into a non-metallic container of suitable size. Mix the marinade ingredients and pour over the rabbit, tossing to coat all sides. Marinate in the refrigerator overnight or longer.

Build a hot charcoal fire. Remove the rabbits from the marinade. Retain the marinade, heating it to a simmer in a saucepan. Brush the rabbit pieces with bacon drippings, then salt and pepper them. Put the rabbit halves onto a greased rack about 6 inches over the coals. Cook for about 30 minutes, turning and basting with warm bacon drippings from time to time. When the pieces are almost done, start basting with the leftover marinade instead of bacon drippings. Before serving, cut well into the thickest part of a thigh to test for doneness.

Big-Game Ribs with Beer and Honey

The measures below work with a rack of ribs from a whitetail of normal size. The recipe will also work for ribs from mule deer, elk, caribou, moose, bear, or other big game, including alligator. Make more sauce if needed.

> 1 rack of ribs
> 1 can beer (12-ounce size)
> 1 cup honey
> juice of 1 lemon
> 1 tablespoon freshly ground ginger root
> 2 teaspoons salt
> 1 teaspoon dry mustard
> ½ teaspoon pepper
> ½ teaspoon nutmeg

Cut the rack of ribs in half with a saw, then separate them by twos or threes. Steam or simmer the ribs for 1 hour. While waiting, make a sauce by mixing the other ingredients. After the ribs have steamed, put them into a nonmetallic container and pour the sauce over them. Marinate for 4 hours, turning several times.

Build a charcoal fire in a large grill with a hinged cover. Lay the ribs on heavy-duty aluminum foil and pour ¼ cup of the sauce over them. Cover with another sheet of foil and seal with double folds. Being careful not to puncture the foil with a sharp rib bone, place the package in the grill, close the cover, and cook for 30 minutes. Then open the lid, remove the foil from the coals, and put the ribs on the rack directly over the coals. Cook until the ribs are nicely browned, basting several times with the sauce left in the aluminum foil. Place ribs on a serving platter. If you've got any sauce left over, pour it over them.

Note: If you are working with tender ribs that tend to come apart, put them into a hinged wire rack for the final browning over open coals.

Grilled Filet Mignon

Many people consider filet mignon to be the ultimate in meat cookery. Essentially, it is a fillet of meat wrapped in bacon and grilled or broiled. Use tenderloin or loin from deer, elk, or other big game—but I do not recommend that you use fresh bear or pork because these meats, for safety's sake, should be cooked until well done, whereas the filet mignon used in this recipe should be eaten rather rare. To get the onion juice for the recipe, cut the onion into 8 pieces and squeeze in a sturdy garlic press.

> tenderloin from deer or other big game
> thinly sliced bacon
> 1 cup cooking oil
> ½ cup red wine
> juice from 1 medium to large onion
> 3 crushed cloves garlic
> salt and pepper
> Hungarian paprika

Cut the fillets of tenderloin ¾ to 1 inch thick. Wrap each piece with part of a strip of bacon, pin with a round toothpick or skewer, and place in a nonmetallic container. Mix the onion juice, crushed garlic, wine, and oil. Pour this mixture over the fillet pieces, then refrigerate for at least 2 hours.

Build a charcoal fire and adjust the rack so that it is about 4 inches above the heat. Drain the fillet pieces. Put the leftover marinade into a saucepan, bring it almost to a boil, and keep warm. When the coals are hot, broil the fillet pieces quickly, being careful to keep them out of fires from the bacon drippings. It's best to have a large grilling area and move the pieces about with tongs. Baste with the leftover marinade when the meat begins to look ready. Sprinkle with salt, pepper, and paprika. Serve hot. Allow ⅓ to ½ pound of meat per person, depending on their appetites and what you've got to go with the meat.

Hot Smoked Venison and Dove Breasts

Here's a good combination of game that can be cooked on a large covered grill, or perhaps on one of the silo cooker-smokers. It's best to cut the venison into chunks about the same size as the dove breasts.

dove breasts
venison chunks
bacon
bacon drippings
garlic salt
pepper
hickory chips
meat tenderizer (if necessary)

Digging a Pit

For some reason, cooking game or meat in a pit seems to strike man's fancy. The method can produce some very good eating, and it can be fun. Building a wood fire instead of using charcoal seems to add to the fun.

There are exceptions, of course, but the place to dig a pit is usually in your backyard, or perhaps in the corner of your garden, rather than in the woods. For easy digging, find a spot that is soft and free of roots and telephone cables. If possible, use the same spot each time you cook, so that the ground will be rather soft. A good, sharp scoop helps. So does a posthole digger. It also helps to soften the ground by soaking it with water before digging; to this end, put a garden hose on the spot, crack the valve open just a bit, and let the water ooze out for half a day. Don't worry—the fire will dry out the dirt long before you are ready to cook.

If the venison is tough, sprinkle it with meat tenderizer, following the directions on the package. Fire up the smoker with charcoal and have hickory chips ready, either soaked or green. Put the venison chunks and dove breasts in a glass bowl and drizzle bacon drippings over them. Sprinkle liberally with pepper and garlic salt, tossing to coat all surfaces. Wrap each chunk of venison and each dove breast with half a strip of bacon, and pin with a toothpick or skewer or tie off with cotton twine.

When the charcoal is ready, cover it with hickory chips. Close the cover. Adjust the temperature to about 200 degrees. Grease the rack and place the bacon-wrapped venison and dove breasts on it. Smoke for 1 hour, then test for doneness. Smoke longer if necessary, but do not overcook.

Note: Gas or electric smokers can also be used. The tall silo-shaped smoker-cookers work fine with or without water in the pan.

Game Kabobs

Kabobs are fun to cook and eat inside or outside the house. The key is in using good meat and not overcooking it. There are a thousand excellent kabob recipes that will work for game, but I like to keep it simple, using what I call "good ol' boy" marinade: Zesty Italian salad dressing. Although the ingredients below call for tenderloin or loin, I don't hesitate to use cubed shoulder meat for kabobs, if the meat isn't too tough.

>   tenderloin or loin, cut into kabob-size
>   chunks
>   Zesty Italian salad dressing
>   thinly sliced bacon
>   onion
>   tomato
>   green pepper
>   red pepper
>   salt and pepper

Put the chunks of meat into a nonmetallic container, then pour some Zesty Italian dressing over them, cover, and refrigerate for several hours. An hour before you are ready to cook, quarter the green pepper, red pepper, onion, and tomato. Wrap each piece of meat with part of a strip of bacon. Skewer the meat pieces and vegetables, alternating in the usual kabob fashion.

Put the kabobs into a suitable baking tray, or some such container, and pour some of the Zesty Italian dressing over them. Turn the kabobs around to coat all sides. Let sit while you build a charcoal fire and burn it down to coals.

Grill the kabobs about 6 inches from the heat, turning from time to time, until they are done. This should take about 20 minutes, but a good deal depends on the thickness of the meat, the fire, and the distance of the rack to the coals.

Note: Cooking kabobs is easier if you can rig a way to eliminate the rack from the process. Try building a wood fire on the ground, burning it down to coals. Put the coals between two rows of bricks, then rest the ends of the skewers on the bricks. The kabobs are easier to turn since there is no rack for the meat to stick to.

Patio-Grilled Rib Chops

For a combination of tender bites and tasty gnawing, rib chops from deer, antelope, and such game are hard to beat. Allow 3 or more chops per person.

>   2 pounds rib chops
>   3 strips bacon
>   1 can tomato paste (6-ounce size)
>   1 medium onion, finely chopped
>   2 cloves garlic, minced
>   juice of 1 lemon
>   1 cup water
>   1/4 cup red wine vinegar
>   2 tablespoons brown sugar
>   1/2 teaspoon dry mustard
>   salt and pepper

Cook the bacon in a skillet. Drain. Sauté the onion and garlic in the bacon drippings for

5 minutes. Stir in the remaining ingredients. Simmer the sauce for 15 minutes.

Cook the chops about 6 inches over hot coals for 10 minutes. Baste heavily. Turn and cook for 8 more minutes. Turn again, baste, and cook for a few more minutes, or until done. Do not overcook. Serve any leftover sauce with the chops.

Grilled Game Ribs

Ribs can be very good when cooked on a grill, but most game ribs tend to be on the lean side. I often poach or steam them before grilling, which makes them much easier to eat.

The Ribs
    4 pounds ribs, more or less
    3 bay leaves
    water
    salt and pepper
The Sauce
    1 can tomato sauce (8-ounce size)
    1 cup red wine vinegar
    ½ cup catsup
    ¼ cup Worcestershire sauce
    ¼ cup cooking oil
    1 bell pepper, minced
    1 large onion, minced
    3 cloves garlic, minced
    salt and pepper

Cut the ribs into serving-size pieces. Put them into a large pot, cover with water, add the bay leaves, and simmer for 1 hour, or until tender. While waiting, mix all the sauce ingredients, simmer in a skillet for 10 minutes, and keep warm. Also, build a medium hot charcoal fire in your grill and let the coals burn down.

Drain the ribs, then salt and pepper them. Grease the rack, arrange the ribs on it, and cook for 20 minutes, turning from time to time. Baste heavily with the barbecue sauce, then cook for 15 minutes, turning and basting 2 or 3 times.

I usually allow 1 pound of game ribs per person. Serve with baked beans or thick Brunswick stew, sliced Vidalia onions, and barbecue bread.

Grilled Gameburgers

If you like to cook hamburgers on a grill, try gameburgers over the coals or in your smoker-cooker. You can use your favorite burger recipe and cooking technique, but you may need to add some beef suet or other fat to venison, or your burgers may be too dry and tend to fall apart when you turn them. To make gameburger from scratch, I recommend adding 1 pound of beef suet to 3 pounds of venison or similar game. You can grind a little bacon in with your game meat instead of beef suet.

If you don't have a favorite recipe, try adding a little finely chopped onion, Worcestershire sauce, salt, and pepper. Shape the meat into patties and put them into a well-greased, hinged grilling or burger basket. Cook over hot coals until done, turning the whole basket from time to time. Do not overcook.

Grilled Game Roast

One of the best venison roasts I've ever eaten was cooked on a patio grill with a hinged cover. The fellow who cooked it made deep slits into the meat with a fish fillet knife and poked chunks of salt pork deep into the meat. Then he sprinkled the roast with lots of pepper and garlic salt. He wrapped it in heavy-duty aluminum foil and cooked it all morning over low coals, along with some other meat he was preparing for a Thanksgiving dinner. He turned the roast once, very carefully, about midmorning.

It was delicious.

Rotisserie Roasts

All manner of rotisserie units are available for home and patio use. In principle, they are ideal for cooking roasts and other large chunks of meat. But in practice, the smaller units, seldom heavy-duty, tend to tear up when used with large pieces of meat, partly because the roast is difficult to center properly, putting a strain on the motor and gears.

Because proper spitting is so important, your best bet is to read the instruction booklet that comes with each unit.

I also recommend that you use a meat thermometer inserted into the thickest part of the meat. Venison is medium rare at about 140 to 145 degrees. A recipe? Baste the roast from time to time with bacon drippings. After each basting, sprinkle it with lemon-pepper seasoning.

Pit Roast

When studying a book on outdoor cooking many years ago, I was more than a little puzzled by the directions. First, the book said, you dig a hole, build a fire, and build up a good bed of coals. Fine. Baste the meat, wrap it in a wet burlap bag or banana leaves, put it into the hole, cover it with a layer of coals, and pile on the dirt. Fine. Then the book said to check it

from time to time to see whether more coals were needed! Back to the drawing board.

I've always been uncomfortable about the coals burning out, the meat burning up, or both. All of the pit-cooked meat I've ever eaten, however, turned out to be very good, but I did cook one batch that didn't get done. My wife had to help it along in the microwave, as reported elsewhere in this book. The problem, I have concluded, was that I didn't get the pit hot enough.

If you want to try this method, I recommend that you use a fairly large chunk of meat. Try the whole ham from a wild pig, or a large shoulder roast of venison made by boning both shoulders then rolling and tying them together with cord. Or try a whole venison hindquarter.

Use the same method that was described for cooking pit turkey in chapter 22. If you use boar, try the barbecue sauce that was recommended in the turkey text. With venison, elk, moose, and so on, instead of using barbecue sauce, try a mixture of prepared mustard, brown sugar, and good black pepper. You'll need lots of mustard if you soak the cheesecloth properly, so buy a gallon—which is surprisingly cheap in some stores. And use plenty of cheesecloth, or a few layers of cheesecloth followed by burlap.

Have plenty of good hardwood at hand, or else have very large bags of charcoal ready. Dig the pit and build the fire before sundown. Keep the fire going, while telling stories with the boys, until midnight. Put the well-wrapped meat onto the coals and cover it up. Then sleep on it. At about 11 o'clock the next morning, uncover the meat and get it ready for dinner. If you had enough coals and covered the hole properly, the meat will be hot, tender, moist, and delicious. If not . . . I don't want to hear about it.

44

COOKING GAME
IN CAMP

Something romantic fills our souls when we envision the hunter in camp. In our mind's eye we see meat frying over wood coals or a venison rump roast cooking in a Dutch oven. It's all true. Some of the most enjoyable meals available to the outdoorsman are in the woods or along a stream. Or at the seashore.

Indeed, one of my fondest memories of boyhood was of setting out afoot on a Saturday morning, hunting first across our small farm, and then beyond and into the countryside pretty much where my fancy led. More often than not, I shot birds or a rabbit for a noonday meal, stopping to rest while a fire burned. I went lightly, already loaded, I felt, with a gun, and usually did not carry cooking gear. A good knife to help dress the game and to cut a forked spit was about all I needed, along with a little bacon and salt. I wrapped the bacon around the meat and roasted it, just as many people today wrap bacon around meat to be cooked on the patio, kabob-style.

I also remember eating fried quail, cooked on the tailgate of a pickup truck, that were simply wonderful. These meals I enjoyed with my father and some older men, who smoked and told jokes and tales of fox hunting. I suspect that the company and the circumstances made the birds taste better!

Even so, game is not usually the best meat to eat in camp. For one thing, game meat, almost without exception, is better if it is allowed to cure, under refrigeration, for a few days before cooking it. Also, it is more difficult to cook most game meat, and the kitchen might be better because you have more equipment and better control of your heat.

But I repeat that game *can* be cooked successfully in camp, and should be enjoyed at every opportunity. Some cuts, such as venison

417

Campfires

The best campfires I've ever made were on the banks of an inside bend in the Choctawhatchee River. We camped on the spot several times a year, and we took the trouble to cut an oak tree each summer for use the following fall and winter. After sawing and splitting the wood, we stacked it between two trees so that most of it would be off the ground. Before long, it was seasoned just right for making a good campfire.

Getting good wood is not always easy, and, of course, dry seasoned wood burns much better than green or rotten wood. It also produces good coals faster—and less smoke, an important consideration unless you're being pestered by mosquitoes.

Rotten wood is not much good for anything, but freshly cut green hardwood will make a very good, hot fire if you can get it started. The coals from green wood glow for a long time. When using green wood, build a larger than normal fire and wait for it to burn down.

Because it's often difficult to find good wood quickly, and because of the restrictions in some state and federal parks, some people are hauling store-bought charcoal or briquettes into the woods. Charcoal and briquettes are certainly convenient and really make cooking easier simply because they don't get as hot as wood coals and don't put out much smoke. Still, a wood fire is hard to beat for atmosphere.

There are various schemes for building a good campfire, and I lean toward the keyhole concept. The keyhole is made with rocks. The fire is built in the main part, and the coals are raked into the smaller part for cooking. The rocks in the smaller part should be steady and should be laid to accommodate your cooking pan or pot, or a grill.

Parallel green logs, or logs placed in a V shape, can also be used successfully. It's best to build a fire in one end, then rake some hot coals down to the other end for cooking. Arrange the logs carefully before building the fire, and make sure your skillet or pot will fit and stay level.

Finding suitable rocks or logs is not always easy, so your best bet for cooking over a campfire is to bring along a portable grill with folding legs. If you've got the money and don't mind the extra weight, look into one of the grills that swing away from the fire. I've got a Big Foot grill, which I consider to be perfect. It can be raised or lowered easily, or swung away from the fire if need be. There are cheaper swing-away models available through camping and outdoor catalogs.

If you are using a pot instead of a skillet, you'll need a good camp tripod and a chain with an S hook, as described in a separate sidebar. Or rig a super dingle stick, also described separately.

tenderloin and deer liver, are rather traditional camp foods. Note also that the fried dishes and some of the more elaborate recipes set forth in other chapters can also be cooked in camp merely by packing in all the ingredients and bringing along a suitable pan—and paying close attention to your fire.

In any case, be sure to try the following:

Camp Stew

Here's a no-frills squirrel stew, hearty and good, that can be cooked in camp with only a few ingredients.

> 8 gray squirrels or 5 fox squirrels
> 8 medium potatoes, quartered
> 4 medium to large onions, quartered
> 4 carrots, cut into chunks
> branch water
> 1 teaspoon red pepper flakes
> salt and black pepper
> stone-ground cornmeal (optional)

Skin, draw, and disjoint the squirrels. Put the pieces into a pot, carefully cover with water, bring to a boil, add the red pepper flakes, and simmer until tender. Old squirrels will require longer cooking than younger ones; cook them in 2 batches, or keep up with what's what and remove the tender pieces while the others cook longer. Pull the meat from the bones with a fork. Discard the bones. Put all the meat back into the pot along with the potatoes, onions, carrots, salt, and black pepper. Add enough water to barely cover everything. Bring to a boil, reduce heat, cover, and simmer for 20 minutes, or until the potatoes and carrots are tender.

If you've got fine-ground cornmeal in camp, try some corn dodgers in with the stew. Simply mix some of the meal with water and some broth from the pot until you have a soft mush that will hold together. Add a little salt to taste. Shape the mush into patties about 2 inches in diameter and ¾ inch thick. Gently place these corn dodgers on top of the stew and simmer (or steam) for 20 minutes. If you cover the pot, it will not be necessary to submerge the corn dodgers, although they should be wet with the pot liquor before serving.

These measures make a full meal for 6 to 8 hunters.

Variation: Use 2 cottontails or marsh rabbits instead of squirrels, or mix squirrels and rabbits. Also, cook the hearts and livers along with the other pieces, unless you want to save these for breakfast.

Camp Stew with Canned Vegetables

I designed this recipe for cooking rabbit, squirrel, or similar small game in camp. It provides several vegetables and a grain, making a complete meal for the hunter. The idea, of course, is to eat well with game meat and ingredients that don't require refrigeration and are easy to pack.

1 rabbit, disjointed (or 2 or 3 young squirrels)
1 can tomatoes (16-ounce size)
1 can mixed vegetables (16-ounce size)
1 can onions (12-ounce size)
½ cup cooking oil
¼ cup long-grain rice
1 envelope chicken soup mix (1.2-ounce size)
flour
water
salt and pepper
meat tenderizer (optional)

If you've got a young rabbit or young squirrels, omit the meat tenderizer. If your meat is tough, you may want to sprinkle it with meat tenderizer and let it stand awhile. (Follow the directions on the package.) Or you can simmer the meat on very low heat until it is tender, drain it, and proceed with the recipe.

Brunswick Stew in Camp

If you've got the time, ingredients, and facilities, a Brunswick stew is hard to beat in camp. It provides a complete meal, and the vegetables can be brought to camp in easy-to-store cans. The basic recipe for squirrel (see page 276) can be used, or it can be modified to fit the game and ingredients on hand. Use rabbit or pheasant, for example, or use a combination of jackrabbit, armadillo, and so forth.

Heat 2 cups of water, add the chicken soup mix, and simmer for a few minutes, according to the directions on the package. Salt and pepper each piece of meat, coat with flour, and set aside for a few minutes. Open and drain all the canned vegetables. Rake out a few coals from the campfire and heat the oil in a large skillet or Dutch oven. Lightly brown the meat on both sides, add the onions, and cook for 5 minutes. Add the chicken soup, rice, canned vegetables, salt, and pepper. Cover and simmer for 25 minutes. Serve hot. Feeds 2 to 4. If you've got hot bread, serve it with the stew.

Deer Liver Camp Stew

Venison liver is a traditional deer camp meat because it can and should be eaten fresh. Here's a recipe that makes a complete meal:

1 pound venison liver
3 medium potatoes
3 carrots
1 medium to large onion
1 can tomato paste (6-ounce size)
3 tablespoons bacon drippings or oil
water
salt and pepper

Chop the potatoes, carrots, and onion. Heat the oil in a Dutch oven or skillet, then sauté the vegetables for 5 minutes, stirring as you go. Cut the liver into 1-inch chunks. Stir these into the pot and cook for another 5 minutes. Mix the tomato paste with 5 cans of water, then stir it into the pot contents, along with salt and pepper to taste. Cover and simmer on very low heat for 1 hour. Serve with skillet bread or camp biscuits.

Rigging a Super Dingle Stick

Everybody knows that a dingle stick is used for suspending a cooking pot over a campfire. It is usually made by first cutting and trimming a green sapling to get a pole 7 or 8 feet long. The big end is sometimes sharpened for jabbing into the ground at an angle, and the other end is always trimmed at a fork for holding the pot. The dingle stick is braced more or less in the middle by a forked stick (or by a flat rock), as shown in the drawing.

Dingle stick

Super dingle stick

In any case, the important thing about a dingle stick, as compared to other methods of suspending a pot over the fire, is that it can be swung away from the fire very quickly for temperature control. Sometimes it comes in handy to shift the pot in case the wind changes.

The super dingle stick works even better, but it requires a longer pole. Usually, a ten footer will be just right. From the super dingle stick, the pot hangs not from the end but from a point more or less in the middle, as shown in the drawing. The butt end rests on the ground and serves as a pivot point. The support post can be a forked stick of suitable stiffness, but it's better to have several notch settings to hold the end of the dingle stick. Such a post can be made by trimming a bush that grows near the fire, or by embedding a suitable limb in the ground. The advantages of the super dingle stick design are considerable. First, the pot can be swung away from the fire by merely lifting the end off the post and swinging it around, without having to dislodge the butt of the pole as with the regular dingle stick. (The super dingle stick can also be worked by lifting or sliding the butt end around.) Second, the several stops on the post make it easy to adjust the distance of the pot from the fire. This feature can be very important for temperature adjustments made as the coals burn down.

—Anderson DuPree, *Sports Afield*

Camp Fried Tenderloin

I don't normally recommend that big game be fried in camp, but the tenderloin can be very, very good. It is usually a tender, mild-tasting cut of meat that needs no aging, and it can be cut from a deer or elk from the inside of the body cavity, without having to skin the animal. I allow from ¼ to ½ pound per person, depending on who I am feeding. An old buddy of mine told me it was so good that he "can't hardly get enough of it."

The Chain and S Hook

There are dozens of ways of suspending a pot over a fire or coals, but the best one I've ever seen is the camp tripod. A chain drops down from the apex, and the pot handle is attached to the chain by an S hook.

The chain and the S hook are really the key elements and can be suspended from three poles, a tree limb, or other overhead structure of suitable strength. The nice thing about this rig, of course, is that the height can be easily adjusted—especially if you install a second S hook higher up the chain just in case the bottom one gets too hot to handle during cooking.

The chain should be fairly long, allowing you to swing the pot away from the fire in case things get too hot or you need to stir the contents. A stick with a hook, or hook-shaped fork, on one end should be kept handy.

But bear in mind that fried meat can become tough if it is cooked too long. In my opinion, it's best to cook it fast in very hot oil. If the oil starts to smoke, it's too hot; move the skillet or Dutch oven away from the coals quickly, preferably with the aid of camp gloves (asbestos) or by using a swing-away grill. Be careful—hot oil is dangerous.

In any case, here's all you'll need to fry delicious tenderloin in camp:

tenderloin, cut across the grain into ½-inch rounds
peanut oil
flour
water
salt and pepper

Salt and pepper each piece of meat, coat with flour, and let sit for a few minutes. Rake some coals from the fire. Heat the oil in a skillet or Dutch oven. Carefully drop in a piece of tenderloin to see if the oil is hot enough. There ought to be a word to describe the reaction of floured meat to just-right oil, but I can't think of one. My wife says that it "sputters." So, when the oil sputters upon receiving a piece of tenderloin, cook several pieces, being careful not to crowd them too much. Drain these pieces while you cook another batch.

After all the tenderloin has been cooked, pour off most of the oil and scrape up any pan dredgings. Mix a paste with a little water and flour, then slowly add this paste to the skillet, stirring as you go until you have a good gravy. The gravy can be thickened with more flour paste or thinned with water, as needed. Serve the gravy over the tenderloin or, better, over biscuit halves, if you've got them. The gravy also goes nicely with rice or boiled potatoes.

Note: Young squirrels, rabbits, and other tender meats can be cooked in same manner. Larger pieces, however, should not be cooked on high heat because the outside will burn before the inside gets done. Most frying over hot coals goes better with a cast-iron or heavy aluminum skillet. Thin skillets burn the meat and tend to warp.

Moose Fries

Some of the French Canadians are fond of fried moose testicles, and, of course, similar parts from other animals are also eaten.

testicles
butter, cooking oil, or bacon
salt and pepper
water

To prepare these parts for cooking, scald, skin, wash, thinly slice, and soak them in water for several hours. Drain the slices, then salt and pepper them. Heat a little oil or butter in a skillet, then sauté the slices for a few minutes, browning them on both sides. Do not overcook. Allow at least ¼ pound per person, unless this recipe is used as a side dish, as is often the case. You can also cook some bacon, then fry the moose pieces in the pan drippings. Serve the bacon along with the fries.

For fancier recipes along this line, see chapter 42.

Camp Liver and Heart

If you are as fond as I am of the so-called variety meats from beef, lamb, and so on, then this dish, or something close to it, will probably be your favorite camp eating. Of course, one advantage is that these parts are obtained during the field-dressing operation and should be eaten right away. Although this recipe calls for venison heart and liver, those parts from most other game or fowl, large or small, can also be used. See chapters 10 and 42 for fuller discussions of variety meats.

venison heart and liver
bacon
flour
sliced onions
salt and pepper
water

Cut the liver and heart into strips about ½ inch thick. Salt and pepper the pieces, then dust them with flour. Rake some coals from the fire and cook the bacon in a skillet until crisp. Set the bacon aside to drain. Sauté the onions for 5 minutes. Set aside to drain. Quickly brown the liver and heart pieces, then add just enough water to cover the meat. Cover the skillet and simmer on very low heat for 30 minutes, stirring from time to time, and adding more water if needed. Thicken the gravy with a little flour, and add more salt and pepper if needed. Return the onions and bacon (crumbled) to the skillet and heat through. Serve hot with whatever vegetables you've got. The gravy goes nicely with rice, mashed potatoes, egg noodles, or biscuits, if you've got them.

The liver and heart from a white-tailed deer of average size will feed 4 people of normal appetite.

The Camp Skillet

I much prefer thick cast-iron skillets, but they are a bit heavy for use in camp. Heavy-duty aluminum skillets are my next choice. Skillets of thin metal come in last. A long-handled skillet is sometimes helpful, but more and more I use asbestos gloves and regular handles.

Variation: If you've got edible wild mushrooms in camp, be sure to use some, slicing and sautéing them along with the onions.

Easy Neck Roast

If you've got an oven in your deer camp or cabin, this is a good, easy recipe to try. Any good roast, not too tough, can be used for this method, but a neck roast is usually juicier than the other cuts of venison and can therefore be cooked without pampering it. Also, the neck can be eaten without being aged. I like the recipe for camp because you don't need lots of stuff to cook it. Just pack a few envelopes of dry soup mix. If you don't bag some meat, eat the soup, maybe with a handful of rice in it.

> 1 neck roast
> 2 envelopes onion soup mix (1.2-ounce size)
> ¼ cup water
> salt and pepper

Preheat the oven to about 300 degrees. Tear off a suitable length of wide, heavy-duty aluminum foil. Dump the soup mix in the center, add some salt and pepper, spread it, and roll the roast in it. Fold in the edges of the aluminum foil and add the water. Cover the roast with a twin sheet of foil, making double folds along the edges to seal in the steam, and cook in the oven for 3 hours. This dish can also be cooked in a camp Dutch oven (as described in the next recipe), or you can bury the package for several hours under hot ashes and coals—and hope to hell it's done when you dig it out.

Easy Dutch-Oven Antelope Roast

Antelope is a fine meat, and, if properly handled before it gets to the cook, it needs very little pampering. It can be cooked successfully in a camp Dutch oven. Here's a basic recipe and technique, which can be modified somewhat if you've got onions, carrots, mushrooms, and so on in camp. You can also cook other meats by this recipe and method, especially a roast from a young buck or a tender doe. It is, however, best to gain some experience with a Dutch oven before you rely on it. Try cooking a few roasts on your patio or in your fireplace. That way, you can order pizza if all doesn't go as planned.

To cook this dish, you'll need a genuine old-

Grills or Racks for Camp

A grill is one of the most useful items you can have for cooking over a campfire or hot coals. Unless transportation is a problem, the best ones are large and steady, such as the racks from a refrigerator, so that they can be put atop rocks around the fire. But smaller racks with legs can also be used.

My favorite rack for light cooking is a hinged double wire grill, or basket, with two handles fitted together, such as those used for cooking hamburgers on the patio. The basket can be rested atop properly spaced rocks or green logs, or it can be hand-held, or, as often as not, a combination of the two. Long handles are highly recommended for such double racks for use over a campfire.

Dutch Ovens

Once I knew a tall girl who was going through college on short money. The only thing she had to cook in was a stove-top Dutch oven, and she prepared everything in it. There is no doubt that the Dutch oven is one of the best and most versatile cooking tools ever invented. It is, however, a little heavy for many camp cooks to lug around. It all depends on your transportation, how long you will be in camp, and so on.

A camp Dutch oven is different from the stove-top kind. It has three legs on it, and the cover is flanged so that it will hold coals on top of the main part. This type of lid makes it easy to keep stews and stuff hot, and it is an aid in baking bread in camp. The lid itself can be used as a griddle of sorts.

The Dutch oven is sometimes put into a hole in the ground over hot coals, and more coals are piled on top of the lid. Then the whole works is covered with dirt. For best results with this method, or for other no-peek long simmering, it's best to have a tight-fitting lid. If in doubt, seal the lid with a paste made of flour and water.

timey camp Dutch oven, as described in the sidebar above.

> antelope roast, 3 to 5 pounds
> salt and pepper
> 1 envelope onion soup mix (1.2-ounce size)
> 1 cup water

Build two separate fires or one long fire and let burn down to coals. (The idea is to have coals under, around, and on top of the Dutch oven.) Put a shallow rack in the bottom of the Dutch oven to keep the roast from resting directly on the metal. If you don't have a suitable rack, use carrots or trimmed tree branches—try sassafras if you want a nice spicy roast. Pour the water into the Dutch oven. Sprinkle the roast all over with salt, pepper, and soup mix; place it on the rack, and cover the Dutch oven tightly. Rake out a bed of coals, place the Dutch oven on top, and settle it in. Move some coals around the sides, and pile some coals on top of the lid. Keep a good fire going away from the Dutch oven, and replenish the coals on the lid and around the sides from time to time. Cook for 2 to 3 hours. Feeds 6 to 10.

Camp Rabbit or Squirrel

Here's a recipe that works with rabbit or squirrel and ingredients that are easy to tote into camp and to store. Also try it with armadillo or other small game, as well as with venison tenderloin.

> 1 cottontail or 2 squirrels
> ½ cup Coffee-Mate
> 2 tablespoons cooking oil or bacon
>   drippings
> flour
> 2 beef bouillon cubes
> salt and pepper
> water
> rice or egg noodles (cooked separately)

Skin and dress the rabbit or squirrels. If the game is young and tender, it can be used without parboiling. Old or tough game, however, should be simmered in water until tender. Cut the game into pieces, sprinkle with salt and pepper, then roll in flour. Heat the oil in a skillet that has a cover or in a Dutch oven. Brown the pieces. Heat 1 cup of water, mix in the Coffee-Mate, and then pour it over the game. Cover the pan and simmer for 1 hour. (If your skillet doesn't have a cover, add a little water from time to time.) Remove the game from the skillet. Add a little water to the skillet, stir in the bouillon cubes, and simmer until the gravy reaches the consistency you want. Put the meat back into the skillet and cover with gravy. Simmer for a few minutes, then serve over noodles, rice, or camp biscuits.

Roast Beaver Tail

The old mountain men, some say, liked beaver tail roasted over a campfire. The trick is to hold the tail over an open flame until the skin blisters and cracks. Then let the tail cool off. Peel away the skin. Then roast the tail over coals. Try it—but be warned that a beaver tail is, for the most part, a sort of edible gristle. Some people like it, some don't.

Kiwi and Meat

If you want to travel light but want some fresh fruit along on your trip, consider the kiwi. This little fruit is now widely available in the United States, and it keeps for a long time

Survival Cooking

I've read several accounts of game being cooked in open fires. For example, the Indians of the Southwest are said to have thrown prairie dogs into a fire whole, skin and all, and stirred them about with a stick. They were said to be done when they "popped open." The prairie dogs were raked out of the coals, cooled a bit, and skinned before eating whatever parts the Indians wanted to eat.

Also, the Gypsies of Europe were once fond of cooking hedgehogs in an open fire. These were first encased with mud, then put onto the coals. When cracked open and peeled off, the clay also took away the quills and the skin. In Russia, birds are cooked by the same method.

Cooking animals with the fur on them doesn't sound appetizing, but it does make a point: You don't have to have tools and equipment in order to cook. If you've got a knife to help clean and skin the game or fish, your fare can be made more appetizing (psychologically speaking) by wrapping it in wet leaves or wet clay before cooking, or by skinning the game and holding it over a fire with a stick. Some small animals, such as the crawfish, can be cooked quite successfully in their shells. If you have water and a suitable container, you can cook meat by putting hot rocks into the water, as the American Indians did. And don't forget that a flat rock can be heated and used as a cooking surface. So if you find yourself in a survival situation, remember that a fire is all you need in order to cook meat, fish, and shellfish.

without special care, provided that it isn't mashed or bruised. Also, it has a thin skin and edible core, so almost all of it can be eaten. The skin can even be used to tenderize meat. Just put the skin, fruit side down, onto the meat and let it sit in a cool place for an hour or so. Also, you can mash up the meat of the kiwi and spread it over the meat to tenderize it.

Or slice up the fruit and put it between slices of meat on a skewer, or in a double rack. Let it sit for an hour or so, then grill over hot coals or even over an open flame until the meat is done. Sprinkle on a little salt. Eat the kiwi right along with the meat.

Big-Game Ribs in Camp

Most of the meat on your deer or other big game should be aged for several days before you eat it. But not all. Liver and tenderloins, for example, are traditional meats for cooking in camp. Ribs from deer, antelope, elk, caribou, and so on can also be cooked without aging. Your best bet is to cook the whole rack atop a

Aluminum Foil

A little aluminum foil can save the day on camping trips. With it you can wrap food for cooking in or under the coals, or you can fashion a reflector oven. The extra-heavy type can even be shaped into a pan or cooking utensil of sorts.

large wire grill positioned over the coals. But you can also devise ways to prop a rack of ribs alongside hot coals, then cook them for a long time, turning them over as well as around from time to time.

Salt and pepper the ribs. Baste them with bacon drippings, or use some sort of barbecue sauce if you've got it in camp. Some of the best ribs I ever ate had nothing but lemon juice squeezed on them.

I'll normally allow 1 pound or so of game ribs for each person, but a lot depends on how much meat is on them.

45

LEFTOVERS

I don't like to throw good food out, and at our house we frequently save leftover meats, vegetables, rice, and gravy for use in soup. A helpful recipe for soup made with leftovers is, of course, impossible simply because the ingredients on hand are always different.

I might add that some of our best eating has come from mixing leftovers of one sort or another, and I assume that anyone knows what to do with leftover roast venison. (If not, try sautéing some chopped onions and fresh mushrooms in butter, add some chopped venison, and serve over freshly cooked rice.) In any case, here are some recipes you may want to try:

Leftover Pot Roast Pie

This dish is easy to prepare and makes good use of leftover roast—especially when the vegetables were cooked along with the meat. Other leftover or fresh vegetables, such as onions or celery, can also be put into the pie.

2 cups cubed leftover roast
2 cups leftover gravy
2 cups diced leftover potatoes
2 cups diced leftover carrots
1 package of refrigerator biscuits

Preheat the oven to 450 degrees. Mix the meat and vegetables. Put the mixture into a greased casserole dish. Place the biscuits on top. Bake for 20 minutes, or until the biscuits are browned on top and done on the bottom.

I recommend using regular-size biscuits for this recipe. The large, Texas-style biscuits may brown nicely on top but will stay gooey on the bottom.

Feeds 4 to 6.

Venison Curry

Although curry powder is not one of my favorite ingredients, I have found this dish to be quite good. (If you aren't certain of your taste for curry, cut the measure in half the first time you try the dish.) The recipe has been adapted from *Game and Fish Cookbook,* by Harriet and James Barnett.

> 2 cups cooked venison, cubed
> 3 medium onions, diced
> 1 cup diced tart apple
> 1 cup beef stock (or 1 cup water and 1 bouillon cube)
> ½ cup Madeira
> ¼ cup butter
> 2 tablespoons flour
> 1 tablespoon curry powder
> 1½ tablespoons fresh lemon juice
> ⅛ teaspoon nutmeg
> salt and pepper
> rice (cooked separately)

Heat the beef stock in a saucepan, reduce heat to very low, and simmer. Melt the butter in a skillet, sauté the onions and apple, then remove with a slotted spoon, setting them aside to drain. Using a wooden spoon, slowly stir the flour into the butter left in the skillet. (Add a little more butter if needed.) Cook and stir for 10 minutes or longer. When the flour browns, slowly stir in the heated beef stock, Madeira, lemon juice, nutmeg, curry powder, salt, and pepper.

Leave the mixture over low heat and stir constantly until it starts to thicken. Add the sautéed onions and apple. Bring to a new simmer, then stir in the diced venison. Simmer for a few minutes, then serve over rice. Feeds 3 or 4.

Leftover Venison Salad

Here's a nice lunch to prepare when you have a cup or so of leftover venison roast or other game. Increase the measures if you've got lots of people to feed.

> 1 cup leftover venison roast or other game meat
> ¼ red bell pepper, finely chopped
> ¼ green bell pepper, finely chopped
> 2 tablespoons salad pickle relish
> 2 tablespoons finely chopped onion
> mayonnaise

Mix the venison, pickle relish, onion, and peppers. Add mayonnaise, stirring, until the desired consistency is reached. For lunch, serve on lettuce leaves or eat with wheat crackers. Feeds 2.

Variation: If your wife is on a diet, try low-fat sour cream or low-fat yogurt instead of mayonnaise.

Leftover Roast with Brandy and Mushrooms

This happens to be one of my favorite meals, but I seldom cook it exactly the same way more than once. To proceed, have a good sourdough bread ready, hot and well buttered. Slice the leftover roast into thin strips, about 1 inch wide and ⅛ inch thick. Salt and pepper these strips to taste. Melt a little butter in a skillet. Sauté some fresh mushrooms until tender. (I like portabellas, sliced.) Add the meat strips and bring to heat. In a small saucepan, heat a little brandy. Flame the brandy and pour it, burning, into the skillet with the meat and mushrooms. When the flame dies down, stir the dish and serve it with the hot sourdough bread. Allow ⅓ to ½ pound of meat per person.

Leftover Elk Sandwich Spread

If you've got a meat grinder, use it to prepare the leftover meat. If not, chop it finely with a chef's knife. Of course, you can use any good meat in lieu of elk.

2 cups ground elk roast
¾ cup mayonnaise
¼ cup finely chopped onion
¼ cup finely chopped celery with green
    tops
¼ cup salad pickle relish
salt

Mix everything and spread it over thin white sandwich bread or atop crackers.

Leftover Game Meat Barbecue

This dish is an excellent way to use leftover roasts and other cooked meats.

3 pounds cooked venison roast
1 large onion, chopped
3 cloves garlic, chopped
1 can tomato sauce (15-ounce size)
¼ cup Worcestershire sauce
¼ cup red wine vinegar
¼ cup brown sugar
1½ teaspoons salt
1 teaspoon pepper
1 teaspoon paprika
1 teaspoon dry mustard
cooking oil

Put a little oil in a Dutch oven or large skillet. Sauté the chopped onions until tender. Add all other ingredients except meat, stir, and simmer for 30 minutes. Chop the cold meat and add to sauce. Cover and simmer for 20 minutes. Serve with rice or mashed potatoes, along with vegetables of your choice. Barbecue freaks might prefer baked beans. This barbecue can also be served over open-face hamburger bun halves. Feeds 6 to 8.

Jerky

Drying meat in the sun is the oldest way of preserving it, and the process is known to all cultures. In Africa it is known as *biltong*, a corruption of the words for buttocks and tongue. Apparently this refers to where the meat came from (the hindquarters), and what it looks like after the long strips have been dried.

In the West Indies, the French-African inhabitants of the early 17th century lived on a diet of dried beef made from the wild cattle which roamed the islands. In French these dried-beef eaters were called *boucaniers*, and since many of the islanders were pirates who preyed on Spanish shipping, you now know where the word "buccaneer" comes from.

The Spanish word for dried meat is *charqui*, and it is from this word that we get our word "jerky."

—Art Boebinger
Kentucky Happy Hunting Ground

46

GAME FROM FIELD
TO TABLE

The first step to getting very good game meat is to select a healthy animal. Age is not always a good guide, but in general a fully grown but young animal in its prime is better than an old one. Also, does are usually better eating than bucks. This often creates a conflict between hunting for the table and hunting for a trophy. In fact, many states that have a doe season (and want the doe population thinned down) have trouble getting hunters to take advantage of it.

After you have selected the right animal, your job is to kill it cleanly. A wounded animal that runs a long distance, or an animal that has been chased by dogs, simply does not taste as good as one that has not been pumping adrenaline. Any farm boy that has ever helped butcher hogs or goats or other farm animals knows that they should be calm at the time of slaughter. I remember having breakfast before daylight one chilly morning in a small café in Williston, Florida, where a group of deer hunters were talking to a local farmer who was getting ready to kill hogs. The farmer said that a big boar ought to be scratched down before hitting it in the head with a ball peen hammer! By scratching down, he meant scratching the hog's back until it lay down and went to sleep. It's a good image to remember if you want the best possible wild game meat. Kill your animal the first time you shoot at it. Some hunters like a head shot or a neck shot, but most experts these days go for a lung shot. A good deal depends on the situation at hand, or what and how you are hunting, but in general I endorse the lung shot.

In any case, after you have dropped your animal, approach it carefully to make sure that it is dead. Once you have determined that fact, proceed with field-dressing the animal as soon as possible. The main purpose in doing so is not to remove the guts and innards per se. The idea is to remove these parts, *and the heat they contain,* so that the body of the animal can cool down faster.

431

FIELD-DRESSING GAME

Deer

There are different methods of dressing out a deer. I recommend the following method for beginners. Experienced hunters may want to change the sequence or combine some of the steps.

1. If possible, place the deer on its back with its head pointed slightly uphill. Brace the body with stones or tree limbs to keep it from rolling over. Straddle the body and make a cut into the deer's skin at a point in the boneless area just below the rib cage, as shown by the + in the drawing. Make this initial cut by bunching up some of the skin in your left hand and slicing into it with your knife blade. Try to cut through the skin only, not into the muscle tissue. Of course, your blade should be sharp.

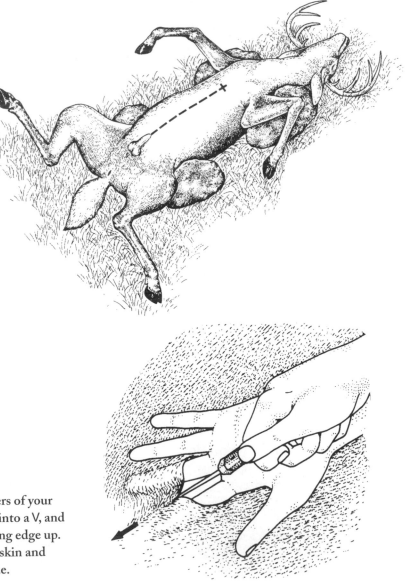

2. Insert the index and middle fingers of your left hand into the cut, spread them into a V, and insert the knife blade with the cutting edge up. The blade should be just under the skin and should not cut into the muscle tissue.

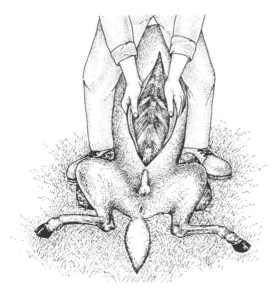

3. Working your way down with your finger V and following with the blade, cut the skin all the way to the pelvic area. Then pull back some of the skin from either side of the cut, opening up the area. Note that the tissue has not yet been cut, but the skin is now out of the way so that you won't be as likely to get hair on the meat. (Some people will want to cut the other way, going from the pelvic area to the chest. But I prefer to cut with the natural lay of the hair instead of against it.)

4. Starting at the rib cage, make an insertion into the muscle tissue. Then, using the same V technique, cut through the muscle tissue to the pelvic area. Avoid cutting into the organs or intestines. If you have bagged a doe, carefully cut a circle around the anus and the vagina. Work with this circle of flesh until you can see the two tubes (rectum and urethra). Loosen these tubes and pull them back enough to tie them off with a piece of string.

5. If you have a buck, note that the urethra curves over the pelvic arch to the penis. Hold the penis with one hand, pulling on it, and cut down toward the rectum with your knife. Do not cut it or the scrotum off completely. Instead, cut a circle around the penis and the rectum so that both can be tied off and removed together. Make sure that the tubes will go through the pelvic bones. It is not necessary to saw or hack through the pelvic bones, if you have cut around the anus deeply enough.

6. Turn the animal on its side and empty the contents onto the ground. This should pull the tubes (urethra and rectum) through the pelvic bone, and it should also clear the bladder and small intestines.

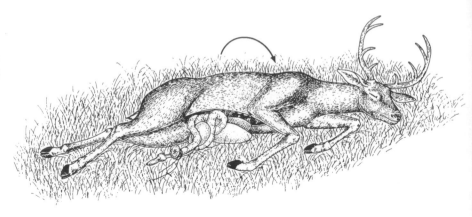

7. Work on the chest cavity. The diaphragm, which separates the chest cavity from the lower part of the body, must be cut. Reach into the chest cavity with your knife and cut along the rib cage, thereby slicing the diaphragm.

8. Reach up into the throat area with both hands to remove the windpipe and the gullet. Grasp these tubes with one hand, then cut them with the other. Pull down on the windpipe and gullet, which should loosen the heart and lungs. Pull all these organs free and dump them onto the ground.

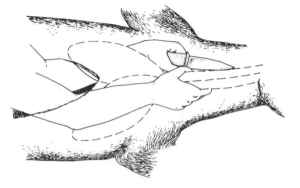

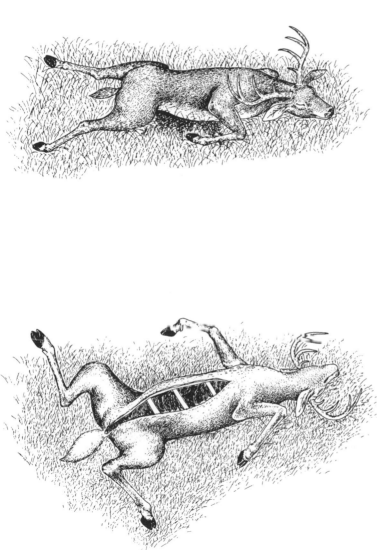

9. Turn the animal over on its stomach, away from the innards, so that it will drain. Prop the body if necessary so that it will not roll back over. While the body cavity is draining, separate the heart, liver, kidneys, and other parts that you want to eat. Note that the deer liver does not have a gallbladder attached to it. Trim off any blood vessels and place the parts into plastic bags.

10. Turn the deer over on its back and wipe out the inside of the cavity with a dry cloth. Prop the cavity open with two or three sticks, which will help the body to cool down.

The field dressing is now complete, unless you choose to remove the tenderloin from either side of the inner back and put the two pieces into a plastic bag. These choice pieces are not covered by skin and will tend to dry out if your deer is to be left hanging or will be in transport for some time. (See page 450 for a further discussion of the tenderloin and the loin.)

If there will be any delay in transporting the deer, it should be hung up, if possible. If hanging is not feasible, put the deer onto a ventilated bed of limbs or stones.

Elk

Generally, dressing out an elk is quite similar to dressing a deer. Of course, an elk is much larger and presents bigger problems of handling and transport. Also, the larger volume makes it even more important to field-dress the animal quickly. If possible, position the animal so that its head is elevated more than the rump. Then proceed as follows:

1. Make the first incision in the middle of the breast, starting at a point halfway between the legs and ending at the rear end. Cut through the skin first, as discussed in the section on deer, and pull the skin back on either side. Next, cut through the tissue layer. Do not cut into the intestines or organs.

2. Cut free and tie off the rectal tubes and the urethral tubes, as described for deer. Make sure that the flesh around the tubes is cut deeply enough to free the tubes for removal through the opening in the pelvic bone.

3. Turn the animal on its side and empty out the organs and intestines.

4. If you want to save the cape for a mount, you must now skin out the neck and the brisket area.

5. Reaching through the rib cage, grasp the windpipe and gullet. Cut them as high up as you can reach. Then cut the diaphragm free of the rib cage and remove the organs.

6. Now get your elk to a meat processor as soon as possible, or take it to your home or camp if you are going to butcher it yourself. If you have transportation problems at this time, it is best to cut the elk into six parts, as shown in the drawing on page 449. This is much easier to accomplish if you have a block and tackle or some other means of hanging the animal. You'll also need a saw. Use the same procedure as for butchering deer, discussed later in this chapter.

You can either skin the elk before you cut it into pieces or leave the skin on. If the weather is warm, it may be best to skin the animal entirely to help cool the meat. Also, the hide is heavy and may become a factor if you are backpacking.

When transporting the meat, use game bags or wrap it in cheesecloth.

Moose

Dressing a moose is similar to dressing an elk or a deer, and the same directions apply. A moose, of course, is very large—it can weight almost a ton. You need heavy-duty equipment to manage a moose, and you should have this equipment along, or nearby, when you are hunting the animal. You should also consider the animal's size when you choose an area to hunt, and remember that a moose shot in the water will be almost impossible to handle.

Since the animal is so large, it is important that you gut it as soon as possible. Removing the innards will also remove much of the internal heat and will open up the body cavity to promote better cooling. Getting the skin off as soon as possible also helps in cooling the meat.

In most cases, the moose will have to be cut into parts before it can be removed. After

Watch for Glands?

A number of people who have written about dressing game have warned readers about glands, and they have recommended that the glands be removed from squirrels, raccoons, deer, and other animals. I don't agree. For the most part, in my opinion, the hunter who dresses out game reasonably well is better off ignoring the glands. This is especially true of the tarsal glands on the hind legs of deer; let them be, since they are on the part of the leg that is normally thrown away anyhow. These glands stop functioning when the deer dies. They will cause no harm to the meat unless the hunter cuts into them while trying to remove them, and then spreads the gland oil to some of the meat. In short, forget about the tarsal glands.

I feel pretty much the same way about the glands in other animals. The javelina, for example, has a potent gland on the rump, but it will usually come off when the animal is skinned. Therefore, trying to remove it before skinning is usually unnecessary, and could ruin the meat. The best policy is to be aware that the gland is there, then check after skinning to see that it is gone. If necessary, cut it out after skinning.

Another animal that has a bad gland is the pronghorn antelope. As with the javelina, this gland is on the rump, just under a white patch of hair. The gland will usually come off with the hide, but watch for it. If you use a skinning knife on either the javelina or the pronghorn, be careful when you are in the rump area.

I've never had any trouble with glands from small game, but be aware that the glands in an opossum (just under the forelegs and along the top of the rear back or rump) might need attention if you scald and scrape the animal instead of skinning it. In rabbits, the glands are under the forelegs, and in the beaver, opossum, muskrat, and raccoon, the glands are under the forelegs as well as on the rump. The glands are waxy little nodules, usually reddish in color.

butchering, keeping the meat off the ground will help cool it. If the parts can't be hung, put them on a ventilated bed made of limbs or brush.

Caribou
Although a caribou can have a set of antlers as wide as an elk's and hooves the size of a moose's, dressing out the animal, which weighs about 600 pounds, doesn't usually present as much of a problem as dressing out an elk or a moose simply because it is smaller. Follow the instructions for elk if you want to save the cape for mounting. In general, follow the field-dressing instructions for deer.

Bighorn Sheep and Mountain Goat
Both sheep and goats usually live in rugged country, and that fact can present transportation problems. If you are after only the meat, then proceed to field dress the sheep or goat just as you would a deer.

If you want to keep the cape for a trophy, start by cutting through the skin all the way around the upper part of the body. The cut should be made entirely around the body, just behind the front legs, above the knees. Next, cut along the back of the neck, up to a point about 4 inches behind the horns. Then cut to the base of each horn. Skin the cape. Then cut through the neck at the base of the skull.

Proceed with the field dressing, following the general instructions given for deer.

Both sheep and goats are easier to field-dress if you don't want to keep the horns or cape. Dress either animal like a deer. But be warned that the bighorn has a bad gallbladder attached to the liver. If you puncture it, you will likely ruin some good meat.

Pronghorn

The pronghorn antelope is easy to field-dress as compared with a moose or an elk, as its maximum weight is about 140 pounds. On the other hand, it is an animal of the plains, where the temperature is usually much warmer than at the higher elevations where the elk is found. In short, field-dress the antelope as quickly as possible, following the instructions given for deer. On your initial cut from the chest to the rear end, you can usually make do with one cut instead of making separate cuts of the skin and tissue. Use the finger V cut. If possible, get your pronghorn into a shady area as soon as possible after field-dressing it.

Be warned that the antelope has a powerful scent gland, used to alert the herd in case of danger, and this thing can cause some problems. The gland is located just under the white patch of skin on the rump. It's best to leave the gland alone and hope it comes off with the skin, as it often will. Inspect the spot after skinning, however, looking for a group of yellowish nodules. If necessary, cut the gland out, working around it very carefully with your knife. Then wash your knife before cutting meat.

Wild Hog

There are two kinds of wild hogs in North America, in addition to the javelina (which isn't really a pig). The European wild boar can weight up to 400 pounds, whereas the smaller "feral hog" usually averages about 100 pounds. The wild boar is harder to dress out simply because it is bigger.

Either type of hog should be scalded and scraped before it is dressed out. This is accomplished by dipping the dead hog in hot water, and then scraping the hair off the hide. A large barrel or some sort of vat is highly desirable for scalding. You really need lots of very hot water. If necessary, you can pour hot water on parts of the hog with a bucket, then scrape the hair off the scalded area. Boiling water isn't necessary, but it should be at least 150 degrees, especially in cold weather. Domestic hogs are treated in this manner, and scalding and scraping are the first order of business after the animal is killed. Of course, when dressing out domestic animals, the hot water and some sort of vat can be at hand, but this is usually a problem in the woods. Unless you are close to camp, it may be best to field-dress the hog first and worry about the hair later.

To field-dress a hog, cut it open from the rib cage to the rear, then remove the organs and intestines just as you would with a deer or other animal. After you have gutted the hog, get it out of the woods and to a spot where the scalding operation can be performed. Or take it to a good meat processor.

I might add that feral hogs offer some very good eating, and they are widely available in some areas. Since they are not classified as game animals, they may not be subject to game laws, so you may have no seasons or bag limits to worry about. My daughter and her husband live in Sopchoppy, Florida, next to the huge Apalachicola National Forest, and they often have wild pigs rooting in their driveway and around their house. They, along with their neighbors, eat one from time to time, finding them to be delicious when smoked. In that neck of the woods, the feral pigs are called "piney woods rooters."

If you don't want to scald and scrape the hog, you might consider skinning it as best you can. I might point out, however, that you don't have to do both, as was directed in a book released a few years ago by a well-known out-door publisher. That's right—the book advised you to scald the pig in a barrel in the woods, scrape off the hair—and then skin it!

Javelina

The javelina, or collared peccary, isn't really a pig and it isn't normally scalded and scraped like a boar. It seldom gets larger than 50 pounds and should be dressed out like a small deer. One potential problem is a musk gland located on the animal's rump. Usually, this gland will come off with the skin and therefore will not present a problem. If it doesn't come off,

The Best Way to Freeze

A lot of us bring home more fish and game than can be fit into our freezers. Often, reducing the meat to small packages works much better than trying to freeze large chunks. Also, many people who don't know much about butchering meat can solve a lot of problems by reducing the animal to small parts.

I have known hunters who grind up a whole deer or even an elk into hamburger meat or sausage. Following one formula or another, they usually add a certain percentage of beef fat, sometimes called suet, or pork. The resulting mix is often quite tasty—but remember that the method adds both fat and cholesterol to one of nature's most healthy red meats.

I suggest a different and more versatile approach, and one that leads to better eating. Instead of grinding the meat, cut it into cubes like supermarket stew meat. Such meat can be easily wrapped and frozen in small packages, and it is easy to cook. Cutting the meat into chunks doesn't require special meat-cutting equipment, grinders, or a trade school degree in butchering. Remember that stew meat itself can be ground into hamburger meat before it is cooked making it even more versatile.

In any case, the stew meat is best wrapped tightly in white paper and properly marked. Units of 1 pound work best for me simply because I most often use either 1- or 2-pound units in recipes, not the 1.41-pound or 2.37-pound packages of stew meat found in our supermarkets. Of course, the home butcher can also trim all the fat and connective tissue from the venison before freezing it. If ½ pound of meat is needed, it's easy to score and break a package in half. The remainder can be wrapped again and put back into the freezer for future use.

—Adapted from *Venison Cookbook*

remove it carefully with your knife. In my opinion, you should not try to remove the gland before you skin the animal. There are other opinions on this matter, however, and some people recommend that the gland be cut out before the animal is skinned. Either way, be careful not to cut into the gland.

Black Bear

A large black bear can weigh more than 600 pounds, and some of the other bears are much larger. The average adult male black, however, will weigh in at 300 to 400 pounds. That's a big chunk of meat—and it is covered with very thick, black hair, which holds in the body heat. It is therefore important that the bear be field-dressed as soon as possible.

The instructions presented here are based in large part on a booklet that was published by the Ontario Federation of Anglers and Hunters. Proceed as follows:

1. Turn the bear on its back. Cut into the skin at a point just beneath the lower jaw, being careful not to cut into the meat. Insert two fingers and, holding the blade edge pointed upward, start cutting through the skin toward the tail. The cutting edge of the knife should follow along as you work your fingers down the skin. Proceed slowly, being careful not to cut into the abdominal cavity, until you reach the top of the tail. Next, cut the skin on the inside of each leg all the way to the paw pads. Pull the skin away from the tissue a ways, but do not skin the animal yet.

2. Working in the cut that you have made in the skin, carefully insert the knife, cutting edge up, into the abdominal cavity near the pelvic bone. Cutting with the blade between your two fingers, work carefully all the way up to the breastbone. Try to avoid cutting into the intestines or organs. Do not waste time at this point trying to cut through the breastbone or the pelvic bone.

3. Reach into the cavity and locate the diaphragm or membrane that separates the heart and lungs from the liver and stomach. Cut this diaphragm away from the rib cage.

4. Reach up under the rib cage and cut the windpipe, gullet, and arteries.

5. Cut around the vent with your knife as deeply as you can, pretty much as shown in the illustrations for dressing deer. Tie off the tube and pull it from the body cavity. If you have a male bear, cut off the penis at its base and pull it from the body cavity.

6. Roll the bear on its side. Pull all the organs and innards out of the body cavity, using your knife to help free any connective tissue.

7. Insert several sticks into the edge of the body cavity, propping it open to help ventilation.

8. Separate the heart, liver, kidneys, and other innards that you want to keep. Put these parts into plastic bags or other containers, and leave them in a cool place.

9. If possible, skin the bear as a final part of the field dressing. This will help cool the meat more quickly. It will, of course, be easier to skin the bear if you hang it up, preferably with the aid of a small block and tackle. Hanging will also help cool the carcass. It is easier to hang the bear from the hind legs, first inserting a strong limb between the tendon and the leg bone, as shown in the drawing.

10. Unless you have plenty of help, you might have to cut the bear into pieces before you can transport it. To do so, you'll need a saw. First, cut through the neck. Then saw down the middle of the bear, starting at the pelvic bone. Next, cut off the hindquarters. Cut through the back where it joins the front quarters.

Get your bear to a meat processer as soon as possible. I don't recommend that you try

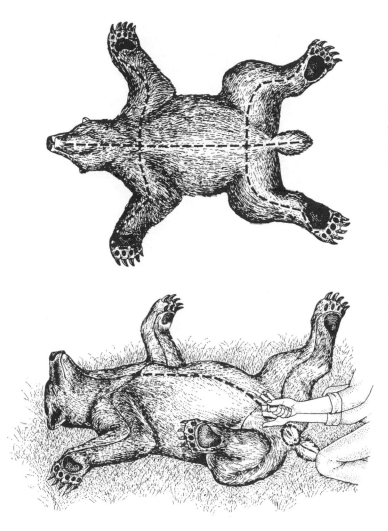

Dashed lines show cuts to be made when dressing out a black bear. Cuts along legs are for skinning the bear after field dressing is completed.

After making first cut from jaw to tail, work in the same cut from pelvic bone to breast bone, cutting into the abdominal cavity.

Hanging a black bear from the hind legs. A strong limb should be inserted between the tendon and the leg bone.

to hang or otherwise cure bear meat. If you butcher it yourself, cut the meat into whatever cuts you want, wrap them, and freeze them as soon as possible. (But don't put all the meat into a small freezer at the same time; freeze it in small batches so that it won't lower the temperature of the freezer too much.)

Cut the fat from the meat before freezing, as fat has a much lower freezing point. If you want the fat for cooking, cut it into small chunks and fry these in a large cast-iron skillet. As the fat fries out, the chunks will turn into small, nicely browned, crisp nuggets. These are very tasty and can be eaten on the spot, saved for crackling bread, or perhaps crumbled and served over salads or over sour cream on baked potatoes.

Small Game

Generally, small game is easier to dress out than big game. It doesn't hold the heat as long, and there isn't as much heat to hold. Consequently, field dressing is not as critical. Even so, for maximum quality, any game, fish, or fowl should be field-dressed as soon as possible or at least as soon as practical. Too many people put small game into rubberized game compartments of

> ## Dressing a Rattlesnake
>
> Snakes are very easy to dress out. First, nail the head to a tree or the barn wall, or hold it (carefully) with pliers. Make a cut around the body, near the head, and start the skin down. Grab the skin with pliers and pull. It comes off easily. Then gut the snake down the middle of the belly, and pull out the innards. Cut the snake into 4-inch segments.
>
> Put the snake into plain water and refrigerate for 2 days or longer before eating. The snake can also be frozen, preferably in water as described for fish.

hunting jackets and leave them there, unventilated, for the length of the hunt.

When dressing any small game, I normally skin it first, then gut it. Other people may want to gut the game and skin it later, but not me. I put my dressed game in plastic bags (one squirrel or rabbit per bag) and try to keep it in a cool place. I always like to wash small game

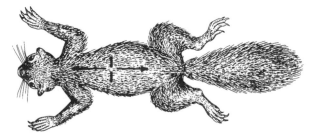

Skinning a squirrel. Cut at dotted line, then pull with fingers in opposite directions.

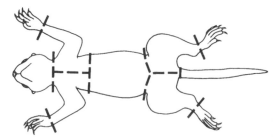

After pulling skin all the way to feet and head, cut them off, plus the tail. Then cut up squirrel as shown by dashed lines.

in a stream when it is field-dressed, but many hunters and outdoor writers object to this practice. Suit yourself.

There are many ways to skin small game. I always begin by making a cut across the back with a very sharp knife. (A short knife is especially important for cutting into squirrel skin, but not so much for rabbit.) Then I loosen the skin a bit with the point of the knife. Next, I work my index fingers into each side of the hole, crook the fingers, and pull in opposite directions. This gets the skin to the front legs and rear legs. Holding the head and front feet with one hand, I pull the skin over the hind legs down to the feet. Next, I hold the hind feet and pull the skin over the front legs down to the feet. I then cut off the feet, head, and tail with a sharp knife. Finally, I gut the animal and fish out the liver if I want to keep it. I've read about other methods of skinning squirrels and such, but none of these work any better or faster, at least not for me.

If you want to save the hide of the animal, however, you need to proceed differently. Cut the skin on the underside of the animal, working from chin to tail. Then make crosscuts along each leg to the feet. This method makes skinning harder, but it gives you a hide that can be tacked to a barn wall. (If you are selling hides from a trap line, follow the procedure recommended by the people who traffic in hides. This could be very, very important.)

Exceptions to the above method include dressing the opossum and the armadillo. I have no advice on the latter, except to turn it on its back and work from the bottom, much like dressing a turtle. The possum can be skinned like a rabbit, or scalded and scraped like a hog. The latter method works fine, but it does leave a lot of fat on the possum. For roasting the possum whole, leave the skin on. For cutting it into pieces for frying or stewing, skin it.

TRANSPORTING GAME

Often the hunter can save himself a lot of work, and end up with better meat, if he considers before the hunt how he will pack an animal out if he does kill one. Once, for example, a young friend of mine had a map of a game management area and pointed out the spot where he wanted to make a deer stand. He had good reason for choosing the spot, but he had to walk some 3 miles to get to it. Wanting him to get close to the road, I asked him how he was going to get a big buck out. He hadn't thought of that. But he didn't want to get near the road because he thought that, as it was late in the season, the deer would be deeper in the woods during the day. He also knew that there would be too many hunters in the area. He was right on both counts.

Finally, he chose a stand even farther into

Warning

Transporting a deer or other animal, especially bear, elk, or moose, can be very hard work. Moreover, the hunter may be heavily dressed. This combination is dangerous for people who are not in good shape. Having a heart attack while shoveling snow in your driveway is indeed dangerous—but not as dangerous as having one while trying to move a moose out of the deep woods, many miles away from a hospital.

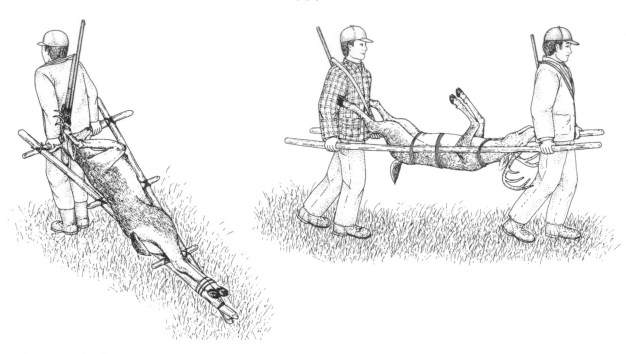

Two methods of transporting a deer out of the woods. If you're alone, you can make a framework of poles and drag the deer out. With a partner, you can make a pole stretcher.

the forest, near a very small stream. He got to the stand by canoe—and he got his buck out by canoe. In short, he floated in, bagged his buck, field-dressed it, and floated on down to the next bridge, where he got another hunter to give him a lift back to his own truck. Thus, a little planning paid off.

Of course, it is often necessary to transport game on your back, on a pack horse, or in a backpack. (I do not recommend that good meat be dragged on the ground for any distance.) Consider all this *before* you go hunting. Get topo maps of the area and study them. A backpack frame is often a big help in getting meat out—but be careful about sticking antlers up over the top, unless you want your head shot off. If you pack out antlers, or whole animals, be

sure to make good use of bright orange tape. And lots of it.

If you are alone, you can make a frame of two poles and drag the deer so that it isn't touching the ground. This method works even better with two people. Also, if you've got help, you can transport the deer on a makeshift stretcher.

If you do have to drag the deer, it's best to tie a rope or cable to the base of the antlers. Tie the front legs to the antlers so that the feet won't drag. Have a comfortable handle, if possible, or a short rope. The antlers should be lifted slightly so that they won't stick into the ground while you drag the body.

Sometimes the best bet is to leave the animal and go for help. If at all possible, field-dress it before you leave and hang it so that it clears the ground. If you don't have a small block and tackle with you, consider lifting it with a tripod made from poles.

Usually, you will move your animal from the point of kill to some sort of vehicle. Your problems may not be over once you reach the vehicle. Never put a deer or other animal across the hood of a car if you have other options. The heat from the engine will not be good for the meat. The longer you have to travel, the worse this problem will be.

Weather can compound your problems. In relatively warm weather, it's best to travel after sunset. If you are traveling in very cold weather, however, it may be better to travel by sunlight to help prevent the meat from freezing. Snow packed into the body cavity may help keep the meat cool by day—and may help keep it from freezing by night.

In any case, get the animal home or, better, to a professional meat processor as soon as you can.

HANGING OR AGING MEAT

Most meat is better, no doubt, if it is aged properly. This is especially true of deer, elk, beef, and similar animals. For the larger animals, aging is best accomplished at a meat processor's facility, where the animal is hung up in a controlled, refrigerated environment.

Many hunters will want to hang their deer at home, but this is seldom advisable unless you have the facilities. It is usually a mistake to hang the deer outside at night in freezing temperatures and then have it thaw out as the sun comes up during the day.

If you don't have adequate facilities, your best bet is to cool the deer or other animal off as much as possible and butcher it. Then put the pieces on ice for 5 days. I know some local deer hunters who always butcher their meat as soon as possible, then put it into large ice chests. They ice the meat and drain off the water every day for 5 days. I have tried this method and I like it. Such ice chests can often be carried along on a hunting trip, so that the deer can be butchered or packed down in camp or near the back of a pickup truck. It is important that the water be drained from the chest.

Still another method is to butcher the animal, wrap the pieces, and freeze them as soon as possible. Freezing the meat for a month or so has an effect quite similar to aging. Often, it is best to proceed with a combination of ice chest and freezer methods, simply because most home units won't quick-freeze a lot of meat at a time. In any case, there is no doubt that cured venison is better in texture as well as flavor if it is cured by hanging, icing, or freezing.

To Bleed or Not to Bleed

A few years back, most hunters and most authorities on the subject recommended that deer and other big-game animals be bled before field dressing. Although the practice is still widespread, it is not recommended by most up-to-date books and magazines. Modern thinking has it that a shot in the lungs with modern ammunition, along with normal field dressing, is all the bleeding that is required. It is more important to remove the organs and open the body up as soon as possible. Don't waste time with bleeding.

Hanging a deer from a tripod of poles.

Small game is also better if it is aged. A few days in the refrigerator will help the meat of squirrels, rabbits, muskrats, and others.

SKINNING

It is difficult, in a book like this, to get first things first simply because there is more than one way to skin a deer or other big game. Except possibly for the bear and very large game such as a full-grown moose or elk, I recommend that skinning be delayed until the animal has been transported to the place where it will be butchered. The hide will protect the animal during transport and will keep the meat from drying out while the animal is hanging. On the other hand, the animal is much easier to skin while the body is still warm, so many people will want to skin it as a part of field dressing.

Special skinning knives have been designed, but a good general-purpose blade will do the job. The drop-point design is a good choice for field dressing as well as skinning if the blade is kept sharp.

In the field or at home, it is much easier to skin deer and similar animals if you first hang them by the head. Unless you want to mount the head, start by cutting completely around the top of the neck with your knife. First insert the blade, then work around the neck with the finger V technique that was used to field-dress the animal. Do not cut into the meat if you can avoid it. Then cut off each leg at the knee joint.

Start working at the neck, pulling down on the hide with one hand while working the skinning blade with the other. The knife helps in slicing the tissue, freeing the skin from the meat. Do not cut into the meat. The knife is an *aid* in skinning and should not be used to cut off the hide. If the hide comes freely, you may not need the skinning knife at all after you get started. Try working with both hands, rolling the hide as you go. You can skin and roll the hide all the way down to the tail, bringing it all off in one piece. (At the shoulders, you'll have to work on each front leg as well as the body.) It is easier to cut the tail off, leaving the bone in the hide. But if you want the bucktail to tie jigs or flies, you might carefully split the hide on the underside before skinning the tail.

Typical drop-point knife design—good for skinning and field dressing.

The above procedure works if you are interested only in saving the meat. But you may wish to save the hide or cape.

Skinning to Save the Hide

If you want to save the hide, the above procedure should be modified as follows: Cut around the neck and remove the legs at the knees, as described above. Next, go to the cut you made in the first step of field dressing. Extend this cut straight up to the cut around the neck. Next, make a cut underneath each leg, going from the knee joint to the center of the animal. Then skin as usual. This method will give you a hide that can be tacked to a wall or that can be salted and rolled up until it can be delivered to a taxidermist or hide processor.

Skinning to Save the Cape

If you want to save the cape of the animal for a trophy, start by hanging the deer by the hind legs instead of by the head. Skin and remove the cape as soon as possible rather than hanging the animal for several days.

To begin skinning a deer or similar animal for both meat and cape, make cuts in the hide around the hind legs at the knee joints, then down the middle of each leg to the cut made while field dressing. Next, make a cut across the chest or brisket area and down the insides of the legs. On the top side of the cape, make a cut around the shoulder (behind the legs, joining with the similar cut that you made from underneath) and down the center to a point between the base of the antlers. Then skin out the entire neck. Cut off the head at the point where the skull joins the neck bone. Salt the hide thoroughly and pour salt into the neck opening, ears, nose, and mouth. Keep the head in a cool place and get it to your taxidermist as

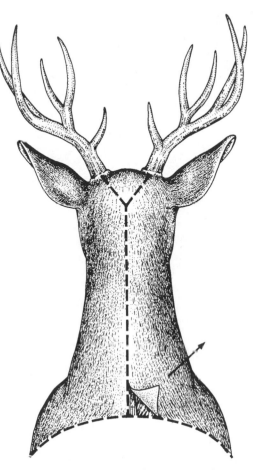

Dashed lines show cuts for caping a deer.

soon as possible. Then skin out the rest of the animal for the meat, starting at the hind legs and working toward the neck.

BUTCHERING YOUR MEAT

I recommend that you take your big-game animals to a professional meat processor for proper aging and butchering, unless you have the facilities to do the job. The average kitchen simply isn't the best place to butcher a large animal, and most homes lack meat saws and

Cold Meat Is Easier to Work

Most butchers and many hunters know that cold meat is easier to slice, dice, or otherwise cut. This information can be especially useful for preparing dishes and recipes that call for thinly sliced meat. Also, when making gameburger or sausage, know that game meat, from javelina to moose, is easier to grind when cold or partially frozen.

other tools. But home butchering can be accomplished, and of course there is nothing wrong with getting a few choice cuts and cutting the rest up into cubes or pieces to be used in stew or ground for gameburger. There are several good books on butchering meat, but there are a thousand different cuts and variations. Consequently, in the end you'll have to make your own decisions anyhow.

It is best to butcher the animal after it has been chilled considerably, simply because cold meat is easier to cut. If your animal is hanging by the head, start butchering it by removing the hind legs. If it is hanging by the hind legs, starting butchering by first removing the neck and front quarters. (Usually, your best guide to butchering any animal is simply to follow the natural divisions in the meat.) At this point, further reduce the primary parts, wrap the meat, label it, and get it ready for freezing.

You can bone the neck for a boneless neck roast, leave it as is for a bone-in neck roast (which I recommend), or trim off the meat for stew, saving the bony part for soup.

The front shoulders can be cut up into three parts: blade roast, arm roast, and shank. Usually, the shank is used for gameburger. If you want a large roast that is easy to bard with bacon, bone both of the shoulders. Put one down flat and lay strips of bacon on it. Then cover the bacon with the second boned piece. Roll both up together with the bacon in the middle, tying off with cotton twine. This makes one of my favorite roasts.

To remove the hind legs, work with your knife blade, cutting along the dotted lines shown in the drawing. Go slowly, working your way around and down to the ball joint. After you have separated the hindquarters, you can slice the large end into round steaks, complete with a little round piece of bone in the middle, if you've got an electric meat saw. Or you can divide the sections up into smaller roasts. The large end of the leg has separate muscles that go around the bone. If you divide the leg muscles into roastlike pieces, these can be sliced or butterflied into chops or small steaks.

The lower part of the hind leg, below the knee, is usually sliced up into stew meat or ground into gameburger.

So . . . we've cut off the neck, the front quarters, and the hindquarters. Decide now whether you want to remove the loin (and the tenderloin if it hasn't been removed during the field dressing operation, as well it should have been) from along the backbone or whether you want to cut it up into chops or steaks. I recommend that you remove the loin, then cut the ribs away from the backbone. With a sharp, stout knife and a good eye you can cut the ribs from the backbone without the aid of a saw; you can also cut each rack of ribs away from the bony plate that joins them. This will give you two whole racks of ribs. A saw will help cut the bones in two, or you can hack them with a cleaver. After you deal with the ribs, you'll have

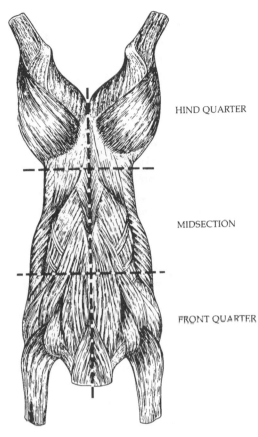

Initial cuts for butchering big game.

HIND QUARTER

MIDSECTION

FRONT QUARTER

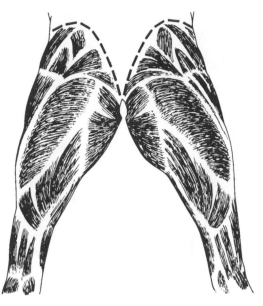

Cuts for removing the hind legs.

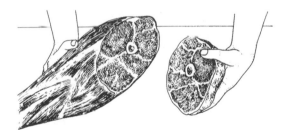

Large end of leg is cut into round steaks.

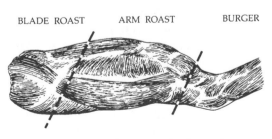

BLADE ROAST   ARM ROAST   BURGER

Shoulder should be cut into three pieces.

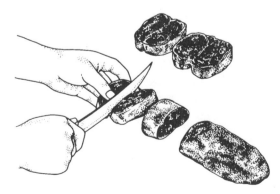

Cutting leg muscle into small steaks.

the backbone left. Cut it into pieces and use it for soup.

Note that the procedure above does not make much use of a saw. If you've got a good saw, you may want to start the whole operation by cutting through the backbone from one end to the other. Many people use this method.

Generally, a muscle that is not used much is better eating, or at least tenderer, than a muscle that is constantly exercised. The loin and the tenderloin, both along the backbone, are not used as much as the muscles in the legs, and therefore are better cuts of meat. Because there is a lot of confusion about these cuts, I am treating them separately.

Besides, it won't hurt a thing to save the best until last.

Loin and Tenderloin

Almost everyone will agree that the loin and tenderloin cuts from almost any animal make the best eating. But there is a lot of misunderstanding, if not downright disagreement, about what, exactly, these cuts are. Some people assume, without really thinking about it, that the loin and the tenderloin are the same thing. Most books about wild game, and meat in general, are vague on the subject.

Both cuts are excellent, coming as they do from along the backbone. Each animal has two loins *atop* the backbone and running parallel to it, and two tenderloins *under* the backbone and running parallel to it. If you took a cross section of the backbone in the loin section (or sawed out a 1-inch segment of the backbone and the surrounding muscles), you would have two T-bone steaks joining each other. Cut the back segment in half, and you have T-bones like you see packaged in the meat market. As every T-bone and pork chop fan knows, there are two main parts to this cut of meat. The larger part is actually a slice of the loin, or top muscle of the back assembly; the small part is a slice of the tenderloin, or bottom muscle of the back assembly. Again, every T-bone fan knows that the smaller side is more tender; hence, the name "tenderloin." In addition to the T-bone, the porterhouse and the sirloin steaks also can contain part of the loin and tenderloin.

Obviously, if you cut the meat up into high-quality steaks, you can't have your tenderloin and eat it too. But you can, by altering the cut of your steaks, cut out both a loin roast and a tenderloin when you butcher an animal. Both of these cuts of meat are very good, with the tenderloin being the better, or at least the more tender.

The tenderloin is best removed during the field-dressing operation. Since it is not covered with hide, it tends to dry out if left intact during hanging. The loins can be cut out with a sharp knife after the animal has been skinned. Each loin is shaped like a long loaf of French bread. The tenderloin is much smaller, but it has the same shape.

If your animal is butchered by a meat processor, you might consider making steaks of the backbone by simply cutting out 1-inch cross sections. Thus, each steak would contain two loin sections and two tenderloin sections. These are perfect for grilling or broiling.

INDEX